THE
WESTERN
EXPERIENCE

VOLUME B:
The Early Modern Era

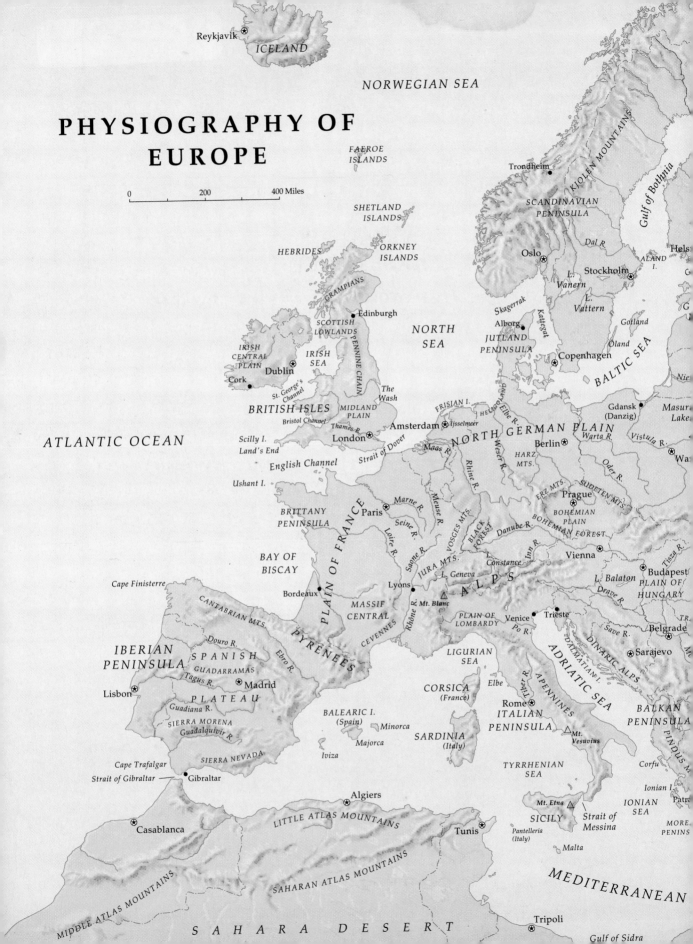

PHYSIOGRAPHY OF EUROPE

Reykjavik
ICELAND

NORWEGIAN SEA

0   200   400 Miles

FAEROE
ISLANDS

SHETLAND
ISLANDS

HEBRIDES

ORKNEY
ISLANDS

GRAMPIANS

Edinburgh

SCOTTISH
LOWLANDS

NORTH
SEA

IRISH
CENTRAL
PLAIN

IRISH
SEA

PENNINE CHAIN

Cork   Dublin

St. George's
Channel

The
Wash

BRITISH ISLES

MIDLAND
PLAIN

Bristol Channel

ATLANTIC OCEAN

Scilly I.
Land's End

Thames R.

London   Amsterdam   Ijsselmeer

FRISIAN I.

Helgoland

Elbe R.

NORTH GERMAN PLAIN

Berlin

Gdansk
(Danzig)

Masur.
Lake

Warta R.

Vistula R.

Wa

Strait of Dover

Maas R.

Rhine R.

Weser R.

HARZ
MTS.

Oder R.

English Channel

Ushant I.

BRITTANY
PENINSULA

Paris

Marne R.

Meuse R.

VOSGES MTS.

BLACK
FOREST

Danube R.

BOHEMIAN
FOREST

ERZ MTS.

Prague

SUDETEN MTS.

BOHEMIAN
PLAIN

Seine R.

Loire R.

Saone R.

JURA MTS.

L.
Constance

Inn R.

Vienna

BAY OF
BISCAY

Bordeaux

PLAIN OF FRANCE

MASSIF
CENTRAL

Lyons

Rhône R.   Mt. Blanc

L. Geneva

ALPS

PLAIN OF
LOMBARDY

Venice   Trieste

Po R.

L. Balaton

PLAIN OF
HUNGARY

Drave R.

Budapest

Save R.

Belgrade

Sarajevo

TR

Cape Finisterre

CANTABRIAN MTS.

IBERIAN
PENINSULA

SPANISH

Douro R.

GUADARRAMAS

Tagus R.   Madrid

Lisbon

PLATEAU

Guadiana R.

SIERRA MORENA

Guadalquivir R.

Ebro R.

PYRENEES

CEVENNES

LIGURIAN
SEA

CORSICA
(France)

BALEARIC I.
(Spain)

Minorca

Majorca

SARDINIA
(Italy)

Elbe

Tiber R.

APENNINES

Rome

ITALIAN
PENINSULA

Mt.
Vesuvius

DALMATIAN I.

DINARIC ALPS

ADRIATIC SEA

PINDUS M.

Corfu

Ionian I.

Patra

BALKAN
PENINSULA

Cape Trafalgar

SIERRA NEVADA

Strait of Gibraltar   Gibraltar

Iviza

TYRRHENIAN
SEA

IONIAN
SEA

MORE
PENINS

Algiers

Casablanca

LITTLE ATLAS MOUNTAINS

Tunis

Pantelleria
(Italy)

Mt. Etna

SICILY

Strait of
Messina

Malta

MIDDLE ATLAS MOUNTAINS

SAHARAN ATLAS MOUNTAINS

MEDITERRANEAN

SAHARA   DESERT

Tripoli

Gulf of Sidra

Trondheim

KIOLEN MOUNTAINS

SCANDINAVIAN
PENINSULA

Dal R.

Gulf of Bothnia

Oslo

Hels

ALAND
I.

L.
Vanern

Stockholm

L.
Vattern

Gotland

Skagerrak

Alborg

Kattegat

Öland

JUTLAND
PENINSULA

Copenhagen

BALTIC SEA

Nie

G

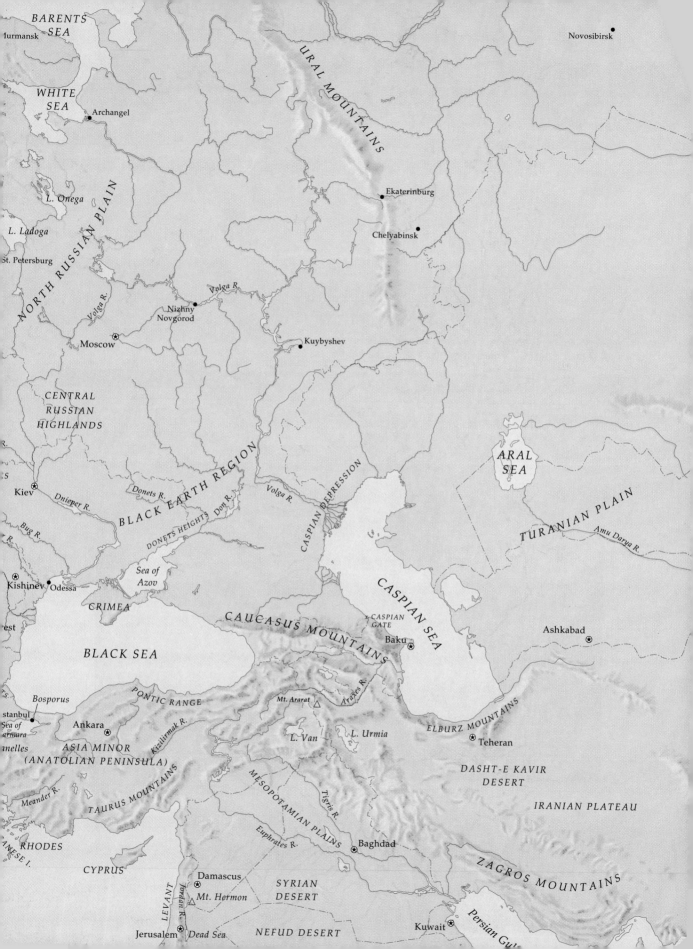

THE WESTERN EXPERIENCE

VOLUME B:
The Early Modern Era

SIXTH EDITION

MORTIMER CHAMBERS
University of California, Los Angeles

RAYMOND GREW
University of Michigan

DAVID HERLIHY
Late Professor of History
Brown University

THEODORE K. RABB
Princeton University

ISSER WOLOCH
Columbia University

McGRAW-HILL, INC.
New York • St. Louis • San Francisco • Auckland • Bogotá • Caracas • Lisbon • London • Madrid
Mexico City • Milan • Montreal • New Delhi • San Juan • Singapore
Sydney • Tokyo • Toronto

THE WESTERN EXPERIENCE
Volume B:
The Early Modern Era

1 2 3 4 5 6 7 8 9 0 VNH   VNH 9 0 9 8 7 6 5 4

ISBN 0-07-011071-9

This book was set in Palatino by CRWaldman Graphic Communications.
The editors were Pamela Gordon and Ira C. Roberts;
the designers were Wanda Lubelska and Wanda Siedlecka;
the production supervisor was Kathryn Porzio.
The cartographer was David Lindroth.
Von Hoffmann Press, Inc., was printer and binder.

Cover art: Pierre-Denis Martin, "Coronation Procession of Louis XV, 1722, at Reims" (detail). Chateau de Versailles ©Photo R.M.N.

About the Authors

Mortimer Chambers is Professor of History at the University of California at Los Angeles. He was a Rhodes scholar from 1949 to 1952 and received an M.A. from Wadham College, Oxford, in 1955 after obtaining his doctorate from Harvard University in 1954. He has taught at Harvard University (1954–1955) and the University of Chicago (1955–1958). He was Visiting Professor at the University of British Columbia in 1958, the State University of New York at Buffalo in 1971, the University of Freiburg (Germany) in 1974 and Vassar College in 1988. A specialist in Greek and Roman history, he is coauthor of *Aristotle's History of Athenian Democracy* (1962), editor of a series of essays entitled *The Fall of Rome* (1963), and author of *Georg Busolt: His Career in His Letters* (1990) and of *Staat der Athener*, a German translation and commentary to Aristotle's *Constitution of the Athenians* (1990). He has edited Greek texts of the latter work (1986) and of the *Hellenica Oxyrhynchia* (1993). He has contributed articles to the *American Historical Review and Classical Philology* as well as other journals, both in America and in Europe.

Raymond Grew is Professor of History at the University of Michigan. He earned both his M.A. (1952) and Ph.D. (1957) from Harvard University in the field of modern European history. He was a Fulbright Fellow to Italy (1954–1955), and Fulbright Travelling Fellow to France (1976, 1990), Guggenheim Fellow (1968–1969), Director of Studies at the Écoles des Hautes Études en Sciences Sociales in Paris (1976, 1987, 1990), and a Fellow of the National Endowment for the Humanities (1979). In 1962 he received the Chester Higby Prize from the American Historical Asso-

ciation, and in 1963 the Italian government awarded him the Unita d'Italia Prize; in 1992 he received the David Pinkney Prize of the Society for French Historical Studies. He is an active member of the A.H.A.; the Society for French Historical Studies; the Society for Italian Historical Studies, of which he has been president; and the Council for European Studies, of which he has twice served as national chair. His books include *A Sterner Plan for Italian Unity* (1963), edited *Crises of Development in Europe and the United States* (1978), and with Patrick J. Harrigan, *School, State, and Society: The Growth of Elementary Schooling in Nineteenth-Century France* (1991); he is also the editor of *Comparative Studies in Society and History* and its book series. He has also written on global history and is one of the directors of the Global History Group. His articles and reviews have appeared in a number of European and American journals.

David Herlihy was the Mary Critchfield and Barnaby Keeney Professor of History at Brown University and the author of numerous books and studies on the social history of the Middle Ages. His most recent publications were *Opera Muliebria: Woman and Work in Medieval Europe* (1990); *Medieval Households* (1985); and, in collaboration with Christiane Klapisch-Zuber, *Tuscans and Their Families: A Study of the Florentine Catasto of 1427* (1985). He received his M.A., from the Catholic University of America in 1952, his Ph.D. from Yale University in 1956, and an honorary Doctor of Humanities from the University of San Francisco in 1983. He was a former president of several historical associations, and in 1990 served as president of the American History Association, the largest historical society in America. He was a fellow of the Guggenheim Foundation (1961–1962), the American Council of Learned Societies (1966–1967), the Center for Advanced Study in the Behavioral Sciences (1972–1973), and the National Endowment for the Humanities (1976). He was a fellow of the American Academy of Arts and Sciences and the American Philosophical Society. His articles and reviews have appeared in numerous professional journals, both here and abroad.

Theodore K. Rabb is Professor of History at Princeton University. He received his Ph.D. from Princeton, and subsequently taught at Stanford, Northwestern, Harvard, and Johns Hopkins universities. He is the author of numerous articles and reviews, and has been editor of *The Journal of Interdisciplinary History* since its foundation. Among his books are *The Struggle for Stability in Early Modern Europe* and *Renaissance Lives*. Professor Rabb has held offices in various national organizations, including the American Historical Association and The National Council for Historical Education. He was the principal historian for the PBS series, *Renaissance.*

Isser Woloch is Professor of History at Columbia University. He received his Ph.D. (1965) from Princeton University in the field of eighteenth- and nineteenth-century European history. He has taught at Indiana University and at the University of California at Los Angeles where, in 1967, he received a Distinguished Teaching Citation. He has been a fellow of the A.C.L.S., the National Endowment for the Humanities, the Guggenheim Foundation, and the Institute for Advanced Study at Princeton. His publications include *Jacobin Legacy: The Democratic Movement under the Directory* (1970), *The Peasantry in the Old Regime: Conditions and Protests* (1970), *The French Veteran from the Revolution to the Restoration* (1979), and *Eighteenth-Century Europe: Tradition and Progress, 1715–1789* (1982), and *The New Regime: Transformations of the French Civic Order, 1789–1820s* (1994).

*This book is dedicated
to the memory of David Herlihy
whose erudition and judgment
were central to its creation
and whose friendship and example
continue to inspire
his co-authors*

Contents

12

THE WEST IN TRANSITION: SOCIETY AND CULTURE 347

13

REFORMATIONS IN RELIGION 383

14

ECONOMIC EXPANSION AND A NEW POLITICS   421

15

WAR AND CRISIS 461

16

CULTURE AND SOCIETY IN THE AGE OF THE SCIENTIFIC REVOLUTION 497

17

THE EMERGENCE OF THE EUROPEAN STATE SYSTEM 533

18

THE WEALTH OF NATIONS 575

19

THE AGE OF ENLIGHTENMENT 607

20

THE FRENCH REVOLUTION 637

21

THE AGE OF NAPOLEON 671

PHOTO AND TEXT CREDITS 703

INDEX 707

LIST OF MAPS

Introduction

[*Publisher's Note:* In order to provide an alternative to the hardcover edition, THE WESTERN EXPERIENCE is being made available in two-volume and three-volume paperbound editions, as well as a paperbound edition that runs from the Renaissance to the Modern Era. Volume I includes Chapters 1–17; Volume II includes Chapters 15–30 and the Epilogue; Volume A includes Chapters 1–12; Volume B includes Chapters 11–21; Volume C includes Chapters 19–30 and the Epilogue; the volume From The Renaissance to the Modern Era includes Chapters 12–30 and the Epilogue. The page numbering and cross-references in these editions remain the same as in the hardcover text.]

Everyone uses history. We use it to define who we are, to connect our personal experience with the collective memory of the groups to which we belong and to attach ourselves to a particular region, nation, or culture. We invoke the past to explain our hopes and ambitions and to justify our fears and conflicts. The Charter of the United Nations, like the American Declaration of Independence, is based on a view of history. When workers strike or armies march, they cite the lessons of their history. Because history is so important to us psychologically and intellectually, historical understanding is always shifting and often controversial.

Some questions must be asked repeatedly; some issues arise again and again. But historical knowledge is cumulative, for while asking new questions, historians integrate the answers learned from previous studies. History is not merely a subjective exercise in which all opinions are equally valid. No matter what motivated a particular historical question, the answer to it stands until overturned by better evidence. We now know more about the past than ever before and understand it as the people we study could not. Unlike them, we know how their history came out; we can apply methods they did not have, and often we have evidence they never saw. This knowledge and the ways of interpreting it are the collective achievement of thousands of historians.

We also use history for pleasure—as a cultivated entertainment. The biographies of admirable or monstrous men and women, dramatic accounts of important events, and colorful tales of earlier times can be fascinating in themselves. Through these encounters with history, we experience the common human concerns of all people; and through the study of European history, we come to appreciate the ideals and conflicts, the failures and accidents, the social needs and human choices that formed the Western world in which we live. When understood in their historical context, the achievements of European civilization are all the more remarkable, hammered out among competing interests and burning controversies.

The Western Experience was designed to provide a reasonably comprehensive and analytic account of the various circumstances within which, and the processes by which, European society and civilization evolved. This is the book's sixth edition, evidence of a long life sustained with the help of prior revisions. Even so, this edition is more completely rewritten and recast than any of its predecessors—our response to changes in students and in historical study. Each cohort of students carries different experiences, interests, and training into the classroom. These changes are easily exaggerated, but they can be important; and the women and men we teach have taught us enough about what currently engages or confuses them, about the impression of European history they bring to college, and about what they can be expected to take from a survey course to make us want to reconsider the way the book presented its material. This led to a rewriting and reordering that we think has made the book clearer and more accessible without sacrificing our initial goals of writing a sophisticated, interpretive, and analytic history.

Adapting the latest developments in historical understanding to a general work presents a problem of a particular kind. From its first edition, this book incorporated more of the results of quantitative and social history than general European histories usually did, an obvious reflection of the several authors' own research. Each subsequent edition provided an occasion to incorporate current methods and new knowledge, an opportunity to reconsider paragraphs, sections, and whole chapters in the light of new approaches and new research, sometimes literally reconceiving part of the past. Recent work—in demographic, economic, diplomatic, and intellectual history as well as social history, and most of all in gender studies and cultural studies—increases those opportunities, and we have sought to convey something of the excitement of this new understanding. At the same time, we have wanted to preserve a special kind of balance. The professional scholar prefers new perspectives to familiar information, but other readers are less likely to make such distinctions. For them, the latest interpretations need to be integrated with a presentation of standard controversies, of the people and events that are part of our cultural lore, and of the basic information necessary to build a framework for the historical understanding that they are begining to form.

Other kinds of balance are important, too. We believe that this history must be interpretive but also that its readers—instructors, students, and general readers—should be free to use it in many different ways and in conjunction with their own interpretive approaches, their own areas of special knowledge, and their own diverse interests and curiosity. Of course, there is no simple standard by which to judge when such a work is comprehensive enough to offer that freedom yet selective enough to be comprehensible. For this edition, the authors once again jointly planned revision of the entire volume, read and criticized each other's drafts, and benefited from the criticisms and suggestions of more than a score of other scholars and teachers. The book carefully includes evidence from which alternative interpretations can be formulated and a platform that allows classroom teachers of any period to emphasize social, political, cultural, economic, or institutional history in lectures and selected readings.

The use of color throughout the book and a new design obviously make it more attractive, and the maps have been completely redrawn. They convey more information more clearly and allow the basic geography of Europe a visual presence throughout the book. The greater range of illustrations has made it possible for them to be more fully integrated into the text than ever before. We have also adopted the common device of including selections from primary sources, choosing samples that expand points made in the text, provide some flavor of the period under discussion, and grant to the reader some of that independence that comes from personal engagement with historical sources.

Throughout the book, from the earliest civilizations to the present, certain themes are pursued. They appear most distinctly in the early chapters, in discussions of how the land is settled, divided among its inhabitants, and put to use; how production and the division of labor are organized and whether there are slaves, classes that do not work at all, and recognized specialists in fighting or crafts or trade; how the family is structured, the gendered roles within and outside the family, and the relationship of that to the overall social structure; how religion and belief systems are sustained and connected to power; how the political system operates, who participates in it, and how it maintains order and makes war; how the institutions of society and the system of law work to permit or constrain social change; and how the forms of cultural expression relate to the social structure and important issues of an era. Attentive readers will note that these themes, introduced early, are then picked up in subsequent sections of the book as changes in these themes are important for understanding other eras of European history.

We think of that history as the history of Western civilization, but the very concept of a Western civilization is itself the result of history. The Greeks gave the names *east* and *west* to the points on the horizon where the sun rises and sets. Because the impressive Persian Empire and India lay to their east, the Greeks thought of themselves as living in the West, on the edge of the continent they called *Europe*. The distinction between Western civilization and others—ethnocentric, often arbitrary, and frequently exaggerated—continued even as that civilization changed and expanded with the Roman Empire, Christianity, and the European conquest of the New World. The view that this is one civilization, with America tied more closely to ancient Greece than Greece is to Egypt or Spain to Islam, can be easily challenged in every respect save cultural tradition.

The Western Experience gives primary attention to a small part of the world and in doing so honors that cultural tradition. The concentration on Europe includes important examples of city and of rural life; of empires and monarchies and republics; of life before and after industrialization; of societies in which labor was organized through markets, serfdom, and slavery; of cultures little concerned with science and of ones that used changing scientific knowledge; of non-Christian religions and of all the major forms of Christianity in action.

To discuss history in this way is to think comparatively and to employ categories of the social history that has greatly affected historical understanding in the last half of the twentieth century. The desire to broaden the scope of historical writing is not new. As early as the eighteenth century many historians (of whom Voltaire was one) called for a history that was more than chronology, more than an account of kings and battles. In the nineteenth century—even while historical studies paid dominant attention to past politics, diplomacy, and war (taking the evidence primarily from official documents found in state archives)—there were important and systematic efforts to encompass the history of intellectual and cultural trends, of law and constitutions, of religion, and of the economy. Social history, as a field of study, emerged as one of these efforts at broader coverage. For some, it was primarily the history of labor movements. For others, it was the history of daily life—in ancient Rome or Renaissance Florence or old New York as reflected in styles of dress, housing, diet, and so on. This "pots and pans history" was the sort of history featured in historical museums and popular magazines. Appealing in its concreteness, it tended (like the collections of interesting objects that it resembled) to lack a theoretical basis.

Modern social history is more systematic. In the theories and methods it employs, it borrows from the social sciences—especially anthropology, sociology, economics, and political science. It seeks to compensate for the fact that most historical writing has been about the tiny minority of the powerful, rich, and educated (who, after all, left behind the fullest and most accessible records of their activities); and it aims to be mindful of popular culture as well as formal or official culture, as interested in the family and living conditions as in the state and political theory.

The growth of social history facilitated a remarkable expansion in the history of women. Stimulated by contemporary feminism as well as by developments within social history, the history of women has in turn grown into gender studies, a set of approaches that has proved enormously revealing about society as a whole, showing how politics and culture together with leisure and work, are shaped by and reproduce assumptions about gender. This new work has affected the historical understanding of every era and nearly every subfield of history. Gender studies have also tended to draw attention to social symbols and to the values expressed in social behavior, drawing history closer to the literary and philosophical theories underlying what is currently called *cultural studies*. These approaches, as well as the renewed interest in intellectual history, emphasize the role of interpretation over objective science and the relativity of all writing on culture and society.

Such interests, theories, and techniques have greatly expanded the range of useful historical sources and the range of issues historians must consider. They also make those mainstays of historical organization—clear chronology and periodization—more complex. The periodization of history based on the rise and fall of dynasties, on the formation of states, and on the duration of wars and revolutions usually does not fit the periodization most appropriate for highlighting changes in culture and ideas, economic production, or science and technology. Historical surveys have therefore frequently been organized topically as well as chronologically, with special chapters on economic or intellectual developments, which can weaken awareness of interconnection.

In *The Western Experience* an effort has been made to combine the newer approaches with more established perspectives. The tradition of the introductory course in European history (and our cultural tradition as well) is recognized by keeping the book's chapters essentially chronological in sequence, sometimes using groups of chapters to cover a whole period. At the same time each chapter is presented as an interpretative essay, introducing a set of historical problems important to the understanding of the period treated. The information within a chapter serves as evidence to illustrate the interpretive argument, but it is also selected to meet the general requirements of a survey of European history, to provide the basis for constructing a coherent picture of the development of Europe, and to exemplify different kinds of historical interest.

Readers of this book may thus use it as an introduction to historical method, find within it a framework to which they can attach whatever else they know about Western society, and discover here some challenge to their preconceptions—about the past, about how societies are organized, and about how people behave. Historical study is an integrative enterprise in which long-term trends and specific moments, as well as social structure and individual actions, are brought together.

A college course is not the only way to build a personal culture. Nor is history the only path to integrated knowledge. Western history is not the only history one should know, nor is an introductory survey necessarily the best way to learn it. Still, as readers consider and then challenge interpretations offered in this text, they will exercise critical and analytical skills; and they will find that the world beyond (and before) our own lives is relevant to our current concerns. They can acknowledge the greatness of their Western heritage and its distinctiveness, which includes injustice, cruelty, and failure. In doing these things, they will experience the study of history as one of those vital intellectual activities by which we come to know who and where we are.

Acknowledgments

We wish to thank the following reviewers, consultants, and users for their helpful suggestions for *The Western Experience:* Catherine Albanese, Wright State University; Thomas M. Bader, California State University–Northridge; B. D. Bargar, University of South Carolina; Edward E. Barry, Montana State University; S. Scott Bartchy, University of California–Los Angeles; Iris Berger, State University of New York–Albany; Alan E. Bernstein, University of Akron; Charles R. Berry, Wright State University; Thomas Blomquist, Northern Illinois University; Stephen Blum, Montgomery County Community College, PA; Jack Bournazian; Elspeth Brown, Hamilton College, NY; Paul Chardoul, Grand Rapids Junior College; Craig A. Czarnecki, Baltimore, MD; Ronnie M. Day, Eastern Tennessee State University; Michael De Michele, University of Scranton; Bradley H. Dowden, California State University–Sacramento; Veron Egger, Georgia Southern College; Nancy Ellenberger, United States Naval Academy; Elfriede Engel, Lansing Community College, MI; Steven Epstein, University of Colorado at Boulder; R. Finucane, Georgia Southern College; Willard C. Frank, Jr., Old Dominion University, VA; Ellen G. Friedman, Boston College; James Friuglietti, Eastern Michigan College; Laura Gellott, University of Wisconsin at Parkside; Robert Gottfried, Rutgers University; Carl Granquist, Jr., Keene State College; Katherine J. Gribble, Highline Community College, WA; Margot A. Haberhern, Florida Institute of Technology; Barbara Hanawalt, University of Minnesota; Drew Harrington, Western Kentucky University; Patricia Herlihy, Brown University; Neil M. Heyman, San Diego State University; Deborah L.

Jones, Lexington, KY; Thomas E. Kaiser, University of Arkansas–Little Rock; Nannerl O. Keohane, Wellesley College; Donald P. King, Whitman College, WA; William J. King, Wright State University; Ellen E. Kittell, University of Oregon; Steven P. Kramer, The University of New Mexico; Lisa Lane, Mira-Costa College; Gordon Lauren, University of Montana; Phoebe Lundy, Boise State University; Gilbert H. McArthur, College of William and Mary; Edward Malefakis, Columbia University; Vesta F. Manning, University of Arizona–Tucson; William Mathews, State University of New York at Potsdam; William Carl Mathews, Ohio State University; Edgar Melton, Wright State University; Carol Menning, University of Toledo; Julius Milmeister, Pittsburgh, PA; Frederick I. Murphy, Western Kentucky University; Sandra Norman, Florida Atlantic University; Peter Pierson, Santa Clara University; Linda J. Piper, The University of Georgia–Athens; Carl Pletsch, Miami University; Phillip Racine, Wof-

ford College; Ronald A. Rebholz, Stanford University; John F. Robertson, Central Michigan University; Louisa Sarasohn, Oregon State College; Judy Sealander, Wright State University; Ezel Kural Shaw, California State University–Northridge; Eileen Soldwedel, Edmonds Community College; Alan Spetter, Wright State University; Richard E. Sullivan, Michigan State University; John Sweets, University of Kansas; George Taylor, University of North Carolina–Chapel Hill; Armstrong Starkey, Adelphi University, NY; Richard Wagner, Des Moines Area Community College; Richard Weigel, Western Kentucky University; Robert H. Welborn, Clayton State College; Michael J. Witt, FSC, Christian Brothers College, TN; and Richard M. Wunderli, University of Colorado.

Mortimer Chambers
Raymond Grew
Theodore K. Rabb
Isser Woloch

SIEGE OF MORTAIGNE
This manuscript illustration from the Hundred Years' War shows a city under siege by both land and sea. The French defender is using a crossbow; the English besiegers are using cannon as well as their famous longbows.

THE WEST IN
ECONOMY AND I

THE vigorous expansion that marked European history from the eleventh to the thirteenth centuries came to an end in the 1300s. Plague, famine, and recurrent wars decimated populations and snuffed out their former prosperity. At the same time, feudal governments as well as the papacy struggled against mounting institutional chaos. But for all the signs of crisis the fourteenth and fifteenth centuries were not merely an age of breakdown. The failures of the medieval economy and its governments prompted change and drove the Western peoples to repair their institutions. By the late fifteenth century the outlines of a new equilibrium were emerging. In 1500 Europeans remained fewer in number than they had been in 1300, but they also had developed a more productive economy and a more powerful technology than they had possessed 200 years before. These achievements were to equip them for their great expansion throughout the world in the early modern period. Some historians refer to the fourteenth and fifteenth centuries as the "autumn of the Middle Ages," and their somber theme is the decline and death of a formerly great civilization. But the study of any past epoch requires an effort to balance the work of death and renewal. In few periods of history do death and renewal confront each other so dramatically as in the years between 1300 and 1500.

...ay have reached 15 million; it, too, was ... to attain this size for 200 years. In Ger... some 170,000 inhabited localities named ...ces before 1300, about 40,000 disappeared ...ng the 1300s and 1400s. Since many of the ...viving towns were also shrinking in size, the ...opulation loss was only greater.

Certain favored regions of Europe—the fertile lands surrounding Paris and the Po valley—did continue to attract settlers and maintain fairly stable populations, but they owed their good fortune more to immigration than to high birthrates or immunity from disease. It can safely be estimated that all of Europe in 1450 had no more than one-half, and probably only one-third, of the population it had had around 1300.

PESTILENCE

The great plague of the fourteenth century, known as the Black Death, provides a dramatic, but not a complete, explanation for these huge human losses. In 1347 a merchant ship sailing from Caffa in the Crimea to Messina in Sicily seems to have carried infected rats. A plague broke out at Messina, and from there it spread throughout Europe (see Map 11.1).

The Persistence of Plague The Black Death was not so much an epidemic as a pandemic, striking an entire continent. Yet it was not the first pandemic in European history. An earlier one had struck in 542, during the reign of Justinian (see Chapter 7). But this was the first in 800 years, and it erupted repeatedly during the century. A city was lucky if more than 10 years went by without an onslaught; the plague was raging in some part of Europe in almost every year (*see box*, p. 316). Barcelona and its province of Catalonia, for example, lived through this record of misery in the fourteenth century: famine, 1333; plague, 1347 and 1351; famine, 1358 and 1359; plague, 1362, 1363, 1371, and 1397.

Some of the horror of the plague can be glimpsed in this account by an anonymous cleric who visited the French city of Avignon in 1348:

To put the matter shortly, one-half, or more than a half, of the people at Avignon are already dead. Within the walls of the city there are now more than

DEMOGRAPHIC CATASTROPHE

A few censuses and other statistical records give us an insight into the size and structure of the European population in the 1300s. Nearly all these records were drawn up for purposes of taxation, and usually they survey only limited geographical areas—a city or a province. They are rarely complete even in limited areas and give us no reliable totals, but they still enable us to perceive with some confidence how the population was changing.

Almost every region of Europe from which we possess such records shows an appalling decline of population between approximately 1300 and 1450. Thus the population of Provence in southern France seems to have shrunk during the century after 1310 from between 350,000 and 400,000 to roughly one-third, or at most one-half, of its earlier size; only after 1470 did it again begin to increase. The city and countryside of Pistoia, near Florence, fell from about 43,000 people in the mid-thirteenth century to 14,000 by the early fifteenth. The nearby city and countryside of San Gimignano has not regained to this day the approximately 13,000 residents it had in 1332.

For the larger kingdoms of Europe the figures are less reliable, but they are similar. England had a population of about 3.7 million in 1347 and 2.2 million by 1377. By 1550 it had no more people than it had had in the thirteenth century. France

Map 11.1 THE BLACK DEATH
For all the impression that the plague spread almost instantly, this reconstruction of its progress reveals that, because it depended on Europe's poor travel conditions and died down each winter, it took three years to move from Sicily to Sweden.

7,000 houses shut up; in these no one is living, and all who have inhabited them are departed. . . . On account of this great mortality there is such a fear of death that people do not dare even to speak with anyone whose relative has died, because it is frequently remarked that in a family where one dies nearly all the relations follow him. . . .[1]

Nature of the Disease Most historians identify the Black Death as the bubonic plague, but this makes it difficult to explain how the disease

could have spread so rapidly and killed so many, since bubonic plague is more a disease of rats and small mammals than human beings. If bubonic plague is to spread to a human, a flea must bite an infected rat, pick up the infection, and carry it to a human host through a bite. The infection causes the lymphatic glands to swell, but recovery is not uncommon. Only if the infection travels

---

[1]*Breve Chronicon clerici anonymi*, quoted in Francis Aidan Gasquet, *The Black Death of 1348 and 1349*, 1908, p. 46.

Boccaccio on the Black Death

*The following eyewitness description of the ravages of the Black Death
in Florence was written by one of its most famous citizens, the writer Giovanni
Boccaccio. This passage comes from his masterpiece,* **The Decameron,** *written
during the three years following the plague.*

"In the year of our Lord 1348, there happened at Florence a most terrible plague, which had broken out some years before in the Levant, and after making incredible havoc all the way, had now reached the west. There, in spite of all the means that art and human foresight could suggest, such as keeping the city clear from filth and the publication of copious instructions for preservation of health, it began to show itself in the spring. Unlike what had been seen in the east, where bleeding from the nose is the fatal prognostic, here there appeared certain tumors in the groin or under the arm-pits, some as big as a small apple, others as an egg, and afterwards purple spots in most parts of the body—messengers of death. To the cure of this malady neither medical knowledge nor the power of drugs was of any effect; whether because the disease was in its own nature mortal, or that the physicians (the number of whom, taking quacks and women pretenders into account, was grown very great) could form no just idea of the cause. Whichever was the reason, few escaped; but nearly all died the third day from the first appearance of the symptoms, some sooner, some later, without any fever or other symptoms. What gave the more virulence to this plague was that it spread daily, like fire when it comes in contact with combustibles. Nor was it caught only by coming near the sick, but even by touching their clothes. One instance of this kind I took particular notice of: the rags of a poor man just dead had been thrown into the street. Two hogs came up, and after rooting amongst the rags, in less than an hour they both turned around and died on the spot."

From Warren Hollister et al., *Medieval Europe: A Short Sourcebook* (2d ed.), McGraw-Hill, 1992, pp. 248–249.

through the bloodstream to the lungs, causing pneumonia, can the disease be spread directly from person to person. The real killer in the 1300s seems to have been pneumonic plague, which infects the lungs directly; it probably was spread through coughing and was almost always fatal.

In spite of the virulence of pneumonic plague, it is hard to believe that medical factors alone can explain the awesome mortalities. After all, Europeans had maintained close contact with the East, where the plague had been endemic, since the eleventh century, but not until 1347 and 1348 did it make serious inroads in Europe. In addition, pneumonic plague is a disease of the winter months, but the plagues of the 1300s characteristically raged during the summer and declined in the cooler weather of autumn. Some scholars

think the weather of the age—it seems to have been unusually cool and humid—somehow favored the disease. Others argue that it was acute, widespread malnutrition that caused starvation and lower resistance to infections.

HUNGER

The second cause of the dramatic fall in population, hunger, was all too common. Even if famines were less lethal than the plague in their initial onslaught, they were likely to persist for several years. In 1315, 1316, and 1317 a severe famine swept the north of Europe; in 1339 and 1340 another struck the south. The starving people ate not only their reserves of grain but also most of the seed they had set aside for planting.

Only a remarkably good harvest could compensate for the loss of grain by providing both immediate food and sufficient seeds for future planting.

Why was hunger so widespread in the early fourteenth century? Some historians see the root of trouble in the sheer number of people the lands had to support by 1300. The medieval population had been growing rapidly since about 1000, and by 1300 Europe, so this analysis suggests, was becoming the victim of its own success. Parts of the continent were crowded, even glutted, with people. Some areas of Normandy, for example, had a population in the early fourteenth century not much below what they supported 600 years later. Thousands, millions even, had to be fed without chemical fertilizers, power tools, and fast transport. Masses of people had come to depend for their livelihood on unrewarding soils, and even in good years they were surviving on the margins of existence. A slightly reduced harvest during any one year took on the dimensions of a major famine.

Even though malnutrition does not directly worsen mortality from plague, it does raise the death rate from respiratory infections and intestinal ailments, which also reached epidemic proportions in the fourteenth century. Furthermore, illness is itself a major cause of malnutrition. Thus hunger, disease, and plague combined to create a grim balance between the numbers of people and the resources that supported them.

▶ **THE TRIUMPH OF DEATH**
The great social disaster of the Black Death left few traces in the visual arts; perhaps people did not wish to be reminded of its horrors. One exception was the *Triumph of Death*, a mural painted shortly after 1348 in the Camposanto (cemetery) of Pisa in Italy. In this detail of the mural, an elegant party of hunters happens upon corpses prepared for burial. Note the rider who holds a handkerchief—scented, undoubtedly—to his nose, to ward off the foul odors.

ECONOMIC EFFECTS

What effects did the fall in population have on the economy of Europe? At first, the losses disrupted production. According to contemporaries, survivors of the plague often gave up toiling in the fields or looking after their shops; presumably, they saw no point in working for the future when it was so uncertain. But in the long run the results were not altogether negative. In agriculture, for example, the contraction of the population enabled the survivors to concentrate their efforts on better soils. Moreover, in both agriculture and industry the shortage of laborers was a challenge to landlords and entrepreneurs to save costs either by adopting productive measures that were less labor intensive or by increasing investment in labor-saving devices. Thus the decline in population eventually encouraged Europeans to find better techniques for making the most of available resources.

AGRICULTURE

Perhaps the best indication of the changes in the European economy comes from the history of prices. This evidence is scattered and rarely precise, but it does reveal roughly similar patterns in prices all over Europe. The cost of most agricultural products—cereals, wine, beer, oil, and meat—shot up immediately after the Black Death and stayed high until approximately 1375 in the north and 1395 in Italy. High food prices in a time of declining population suggest that production was falling even more rapidly than the number of consumers.

The beginnings of an agricultural recovery are apparent in the early fifteenth century. With fewer Europeans to be fed, the demand for cereals (which had long dominated agriculture) lessened perceptibly and their prices declined; with fewer available workers, the cost of labor pushed steadily upward. Landlords had to compete with one another to attract scarce tenants to their lands and did so by offering lower rents and favorable terms of tenancy. The upward movement of wages and the downward price of cereals led to a concentration on commodities that would command a better price in the market or were less expensive to produce. Better wages in both town

▶ **COLLECTING SILKWORMS AND PREPARING SILK** One of the new industries that appeared in Europe in the fourteenth century was the raising of silkworms. Since the spinning of silk was a craft usually associated with women, this scene, from a fifteenth-century manuscript, shows a woman gathering silkworms from the mulberry bushes on which the worms lived, and from whose cocoons the silk threads were unwound.

and country also enabled the population to consume a more varied and expensive diet. While the price of wheat fell, wine, beer, oil, butter, cheese, meat, fruit, and other foods remained relatively expensive, which indicates a strong market demand.

Enclosure One branch of agriculture that enjoyed a remarkable period of growth in the fifteenth century was sheep raising. Labor costs were low, since a few shepherds could guard thousands of sheep; and the prices for wool, skins, mutton, and cheese remained high. In England, landlords sought to take advantage of this situation by fencing large fields and converting them from plowland into sheep pastures and expelling the peasants or small herders who had formerly lived there; this process, called *enclosure*, continued for centuries and played an important role in English economic and social history.

By the middle of the fifteenth century, agricultural prices tended to stabilize, and this suggests that production had become more dependable. Farms enjoyed the advantages of larger size, better location on more profitable soil, and increased capital investments in tools and animals. Agriculture was now more diversified, which benefited the soil, lowered the risk of famine from the failure of a single staple crop, and provided more nourishment for the people. Europeans were consuming a healthier diet by the middle of the fifteenth century than their ancestors had 200 years before.

II. *Depression and Recovery in Trade and Industry*

Although agriculture was the main occupation of the age and also the area of economic activity most directly connected with plague and hunger, there were also profound consequences of the disasters of the 1300s for trade and industry. And here, as in agriculture, there was to be a recovery in the late 1400s that was to have a long-term effect on European history.

PROTECTIONISM

The movement of prices created serious problems for employers in cities. As the labor force contracted, wages in most towns surged to levels as much as four times higher than they had been before 1348. Although the prices of manufactured goods also increased, they did not rise as much as wages, and this worked to reduce profit margins. To offset these unfavorable tendencies, the employers sought government intervention. Between 1349 and 1351, England, France, Aragon, Castile, and other governments tried to fix prices and wages at levels favorable to employers. In enacting the Statute of Laborers, the English Parliament followed a policy typical of the age, forbidding employers to pay more than customary wages and requiring laborers to accept jobs at those wages. Such early experiments in a controlled economy failed. Price and wage ceilings set by law seem to have had little influence on actual prices.

A related problem for businesses was that competition grew as population fell and markets contracted. Traders tried to protect themselves by creating restricted markets and establishing monopolies. Guilds limited their membership, and some admitted only the sons of established masters. Cities, too, imposed heavy restrictions on the importation of foreign manufactures.

The Hanseatic League Probably the best example of this monopolizing trend is the association of northern European trading cities, the Hanseatic League. The league was a defensive association formed in the fourteenth century by the cities that dominated the commerce of the Baltic and North seas, with the aim of excluding foreigners from the Baltic trade. The cities initially sought this protection because the emperor was too weak to defend their interests. At its height, the Hanseatic League included about 70 or 80 cities, stretching from Bruges to Novgorod and led by Bremen, Cologne, Hamburg, and especially Lübeck. Maintaining its own treasury and fleet, the league supervised commercial exchange, policed the waters of the Baltic Sea, and negotiated with foreign princes. By the late fifteenth century, however, it began to decline and was unable to meet growing competition from the Dutch in northern commerce. Although never formally abolished, the Hanseatic League continued to meet—at lengthening intervals—only until 1669.

THE FORCES OF RECOVERY

Attempts to raise the efficiency of workers proved to be far more effective than wage and trade regulation in laying the basis for recovery. Employers were able to counteract high wages by

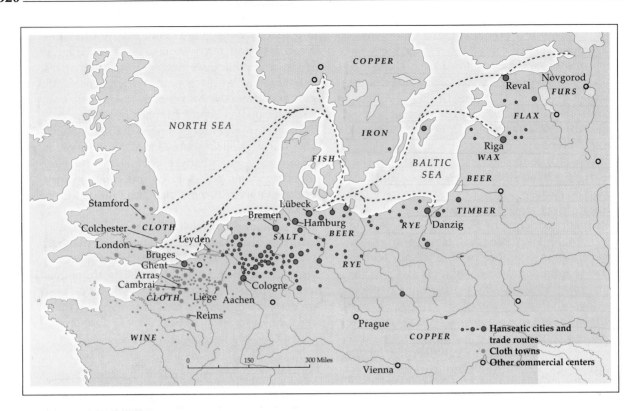

Map 11.2 THE HANSEATIC LEAGUE AND THE GOODS IT TRADED IN THE FOURTEENTH CENTURY Even in the age of the Black Death, international trade remained vigorous in northern Europe. Its leaders were the cities of the Hanseatic League, which shipped a variety of commodities across the continent, though the most sought-after commodity was the cloth produced in England, the Netherlands, and northern France.

adopting more rational methods of production and substituting capital for labor—that is, providing workers with better tools. Though largely inspired by hard times and labor shortages, most of the technical advances of the 1300s and 1400s—both in different industries and in business practices—led workers to practice trade more efficiently, and eventually this helped make Europe a richer community.

METALLURGY

Mining and metallurgy benefited from a series of inventions after 1460 that lowered the cost of metals and extended their use. Better techniques of digging, shoring, ventilating, and draining allowed mine shafts to be sunk several hundred feet into the earth, permitting the large-scale exploitation of the deep, rich mineral deposits of Central Europe. Some historians estimate that the output from the mines of Hungary, the Tyrol, Bohemia, and Saxony grew as much as five times between 1460 and 1530. During this period miners in Saxony discovered a method for extracting pure silver from the lead alloy in which it was often found—an invention that was of major importance for the later massive development of silver mines in America. Larger furnaces came into use, and huge bellows and trip-hammers, driven by waterpower, aided the smelting and working of metals. Simultaneously, the masters of the trade were acquiring a new precision in the difficult art of casting.

By the late fifteenth century, European mines were providing an abundance of silver bullion for coinage. Money became more plentiful, and this stimulated the economy. Exploitation also began in the rich coal deposits of northern Europe. Expanding iron production meant more and stronger pumps, gears and machine parts,

IIIIrrаиик ripiiipiie et ip? c

ptiiitijs foditiii querriitr iii ii;i'iitiim es electiiim. Aiii ;emmas et pieti oiгiitoi;qp

▶ **MINING, 1389**
One does not normally associate miners with
elegant decoration, but in this fourteenth-century
manuscript, a miner provides the subject for the
ornamentation of the capital M that starts the word
metalla (metals). That the artist even considered
such a subject is an indication of the growing
importance of the industry in this period.

tools, and ironwares; such products found wide
application in construction work and shipbuilding. And skill in metalworking contributed to
two other inventions: firearms and movable
metal type.

FIREARMS

Europeans were constantly trying to improve the
arts of war in the Middle Ages, and one weapon
they sought was a device to hurl projectiles with
great force and accuracy. We do not know how
they first learned that certain mixtures of carbon,
sulfur, and saltpeter burn with explosive force

and can be used to hurl boulders at an enemy.
Firearms are first mentioned in 1328, and cannons were used in the early battles of the Hundred Years' War. At first, their effect was chiefly
psychological: the thunderous roar, merely by
frightening the enemy's horses, did far more
damage than the usually inaccurate shots. Still, a
breakthrough had been made, and cannons
gained in military importance. Their development depended primarily on stronger, more precise casting and on proper granulation of the
powder to ensure that the charge burned at the
right speed and put its full force behind the pro-
jectile. With firearms, fewer soldiers could fight
more effectively; capital, in the form of an efficient though expensive tool, was being substituted for labor.

PRINTING

The extension of literacy among laypeople and
the greater reliance of governments and businesses on records created a demand for a cheap
method of reproducing the written word. The introduction of paper from the East was a major
step in reducing costs, for paper is far cheaper
than parchment to produce. A substitute for the
time-consuming labor of writing by hand was
also necessary: Scribes and copiers were skilled
artisans who commanded high salaries. To cut
costs, printing was first tried by pressing woodcuts—inked blocks with letters or designs carved
on them—onto paper or parchment. But these
"block books" represented only a small advance
over handwriting, for a separate woodcut had to
be carved for each page. And the woodcuts were
not durable; they tended to split after being
pressed a number of times.

Gutenberg By the middle of the fifteenth century several masters were on the verge of perfecting the technique of printing with movable
metal type. The first to prove this practicable was
Johannes Gutenberg of Mainz, a former jeweler
and stonecutter. Gutenberg devised an alloy of
lead, tin, and antimony that would melt at a low
temperature, cast well in the die, and be durable
in the press; this alloy is still the basis of the printer's art. His Bible, printed in 1455, is the first major work reproduced through printing.

italic type, modeled on the clear script they found in old manuscripts. They believed this was the style of writing used in ancient Rome, but in fact they were imitating the Carolingian minuscule script.

The immediate effect of the printing press was to multiply the output and cut the costs of books. It made information available to a much broader segment of the population, and libraries could store larger quantities of information at lower cost. Printing also helped disseminate and preserve knowledge in standardized form—a major contribution to the advance of technology and scholarship. Printing produced a revolution in what we would call *information technology*, and indeed it resembles in many ways the profound changes that computers are making in our own lives. Finally, printing could spread new ideas with unprecedented speed—a fact that was not fully appreciated, however, until the 1500s, when print became essential to the propaganda of religious reformers in the Protestant Reformation (see Chapter 13).

NAVIGATION

Ships People as well as ideas began to travel more easily in the fourteenth and fifteenth centuries. Before about 1325 there was still no regular sea traffic between northern and southern Europe by way of the Atlantic, but it grew rapidly thereafter. In navigation, the substitution of capital for labor meant the introduction of bigger ships, which carried more cargo with relatively smaller crews. Large ships were safer at sea; they could sail in uncertain weather, when smaller vessels had to stay in port; they could remain at sea longer; and they did not have to sail close to the coastline in order to replenish their supplies. Their voyages between ports could be more direct and therefore speedier.

The larger vessels required more sophisticated means of steering and navigation. Before 1300, ships were turned by trailing an oar over the side. This provided poor control, especially in sailing ships, which needed efficient steering to take advantage of shifting winds. Some time during the fourteenth century the stern rudder was developed, which enabled a captain to tack effectively against the wind and control his ship closely

▶ **GUTENBERG'S BIBLE**
A page from Johannes Gutenberg's Bible marks one of the most significant technical and cultural advances of the fifteenth century: printing with movable type, a process that made possible a wider dissemination of literature and thought.

Aldus In spite of Gutenberg's efforts to keep the technique a secret, it spread rapidly. By 1500 some 250 European cities had presses (see Map 12.1). German masters held an early leadership, but Italians soon challenged their preeminence. The Venetian printer Aldus Manutius, in particular, published works that are minor masterpieces of scholarship and grace. Aldus and his fellow Italians rejected the elaborate Gothic typeface used in the north and developed their own when entering or leaving ports. Voyages became quicker and safer, and the costs of maritime transport declined.

Instruments Ocean navigation also required a reliable means for estimating course and position, and here notable progress had been made in the late thirteenth century. Scholars at the court of King Alfonso X of Castile compiled the Alfonsine Tables, which showed with unprecedented accuracy the position and movements of the heavenly bodies. Using such tables, captains could take the elevation of the sun or stars with an astrolabe and calculate a ship's latitude, or position on a north-south coordinate. (They could not tell their longitude, or position on an east-west coordinate, until they could carry accurate clocks that could compare their time with that of a basic reference meridian, such as Greenwich in England. Until the 1700s, when the first accurate clocks immune to a ship's swaying were developed, navigators who sailed across the Atlantic could not tell how far they had traveled.)

The origin of the compass is unclear, but it was common on Mediterranean ships by the thirteenth century. By 1300, too, Mediterranean navigators sailed with maps of remarkable accuracy and used *portolani*, or port descriptions, which minutely described harbors, coastlines, and hazards. All these technical developments gave European mariners a mastery of Atlantic coastal waters and helped prepare the way for the voyages of discovery in the fifteenth century.

BUSINESS INSTITUTIONS

Banks The bad times of the fourteenth century also stimulated the development of more efficient business procedures. Merchant houses in the late fourteenth and fifteenth centuries were considerably smaller than those of the thirteenth century, but more flexible. The Medici bank of Florence, which functioned from 1397 until 1498, for example, was not a single monolithic structure; rather, it rested on separate partnerships, which established its various branches at Florence, Venice, Rome, Avignon, Bruges, and London. Central control and unified management were ensured by having the senior partners—members of the Medici family—in all the contracts; but the branches had autonomy, and most important, the collapse of one did not threaten others. This system of interlocked partnerships resembled a modern holding company.

Banking operations also grew more sophisticated. By the late 1300s "book transfers" had become commonplace; that is, a depositor could pay a debt without using coin by ordering the bank to transfer credit from his own account to his creditor's. At first the depositor had to give the order orally, but by 1400 it was commonly written, making it an immediate ancestor of the modern check.

Financial Practices Accounting methods also improved. The most notable development was the adoption of double-entry bookkeeping, which makes errors in arithmetic immediately evident and gives a clear picture of the financial position of a commercial enterprise. Although known in the ancient world, double-entry bookkeeping was not widely practiced in the West until the 1300s. In this, as in other business practices, Italy led the way, but these accounting techniques eventually spread to the rest of Europe.

Another financial innovation was the development of a system of maritime insurance, without which investors would have been reluctant to risk their money on expensive vessels. There

▶ **EARLY BANKERS**
This illustration from a printed Italian handbook, which gives instructions to merchants and is dated circa 1496, shows the interior of a bank or accounting house.

are references to the practice of insuring ships in the major Italian ports as early as 1318. In these first insurance contracts the broker bought the ship and cargo at the port of embarkation and agreed to sell them back at a higher price once the ship reached its destination. If the ship sank, it was legally the broker's and he assumed the loss. In the 1300s the leading companies of Florence abandoned the clumsy device of conditional sales and wrote explicit insurance contracts. By 1400 maritime insurance had become a regular item of the shipping business, and it was to play a major role in the opening of the Atlantic.

Insurance for land transport developed in the 1400s but was never common. The first life insurance contracts appeared in fifteenth-century Italy and were limited to particular periods (the duration of a voyage) or particular persons (a wife during pregnancy). But without actuarial tables, life insurance of this sort was far more of a gamble than a business.

THE ECONOMY IN THE LATE FIFTEENTH CENTURY

In the last half of the fifteenth century Europe had recovered fairly well from the economic blows of a hundred years before, and the revived economy differed greatly from what it had been. Increased diversification, capitalization, and rationalization aided production and enterprise in both countryside and city. Europe in 1500 was certainly a much smaller community than it had been in 1300. Possibly, too, the gross product of its economy may not have equaled the output of the best years of the thirteenth century. But in the end the population had fallen more drastically than production. After a century of difficult readjustment Europe emerged more productive and richer than it had been at any time in its history.

III. Popular Unrest

The demographic collapse and economic troubles of the fourteenth century deeply disturbed the social peace of Europe. European society had been remarkably stable and mostly peaceful from the Early Middle Ages until around 1300, and

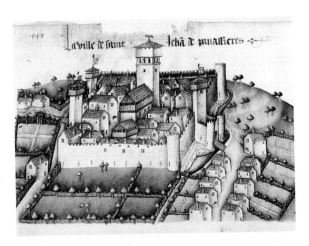

▶ VIEW OF PANISSIÈRES, FROM A FIFTEENTH-CENTURY ARMORIAL
As the population of Europe began to recover from the Black Death, one can see signs of expansion and prosperity in its most fertile regions. This fifteenth-century view of the town of Panissières, in the rich Loire valley in France, indicates that houses were again springing up and fields were being cultivated outside the walls of the fortified heart of the town.

there is little evidence of uprisings or social warfare. The 1300s and 1400, however, witnessed numerous revolts of peasants and artisans against what they believed to be the oppression of the propertied classes.

RURAL REVOLTS

One of the most spectacular fourteenth-century rural uprisings was the English Peasants' War of 1381. This revolt originated in popular resentment against both the policies of the royal government and the practices of the great landlords. The royal government through the Statute of Laborers (1351) had sought to freeze wages and keep the workers bound to their jobs. Although this policy had little practical success, the mere effort to implement it aggravated social tensions, especially in the countryside, where it would have imposed a kind of serfdom on the peasants. Concurrent attempts to collect poll taxes (flat charges on each member of the population), which by their nature demanded less from the prosperous than the humble, crystallized resentment against the government. Rich landlords did nothing to help the situation by trying to revive many half-forgotten feudal dues, which had been allowed to lapse when rents were high in the thirteenth century.

Under leaders of uncertain background—Wat Tyler, Jack Straw, and a priest named John Ball—peasant bands, enraged by the latest poll tax, marched on London in 1381. They called for the abolition of serfdom, labor services, tithes, and other feudal dues, and demanded an end to the poll taxes. The workers of London, St. Albans, York, and other cities, who had similar grievances, rose in support of the peasants. After mobs burned the houses of prominent lawyers and royal officials, King Richard II, then aged 15, bravely met with the peasants in person and was able to placate them by promising to accept their demands. But as the peasants dispersed, the great landlords reorganized their forces and violently suppressed the last vestiges of unrest in the countryside; the young king also reneged on his promises.

The peasant uprising in England was only one of many rural disturbances between 1350 and 1450, including revolts near Paris and in Languedoc, Catalonia, and Sweden. There were also such disturbances in Germany in the fifteenth century and a major peasant revolt in 1524, which was to feed into the tensions of the early days of the Protestant Reformation.

URBAN REVOLTS

The causes of social unrest within the cities were similar to those in the countryside. Governments controlled by the propertied classes tried to prevent wages from rising and workers from moving and also sought to impose a heavier share of the tax burden on the poorer segments of society. In the 1300s and early 1400s, Strassburg, Metz, Ghent, Liège, and Paris were all scenes of riots. Though not entirely typical, one of the most interesting of these urban revolts was the Ciompi uprising at Florence in 1378.

The Ciompi Florence was one of the wool-manufacturing centers of Europe; the industry employed probably one-third of the working population of the city, which shortly before the Black Death may have risen to 120,000 people.

▶ FEBRUARY, *LES TRÈS RICHES HEURES*, 1413–1416
The different labors of the 12 months of the year are depicted in this fifteenth-century book of hours commissioned by the French Duke of Berry.
Despite the snowy, barren season, the rural laborers still have to work. They gather sticks and wood and then carry them to the distant village.

The wool industry, like most, entered bad times immediately after the plague. To protect themselves, employers cut production, thereby spreading unemployment. Since many of the employers were also members of the ruling oligarchy, they had laws passed limiting wages and manipulating taxation and monetary policy to benefit the rich. The poorest workers were denied their own guild and had no collective voice that could influence the government. In all disputes they were subject to the bosses' judges and the bosses' law.

▶ **CLOTH MARKET IN BOLOGNA**
**The manufacture and marketing of textiles was one
of the main sources of wealth for the cities of
northern Italy. This scene, from a manuscript dated
1411, gives us a sense of what the cloth market in
Bologna must have been like as merchants
examined, bought, and sold various fabrics. But
ordinary cloth workers like the Ciompi rarely
shared in the wealth.**

The poorest workers—mainly the wool card-
ers, known as Ciompi—rose in revolt. They demanded, and for a short time got, several reforms. The employers would produce at least
enough cloth to ensure work, they would refrain
from monetary manipulations considered harm-
ful to the workers, and they would allow the
workers their own guild and representation in
communal government. This was hardly power
for the workers, but it was nevertheless intoler-

able to the ruling oligarchy. Because the Ciompi
did not have the leaders to maintain a steady influence on government policy, the great families
regained full authority in the city by 1382 and
quickly ended the democratic concessions. Although the Ciompi revolt was short-lived and ultimately unsuccessful, the incident is one of the
first signs of the urban class tensions that would
be a regular disturbance in future centuries.

THE SEEDS OF DISCONTENT

Each of the social disturbances of the 1300s and
1400s was shaped by circumstances that were local and unique. Yet there were similarities in
these social movements: for example, the fact that
misery does not seem to have been the main
cause of unrest. Indeed, the evidence suggests
that the conditions of the working classes in both
countryside and city were improving after the
Black Death. The prosperity of the thirteenth century, which was chiefly a prosperity of landlords
and employers, had been founded in part upon
the poor negotiating position, and even exploitation, of the workers. The depopulation of the
fourteenth century radically altered this situation. The workers, now reduced in number, were
better able to bargain for lower rents, higher
wages, and a fairer distribution of social benefits.

With the possible exception of the Ciompi, the
people who revolted were rarely the desperately
poor. In England, for example, the centers of the
peasant uprising of 1381 were in the lower
Thames valley—a region that was more fertile,
more prosperous, less oppressed and with less
serfdom than other parts of the kingdom. Also,
the immediate provocation for the revolt was the
imposition of a poll tax, and poll taxes (or any
taxes) obviously do not alarm the truly destitute,
whereas they do alarm people who have recently
made financial gains and are anxious to hold on
to them.

Causes of Revolt The principal goad to revolt
in both town and country seems to have been the
effort of the propertied classes to retain their old
advantages and deny the workers their new ones.
In the first decades after the Black Death, governments failed in their efforts to increase taxes and
to peg rents, wages, and prices at levels favorable

to landlords and employers; meanwhile, they spread hostility among the workers, who felt that their improving social and economic status was being threatened.

The impulse to revolt also drew strength from the psychological tensions of this age of devastating plagues, famines, and wars. The nervous temper of the times predisposed people to take action against real or imagined enemies. When needed, justifications for revolt could be found in Christian belief, for the Christian fathers had taught that neither the concept of private property nor social inequality had been intended by God. In a high-strung world many of these uprisings involved an emotional effort to attain the millennium, to reach that age of justice and equality that Christian belief saw in the past, expected in the future, and put off for the present.

A New Stability In the end, as labor became scarce, the rich had to offer favorable terms if they wanted tillers for their lands and workers for their shops. Thus, by about 1450, after a century of instability, a new equilibrium was emerging in European society, even if slowly and never completely. The humblest classes improved their lot and were fairly secure in their gains. Serfdom all but disappeared in the West; wages remained high and bread cheap. Life, of course, was still very hard for most workers, but it was better than it had been two centuries before. Perhaps reflective of better social conditions for the masses, the population once more began to grow, equipping Europe for its great expansion in the sixteenth century.

IV. The Governments of Europe

War was a frequent occurrence throughout the Middle Ages but was never so widespread or long-lasting as in the conflicts of the 1300s and 1400s. The Hundred Years' War between England and France is the most famous of these struggles, but there was fighting in every corner of Europe. The inbred violence of the age indicated a partial breakdown in governmental systems, which failed to maintain stability at home and peace with foreign powers.

THE FEUDAL EQUILIBRIUM

The governmental systems of Europe were founded on multiple partnerships that exercised power under feudal constitutions. The king enjoyed supreme dignity and even a recognized sacred character, but he was far from being an absolute ruler. In return for loyalty and service, he conceded a large share of the responsibility for government to a wide range of privileged persons and institutions: the great secular and ecclesiastical princes, the nobles, religious congregations, powerful military orders such as the Templars, free cities or communes, and even favored guilds such as the universities.

The growth of the feudal constitution in the eleventh and twelfth centuries had been a major step toward a more ordered political life, but it rested on a delicate equilibrium. To keep internal peace, which often meant international peace because of the confused borders of most feudal states, all members of the feudal partnership had to remain faithful to their obligations. This governmental system worked well until the early 1300s, but it could not sustain the blows it suffered during the period of social crisis. Governments had to be slowly rebuilt, though still along feudal lines and still based on shared authority. Nevertheless, many of the new governments that came to dominate the European political scene in the late 1400s conceded far more power to the senior partner in the feudal relationship, the king or prince.

DYNASTIC INSTABILITY

The forces that upset the equilibrium of feudal governments were many. One of the most obvious, itself rooted in the demographic instability of the age, was the failure of dynasties to perpetuate themselves. The Hundred Years' War, or at least the excuse for it, arose from the inability of the Capetian kings of France, for the first time since the tenth century, to produce a male heir in direct line. The English War of the Roses resulted from the uncertain succession to the crown of

▶ *Ambrogio Lorenzetti*
**THE PEACEFUL CITY (detail from GOOD
GOVERNMENT), 1338–1341**
**The effects of good government, seen in this
idealized representation of the *Peaceful City*, by
Ambrogio Lorenzetti, include flourishing
commerce, dancing maidens, and lavish residences,
as opposed to the protective towers of feudal
warfare. This fresco in the city hall of Siena was a
constant reminder to the citizens of the advantages
of living in their city.**

England and the claims of the two rival houses
of Lancaster and York. In Portugal, Castile,
France, England, Naples, Hungary, Poland, and
the Scandinavian countries, the reigning monarchs of 1450 were not the direct, male, legitimate
descendants of those reigning in 1300. Most of
the founders of new lines had to fight for their
positions.

FISCAL PRESSURES

War The same powerful economic forces that
were creating new patterns of agriculture and
trade were also reshaping the fiscal policies and
financial machinery of feudal governments. War
was growing more expensive, as well as more
frequent. Better-trained armies were needed to
fight for longer periods of time and with more
complex weaponry. Above all, the increasing use
of firearms was adding to the costs of war. To
replace the traditional, undisciplined, unpaid,
and poorly equipped feudal armies, governments came more and more to rely on mercenaries, who were better trained and better armed
than the vassals who fought to fulfill their feudal
obligations. Many mercenaries were organized
into associations known as companies of adventure, whose leaders were both good commanders
and businesssmen. They took their enterprise
where the market was most favorable, sold their
services to the highest bidder, and turned substantial profits. To hire mercenaries, and win battles, was increasingly a question of money.

Taxes While war went up in price, the traditional revenues upon which governments depended sank. Until the fourteenth century, the
king or prince was expected to meet the expenses
of government from ordinary revenues, chiefly
rents from his properties; but his rents, like
everyone else's, were falling in the Late Middle
Ages. Governments of all types—monarchies,
the papacy, cities—desperately sought to develop new sources of revenue. For example, the
papacy, because it could not rely on the meager
receipts from its lands, built a huge financial apparatus that sold ecclesiastical appointments, favors, and dispensations from normal canonical
requirements; imposed tithes on ecclesiastical
revenues; and sold remissions of sin known as
indulgences. In France the monarchy established

a monopoly over the sale of salt. In England the king at various times imposed direct taxes on hearths, individuals (the poll tax), and plow teams, plus a host of smaller levies. The Italian cities taxed a whole range of items from windows to prostitutes. Under acute fiscal pressures, governments scrutinized the necessities, pleasures, and sins of society to find sources of revenue; and surviving fiscal records indicate that, in spite of the disturbed times, they managed to increase their incomes hugely through these taxes. For example, the English monarchy never collected or spent more than £30,000 per year before 1336; thereafter, the budget rarely sank below £100,000 and at times reached £250,000 in the late fourteenth century.

This new reliance on extraordinary taxes had important political consequences. The most lucrative taxes were not limited to the ruler's own lands but extended over all the realm. Since he had no established right to these demands, he had to seek the consent of his subjects, and he therefore had to summon territorial or national assemblies of estates, such as Parliament in England or the Estates General in France, to grant new taxes. But these assemblies, in turn, often balked at the demands or offered taxes only in return for political concessions. Even in the Church many reformers maintained that a general council should have ultimate control over papal finances. The extraordinary expansion of governmental revenues thus raised profound constitutional questions in both secular and ecclesiastical governments.

FACTIONAL CONFLICTS

The nobility that had developed nearly everywhere in Europe also entered a period of instability in the Late Middle Ages. Birth was the main means of access to this class, and membership offered legal and social privileges—exemption from most taxes, immunity from certain juridical procedures (such as torture), and so forth. The nobles saw themselves as the chief counselors of the king and his principal partners in the conduct of government.

By the 1300s, however, the nobles had long since lost whatever economic homogeneity they might once have possessed. Their wealth was chiefly in land, and they, like all landlords, faced the problem of declining rents. They often lacked the funds needed for the new systems of agriculture, and they were further plagued by the continuing problem of finding income and careers for their younger sons. In short, the nobles were not immune from the acute economic dislocations of the times, and their class included men who lived on the brink of poverty as well as holders of enormous estates.

Factions To maintain their position, some of the nobles joined the companies of adventure to fight as mercenaries. Others hoped to buttress their sinking fortunes through marriage or by winning offices, lands, pensions, or other favors from governments. But as the social uncertainties intensified, the nobles tended to coalesce into factions, which disputed with one another over the control of government and the distribution of its favors. From England to Italy, factional warfare constantly disturbed the peace. A divided and grasping nobility added to the tensions of the age and to its violence.

Characteristically, a faction was led by a great noble house and included people of varying social station—great nobles in alliance with the leading house, poor knights, retainers, servants, sometimes even artisans and peasants. Some of the factions encompassed scores of families and hundreds of men and could almost be considered little states within a state, with their own small armies, loyalties, and symbols of allegiance in the colors or distinctive costumes (livery) worn by their members.

ENGLAND, FRANCE, AND THE HUNDRED YEARS' WAR

All the factors that upset the equilibrium of feudal governments—dynastic instability, fiscal pressures, and factional rivalries—helped to provoke the greatest struggle of the epoch, the Hundred Years' War.

Causes The issue over which the Hundred Years' War was supposedly fought was a dispute over the French royal succession. After more than 300 years of extraordinary good luck, the last three Capetian kings (the brothers Louis X, Philip

V, and Charles IV) failed to produce male heirs. With Charles's death in 1328, the nearest surviving male relative was his nephew King Edward III of England, son of his sister Isabella. But the Parlement of Paris—the supreme court of France—declared that women could not transmit a claim to the crown. In place of Edward, the French Estates chose Philip of Valois, a first cousin of the previous kings. Edward did not at first dispute this decision, and as holder of the French fiefs of Aquitaine and Ponthieu, he did homage to Philip.

More important than the dynastic issue was in fact the clash of French and English interests in Flanders, an area whose cloth-making industry relied on England for wool. In 1302 the Flemings had rebelled against their count, a vassal of the French king, and had remained virtually independent until 1328, when Philip defeated their troops and restored the count. At Philip's insistence, the count ordered the arrest of all English merchants in Flanders; Edward retaliated by cutting off the export of wool, which spread unemployment in the Flemish towns. The Flemings revolted once more and drove out the count. To give legal sanction to their revolt, they persuaded Edward to assert his claim to the French crown, which held suzerainty over Flanders.

The most serious point of friction, however, was the status of Aquitaine and Ponthieu. Edward had willingly performed ordinary homage for them, but Philip then insisted on liege homage, which would have obligated Edward to support Philip against all enemies. Edward did not believe that, as a king, he could undertake the obligations of liege homage to any man, and refused. Philip began harassing the frontiers of Aquitaine and declared Edward's fiefs forfeit in 1337. The attack on Aquitaine pushed Edward into supporting the Flemish revolt and was thus the main provocation for the Hundred Years' War.

Philip, a new king eager for glory, had clearly embarked on a dangerous adventure by harassing Aquitaine; and Edward, in supporting the Flemings, reacted perhaps too strongly. Their minimal concern for traditional obligations suggests that the war was mainly the result of a breakdown of the feudal constitution of medieval France in both its institutions and its spirit.

THE TIDES OF BATTLE

The French seemed to have a decisive superiority over the English at the outset of the war. The population of France was perhaps 15 million; England had between 4 and 7 million. But the war was hardly ever a national confrontation, because French subjects (Flemings, Gascons, Burgundians) fought alongside the English against other French subjects. The confused struggle may, however, be divided into three periods: initial English victories from 1338 to 1360; French resurgence, then stalemate, from 1367 to 1415; and a wild denouement with tides rapidly shifting from 1415 to 1453.

First Period   The English never fully exploited their early victories, nor did the French ever manage to undo them. An English naval victory at Sluys in 1340 ensured English communications across the Channel and determined that France would be the scene of the fighting. Six years later Edward landed in France on what was more a marauding expedition than a campaign of conquest. Philip pursued the English and finally overtook them at Crécy, where the French knights attacked before their own forces could be fully marshaled and organized. The disciplined English, making effective use of the longbow, cut the confused French army to pieces. The victory also ensured the English possession of Calais, which they took in 1347. The scenario was repeated in 1356 at Poitiers when John II, who had succeeded Philip, attacked an English army led by Edward's son, the Black Prince, and suffered an even more crushing defeat. English victories, the Black Death, and mutual exhaustion led to the Peace of Brétigny in 1360. The English were granted Calais and an enlarged Aquitaine, and Edward, in turn, renounced his claim to the French crown.

Second Period   But the French were not willing to allow so large a part of their kingdom to remain in English hands. In 1369, under John's successor, Charles V, they opened a second phase of the war. Their strategy was to avoid full-scale battles and wear down the English forces, and they succeeded. By 1380 they had pushed the English nearly into the sea, confining them to Ca-

CHRONOLOGY OF THE HUNDRED YEARS' WAR

1351 Charles IV, last Capetian king in direct line, dies; Philip of Valois elected king of France as Philip VI; Philip defeats Flemings at Cassel; unrest continues in Flemish towns.

1329 Edward III of England does simple homage to Philip for continental possessions but refuses liege homage.

1336 Edward embargoes wool exports to Flanders.

1338 Philip's troops harass English Guienne; Edward, urged on by the Flemings, claims French crown; war begins.

1346 Major English victory at Crécy.

1347–1351 Black Death ravages Europe.

1356 Black Prince defeats French at Poitiers.

1358 Peasants' uprising near Paris.

1360 Peace of Brétigny; English gain major territorial concessions but abandon claim to French crown.

1369 Fighting renewed in France.

1370 Bertrand du Guesclin, constable of France, leads French resurgence.

1381 Peasants' Revolt in England.

1392 Charles VI of France suffers first attack of insanity; Burgundians and Armagnacs contend for power over king; fighting wanes as both sides exhausted.

1399 Henry IV of Lancaster takes English throne.

1415 Henry V wins major victory at Agincourt.

1420 Treaty of Troyes; Charles VI recognizes Henry V as legitimate heir to French crown; high-water mark of English fortunes.

1429 Joan of Arc relieves Orléans from English siege; Dauphin crowned king at Reims as Charles VII.

1431 Joan burned at the stake at Rouen.

1435 Peace of Arras; Burgundy abandons English side.

1436 Charles retakes Paris.

1453 Bordeaux falls to French; English retain only Calais on Continent; effective end of war, though no treaty is signed.

lais and a narrow strip of the Atlantic coast from Bordeaux to Bayonne. Fighting was sporadic from 1380 until 1415, with both sides content with a stalemate.

Third Period   The last period of the war, from 1415 to 1453, was one of high drama and rapidly shifting fortunes. Henvy V of England invaded France and shattered the French army at Agincourt in 1415. His success was confirmed by the Treaty of Troyes in 1420, an almost total French capitulation. King Charles VI of France declared his son the Dauphin (the future Charles VII) illegitimate, named Henry his successor and re-

gent of France, and gave him direct rule over all French lands as far south as the Loire River (see Map 11.3). Charles also gave Henry his daughter Catherine in marriage.

The Dauphin could not accept this forced abdication, and from his capital at Bourges he led an expedition across the Loire River. The English drove his forces back and systematically took the towns and fortresses north of the river that were loyal to him. In 1428 they finally laid siege to Orléans, a city whose fall would have given them a commanding position in the Loire valley and would have made the Dauphin's cause desperate.

Map 11.3 THE HUNDRED YEARS' WAR
Because of their closeness to the continent and their naval power, the English were able to dominate northern France, the area which traditionally had been that kingdom's heartland. As a result, Joan of Arc's decisive victory came not in Paris but in Orléans on the Loire River—which proved to be a crucial boundary between the two sides.

JOAN OF ARC

The intervention of a young peasant girl, Joan of Arc, saved the Valois dynasty. Convinced that heavenly voices were ordering her to rescue France, Joan persuaded several royal officials, and finally the Dauphin himself, of the authenticity of her mission and was given command of an army. In 1429 she marched to Orléans and forced the English to raise the siege. She then escorted the Dauphin to Reims, the historic coronation city of France, where his crowning confirmed his legitimacy and won him broad support as the embodiment of French royalist sentiment. The tide had turned.

Joan passed from history as quickly and as dramatically as she had arrived. The Burgundians, allies of the English, captured her in 1430 and sold her to the English, who put her on trial for witchcraft and heresy (*see box*, p. 334). She was burned at the stake at Rouen in 1431. Yet Joan's commitment was one sign of an increasingly powerful feeling among the people. They had grown impatient with continuing destruction and had come to identify their own security with the expulsion of the English and the establishment of a strong Valois monarchy. This growing loyalty to the king finally saved France from its long agony. A series of French successes followed Joan's death, and by 1453 only Calais was left in English hands. No formal treaty ended the war, but both sides accepted the outcome: England was no longer a continental power.

THE EFFECTS OF THE HUNDRED YEARS' WAR

Like all the disasters of the era, the Hundred Years' War accelerated change. It stimulated the development of firearms and the technologies needed to manufacture them, and it helped establish the infantry—armed with longbow, pike, or gun—as superior in battle to mounted knights.

Parliament The war also had a major effect on government institutions in England and France. The expense of fighting forced the kings on each side to look for new sources of revenue through taxation. In England the king willingly gave Parliament a larger political role in return for grants

▶ JOAN OF ARC, 1484
Surrounded by the clerics who had condemned her, Joan of Arc is bound to the stake in this scene from a manuscript that was prepared half a century after she was executed in 1431. Despite Joan's own preference for short hair and manly costume, she is here shown as a conventionally idealized female figure.

of new taxes. The tradition became firmly established that Parliament had the right to grant or refuse new taxes, to agree to legislation, to channel appeals to the king, and to offer advice on important decisions such as peace and war. The House of Commons gained the right to introduce all tax legislation, since the Commons, unlike the Lords, were representatives of shires and boroughs. Parliament also named a committee to audit tax records and supervise payments. Equally important, the Commons could impeach high royal officials, a crucial step in establishing the principle that a king's ministers were responsible to Parliament as well as to their royal master. By the end of the Hundred Years' War, Parliament had been notably strengthened at the expense of royal power.

French Government The need for new taxes had a rather different outcome in France, where it enhanced the power of the monarchs while weakening the Estates General, the national representative assembly. In 1343 Philip VI established a monopoly over the sale of salt, laying down in many areas of France how much it cost and how much each family had to consume. The tax on salt, called the *gabelle,* was to be essential to

The Trial of Joan of Arc

The records of the trial of Joan of Arc in Rouen in 1431 give us a rare opportunity to hear her directly, or at least the words a secretary heard. Whether recorded accurately or not, her testimony does give us a glimpse of her extraordinary spirit and determination.

"When she had taken the oath the said Jeanne was questioned by us about her name and her surname. To which she replied that in her own country she was called Jeannette. She was questioned about the district from which she came.

"She said she was born in the village of Domrémy. Asked if in her youth she had learned any craft, she saw yes, to sew and spin; and in sewing and spinning she feared no woman in Rouen.

"Afterwards she declared that at the age of 13 she had a voice from God to help her and guide her. And the first time she was much afraid. And this voice came towards noon, in summer, in her father's garden. Asked what instruction this voice gave her for the salvation of her soul, she said it taught her to be good and to go to church often; and the voice told her that she should raise the siege of the city of Orléans.

"Asked whether, when she saw the voice coming to her, there was a light, she answered that there was a great deal of light on all sides. She added to the examiner that not all the light came to him alone!

"Asked whether she thought she had committed a sin when she left her father and mother, she answered that since God commanded, it was right to do so. She added that since God commanded, if she had had a hundred parents, she would have gone nevertheless.

"Jeanne was admonished to speak the truth. Many of the points were read and explained to her, and she was told that if she did not confess them truthfully she would be put to the torture, the instruments of which were shown to her.

"To which Jeanne answered in this manner: 'Truly if you were to tear me limb from limb and separate my soul from my body, I would not tell you anything more; and if I did say anything, I should afterwards declare that you had compelled me to say it by force.'"

From *The Trial of Jeanne d'Arc,* as cited in Leonard Bernard and Theodore B. Hodges (eds.), *Readings in European History* (New York: Macmillan, 1958), pp. 181–182.

French royal finance until 1789. In gaining support for this and other taxes, Philip and his successors sought the agreement of regional assemblies of estates as well as the national Estates General. The kings' reliance on the local estates hindered the rise of a centralized assembly that could speak for the entire kingdom. By the reign of Charles VII, during the last stages of the war, the monarchy obtained the right to impose national taxes (notably the *taille,* a direct tax from which nobles and clerics were exempt) without the consent of the Estates General. By then, too, the royal government was served by a standing professional army—the first in any European country since the fall of the Roman Empire.

The War of the Roses Both England and France experienced internal dissension during the Hundred Years' War. After the death of Edward III in 1377, England faced over a century of turmoil, with nobles striving to maintain their economic fortunes through factional conflicts—that is, by preying on one another. In time, these conflicts led to a struggle between two factions, the Lancastrians and the Yorkists, over the throne itself, with all English nobles aligning themselves on one side or the other. The civil war that followed is known to historians as the War of the Roses (the Lancastrians' emblem was a red rose, the Yorkists' a white rose). It lasted some 35 years, ending in 1485, when Henry Tudor defeated the

Yorkists at Bosworth Field and came to the throne as Henry VII. By this time, prosperity had relieved the pressures on the English nobles, and the people in general, weary of war, welcomed the strong and orderly regime that Henry established.

Burgundy In France, too, the power of the monarchy was threatened by rival factions of nobles, the Armagnacs and the Burgundians. The Armagnacs wanted the war with England vigorously pursued, while the Burgundians favored accommodation. The territorial ambitions of the Burgundians also posed a threat to the French monarchy. King John the Good of France had granted the huge Duchy of Burgundy to his younger son, Philip the Bold, in 1363. Philip and his successors greatly enlarged their possessions in eastern France, the Rhône and Rhine valleys, and the Low Countries (see Map 11.3). They were generous patrons of literature and the arts, and they made their court at Dijon the most brilliant in Europe. The dukes seem to have sought to establish a Burgundian "middle kingdom" between France and the Holy Roman Empire; such a state would have affected the political geography of Europe permanently and undermined the position of the French monarch. But the threat vanished in 1477 when the last duke, Charles the Bold, was killed in battle with the Swiss at Nancy. His daughter and heir, Mary of Burgundy, could not hold her scattered inheritance together, and a large part of it came under French control.

The English and French States With the loss of most of its continental possessions, England emerged from the war geographically more consolidated. It was also homogeneous in its language (English now replaced French as the language of the law courts and administration) and more conscious of its cultural distinctiveness and national identity. Freed from its continental entanglements, England was ready for its expansion beyond the seas and for a surge in national pride and self-consciousness.

France never achieved quite the territorial consolidation of England, but with the expulsion of the English from his lands and the sudden disintegration of the Duchy of Burgundy, the French king was without a major rival among his feudal

princes. The monarchy emerged from the war with a permanent army, a rich tax system, and no clear constitutional restrictions on its exercise of power. Most significantly, the war gave the French king high prestige and confirmed him as the chief protector and patron of the people.

In both France and England, government at the end of the Middle Ages was still decentralized and "feudal," if we mean by that term that certain privileged persons and institutions (nobles, the Church, towns, and the like) continued to hold and to exercise some form of private jurisdiction. They retained, for example, their own courts. But the king had unmistakably emerged as the dominant partner in the feudal relationship. Moreover, he was prepared to press his advantages in the sixteenth century.

▶ **CHRISTINE DE PISAN PRESENTS POEMS TO ISABEAU OF BAVARIA**
Christine de Pisan (1364–1430) was the author of several important historical and literary works, including a biography of King Charles V of France and *The Book of the Three Virtues*, a manual for the education of women. She is here depicted presenting a volume of her poems to the queen of France, who is surrounded by ladies in waiting and the symbol of the French royal family, the fleur-de-lis. It is significant that there were such scenes of elegance and intellectual life even amidst the chaos and destruction of the Hundred Years' War.

THE HOLY ROMAN EMPIRE

With the death of Emperor Frederick II of Hohenstaufen (1250), the Holy Roman Empire ceased to function as a major power in European affairs. The empire continued to link Germany and Italy, but real authority fell to the princes in Germany and the city republics in Italy. In 1273, after a tumultuous period known as the Interregnum, during which several rivals contended for the title, the princes chose as emperor Rudolf of Habsburg, the first of that long-enduring family to hold the office. Instead of rebuilding the imperial authority, Rudolf sought to advance the interests of his own dynasty and its ancestral possessions. His successors also tended to use the office of emperor for their own narrow dynastic advantage.

The most significant event of the fourteenth century was the issuance in 1356 of the Golden Bull, which essentially defined the constitution of the empire until 1806. Although issued by the pope, the bull reflected the interests of the leading German princes. The right of naming the emperor was given to seven electors—the archbishops of Mainz, Trier, and Cologne; the count palatine of the Rhine; the duke of Saxony; the margrave of Brandenburg; and the king of Bohemia. As the bull assigned the papacy no role in naming or crowning the emperor, it was a victory for imperial autonomy.

The Swiss An indication of the growing autonomy of regions within the empire was the emergence of the Swiss Confederation of cantons (districts), which won virtual independence in the Late Middle Ages. In the early 1200s Emperor Frederick II of Hohenstaufen had recognized the autonomy of two cantons, Uri and Schwyz, and had given them the responsibility of guarding the Saint Gotthard Pass through the Alps, the shortest route from Germany to Italy. The lands of the cantons were technically part of the ancient Duchy of Swabia, and in the late thirteenth century the Habsburg princes, seeking to consolidate their possessions in the duchy, attempted to subjugate the Swiss lands as well. To resist the Habsburg threat, the cantons of Uri, Schwyz, and Unterwalden joined in a Perpetual Compact in 1291. They formed the nucleus of what was eventually to become the 22 cantons of present-day Switzerland.

The Swiss had to fight for their autonomy, and they acquired a reputation as the best fighters in Europe. At the same time, their confederated system of government, which allowed each canton to run its own affairs, was a notable exception to the tendency, evident elsewhere in Europe, for central governments to grow stronger in the 1300s and 1400s.

THE STATES OF ITALY

Free cities, or communes, dominated the political life of central and northern Italy in the early fourteenth century. The Holy Roman Empire claimed a loose sovereignty over much of the peninsula north of Rome, and the papacy governed the area around Rome; but in fact most of the principal cities, and many small ones too, had gained the status of self-governing city-states.

However, the new economic and social conditions of the 1300s worked against the survival of the smaller communes. The economic contraction made it increasingly difficult for industries and merchant houses in the smaller cities to compete with their rivals in the larger ones. And the rising costs of war made it hard for small communes to defend their independence. In addition, all of Italian society, in both large and small towns, was deeply disturbed by factional strife that often made political order impossible.

In response to these pressures, two major tendencies became evident. Much stronger governments, amounting at times to despotisms, tended to replace the weak governments of free communes. And regional states, dominated politically and economically by a single metropolis, replaced the numerous, free, and highly competitive communes.

Milan Perhaps the most effective Italian despot was the ruler of Milan, Gian Galeazzo Visconti (1378–1402), who set about enlarging the Visconti inheritance of 21 cities in the Po valley. Through shrewd negotiations and opportune attacks, he secured the submission of cities to his east, which gave him an outlet to the Adriatic Sea. He then seized Bologna, purchased Pisa, and through a variety of methods was accepted as ruler of Siena, Perugia, Spoleto, Nocera, and Assisi. In the course of this advance deep into central Italy,

▶ **FAMILY TOWERS AT LUCCA**
This fourteenth-century view of the Italian city of Lucca testifies to the violence of factional conflict within these cities. Each major family and its leading supporters built a defensible structure, topped by an identifiable tower. Here, in a large building that surrounded a central courtyard and had its own chapel, they could find refuge from rival families and factions.

Gian Galeazzo kept his chief enemies, the Florentines and the Venetians, divided, and he seemed ready to create a united Italian kingdom.

To establish a legal basis for his power, Gian Galeazzo secured from the emperor an appointment as imperial vicar in 1380 and then as hereditary duke in 1395. This made him the only duke in all Italy, and it seemed a step toward a royal title. He revised the laws of Milan, but the chief administrative foundation of his success was his ability to wring enormous tax revenues from his subjects. Gian Galeazzo was also a generous patron of the new learning of his day; and with his conquests, wealth, and brilliance, he seemed to be awaiting only the submission of the Florentines before adopting the title of king. But he died unexpectedly in 1402, leaving two minor sons, who were incapable of defending their inheritance.

Venice Even those states that escaped the despotism of a Gian Galeazzo moved toward stronger governments and the formation of territorial or regional states. In Venice the government came to be run by a small and closed oligarchy—a group of families that dominated the Council of Ten, the body that controlled the Venetian state. Its policies were geared to preserving oligarchic rule and suppressing opposition to the government.

Whereas Venice had long devoted its main energies to maritime commerce and overseas possessions, it could not now ignore the growth of territorial states on the mainland, which might threaten its agricultural imports or jeopardize its inland trade routes. From the early fifteenth century onward, Venice, too, initiated a policy of territorial expansion on the mainland. By 1405, Padua, Verona, and Vicenza had become Venetian dependencies.

Florence While retaining the trappings of republican government, Florence also came under stronger central control. In 1434 a successful banker named Cosimo de Medici established a form of boss rule over the city. His tax policies favored the lower and middle classes, and he also gained the support of the middle classes by appointments to office and other forms of political patronage. He made peace in Italy his supreme goal and started his family's brilliant tradition of patronage of learning and the arts.

▶ INVESTITURE OF GIAN GALEAZZO VISCONTI,
CA. 1395
This contemporary depiction of the investiture of
Gian Galeazzo Visconti as duke of Milan is from
a manuscript he commissioned to commemorate
the occasion. The picture on top shows Visconti
in a white cape seated next to the emperor's
representative, who in the picture below places the
diadem on the kneeling Visconti's head. The
spectators come from all walks of life, including
bishops and soldiers carrying cannon, but the
ceremony itself takes place in front of an altar. The
margins contain such Visconti family symbols as
the eagle, the cheetah, and various fruit trees; and
the entire manuscript leaf is a rich and colorful
glorification of a central event in Visconti's life.

This tradition was enhanced by Cosimo's
grandson, Lorenzo the Magnificent (1469–1492),
who beat back the plots of other powerful Florentine families and strengthened centralized control over the city. Lorenzo's Florence came to set
the style for Italy, and eventually for Europe, in
the splendor of its festivals, the elegance of its
social life, the beauty of its buildings, and the lavish support it extended to scholars and artists.

THE PAPAL STATES
AND THE KINGDOM OF NAPLES

The popes were as concerned as the leaders of
city-states to consolidate their rule over their possessions in central Italy, but they faced formidable obstacles because the papacy was now
located in Avignon in southern France. The difficult terrain of the Italian Papal States—dotted
with castles and fortified towns—enabled communes, petty lords, and plain brigands to defy
papal authority. Continuing disorders discouraged the popes from returning to Rome, and their
efforts to pacify their tumultuous lands were a
major drain on papal finances. Even after its return to Rome in 1378 the papacy had difficulty
maintaining authority. Not until the pontificate
of Martin V (1417–1431) was a stable administration established, and Martin's successors still
faced frequent revolts throughout the fifteenth
century.

The political situation was equally confused in
the Kingdom of Naples and Sicily. With papal
support, Charles of Anjou, younger brother of St.
Louis of France, had established a dynasty of An-
gevin rulers over the area. But in 1282 the people
of Sicily revolted against the Angevins and appealed for help to the king of Aragon. For the
next 150 years the Aragonese and the Angevins
battled for dominion over Sicily and Naples.
Then in 1435 the king of Aragon, Alfonso V, the
Magnanimous, reunited Sicily and southern Italy
and made the kingdom the center of an Aragonese empire in the Mediterranean. Alfonso
sought to suppress the factions of lawless nobles
and to reform taxes and strengthen administration. His efforts were not completely successful,
for southern Italy and Sicily were rugged, poor
lands and difficult to subdue; but he was at least
able to overcome the chaos that had prevailed
earlier. Alfonso thus extended to the Mediterra-

nean the strengthening of central governments that took place elsewhere in Europe in the 1400s. The court he created at Naples was one of the most brilliant centers of art and literature of the age.

DIPLOMACY

By about 1450, Italy was no longer a land of numerous, tiny free communes. Rather, it was divided among five territorial states: the Duchy of Milan, the republics of Venice and Florence, the Papal States, and the Kingdom of Naples (see Map 11.4). To govern the relations among these states, the Italians conceived new methods of diplomacy. Led by Venice, they began to maintain permanent embassies at important foreign courts. Moreover, largely through the political sense of Cosimo de Medici, these states were able to pioneer a new way of preserving stability. The

▶ *Benozzo Gozzoli*
**PROCESSION OF THE THREE KINGS
TO BETHLEHEM (detail)**
This enormous fresco in the Medici palace in Florence, completed in 1459, gives place of honor in the biblical scene of the procession of the Magi to the future ruler of Florence, the ten-year-old Lorenzo de Medici, riding a white horse, and to his grandfather Cosimo de Medici, the founder of the dynasty's power, who is behind Lorenzo, also on a white horse.

Peace of Lodi in 1454 ended a war between Milan, Florence, and Venice; and Cosimo sought to make the peace lasting by creating alliance systems that would balance one another. Milan, Naples, and Florence held one side of the balance; and Venice and the Papal States, the other. Each state felt sufficiently secure in its alliances to have no need to appeal to non-Italian powers for support. During the next 40 years, until the French

Map 11.4 THE ITALIAN STATES IN 1454
Five major states dominated Italy after the Peace of Lodi in 1454. For the next 40 years they maintained a balance of power among themselves, dominating the few independent areas—such as Siena, Genoa, Savoy—and a number of principalities too tiny to be shown on this map.

invaded the peninsula in 1494, the balance was occasionally rocked but never overturned, and it gave Italy an unaccustomed period of peace and freedom from foreign intervention. This system represents one of the earliest appearances in European history of a diplomatic balance of power maintaining international security and peace.

V. The Church

▼

The Church as an institution also experienced major transformations in the 1300s and 1400s. It continued to seek a peaceful Christendom united in faith and obedience to Rome. But the international Christian community was in fact beset by powerful forces that undermined its cohesiveness and weakened papal authority and influence. Although the culmination of these disruptions did not come until the Reformation in the 1500s, the history of the previous two centuries made it clear that the institution was profoundly troubled.

THE AVIGNON EXILE

The humiliation of Pope Boniface VIII by the agents of Philip IV of France at Anagni in 1303 opened the doors to French influence at the Curia. In 1305 the College of Cardinals elected a French pope, Clement V, who because of the political disorders in the Papal States eventually settled at Avignon (1309). Though technically a part of the Holy Roman Empire, Avignon was in language and culture a French city. The popes who followed Clement expressed an intention to return to Rome but remained at Avignon, claiming that the continuing turmoil of central Italy would not permit the papal government to function effectively. These popes were skilled administrators who expanded the papal bureaucracy enormously—especially its fiscal machinery—but the long absence from Rome clearly harmed papal prestige.

FISCAL CRISIS

Like many secular governments, the papacy at Avignon faced an acute fiscal crisis. But unlike the major powers of Europe, its territorial base could not supply it with the funds it needed, because controlling the Papal States usually cost more money than they produced. The powers of appointment, dispensation, tithing, and indulgences were the only resources the papacy had, and it was thus drawn into the unfortunate practice of exploiting these powers for financial gain. Thus the popes insisted that candidates appointed to high ecclesiastical offices pay a special tax, which usually amounted to a third or a half of the first year's revenues. The popes also claimed the income from vacant offices and even sold future appointments to office when the incumbents were still alive. Dispensations, which were also sold, released a petitioner from the normal requirements of canon law. A monastery or religious house, for example, might purchase from the pope an exemption from the visitation and inspection of the local bishop. Tithes paid to the pope amounted to one-tenth of the revenues of ecclesiastical benefices or offices throughout Christendom. And indulgences, remissions of the temporal punishment for sin, were given in return for monetary contributions to the papacy.

These fiscal practices enlarged the popes' revenues, but they had deplorable results. Prelates who paid huge sums to Avignon tended to pass on the costs to the lower clergy. Parish priests, hardly able to live from their incomes, were more easily tempted to lower their moral standards. The flow of money to Avignon angered rulers and prompted demands for a halt to such payments and even for the confiscation of Church property. Dispensations gravely injured the authority of the bishops, since an exempt person or house all but escaped their supervision. The bishops were frequently too weak, and the pope too distant, to deal effectively with abuses on the local level. The fiscal measures thus helped sow chaos in many parts of the Western Church.

THE GREAT SCHISM

The end of the 70-year Avignon exile led to a controversy that almost split the Western Church. Pope Gregory XI returned reluctantly to Rome in 1377 and died there a short time later. The Roman people, fearing that Gregory's successor would once more remove the court to Avignon and

Map 11.5 THE GREAT SCHISM 1378–1417
The antagonisms in Europe during the Great
Schism set neighboring regions against one another
and created divisions from which the Church never
fully recovered.

thereby deprive Rome of desperately needed revenues, agitated for the election of an Italian pope.
Responding to this pressure, the College of
Cardinals found a compromise candidate who
satisfied both French and Italian interests, but the
new pope, Urban VI (1378–1389), soon antagonized the French cardinals by seeking to limit
their privileges and by threatening to pack the
College with his own appointments. Seven

months after choosing Urban, a majority of the
cardinals declared that his election had taken
place under duress and was therefore invalid;
they then named a new pope, who returned to
Avignon. Thus began the Great Schism of the
West (1378–1417), the period when two, and later
three, popes fought over the rule of the Church.

Christendom was now confronted with the
spectacle of two pretenders to the throne of Peter,
one in Rome and one in Avignon. Princes and
peoples quickly took sides (see Map 11.5), and
the troubles of the papacy multiplied. Each pope
had his own court and needed yet more funds,
both to meet ordinary expenses and to pay for
policies that he hoped would defeat his rival.
And since each pope excommunicated the other
and those who supported him, everyone in

Christendom was at least technically excommunicated.

THE CONCILIAR MOVEMENT

Theologians and jurists had long speculated on who should rule the Church if the pope were to become heretical or incompetent; some concluded that it should be the College of Cardinals or a general council of Church officials. Since the College of Cardinals had split into two factions, each backing one of the rival popes, many prominent thinkers supported the theory that a general council should rule the Church. These conciliarists, as they were called, went further. They wanted the Church to have a new constitution to confirm the supremacy of a general council. Such a step would have reduced the pope's role to that of a limited monarch, but the need to correct numerous abuses, particularly in the fiscal support and morality of the clergy, lent strength to the idea that a general council should rule and reform the Church.

Pisa and Constance   The first test of the conciliarists' position was the Council of Pisa (1409), convened by cardinals of both Rome and Avignon. This council asserted its supremacy within the Church by deposing the two popes and electing another. But this act merely compounded the confusion, for it left Christendom with three rivals claiming to be the lawful pope.

A few years later another council finally resolved the situation. Some 400 ecclesiastics assembled at the Council of Constance (1414–1418), the greatest international gathering of the Middle Ages. The council was organized in a new way, with the delegates voting as nations to offset the power of the Italians, who constituted nearly half the attendance. This procedure reflected the new importance of national and territorial churches. It enabled the assembled delegates immediately to depose both the Pisan pope and the pope at Avignon and to persuade the Roman pope to resign. In his stead they elected a Roman cardinal, who took the name Martin V. Thus the Great Schism was ended, and the Western Church was once again united under a single pope.

As the meetings continued, the views of the conciliarists prevailed. The delegates formally declared that a general council was supreme within the Church. To ensure continuity in Church government, the delegates further directed that new councils be summoned periodically.

The Revival of the Papacy   In spite of this assertion of supremacy, the council made little headway in reforming the Church. The delegates, mostly great prelates, were the chief beneficiaries of the fiscal system and were reluctant to touch their own privileges and advantages. The real victims of the fiscal abuses, the lower clergy, were poorly represented. As a result, the council could not agree on a general program of reform—a failure that illustrated the fatal flaw in the vision of conciliar rule over the Church. The council was too large, too cumbersome, and too divided to maintain an effective ecclesiastical government. The restored papacy quickly reclaimed its position as supreme head of the Western Church (*see box*, p. 344).

The practical weaknesses of the conciliar movement were amply revealed at the Council of Basel (1431–1449). Because disputes broke out almost at once with the pope, the council deposed him and elected another, Felix V, to replace him. The conciliar movement, designed to heal the schism, now seemed responsible for renewing it. Recognizing the futility of its actions, the council at the death of Felix tried to rescue its dignity by endorsing the election of a new pope, Nicholas V, in 1449 and then disbanding. This action ended efforts to reform the Church by giving supreme authority to councils. But the idea of government by representation that they advanced was to have an important influence on later political developments in Europe.

Territorial Independence   Although the popes remained suspicious of councils, they had much more serious rivals to their authority in the powerful lay princes, who were exerting ever tighter control over territorial churches. Both England and France issued decrees that limited papal powers within their kingdoms, and this policy was soon imitated in Spain and the stronger principalities of the Holy Roman Empire. Although such decrees did not establish national or territorial churches, they do document the decline of papal control over the international Christian community.

The Papacy Condemns Conciliarism

By 1460, the papacy was firmly back in command of the Church, and in that year, Pope Pius II issued a decree forbidding all further appeals above his head to a council. Decrees are known by their first Latin words, and it is appropriate that this angry denunciation of conciliarism should have been called "Execrabilis"—that is "execrable."

"The execrable and hitherto unknown abuse has grown up in our day, that certain persons, imbued with the spirit of rebellion, and not from a desire to secure a better judgment, but to escape the punishment of some offence which they have committed, presume to appeal from the pope to a future council, in spite of the fact that the pope is the vicar of Jesus Christ and to him, in the person of St. Peter, the following was said: 'Feed my sheep' [John 21:16] and 'Whatsoever thou shalt bound on earth shall be bound in heaven' [Matthew 16:18]. Wishing therefore to expel this pestiferous poison from the church of Christ and to care for the salvation of the flock entrusted to us, and to remove every cause of offence from the fold of our Savior, with the advice and consent of our brothers, the cardinals of the holy Roman church, and of all the prelates, and of those who have been trained in the canon and civil law, who are at our court, and with our own sure knowledge, we condemn all such appeals and prohibit them as erroneous and detestable."

From Warren Hollister et al., *Medieval Europe: A Short Sourcebook* (2d ed.), McGraw-Hill, 1992, p. 245.

THE REVIVAL OF ROME

When Martin V returned to Rome in 1417, the popes faced the monumental task of rebuilding their office and their prestige as both political and cultural leaders of Europe. They wanted Rome to be a major capital, a worthy home for the papacy, and not dependent on French rulers or culture as they had been for the past century. To this end, they adopted enthusiastically the new literary and artistic ideas of the Renaissance that were beginning to come out of Florence in the 1400s (see Chapter 12). The result was a huge rebuilding program that symbolized the restored authority of the popes. They sought, as one contemporary put it, "by the construction of grand and lasting buildings to increase the honor of the Roman Church and the glory of the Apostolic see, and widen and strengthen the devotion of all Christian people." One of the popes even proclaimed that if any city "ought to shine by its cleanliness and beauty, it is above all that which bears the title of capital of the universe." The building of a new St. Peter's Church in the 1400s was but the climax of this campaign of beautification, designed to assert a cultural supremacy that went along with the supremacy of the Pope's authority. At the same time, vigorous military campaigns in the Papal States subdued that difficult territory and established the papacy as a major Italian power.

It could be argued, however, that in identifying itself so closely with Rome and with Italian politics, the papacy became less universal. For all its splendor and its renewed control over the institution of the Church, it was failing to retain the spiritual allegiance of Europe, especially in the north. The popes may have succeeded in reshaping the Church into a powerful and centralized body, and in making Rome once again a cultural capital of the Western world, but the new cultural and intellectual forces that were at work in the 1400s were ultimately to undermine the centrality of the papacy to the life of Europe.

Recommended Reading

▼

Sources

Council of Constance. Louise R. Loomis (tr.). 1961.

*Froissart, Jean. *The Chronicles of England, France, Spain and Other Places Adjoining.* 1961.

*Vespasiano da Bisticci. *Renaissance Princes, Popes and Prelates.* 1963.

Studies

Allmand, Christopher. *The Hundred Years War: England and France at War, c. 1300–1450.* 1988.

———. *Florentine Politics and Society, 1373–1378.* 1962.

Brucker, Gene A. *The Civic World of Early Renaissance Florence.* 1977. Important studies of Florentine politics and society from about 1300 to 1430.

Burne, Alfred H. *The Agincourt War: A Military History of the Latter Part of the Hundred Years War, from 1369 to 1453.* 1991.

De Roover, Raymond. *The Rise and Decline of the Medici Bank.* 1963.

Eisenstein, Elizabeth L. *The Printing Press as an Agent of Change in Early-Modern Europe* (2 vols.). 1979. Provocative interpretation of the place of printing in European history.

Gillingham, John. *The Wars of the Roses: Peace and Conflict in Fifteenth-Century England.* 1981. Readable political and military history.

Gottfried, Robert S. *The Black Death: Natural and Human Disaster in Medieval Europe.* 1983. With particular emphasis on the medical consequences.

Harvey, L. P. *Islamic Spain 1250–1500.* 1990. A survey of the one non-Christian territory in Western Europe and its steady decline.

Hatcher, John. *Plague, Population and the English Economy.* 1977. Economic effects of the great mortality in England.

*Hilton, Rodney. *Bond Men Made Free.* 1979. A study of peasant unrest in the Late Middle Ages.

*Hilton, Rodney, and T. H. Aston (eds.). *The English Rising of 1381.* 1987. Collected essays.

Kaeuper, Richard W. *War Justice and Public Order: England and France in the Late Middle Ages.* 1988.

Mallett, M. E., and J. R. Hale. *The Military Organization of a Renaissance State: Venice c. 1400 to 1617.* 1984.

*Mattingly, Garrett. *Renaissance Diplomacy.* 1964.

Miskimin, Harry A. *The Economy of Early Renaissance Europe, 1300–1460.* 1969.

———. *The Economy of Later Renaissance Europe, 1460–1600.* 1977.

Monahan, Arthur P. *Consent, Coercion and Limit: The Medieval Origins of Parliamentary Democracy.* 1987.

Oakley, Francis. *The Western Church in the Later Middle Ages.* 1979.

*Perroy, Edouard. *The Hundred Years' War.* 1965. An excellent survey.

Russell, J. C. *British Medieval Population.* 1948.

Seward, Desmond. *The Hundred Years War.* 1978. Short and readable.

Unger, Richard W. *The Ship in the Medieval Economy.* 1980. The evolution of medieval ship design.

Vaughan, Richard. *John the Fearless: The Growth of Burgundian Power.* 1979.

———. *Philip the Bold: The Formation of the Burgundian State.* 1979.

*Available in paperback.

Jan Van Eyck
PORTRAIT OF GIOVANNI ARNOLFINI AND HIS WIFE, 1434
The symbolism that permeates this depiction of a husband and wife has led to the suggestion that it is a wedding picture. The bed and seeming pregnancy are symbols of marriage, and the husband blesses his wife as he bestows the sacrament of marriage (for which the Church did not yet require a priest). On the back wall, the mirror reflects the witnesses attending the wedding. Van Eyck's use of the new medium of oil paint allowed him to reproduce vividly the texture of the fur-edged robe and the glimmer of the mirror's glass.

CHAPTER TWELVE

THE WEST IN TRANSITION: SOCIETY AND CULTURE

B Y 1300 the civilization of Europe appeared to have settled into stable and self-assured patterns. The division of society into the vast majority who labored, the knights and nobles who fought, and the clergy who prayed for the salvation of all seemed accepted and secure. If this was primarily a rural pattern, into which city dwellers did not easily fit, they were no more than a minor exception. The whole society shared assumptions about religious beliefs, about the appropriate way to integrate the heritage of the ancient world with faith, about the purposes of scholarship, and about the forms of literature and art; and this has led historians to describe the outlook of the age as "the medieval synthesis." But such moments of stability or apparent stability rarely last long. Within a few generations, major changes had overtaken European society, and profound doubts had arisen on such fundamental questions as the nature of religious faith, the authority of the Church, the aims of scholarship, the source of moral ideals, and the standards of beauty in the arts. As challenges to old ideas arose in each of these areas, there was an outpouring of creativity that has dazzled us ever since. Because those who sought new answers tended to look for guidance to what they considered a better past—the ancient world, or the early days of Christianity—and sought to revive those long-lost values, their efforts, and the times in which they lived, have been called an age of rebirth, or Renaissance.

I. Italian Society

In the fourteenth and fifteenth centuries the ideas that we associate with the Renaissance flourished mainly in Italy. Before looking at those ideas, therefore, we need to understand the elements that made Italy distinctive. What possibilities arose when, in the 1300s, the two major international powers that had dominated the peninsula for centuries—the pope and the emperor—turned their attention elsewhere and gave the Italians the opportunity to shape their own destinies?

CITIES

One basic social characteristic clearly distinguished Italy from most European areas: the number and size of its cities, particularly in the northern regions of Tuscany and the Lombard plain. In 1377, for example, only 10 percent of the people in England lived in urban centers with a population greater than 3200—a percentage fairly typical for most of northern Europe—whereas in Tuscany about 26 percent lived in urban centers. The cities were large. Venice, for instance, probably had 120,000 inhabitants in 1338, and despite the plagues of the next two centuries, the city had grown to 169,000 by 1563—a figure it was not to reach again until the twentieth century.

This remarkable urban concentration affected Italian culture. The large nonagrarian population depended for its support on a vigorous commerce and active urban industries. All levels of society participated in commerce, including the great landlords, nobles, and knights—classes that in northern Europe remained mainly on their rural estates. Moreover, success in urban occupations required a level of training higher than that needed in agriculture; therefore, many Italian cities supported public schools to assure themselves of an educated citizenry. Frequently even girls were given an elementary education, since literacy was a nearly essential skill for the wives of shopkeepers and merchants. Finally, many towns were politically independent and offered their affluent citizens the opportunity to participate in governmental decisions. To many great families, such participation was essential to the protection of their interests and required a mastery of the arts of communicating with their fellow citizens. In sum, Italian urban society in the fourteenth and fifteenth centuries was remarkably well educated and committed to active participation in the affairs of business and of government.

FAMILIES

The cities were populous, but the households within them tended to be small and unstable. The average household size in Florence in 1427 was only 3.8 persons, and in some other cities it was even smaller. The low numbers reflected the numerous deaths in a time of plagues, but marital customs also had an effect. For urban males tended to be much older than their brides when they married. In fifteenth-century Florence, men tended to postpone marriage until they were 30, and some did not marry at all. Economic factors—the lengthy apprenticeships men served in urban trades, their extended absences from home on commercial ventures, and their need to accumulate capital before starting a family—delayed and sometimes prevented marriage. Florentine women, on the other hand, were, on the average, less than 18 years old when they married for the first time; the modal (most common) age of first marriage for these women in 1427 was 15 years.

Gender Roles   The result of this distinctive marriage pattern, when combined with high mortality, was that the pool of prospective grooms (men approximately 30 years old) was distinctly smaller than the pool of eligible young women (in their middle and late teens). A girl faced acute competition in the search for a husband; young women, in consequence, often entered marriage under unfavorable terms. Their families had to pay substantial dowries, and families with many daughters faced financial ruin. This was one reason why girls were married so young; their fathers or families were eager to settle their uncertain futures as soon as possible. Those who could not be married before the age of 20 had no honorable alternative but to enter a convent—which many did reluctantly. A contemporary saint, Bernardino of Siena, called the unwilling nuns "the scum and vomit of the world."

Given the wide age difference separating the spouses, urban marriages were not likely to last long before the death of the husband. Often, too, the young widow did not remarry. Florentine husbands typically tried to discourage their spouses from remarrying because widows, once remarried, might neglect the offspring of earlier unions. Thus the wills of Florentine husbands often gave their widows special concessions that would be lost on remarriage: use of the family home, the right to serve as guardians over their children, sometimes a pension. In general, after the death of a husband a woman tended to find herself suddenly in control of significant assets. The dowry that her family had paid at her marriage became her own property as a widow, and for the first time in her life she was freed from the male tutelage of a father, brother, or husband. Many widowed women relished this newfound freedom. At Florence in 1427, more than one-half of the female population, age 40 or over, were widowed. Thus the city teemed with mature women, many of them widows and some wealthy enough to influence urban culture.

Even while her husband lived, the Florentine woman was of great importance within the household. Men were likely to be occupied by affairs of business or politics, and the wife was responsible for running the household and bringing up the children. She was also usually destined for longer contact with her children. The average baby in Florence in 1427 was born to a mother of 26 and a father of 40. To many Florentines of the fourteenth and fifteenth centuries, the father was a distant figure, routinely praised but rarely intimately known; the mother dominated the formative years of the children. A friar named Giovanni Dominici, writing in the 1410s, complained that Florentine mothers were spoiling their children. They dressed them in elegant clothes and taught them music and dancing, but not rough games or sports. The result, Dominici implied, was an effeminization of Florentine culture because women, as crucial intermediaries between the generations, shaped the values and attitudes of the young. Thus the elegance and refinement that were essential attributes of Renais-sance culture seem to have been nurtured within the bosom of the urban family.

Migration The short duration of urban marriage, the reluctance of many widows to remarry, and the commitment of many girls to the convent limited the number of pregnancies. In the countryside, men characteristically married in their middle twenties and took as brides women nearer in age to themselves. Rural marriages lasted longer, and couples had more children. The city thus ran a demographic deficit in relation to the countryside. This, too, had important social consequences. The city was forced to replenish its numbers by encouraging immigration from the countryside and small towns, and this promoted both physical and social mobility, because the city often attracted and rewarded skilled and energetic immigrants. Many of the leaders of the Renaissance—Boccaccio and Leonardo da Vinci, to name but two—came from rural or small-town origins to the city to meet its constant need for immigrants. The Renaissance city was highly successful in identifying the talented and in using its human capital to best effect.

Theories of Family Life The unstable character of the urban household and of human relations within it prompted much reflection on the family. Earlier, social thinkers had viewed the family in the abstract, in terms of humanity's ultimate destiny; they said it accorded with nature and was a training ground for faith and morality, but they did not examine how it functioned in the real world. In contrast, writers of the fifteenth century in Italy were concerned about the welfare, even the survival, of families. Foremost among them was the Florentine scholar, artist, and architect Leon Battista Alberti, who in the 1430s wrote a tract entitled *Four Books on the Family*. He suggested how children should be reared, wives chosen, domestic affairs managed, and friends cultivated—all to ensure the survival of threatened lineages. There were also many books on the education of children and attempts to reform schools, all of which showed a new awareness of the special psychology of children. And the artists of the period presented young people, even the infant Christ, not as miniature adults but authentically as children, looking and acting as children do. The playful baby angels known as *putti* appear in even the most solemn religious paintings. The very fragility of the Italian urban family thus seems to have inspired a deeper appreciation for the values of family life and the contributions that are made by every one of its members, even the youngest.

LIFE EXPECTANCY

A major reason for the instability of the urban family was the high mortality in Europe during the fourteenth and fifteenth centuries. The family memoirs of Florentine merchants, which record births and deaths, suggest that life expectancy from birth for these relatively affluent persons was 40 years in about 1300, dropping to only 18 years in the generation of the Black Death, and rising to 30 years in the fifteenth century as the plagues declined in virulence. (Today in the United States a newborn may be expected to survive for over 70 years.) To be sure, the high death rates attributable to plague were strongly "age specific"; that is, they varied considerably by age. The principal victims were the very young. In many periods, between a half and a third of the babies born never reached 15. Society swarmed with little children, but their deaths were common occurrences in almost every family.

The plague took a greater toll among young adults than among the aged. In effect, a person who survived one or more major epidemics had a good chance of living through the next onslaught. Thus a favored few did reach extreme old age, despite horrendous mortalities. But young adults always faced high risks of dying. Friars who entered the convent of Sta. Maria Novella at Florence in the last half of the fourteenth century, for example, lived an average of only 20 years after entering their order (which they usually did in their late teens). Although there are exceptions, the normal adult career was short.

Leadership of the Young For this reason, in every activity of life, the leaders of the 1300s and 1400s were often very young and were subject to rapid replacement. The young were not frustrated by the survival of their immediate elders, who in other times would have clung to the available jobs. There was far less of the generational tensions and conflicts that have disturbed modern societies. Indeed, the leaders of the age show psychological qualities that may be attributed, in part at least, to their youth: impatience and imagination; a tendency to turn quickly to violence; a love of extravagant gesture and display; and a rather small measure of prudence, restraint, and self-control. High mortality and a rapid turnover of leaders contributed to making this an age of opportunity, especially within cities. Early death created room at the top for the energetic and the gifted, especially in business and the arts, where birth mattered little and skill counted for much.

The power given to the young, the rapid replacement of leaders, the openings for talent, and the thin ranks of an older generation that might counsel restraint intensified the pace of cultural change. To be sure, poor communications hampered the spread of ideas. The quickest a person or a letter could travel on land was between 20 and 30 miles per day: To get to Bruges by sea from Genoa took 30 days; from Venice, 40 days. The expense and scarcity of manuscripts before the age of printing further restricted intellectual dialogue. Nevertheless, new generations pressed upon the old at a much more rapid rate than in our own society, and they brought with them new preferences and ideas—or at least a willingness to experiment—because the individual had his or her main chance early in life and passed early from the scene.

FLORENCE AND VENICE

The two chief sources of the new ideas and art of the Italian Renaissance were its richest cities, Florence and Venice. Both were governed by oligarchies of leading families, but it was their wealth rather than their political system that set them apart, because in one city the families were in constant competition, while in the other they ruled cooperatively.

Florence Florence by the mid-1300s was the principal banking center in Europe and one of the most important producers of luxury goods. Its silks, textiles, fine leather, and silver and gold ob-

Map 12.1 **THE SPREAD OF PRINTING BEFORE 1500**
After its invention in the Rhineland, printing first spread along the rivers that were Europe's main highways. By 1500 it was concentrated mainly in southern Germany, the Netherlands, and northern Italy.

jects were much prized, and the training its guilds offered in design and craftsmanship was a major reason for the high skills of its artists. The florin, the city's gold coin, had international standing as one of the most reliable currencies of the time, and the broad contacts of its merchants gave Florence a cosmopolitan air. The citizens took special pride in the fame of two of their sons, Dante and Giotto, who during the first decades of the fourteenth century had become, respectively, the most famous poet and the most famous artist in Italy.

It was ironic that the Florentines should have taken credit for Dante, because he had been ex-iled from the city as a result of its vicious factional divisions. By the 1300s Florence had been a self-governing commune for two centuries, but it had rarely enjoyed political stability. It was ruled by a series of councils, whose members were drawn from the leading families. From time to time, however, as movements for wider representation

▶ *Giotto*
LAMENTATION
The Florentine Giotto di Bondone (1266?–1337) was the most celebrated painter of his age. He painted fresco cycles in a number of Italian cities, and this segment from one of them indicates the qualities that made him famous: the solid bodies, the expression of human emotion, and the suggestion of landscape, all of which created an impact that was without precedent in medieval art.

arose, such as the Ciompi revolt of 1378, places on the councils were opened to a broader segment of the citizenry—at times, as many as 20 percent of adult males may have been eligible for office. The volatile fortunes of the different groups did not give way to a more stable regime until the rich Medici banking family gained control of the city's government in 1434 and made sure that only people they favored were defined as eligible for government positions. Even amidst the disputes, however (and partly *because* of their competitive instincts), Florence's wealthy families eagerly provided the patronage that enabled this city of some 60,000 people to become one of Europe's most influential cultural centers in the fifteenth century.

Venice The city of Venice reached its greatest power and influence at the same time. Already independent for over 500 years, by 1400 it controlled a far-flung empire in northern Italy and the eastern Mediterranean and kept a large army and navy. Venice's wealth came from its dominance of the import of goods from Asia, notably spices like pepper and cloves, which were probably the most expensive commodities, per ounce, sold in Europe. Its wealthiest citizens also controlled its government; unlike Florence, Venice was ruled by a cohesive, rather than faction-ridden, group of some 150 families, who inherited this dominance from generation to generation. From among their number they elected the *doge*, the head of the government, who held that position for life. (To increase turnover, older men were usually elected.)

Venice enjoyed remarkable political stability. There were occasional outbursts of discontent, but usually the patricians—who stayed united, relied on informers, made decisions in secret, and were ready to punish troublemakers severely—were able to maintain an image of orderliness and justice in goverment. They were also careful to show a concern for public welfare. The chief

▶ *Antonio Natale*
VENICE ARSENAL
This eighteenth-century depiction of the huge complex that made up the Arsenal in Venice indicates some of the specialized buildings that formed the production line around the pools where the ships were built. At the back, hulls are being laid, and in the foreground, a ship is being scuttled. At the very front are the two towers that flanked the entrance gate to the Arsenal.

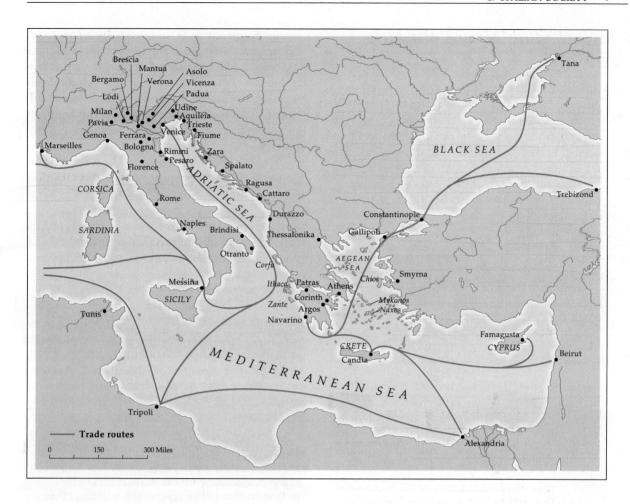

Map 12.2 THE VENETIAN EMPIRE IN THE 1400s
Thanks to its trade, Venice became a major power, controlling dozens of cities in northern Italy and the eastern Mediterranean.

support of the navy, for instance—an essential asset for a city that, though containing over 100,000 people, was built on a collection of islands in a lagoon—was a unique ship-building and arms manufacturing facility, the Arsenal. This gigantic complex, which employed over 5 percent of the city's adult population, was not only the largest industrial enterprise in Europe but also a crucial source of employment. The Arsenal could build a fully equipped warship, starting from scratch, in just one day, and the skills it required helped maintain Venice's reputation as a haven for the finest artisans of the day. Not only men but entire families came to work there; one visitor described a "hall where about 50 women were making sails for ships" and another where 100 women were "spinning and making ropes and doing other work related to ropes."

An institution like the Arsenal promoted economic and social stability by offering so many jobs and also helped improve the craftsmanship and skills of the city's artisans. In addition, because of its location and its easy openness to all who wished to trade, Venice was a meeting ground for Slavs, Turks, Germans, Jews, Muslims, Greeks, and other Italians. It was a favorite tourist spot for travelers and for pilgrims on the way to the Holy Land; it was a major center of the new international art of printing (see Map 12.1); and it was famous for its shops and entertainments. By the mid-1400s, its coin, the ducat, was replacing the florin as a standard for all Europe; and its patrons, often interested in more earthy themes than the Florentines, were promoting a flowering of literature, learning, and the arts that made Venice a focus of Renaissance culture.

II. The New Learning

▼

Although traditional forms of learning retained considerable vitality in the fourteenth and fifteenth centuries, medieval Scholasticism, with its highly refined forms of reasoning, did not adequately serve the literate lay population. The curriculum remained largely designed for the training of teachers and theologians, whereas increasingly the demand was for practical training in the arts of persuasion and communication: good speaking and good writing. Moreover, many laypeople believed that Scholastics failed to offer moral guidance. As Petrarch was to note, education should train people in the art of leading a wise, pious, and happy life. A central concern of the Renaissance was to develop a system of education that would do exactly that.

HUMANISM

One minor branch of the medieval educational curriculum, rhetoric, was concerned with the art of good speaking and writing. Increasingly, its practitioners in Italy began to turn to the Latin classics for models of good writing. This interest in the Classical authors was helped by the close relationship between the Italian language and Latin, by the availability of manuscripts, and by the presence in Italy of countless Classical monuments. It was rhetoricians who first began to argue, in the late thirteenth century, that education should be reformed to give more attention to the classics and to help people lead more moral lives.

These rhetoricians were to found an intellectual movement known as Humanism. The term *Humanism* was not coined until the nineteenth century. In fifteenth-century Italy, *humanista* signified a professor of humane studies or a Classical scholar, but eventually Humanism came to mean Classical scholarship—the ability to read, understand, and appreciate the writings of the ancient world. The aim of a humanist education was to train individuals in the classics, which offered models both of the wisdom a person needed to follow the right path in any situation and of the eloquence necessary to persuade others to that path. The modern use of the word *Hu-*

manism to denote a secular philosophy that denies an afterlife has no basis in the Renaissance. Most Renaissance humanists read the Church fathers as avidly as they read pagan authors and believed that the highest virtues included piety. Humanism was far more an effort to enrich traditional religious attitudes than a revolt against them.

Petrarch   The most influential early advocate of Humanism was Francesco Petrarca, known as Petrarch (1304–1374). He was a lawyer and cleric who practiced neither of those professions but rather devoted his life to writing poetry, scholarly and moral treatises, and letters. He became famous for his Italian verse—his sonnets inspired poets for centuries—but he sought above all to emulate Virgil by writing a Latin epic poem. A master of self-promotion, he used that work as the occasion for reviving the ancient title of "poet laureate" and having himself crowned in Rome in 1341. But he was also capable of profound self-examination. In a remarkable work, which he called *My Secret*—a dialogue with one of his heroes, St. Augustine—he laid bare his struggles to achieve spiritual peace despite the earthly temptations of fame and love. Increasingly, he became concerned that nowhere in the world around him could he find a model of virtuous behavior that he could respect. The leaders of the Church he considered poor examples, for they seemed worldly and materialistic. Convinced that no guide from his own times or the immediate past would serve, Petrarch concluded that he had to turn to the Church fathers and the ancient Romans to find worthy examples of the moral life (*see box*, p. 355).

How, then, could one be a good person? By imitating such figures from antiquity as Cicero and Augustine, who knew what proper values were and pursued them in their own lives, despite temptations and the distractions of public affairs. The period between their time and his own—which Petrarch regarded as the "middle" ages—he considered contemptible. His own world, he felt, would improve only if it tried to emulate the ancients, and in fact a central purpose of education ought to be to teach what they did and said. In particular, like the good rheto-

Petrarch on Ancient Rome

Petrarch was so determined to relive the experience of antiquity that he wrote letters to famous Roman authors as if they were acquaintances. In one letter, he even described Cicero coming to visit him. While he was passing through Padua in February 1350 he recalled that the city was the birthplace of the Roman historian Livy, and he promptly wrote to him.

"I only wish, either that I had been born in your time or you in ours. If the latter, our age would have benefited; if the former, I myself would have been the better for it. I would surely have visited you. As it is, I can merely see you reflected in your works. It is over those works that I labor whenever I want to forget the places, times, and customs around me. I am often filled with anger at today's morals, when people value only gold and silver, and want nothing but physical pleasures.

"I have to thank you for many things, but especially because you have so often helped me forget the evils of today, and have transported me to happier times. As I read you, I seem to be living with Scipio, Brutus, Cato, and many others. It is with them that I live, and not with the ruffians of today, among whom an evil star had me born. Oh, the great names that comfort me in my wretchedness, and make me forget this wicked age! Please greet for me those older historians like Polybius, and those younger than you like Pliny.

"Farewell forever, you unequalled historian!

"Written in the land of the living, in that part of Italy where you were born and buried, in sight of your own tombstone, on the 22nd of February in the 1350th year after the birth of Him whom you would have seen had you lived longer."

Petrarch, *Epistolae Familiares*, XXIV, 8. Passages selected and translated by Theodore K. Rabb.

---

rician he was, he believed that only by restoring the mastery of the written and spoken word that had distinguished the great Romans—an imitation of their style, of the way they had conveyed their ideas—could his contemporaries learn to behave like the ancients.

Boccaccio The program Petrarch laid out soon caught fire in Florence, the city from which his family had come and where he found influential friends and disciples. The most important was the poet and writer Giovanni Boccaccio (1313–1375). He became famous in Florence for a collection of short stories known as *The Decameron*, written between 1348 and 1351. It recounts how a group of young Florentines—seven women and three men—fled during the Black Death of 1348 to a secluded villa, where for 10 days each told a story. The first prose masterpiece in Italian, *The Decameron*'s frank treatment of sex and its vivid creation of ordinary characters make it one of the first major works in Western letters intended to divert and amuse rather than edify. But in his later years Boccaccio grew increasingly concerned with the teaching of moral values, and he became a powerful supporter of Petrarch's ideas.

THE CIVIC HUMANISTS

In the generation after Petrarch and Boccaccio, Humanism became a rallying cry for the intellectual leaders of Florence. They argued that, by associating their city with the revival of antiquity, Florentines would be identified with a distinctive vision that would become the envy of their rivals among the cities and states of Italy. And that was indeed what happened. The campaign for a return to the classics started a revolution in education that soon began to take hold throughout

Italy; the writing and speaking skills the humanists emphasized came to be in demand at every princely court (including that of the papacy); and the crusade to study and imitate the ancients transformed art, literature, and even political and social values.

Led by the chancellor of Florence, Coluccio Salutati (whose position, as the official who prepared the city's official communications, required training in rhetoric), a group of humanists began to collect ancient manuscripts and form libraries, so as to make accessible to scholars virtually all the surviving writings of Classical Latin authors. These Florentines also sought to reestablish in Italy a command of the Greek language, and in 1396 they invited the Byzantine scholar Manuel Chrysoloras to lecture at the University of Florence. In the following decades—troubled years for the Byzantine Empire—other Eastern scholars joined the exodus to the West, and they and Western visitors returning from the East brought with them hundreds of Greek manuscripts. By the middle of the fifteenth century Western scholars had both the philological skill and the manuscripts to establish direct contact with the most original minds of the Classical world and were making numerous Latin and Italian translations of Greek works. Histories, tragedies, lyric poetry, the dialogues of Plato, many mathematical treatises, and the most important works of the Greek fathers of the Church fully entered Western culture for the first time.

Salutati and his contemporaries and successors in Florence are often called *civic humanists*, because they stressed that participation in public affairs is essential for full human development. Petrarch had wondered whether individuals should cut themselves off from the larger world, with its corruptions and compromises, and focus only on what he called (using its Latin name) the *vita contemplativa*—the contemplative life—or try to improve that world through the *vita activa*—the active life. Petrarch's models had offered no clear answer. Cicero had suggested the need for both lives, but Augustine had been fearful of outside temptations. In the generations following Petrarch, however, the doubts declined, and the humanists argued that only by participating in public life, seeking higher ends for one's society

as well as oneself, could an individual be truly virtuous. Republican government was the best form, they argued, because unless educated citizens made use of their wisdom for the benefit of all, their moral understanding would remain socially barren. These were lessons exemplified by the ancient classics, and thus in one connected argument the civic humanists defended the necessity of studying the ancients, the superiority of the active life, and the value of Florentine republican institutions.

HUMANISM IN THE FIFTEENTH CENTURY

As the humanist movement gained in prestige, it spread from Florence to other cities of Italy. Pope Nicholas V (1447–1455), for example, founded a library in the Vatican that was to become the greatest repository of ancient manuscripts in Italy. And princely courts, such as those of the Gonzaga at Mantua and the Montefeltro at Urbino, gained fame because of their patronage of humanists. Moreover, the influence of antiquity was coming to be felt in all areas of learning and writing. Literature was profoundly influenced by the ancients, as a new interest in Classical models reshaped the form and content of both poetry and drama, from the epic to the bawdy comedy. Purely secular themes, without religious purpose, became more common. And works of history grew increasingly analytic, openly acknowledging such ancients as Thucydides, Livy, and Tacitus as their inspiration.

Education Perhaps the most direct effect was on education itself. Two scholars from the north of Italy, Guarino da Verona and Vittorino da Feltre, succeeded in turning the diffuse educational ideas of the humanists into a practical curriculum. Guarino argued for a reform of traditional methods of education, and Vittorino brought the new methods to their fullest development in the various schools he founded, especially his Casa Giocosa ("Happy House") at Mantua. The pupils included boys and girls, both rich and poor (the latter on scholarships). All the students learned Latin and Greek, mathematics, music, and philosophy; in addition—because Vittorino believed that education should aid physical, moral, and social development—they were taught social graces, such as dancing and courteous manners, and received instruction in physical exercises like riding and fencing. Vittorino's school attracted pupils from all over Italy, and his methods were widely imitated.

Ultimately, a humanist education was to give the elite throughout Europe a new way of measuring social distinction. It soon became apparent that the ability to quote Virgil or some other ancient writer was not so much a sign of moral seriousness as a badge of superiority. What differentiated people was whether they could use or recognize the quotations, and that was why the new curriculum was so popular—even though it seemed to consist, more and more, of endless memorizations and repetitions of Latin texts.

New Standards of Behavior The growing admiration for the humanists and their teachings also gave an important boost to the patronage of arts and letters. In the age of gunpowder, it was no longer easy to claim that physical bravery was the supreme quality of noblemen. Instead, nobles began to set themselves apart not just by seeking a humanist education but by winning fame through the patronage of artists and writers whose praise made their benefactors famous. Thus a new image of gentlemanly behavior, which included the qualities that Guarino fostered—a commitment to refinement, taste, and elegance as well as to courage—became widely accepted. This new life style was to be summarized and promoted in a book, *The Courtier*, written in 1516 by Baldassare Castiglione, that became a manual of proper behavior for gentlemen and ladies for centuries. Castiglione's patron, duke Federigo Montefeltro of Urbino, even had his portrait painted sitting in his study reading a book, but dressed in armor.

By the mid-1400s Humanism was a dominant intellectual force throughout Italy, and by the end of the century it was sweeping all of Europe, transmitted not only by its devoted adherents but also by a recent invention, printing, which made the texts of both humanists and ancients far more easily available. Dozens of new schools and universities were founded, and no court of any significance was without its roster of artists and

▶ *Raphael*
BALDASSARE CASTIGLIONE
Raphael painted this portrait of his friend, the count Baldassare Castiglione, around 1514. Castiglione's solemn pose and thoughtful expression exude the dignity and cultivation that were described as essential attributes of the courtier in Castiglione's famous book on courtly behavior.

writers familiar with the latest ideas. Even legal systems were affected, as the principles of Roman law (which tended to endorse the power of the ruler) were adopted in many countries. But in the late fifteenth century the revival of antiquity took a direction that qualified the commitment to the *vita activa* that had been the mark of the civic humanists. A new movement, Neoplatonism, brought to the fore the interest in spiritual values that was the heart of the *vita contemplativa*.

▶ *Joos van Wassenhove and Pedro Berruguete*
FEDERIGO DA MONTEFELTRO
This remarkable painting embodies the new ideal of the gentleman that emerged in the Renaissance. Federigo da Montefeltro was both one of the most notable warriors and one of the most distinguished patrons of learning of the age, and this portrait captures both sides of his princely image. Sitting in his study with his richly clothed son, Guidobaldo, Duke Federigo is reading a book but is also dressed in armor.

THE FLORENTINE NEOPLATONISTS

The turn away from the practical concerns of the civic humanists toward a renewed exploration of grand ideals of truth and perfection was a result of the growing interest in Greek as well as Roman antiquity—especially the works of Plato. A group of Florentine philosophers, active in the last decades of the fifteenth century and equally at home in Greek and Latin, led the way.

Ficino The most gifted of these Neoplatonists, as they are called—"new" followers of Plato—was the physician Marsilio Ficino. His career is a tribute to the cultural patronage of the Medici family, which spotted his talents as a child and gave him the use of a villa and library near Florence. In this lovely setting a group of scholars and statesmen met frequently to discuss philosophical questions. Drawn to the idealism of Plato, Ficino and his colleagues argued that Platonic ideas demonstrated the dignity and immortality of the human soul. To spread these views among a larger audience, Ficino translated into Latin all Plato's dialogues and the writings of Plato's chief followers. In his *Theologica Platonica* (1469), he made an ambitious effort to reconcile Platonic philosophy and the Christian religion.

Pico Another member of the group was Count Giovanni Pico della Mirandola, who thought he could reconcile all philosophies in order to show that there was a single truth that lay behind every quest for the ideal. In 1486 Pico sought to defend publicly, in Rome, some 900 theses that would show the essential unity of all philosophies. The pope, fearful that the theses contained several heretical propositions, forbade the disputation, but Pico's introductory "Oration on the Dignity of Man" remains one of the supreme examples of the humanists' optimism about the potential of the individual.

The message of both Ficino and Pico was founded on two essential assumptions. First, the entire universe is arranged in a hierarchy of excellence, with God at the summit. Second, each being in the universe, with the exception only of God, is impelled by "natural appetite" to seek perfection; it is impelled, in other words, to achieve—or at least to contemplate—the beauti-

Map 12.3 THE SPREAD OF UNIVERSITIES IN THE RENAISSANCE
A significant indication of the rising status accorded to learning, and the growing importance of education in general during the Renaissance, is the opening of major new universities. Even where earlier universities existed, as at Oxford, many new colleges were founded, and the number of graduates increased rapidly in the fifteenth and sixteenth centuries.

ful. As Pico expressed it, man is unique in that he is placed in the middle of the universe, linked with both the spiritual world above and the material one below. His free will enables him to seek perfection in either direction; he is free to become all things. A clear ethic emerges from this scheme: The good life should be an effort to achieve personal perfection, and the highest human value is the contemplation of the beautiful.

These writers believed that Plato had been divinely illumined and therefore that Platonic philosophy and Christian belief were two wholly reconcilable faces of a single truth. Because of this synthesis, and also its passionate idealism, Neoplatonic philosophy was to be a major influence on artists and thinkers for the next two centuries.

THE HERITAGE OF HUMANISM

Although its scholarship was often arid and difficult, fifteenth-century Italian Humanism left a deep imprint on European thought and education. The humanists greatly improved the command of Latin; they restored a large part of the Greek cultural inheritance to Western civilization; their investigations led to a mastery of other languages associated with great cultural traditions, most notably Hebrew; and they laid the basis of modern textual criticism. They also developed new ways of examining the ancient world—through archaeology, numismatics (the study of coins), and epigraphy (the study of inscriptions on buildings, statues, and the like), as well as through the study of literary texts. As for the study of history, while medieval chroniclers had looked to the past for evidence of God's providence, the humanists used the past to illustrate human behavior and provide moral examples. They also helped standardize spelling and grammar in vernacular languages; and the Classical ideals of simplicity, restraint, and elegance of style that they promoted helped reshape Western literature.

No less important was the role of the humanists as educational reformers. The curriculum they devised spread throughout Europe in the sixteenth century, and until our own century it continued to define the standards by which the lay leaders of Western society were trained. In the thirteenth century, learning was largely a monopoly of monks and Scholastics; during the Renaissance, the humanists introduced a narrow but still important segment of lay society to the intellectual treasury of the European past, both ancient and medieval. Simultaneously, they reinterpreted that heritage and enlarged the function of education and scholarship to serve human beings in their present lives by teaching them, as Petrarch recommended, the art of living wisely and well. Moreover, the fact that, regardless of religious and other divisions, men and women throughout Europe were steeped in the same classics meant that they thought and communicated in similar fashion. In spite of the continent's bitter conflicts, this common humanistic education helped preserve the fundamental cultural unity of the West.

III. Art and Artists in the Italian Renaissance

The most visible effect of Humanism and its admiration for the ancients was on the arts. Since the movement first took hold in Florence, it is not too surprising that its first artistic disciples appeared among the Florentines. They had other advantages. First, the city was already famous throughout Italy for its art, because the greatest painters of the late 1200s and 1300s, Cimabue (1240–1302) and his pupil Giotto (1276–1336), were identified with Florence. Giotto, in particular, had decorated buildings from Padua to Naples and thus gained a wide audience for the sense of realism and powerful emotion that he created; he became celebrated for an immediacy that had never been seen in the formal and restrained styles of earlier artists. Second, Florence was full of wealthy citizens who were ready to patronize art; and third, the city had a long tradition of excellence in the design of luxury goods such as silks and gold objects. Many leading artists of the 1400s and 1500s started their careers as apprentices to goldsmiths, in whose workshops they mastered creative techniques as well as aesthetic principles that informed their work when they turned to painting, sculpture, & architecture.

THREE FRIENDS

The revolution in these three disciplines was started by three friends, who were united by a determination to apply the humanists' lessons to art. They wanted to break with the styles of the immediate past and create paintings, statues, and buildings that would not merely imitate the glories of Rome but actually bring them back to life. All three went to Rome in the 1420s, hoping by direct observation and study of ancient master-

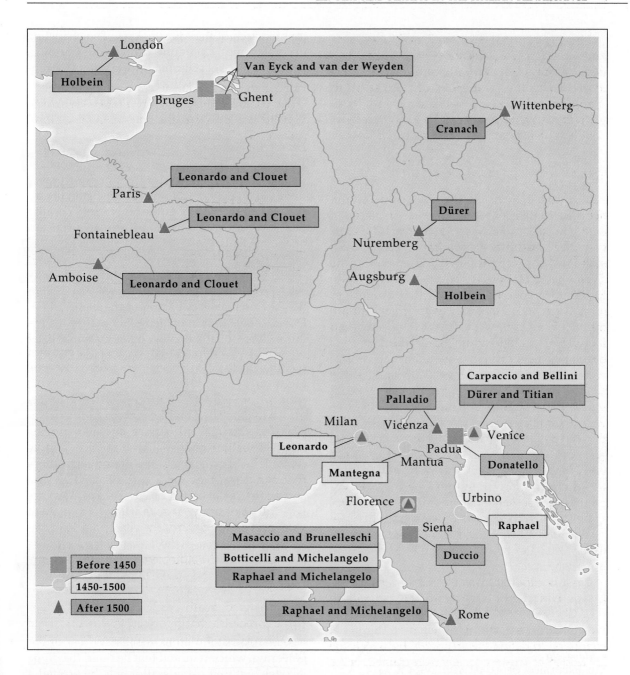

Map 12.4 MAJOR CENTERS OF RENAISSANCE ART
From its beginnings in Florence, Renaissance art spread throughout Italy, while in northern Europe, after the pioneering work of Van Eyck, the Italian influence took hold mainly in Germany and France.

pieces to re-create their qualities and thus fulfill the humanists' goal of reviving the spirit of Classical times. The locals regarded the three as rather strange, for they went around measuring, taking notes, and calculating sizes and proportions. But the lessons they learned enabled them to transform the styles and purposes of art.

Masaccio   The painter among the three, Masaccio (1401–1428), used the inspiration of the an-

cients to put a new emphasis on nature, on three-dimensional human bodies, and on perspective. In showing Adam and Eve, he not only depicted the first nudes since antiquity but showed them coming through a rounded arch that was the

▶ *Masaccio*
THE EXPULSION OF ADAM AND EVE, CA. 1425
Masaccio shows Adam and Eve expelled from paradise through a rounded archway that recalls ancient architecture. Also indicative of the influence of Roman art is the attempt to create what we would consider realistic (rather than stylized) human beings and to portray them nude, displaying powerful, recognizable emotions. This was one of the paintings that made the Brancacci Chapel an inspiration to generations of artists.

pointed arch of the Middle Ages. The chapel he decorated in a Florentine church, the Carmine, became a place of pilgrimage for painters for centuries, for here the values of ancient art—especially its emphasis on the individual human figure—were reborn.

Donatello   Masaccio's friend Donatello (1386–1466) was primarily a sculptor, and the figures he created in three dimensions had the same qualities as Masaccio's had in two. Once again the focus was on the beauty of the body itself, because that had been a notable and distinctive concern of the ancients. The interest in the nude, accurately displayed, transformed the very purpose of art, for it led to an idealized representation of the human form that had not been seen in centuries. Donatello's depiction of the biblical hero David shows him in contemplation after his triumph over Goliath. Because his story symbolized vigor and youth, the Florentines made David a favorite subject.

Brunelleschi   The most spectacular of these three pioneers was the architect Brunelleschi (1377?–1446). For decades, his fellow citizens had been building a new cathedral, which, as a sign of their artistic superiority, was going to be the largest in Italy. Seen from above, it was shaped—as was traditional—like a cross. The basic structure was in place, but the huge space where the horizontal and vertical met, the crossing, had not yet been covered. In response to a competition for a design to complete the building, Brunelleschi, inspired by what he had learned in Rome, proposed covering the crossing with the largest dome built in Europe since antiquity. Although the first reaction was that it was impossible, eventually he got the commission. In an extraordinary feat of engineering, which required that he build the dome in rings, without using scaffolding, he erected a structure that became not only a fitting climax to the cathedral but also the hallmark of Renaissance Florence and an inspiration for all architects. And the symmetrical simplicity of his other buildings shaped a new aesthetic of harmony and balance that matched what Masaccio and Donatello accomplished in painting and sculpture. In all three, the imitation of ancient Rome inspired subjects and styles that broke decisively with their immediate medieval past.

During the remaining years of the 1400s, a succession of artists, not just in Florence but increasingly in other parts of Italy as well, built on the achievements of the pioneer generation. They experimented with perspective and the modeling of bodies and drapery, so as to recapture the an-

▶ *Donatello*
DAVID, CA. 1430–1432
Like Masaccio, Donatello imitated the Romans by creating idealized nude bodies. His *David* has just killed and decapitated Goliath, whose head lies at his feet. Goliath's helmet recalls those worn by Florence's enemies, which makes this sculpture a work of patriotism as well as art. It happens also to have been the first life-size bronze figure cast since antiquity.

▶ *Brunelleschi*
DOME OF FLORENCE CATHEDRAL, 1420–1436
Brunelleschi's famous dome—the first built in Italy since the fall of the Roman Empire—embodied the revival of Classical forms in architecture. The contrast with the bell tower designed a century earlier by Giotto, with its suggestion of pointed Gothic arches, is unmistakable. The dome was a feat of engineering as well as design: Its 135-feet diameter was spanned without scaffolding, and Brunelleschi himself invented the machines that made the construction possible.

cients' mastery of depth, and they made close observations of nature. The sculptors created monumental figures, some on horseback, in imitation of Roman models. And the architects perfected the use of the rounded arches and symmetrical forms they saw in antique buildings. Subject matter also changed, as artists produced increasing numbers of portraits of their contemporaries and depicted stories out of Roman and Greek myths as well as traditional religious scenes. By the end of the 1400s, the leading Florentine painter of the day, Botticelli (1444?–1510), was presenting ancient subjects like the Birth of Venus, goddess of love, in exactly the way a Roman might have fashioned them.

THE HIGH RENAISSANCE

The artists at work in the early years of the 1500s are often referred to as the generation of the High Renaissance. Four, in particular—Leo-

▶ *Sandro Botticelli*
BIRTH OF VENUS, CA. 1480
Sandro Botticelli was a member of the intellectual circle of Lorenzo de Medici, and this painting is evidence of the growing interest in Neoplatonism at the Medici court. The wistful, ethereal look on Venus' face reflects the otherworldliness that was emphasized by the Neoplatonists; moreover, their belief in the analogies that link all ideas suggests that Botticelli may have been implying that Venus resembled the Virgin Mary as a source of divine love. In depicting an ancient myth as ancient painters would have shown it, Botticelli represents the triumph of Renaissance ambitions, and the idealized beauty of his work helped shape an aesthetic standard that has been admired ever since.

▶ *Leonardo da Vinci*
MONA LISA, CA. 1503–1505
This is probably the most celebrated image in Renaissance art. The famous hint of a smile and the calm and solid pose are so familiar that we all too easily forget how striking it seemed at the time and how often it inspired later portraits. As in his *Last Supper*, however, Leonardo was experimenting with his materials, and the picture has therefore faded over the years.

nardo, Raphael, Michelangelo, and Titian—are thought of as bringing the new movement that had begun a hundred years before to a climax.

Leonardo The oldest, Leonardo (1452–1519), was the epitome of the experimental tradition. Always seeking new ways of doing things, whether in observing anatomy or designing fortifications, he was unable to resist the challenge of solving practical problems, even in his paintings. They are marvels of technical virtuosity, which make difficult angles, tricks of perspective, and bizarre geological formations look easy. His portrait of the *Mona Lisa*, for example, is famous not only for her mysterious smile but for the incredible rocky landscape in the background. Unfortunately, Leonardo also experimented with methods of painting; as a result, one of his masterpieces, the *Last Supper*, has almost completely disintegrated.

Raphael By contrast, Raphael (1483–1520) used the mastery of perspective and ancient styles that had been achieved in the 1400s to produce works of perfect harmony, beauty, and serenity. His paintings give an impression of utter relaxation, of an artist in complete command of his materials and therefore able to create sunny scenes that are

▶ *Raphael*
SCHOOL OF ATHENS
Painted in 1510 and 1511, this fresco celebrating the glories of Greek philosophy represents the triumph of the Renaissance campaign to revive antiquity. That the Classical setting and theme could have been accepted as appropriate for a wall of the Vatican suggests how completely Humanism had captured intellectual life. A number of the figures are portraits of artists whom Raphael knew: Plato, pointing to heaven at the back, has the face of Leonardo, and the notoriously moody Michelangelo broods, with his head on his arm, at the front.

▶ *Michelangelo*
THE CREATION OF MAN
Michelangelo worked on the ceiling of the Sistine Chapel in the Vatican from 1508 to 1512 and painted hundreds of figures. None has come to symbolize the rebirth associated with the Renaissance and the power of creative genius so forcefully as the portrayal of God extending a finger to bring the vigorous body of Adam to life. Tucked under God's other arm is the figure of Eve, ready to join Adam in giving birth to mankind.

balanced and at peace. His tribute to the ancient world, *The School of Athens*, places in a Classical architectural setting the great philosophers of Greece, many of whom are portraits of the artists of the day: Aristotle, for instance, has Leonardo's face. If the philosophers were the chief glory of Athens, Raphael seems to be saying, then the artists are the crowning glory of the Renaissance.

Michelangelo For Michelangelo (1475–1564), painting was but one means of expression. Equally at home in poetry, architecture, and sculpture, he often seems the ultimate embodiment of the achievements of his age. Yet there are few of Raphael's relaxed qualities in his work. He once said that no two of the thousands of figures he depicted were the same, and one might add that just about every one of them conveys the sense of latent strength, of striving, that was

Michelangelo's signature. Although Adam, shown at the moment of his creation, has not yet received the gift of life from God, he already displays the vigor that Michelangelo gave to every human body. The same is true of his version of David, seemingly tranquil but showing his potential power in his massive, oversized hand. The sculptor relishes his ability to show the human being in full majesty, as an independent and potent individual.

Titian In Venice, the developments in art took a slightly different form. This was also a rich trading city, sophisticated, with broad international connections. But here Humanism was not so central, and the art—as befitted this most down-to-earth and cosmopolitan of Europe's cities—was more sensuous. The most famous Venetian painter, Titian (1482?–1576), depicted rich velvets, lush nudes, stormy skies, and dogs with wagging tails with a directness and immediacy that enable the viewer almost to feel them. His friend Aretino said of one of his pictures: "I can say nothing of the crimson of the garment nor of its lynx lining, for in comparison real crimson and real lynx seem painted, and these seem real." Titian was Europe's most sought-after portraitist, and to this day we can recognize the leading figures of his time, and sense their character, because of the mastery of his depictions.

STATUS AND PERCEPTION

The Artist as Craftsman To the generation of Masaccio, a painter was merely one of the many craftsmen in a city, not inherently more admired than a skilled leather finisher or mason. Like them, he was a member of a guild, he had to pass a carefully regulated apprenticeship, and he was subject to the rules that controlled his trade. Both Donatello and Brunelleschi were trained as goldsmiths, and the latter was even briefly imprisoned by his guild for not paying his dues while he was working—as an independent person, so he thought, and thus outside the guild structure—on the cathedral dome.

Given the Florentines' interest in gaining fame by beautifying their city, it was not surprising that the work of these artists should have at-

▶ *Titian*
BACCHANAL, CA. 1518
The earthy realism of Venice contrasted sharply with the idealization common in Florentine art. The setting and even the sky seem more tangible, and Titian's lush nude in the foreground (who was to be much copied) is the essence of sensuality. It has been suggested that the painting represents the different stages of life, from the incontinent child through the vigorous youths and adults to the old man who has collapsed in the back.

tracted considerable attention. But it rarely occurred to anyone in the early 1400s—as Brunelleschi discovered from his guild—that they might deserve special respect or be considered anything more elevated than middle-class tradesmen. It was true that some of them were becoming famous throughout Italy, but would that lead to a change in their social status?

Humanism and the Change in Status The answer was that it did, and again the impetus came from the humanist movement. Three consequences of the revival of antiquity, in particular, began a reevaluation of the position of the artist. First was the recognition that the most vivid and convincing re-creations of the achievements of the ancient world were being produced in the visual arts. No letter written like Cicero's could compare with a painting, a statue, or a building as a means of bringing Rome back to life for all to see—as an open and public display of the virtues of Classical times.

A second influence was the humanists' new interest in personal fame. This had been an acceptable aspiration in antiquity, but during the Middle Ages spiritual concerns encouraged a disdain for worldly matters, and so it was a problem for Petrarch to admit that, like the ancients he admired, he wanted to be famous. In the book he called *My Secret* he struggled to justify his ambition, but he could never shake free of the guilt it aroused in him. For later humanists, the doubts receded, and the princes who valued their ideas eagerly accepted the notion that they should devote their lives to attaining fame. That was what nobles had won as warriors, but now there was a more reliable way to ensure that one's name lived forever.

The New Patrons That way was provided by the third of the humanists' lessons: that the truly moral person had to combine the contemplative with the active life. A prince, therefore, ought to cultivate the fine as well as the martial arts. No aristocratic court could be complete without its poets and painters, who sang their patron's praises while fashioning the masterpieces that not only brought prestige but also endured far longer than a brief human life. As a result, if a duke or a count wanted to be remembered, it was

no longer enough to be a famous warrior; increasingly, it became essential to build a splendid new palace or have his portrait done by a famous painter. To be most like the virtuous heroes of Rome who were the society's ideal, he had to be a patron of culture as well as a vigorous leader. And this outlook was not confined to the males who now tried to unite artistic and military glory. Noble women, whose chief role had long been to offer an idealized object of chivalric devotion and who continued to struggle to gain access to education, occasionally won that struggle, and the result was a refined patronage that could be crucial in fashioning a princely image. Without Isabella d'Este, for example, the court in Mantua would not have achieved all the fame it won as a center of painting, architecture, and music. That both Leonardo and Titian did her portrait was a reflection not of her husband's importance but of her own independent contribution to the arts. Her rooms, surrounding a lovely garden, remain one of the wonders of the palace at Mantua and a worthy testimony to the fame she achieved as a patroness (*see box*, p. 369).

The effect of this new attitude was to transform the status of artists. They became highly prized at the courts of aristocrats, who saw them as extraordinarily effective image makers. Perhaps the most famous family of patrons in Italy, the Medici of Florence, were envied throughout Europe mainly because, for generations, they seemed always to be surrounded by the finest painters, sculptors, and architects of the age. Two of the Medici became popes, and they brought Raphael and Michelangelo to Rome, just as their ancestors had patronized Brunelleschi, Donatello, and Botticelli in Florence. The Church as an institution had been the main sponsor of art in the Middle Ages, but now it was the papacy in particular that promoted and inspired artistic production. In their determination to rebuild and beautify Rome as a worthy capital of Christendom, the popes gave such artists as Raphael and Michelangelo their most famous commissions—notably Michelangelo's Sistine Chapel within the Vatican. It was thus as a result of shifting patterns in the commissioning and buying of art that, as honored members of papal as well as princely courts, Renaissance artists created both a new aesthetic and a new social identity.

Isabella d'Este's Quest for Art

As the passion for art took hold, the great patrons of the Renaissance became relentless in their search for new works. None was more avid than Isabella d'Este (1474–1539), who became the wife of the Gonzaga prince of Mantua at the age of 16 and made her private suite of rooms (which she called her studio) a gathering place for artists, musicians, and poets for nearly 50 years. Her passion for art shines through her letters; in these extracts, she is pursuing both the Venetian painter Bellini and Leonardo da Vinci.

"*To an agent, 1502:* 'You may remember that many months ago we gave Giovanni Bellini a commission to paint a picture for the decoration of our studio, and when it ought to have been finished we found it was not yet begun. We told him to abandon the work, and give you back the 25 ducats, but now he begs us to leave him the work and promises to finish it soon. As till now he has given us nothing but words, tell him that we no longer care to have the picture, but if instead he would paint a Nativity, we should be well content, as long as he does not keep us waiting any longer.'

"*Two months later:* 'As Bellini is resolved on doing a picture of the Madonna and Child and St. John the Baptist in place of the Nativity scene, I should be glad if he would also include a St. Jerome; and about the price of 50 ducats we are content, but above all urge him to serve us quickly and well.'

"*Three years later, to Bellini himself:* 'You will remember very well how great our desire was for a picture painted by your hand, to put in our studio. We appealed to you for this in the past, but you could not do it on account of your many other commitments. [We recently heard you might be free,] but we have been ill with fever and unable to attend to such things. Now that we are feeling better it has occurred to us to write begging you to consent to painting a picture, and we will leave the poetic invention for you to make up if you do not want us to give it to you. As well as the proper payment, we shall be under an eternal obligation to you. When we hear of your agreement, we will send you the measurements of the canvas and an initial payment.'

"*In the meantime, in May 1504, she wrote to Leonardo da Vinci:* 'Hearing that you are staying in Florence, we have conceived the hope that something we have long desired might come true: to have something by your hand. When you were here and drew our portrait in charcoal, you promised one day to do it in color. Since it would be inconvenient for you to move here, we beg you to keep your good faith with us by substituting for our portrait a youthful Christ of about twelve years old, executed with that sweetness and soft ethereal charm which is the peculiar excellence of your art.'

"*Five months later she wrote again:* 'Some months ago we wrote to you that we wanted to have a young Christ, about twelve years old, by your hand. You replied that you would do this gladly, but owing to the many commissioned works you have on your hands, we doubt whether you remembered ours. Wherefore it has occurred to us to send you these few lines, begging you that you will turn to doing this little figure for us by way of recreation, which will be doing us a very gracious service and of benefit to yourself.' "

From D. S. Chambers (ed.), *Patrons and Artists in the Italian Renaissance* (London: Macmillan, 1970), pp. 128–130 and 147–148.

Vasari In the mid-1500s, a leading protégé of the Medici, an architect and painter named Giorgio Vasari (1511–1574), decided to try and figure out how and why it was that artists like him were being showered with privileges. He himself had been given the responsibility to design, build, and decorate a large new building in the center of the city for the government's offices—or, in

▶ *Benvenuto Cellini*
Salt Cellar for Francis I
Benvenuto Cellini, a Florentine goldsmith who challenged Giorgio Vasari's distinction between artisan and artist in his lively *Autobiography* (1562), executed this work for the French king Francis I in 1543. Juxtaposing allegorical images of the Earth and the Sea, which he presented as opposing forces, Cellini created figures as elegant as any sculpture and set them on a fantastic base of gold and enamel. His extraordinary skills indicate why so many Renaissance artists began their careers in goldsmiths' workshops.

Italian, Uffizi (now the main museum of Renaissance art in Florence). He had been knighted for his services, and he was a significant figure at the court ruled over by the Medici, who in 1530 had been named Grand Dukes of Tuscany. To understand his own good fortune, he looked to the past and wrote the first major work of what became, in his hands, a new field of study: the history of art.

Vasari put forward the idea that certain artists were filled with a special spirit, which he called genius, that set them apart from—and above—other people. The status artists had achieved was, in Vasari's account, richly deserved. They were appropriate courtiers, and even minor aristocrats, because of their genius and their fame. He wrote of them as if it were impossible to remember that, just a century before, they had been considered mere craftsman. Titian, for example, lived like a member of one of the finest families in Venice. He had a splendid house and was wel-

comed at the grandest occasions. Although he was in huge demand throughout Europe, he chose not to leave his native city. He might visit a king or an emperor, but he did not need to be attached to their court—as Botticelli was, for instance, to the Medici—in order to maintain his high standing. The acceptance of artists into the uppermost levels of society was one of the most remarkable transformations produced by the Italian Renaissance.

IV. The Culture of the North

North of the Alps the transformations of the 1300s and 1400s were not as dramatic as those that took place in Italy, but they were to have consequences after 1500 that were no less dramatic than the effects of Humanism, Neoplatonism, and the social changes of the south. This area of Europe did not have the many large cities and the high percentages of urban dwellers that were crucial to the humanist movement in Italy. Nor did the physical monuments and languages of northern Europe offer ready reminders of the Classical heritage. Humanism and the revival of Classical learning—with its literate, trained laity—did not come to the north until the last decade of the fifteenth century. But here, where the princely court rather than the city, and the knight rather than the merchant, dominated cultural life, there were other vital shifts in outlook.

CHIVALRY

In 1919 a Dutch historian, Johan Huizinga, described northern European culture in the 1400s and 1500s not as a renaissance but as the decline of medieval civilization. The stimulating book in which he made that argument, *The Waning of the Middle Ages*, focused primarily on the court of the dukes of Burgundy, who were among the wealthiest and most powerful princes of the north. Huizinga found tension and frequent violence in this society, with little of the serenity that had marked the thirteenth century. Instead, writers and artists seemed to have little grasp on reality and displayed deep emotional instability. Although many now consider Huizinga's interpretation exaggerated, his analysis clearly contains much that is accurate.

The poor grasp of reality that Huizinga noted is evident in the extravagant cultivation of the notion of chivalry. Militarily, the knight was becoming less important than the foot soldier armed with longbow, pike, or firearms. But the noble classes of the north continued to pretend that knightly virtues governed all questions of state and society; they discounted such lowly considerations as money, arms, number of forces, supplies, and the total resources of countries in deciding the outcome of wars. For example, before the Battle of Agincourt, one knight told the French King Charles that he should not use contingents from the Parisian townsfolk because that would give his army an unfair numerical advantage; the battle should be decided strictly on the basis of chivalrous valor.

Bravery and Display   This was the age of the perfect knight and the "grand gesture." King John of Bohemia insisted that his soldiers lead him to the front rank of battle, so that he could strike at the enemy even though he was blind. The feats of renowned knights won the admiration of chroniclers but affected the outcome of battle hardly at all. And the reason for the foundation of new orders of chivalry—notably the Knights of the Garter in England and the Burgundian Knights of the Golden Fleece—was that these orders would reform the world by cultivating knightly virtues.

Princes rivaled one another in the sheer glitter of their arms and the splendor of their tournaments. They waged wars of dazzlement, seeking to confound rivals and confirm friends with spectacular displays of gold, silks, and tapestries. Court ceremony was marked by excess, as were the chivalric arts of love. A special order was founded for the defense of women, and knights frequently took lunatic oaths to honor their ladies, such as keeping one eye closed for weeks. Obviously people rarely made love or war in this artificial way. But they still drew satisfaction in dreaming about the possibilities for love and war if this sad world were only a perfect place.

THE CULT OF DECAY

Huizinga called the extravagant life style of the northern courts the "cult of the sublime," or the impossibly beautiful. But he also noted that both knights and commoners showed a morbid fascination with death and its ravages. Reminders of the ultimate victory of death and treatments of decay are frequent in both literature and art. One popular artistic motif was the *danse macabre*, or dance of death, depicting people from all walks of life—rich and poor, clergy and laity, good and bad—dancing with a skeleton. Another melancholy theme favored by artists across Europe was the Pietà—the Virgin weeping over her dead son.

This morbid interest in death and decay in an age of plague was not the result of lofty religious sentiment. The obsession with the fleetingness of material beauty in fact indicated how attached people were to earthly pleasures; it was a kind of inverse materialism. Above all, the gloom reflected a growing religious dissatisfaction. In the 1200s Francis of Assisi addressed death as a sister; in the fourteenth and fifteenth centuries people apparently regarded it as a ravaging, indomitable fiend. Clearly (as Petrarch, too, had noted) the Church was failing to provide consolation to many of its members, and a religion that fails to console is a religion in crisis.

The Devil   Still another sign of the unsettled religious spirit of the age was a fascination with the devil, demonology, and witchcraft. The most enlightened scholars of the day argued at length about whether witches could ride through the air on sticks and about their relations with the devil. One of the more notable witch trials of Western history was held at Arras in 1460, when scores of people were accused of participating in a witches' sabbath, giving homage to the devil, and having sexual intercourse with him. In 1486 two inquisitors who had been authorized by the pope to prosecute witches published the *Malleus Maleficarum* (hammer of witches), which defined witchcraft as heresy and became the standard handbook for prosecutors. This fear of the devil and interest in occult arts among all levels of society were departures from the serene, confident religion of the thirteenth century.

Relics At the same time, there was a growing fascination with concrete religious images. The need to have immediate, physical contact with the objects of religious devotion added to the popularity of pilgrimages and stimulated the obsession with the relics of saints. These were usually fake, but they became a major commodity in international trade. Some princes accumulated collections of relics numbering in the tens of thousands.

Huizinga saw these aspects of northern culture as signaling the disintegration of the cultural synthesis of the Middle Ages. Without a disciplined and unified view of the world, attitudes toward war, love, and religion lost balance, and disordered behavior followed. This culture was not young and vigorous but old and dying. However, this concept of decadence must be used with caution. Certainly this was a psychologically disturbed world that had lost the self-confidence of the thirteenth century; but these supposedly decadent people, though dissatisfied, were also passionately anxious to find solutions to the tensions that unsettled them. We need to recall that passion when trying to understand the appeal and the power behind other cultural movements—lay piety, northern Humanism, and efforts for religious reform.

CONTEMPORARY VIEWS OF NORTHERN SOCIETY

Froissart Huizinga wrote about chivalric society from the perspective of the twentieth century. One of the best contemporary historians of that society was Jean Froissart (1333?–1400?) of Flanders, who traveled widely across England and the continent, noting carefully the exploits of valiant men. His chronicles, which survey the years 1325 to 1400, give the richest account of the first half of the Hundred Years' War, and he has no equal among medieval chroniclers for colorful, dramatic narration. Nonetheless, Froissart seems overly preoccupied with chivalric society; his narrative treats peasants and townspeople with contempt, or simply ignores them. Yet these emphases suited his purpose, which was, as he put it, to record the wars of his day, lest "the deeds of present champions should fade into oblivion."

Langland The works of two contemporary English writers give a broader picture of northern society in the fourteenth century. One of them, a poet known as William Langland, offered the viewpoint of the humbler classes. His *Vision of Piers Plowman*, probably written about 1360, is one of the most remarkable works of the age. The poem gives a loosely connected account of 11 visions, each of which is crowded with allegorical figures and is filled with spirited comment about the various classes of people, the impact of plague and war on society, and the failings of the Church.

Chaucer Geoffrey Chaucer (1340?–1400) came from a middle-class background; his father was a London vintner, and he himself was a soldier, diplomat, and government official. His *Canterbury Tales*, written in the 1390s, is the greatest work of imaginative literature of the late fourteenth century. It recounts the pilgrimage of some 30 persons to the tomb of St. Thomas Becket at Canterbury. For entertainment on the road, each pilgrim agrees to tell two stories. Chaucer's lively portraits provide a rich tapestry of English society, especially in its middle ranges. The stories also sum up the moral and social ills of the day. His robust monk, for example, ignores the Benedictine rule; his friar is more interested in donations than in the cure of souls; his pardoner knowingly hawks fraudulent relics; and the wife of Bath complains of prejudice against women. But Chaucer's picture remains balanced and good-humored; he praises the student of Oxford, who would gladly learn and gladly teach, and the rural parson, who cares for his flock while others search out benefices to the neglect of the faithful. Apart from the grace of his poetry, Chaucer had the ability to delineate character and spin a lively narrative. The *Canterbury Tales* is a masterly portrayal of human personalities and human behavior that can delight readers in any age.

THE FINE ARTS

The leaders of the transformation in both the style and the status of artists in the 1400s were mainly Italians. But there were also major advances in northern Europe. Indeed, oil painting—

on wood or canvas—was invented in the Netherlands, and its first great exponent, Jan Van Eyck, a contemporary of Donatello, revealed both the similarities and the differences between north and south. Van Eyck was less interested in idealization than the Florentines and more fascinated with the details of the physical world. One sees almost every thread in a carpet. But his portrait of an Italian couple, the Arnolfinis, is shot through with religious symbolism as well as a sly sense of humor about sex and marriage. The dog is a sign of fidelity, and the carving on the bedpost is of St. Margaret, the patron saint of childbirth; but the single candle is what newlyweds are supposed to keep burning on their wedding night, and the grinning carved figures behind their clasped hands are a wry comment on their marriage. The picture displays a combination of earthiness and piety that places it in a tradition unlike any that one finds in Italy (see p. 346).

Dürer The leading northern artist of the period of the High Renaissance was a German, Albrecht Dürer, who deliberately sought to blend southern and northern styles. He made two trips to Venice, and the results were clear in a self-portrait that shows him as a fine gentleman, painted in the Italian style. But he continued, especially in the engravings that made him famous, to emphasize the detailed depiction of nature and the religious purposes that were characteristic of northern art.

Dürer refused to break completely with the craft origins of his vocation. He knew, from his visits to Venice, that Italian painters could live like lords, and he was invited by the Holy Roman Emperor to join his court. But he preferred to remain in his home city of Nuremberg, earning his living more through the sale of his prints than from the stipends he was offered by patrons. Indeed, he became a highly successful entrepreneur, creating different kinds of prints for different markets—the elite liked elegant and expensive copper engravings, while others preferred cruder but cheaper woodcuts—and producing a best-seller in a book of illustrations of the Apocalypse. Working with his wife, who was a highly effective seller of his prints, he seemed as much engaged in business as in art.

▶ *Albrecht Dürer*
THE FOUR HORSEMEN
OF THE APOCALYPSE
The best-seller Dürer published in 1498, *The Apocalypse*, has the text of the biblical account of the apocalypse on one side and full-page woodcuts on the other. The four horsemen who will wreak vengeance on the damned during the final Day of Judgment are Conquest holding a bow, War holding a sword, Famine or Justice holding scales, and Death or Plague riding a pale horse and trampling a bishop.

MUSIC

Interestingly, the process that was at work in the visual arts had similar effects in music, which again had been created primarily for liturgical purposes in the Middle Ages. In the Renaissance, musicians became as prized as artists at princely courts, and their growing professionalism was demonstrated by the organists and choir singers hired by churches, the trumpeters employed by cities for official occasions, and the composers and performers who joined the households of the wealthy. Musical notation became standardized, and instruments became more diverse as old ones were improved and new ones—such as the viol, the oboe, and the clavichord—were invented.

Unlike the visual arts, the chief musical center of Europe around 1500 was in the Low Countries, not Italy. The choirmasters of cathedral towns like Bruges employed professional singers who brought the traditional choral form of four-part polyphony (that is, four different lines playing against one another) to new levels. This complex vocal harmony had no need of instrumental accompaniment; as a result, freed from their usual subservience to the voice, instruments could be developed in new ways. The greatest masters of the time, Guillaume Dufay and Josquin des Prez, excelled in secular as well as religious music, and theirs was one field of creativity in which new techniques and ideas flowed mainly from the north to Italy, not the other way around.

V. Scholastic Philosophy, Religious Thought, and Piety

In theology, Scholasticism retained its hold even as Humanism swept the literary world. But it was not the Scholasticism of the thirteenth century, of Thomas Aquinas, which asserted that human reason could construct a universal philosophy that did justice to all truths and reconciled all apparent conflicts among them. Nor did the traditional acceptance of ecclesiastical law continue, with its definition of Christian obligations and the Christian life in terms of precise rules of behavior rather than interior spirit. This style of thinking changed as the Scholastics of the 1400s and 1500s were drawn to analysis (breaking apart) rather than synthesis (putting together) in

their examinations of philosophical and theological statements. Many of them no longer shared Aquinas' confidence in human reason, and they hoped to repair his synthesis or to replace it with new systems that, though less comprehensive, could at least be more easily defended in an age growing increasingly doubtful about reason. Piety changed too, as more and more Christian leaders sought ways of deepening interior, mystical experience.

THE "MODERN WAY"

The followers of Aquinas remained active in the schools, but the most original of the Scholastics in the fourteenth century took a different approach to their studies. They were known as *nominalists*, because they focused on the way we describe the world—the names (in Latin *nomina*) that we give to things—rather than on its reality. The nominalists denied the existence, or at least the knowability, of universal forms—"manness," "dogness," and the like. The greatest among them was the English Franciscan William of Ockham (1300?–1349?), and the fundamental principle of his logical analysis later came to be called *Ockham's razor*. It can be stated in various ways, but essentially it affirms that between alternative explanations for the same phenomenon, the simpler is always to be preferred.

Ockham   On the basis of this "principle of parsimony," Ockham attacked the traditional focus of philosophy on ideal forms, which required Aquinas to argue that all individual beings had to be understood as reflections of their universal forms. The simplest way to explain the existence of any specific object, Ockham said, is just to affirm that it exists. The mind can detect resemblances among objects and form general concepts about them; these concepts can then be examined in coherent and logical ways. But they offer no certainty that Aquinas' ideal forms—the grand principles of unity like "manness" that all individual beings and objects reflect—actually exist.

The area of reality in which the mind functions is thus severly limited. The universe, as far as human reason can detect, is a collection of separate individual beings, not a hierarchy of ideal forms. The proper way to deal with this universe is by direct experience, not by speculating about ideal or abstract natures. This theology, based on observation and reason, was obviously rather limited. Ockham believed that one could still prove the existence of some necessary principles in the universe, but he thought human beings could know very little about the ultimate necessary principle, God.

Nominalist Theology   Ockham and many of his contemporaries insisted on the total power of God and emphasized humanity's absolute dependence on him. God's freedom allowed him, if he chose, to reward vice or punish virtue. But if God was free to act in erratic ways, how could there be a stable system of dogma, a fixed theology or ethics? To escape this dilemma, the nominalists made a crucial distinction between the absolute and the ordained power of God. With his absolute power, God could act in any way he chose. But through a covenant, or agreement, God assures people that he will act in consistent and predictable ways. Given these assumptions, theology becomes the study not of metaphysics but of God's will and covenant regarding the human race.

Nominalists thus rejected Aquinas' high assessment of human powers and his confident belief in the ordered and knowable structure of the natural world. Living in a disturbed, pessimistic age, they reflected the crisis of confidence in natural reason and human capability that is a major feature of the cultural history of the north in these years.

Nominalists enjoyed wide popularity in the universities, and Ockhamite philosophy, in particular, came to be known as the *via moderna* ("modern way"). Although nominalists and humanists were frequently at odds, they did share a dissatisfaction with aspects of the medieval intellectual tradition, especially the speculative abstractions of medieval thought; and both advocated approaches to reality that concentrated on the concrete and the present and demanded a strict awareness of method.

SOCIAL AND SCIENTIFIC THOUGHT

Marsilius   The belief of the nominalists that reality was to be found not in abstract forms but in concrete objects had important implications for social thought. Among social thinkers influenced by nominalism, the most remarkable was Marsilius of Padua, an Italian lawyer who served at the French royal court. In 1324 he wrote a book, *Defender of Peace*, which attacked papal authority and supported lay sovereignty within the Church. His purpose was obviously to endorse the independent authority of his patron, the king of France, who was engaged in a running battle with the pope. But his work had wider implications. Using nominalist principles, Marsilius argued that the reality of the Christian community, like the reality of the universe, consists of the aggregate of all its parts. The sovereignty of the Church thus belongs to its membership, which alone can define the collective will of the community.

Marsilius is sometimes described as one of the first theorists of the modern concept of sovereignty, and he certainly endorsed secular authority. He maintained that only regulations supported by force are true law, and that therefore the enactments of the Church do not bind because they are not supported by coercive force. The Church has no right to power or to property and is entirely subject to the sovereign will of the state, which is indivisible, absolute, and unlimited. *Defender of Peace* is noteworthy not only for its radical ideas but also for its reflection of the deep dissatisfactions in medieval society. Marsilius and others revealed a hostile impatience with the papal and clerical domination of Western political life. They wanted the guidance of the Church and the Christian community to rest with laypeople. In this respect at least, the book was a prophecy of things to come.

Nature   In studies of nature, a few nominalists at Paris and Oxford in the fourteenth century took the first hesitant steps toward a criticism of the Aristotelian world system that had dominated European studies of physics since antiquity. At the University of Paris, for example, Jean Buridan proposed an important revision in Aristotle's theory of motion. If, as Aristotle had said, all objects are at rest in their natural state, what keeps an arrow flying after it leaves the bow? Aristotle had reasoned rather lamely that the arrow disturbs the air through which it passes and that it is this disturbance that keeps pushing the arrow forward.

But this explanation did not satisfy the nominalists. Buridan suggested that the movement of the bow lends the arrow a special quality of motion, an "impetus," which stays with it permanently unless removed by the resistance of the air. In addition, Buridan and other fourteenth-century nominalists theorized about the acceleration of falling objects and made some attempt to describe this phenomenon in mathematical terms. Although they were often inadequate or inaccurate, these attempts at new explanations started the shift away from an unquestioned acceptance of ancient systems (such as Aristotle's) that was to climax, 300 years later, in the scientific revolution.

The humanists also helped to prepare the way for scientific advance. Not only did they rediscover important ancient writers whose works had been forgotten, but their skills in textual and literary criticism taught people to look with greater precision at works inherited from the past. As more of the classics became available, it became apparent that ancient authors did not always speak in unison. Could they, therefore, always be correct? Furthermore, the idealism of Plato and the number mysticism of Pythagoras suggested that unifying forms and harmonies lay behind the disparate data of experience and observation. Once this assumption took hold, it was soon being argued that perhaps the cosmic harmonies might be described in mathematical terms.

STYLES OF PIETY

The natural world was never a central object of study in the fourteenth and fifteenth centuries, because theology remained the queen of the sciences. Within the world of faith, however, important changes began to take place as new forms of piety and religious practice appeared in order to meet the needs of laypeople. Where once praying for the salvation of the community had been considered the province of the clergy, it was now increasingly felt that each individual ought to take responsibility for seeking the favor of God.

Lay Mysticism and Piety One consequence was that mysticism—an interior sense of the direct presence and love of God—which previously had been characteristic only of monastic religious life, began to move out of the monasteries in the thirteenth century. The prime mission of the Franciscans and the Dominicans was preaching to the laity, and increasingly they were communicating some of the satisfactions of mystical religion. Laypeople wishing to remain in the outside world could join special branches of the Franciscans or Dominicans known as third orders. Confraternities, which were religious guilds founded largely for laypeople, grew up in the cities and, through common religious services and programs of charitable activities, tried to deepen the spiritual lives of their members. Humanism had strong overtones of a movement for lay piety. And hundreds of devotional and mystical works were written for laypeople to teach them how to feel repentance, not just how to define it. Translations of the Scriptures into vernacular languages also appeared, though the Church disapproved of such efforts and the high cost of manuscripts before the age of printing severely limited their circulation.

This growth of lay piety was, in essence, an effort to put at the disposal of all what hitherto had been restricted to a spiritual elite. Frightened by the disasters of the age, people hungered for emotional reassurance, for evidence of God's love and redeeming grace within them. Moreover, the spread of education among the laity, at least in the cities, made people discontented with empty forms of religious ritual.

FEMALE PIETY

The commitment to personal piety among the laity was particularly apparent among women. It is significant that, whereas male saints outnumbered females in the years between 1000 and 1150 by 12 to 1, in the years 1348 to 1500 the ratio dropped to 2.74 to 1. Moreover, the typical female saints of the later Middle Ages were no longer queens, princesses, and abbesses. They were mystics and visionaries, ordinary yet charismatic people who gained the attention of the Church and the world by the power of their message and the force of their own personalities. Catherine of Siena (1347–1380), for example, was the youngest of the 25 children of a humble Italian dyer. Her reputation for holiness attracted a company of followers from as far off as England, and she wrote (or dictated, for she probably couldn't write) devotional tracts that are monuments of Italian literature. Similar charismatic qualities made a simple Englishwoman, Margery Kempe, famous for her visions and her piety.

Women who out of poverty or preference lived a religious life outside convents became numerous, especially in towns. Some lived with their families, and others eked out a living on the margins of society. Still others lived in spontaneously organized religious houses—called Beguines in northern Europe—where they shared all tasks and property. The Church was suspicious of these women professing a religious life outside convents, without an approved rule. But the movement was too large for the Church to suppress or control. And many of them came to be particularly identified with one of the most powerful forms of lay piety in this period, mysticism.

THE MYSTICS

It was appropriate that one of the most active centers of the new lay piety should have been the Rhine valley, a region that was especially noted for its remarkable mystics. The most famous was the Dominican Meister Eckhart (1260?–1327?), a spellbinding preacher and a devoted student of Aquinas, who sought to bring his largely lay listeners into a mystical confrontation with God. Believers, he maintained, should cultivate the "divine spark" that is in every soul. To achieve this, they had to banish all thought from their minds and seek to attain a state of pure passivity. If they succeeded, God would come and dwell within them. Eckhart stressed the futility of dogma and, implicitly, traditional acts of piety. God is too great for such categories and cannot be moved by conventional piety.

Brethren of the Common Life Just as the nominalists argued for philosophical reasons that God is unknowable, so the mystics dismissed the value of formal knowledge and stressed the need

▶ *Pisan Artist of XIV Century*
THE MYSTIC MARRIAGE OF CATHERINE OF SIENA
Catherine of Siena was a nun who was known for her efforts to return the papacy to Rome. Part of the reason for her sainthood was that, like Joan of Arc, she experienced visions from an early age. She is shown here with her symbol, the lily, in a scene from one of her visions. About to enter into a mystic marriage with Christ, she is accepting the wedding ring directly from him. Note that in the Renaissance, wedding rings were often placed on the third finger.

for love and an emotional commitment to God and his attributes. Perhaps the most influential of them was Gerhard Groote of Holland. Groote wrote sparingly, exerting his influence over his followers largely through his personality. After his death in 1384 his disciples formed a religious congregation known as the Brethren of the Common Life. Taking education as their principal task, they founded schools in Germany and the Low Countries that imparted a style of lay piety known as the *devotio moderna* (modern devotion). Later reformers, such as Erasmus of Rotterdam and Martin Luther, were to be among their pupils.

Thomas à Kempis   The richest statement of the *devotio moderna* appeared about 1425 in *The Imitation of Christ*, a small devotional manual attributed to Thomas à Kempis, a member of the Brethren of the Common Life. *The Imitation of Christ* says almost nothing about fasting, pilgrimages, or other traditional acts of private piety. Instead, it emphasizes interior experience as essential to religious life. The believer, it argued, needed only to emulate the life of Jesus. The book's ethical and social consciousness is also unusual. Powerful interior faith leads not to extreme acts of personal expiation but to highly ethical behavior: "First, keep yourself in peace, and then you shall be able to bring peace to others."

Features of Lay Piety   The new lay piety was by no means a revolutionary break with the medieval Church, but it implicitly discounted the importance of many traditional institutions and practices. In this personal approach to God there was no special value in the monastic vocation. As Erasmus would later argue, what was good in monasticism should be practiced by every Christian. Stressing simplicity and humility, the new lay piety was reacting against the pomp and splendor that had come to surround popes and prelates and to mark religious ceremonies. Likewise, the detailed rules for fasts, abstinences, and devotional exercises; the cult of the saints and their relics; and the traffic in indulgences and pardons all seemed peripheral to true religious needs. Without the proper state of soul, these traditional acts of piety were meaningless; with the proper state, every act was worship.

This new lay piety, emerging as it did out of medieval religious traditions, was clearly a preparation for the reformations of faith that took place in the sixteenth century among both Protestants and Catholics. It helped produce a more penetrating faith at a time when the formal beliefs of the Middle Ages, for all their grandeur and logical intricacies, no longer fully satisfied the religious spirit and were leaving hollows in the human heart.

Although the *devotio moderna* was a religious movement and had little regard for humanist learning, it shared Humanism's distaste for the abstractions and intellectual arrogance of the Scholastics and the humanists' belief that a wise and good person will cultivate humility and maintain toward the profound questions of religion a "learned ignorance." Moreover, both movements addressed their message primarily to laypeople, in order to help them lead a higher moral life. The humanists, of course, drew their chief inspiration from the works of pagan and Christian antiquity, whereas the advocates of the new lay piety looked almost exclusively to Scripture. But the resemblances were close enough for scholars like Erasmus and Thomas More, writing in the early 1500s, to combine elements from both in the movement known as Christian Humanism.

MOVEMENTS OF DOCTRINAL REFORM

The effort to reform the traditions of medieval Christianity also led to open attacks on the religious establishment—fueled, of course, by antagonism toward the papacy and corruption in the Church and by the larger tensions of this troubled epoch. Above all, these attacks gained support because the Church remained reluctant to adapt its organization and teachings to the demands of a changing world.

Wycliffe   The most prominent of the assaults of the 1300s was launched by an Englishman, John Wycliffe (1320?–1384), a clergyman who taught at Oxford University. He argued that the Church had become too remote from the people, and he wanted its doctrines simplified. To this end, he sought a more direct reliance on the Bible itself (which he suggested having translated into English so as to make it easier to understand) and less power for priests. Beyond his unease over the Church's remoteness from ordinary believers, he may have had political reasons (and thus support) for his stand. He was close to members of the royal court, who were increasingly resistant to papal demands and who were troubled that, in the midst of England's war with France, the papacy should have come under French influence when it moved from Rome to Avignon. In 1365 Wycliffe denounced the payment of Peter's pence, the annual tax given by English people to the papacy, and shortly thereafter he publicly denounced the papal Curia, monks, and friars for their vices.

Wycliffe argued that the Scriptures alone declared the will of God and that neither the pope and the cardinals nor the Scholastic theologians could tell Christians what they should believe. In particular, he questioned one of the central dogmas of the Church that emphasized the special power of the priest: *transubstantiation*, which asserts that priests at the Mass work a miracle when they change the substance of bread and wine into the substance of Christ's body and blood. Besides attacking the exalted position and privileges of the priesthood in such rites as transubstantiation, Wycliffe denied the authority of the pope and the hierarchy to exercise jurisdiction or to hold property. He claimed that the true Church was that of the predestined—that is, those whom God would save and were thus in a state of grace. Only these elect could rule the elect; therefore, popes and bishops who had no grace could have their properties removed and had no right to rule. Responsibility for ecclesiastical reform rested with the prince, and the pope could exercise only as much authority as the prince allowed.

The Lollards Many of Wycliffe's views were branded heretical, but even though he was forced to leave Oxford when he offended his protectors at the royal court, they did keep him unharmed until he died. His followers, mostly ordinary people who were known as Lollards—a name apparently derived from "lollar" (idler)—were not so lucky. They managed to survive as an underground movement in the countryside until the Protestant Reformation exploded more than a century later, but they were constantly hounded, and in 1428 the Church had Wycliffe's remains dug up, burned, and thrown into a river.

Hus An even harsher fate awaited Wycliffe's most famous admirer, a Bohemian priest named Jan Hus (1369–1415), who started a broad and even more defiant movement in his homeland. Hus was a distinguished churchman and scholar. He served as rector (the equivalent of president) of the Charles University in Prague, one of Europe's best-known institutions, and he was the main preacher at a fashionable chapel in Prague. Like Wycliffe, he argued that priests were not a holy and privileged group, set apart from laymen, but that the Church was made up of all the

Hus at Constance

A few weeks before he was executed, Jan Hus wrote to his Czech followers to tell them how he had responded to his accusers at the Council of Constance:

"Master Jan Hus, in hope a servant of God, to all faithful Czechs who love God: I call to your attention that the proud and avaricious Council, full of all abomination, condemned my Czech books having neither heard nor seen them; even if it had heard them, it would not have understood them. O, had you seen that Council which calls itself the most holy, and that cannot err, you would have seen the greatest abomination! I have heard it commonly said that Constance would not for thirty years rid itself of the sins which that Council has committed. That Council has done more harm than good.

"Therefore, faithful Christians, do not allow yourselves to be terrified by their decrees, which will profit them nothing. They will fly away like butterflies, and their decrees will turn into a spiderweb. They wanted to frighten me, but could not overcome God's power in me. They did not dare to oppose me with Scripture.

"I am writing this to you that you may know that they did not defeat me by any Scripture or any proof, but that they sought to seduce me by deceits and threats to recant and abjure. But the merciful Lord God, whose law I have extolled, has been and is with me, and I hope that He will be with me to the end and will preserve me in His grace until death.

"This letter was written in chains, in the expectation of death."

From Matthew Spinka (ed.), *The Letters of John Hus* (Manchester University Press, 1972), pp. 195–197.

faithful. To emphasize this equality, he rejected the custom of allowing the congregation at a Mass to eat the wafer that symbolized Christ's body but allowing only the priest to drink the wine that symbolized his blood. In a dramatic gesture, Hus shared the cup of wine with all worshipers, thus reducing the distinctiveness of the priest. His followers adopted a chalice, or cup, as the symbol of their movement.

Hus was not hesitant about defying the leadership of the Church. Denounced for the positions he had taken, he replied by questioning the authority of the pope himself:

> If a Pope is wicked, then like Judas he is a devil and a son of perdition and not the head of the Church militant. If he lives in a manner contrary to Christ he has entered the papacy by another way than through Christ.

In 1415 Hus was summoned to defend his views before the Church Council at Constance. Although he had been guaranteed safe passage if he came to answer accusations of heresy,

the promise was broken. He was condemned, handed over to the secular authorities, and executed (*see box*, p. 379). But his followers, unlike the Lollards who stayed out of sight in England, refused to retreat in the face of persecution.

The Hussites   A new leader, Jan Žižka, known as John of the Chalice, raised an army and led a successful campaign against the emperor, who was also king of Bohemia and the head of the crusade that was now mounted against the Hussites. The resistance lasted 20 years, outliving Žižka, but sustained by Bohemian nobles, and eventually the Hussites were allowed to establish a special church, the Utraquist Church, in which both cup and wafer were shared by all worshipers at Mass. But Hus's other demands, such as the surrender of all personal possessions by the clergy (an echo of St. Francis), were rejected. Those who tried to fight on for these causes were defeated in battle, and after a long struggle the resistance came to an end, having made only a minor dent in the unity of the Church.

The popular appeal of Wycliffe and Hus reflected the widespread dissatisfaction with official teachings in the late 1300s and 1400s—a dissatisfaction that Petrarch, too, had shown, although in his case there was no question of challenging traditional doctrine. Instead of trying to change the Church itself, he merely sought moral guidance elsewhere. And yet, when Wycliffe and Hus chose to risk an open confrontation, they demonstrated that reform ideas, advanced by charismatic leaders, could find a following among those who resented the authoritarian and materialistic outlook of the Church. At the same time, however, it became clear that such dissent could not survive without support from nobles, princes, or other leaders of society. Even with such help, the Hussites had to limit their demands; without it, they would have gained nothing. It was 100 years after Hus's death before a new reformer arose who had learned these lessons, and he was to transform Western Christianity beyond recognition.

Recommended Reading

Sources

*Brucker, Gene A. (ed.). *The Society of Renaissance Florence: A Documentary Study.* 1971.

*Available in paperback.

*Cassirer, Ernst, P. O. Kristeller, and J. H. Randall, Jr. (eds.). *The Renaissance Philosophy of Man.* 1953. Selections from Petrarch, Ficino, Pico, and others.

*Chambers, David, and Brian Pullan (eds.). *Venice: A Documentary History. 1450–1630.* 1992.

Eckhart. *Meister Eckhart, a Modern Translation.* R. B. Blakney (tr.). 1956.

Kempe, Margery. *The Book of Margery Kempe (1436)*. B. A. Windeatt (tr.). The autobiography of an extraordinary woman. 1985.

*Kohl, Benjamin G., and Ronald G. Witt (eds.). *The Earthly Republic: Italian Humanists on Government and Society*. 1978.

*Marsilius of Padua. *Defender of Peace*. Alan Gerwith (tr.). 1986.

Studies

*Baron, Hans. *The Crisis of the Early Italian Renaissance: Civic Humanism and Republican Liberty in the Age of Classicism and Tyranny*. 1966. Fundamental analysis of Florentine "civic humanism."

Becker, M. B. *Civility and Society in Western Europe. 1300–1600*. 1988.

*Berenson, Bernard. *The Italian Painters of the Renaissance*. 1968. Classic essays on the history of art.

Bergin, Thomas G. *Boccaccio*. 1981. Learned and readable.

Brucker, Gene A. *Renaissance Florence*. 1983. The standard introduction.

*Burckhardt, Jacob. *The Civilization of the Renaissance in Italy*. 1958. One of the pioneering works of European history, first published in 1860.

Clark, J. M. *The Great German Mystics: Eckhart, Tauler and Suso*. 1949.

Cole, Bruce. *The Renaissance Artist at Work: From Pisano to Titian*. 1983.

Crombie, Alistair C. *Medieval and Early Modern Science*. 1961.

Funkenstein, Amos. *Theology and the Scientific Imagination from the Middle Ages to the Seventeenth Century*. 1986.

*Goldthwaite, Richard A. *The Building of Renaissance Florence: An Economic and Social History*. 1980. Imaginative examination of the relations between society and architecture.

Grendler, Paul F. *Schooling in Renaissance Italy: Literacy and Learning. 1300–1600*. 1989. A recent survey.

Hanning, Robert W., and David Rosand (eds.). *Castiglione: The Ideal and the Real in Renaissance Culture*. 1983.

*Herlihy, David, and Christiane Klapisch-Zuber. *Tuscans and Their Families*. 1985. A study of a Florentine census of 1427.

Holmes, George. *Florence, Rome and the Origins of the Renaissance*. 1986.

*Huizinga, Johann. *The Waning of the Middle Ages*. 1954.

Hutchison, Jane C. *Albrecht Dürer: A Biography*. 1990.

*Keen, Maurice. *Chivalry*. 1984. Sympathetic survey of knightly culture.

Kent, F. W., and Patricia Simons (eds.). *Patronage, Art and Society in Renaissance Italy*. 1987. A collection of interesting essays.

Klapisch-Zuber, Christiane. *Women, Family and Ritual in Renaissance Italy*. 1985. Collected essays.

*Kristeller, Paul O. *Renaissance Thought and Its Sources*. 1979. By a leading historian of Renaissance thought.

Leff, Gordon. *William of Ockham*. 1975. Authoritative examination of a difficult philosopher.

Martines, Lauro. *The Social World of the Florentine Humanists*. 1963. The humanists examined in the light of their social background.

Rosand, David (ed.). *Titian, His World and His Legacy*. 1981.

Tobin, Frank. *Meister Eckhart: Thought and Language*. 1986.

Wilkins, Ernest Hatch. *Life of Petrarch*. 1961.

Lucas Cranach the Elder
LUTHER IN THE VINEYARD
This work of propaganda uses the biblical image
of Christians toiling in the vineyard of the Lord
to contrast the seriousness and fruitfulness of
the Protestants on the left with the greed and
destructiveness of the Catholics on the right. Luther
himself rakes in the center, while Melanchthon at
the far left goes to the source (the Bible) and draws
from the well; meanwhile, on the right, bishops and
monks ruin the crops, burn the wood, and fill the
well with stones.

CHAPTER THIRTEEN

REFORMATIONS IN RELIGION

ALTHOUGH it may have seemed monolithic and all-powerful, the Roman Church in the fifteenth century was neither a unified nor an unchallenged institution. It had long permitted considerable variety in individual beliefs, from the analytic investigations of canon lawyers to the emotional outpourings of mystics. There were local saints, some of whom were recognized as holy only by a few villages; and for many Europeans the papacy remained a distant and barely comprehensible authority. To assume that its theological pronouncements were understood by the average illiterate Christian is to misrepresent the loose, fragmentary nature of the medieval Church. Moreover, doubts had been raised, by the political disputes and reform movements of the fourteenth and fifteenth centuries, about the central structure and doctrines of the Church. That the papacy had weathered these storms by 1500 indicated both how flexible and how powerful it was. What was to be remarkable in the years that followed was the sudden revelation of the Church's fragility, as a protest by a single monk snowballed into a movement that shattered the thousand-year unity of Western Christendom.

I. Piety and Dissent

DOCTRINE

The fundamental question all Christians face is: How can sinful human beings gain salvation? In 1500, the standard official answer was that the Church was an essential intermediary. Only through participation in its rituals, and particularly through the seven sacraments its priests administered—baptism, confirmation, matrimony, the eucharist, ordination, penance, and extreme unction—did the believer have access to the grace that God offered as an antidote to sin. But there was another answer, identified with distinguished Church fathers such as St. Augustine: People can be saved by their faith in God and love of him. This view emphasized inward and personal belief and focused on God as the source of grace.

The two traditions were not incompatible; for centuries they had coexisted without difficulty. Yet the absence of precise definition in many areas of Christian doctrine was a major problem for theologians, because it was often difficult to tell where orthodoxy ended and heresy began. The position taken by the papacy, however, had grown less inclusive and adaptable over the years; by 1500 it was stressing the outward and institutional far more than the inward and personal route to salvation. The aim of reformers for over a century had been to reverse this trend, and it remained unclear whether the change would be accomplished by reform from within or by a revolution and split in the Church.

FORMS OF PIETY

The root of the demand for change was the need of many laypeople for a more personal way of expressing their piety than official practices offered. Church rituals meant little, they felt, unless believers could cultivate an interior sense of the love and presence of God. They looked for nourishment, therefore, to those who emphasized religious individualism. Rejecting the theological subtleties of Scholasticism, they sought divine guidance in the Bible and the writings of the early Church fathers, especially St. Augustine. Lay religious fraternities dedicated to private forms of worship and charitable works proliferated in the cities, especially in Germany and Italy. The most widespread of them in Germany, the Brotherhood of the Eleven Thousand Virgins, consisted of laypeople who gathered together, usually in a church, to sing hymns. In the mid-fifteenth century, more than 100 such groups had been established in Hamburg, a city of slightly more than 10,000 inhabitants. Church leaders, unhappy about a development over which they had no control, had tried to suppress them but to no avail.

Savonarola The most spectacular outburst of popular piety around 1500 occurred in seemingly materialist Florence, which embraced Girolamo Savonarola, a zealous friar who wanted to banish the irreligion and materialism he saw everywhere about him. The climax of his influence came in 1496, when he arranged a tremendous bonfire in which the Florentines burned cosmetics, light literature, dice, and other such frivolities. Savonarola embodied the desire for personal renewal that had long been a part of Western Christianity but seemed to be gaining intensity in the 1400s. His attempts at reform eventually brought him into conflict with the papacy, which rightly saw him as a threat to its authority. The Church therefore denounced him and gave its support to those who resented his power in Florence. His opponents had the friar arrested in 1498 and then executed on a trumped-up charge of treason.

The widespread search for a more intense devotional life was a sign of spiritual vitality. But Church leaders in the age of Savonarola gave little encouragement to ecclesiastical reform and the evangelization of the laity. Only in Spain was there a deliberate attempt to eradicate abuses and encourage religious fervor, and there the leadership in the effort came not from Rome but from the head of the Spanish Church, Cardinal Francisco Ximenes. Elsewhere, the hierarchy reacted harshly when such movements threatened its authority.

THE LEGACY OF WYCLIFFE AND HUS

Such threats had arisen from time to time, notably at universities, where the basic method of

▶ *Anonymous*

THE MARTYRDOM OF SAVONAROLA, CA. 1500
This painting still hangs in the monastery of San Marco where Savonarola lived during his years of power. It shows the city's central square—a setting that remains recognizable to anyone who visits Florence today—where the bonfire of the "vanities" had been held in 1496, and where Savonarola was executed in 1498. The execution is depicted here as an event that the ordinary citizens of Florence virtually ignore as they go about their daily routines.

instruction, the disputation, encouraged the discussion of unorthodox ideas. At disputations, students learned by listening to arguments for and against standard views. It was not impossible for someone taking the "wrong" side in such a debate to be carried away and cross the line between a theoretical discussion and open dissent.

That is what had happened with the Englishman John Wycliffe, who taught at Oxford University in the late 1300s, and with the Bohemian Jan Hus, a professor at the University of Prague a few years later. They had demanded a simplification of doctrines, more reliance on the Bible, and less power for priests. Both had been condemned by the Church, and Hus had been burned at the stake in 1415. But their disciples had kept their ideas alive. Known in England as "Lollards," Wycliffe's followers managed to survive as an underground movement in the countryside. In Bohemia the Hussites had raised an army and won acceptance for their own church, which allowed worshipers greater participation in the Mass than did the Roman Church.

These protests revealed the extent of the dissatisfaction with official teachings. Charismatic leaders could find a following for unorthodox ideas if they could tap popular piety and resentment toward the Church. It was not easy for dissent to survive without support from nobles or princes; aristocrats had protected Wycliffe, and they had formed and led the Hussite army. Even without such patronage, however, the concerns persisted.

CAUSES OF DISCONTENT

By 1500 the spiritual authority of the papacy had been declining for more than two centuries. During the 70 years of the Babylonian captivity, when the pontiffs had lived in Avignon, they had seemed to be captives of the French monarchy rather than symbols of the universal Church. Far more demoralizing, the Great Schism that followed had threatened to undermine the unity of Western Christendom, as two and then three pretenders each claimed to be the true pope. The Council of Constance had closed this breach by 1418 but had also encouraged the conciliar movement. This attempt to subordinate papal power to the authority of Church councils ultimately failed, but it was yet another direct challenge to the pope's supremacy.

Secular Interests The papacy had also lost spiritual influence because of its secular interests. Increasingly, popes conducted themselves like princes. With skillful diplomacy and even military action, they had consolidated their control over the papal lands in the Italian peninsula. They had surrounded themselves with an elaborate court, had become patrons of the arts, and for a time had taken over the cultural leadership of Europe. This concern with political power and grandeur had eclipsed religious duties to the point that some popes used their spiritual powers to raise funds for their secular activities. The fiscal measures developed at Avignon, which furnished the papacy with income from appointments to Church offices and from various fees, had enlarged revenues but led to widespread abuses. High ecclesiastical offices could be bought and sold, and men (usually sons of nobles) were attracted to these positions by the opportunities they provided for wealth and power, not by a religious vocation.

Abuses were widespread at lower levels in the Church as well. Some prelates held several offices at a time and could not give adequate attention to any of them. The ignorance and moral laxity of the parish and monastic clergy also aroused antagonism. Even more damaging was the widespread impression that the Church was failing to meet individual spiritual needs because of its remoteness from the day-to-day needs of the average believer, its elaborate and incomprehensible system of canon law and theology, and its formal ceremonials. Above all, there was a general perception that priests and monks were profiting from their positions, exploiting the people, and giving minimal moral leadership or religious guidance in return.

Anticlericalism These concerns provoked anticlericalism (hostility to the clergy) and calls for reform which, except in the Spain of Cardinal Ximenes, went unheeded. For increasing numbers of deeply pious people, the growing emphasis on ritual and standardized practices seemed irrelevant to their personal quest for salvation. And their reaction was symptomatic of the broad commitment to genuine piety that was apparent, not only in the followers of Wycliffe, Hus, and Savonarola but in many segments of European society in the early 1500s.

POPULAR RELIGION

It was not only the educated elite and the city dwellers (a minority of Europe's inhabitants) who sought to express their faith in personal terms. The yearning for religious devotion among ordinary villagers, the majority of the population, was apparent even when the local priest—who was often hardly better educated than his parishioners—did little to inspire spiritual commitments. People would listen avidly to news of distant places brought by travelers who stopped at taverns and inns (a major source of information and ideas), and increasingly the tales they told were of religious upheaval. In addition, itinerant preachers roamed some regions, notably Central Europe, in considerable numbers, and they drew crowds when they started speaking—on street corners in towns or out in the fields—and described the power of faith. They usually urged direct communication between believers and God, free from ritual and complex doctrine. To the vast crowds they often drew, many of them seemed to echo the words of St. Augustine: "God and the soul I want to recognize, nothing else."

Equally important as a means of learning about and discussing the latest religious issues were the gatherings that regularly brought villagers together. Throughout the year, they would assemble to celebrate holidays—not only the landmarks of the Christian calendar like Christmas and Easter but also local festivals. Religion was always essential to these occasions. When, for example, the planting season arrived, the local priest would lead a procession into the countryside to bless the fields and pray for good crops. Family events, too, from birth to death, had important religious elements.

The Veillée The most common occasion when the community's traditional beliefs and assumptions were discussed, however, was the evening gathering—generally referred to by its French name, *veillée*, which means staying up in the evening. Between spring and autumn, when the weather was not too cold, a good part of the village came together at a central location after each day's work was done. There was little point in staying in one's own home after dark, because making a light with candles or oil was too expensive. Instead, sitting around a communal fire, people could sew clothes, repair tools, feed babies, resolve (or start) disputes, and discuss news. It was one of the few times when women were of no lesser status than men; the views they expressed were as important as any in shaping the common outlook of the villagers.

A favorite occupation at the *veillée* was listening to stories. Every village had its storytellers, who recounted wondrous tales of local history, of magical adventures, or of moral dilemmas, as the mood required. Biblical tales and the exploits

▶ *Hans Sebald Beham*
Church Festival, Woodcut, 1535
The celebration of the anniversary of a church's consecration was one of the most important holidays in a village. Not everyone, however, used this opportunity for spiritual ends, like the couple getting married in front of the church. Some overindulged at the tavern (lower right); some had a tooth extracted (center left); and some, as the chickens in the center and various couples in the scene suggest, used the occasion for pleasure alone. (Hans Sebald Beham, *Large Peasant Holiday*, 1535, Art Institute of Chicago.)

▶ *Peter Brueghel*
THE PEASANT DANCE, CA. 1567
The most vivid images of life in the village during the sixteenth century were created by the Flemish artist Peter Brueghel. The different human types, and the earthiness of country life, are captured in scenes that show the villagers both at work and, as here, at ease and relaxed.

of Christian heroes like the Crusaders had always drawn an attentive audience. Now, however, in addition to entertainment and general moral up-lift, peddlers and travelers who attended the *veillée* brought news of challenges to religious traditions. They told of attacks on the pope and Church practices, and of arguments for a simpler and more easily understood faith. This was how the ideas of religious reformers spread and how those with unorthodox views like the Lollards kept their faith alive. In some cases, the beliefs that were described made converts of those who heard them, and traveling preachers came to regard the gatherings at the *veillées* as ready-made

congregations. They were usually far more knowledgeable, better trained, and more effective than local priests.

The response of the traditional Church to this challenge, after decades of indifference, was to insist that the local priest be better educated and more aware of what was at stake in the religious struggles of the day. As long as he had the support of the local authorities, he could make sure that his views dominated the *veillée* and that contrary beliefs were not expressed. Whichever way the discussions at these communal gatherings went, however, they demonstrated the power of popular piety in the tens of thousands of villages that dotted the European countryside.

THE IMPACT OF PRINTING

The expression of this piety received unexpected assistance from technology: the invention of a printing press with moveable type in the mid-1400s. At least a hundred years earlier, Europeans had known that by carving words and pictures into a wood block, inking them, and pressing the block onto paper, they could make an image that could be repeated on many sheets of paper. We do not know exactly when they discovered that they could speed up this cumber-some process and therefore change the text from page to page, if they used individual letters and put them together within a frame. We do know, however, that a printer named Johannes Gutenberg, who lived in the city of Mainz on the Rhine, was producing books this way by the 1450s. The technique spread rapidly (see table below) and made reading material available to a much broader segment of the population.

As a result, new ideas could travel with unprecedented speed. Perhaps a third of the trading and upper classes—townspeople, the educated, and the nobility—could read, but books could reach a much wider audience, because peddlers began to sell printed materials throughout Europe. They were bought everywhere and became favorite material for reading out loud at *veillées*. Thus people who had had little contact with written literature in the days of manuscripts now gained access to the latest ideas of the time.

Printing and Religion   Printers were not slow to take advantage of the popular interest in books

Der Buchdrucker.

▶ *Jost Amman*
"THE PRINTER" FROM DAS STÄNDEBUCH
(THE BOOK OF TRADES), 1568
This is the first detailed depiction of a printer's shop, showing assistants taking type from large wooden holders in the back, the press on the right, the pages being prepared and inked in the foreground, and finally the sheets of paper before and after they are printed. The caption notes that printing had been invented in the German city of Mainz.

THE SPREAD OF PRINTING THROUGH 1500
Number of towns in which a printing press was established for the first time, by period and country

Period	German-Speaking Areas	Italian-Speaking Areas	French-Speaking Areas	Spain	England*	Netherlands	Other	Total
Before 1471	8	4	1	1	—	—	—	14
1471–1480	22	36	9	6	3	12	5	93
1481–1490	17	13	21	12	—	5	4	72
1491–1500	9	5	11	6	—	2	8	41
Total by 1500	56	58	42	25	3	19	17	220

*In order to try to control the printers, the English government ordered that they work only in London and at Oxford and Cambridge universities.

Adapted from Lucien Febvre and Henri-Jean Martin, *The Coming of the Book: The Impact of Printing 1450–1800*, translated by David Gerard, London, NLB, 1976, pp. 178–179 and 184–185.

by publishing almanacs filled with home-spun advice about the weather and nature that were written specifically for simple rural folk. Even the almanacs, however, carried religious advice; and, more importantly, translations of the Bible made it available to ordinary people in a language that, for the first time, they could understand. Books thus became powerful weapons in the religious conflicts of the day. Devotional tracts, lives of the saints, and the Bible were the most popular titles—often running to editions of around 1000 copies. They became means of spreading new ideas, and the ready markets they found reflected the general interest of the age in spiritual matters.

Printing clearly lessened laypeople's dependence on the clergy; whereas traditionally the priest had read and interpreted the Scriptures for his congregation, now people could consult their own copies. By 1522, 18 translations of the Bible had been published. Some 14,000 copies had been printed in German alone, enough to make it easy to buy in most German-speaking regions. The Church frowned on these efforts, and governments tried to regulate the numbers and locations of presses; but in the end it proved impossible to control the effects of printing.

PIETY AND PROTEST IN LITERATURE AND ART

The printing press broke the Church's monopoly over the public discussion of religious teachings. Authorities might be dismayed by, but could not totally prevent, the publication of writings that criticized doctrines or practices. Thus the most gifted satirist of the sixteenth century, the French humanist François Rabelais, openly ridiculed the clergy and the morality of his day. Rabelais was a monk (as well as a doctor), and he was deeply unhappy that traditional religious practices had diverged so far from the ideals of Jesus. He was most famous for his earthy bawdiness, but again and again he returned to clerical targets, as in this passage from his *Gargantua* (1533):

"Don't monks pray to God for us?" "They do nothing of the kind," said Gargantua. "All they do is keep the whole neighborhood awake by jangling their bells. . . . They mumble over a lot of legends and psalms, which they don't in the least under-

stand; and they say a great many paternosters . . . without thinking or caring about what they are saying. And all that I call a mockery of God, not prayer."

Scurrilous broadsides no less stinging in tone became very popular during the religious disputes of the 1500s. These single sheets often contained vicious attacks on religious opponents and were usually illustrated by cartoons with obscene imagery. The broadsides were examples of par-

▶ *Hans Baldung Grien*
THE THREE AGES OF WOMAN AND DEATH, CA. 1510
The preoccupation with the transitoriness of life and the vanity of earthly things took many forms in the sixteenth century. Here the point is hammered home unmistakably, as the central figure—a young woman at the height of her beauty between infancy and old age—is reminded of the passage of time (the hourglass) and the omnipresence of death even as she admires herself in a convex mirror.

▶ *Matthias Grünewald*

THE TEMPTATION OF ST. ANTHONY, CA. 1510
This detail from a series of scenes Grünewald painted for the Isenheim Altar suggests the power the devil held over the imagination of sixteenth-century Europeans. The gentle, bearded St. Anthony is not seated in contemplation, as in Dürer's portrayal (see plate on p. 392). Instead, he is surrounded by the monsters the devil has sent to frighten him out of his faith. This was a favorite subject of the period, and provided artists like Bosch and Grünewald the opportunity to make vivid and terrifying the ordinary Christian's fear of sin.

tisan hostility, but their broader significance should not be ignored. Even the most lowly of hack writers could share with a serious author like Rabelais a sense of outrage at indifference in high places and a dismay with the lack of spiritual leadership of the time.

Art This emphasis on the importance of religious belief, so evident in European literature, also permeated the work of northern artists in the late fifteenth and early sixteenth centuries (see plates on p. 390 and above). The gruesome paintings of Hieronymus Bosch, for example, depicted the fears of devils and of hell that his contemporaries felt endangered them at all times. He put on canvas the demons, the temptations, the terrible punishments for sin that people considered as real as their tangible surroundings. Bosch's younger contemporary Matthias Grünewald conveyed the same mixture of terror and devotion. Like Bosch, he painted a frightening *Temptation of St. Anthony*, showing the travails of the saint who steadfastly resisted horrible attacks by the devil. These artists explored the darker side of faith, taking their inspiration from the fear of damnation and the hope for salvation—the first seen in the demons, the second in the redeeming Christ.

Dürer The most famous northern artist of this period was Albrecht Dürer, and it is significant that his fame began when he produced an illustrated edition of a biblical book, *The Apocalypse*, which describes God's punishment of sinners on the final Day of Judgment. The book became a best-seller and made Dürer a rich man. He was sought after throughout Europe, and he became known at all levels of society because he was a master of the art of the woodcut. Dürer enjoyed this medium more than painting because, as he noted, many copies could be sold quite cheaply, and his fame and his finances profited accordingly. His wife Agnes was a shrewd businesswoman who accompanied her husband on his travels and set up a stall to sell his works whenever she found a convenient marketplace. Dürer's subjects were largely religious—the life of Christ, portraits of saints, and scenes with the Virgin Mary—which ensured that they had the widest possible appeal.

The depth of piety conveyed by artists like Dürer reflected the temper of Europe. In art and literature, as in lay organizations and the continuing popularity of itinerant preachers, people showed their concern for individual spiritual values and their dissatisfaction with a Church that was not meeting their needs.

▶ *Albrecht Dürer*
ST. ANTHONY, ENGRAVING, 1519
The ease and mastery Dürer brought to the art of engraving made it as powerful and flexible a form as painting. Here the massive figure of the saint, deep in study, is placed in front of a marvelously observed city. The buildings display Dürer's virtuosity—their shapes echo the bulk and solidity of the figure—and they may have symbolized the temptations of city life for a saint who was revered for his solitary piety in the desert.

CHRISTIAN HUMANISM

No segment of society expressed the strivings and yearnings of the age more eloquently than the northern humanists. The salient features of the humanist movement in Italy—its theory of education, its emphasis on eloquence, its reverence for the ancients, and its endorsement of active participation in affairs of state—began to win wide acceptance north of the Alps in the late 1400s. But the northerners added a significant religious dimension to the movement by devoting considerable attention to early Christian literature: the Bible and the writings of the Church fathers. As a result, they have been called *Christian humanists.*

The first major center of humanism in the north was at the University of Heidelberg; but by the end of the fifteenth century the movement's influence, carried by the printing press, was European-wide. The northern humanists were particularly determined to probe early Christianity for the light it could throw on the origins and accuracy of current religious teachings. Indeed, northern humanism's broad examination of religious issues in the early 1500s helped create an atmosphere in which much more serious criticism of the Church could flourish.

The Christian humanists did not abandon the interest in classical authors or the methods for analyzing ancient texts, language, and style that had been developed by Italian humanism. But they put these methods to a new use: analysis of the Bible in order to explain more clearly the message of Jesus and his apostles, and thus to provide a better guide to true piety and morality. This deeply religious undertaking dominated the writings of the two most famous Christian humanists, one English and one Dutch.

MORE AND ERASMUS

More Sir Thomas More (1478–1535), a lawyer and statesman, was the central figure of English humanism. His reputation as a writer rests primarily on a short work, *Utopia,* published in Latin in 1516, which describes an ideal society on an imaginary island. In it, More condemned war, poverty, intolerance, and other evils of his day and defined the general principles of morality that he felt should underlie human society.

The first book of *Utopia* returns to the conflict between the *vita contemplativa* and the *vita activa* that Petrarch had emphasized, and asks whether a learned person should withdraw from the world to avoid the corruptions of politics or actively participate in affairs of state so as to guide policy. In his own career, More chose the latter path, with fatal results. The second, more famous book of *Utopia* leaves such practical issues aside and describes what an ideal commonwealth might be like. In political and social organization, Utopia is a carefully regulated, almost monastic community that has succeeded in abolishing private property, greed, and pride—and thus has freed its inhabitants from some of the worst sins of More's day. The Utopians have accomplished all this without Christianity, and More implies that a society based on Christian principles can attain even greater good. Well-designed institutions, education, and discipline are his answer to the fall of Adam and Eve: Weak human nature can be led to virtuousness only if severely curbed.

Deeply devout and firmly attached to the traditional Church, More entered public life as a member of Parliament in 1504. He rose high in government service, but eventually he gave his life for remaining loyal to the pope and refusing to recognize the decision of his king, Henry VIII, to reject papal authority and become head of the English Church. When Henry determined to break with Rome, he found it intolerable that this prominent political figure rejected his actions and would not compromise; and so, to discourage any further disobedience, Henry had him beheaded. More's last words revealed his unflinching adherence to the Christian principles he pursued throughout his life: "I die the King's good servant, but God's first."

Erasmus The supreme representative of Christian humanism was the Dutchman Desiderius Erasmus (1466?–1536). Erasmus early acquired a taste for ancient writers, and he determined to devote himself to classical studies. For the greater part of his life, he wandered through Europe, writing, visiting friends, and occasionally working for important patrons. He always retained his independence, however, for unlike More, he answered the question of whether a scholar should

▶ *Hans Holbein the Younger*
PORTRAIT OF ERASMUS, 1523
The leading portraitist of the age, Hans Holbein, painted his friend Erasmus a number of times. Here he shows the great scholar at work, possibly writing one of the many elegantly constructed letters that he sent to colleagues throughout Europe. The richness of the scene bears noting—the gold ring, the fine coat with a fur collar, and the splendid tapestry hanging over the paneled wall.

enter public life by avoiding the compromises that would be necessary in the service of a ruler.

Erasmus was so famous for his learning and his literary skills that he dominated the world of letters of his time. Constantly consulted by scholars and admirers, he wrote magnificently composed letters that reflected every aspect of the culture of his age. He became known throughout Europe, however, as a result of a little book, *The Praise of Folly* (1509), which was one of the first best-sellers created by the printing press. Some of it is gay, lighthearted banter that pokes fun at the author himself, his friends, and the follies of everyday life, and suggests that a little folly is essential to human existence. The book also points out that Christianity itself is a kind of folly, a belief in "things not seen." In many passages, though, Erasmus launches sharply satirical attacks against monks, the pope, meaningless ceremonies, and the many lapses from what he perceived to be the true Christian spirit.

The Philosophy of Christ   At the heart of Erasmus' work was the message that he called the "philosophy of Christ." He believed that the life of Jesus and, especially, his teachings in the Sermon on the Mount should be models for Christian piety and morality. For the Church's ceremonies and for rigid discipline he had only censure: Too often, he said, they served as substitutes for genuine spiritual concerns. People lit thousands of candles for Mary but cared little about the humility she is supposed to inspire. They forgot that what counts is the spirit of religious devotion, not the form. By simply following the precepts of Jesus, he argued, a Christian could lead a life guided by sincere faith. Because of his insistence on ethical behavior, Erasmus could admire a truly moral man even if he was a pagan. "I could almost say, 'Pray for me, St. Socrates!'" he once wrote.

Erasmus believed that the Church had lost sight of its original mission. In the course of 15 centuries, traditions and practices had developed that obscured the intentions of its founder, and purity could be restored only by studying the Scriptures and the writings of the early Church fathers. Here the literary and analytic tools of the humanists became vitally important, because they enabled scholars to understand the meaning and intention of ancient manuscripts. Practicing what he preached, Erasmus spent 10 years preparing a new edition of the Greek text of the New Testament so as to correct errors in the Latin Vulgate, which was the standard version, and he revised it repeatedly for another 20 years.

But the calm, scholarly, and tolerant moderation Erasmus prized was soon left behind by events. The rising intensity of religious reformers and their opponents destroyed the effort he had led to cure the ills of the Church quietly, from within. Erasmus wanted a revival of purer faith, but he would never have dreamed of rejecting the traditional authority of the Church. As Europe entered an age of confrontation, he found it impossible to preserve a middle course between the two sides. Unable to choose, Erasmus was swept aside by revolutionary forces that he himself had helped build but that Martin Luther was to unleash.

II. The Lutheran Reformation

THE CONDITIONS FOR CHANGE

That a major religious conflict should have erupted in the Holy Roman Empire is not surprising. In this territory of fragmented government, with hundreds of independent local princes, popular piety was noticeably strong. Yet anyone who was unhappy with Church leadership had all the more reason to resent the power of bishops, because in the empire they were often also princes—such as the aristocratic bishop who ruled the important city of Cologne on the Rhine. There were few strong secular princes who could protect the people from the fiscal demands of the Church, and the popes therefore regarded the empire as their surest source of revenue.

This situation was made more volatile by the ambitions of the secular princes. Their ostensible overlord, the emperor, had no real power over them, and they worked tirelessly to strengthen their control over their subjects and to assert their independence from all outside authority. A number of them were in fact to see the religious upheavals of the 1500s as a means of advancing their own political purposes. Their ambitions help explain why a determined reformer, Martin Luther, won such swift and widespread support.

MARTIN LUTHER

Martin Luther (1483–1546) was born into a miner's family in Saxony in central Germany. The household was dominated by the father, whose powerful presence some modern commentators have seen reflected in his son's vision of an omnipotent God. The boy received a good education and decided to become a lawyer, a profession that would have given him many opportunities for advancement. But in his early twenties, shortly after starting his legal studies, he had an experience that changed his life. Crossing a field during a thunderstorm, he was thrown to the ground by a bolt of lightning, and in his terror he cried out to St. Anne that he would enter a monastery.

Luther as a Monk   Although the decision may well have been that sudden, it is clear that there was more to Luther's complete change of direction than this one incident, however traumatic. A highly sensitive, energetic, and troubled young man, he had become obsessed with his own sinfulness, and he joined a monastery in the hope that a penitential life would help him overcome his sense of guilt. Once he became a monk, he pursued every possible opportunity to earn worthiness in the sight of God. He overlooked no means of discipline or act of contrition or self-denial, and for added merit he endured austerities, such as self-flagellation, that went far beyond normal requirements. But it was all to no avail: When called upon to officiate at his first Mass after his ordination in 1507, he was so terrified at the prospect of a sinner like himself administering the sacrament—that is, transforming the wafer and wine of the Mass into the body and blood of Christ—that he almost failed to complete the ritual.

Fortunately for Luther, his superiors took more notice of his intellectual gifts than of his self-doubts and in 1508 assigned him to the faculty of a new university in Wittenberg, the capital of Saxony. It was from his scholarship, which was excellent, and especially from his study of the Bible that he was able at last to draw comfort and spiritual peace.

This second crucial turning point in Luther's life, as important as the lightning bolt, occurred while he was preparing his university lectures. Until this point, which is known as "the experience in the tower," he could see no way that he, a despicable mortal, could receive anything but the fiercest punishments from a God of absolute

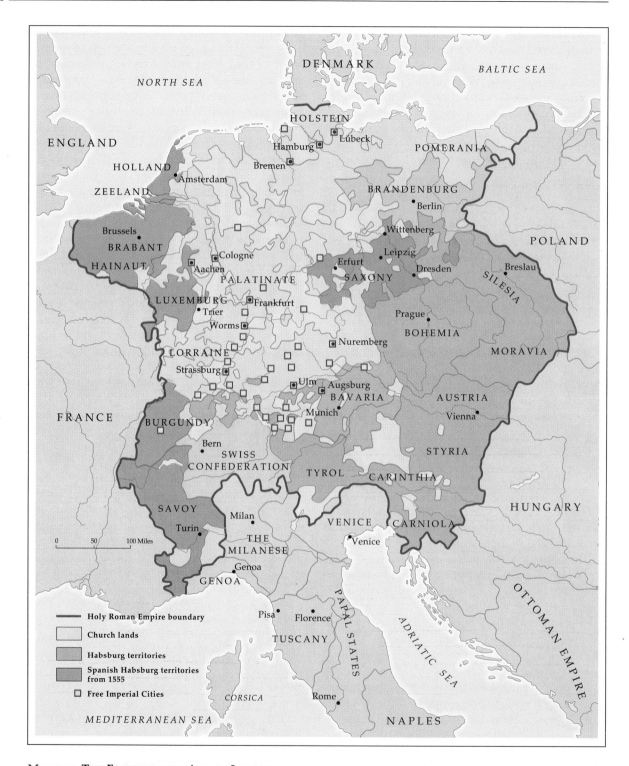

Map 13.1 THE EMPIRE IN THE AGE OF LUTHER
The fragmentation that divided the empire into dozens of distinct principalities, independent cities, and autonomous territories enabled Luther to find the political support that kept his religious reform alive.

justice. Now, however, he had an insight that led him to understand that he needed only to rely on God's mercy, a quality as great as divine justice (*see box*, below). The many advances in Luther's thinking thereafter came from this insight: that justification—which removes sin and bestows righteousness through a gift of grace—is achieved by faith alone.

THE INDULGENCE CONTROVERSY

In 1517 an event occurred that was ultimately to lead Luther to an irrevocable break with the Church. In the spring, a friar, Johann Tetzel, began to peddle indulgences a few miles from Wittenberg as part of a huge fund-raising effort to pay for the new Church of St. Peter in Rome. Originally, an indulgence had been granted to anyone going on a crusade. It was then extended to those who, though unable to join a crusade, gave enough money for a poor crusader to be able to reach the Holy Land. Indulgences released sinners from a certain period of punishment in purgatory before they went on to heaven and were justified doctrinally as a sort of credit that could be drawn from the treasury of merit built up by Jesus and the saints. But neither the doctrine nor the connection with money had been fully defined, and clerics had taken advantage of this vagueness simply to sell indulgences. Tetzel, an expert peddler, was offering complete releases from purgatory without bothering to mention the repentance that, according to Church teachings, was essential if a sinner was to be forgiven or absolved.

The 95 Theses The people of Wittenberg were soon flocking to Tetzel to buy this easy guarantee

Luther's "Experience in the Tower"

The following passage was written by Luther in 1545, at least 25 years after the experience it described. As a result, scholars have been unable to decide (a) whether the breakthrough was in fact as sudden as Luther suggests; (b) when it took place—possibly as early as 1512, five years before the indulgence dispute, or as late as 1519, when Luther was already under attack for his views; or (c) how it should be interpreted—as a scholar's insight, as a revelation from God, or as Luther's later crystallization into a single event of a process that had taken many years.

I wanted very much to understand Paul's Epistle to the Romans, but despite my determination to do so I kept being stopped by the one word, "the *righteousness* of God." I hated that word, because I had been taught to understand it as the active righteousness by which a just God punishes unjust sinners. The trouble was that, although I may have been an impeccable monk, I felt myself to be a sinner before God. As a result, not only was I unable to love, but I actually hated this just God, who punishes all sinners. And so I raged, yet I still longed to understand St. Paul.

At last, as I grappled with the words day and night, God had mercy on me, and I saw the connection between the words "the righteousness of God" and "The righteous shall live by faith" (Romans 1:17). I understood that the righteousness of God refers to the gift by which God enables the just to live—that is, by faith. A merciful God justifies us by faith, as it is written: "The righteous shall live by faith." At that point, I felt as if I had been reborn and had passed through open doors into paradise. The whole of Scripture took on new meaning. As I had previously hated the phrase, "the righteousness of God," so now I lovingly praised it.

Translation from the Latin by Theodore K. Rabb of Luther's Preface to the 1545 edition of his writings, in Otto Scheel (ed.), *Dokumente zu Luthers Entwicklung* (Tübingen: Mohr, 1929), pp. 191–192.

▶ *Jörg Breu*
ENGRAVING DEPICTING THE SALE OF INDULGENCES, CA. 1530
This would have been a familiar scene in Europe until Luther's attacks brought it to an end. The clerics on their fine horses on the right bring a cross and the papal bull, which is authenticated by the elaborate seals and ribbons that hang from it. The faithful put money in the barrel in the middle or hand it to the dispenser of certificates on the left, who sits near the large locked chest that will hold the revenues from the sales.

of salvation. For Luther, a man groping toward an evangelical solution of his own doubts, it was unforgivable that people should be deprived of their hard-earned money for spurious, worthless promises. On October 31, 1517, he published in Wittenberg 95 theses, or statements, on indulgences that he offered to debate with experts in Christian doctrine.

This was no revolutionary document. It merely described what Luther believed to be correct teachings on indulgences: that the pope could remit only the penalties that he himself or canon law imposed; that therefore the promise of

a general pardon was damnable; and that every true believer shared in the treasury of merit left by Jesus and the saints, whether or not he or she obtained an indulgence. Within a few weeks the story was all over the empire that a monk had challenged the sale of indulgences. The proceeds of Tetzel's mission began to drop off; and other members of his order, the Dominicans, rallied to their brother by attacking his presumptuous critic, Luther, who happened to belong to a rival order, the Augustinians.

Luther Elaborates The controversy soon drew attention in Rome. At first, Pope Leo X regarded the affair as merely a monks' quarrel. But, in time, Luther's responses to the Dominicans' attacks began to deviate radically from Church doctrine, and by 1520 he had gone so far as to challenge the authority of the papacy itself in three pamphlets outlining his fundamental position.

In *An Address to the Christian Nobility of the German Nation*, Luther made a frankly patriotic appeal to his fellow Germans to reject the foreign pope's authority. The Church, he said, consisted of all Christians, including the laity; hence the nobles were as much its governors as the clergy, and they had a responsibility to remedy its defects. Indeed, Emperor Charles V had an obligation to call a council to end abuses. In *The Babylonian Captivity*, the most radical of the three works, Luther attacked the system of seven sacraments, the basis of the Church's authority, on the ground that only two are mentioned in the Bible. In *The Liberty of the Christian Man*, a less polemical work, he explained his doctrine of faith and justification by stressing that, although he did not reject good works, only the faith of the individual believer could bring salvation from an all-powerful, just, and merciful God. These three pamphlets had an overwhelming impact on Luther's fellow Germans. His emotional appeal to their resentment of Church power and their wish for a more personal faith made him, almost overnight, the embodiment of a widespread yearning for religious reform.

THE DIET OF WORMS

There could no longer be any doubt that Luther was breaking with the Church, and in 1520 Pope Leo X issued a bull excommunicating him. Luther publicly tossed the document into a bonfire, defending his action by calling the pope an Antichrist. In 1521 Emperor Charles V, who was officially the papacy's secular representative, summoned the celebrated monk to offer his defense against the papal decree at a Diet of the Empire (a meeting of princes, city leaders, and churchmen) at Worms, a city on the Rhine.

The journey across Germany was a triumphant progress for Luther, who now seemed a heroic figure. Appearing before the magnificent assembly dressed in his simple monk's robe, he offered a striking contrast to the display of imperial and princely grandeur. First in German and then in Latin, he made the famous declaration that closed the last door behind him: "I cannot and will not recant anything, since it is unsafe and wrong to go against my conscience. Here I stand. I cannot do otherwise. God help me. Amen." On the following day the emperor gave his reply: "A single friar who goes counter to all Christianity for a thousand years must be wrong."

Luther Protected Charles added legality to the papal bull by issuing an imperial edict calling for Luther's arrest and the burning of his works. At this point, however, the independent power of the German princes and their resentment of for-

▶ *Lucas Cranach the Elder*
PORTRAIT OF MARTIN LUTHER, 1525
One of the first faces made familiar by portraits, but not belonging to a nobleman, was Luther's. Cranach painted the reformer a number of times, so we can see what he looked like at various periods of his life. Luther here is in his early forties, a determined figure who four years earlier had made his stand at the Diet at Worms.

eign ecclesiastical interference came to the reformer's aid. The Elector Frederick III of Saxony,
who had never met Luther and who was never
to break with the traditional Church, nonetheless
determined to protect the rebel who lived in his
territory. He had him taken to the Wartburg castle, one of his strongholds, and here Luther remained for almost a year, safe from his enemies.

LUTHERAN DOCTRINE AND PRACTICE

While at the Wartburg, Luther, together with his
friend Philipp Melanchthon, developed his ideas
and shaped them into a formal set of beliefs that
influenced most of the subsequent variations of
Protestant Christianity. Codified in 1530 in a document known as the Augsburg Confession, these
doctrines have remained the basis of Lutheranism ever since.

Luther's Debt to Nominalism   It is important to
realize that some of Luther's positions had roots
in nominalism, the most influential philosophical
and theological movement of the fourteenth and
fifteenth centuries, which had flourished at his
old monastery. Two nominalist teachings in particular left a lasting impression on Luther and
later reformers. First, in opposition to Thomas
Aquinas and the thirteenth-century attempts to
unite reason and faith, the nominalists stressed
the primacy of faith, the inadequacy of reason,
and the unknowableness of God. Second, as a
natural corollary to God's mystery, they emphasized his overwhelming power and majesty. Both
of these beliefs were to reappear frequently in the
reformers' writings.

Faith and the Bible   The influence of nominalism is apparent in the two fundamental assertions of Luther's teachings. First, faith alone—not
good works or the receiving of the sacraments—
justifies the believer in the eyes of God and wins
redemption. People themselves are helpless and
unworthy sinners who can do nothing to cooperate in their own salvation; God bestows faith
on those he chooses to save. Second, the Bible is
the sole source of religious authority. It alone carries the word of God, and Christians must reject
all other supposed channels of divine inspiration:

Church tradition, commentaries on the Bible,
or the pronouncements of popes and Church
councils.

These two doctrines had far-reaching implications. According to Luther, all people are
equally capable of understanding God's word as
expressed in the Bible and can gain salvation
without the help of intermediaries; they do not
need a priest endowed with special powers or an
interceding church. Luther thus saw God's faithful as a "priesthood of all believers," a concept
totally foreign to the traditional Church, which
insisted on the distinction between clergy and laity. The distinction disappeared in Luther's doctrines, because all the faithful shared the responsibilities formerly reserved for priests.

Sacraments and the Mass   True to his reliance
on biblical authority, Luther denied the efficacy
of five of the sacraments. Only baptism and the
eucharist are mentioned in Scripture; therefore
they alone are the means by which God distrib-
utes grace. Moreover, the ceremony of the eucharist, or Lord's Supper, was now called *communion* (literally, "sharing") to emphasize that all
worshipers, including the officiating clergy, were
equal. Luther also reduced the distinctiveness of
priests by abolishing the sacrament of confession
and by giving them the right to marry.

Luther's teachings on the sacraments transformed the Mass, the ceremony that surrounds
the eucharist, which had caused him such trouble
when he first became a monk. According to traditional dogma, when the priest raises the wafer,
the host, during the Mass and recites the words
Hoc est corpus meum ("This is my body"), the sacrifice of Jesus on the cross is reenacted. The wafer
and the wine retain their outward appearance,
their "accidents," but their substance is transformed into the body and blood of Christ—in
other words, transubstantiation takes place.

Luther asserted that the wafer and wine retain
their substance as well as their accidents and undergo *con*substantiation at the moment the priest
says "This is my body." The real presence of
Christ and the natural substance *coexist* within
the wafer and wine. Nothing suddenly happens;
there is no miraculous moment. Instead, the believer is simply made aware of the real presence

of God, who is everywhere at all times. Again, it is the faith of the individual, not the ceremony itself, that counts.

Luther further reduced the mystery of the Lord's Supper by allowing the congregation to drink the wine, which was reserved for the priest in the traditional ceremony. This change, which undermined the position of the priest, had been demanded by Hus. But Luther went further. He simplified services radically and gave ordinary people a greater role in worship by abolishing the use of Latin, processions, incense, and votive candles.

Translation of the Bible With the priest reduced in stature, it was vital to make God's word more readily available to the faithful, so that they could read or hear the Bible for themselves. To this end, Luther began the long task of translating the Bible. He was to complete the work in 1534, creating a text that is a milestone in the history of the German language. Families were encouraged to read Scripture on their own, and the reformed faith stimulated rising literacy among women as well as men. This was Luther's last major contribution to the religious changes of the sixteenth century. Although he was to live until 1546, henceforth the progress of the revolution he had launched would rely on outside forces: its popular appeal and the actions of political leaders.

THE SPREAD OF LUTHERANISM

It is usually said that Lutheranism spread from above, advancing only when princes and rulers helped it along. Although this view has some merit, it does not adequately explain the growth of the movement. The response to Luther's stand was immediate and widespread. Even before the Diet of Worms, preachers critical of the Church were drawing audiences in many parts of the Holy Roman Empire, and in 1521 there were waves of image smashing, reports of priests marrying, and efforts to reform and simplify the sacraments.

Soon there were congregations following Luther's teachings throughout the empire and neighboring countries. Broadsides and pamphlets fresh from the printing presses disseminated the reformer's message with breathtaking speed, and they stimulated an immediate response from thousands who welcomed the opportunity to renew their faith.

Radical Preachers As long as his own doctrines remained unaltered, Luther was naturally delighted to see his teachings spread. But from the start, people drew inferences that he could not tolerate. Early in 1522, for example, three men from the nearby town of Zwickau appeared in Wittenberg claiming to be prophets who enjoyed direct communication with God. Their ideas were both radical and, in Luther's eyes, damnable. When he returned from the Wartburg, therefore, he preached eight sermons to expose their errors—a futile effort, because the movement to reform the Church was now too dispersed to control. Capitalizing on mass discontent, radical preachers incited disturbances in the name of faith, and soon social as well as religious protest exploded, posing a new challenge for Luther as he struggled to keep his protest alive and under control.

DISORDER AND REVOLT

The first trouble arose in the summer of 1522, started by the weakest independent group in the empire, the imperial knights. The knights occupied a precarious position in the social hierarchy because their holdings rarely consisted of more than a single castle. They accepted no authority but the emperor himself, and they resented the growing power of cities and princes (rulers of large territories) in the empire.

Calling themselves true representatives of the imperial system—that is, loyal supporters of the emperor's authority, in contrast to the cities and princes who wanted to be more independent—and using Lutheranism as further justification, the knights launched an attack on one of the leading ecclesiastical rulers, the archbishop of Trier. The onslaught was crushed within a year, but the Lutherans' opponents could now suggest that the new religious teachings undermined law and order.

Peasant Revolt The banner of the new faith rose

over popular revolts as well. A peasant uprising began in Swabia in 1524 and quickly engulfed the southern and central parts of the empire. Citing Luther's inspiration, and especially his teaching that faith was all the individual needed, the peasants published a list of 12 demands in 1525. Admittedly, 10 of their grievances concerned social, not religious, injustices: They wanted an end to serfdom, tithes, and the restrictions and burdens imposed by their overlords, including prohibitions on hunting and fishing, excessive rents and services, and unlawful punishments. But they also had two religious aims: They wanted the right to choose their own pastors, and they refused to accept any authority other than Scripture to determine if their demands were justified.

Luther sympathized with the last two claims, and at first he considered the peasants' demands reasonable. But when it became apparent that they were challenging all authority, he ignored the oppressions they had suffered and wrote a vicious pamphlet, *Against the Rapacious and Murdering Peasants*, calling on the nobility to cut them down without mercy so as to restore peace. A few months later the rebels were defeated in battle, and thereafter Luther threw his support unreservedly on the side of the princes and the established political and social order. He also grew more virulent in his attacks on Catholics and Jews, and became as insistent as the Roman Church he was defying that his doctrines were not to be questioned.

LUTHERANISM ESTABLISHED

The advance of Lutheranism thus far had depended largely on its appeal to the ordinary believer, and it continued to enjoy wide support. But when Luther was forced to choose between the demands of his humblest followers and the authority of the princes who had protected him, he opted for the princes. It was a decision that enabled his movement to survive and may well have saved him from the fate of Hus—burned at the stake a century before because he defied po-

▶ **CARTOON FROM LUTHERAN WOODCUT BROADSIDE**
Vicious cartoons were a favorite device of religious propaganda during the Age of Religious Reformation. They were especially popular for an illiterate audience, which had to get the message from pictures. The more vivid the image, the easier it was to understand. Here the Protestants show the enemies of Luther as vicious animals. One theologian is a cat eating a mouse; another is a dog holding a bone.

litical as well as religious leaders. Had Luther not condemned the disorders, he would doubtless have been abandoned by the princes, and without their backing he and his followers could not have stood up to the traditional Church or been safe from the power of Charles V.

Luther's Conservatism   One of the reasons the new set of beliefs could attract these princes was its conservatism. Any person who accepted the basic doctrines of justification by faith alone and Scripture as the sole authority could be accepted as a Lutheran. Consequently, the new congregations could retain much from the old religion: most of the liturgy, the sacred music, and, particularly important, a structured church that, though less hierarchical than before, was still organized to provide order and authority.

The Lutheran Princes   Some rulers were swept up by the same emotions that moved their subjects, but others were moved by more material interests. Since the Church lost all its property when reform was introduced, princes could confiscate the rich and extensive ecclesiastical holdings in their domains. Furthermore, they now had added reason for flaunting their independence from Emperor Charles V, an unwavering upholder of orthodoxy. It was risky to adopt this policy, for Charles could strip a prince of his title. On the other side, if a prince promised to remain loyal to the Church, he could blackmail the pope into offering him almost as many riches as he could win by confiscation. Nevertheless, the appeal of the new faith eventually tipped the balance for enough princes to create a formidable party capable of resisting Charles's power. While they were attending an imperial Diet at Speyer in 1529, they signed a declaration "protesting" the Diet's decree that no religious innovations were to be introduced in the empire. Thereafter all who accepted religious reform, including the Lutherans, were known as Protestants; and adherents of the traditional Church, which was led from Rome and continued to claim that it was universal (or catholic), came to be known as Roman Catholics.

The following year, at another imperial Diet, the Lutheran princes announced their support of the Augsburg Confession, the official statement of Lutheran doctrines that had been prepared by Melanchthon and Luther. Charles V now threatened to use military force to crush the heresy, and in the face of this danger, the Lutherans formed a defensive league in 1531 at the small Saxon town of Schmalkalden. Throughout the 1530s this alliance consolidated Protestant gains, brought new princes into the cause, and, in general, amassed sufficient strength to deter Charles from immediate military action.

War over Religion   The reform party became so solidly established that it negotiated with the pope on equal terms about the possibility of reconciliation in 1541, but the talks collapsed, and the chances for a reunification of Christendom evaporated. Not until 1546, the year of Luther's death, however, did open war begin. Then, after a brief campaign, Charles won a crushing victory over the Lutherans in 1547. But matters had advanced too far for their movement to collapse merely because of a single defeat on the battlefield. The new faith had won the devotion of a large part of the German people, particularly in the north and the east, farthest away from the center of imperial power. Some of the great cities of the south, such as Nuremberg, which had been centers of humanism, had also come over to the Lutheran side. By the 1550s Lutheranism had captured about half the population of the Empire.

The Catholic princes also played a part in ensuring the survival of the new faith. Fearful of Charles V's new power, they refused to cooperate in his attempt to establish his authority throughout the empire, and he had to rely on Spanish troops, who further alienated him from his subjects. The Lutherans regrouped after their 1547 defeat, and in 1555 the imperial Diet at Augsburg drew up a compromise settlement that exposed the decline of the emperor's power. Henceforth each prince was allowed to determine the religion of his own territory, Lutheran or Catholic. Religious uniformity was at an end, and the future of Lutheranism was secure.

The Heritage of Lutheranism   The influence that this first Protestant Church was to exert on all of European life was immense. The idea that all believers were equal in the eyes of God inspired revolutionary changes in thought and society. It justified antimonarchical constitutional theories,

▶ ENGRAVING OF THE DIET OF AUGSBURG, 1530
At the Diet—the meeting of the princes and cities of the Holy Roman Empire—in Augsburg in 1530, the Lutherans presented to the emperor, Charles V, a statement, or "confession," of their faith. This "Confession of Augsburg" became the founding doctrine of the Lutheran church. It was rejected as heretical by Charles, but he could not suppress it. One of the Lutheran princes told him in 1530 that he would rather have his head cut off than attend a Catholic mass. And Charles was unable to crush such defiance.

it allowed people to feel that all occupations were equally worthy and that there was nothing wrong with the life of the merchant or even the moneylender, and it undermined the hierarchic view of the universe. One can easily overstate the notion that Lutheranism made people more self-reliant, because independent and pioneering behavior was far from new. Nevertheless, there is no question that, by condemning the traditional reliance on priests and the Church and by mak-

ing individuals responsible for their own salvation, Luther did encourage his followers to act on their own. Yet the new faith had its most immediate effect on religious life itself: Before the century was out, the dissent started by Luther inspired a multitude of sects and a ferment of ideas without precedent in the history of Europe.

III. The Growth of Protestantism

ZWINGLIANISM

Hardly had Luther made his protest in 1517 when religious dissent in many different forms suddenly appeared. It was as if no more was needed than one opening shot before a volley of discontent broke out—testimony to the deep and widespread desire for individual piety of the times. The most influential of these new initiatives began in the Swiss city of Zurich.

Zwingli   This new reformer, Ulrich Zwingli (1484–1531), was a priest, a learned humanist, and a disciple of Erasmus. The doctrines he began to develop between 1519 and 1522 were similar to Luther's. Like the Saxon reformer, Zwingli based his ideas entirely on Scripture and emphasized faith alone. He rejected the Church's role as the channel of God's grace to believers, the idea that the clergy should be celibate, and the belief in purgatory after death. Suspicious of any reliance on Church rituals, Zwingli, even more than Luther, wanted to simplify religious belief and practice. In his view, none of the sacraments bestowed grace; they were merely signs of grace already given. Thus, baptism is symbolic, not a ceremony that regenerates the recipient; and communion is no more than a memorial and thanksgiving for the grace given by God, who is present only symbolically—not in actuality, as Luther believed.

Despite his obvious debt to Luther, Zwingli's divergences were significant. When the two reformers met in 1529, hoping to iron out differences in order to present a united front, their inability to agree on a doctrine of communion kept them apart. Zwingli had founded a new form of Protestantism, more thoroughly dependent on the individual believer and more devoid of mystery and ritual than anything Luther could accept.

Zwingli held that people need constant correction to lead godly lives. Since he recognized no distinction between secular and religious authority, he established a tribunal of clergy and secular officials to enforce discipline among the faithful. They supervised all moral issues, from compulsory church attendance to the public behavior of amorous couples. The court could excommunicate flagrant transgressors, and it maintained constant surveillance—through a network of informers—to keep the faithful moral and godly.

Because Zwingli considered it vital for discipline that the faithful receive a continuing education, he founded a theological school and authorized a new translation of the Bible. He also insisted on lengthy sermons at each service. Wor-

ship was stripped bare, as were the churches, and preaching began to assume tremendous importance as a means of instructing believers and strengthening their faith. Zwingli also revived the ancient Christian practice of public confession of sin—yet another reinforcement of discipline.

Zwingli's Church   Zwingli's ideas spread rapidly in the Swiss Confederation, helped by the virtual autonomy of each canton, or region. By 1529 a number of cantons had accepted Zwinglianism. As a result, two camps formed in the country, and a war broke out in 1531 in which Zwingli himself was killed. Thereafter the Swiss Confederation remained split between Catholics and reformers. Zwinglianism never grew into a major religion, but it had a considerable effect on later forms of Protestantism, particularly Calvinism.

THE RADICALS

Both Luther and Zwingli wanted to retain church authority, and both therefore insisted that infant baptism was the moment of entry into the church, even though this belief had no scriptural sanction. Some radical reformers, however, insisted on taking the Bible literally and argued that, as in biblical times, baptism should be administered only to mature adults who could make a conscious choice to receive grace, not to infants who could not understand what was happening. Soon these reformers were being called *Anabaptists* ("rebaptizers") by their enemies. The term is often applied to all radicals, though in fact it described only one conspicuous group.

Sects   Diversity was inevitable among the radical reformers, most of whom refused to recognize church organization, rejected priests, and gave individual belief free rein, sometimes to the point of recognizing only personal communication with God and disregarding Scripture. Many groups of like-minded radicals formed small sects—voluntary associations which rarely included more than 100 or so adults—in an effort to achieve complete separation from the world and avoid compromising their ideals. They wanted to set an example for others by adhering fervently to the truth as they saw it, regardless of the consequences.

Some sects established little utopian communities, holding everything in common, including property and spouses. Others disdained all worldly things and lived only for the supreme ecstasy of a trance in which they made direct contact with God himself. Many, believing in the imminent coming of the Messiah, prepared themselves for the end of the world and the Day of Judgment.

PERSECUTION

Such variety in the name of a personal search for God was intolerable to major reformers like Luther and Zwingli, who believed that their own doctrines were the only means of salvation. Once these branches of Protestantism were firmly entrenched, they, like the Catholic Church, became deeply committed to the status quo and to their own hierarchies and traditions. The established reformers thus regarded the radicals' refusal to conform as an unmistakable sign of damnation; Heinrich Bullinger, Zwingli's successor, put it bluntly when he wrote that individual interpretation of the Bible allowed each man to carve his own path to hell. Indeed, Lutherans were just as ready as Catholics to persecute those who rejected their particular brand of salvation.

Münster The assault on the radicals began in the mid-1520s and soon spread through most of Europe. The imperial Diet in 1529 called for the death penalty against all Anabaptists, and indeed, most members of a group of more than 30 Anabaptist leaders who met to discuss their ideas in 1533 eventually met a violent death. Finally, in the northwest German city of Münster, a particularly fiery sect, inspired by a "prophet" named Melchior and known as Melchiorites, provoked a reaction that signaled doom even for less radical dissenters.

The Melchiorites had managed to gain considerable influence over the ordinary workers of Münster and over the craft guilds to which many belonged. They gained political control of the city early in 1534 and began to establish their "heavenly Jerusalem" on earth. They burned all books except the Bible, abolished private property, introduced polygamy, and, in an atmosphere of abandon and chaos, dug in to await the coming of the Messiah.

Here was a threat to society sufficient to force Protestants and Catholics into an alliance, and they captured the city and brutally massacred the Melchiorites. Thereafter the radicals were savagely persecuted throughout the empire. To survive, many fled first to Poland, then to the Low Countries and England, and eventually to the New World.

JOHN CALVIN

During the 1530s, Protestantism began to fragment. Neither Lutherans nor Zwinglians expanded much beyond the areas where their reforms had begun, radicals multiplied but gained few followers, and it might have seemed that the original energy had left the movement. In the early 1540s, however, a new dynamism and also a more elaborate and systematic body of doctrine were brought to Protestantism by a second-generation reformer, John Calvin (1509–1564). Born in Noyon, a small town in northern France, Calvin studied both law and the humanities at the University of Paris. In his early twenties he apparently had a shattering spiritual experience that he later called his "sudden conversion," an event about which he would say almost nothing else. Yet from that moment on, all his energy was devoted to religious reform.

In November 1533 Calvin was indicted by French Church authorities for holding heretical views, and after more than a year in hiding, he took refuge in the Swiss city of Basel. There in 1536 he published a little treatise, *Institutes of the Christian Religion*, outlining the principles of a new system of belief. He would revise and expand the *Institutes* for the remainder of his life, and it was to become the basis of Calvinism, the most vigorous branch of Protestantism in the sixteenth century.

Geneva Later in 1536 Calvin settled in Geneva, where, except for a brief period, he was to remain until his death and where he was to create a new church in the 1540s. The citizens of this prosperous market center had just overthrown their prince, a Catholic bishop. In achieving their independence, they had allied with other Swiss cities, notably Bern, a recent convert to Zwinglianism. Rebels who, with the help of Protestants, had just freed themselves from an ecclesiastical over-

CALVINISM

lord were understandably receptive to new religious teachings, and they welcomed the beliefs that Calvin proclaimed.

CALVINISM

Outwardly, Calvinism seemed to have much in common with Lutheranism. Both emphasized people's sinfulness, lack of free will, and helplessness; both rejected good works as a means of salvation; both accepted only two sacraments, baptism and communion; both regarded all occupations as equally worthy in the sight of God; both strongly upheld established political and social authority; and both leaned heavily on St. Paul and St. Augustine in their views of faith, people's weaknesses, and God's omnipotence. But the emphases in Calvinism were very different.

Predestination In arguing for justification by faith alone, Luther assumed that God can predestine a person to be saved but rejected the idea that damnation can also be preordained. Calvin's faith was much sterner. He recognized no such

▶ **AN ENGRAVING OF THE ARMY FROM BERN INVADING A NEIGHBORING PROVINCE IN 1536, FROM JOHANNES STUMPF'S CHRONICLE, 1548**
These are the soldiers who helped Geneva win its independence from the bishop who was the city's ruler. The Bernese also encouraged the acceptance of Protestantism, which John Calvin was soon to help establish in Geneva.

distinction: If people are damned, they should praise God's justice, because their sins certainly merit such a judgment; if people are saved, they should praise God's mercy, because their salvation is not a result of their own good deeds. Either way, the outcome is predestined, and nothing can be done to affect an individual's fate. It is up to God to save a person; he then perseveres in his mercy despite the person's sins; and finally, he alone decides whether to receive the sinner into the small band of saints, or elect, whom he brings into heaven. Calvin's was a grim but powerful answer to the age-old Christian question: How can sinful human beings gain salvation?

Calvin believed that our behavior here on

earth, whether good or bad, is no indication of our fate. He did suggest that someone who is to be saved by God is likely to be upright and moral, but such conduct is not necessarily a sign of salvation. However, because we should try to please God at all times, and because our communities ought to be fitting places for the elect to live, we must make every effort to lead lives worthy of one of the elect.

Morality and Discipline Calvin therefore developed a strict moral code for the true believer that banned frivolous activities, like dancing, in favor of constant self-examination, austerity, and sober study of the Bible. To help the faithful observe such regulation, he reestablished public confessions, as Zwingli had, and required daily preaching. He made services starkly simple: Stripped of ornaments, worship concentrated on uplifting sermons and the celebration of communion. His doctrine of communion occupied a middle ground between Luther's and Zwingli's. He rejected Zwingli's interpretation, saying instead that Christ's body and blood were actually and not just symbolically present. But unlike Luther, he held that they were present only in spirit and were consumed only spiritually, by faith.

To supervise the morals of the faithful and ensure that the community was worthy of the elect, Calvin gave his church a strict hierarchical structure. It was controlled by church officials called deacons and by lay elders, who were able to function even in the hostile territories where many Calvinists found themselves. A body of lay elders called the *consistory* served as the chief ecclesiastical authority. They enforced discipline and had the power of excommunication, though they always worked with local officials, who imposed the actual punishments for failures in religious duties.

Church Organization Calvin's system produced a cohesiveness and organization achieved by no other Protestant church. The *Institutes* spelled out every point of faith and practice in detail—an enormous advantage for Calvin's followers at a time when new religious doctrines were still fluid. The believer's duties and obligations were absolutely clear, as was his or her position in the very carefully organized hierarchy

of the church. In France, for example, there was a small community (or cell) in each town, a governing synod (or council) in each local area, a provincial synod in each province, and a national synod at the top of the pyramid. Tight discipline controlled the entire system, with the result that Calvinists felt themselves to be setting a moral and religious example that all the world would eventually have to follow. They were part of a very privileged community from whom the elect would be drawn. Thus they could be oppressive when they had power, yet holy rebels when they were a minority. After all, since they were freed of responsibility for their own salvation, they were acting selflessly at all times. Like the children of Israel, they had a mission to live for God, and this sense of destiny was to be one of Calvinism's greatest strengths.

Preachers from Geneva traveled through Europe to win adherents and organize the faithful wherever they could. In 1559 the city opened a university for the purpose of training preachers, because Calvin regarded education as an essential means of instilling faith. From Geneva flowed a stream of pamphlets and books, which strengthened the faith of all believers and made sure that none who wished to learn would lack the opportunity. A special target was Calvin's homeland, France, where his preachers had their first successes, especially in the cities. Calvinism also won important support in the nobility, notably among women aristocrats who often influenced their families to adopt the new beliefs.

By 1564, when Calvin died, his church was well established: more than a million adherents in France, where they were called Huguenots; the Palatinate converted; Scotland won; and considerable groups of followers in England, the Low Countries, and Hungary. Despite its severity, Calvin's coherent and comprehensive body of doctrine proved to have wide appeal in an age of piety that yearned for clear religious answers. To whom, however, did it appeal?

The Appeal of Calvinism When those who adopted the new faith explained their conversion, they usually did so in terms of a slow or sudden revelation—God had finally shown them the truth. But historians have noted that there were certain groups who seemed especially open to Protestant, and particularly Calvinist, teachings. All the reformed faiths did particularly well in cities, and it has been suggested that the long history of independence among townspeople made them more inclined to challenge traditional authorities. In addition, they tended to be more literate, and thus were drawn to beliefs that emphasized reading the Bible for oneself. And Calvinism put an emphasis on sobriety, discipline, and communal responsibility that would have appealed strongly to the increasingly self-confident merchants and artisans of the cities. That the Calvinists were also successful in the areas of southern France farthest away from central authority in Paris only reinforces the connection with an inclination toward independence and self-reliance.

Geneva itself became a determinedly independent place—the only city in Europe that successfully resisted becoming part of a territorial state and remained an autonomous political force during the two centuries following Calvin's death. Because of the dominance of Calvinism, morals were strictly supervised, and there was an aura of public discipline that all visitors noted. At the same time, artisans and merchants made Geneva an important economic center, and the university achieved an international reputation. Gradually in the seventeenth century the atmosphere of austerity softened, but the city continued to be seen as a model community for all Calvinists.

Women and Reform   Cities were not the only centers of religious reform. In some parts of Europe, such as Scotland, new beliefs flourished outside towns because they won political support. But in all areas, the importance of women to the spread of Protestantism was unmistakable. Calvin's earliest significant converts were aristocratic women, whose patronage helped his faith take root at the highest levels of society. Like the literate women of the cities, they saw in its message an opportunity to express themselves and to work for others in ways that had not been possible before. They were often the main readers of the Bible in family gatherings; they took the lead in demanding broader access to education, especially for girls; and they were regularly prominent in radical movements.

One theologian who despaired at the results of Luther's translation of the New Testament reserved his most bitter complaints for the women who were studying the Bible for themselves. And the results were apparent not only among the literate. The records of the Inquisition, the Catholic tribunal charged with rooting out heresy, are full of the trials and executions of women who were martyrs for their beliefs and who died defending doctrines they had learned from preachers or other women. Again and again, they rejected the authority of priests and asserted their right to individual faith. It was determination like this that enabled the Reformation to establish itself and to spread until it posed a major challenge to the traditional Church (*see box*, p. 410).

IV. *The Catholic Revival*

REFORM AND COUNTER REFORM

Those with Protestant sympathies usually refer to the Catholic revival that started in the 1530s as the Counter Reformation, implying that the Roman Church acted only as a result of criticisms by Luther and others. Catholic historians call it the Catholic Reformation, implying that the movement began within the Church and was not merely a reaction to Protestantism. There is justification for both views. Certainly the papacy was aware of its loss of control over millions of Christians, but a great deal of the effort to put the Catholic Church's house in order was a result of deep faith and a determination to purify the in-

Although a major effort was certainly needed, and serious problems had to be addressed, one must not forget that there was a vast reserve of loyalty and affection that the Church could draw on. Many more Europeans remained Catholic in the long run than converted to Protestantism. They took comfort from tradition and from priests who, rather than demanding that believers achieve salvation on their own, offered the Church's mediation, beautiful ceremonies, and rituals to help people overcome their sins. Catholicism had a long history of charity for the

The Trial of Elizabeth Dirks

In radical groups, women often occupied central roles they never achieved in the larger churches. Since the most important attributes of a believer in these groups were faith, commitment, and the presence of the holy spirit, there was frequently an egalitarianism not found elsewhere in sixteenth-century society. Thus it was that the radical "teacher" (or leader) whom the Inquisition in the Netherlands interrogated in January 1549 was a woman named Elizabeth Dirks. Her replies give us a vivid sense of the beliefs the Reformation was stimulating among ordinary people—though in this case they were put forward with a clarity and a conviction that would lead to Elizabeth's execution two months later.

Examiner: We understand you are a teacher and have led many astray. Who are your friends?

Elizabeth: Do not press me on this point. Ask me about my faith and I will answer you gladly.

Examiner: Do you not consider our Church to be the house of the Lord?

Elizabeth: I do not. For it is written that God said "I will dwell with you."

Examiner: What do you think of our mass?

Elizabeth: I have no faith in your mass, but only in the word of God.

Examiner: What do you believe about the Holy Sacrament of the Eucharist?

Elizabeth: I never in my life read in Scripture about a Holy Sacrament, but only of the Supper of the Lord.

Examiner: You speak with a haughty tongue.

Elizabeth: No. I speak with a free tongue.

Examiner: Do you not believe that you are saved by baptism?

Elizabeth: No: all the water in the sea cannot save me. My salvation is in Christ, who commanded me to love my God and my neighbor as myself.

Examiner: Do priests have the power to forgive sins?

Elizabeth: How should I believe that? Christ is the only priest through whom sins are forgiven.

As torture was applied:

Examiner: You can recant everything you have said.

Elizabeth: No, I will not, but I will seal it with my blood.

Adapted from Thieleman von Bracht, *The Bloody Theater or Martyr's Mirror*, Daniel Rupp (trans.) (Lancaster, Pa.: David Miller, 1837), pp. 409–410.

poor, and this was strengthened during the sixteenth century. For ordinary Christians, the familiarity, support, and grandeur they found in the Church were often more than enough reason to resist the appeals of reformers.

CRISIS AND CHANGE IN THE CHURCH

Yet there was no doubt that the first half of the sixteenth century was the lowest point in the history of the Catholic Church and that few would have expected the recovery that followed. By 1550 many areas of Europe had been lost to the Protestants, and even in regions that were still loyal, the papacy was able to exercise little control. The French Church, for example, had a well-established tradition of autonomy, exemplified by the right France's kings had had since 1516 to make ecclesiastical appointments. In Spain, too, the monarchy retained its independence and even had its own Inquisition. In the Holy Roman Empire, those states that had rejected Protestantism gave the pope no more than token allegiance.

Moreover, there was still no comprehensive

definition of Catholic doctrine on justification, salvation, and the sacraments. Worse yet, the Church's leadership was far from effective. Although one pope, Leo X, had attempted to correct notorious abuses such as simony, the sale of church offices, in the early sixteenth century, Rome simply did not have the spiritual authority to make reform a vital force in the Catholic Church.

Paul III   The situation changed with the pope elected in 1534: Paul III, a man not renowned for saintliness but a genius at making the right decisions for the Church. By the end of his reign, in 1549, the Catholic revival was under way. The heart of Paul's strategy was his determination to assert papal responsibility throughout the Church. Realizing that uncertainties in Catholic doctrine could be resolved only by a reexamination of traditional theology, he decided within a few months of taking office to call a Church council for that purpose, despite the danger of rekindling the conciliar movement. It took 10 years to overcome resistance to the idea, but in the meantime Paul attacked abuses throughout the

▸ *Titian*
POPE PAUL III AND HIS NEPHEWS, ALESSANDRO AND OTTAVIO FARNESE, 1546
The psychological tension Titian created in this family portrait is extraordinary. The shrewd 77-year-old pope who had launched the Church's vigorous response to Protestantism looks benignly on Ottavio, whose seemingly calculated gesture of deference hints at the aggressiveness that was soon to cause a major family quarrel over land and money. And Cardinal Alessandro, standing apart, was already a famous patron of art with little concern for Church affairs. Perhaps because of its revelation of character, the painting was never finished.

Church, disregarding both vested interests and tradition. He aimed his campaign at all levels of the hierarchy, undeterred by powerful bishops and cardinals long used to a lax and corrupt regime. In addition, he founded a Roman Inquisition, a decision that reflected the era's growing reliance on persecution as a means of destroying dissent.

Paul realized that, in the long run, the revival of Catholicism would depend on whether his successors maintained his efforts. During his 15-year reign, therefore, he made a series of superb appointments to the College of Cardinals (the body that elects the popes); the result was the creation of possibly the most illustrious College in history. Many of its members were famous for their piety, others for their learning. They came from all over Europe, united by their devotion to the Church and their resolve to see it once again command admiration and reverence. The result of Paul's farsighted policy was to be a succession of popes through the early seventeenth century who would fully restore the atmosphere of spirituality and morality that had long been missing from the papacy.

THE COUNCIL OF TRENT

The ecumenical, or general, council of Church leaders called by Paul finally assembled at Trent, a northern Italian city, in 1545, and met irregularly until the delegates managed to complete their work in 1563. The council's history was one of stormy battles between various national factions. The non-Italians pressed for decentralization of religious authority; the Italians, closely tied to the papacy, advocated a consolidation of power. For both sides, the divisions were political as well as ecclesiastical, because at issue was the independence not only of bishops but also of local princes and kings. A large majority of the delegates were Italians, however, and their conclusions almost always reinforced the dominance of the pope. The threat of a revival of conciliarism never materialized.

Doctrine In keeping with Paul's instructions, the Council of Trent gave more of its time to the basic issue of Church doctrine than to the problem of reform. Nearly all its decisions were intended to establish clear definitions of practice and belief, and to bring to an end long-standing theological uncertainties or differences of opinion. The main sources for these decisions were the interpretations put forward by Thomas Aquinas, who now became the central theologian of the Catholic Church. At the same time, Trent's decrees were designed to affirm precisely those teachings that the Protestants had rejected. Catholicism from then on would be committed primarily to the outward, sacramental heritage of Christianity. In this view, the Bible is not the exclusive authority for the believer: Church tradition holds an equal place in establishing religious truth. Human will is free, good works as well as faith are a means of salvation, all seven sacraments are channels of grace, and Christ's sacrifice is reenacted in every Mass. The Council of Trent endorsed the special position of the priest and insisted that God be worshiped with appropriately elaborate ceremonies and rites.

These were the principal decisions at Trent, but hundreds of minor matters were also settled: For the first time, the priest's presence was declared to be essential at the sacrament of marriage, a further reinforcement of his importance; the Vulgate, the Latin translation of the Bible prepared chiefly by St. Jerome, was decreed to be a holy text, a decision which rebutted humanists and other scholars who had found mistranslations of Greek and Hebrew in Jerome's work; and in direct contrast to the Protestants, gorgeous ritual was heavily stressed, which encouraged artists to beautify church buildings and ceremonies.

Restoring the Church The achievement of the council was to adjust the Church to the world. Many ordinary people, troubled by the stern self-denial and predestination taught by most Protestant churches and sects, preferred the traditional comfort and support Catholicism had long offered. They were ready to champion their old faith as soon as its leadership restored its sense of purpose by removing abuses and defining doctrines. And the new discipline of the Church was apparent in the council's effort to deal with morality as thoroughly as with belief. When it gave its approval to the Inquisition and to the "Index of Forbidden Books," which informed all Catholics of the heretical works they were not allowed to read, the council signaled the determination of the Church to recover the ground it had lost.

THE AFTERMATH OF TRENT

The new atmosphere of dedication swept through the Catholic Church, inspiring thinkers and artists throughout Europe to lend their talents to the cause. In many ways, Baroque art was to be the genre of the Counter Reformation: Painters, architects, and musicians caught up by the new moral fervor in Catholicism expressed their faith in brilliant and dramatic portrayals of religious subjects and in churches that were designed to dazzle the observer in a way that most Protestants could not allow.

This artistic outpouring was, of course, far more than a reflection of the decisions of a few hundred prelates assembled in a council. It was also one of many indicators of the new vigor of Catholicism. In France the new generation of Church leaders who appeared in the late sixteenth century was distinguished for its austerity, learning, and observance of duties. The inheritors of the traditional Scholastic philosophy multiplied, and in the late sixteenth and early seventeenth centuries they were to become influential throughout Europe.

▶ *Titian*
The Council of Trent, ca. 1564
The splendor of the gathering of representatives of the Catholic Church from all of Europe is conveyed by this scene, attributed to Titian. The ranks of bishops in their miters, listening to one of their number address the assembly from the pulpit on the right, visibly embodied a Church putting itself in order as it faced the challenge of Protestantism.

Women in the Church Moreover, the crucial contribution to Protestantism of its women adherents was echoed in the revival of Catholicism. There was a remarkable flowering of new religious orders for women in the sixteenth and seventeenth centuries, many of which became identified with charitable works. Since one of the most important ways the Church set about winning back the faithful was by expanding its philanthropic activities—through new hospitals and expanded assistance to the poor, to orphans, and to other unfortunates—its female orders played an essential role in the Counter Reformation. And nowhere was their devout spirituality more apparent than in Spain, the most fiercely Catholic of all European countries.

The Spaniards expressed their religious passion in many ways—by insisting on converting the native peoples they conquered overseas, by giving great power to the Inquisition that guarded orthodoxy from large Muslim and Jewish communities at home, by encouraging lay as well as clerical piety, and by founding the most famous new order of the age, the Jesuits (see below). But no indication of their devotion was as distinctive as the great flowering of mysticism, which was most famously represented by St. Teresa (1515–1582).

St. Teresa The mystic seeks to worship God directly and immediately, in an encounter that usually takes place in a trance and without the intervention of a priest. Because this is an entirely personal religious experience, which does not require the mediation of the Church, it has always been looked on with suspicion by the authorities. St. Teresa was no exception. As a rich and spoiled young girl, she had led a rather loose life, and her concerned father had sent her to a convent to instill some discipline. Perhaps because the family had only recently converted from Judaism, considerable attention was also given to Teresa's religious education. She later recalled a time when, after reading the lives of saints, she decided to become a martyr for Christ. She set out with her brother for North Africa, where she was determined to die fighting Muslims but was caught by an uncle. Of more lasting effect were the visions of God she began to have, which gradually convinced her that she had a special religious mission (*see box*, p. 415).

Church authorities became worried when, after becoming a nun, Teresa began to attract a following as a spiritual adviser to a number of women in her native city of Avila. Some churchmen suggested that her visions were the work of the devil, not God. After many examinations, however—and finally an interview with the king of Spain himself, who was deeply impressed by her holiness—the doubts evaporated. Teresa founded a strict new order of nuns and traveled all over Spain establishing convents. She soon became a legendary figure and was made a saint only 40 years after her death. To Spaniards she

has remained a heroine, the subject of many affectionate stories. Once, when her carriage got stuck in the mud, she apparently looked heavenward and said: "If this is the way you treat your friends, God, no wonder you have so few of them." Above all, she came to embody the deep religious devotion of Counter Reformation Spain.

The Papacy The most conspicuous embodiments of the new energy of the Church, however, were the popes themselves. Paul III's successors used their personal authority and pontifical resources not to adorn their palaces but to continue the enormous cleansing operation within the Church and to lead the counterattack against Protestantism. If a king or prince refused to help, the popes would try to persuade one of his leading subjects (for example, the Guise family in France and the dukes of Bavaria in the empire) to organize the struggle. Their diplomats and agents were everywhere, ceaselessly urging Catholics to stamp out Protestantism wherever it was found. And the pontiffs insisted on strict morality so as to restore their reputation for piety and to set a proper example to the faithful: One pope even ordered clothes painted on the nudes in Michelangelo's *Last Judgment* in the Sistine Chapel.

With the leaders of the Church thus bent on reform, the restoration of the faith and the reconquest of lost souls could proceed with maximum effect. And the popes had at their disposal a religious order established by Ignatius Loyola in 1540 specifically for these purposes: the Society of Jesus.

IGNATIUS LOYOLA

The third of the great religious innovators of the sixteenth century, after Luther and Calvin, was Ignatius Loyola (1491–1556); unlike his predecessors, however, he sought to reform the Catholic Church from within.

Loyola was the son of a Basque nobleman, raised in the chivalric and intensely religious atmosphere of Spain, and he was often at the court of Ferdinand of Aragon. In his teens he entered the army, but when he was 30, a leg wound ended his military career. While convalescing, he was deeply impressed by a number of popular

St. Teresa's Visions

These two are among the most famous passages from the autobiography St. Teresa began writing in 1562, when she was 47 years old. The book is essentially the story of a spiritual journey, as a restless young woman gains purpose and strength through mystical visions and unwavering faith. Her account of a mystical transport in the second passage quoted here was the inspiration for a famous sculpture by Gian Lorenzo Bernini, **The Ecstasy of St. Teresa,** *in the seventeenth century.*

I: One day, when I was at prayer, the Lord was pleased to reveal to me nothing but His hands, whose beauty was so great as to be indescribable. This made me very fearful. A few days later I also saw the Divine face. On St. Paul's Day, I saw a complete representation of his sacred Humanity. If there were nothing else in Heaven to delight the eyes but the extreme beauty of the glorified bodies there, that alone would be the greatest bliss. If I were to spend years and years imagining how to invent anything so beautiful, I could not do it. In its whiteness and radiance, it exceeds all we can imagine. It is a soft whiteness which, without wearying the eyes, causes them the greatest delight. By comparison with it, the brightness of our sun seems quite dim.

II: It pleased the Lord that I sometimes saw beside me an angel in bodily form. He was not tall, but short, and very beautiful, his face aflame. In his hands I saw a long golden spear, and at the end of the iron tip I seemed to see a point of fire. With this he seemed to pierce my heart several times. When he drew it out, he left me completely afire with a great love for God. During the days when this continued, I went about as if in a stupor.

From E. Allison Peers, *The Life of Teresa of Jesus* (London: Sheed & Ward, 1944; reprinted New York: Doubleday, 1960), pp. 258–260 and 273–274.

lives of the saints he read, and soon his religious interests began to take shape in chivalric and military terms. He visualized Mary as his lady, the inspiration of a Christian quest in which the forces of God and the devil fight in mighty battle. This was a faith seen from the perspective of the knight, and though the direct parallel lessened as Loyola's thought developed, it left an unmistakable stamp on his future work.

In 1522 Loyola gave up his knightly garb and swore to go on a pilgrimage to Jerusalem. He retired to a monastery for 10 months to absolve himself of the guilt of a sinful life and to prepare spiritually for the journey to the Holy Land. At the monastery he had a momentous experience that, like Luther's and Calvin's, dominated the rest of his life. According to tradition, he had a vision lasting eight days, during which he saw in detail the outline of a book, the *Spiritual Exercises*, and a new religious order, the Society of Jesus.

The **Spiritual Exercises** The first version of the *Spiritual Exercises* certainly dated from this period, but like Calvin's *Institutes*, it was to be thoroughly revised many times. The book deals not with doctrines or theology but with the discipline and training necessary for a God-fearing life. Believers must undertake four weeks of contemplation and self-examination that culminate in a feeling of union with God, in which they surrender their minds and wills to Christ. If successful, they are then ready to submit completely to the call of God and to pursue the Church's commands without question.

The manual was the heart of the organization of the Society of Jesus, and it gave those who followed its precepts (known as Jesuits) a dedication and determination that made them seem the Church's answer to the Calvinists. But while the end might be similar to Luther's and Calvin's— the personal attainment of grace—the method,

Map 13.2 RELIGIOUS DIVISIONS IN EUROPE AT THE END OF THE SIXTEENTH CENTURY
By the late sixteenth century, the division of Europe into distinct areas, each committed primarily
to one church, was virtually complete. Now that they were solidly established, the major faiths
became associated with universities that elaborated and promoted their beliefs.

with its emphasis on individual effort and concentration, could not have been more different. For the *Spiritual Exercises* emphasize that believers can *act* for themselves; they do not have to depend on faith alone to gain salvation, as Protestants assert. One can prepare for grace through a tremendous act of will and not depend solely on a gift from God. Loyola makes immense demands precisely because he insists that the will is free and that good works are efficacious.

Loyola's Followers During the 16 years after he left the monastery, Ignatius led a life of poverty and study. Though lame, he traveled to Jerusalem and back barefoot in 1523–1524, and two years later he found his way to the University of Alcalá, where he attracted his first disciples, three fellow students. Suspected by the Inquisition of being rather too independent in their beliefs, the little band walked to Paris, where they were joined by six more disciples. Ignatius now decided to return to the Holy Land, but the companions found themselves unable to travel beyond Venice because of war. Instead, they preached in the streets, visited the poor and the sick, urged all who would listen to rededicate themselves to piety and faith, and in 1537 achieved ordination as priests. Their activities were beginning to take definite shape, and so they decided to seek the pope's blessing for their work. They saw Paul III in 1538, and two years later, despite opposition from those who saw it as a threat to the authority of local bishops, the pope approved a plan Ignatius submitted for a new religious order that would owe allegiance only to the papacy.

THE JESUITS

The Society, or Company, of Jesus had four principal functions: preaching, hearing confessions, teaching, and founding and maintaining missions. The first two were the Jesuits' means of strengthening the beliefs of individual Catholics or converting Protestants. The third became one of their most effective weapons. Loyola, much influenced by the Christian humanists he had encountered, was convinced of the tremendous power of education. The Jesuits therefore set about organizing the best schools in Europe and

were so successful that some Protestants sent their children to the Society's schools despite the certainty that the pupils would become committed Catholics. The instructors followed humanist principles and taught the latest ideas, including the most recent advances in science. The Jesuits' final activity, missionary work, brought them their most spectacular successes among both non-Christians and Protestants.

▶ *Peter Paul Rubens*
THE MIRACLE OF ST. IGNATIUS, 1619
Loyola quickly became one of the major heroes of the Catholic revival. Within less than 60 years of his death (1556), he was to become a saint of the Church. He became one of the heroes of Baroque art, as is apparent in this painting by Peter Paul Rubens, which creates a powerful image that represents Loyola at the moment when he cures a man and a woman who have been possessed by the devil.

A number of qualities combined to make the Jesuits extraordinarily effective in winning converts and turning Catholics into militant activists. First, the order demanded very high intellectual abilities. It selected recruits carefully (turning many applicants away) and gave them a superb

education. Jesuits were famous for their knowledge of Scripture and traditional teachings and their ability to out-argue opponents. In addition, they were trained to be highly effective preachers and excellent educators. And their discipline, determination, and awareness of the contemporary world soon won them a fearsome reputation. They had no equal in the forcefulness with which they advanced the aims of the Council of Trent and the papacy.

There is every reason to regard the Jesuits as the striking arm of the Counter Reformation; indeed, their organization was to some extent modeled on the medieval military orders. A Jesuit at a royal court was often the chief inspiration for a ruler's militant support of the faith, and in many areas the Society was the main conqueror of rival beliefs—for example, in Poland, where Jesuits in the late sixteenth century led a campaign that eradicated widespread Protestantism and created a devotedly Catholic country. Yet it must be noted that in an age that took persecution for granted, the Jesuits always opposed execution for heresy; they far preferred to win a convert than to kill a heretic. Their presence was soon felt all over the world: As early as the 1540s, one of Loyola's first disciples, Francis Xavier, was conducting a mission to Japan. Despite the many enmities they aroused by their single-mindedness and their self-assurance, their unswerving devotion was a major reason for the revival of the Roman Church.

RELIGION AND POLITICS

As a revived Catholic Church confronted the Protestants, religious warfare of unprecedented ferocity erupted throughout Europe (see Chapter 15). More people seemed to feel more passionately about faith than at any other time in Western history. But the conflict would not have continued as long as it did without the armies and resources provided by princes and monarchs. Both sides drew crucial support from rulers who were determined either to suppress any sign of heresy (that is, any faith other than their own) in their territories or to overthrow heretical regimes in neighboring lands. The struggle over religion was, for these rulers, a means of establishing their authority in their own realms and a justification for aggression abroad.

CHRONOLOGY OF THE REFORMATION AND COUNTER REFORMATION

1517	Luther's protest begins: the 95 Theses on indulgences.
1521	Diet of Worms: Luther condemned by Emperor Charles V.
1524–1525	Peasants' Revolt in Germany. Zürich adopts Zwingli's Reformation.
1531	Protestant League of Schmalkalden formed in Germany. Death of Zwingli. King Henry VIII proclaims himself head of the Church of England.
1534	Paul III becomes pope. Anabaptists take over the city of Münster in Germany.
1535	Thomas More executed for not accepting Henry VIII as head of the Church of England.
1536	Calvin comes to Geneva; first edition of his *Institutes*. Death of Erasmus.
1540	Pope Paul III approves the Jesuit Order.
1541	Calvin settles in Geneva permanently.
1545	Council of Trent begins.
1546	Death of Luther.
1556	Death of Loyola.
1559	First "Index of Forbidden Books" published. Execution of Protestants after Inquisition trials in Spain.
1564	Publication of the Decrees of the Council of Trent. Death of Calvin.

The strong connection between politics and belief, and its dire consequences, was the result of a transformation that was almost as far-reaching as the Reformation itself. Just as Western Christianity was changed forever in the sixteenth century, so too were the power and the ambition of the territorial state. At the same time as a handful of reformers, building on powerful social and intellectual forces, reshaped religious structures and practices, a handful of political leaders—building on no less powerful military, social, and economic forces—created armies, systems of taxation, and bureaucratic organizations that reshaped the structures and practices of central governments throughout Europe.

Recommended Reading

Sources

*Calvin, John. *On God and Political Duty.* J. T. McNeill (ed.). 1950.

*Erasmus, Desiderius. *Essential Works of Erasmus.* W. T. H. Jackson (ed.). 1965.

Loyola, Ignatius. *The Spiritual Exercises of St. Ignatius.* R. W. Gleason (ed.). 1964.

*Luther, Martin. *Martin Luther: Selections from His Writings.* John Dillenberger (ed.). 1961.

Studies

*Bainton, Roland H. *Here I Stand: A Life of Martin Luther.* 1955. A classic biography in English, with many quotations from Luther's writings.

Bangert, William. *A History of the Society of Jesus.* 1972. The best basic history in English of the work of Loyola and the Jesuits.

*Bossy, John. *Christianity in the West. 1400–1700.* 1985. An overview of the religious history of Europe by one of the leading historians of Catholic thought and practice.

*Bouwsma, William J. *John Calvin: A Sixteenth-Century Portrait.* 1988. The standard biography.

*Davis, Natalie Zemon. *Society and Culture in Early Modern France.* 1975. A collection of essays about popular beliefs and attitudes, particularly on religious matters, during the sixteenth century.

Delumeau, Jean. *Catholicism between Luther and Voltaire: A New View of the Counter-Reformation.* 1977. The standard introduction.

Hillerbrand, Hans J. (ed.). *Radical Tendencies in the Reformation: Divergent Perspectives.* 1986. Important essays on the emergence of radical ideas and sects in the Reformation.

*Huizinga, Johan. *Erasmus and the Age of Reformation.* 1957. A warm and sympathetic biography, beautifully written.

*Kenny, Anthony. *Thomas More.* 1983. An excellent brief introduction to the life and work of the humanist-statesman.

Kittelson, James M. *Luther the Reformer: The Story of the Man and His Career.* 1986. The best introduction to Luther's life and thought.

Moeller, Bernd. *Imperial Cities and the Reformation.* H. C. E. Midelfort and M. U. Edwards (trs.). 1972. Three stimulating essays about the special role of cities in establishing the Reformation in Germany.

Po-chia Hsia, R. (ed.). *The People and the German Reformation: Approaches in the Social History of Religion.* 1988. A set of essays that reflects recent trends in the social interpretation of the Reformation.

Scribner, Robert. *For the Sake of Simple Folk: Popular Propaganda for the German Reformation.* 1981. A pathbreaking analysis of how the Reformation was spread.

Scribner, Robert, and Gerhard Benecke (eds.). *The German Peasant War of 1525: New Viewpoints.* 1979. A stimulating set of essays about the social upheaval that accompanied the Reformation.

*Weber, Max. *The Protestant Ethic and the Spirit of Capitalism.* Talcott Parsons (tr.). 1958. Originally published in 1904 and 1905, this study of the way in which the Reformation helped create the modern world has influenced much of the historical thinking about the Reformation.

Williams, George H. *The Radical Reformation.* 1962. The most comprehensive account of the sects and their founders.

*Available in paperback.

Hans Holbein the Younger
THE AMBASSADORS, 1533
Hans Holbein the Younger's *The Ambassadors*
shows the worldliness that was expected of
diplomats (many of whom were also soldiers) in the
sixteenth century. The two men are surrounded by
symbols of the skills, knowledge, and refinement
their job required—geography, mathematics,
literature, and music. But despite this emphasis on
material concerns, Holbein reminds us (in the
optically distorted skull across the bottom of the
painting) that death and spiritual needs cannot be
forgotten.

CHAPTER FOURTEEN

ECONOMIC EXPANSION AND A NEW POLITICS

EUROPE in 1400 was a poor, technologically backward, and politically disorganized area compared to the realms of the Indian moguls or Chinese emperors. And yet within little more than a century, Europeans were expanding aggressively into Asia and the Americas. Their numbers were growing, their economy was booming, their technological advances were making possible the creation of new markets and new empires, and their political leaders were developing structures of government and authority more elaborate than any that had been seen since the fall of the Roman Empire. The emergence of this new world power was one of the most astonishing transformations in Western history, and historians have long debated its causes. Their suggestions have ranged from the personal (the initiatives of specific kings, entrepreneurs, or explorers) to the abstract (such forces as demographic change or a gradual warming of the climate). Like the fall of the Roman Empire, however, this was so profound a reshaping of Europe that one cannot suggest a single comprehensive explanation. Indeed, it is only by looking at the individual changes in some detail that one can understand how far-reaching was the reordering that had taken place by the late sixteenth century.

I. Expansion at Home

POPULATION INCREASE

It was during the last third of the fifteenth century that signs of change appeared in the demographic, economic, and political history of Europe. Some have argued that the root cause lay in politics: Because assertive regimes restored order and authority in a number of states, confidence rose, trade quickened, and populations grew. Others regard either economic or demographic advance as the source of change. In fact, it is clear that all three were connected and that all three reinforced one another. Thus, although we are not certain why the number of Europeans began to increase after more than 100 years of decline, we can see the effects of the increase in many areas of life.

Exact measurements are not possible, but it seems likely that the loss of population that began with the Black Death in the 1340s had run its course by the 1460s. Plagues, though recurrent, began to take less of a toll (perhaps because immunities developed); bad harvests became less frequent (perhaps because of a warming climate); and families were thus able to produce more surviving children. As a result, Europe's population rose by some 50 percent between 1470 and 1620. And cities expanded even faster: London had fewer than 50,000 inhabitants in the early sixteenth century but over 200,000 a hundred years later. There was also extensive reoccupation of marginal farmland, which had been abandoned in the fourteenth and fifteenth centuries because a shrinking population had provided no market for its produce. Now there were more mouths to feed, and the extra acres again became profitable.

Consequences of the Increase The rise in population was followed by a staggering jump in food prices. By the early 1600s wheat cost approximately five times more than in the late 1400s, an increase that far outpaced the movement of prices in general. It is not surprising, therefore, that this period witnessed the first wave of enclosures in England: Major landowners put up fences around common tilling or grazing ground, traditionally open to all the animals of the locality, and reserved it for their own crops or their sheep, whose wool was also in increasing demand. By 1600 about one-eighth of England's arable land had been enclosed. The only answer, when changes like these made a village incapable of supporting its growing population, was for people to move to towns and cities.

ECONOMIC GROWTH

As markets began to grow in response to population pressures, the volume of trade also shot upward; commercial profits thus kept pace with those of agriculture. Customs receipts rose steadily, as did the yield of tolls from ships entering the Baltic Sea, one of the main routes of European trade. In many areas, too, shipbuilding boomed. This was the heyday of the English cloth trade and the great Spanish sheep farms, of the central German linen industry and the northern Italian silk industry. Printing became a widespread occupation, and gun making and glassmaking also expanded rapidly. Glassmaking had a major effect on European society because the increasing use of windows allowed builders to divide houses into small rooms, thus giving many people a little privacy for the first time.

Leading financiers who invested in the growing volume of trade accumulated large fortunes. For centuries the Italians had been in the vanguard of economic advance, but in the sixteenth century firms of other nations were achieving international prominence. The most successful of the new enterprises was run by a family descended from a fourteenth-century weaver, Johannes Fugger of Augsburg. The sixteenth-century Fuggers financed the Spanish King Charles I's quest for the throne of the Holy Roman Empire and his later wars after he became the Emperor Charles V. Great bankers were thus often closely allied with monarchs, and like all merchants, they gained from the mounting power of central governments. Rulers encouraged commerce in the hope of larger revenues from customs duties and taxes, and they gave leading entrepreneurs valuable privileges. Such alliances were eventually the undoing of some firms, which were ruined when kings went bankrupt, but until the late sixteenth century, Italian and German bankers controlled Europe's finances.

Almost every level of commercial activity offered opportunities for advancement. The guild system expanded in the sixteenth century to incorporate many new trades, and the structure of merchant enterprises became more elaborate. The idea took hold that a business firm was an impersonal entity—larger than the person who owned it—with an identity, legal status, permanence, and even profits that were not the same as those of its members. Here was yet another indication of the changes taking place in economic affairs.

INFLATION AND SILVER

The surest sign of growth, however, was the slow inflation of prices, which began around 1500 after some 150 years of either stagnant or falling prices. By modern standards, the increase was tiny—1 or 2 percent a year, totaling 75 percent in Spain by 1600 and slightly less elsewhere in Europe—but it prompted bitter protests from those who thought a loaf of bread had a "just" price and that any increase was mere exploitation by the baker. In general, however, the modest inflation was an indication that demand was rising, and it not only boosted profits but also reduced people's debts (because the amount that had been borrowed was worth less each year).

Silver Imports   A major reason for the inflation was the growth of the population, but it was also propelled by the huge quantities of silver the

▶ *Anonymous French Miniature*
MERCHANTS CLEARING ACCOUNTS
This sixteenth-century depiction of a group of people in a fine house calculating accounts gives a sense of the increasingly complicated exchanges that became necessary as commerce expanded. Books had to be checked and moneys counted, and it is noteworthy that the transactions involve the monk on the left and the woman holding her purse on the right.

IMPORTS OF TREASURE TO SPAIN FROM THE NEW WORLD, 1511–1600	
Decade	Total Value*
1511–1520	2,626,000
1521–1530	1,407,000
1531–1540	6,706,000
1541–1550	12,555,000
1551–1560	21,437,000
1561–1570	30,418,000
1571–1580	34,990,000
1581–1590	63,849,000
1591–1600	85,536,000

*In ducats.

Source: Adapted from J. H. Elliott, *Imperial Spain, 1469–1716* (New York, 1964), p. 175.

Spaniards imported from the New World, which made money more readily available (see accompanying table). Most of the silver passed from Spain to the Italian and German merchants who financed Spanish wars and controlled the American trade, and it thus affected all of Europe. Other sources of supply, notably silver mines in Austria, were appearing at this time; but the flow of New World silver was the main reason for the end of the crippling shortage of precious metals and, hence, of coins that had plagued Europe for centuries. By the middle of the seventeenth century, the continent's holdings in gold had increased by one-fifth and, more important, its stock of silver had tripled.

With money circulating more freely and markets growing, the profits of traders and financiers improved dramatically. They could invest more widely (for example, in overseas ventures), and they could achieve new levels of wealth.

THE COMMERCIAL REVOLUTION

As the volume of trade rose, new mechanisms for organizing large-scale economic activity were put in place—a process that has been called Europe's *commercial revolution*. Bookkeepers devised new, standardized principles for keeping track of a firm's accounts, bankers created elaborate systems of agents and letters of credit to transfer funds across large distances, merchants developed more effective means of forming broad partnerships that were capable of major investments and of ensuring against losses, and governments gave increased support to new ventures and to the financial community in general. Essential to these activities was an attitude and a way of conducting business that is known as *capitalism.*

Capitalism   Capitalism was both a product of economic change and a stimulus to further change. It is often thought of as a system, but it refers primarily to the distinct outlook and kinds of behavior displayed by certain people as they make, buy, and sell goods. At its root capitalism means the accumulation of capital—that is, tangible wealth—for its own sake. In practice, this requires taking risks and also reinvesting whatever one earns so as to enlarge one's profits. Those who undertook long-distance trade had many capitalist traits: They took great risks, and they were prepared to wait months and even years in order to make as large a financial gain as possible. Similarly, bankers were prepared to lend their capital, despite the danger that the loan might not be repaid, in the hope of profit; and if

▶ *Jost Amman*
ALLEGORY OF TRADE, WOODCUT
This late-sixteenth-century celebration of the world of the merchant shows, around the sides, the shipping of goods, the keeping of accounts, and the exchange of money that were transforming economic life. In the center, the virtues of the merchant are symbolized: integrity (a man looking over his shoulder), taciturnity (two men on his right), and a knowledge of languages (two men in turbans) in front of judiciousness on a throne and a book representing invention.

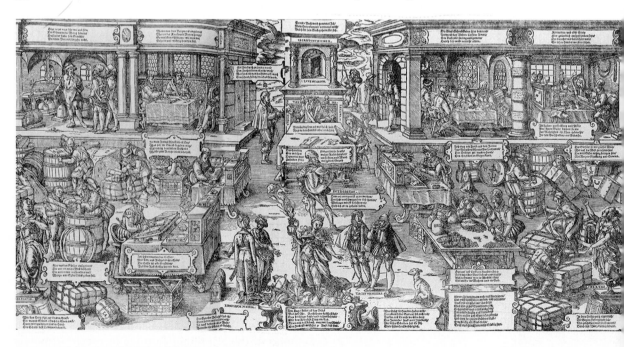

they succeeded, they continually plowed their earnings back into their businesses to make them ever larger. The fortunes that these capitalists accumulated, and the desire for worldly riches that they displayed, became an essential stimulus to economic growth. Far from the rural world where food was grown primarily for survival, not for profit, they were forging a new way of thinking about money and wealth. Although their outlook had existed before, only in the sixteenth century did it come to dominate Europe's economy. As a result, traditional religious prohibitions on the charging of interest began to weaken, and materialist ambitions became more open and accepted.

Unease over this new outlook did not disappear. Shakespeare's play *The Merchant of Venice*, written in the 1590s, attacked the values that capitalism was coming to represent. He contrasted unfavorably the quest for profit with more tra-

▶ *Petrus Christus*
ST. ELIGIUS AS A GOLDSMITH, 1449
Goldsmiths played a vital financial role in the early days of capitalism. Because of the value of the merchandise they made and sold, their shops—like the one here, with customers looking in the window, as one can see in the convex mirror on the right—were sources of capital as well as goods. In addition to providing such items as the ring he is handing to the young woman, the goldsmith might well have provided investments for the traders in his city.

ditional commitments, such as charity and mercy. And his choice of Venice as a setting was appropriate because the large empire this city built in the eastern Mediterranean was mainly the result of a single-minded pursuit of trade. But criticism had no effect. The spread of capitalism was now irresistible.

SOCIAL CHANGE: THE COUNTRYSIDE

Not everyone shared in the new prosperity of the sixteenth century. Landowners, food producers, artisans, and merchants benefited most from the rising population and could amass fortunes. Tenants who were able to harvest a surplus beyond their own needs did well, because for a while rents did not keep pace with food prices. But the wages of ordinary laborers lagged miserably. By the early seventeenth century, a laborer's annual income had about half the purchasing power it had had at the end of the fifteenth century, a decline that had its most drastic impact in Eastern Europe, where serfdom reappeared.

In the West, the large numbers of peasants who were forced off the land as the population rose turned to begging and wandering across country, often ending up in towns, where crime became a serious problem. Peasant uprisings directed at tax collectors, nobles, or food suppliers were almost annual affairs in one region or another of France after the mid-sixteenth century, and in England the unending stream of vagrants gave rise to a belief that the country was overpopulated. The extreme poverty was universally deplored, particularly as it promoted crime and disorder.

Relief of Distress Nobody could understand, much less control, the forces that were transforming society. Some governments tried to relieve the economic distress, but their efforts were not always consistent. English legislation in the sixteenth century, for example, treated beggars sometimes as shirkers who should be punished and at other times as unfortunates who needed to be helped. Not until the enactment of the English Poor Law of 1601, which provided work for the poor, did the more compassionate view begin to prevail. In the years that followed, governments in a number of countries began to create institutions that offered basic welfare benefits.

The traditional source of food for the hungry and care for the ill, the monastery, had lost its importance because of the Reformation and because governments were now considered responsible for the needy. Among the remedies they offered were the workhouses established by the English Poor Law where, although conditions

▶ *Hieronymus Bosch*
THE PRODIGAL SON, CA. 1516
Usually known for his horrific paintings of devils and monsters, Bosch here creates a realistic scene of his time to illustrate the biblical story of the prodigal son. He shows the son as one of the many poor peddlers, in torn clothes and ill-matching shoes, who roamed the European countryside. The house he is leaving is hardly in better condition, with holes in the roof and a broken shutter; and the residents show in various ways their indifference to his departure.

could be horrible, the destitute could at least find work, food, and shelter. Other governments founded hospitals, often staffed by nuns, which were especially important as places that looked after abandoned women or children. But these institutions were few and far between, and it was exceptional for a poor person to find such relief. The conditions were especially harsh for women forced off the land, because few trades were open to them even if they got to a town; their choice might be either continued vagrancy or prostitution.

SOCIAL CHANGE: THE TOWN

Vagrancy was only one of the signs that Europeans were witnessing the beginnings of modern urbanization with all its dislocations. Major differences also developed between life in the country and life in the town. Rural workers may have led a strenuous existence, but they escaped the worst hazards of their urban counterparts. Whole sections of most large cities were controlled by the sixteenth-century equivalent of the underworld, which offered sanctuary to criminals and danger to most citizens. Plagues were much more serious in towns—the upper classes soon learned to flee to the country at the first sign of disease—and famines more devastating because of the far poorer sanitation in urban areas and their remoteness from food supplies.

New Opportunities Nevertheless, it was in towns and cities that the economic advances of the age were most visible. As cities grew, they stimulated construction, not only of houses but also of public buildings and city walls. Anyone skilled in bricklaying, in carpentry, or even in carrying heavy loads found ready employment.

Townsfolk needed endless services, from sign painting to the transportation of books, which created jobs at all levels. Given the demand for skills, guilds increasingly allowed the widows of members to take over their husbands' trades, and women shopkeepers were not uncommon. Nobody would have been taken aback, for example, to see an artisan's daughter or wife (like Agnes Dürer, the wife of the famous German artist) take charge of a market stall or a shop. In some trades, such as oil making and baking, women were often essential to production as well as sales, and

▶ *Pieter Brueghel the Elder*
CARNIVAL AND LENT, 1559
This detail from a huge scene shows one of the customary practices during the season of Lent: giving alms to the poor. Beggars were a common subject for Brueghel, who used them to convey a vivid sense of the appearance and behavior of the unfortunate as well as the more comfortable members of his society.

there is also evidence of their growing importance as the keepers of the paperwork and the accounts in family businesses. The expansion of opportunity in the cities, in other words, had social as well as economic consequences.

At the top levels of society—at princely courts and in royal administrations, in the law, among the leaders of the burgeoning cities, and in growing empires overseas—the economic expansion enabled ambitious families to win fortunes and titles and to found new aristocratic dynasties. The means of advancement varied. Once a family had become rich through commerce, it could buy the lands that, in Protestant countries, rulers had confiscated from the Church, or the offices that many governments sold to raise revenue and build bureaucracies. In addition, the New World offered the possibility of acquiring vast estates. Since the possession of land or high office was the key to noble status, the newly rich were soon able to enter the ranks of the nobility. The long boom in commerce thus encouraged a broad spectrum of social change. By the 1620s, when the upward trend of the economy came to an end, a new aristocracy had been born that was destined to dominate Europe for centuries.

II. Expansion Overseas

THE PORTUGUESE

Long before Europe's demographic and economic recovery began in the late fifteenth century, pioneer explorers had taken the first steps that were to lead to the creation of huge empires overseas. Taking farther the voyages beyond Europe of the crusaders and such travelers as Marco Polo, sailors had been inching around Africa seeking a route to the Far East. The riches in goods and lands they eventually found would help fuel the boom of the sixteenth century. But there was little expectation of world-shattering consequences among the Portuguese who began these voyages in the 1410s.

Henry the Navigator The Portuguese lived in an inhospitable land whose seafarers had always been essential to the country's economy. The need for better agricultural opportunities had long turned their eyes toward Atlantic islands like the Canaries and the territories held by the Muslims (Moors) in North Africa. But this ambition had to be organized into a sustained effort if it was to achieve results, and in the early fifteenth century Prince Henry the Navigator, a younger son of the king, undertook that task.

Henry participated in the capture of the North African port of Ceuta from the Muslims in 1415, a crusading expedition that only whetted his appetite for more such victories. At Ceuta he probably heard stories about lost Christians and mines of gold somewhere in the interior of Africa. A mixture of motives—profit, religion, and curiosity—spurred him on; and in 1419 he began patronizing sailors, mapmakers, astronomers (because their contributions to celestial navigation were vital), shipbuilders, and instrument makers who were interested in discovery. They were mainly Italians, and their aim was not merely to make contact with Africans but to find an alternative route to India and the Far East around Africa (in order to avoid the Ottoman Empire, which was coming to dominate the eastern Mediterranean). The early adventurers did not succeed, but during their gradual advance down the West African coast, they opened a rich new trade in ivory, gold, and slaves.

To India and Beyond Then, in 1488, a Portuguese captain, Bartholomeu Dias, returned to Lisbon after making a landfall on the east coast of Africa, beyond the Cape of Good Hope, which previously no one had been able to pass. The way to India now seemed open, but before the Portuguese could send out their first expedition, the news arrived that a sailor employed by the Spaniards, one Christopher Columbus, had apparently reached India by sailing west. To avoid conflicting claims which might interfere with their trade, Portugal and Spain signed the Treaty of Tordesillas in 1494. This gave Portugal possession of all the lands to the east of an imaginary line about 300 miles west of the Azores, and Spain a monopoly of everything to the west. Portugal thus kept the only practical route to India (as well as the rights to Brazil, which one of her sailors may already have discovered). Three years later Vasco da Gama took the first Portuguese fleet across the Indian Ocean.

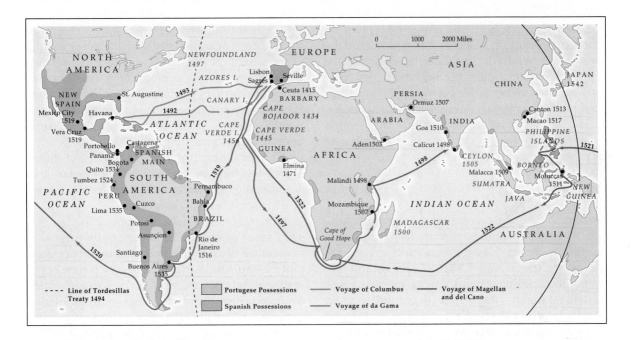

Map 14.1 Exploration and Conquest in the Fifteenth and Sixteenth Centuries
The division of the world between the Portuguese and the Spaniards led to distinct areas of exploration and settlement, demarcated by the line that both sides accepted at the Treaty of Tordesillas.

At first, he found it hard to trade, because the Arabs, who had controlled these waters for centuries, tried to keep out all rivals. Within 14 years, however, the Portuguese merchants had established themselves. The key to their success was naval power, for their ship designers had learned to combine their old square sails, which provided speed, with the Arabs' lateen sails, which increased maneuverability. The Portuguese were also the first to give their fleets effective fire power, realizing that cannon, not soldiers, won battles at sea. In addition, they deployed their ships in squadrons rather than individually, a tactic that further increased their superiority. The result was overwhelming military success. A series of victories reduced Arab naval strength, and bombardments quieted stubborn cities. By 1513 Portugal's trading posts extended beyond India to the rich Spice Islands, the Moluccas.

The Portuguese Empire   The empire Portugal created remained dependent on sea power, not overseas colonies. Except in Brazil, which was virtually unpopulated and where the settlers were able to establish huge estates worked by slave labor, the Portuguese relied on a chain of small trading bases that stretched from West Africa to China. They supplied and defended these bases, which usually consisted of little more than a few warehouses and a fort, by sea; and they tended to keep contacts with the local people to a minimum, so as to maintain friendly relations and missionary and trading rights. The one exception to the isolation was a result of the small numbers of women who traveled to the settlements from Portugal: In these early years there were more marriages with local women than there were in other European empires. But even though their effort remained relatively small-scale, the Portuguese soon began to profit from their explorations—between 1442 and 1446 almost 1000 slaves were brought home from Africa—and in the sixteenth century their wealth grew as they became major importers of luxuries from the East, such as spices, which were in great demand as medicines, preservatives, and tasty delicacies.

By dominating commerce with the Oriental civilizations, which were not only richer but also more sophisticated than their own, Portugal's merchants controlled Europe's most valuable trade. But their dominance was to last less than a century, for their success spurred a competition for empire that was to stimulate new waves of overseas expansion. First Spain determined to emulate her neighbor; and later the Dutch, English, and French sought to outdo their predecessors and one another. This competition gave the Europeans the crucial stimulus that other peoples lacked, and it projected them into a dominance over the rest of the globe that would last for more than 450 years.

THE SPANIARDS

Inspired by the same centuries-old crusading ambitions as the Portuguese, the Spaniards rode the second wave of expansion overseas. Because Spain was much larger than Portugal, and directed its attention toward a more sparsely populated continent, the Spaniards founded their empire on conquest and colonization, not trade. But they got their start from a stroke of luck.

Columbus   Christopher Columbus—an experienced Genoese sailor who was widely read, well versed in Atlantic sailing, and familiar with the leading geographers of his day—seems to have believed (we do not know for certain because he was a secretive man) that Asia lay only 3500 miles beyond the Canary Islands. Thus convinced that sailing west across the Atlantic to the Far East was perfectly feasible, Columbus took his proposal in 1484 to the Portuguese government, which refused to underwrite the venture. With a mystic belief in his own destiny, he persisted, gained the financial backing and blessing of Ferdinand V and Isabella I of Spain, and set sail in 1492. He was an excellent navigator (one of his discoveries on the voyage was the difference between true and magnetic north), and he kept his men going despite their horror of being so long at sea without sight of land. After 33 days he reached the Bahamas. He was disappointed that he found no Chinese or Japanese as he investigated Cuba and the west coast of Hispaniola (today's Haiti), but he was certain that he had reached Asia, even though the few natives he saw did not resemble those whom travelers such as Marco Polo had described.

Columbus crossed the Atlantic Ocean three more times, but he made no other significant discoveries. Yet he did also start the tradition of vi-olence against local people that was to characterize the European conquest of the New World. During his first stay in the Caribbean, his men killed some of the natives they encountered. From the very beginning, therefore, it became clear that the building of empires in the Americas would be a process of destruction as well as creation, of cruelty as well as achievement (*see box*, p. 431). For the victims, the legacy of the brutality, soon intensified by the devastating diseases that accompanied the Europeans, was the eradication of their ancient civilizations.

The Limits of Westward Voyages   By the end of Columbus' life in 1506, it was becoming apparent that he had found islands close by a new continent, not Asia. When, in 1513, the Spaniard Vasco de Balboa saw the Pacific Ocean from Central America, some thought that an easy westward passage to the riches of East Asia might still be found. But the last hope of a quick journey was dashed in 1522, when the one surviving ship from a fleet of five that had set out under Ferdinand Magellan three years before returned to Spain after the ordeal of having sailed around the world.

▶ **WOODCUT OF COLUMBUS**
This picture, by a contemporary, shows King Ferdinand, back in Spain, pointing to Columbus' three ships and the natives greeting the explorer in the New World.

Two Views of Columbus

The following two passages suggest the enormous differences that have arisen in interpretations of the career of Christopher Columbus. The first, by Samuel Eliot Morison, a historian and a noted sailor, represents the traditional view of the explorer's achievements that held sway until recent years. The second, by Kirkpatrick Sale, a writer and environmentalist, indicates how radically the understanding of the effects of exploration has changed in recent years.

1. "Columbus had a Hellenic sense of wonder at the new and strange, combined with an artist's appreciation of natural beauty. Moreover, Columbus had a deep conviction of the sovereignty and the infinite wisdom of God, which enhanced all his triumphs. One only wishes that the Admiral might have been afforded the sense of fulfillment that would have come from foreseeing all that flowed from his discoveries. The whole history of the Americas stems from the Four Voyages of Columbus, and as the Greek city-states looked back to the deathless gods as their founders, so today a score of independent nations unite in homage to Christopher the stout-hearted son of Genoa, who carried Christian civilization across the Ocean Sea."

   From S. E. Morison, *Admiral of the Ocean Sea: A Life of Christopher Columbus* (Boston: Little, Brown, 1942), pp. 670–671.

2. "For all his navigational skill, about which the salty types make such a fuss, and all his fortuitous headings, Admiral Colón [Christopher Columbus] could be a wretched mariner. The four voyages, properly seen, quite apart from bravery, are replete with lubberly mistakes, misconceived sailing plans, foolish disregard of elementary maintenance and stubborn neglect of basic safety—all characterized by the assertion of human superiority over the natural realm. Almost every time Colón went wrong it was because he had refused to bend to the inevitabilities of tide and wind and reef or, more arrogantly still, had not bothered to learn about them.

   "Many of those who know well the cultures that once existed in the New World have reason to be less than enthusiastic about [the 1992 celebrations of] the event that led to the destruction of much of that heritage and the greater part of the people who produced it; others are planning to protest the entire goings-on as a wrongful commemoration of an act steeped in bloodshed, slavery and genocide."

   Kirkpatrick Sale, *The Conquest of Paradise: Christopher Columbus and the Columbian Legacy* (New York: Knopf, 1990), pp. 209–210 and 362.

Magellan's 98-day crossing of the Pacific was the supreme accomplishment of seamanship in the age of discovery. But the voyage persuaded the Spaniards that Portugal had the fastest route to the East, and in 1529 they renounced all attempts to trade with the Spice Islands. Spain could now concentrate on the Americas, those unexpected continents that were to become not an obstacle on the way to the Spice Islands but possessions of unbelievable richness.

The Conquistador Volunteers for empire building were amply available. When the last Muslim kingdom in southern Spain was conquered by the Castilians in 1492, soldiers with long experience of military service found themselves at loose ends. Many were the younger sons of noble families, who were often kept from inheriting land because Spanish law usually allowed only the eldest son to inherit. The prospect of unlimited land and military adventure across the Atlantic appealed to them, as it did to ambitious members of Castile's lower classes, and thus the conquistador, or conqueror, was born. There were not many of them—fewer than 1000—but they overran much of the Americas in search of wealth and glory.

The first and most dramatic of these leaders was Hernando Cortés, who in 1519 landed on the Mexican coast and set out to overcome the rich Aztec civilization in the high plateau of central Mexico. His army consisted of only 600 troops, but in two years, with a few reinforcements, he had won a complete victory. Guns alone made no important difference because Cortés had only 13 muskets and some unwieldy cannon. More effective were his horses, his manipulation of the Aztecs' beliefs (especially after he murdered their ruler) to make them regard him as more powerful than he was, and the unshakable determination of his followers. The conquest of the Mexican Mayas also began under Cortés, while the Incas of Peru fell to Francisco Pizarro. Other conquistadors repeated these successes throughout Central and South America. By 1550 the conquest was over, and the military leaders gave way to administrators who began organizing the huge empire they had won.

THE FIRST COLONIAL EMPIRE

The Spanish government established in the New World the same pattern of political administration that it was setting up in its European territories. Representatives of the throne, viceroys, were sent to administer each territory and to impose centralized control. They were advised by the local *audiencia*, a kind of miniature council that also acted as a court of law, but the ultimate authority remained in Spain.

Real growth did not begin, however, until women pioneers came out to the settlements. In this empire, unlike Portugal's, intermarriage was strongly discouraged. Indeed, the indigenous peoples were treated with a brutality and disdain that set a dismal model for overseas empires. Not only was their labor cruelly exploited (both on farms and especially in silver mines that the Spaniards discovered, where working conditions were dreadful) and not only were families split apart so that men could be put to work, but local beliefs and traditions were actively suppressed

(though many survived despite the oppression). Over the years, there was to be increased intermarriage between Europeans and natives, and the creation of a more united society, but this took centuries to achieve. In the early days, only a few humane voices were raised, mainly by Spanish clergymen, to denounce the oppression. That they were ignored was only one indication of the indifference shown by Europe's colonizers to the well-being of other peoples as the empires were built.

For Spain's neighbors, the colonies were an object of envy because of their mineral wealth. In 1545 a major vein of silver was discovered at Potosí, in Bolivia, and from those mines came the treasure that made fortunes for the colonists, sustained Spain's many wars, and ultimately enriched much of Europe. For the balance of the sixteenth century, however, despite the efforts of other countries, Portugal and Spain remained the only conspicuous participants in Europe's overseas expansion.

THE LIFE OF THE SETTLERS

It took a great deal of determination to board one of the ships that set off across the oceans from Europe. Life at sea offered discomfort and peril: horrible overcrowding, inadequate and often rotting food, disease, dangerous storms, poor navigation, and threats from enemy ships. One cannot determine numbers precisely, but it has been estimated that in some decades of the sixteenth and seventeenth centuries, fewer than two-thirds of those who embarked reached their destination. And their troubles did not end when they came off the ships. Unfamiliar countries, famine, illness, and attacks by natives and European rivals made life precarious at best. Although 5000 people sailed for Virginia between 1619 and 1624, for instance, disease and massacre kept the colony the same size at the end of that period—about 1000 inhabitants—as it had been at the beginning. And yet, despite the difficulties and dangers, people found reasons to keep coming.

The Aims of the Colonists For a few leaders, like the Spanish minor nobles known as *hidalgos* who commanded most of Spain's first missions, the attraction was partly adventure, partly the chance to command a military expedition of con-

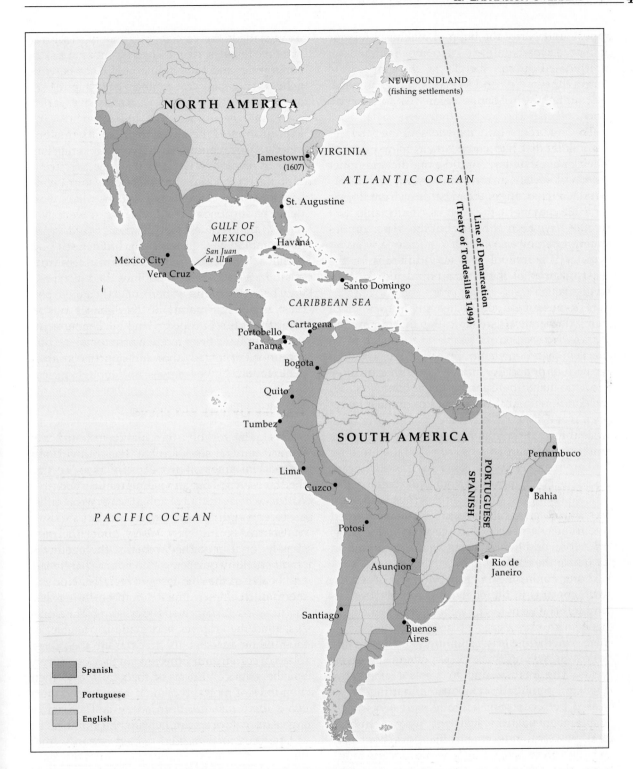

Map 14.2 EMPIRE AND SETTLEMENT IN THE AMERICAS, 1493–1610
The leadership of the Spaniards in expanding into the New World during the century following
the voyages of Columbus is apparent from the territories they dominated. The much smaller area
controlled by the Portuguese, the tentative activities of the English in Virginia, and the occasional
settlements of fishermen in Newfoundland, paled by comparison with the Spanish empire.

quest, and partly the hope of making a fortune which seemed unlikely at home. For another fairly small group, the clergy, the aim was to bring the word of God to people who had never encountered Christianity before. As for government officials and traders, they were usually just following orders, bringing overseas the activities and skills that had earned them their living in their native country. For these middle and upper levels of society, moreover, survival was rarely an issue: They might die in battle or from illness, and life may not have been as comfortable as it would have been at home, but the opportunities to exercise power or to make a fortune were far greater. The outlook was very different for the vast majority of those who populated the new settlements.

For most of the settlers, leaving Europe was a fairly desperate act, an indication that almost any alternative seemed preferable to the bleak prospects in their homeland. If it had not been for the growth of population in the sixteenth century—and the many thousands it made homeless, unable to remain in their villages or make a living in towns—it is unlikely that enough emigrants would have been found to do the work in ports and on the land that was crucial to the building of empires in Asia and America. It is significant that fewer people moved from a rich country like France than from the less prosperous Spain and Portugal. Despite the pressures that persuaded thousands of people to leave their homelands, therefore, additional means had to be found to populate the empires.

Long before the English colonized Australia with convicts in the eighteenth century, for example, they were taking people out of prison to send them overseas to places desperate for settlers. Another tactic was to offer land to anyone who was willing to work for others for seven years. The English, and to a lesser extent the French, permitted religious minorities who feared persecution at home to start a new and more independent existence in America. In general, powerful inducements like poverty or persecution were needed to drive Europeans to accept the hazards of the journey and the subsequent struggles of the pioneer. Some settlers, such as the religious refugees, set out as families, but usually many more men than

women made the voyage. In a society suspicious of single females, women had far more to risk by emigrating, and the chronic imbalance between genders became yet another hardship of life overseas.

Exploitation   When even distress at home provided too few volunteers, the colonizers relied on force to obtain the workers they needed. Just as captains often kidnapped men for a ship's crew, so, too, did the suppliers of settlers. Many woke up at sea surprised to find where they were. And once in the colonies, wage earners could expect their employment to be harsh. Indigenous populations, however, faced the most ruthless treatment: In South America millions died (estimates vary between 25 and 90 percent of the native peoples) as a result mainly of the diseases that accompanied the Europeans, though the susceptibility may have been made worse by the terrible conditions of forced labor and oppression. Even exploitation, however, was not enough to feed the insatiable need for miners, laborers, servants, and farmhands.

Slaves   The solution the colonizers found was slavery, familiar since ancient times but virtually nonexistent among Europeans by 1500. To find the slaves, ships began visiting the west coast of Africa, where the local inhabitants were either captured or purchased from local rulers and then transported to the New World under the most ghastly conditions. They were thrown together in cramped, filthy quarters, often bound, barely fed, and beaten at the slightest provocation. Nor was there much improvement for those—often less than half—who survived the crossing. The slaves sustained the empires and made it possible for their white masters to profit from the silver, tobacco, cotton, and other goods they produced; but the grim conditions of their lives, and their high rates of mortality, would have wiped them out if there had not been a constant stream of slaves from Africa to replenish their numbers.

For those settlers who reaped rewards from the mines and the agricultural products of America, or from the trade with Europe that enriched all the colonies, the hardships did not last long. They created flourishing cities and universities, and made huge fortunes. Their commercial net-

works began to link the entire world together for the first time in history. But for the many who struggled to expand these empires, life on the frontier, despite the promise of new opportunities, remained hard and dangerous for centuries. And for the slaves, there was not the slightest improvement in conditions or even hope of improvement, until revolts and civil wars finally abolished slavery in the nineteenth century.

▶ **SLAVE SHIP**
This picture, made aboard a slave ship, shows the dangerously crowded conditions in which Africans were brought to the New World. It is small wonder that so many of them died of disease even before the end of this miserable voyage.

III. The Centralization of Political Power

THE "NEW MONARCHS"

The economic and social transformations that began around 1500 gained important support from the actions of central governments. Especially in England, France, and Spain, rulers gave vital en-

couragement to the growth of trade, overseas expansion, and attempts to relieve social distress. At the same time, the growing prosperity of the age enhanced the tax revenues that were essential to their power. Both of these mutually reinforcing developments had long-term effects, but it could be argued that the creation of well-organized states, built around strong central governments, was even more decisive than the economic boom in shaping the future of Western Europe.

The rulers of England, France, and Spain in the late fifteenth and early sixteenth centuries were especially successful in accumulating and centralizing power, and historians have therefore called them "new monarchs." The reigns of

Henry VII, Louis XI, and Ferdinand and Isabella, in particular, have come to be regarded as marking the end of more than a century of political fragmentation. They set in motion a revival of royal authority that eventually weakened all rivals to the crown and created the bureaucracies characteristic of the modern state.

TUDOR ENGLAND

The English monarchs had relied for centuries on local cooperation to run their kingdom. Unlike other European countries, England contained only 50 or 60 families who were legally nobles out of a population of perhaps 2.5 million. But many other families, though not technically members of the nobility, had large estates and were dominant figures at the parish, county, and even national levels. They were known as *gentry*, and it was from their ranks that the crown appointed the local officers who administered the realm—notably the justices of the peace (usually referred to as JPs). These voluntary unpaid officials served as the principal public servants in the more than 40 counties of the land.

For reasons of status as well as out of a feeling of responsibility, the gentry had always sought such appointments. From the crown's point of view, the great advantage of the system was its efficiency: Enforcement was in the hands of those who could enforce. As a "great man" in his neighborhood, the justice of the peace rarely had trouble exerting his authority. Thus, the king had at his disposal an administrative structure without rival in Europe because, unlike other rulers, he could count on the cooperation of the leaders of each locality. Since the gentry had been given so much responsibility, they had developed a strong sense of duty over the centuries, and the king had increasingly sought their advice.

Parliament and Common Law   In the sixteenth century an institution that had developed from this relationship, Parliament, began to take on a general importance as the chief representative of the country's wishes; it was increasingly considered to be the only body that could give a ruler's actions a wider sanction than he could draw from his prerogatives alone. Although Parliament remained subordinate to the crown for a long time, England's kings already realized that they could not take such measures as raising extraordinary taxes without its consent.

Just as Parliament served to unify the country, so too did another ancient institution: the common law. This was a system of justice based on precedent and tradition that was the same, or "common," throughout England. In contrast to the Roman law that prevailed on the continent, common law grew out of the interpretations of precedent made by individual judges and the decisions of juries. A court could be dominated by local leaders, but in general this was a system of justice, administered by judges who traveled from area to area, that helped bind England together. Like Parliament, the common law would eventually be regarded by opponents of royal power as an independent source of authority with which the crown could not interfere. In the late 1400s, however, it was an important help to a king who was trying to overcome England's political fragmentation and forge a more unified realm.

HENRY VII

Henry VII (1485–1509), who founded the Tudor dynasty, came to the throne as a usurper in the aftermath of more than 30 years of civil conflict, the Wars of the Roses. England's nobles had caused chaos in these wars, and they had consistently ignored the wishes of the monarchy. The situation hardly looked promising for a reassertion of royal power. Yet Henry both extended the authority of the crown and restored order with extraordinary speed.

Finance   His first concern was finance, because he knew that unless he had sufficient funds to run his government, his ability to control the nobles would remain uncertain. At the same time, he was aware that extra taxes were the surest way to alienate subjects who expected a king to "live of his own," that is, from the income his lands provided, from customs duties, and from the contributions he received at special times, such as the marriage of his daughter. It is a testimony to the care with which Henry nurtured his revenues that by the end of his reign he had paid off the crown's debts and accumulated a substantial reserve. His success came, first, from increases in the profits of justice—fees and fines—which also cowed unruly subjects. In addition, he improved his returns by putting collection and supervision of revenue in the hands of a small, efficient group of officials in his own household. Above all, it was by careful management, and avoidance of foreign entanglements, that he was able to "live of his own."

Restoring Order   Where domestic order was concerned, the revival of royal authority was largely due to the energy of the king and his chief servants. Henry increased the powers of the justices of the peace, thus striking severely at the independence attained by leading nobles during the previous two centuries. Under his leadership, too, the royal Council became a far more active and influential body. Leading officials not only exercised executive powers but also resumed hearing legal appeals—a policy that further undermined the independence of gentry and nobles, who could dominate proceedings in local common law courts. When the royal councillors sat as a court (known as Star Chamber from the decorations on the ceiling of the room where they met), there was no jury, local lords had no influence, and decisions were quick and fair. Eventually, Star Chamber and other so-called royal courts (which derived their jurisdiction from the authority of the king himself) came to be seen as threats to England's traditional common law. Under the Tudors, however, they were accepted as highly effective means of restoring order and asserting the power of the central government.

HENRY VIII AND HIS SUCCESSORS

The first Tudor was a conservative, building up his authority and finances by applying vigorously the traditional methods and institutions that were available to a king. The young man who followed him on the throne, Henry VIII (1509–1547), was an arrogant, dazzling figure, a strong contrast to his careful father. In 1513 he removed a long-standing threat from England's north by inflicting a shattering defeat on an invading Scots army at Flodden. With his prestige thus enhanced, he spent the next 15 years taking little part in European affairs and consolidating royal power at home with the capable assistance of his chief minister, Cardinal Thomas Wolsey.

The Divorce   This successful continuation of Henry VII's policies ended in 1529 when Wolsey fell from power, ruined by the king's wish for a divorce from his wife, who had failed to produce a male heir to continue the dynasty. Henry had married his brother's widow, Catherine of Aragon, under a special papal dispensation from the biblical law that normally prohibited a union between such close relatives. Obsessed with dynastic continuity—and infatuated with a young lady at court, Anne Boleyn—Henry urged Wolsey to ask the pope to declare the previous dispensation invalid. Under ordinary circumstances there would have been no trouble, but at this moment the pope was in the power of Charles V, the Holy Roman Emperor, who was also Catherine's nephew. When Wolsey's efforts to get papal approval for the divorce failed, Henry dismissed him and accused him of treason.

For three years thereafter the king kept trying to get the Church to grant him the divorce. He called Parliament and gave it free rein to express bitter anticlerical sentiments, he sought opinions in European universities in favor of the divorce, he attacked his own clergy for having bowed to Wolsey's authority, and he even extracted a vague recognition from the clergy of his position as "supreme lord" of the Church. Finally, he placed his confidence in Thomas Cromwell, a former servant of Wolsey's and, like Wolsey, a talented man from a humble background who had risen rapidly in royal service. Cromwell suggested a radical but simple solution: that Henry break with the pope, declare himself supreme head of the Church, and divorce Catherine on his own authority. The king agreed, thus unleashing a revolution that dramatically increased the powers of the royal government. At the same time, although he himself had written a book attacking Martin Luther, Henry established the Reformation in England. By identifying his kingdom with Europe's Protestants, in opposition to the Catholics, Henry gave his subjects an emotional cause that eventually stimulated a sense of national pride.

The Reformation Parliament   The instrument chosen to accomplish the break with Rome was Parliament, the only body capable of giving the move legal sanction and an aura of national approval. Henry called the assembly in 1529 and did not dissolve it until 1536. During its sessions it acted on more matters of importance than a Parliament had ever considered before. It forbade litigants from making ecclesiastical appeals to Rome, thus allowing Henry to obtain his divorce and remarry, and in 1534 it took the decisive step: It declared the king supreme head of the Church in England, thus bringing to an end over 1000 years of papal supremacy (*see box*, below). Royal power gained enormously from these acts, but so, too, did the stature of Parliament, thanks to its new responsibilities and the length of its sessions.

Previously, election to Parliament had been considered a chore by the townsmen and landed gentry in the House of Commons, who found the expense of unpaid attendance and the time it took more irksome than did the wealthy nobles in the House of Lords (so named during Henry VIII's reign). But this attitude began to change in the 1530s as members of the Commons, returning to successive sessions, came to know one another and to regard themselves as guardians of Parliament's traditions and privileges. Eventually, they were to make the Commons the dominant house in Parliament.

Royal Power Following his successful suggestion for solving Henry's conflict with Rome, Thomas Cromwell became the king's chief minister. He was a tireless bureaucrat, who reorganized the administration of the country into six departments, each with specific functions, and took the chief executive position, the secretaryship. At the same time, a Privy Council, consisting of the king's principal advisers, was created to coordinate and direct royal administration.

The principal beneficiary of the events of the 1530s was the crown. Royal income rose markedly when Henry became head of the English Church and took over the ecclesiastical fees that previously had gone to the pope. He gained an even larger windfall when he dissolved all Eng-

Henry VIII Claims Independence from the Pope

One of the crucial acts of Parliament through which Henry VIII made the Church of England independent of Rome was the so-called Act in Restraint of Appeals, which became law in 1533. This law forbade Englishmen from appealing court decisions to Rome, which they had been allowed to do when the pope was accepted as the supreme authority. To justify this action, the preamble of the act made a claim for the independence of England and the authority of the king that was typical of the new monarchs of the age.

"Where by divers sundry old authentic histories and chronicles it is manifestly declared that this realm of England is an empire, governed by one supreme head and king, having the dignity and royal estate of the imperial crown of the same, unto whom a body politic be bound and owe next to God a natural and humble obedience; he being also furnished by the goodness of Almighty God with whole and entire power, preeminence, authority, prerogative and jurisdiction to render justice and final determination in all causes, debates and contentions, without restraint to any foreign princes, [and] without the intermeddling of any exterior person, to declare and determine all such doubts. In consideration whereof the King's Highness, his Nobles and Commons, enact, establish and ordain that all causes, already commenced or hereafter coming into contention within this realm or within any of the King's dominions, whether they concern the King our sovereign lord or any other subject, shall be from henceforth heard, examined, discussed, finally and definitely adjudged and determined within the King's jurisdiction and authority and not elsewhere."

From 24 Henry VIII, c. 12, as printed in *Statutes of the Realm*, 11 vols. (London, 1810–1828), vol. III, pp. 427–429.

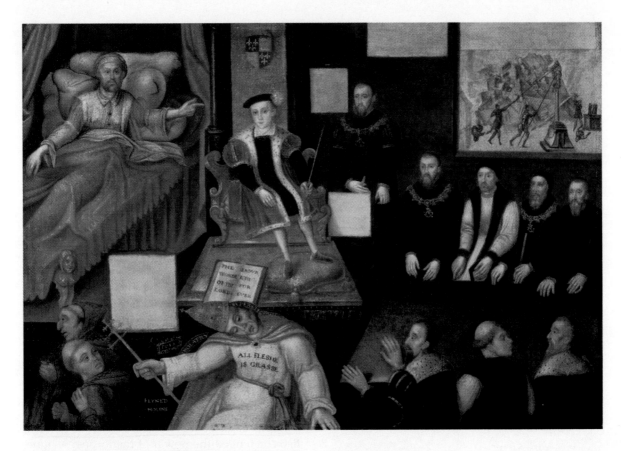

▶ *Unknown Artist*
EDWARD VI AND THE POPE
The anti-Catholic feelings that began to grow in
England during the reign of Edward VI are
expressed in this painting. The young king sits on
his throne. His father, Henry VIII, who started the
Reformation in England, points to him as the victor
over Catholicism. The crushing of the old faith is
symbolized by Christ's conquering of the pope and
monks (below) and the destruction of Roman
churches and images (through the window).

lish monasteries and confiscated their immensely
valuable lands, which were sold over the next
few decades. The result was that fortunes were
made by speculators, and new families rose to
prominence as major landowners.

For all the stimulus he gave to parliamentary
power, Henry now had a much larger, wealthier,
and more sophisticated administration at his disposal; and he left no doubt where ultimate authority lay. He did not establish a standing army,
as some of the continental kings did, because he
had no need for one. He was fully capable of intimidating ambitious nobles or crushing such uprisings as a 1536 revolt against the Reformation.

The English Church   Where doctrine and the
structure of the Church were concerned, Henry
was a conservative; he allowed few changes in
dogma or liturgy and seems to have hoped that
he could simply continue the old ways, changing
only the person at the head of the institution. He
tried to restrain the spread of Reformation beliefs, which travelers and books brought into

England from the continent, and he persecuted
heresy. But it proved impossible to do no more
than expel the papacy. Although many English
men and women clung to tradition, others were
drawn to the new religious ideas, and they pressured Henry to accept Protestant doctrines. Followers of the fourteenth-century reformer John
Wycliffe, known as Lollards, had kept his ideas
alive, and they now joined forces with Protestants inspired by continental reformers to demand services in English and easier access to
Scripture. New translations of the Bible appeared

in the 1530s, as did echoes of the opposition to clerical privilege that had swept Protestant areas on the continent. Perhaps realizing that the pressure would only grow, Henry had his son, Edward, tutored by a committed reformer.

Edward VI and Mary I During the reign of that son, Edward VI (1547–1553), who died while still a minor, the nobility attempted to regain control of the government. There was a relaxation of central authority, and the Reformation advanced rapidly. But Edward's half-sister, Mary I, reestablished Roman Catholicism as England's official religion when she became queen in 1553, forcing many of her subjects into exile and provoking two major revolts during her five-year reign. Royal power, however, was now strong enough to survive both the nobles' ambitions and the revolts. The revival of the nobles was short-lived, and Mary's death, in 1558, brought an end to the reversal of religions. She was succeeded by Henry VIII's last surviving child, Elizabeth, who demonstrated that the growth of the monarchy's authority had been but briefly interrupted under Edward and Mary.

VALOIS FRANCE

The rulers of France in the fifteenth century, unlike their English counterparts, lacked a well-formed organization for local government. Aristocrats dominated many regions, particularly those farthest from Paris, and great nobles had become virtually independent rulers. They had their own administrations and often their own courts and taxation, leaving the crown little say in their affairs. The size of the kingdom also placed restraints on royal power; it took more than a week to travel from Paris to the remoter parts of the realm—almost double the time for the equivalent English journey. Delays of this nature inevitably hampered central authority.

The monarchy had tried to resolve the problem of ruling distant provinces by granting to close relatives large blocs of territory that the crown seized or inherited. Theoretically, these relatives would devote full attention to their lands and execute royal wishes more effectively than the king could from Paris. In practice, however, an ambitious family member often became just as difficult to handle as any powerful noble. After 1469 the crown kept control over such acquisitions—an indication that it now had the resources to exercise authority even in areas far from the capital.

Royal Government The administrative center of the government in Paris was the royal council and its chief departments: the Chancery, which had charge of all formal documents, and the Treasury. The greatest court of law in the land was the Parlement of Paris, which had remained a judicial body, unlike the English Parliament, and whose members were appointed by the crown. As the central administration grew in the fifteenth and early sixteenth centuries, various provinces received their own parlements, a recognition of the continuing strength of the demand for local autonomy. But there was a countervailing force: the dominance of Roman law, which (unlike England's common law) was based on royal decree and which allowed the monarch to govern by issuing ordinances and edicts. These had to be registered by the parlements in order to take effect, but usually that was a formality.

Representative assemblies, known as Estates, also challenged the power of the throne. A number of provinces had such Estates, and they had to approve the level of taxation and other royal policies. But France's chief representative body, the Estates General—consisting of clergy, nobles, and townsmen from every region—never attained the prestige of the English Parliament and was never able to bind the country together or function as an essential organ of government.

For all the threats from nobles and assemblies, therefore, French kings had a degree of independence that English monarchs did not achieve, most notably in one critical area: finances. For centuries they had supplemented their main sources of income, from lands and customs duties, with special levies in the form of a sales tax (*aide*), a hearth tax (*taille*), and a salt tax (*gabelle*). Consequently the average French family that was subject to taxation (all nobles and many towns were exempt) usually bore a heavier burden than its English counterpart. In earlier days the consent of the localities had been required before such levies could be raised, but after 1451 the taxes could be collected on the king's authority alone, although he still had to negotiate the exact rate with provincial Estates and be careful not to go beyond what would seem reasonable to his subjects.

The Army　The most decisive source of power available to the French king (unlike the English king) was his standing army. The upkeep of the troops accounted for more than half the royal expenditures in Louis XI's reign, mainly because their numbers grew as revenues increased. In the 1480s a force probably larger than 15,000 men, chiefly professional mercenaries and military-minded nobles, was held in permanent readiness every campaigning season from spring to fall. Because of the rising costs that were associated with the development of gunpowder weapons, only the central government could afford to maintain such an army. And the troops had to be billeted in various provinces, with support from the local Estates. As a result, the entire French population eventually bore the indirect burden of heavier taxation, while many regions of France had direct contact with royal soldiers. Although frequently short of pay, the troops were firmly under royal control and hence a vital device—rarely used, but always a threat—in the strengthening of royal authority.

LOUIS XI AND CHARLES VIII

When Louis XI (1461–1483) began his reign, he faced a situation as unpromising as that of Henry VII at his succession, for the country had just emerged from the Hundred Years' War and royal authority was generally ignored. English troops, which had been in France for most of the war, had finally departed in the 1450s; but a new and equally dangerous menace had arisen in the east: the conglomeration of territories assembled by successive dukes of Burgundy.

Burgundy　By the 1460s this duke, though a vassal of the French crown in his southern holdings, was among the most powerful lords in Western Europe. He ruled a loosely organized dominion that stretched from the Low Countries to the Swiss Confederation, and his Burgundian capital, Dijon, had become a major cultural and political center. In 1474 Louis XI put together a coalition against Duke Charles the Bold, who had been at war with him for some seven years, and in 1477 Charles was killed in battle with the French king's Swiss allies. Louis then reannexed the duchy of Burgundy itself; but Mary, the duke's daughter, retained the Low Countries, which would later form part of the inheritance of her grandson, the Holy Roman Emperor Charles V.

Diplomacy　The Burgundian lands added considerably to Louis' sphere of authority. His masterly maneuvering in the tortuous diplomacy of his day soon won him other territories; he was appropriately nicknamed "the Spider" because the prizes he caught in his web were the result of waiting or shrewd negotiation rather than victories on the battlefield. Such was the case at the beginning of his reign when, by a typical combination of force and fraud, he pried two provinces on his southern border away from Spain. Simple luck enlarged his realm as well: In 1481 he inherited the three large provinces of Anjou, Maine, and Provence. The result was that by the end of his reign, though government procedures had not noticeably changed, royal power had penetrated into massive areas where previously it had been unknown.

The Invasion of Italy　Louis XI's son and successor, Charles VIII (1483–1498), was equally dedicated to increasing the territories under the Valois dynasty's command. In 1494, he led an army into Italy at the request of the duke of Milan, who was afraid of being attacked by Florence and Naples. After some initial successes the French settled into a prolonged struggle with the Habsburgs for control of the rich Italian peninsula. The conflicts lasted for 65 years, ending in defeat for the French. Although the Italian wars failed to satisfy the territorial ambitions of Charles and his successors, they provided an outlet and distraction for the restless French nobility and gave the monarchs, as commanders in time of war, an opportunity to consolidate royal power at home.

THE GROWTH OF GOVERNMENT POWER

After Charles VIII's reign, France's financial and administrative machinery grew in both size and

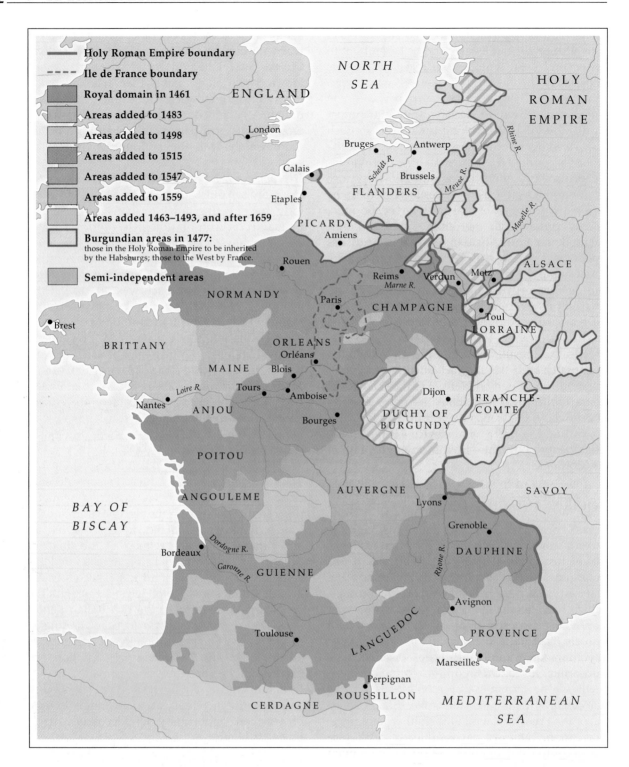

Map 14.3 France in the Fifteenth and Sixteenth Centuries
This map shows in detail the successive stages whereby the monarchy extended its control throughout France.

effectiveness, largely because of the demands of the Italian wars. There was rarely enough money to support the adventure; the kings therefore relied heavily on loans from bankers, who sometimes shaped France's financial policies. At the same time, the crown made a determined effort to increase traditional royal revenues.

Taxes France was a rich country of 15 million people with the most fertile land in Europe; yet the financial needs of the monarch always outstripped his subjects' ability to pay. Nobles, many towns, royal officeholders, and the clergy were exempt from the *taille* and the *gabelle*. Thus the bulk of the taxes had to be raised from the very classes that had the least to give. Other means of raising revenue were therefore needed to supplement royal income. One solution was the sale of offices. Positions were sold in the administration, the parlements, and every branch of the bureaucracy to purchasers eager to obtain both the tax exemption and the considerable status (sometimes a title of nobility) that the offices bestowed. From modest and uncertain beginnings under Louis XII (1498–1515), the system widened steadily; by the end of the sixteenth century, the sale of offices provided the crown with one-twelfth of its revenues.

Many other rulers were adopting this device, and everywhere it had similar effects: It stimulated social mobility, creating dynasties of noble officeholders and a new administrative class; it caused a dramatic expansion of bureaucracies; and it encouraged corruption. The system spread most rapidly, and the effects were most noticeable in France, where the reign of Francis I (1515–1547) witnessed a major increase in the government's power as its servants multiplied. Francis tried hard to continue the expansion of royal control by launching expeditions into Italy, but in fact, he contributed more to the development of the crown's authority by his actions at home.

The Church One of the most remarkable of Francis' accomplishments was the power he gained over his formidable rival, the Church. He was highly successful in his Italian campaigns early in his reign, and he used the power he attained in Italy to persuade the pope in 1516 to give the crown the right to appoint all of France's bishops and abbots. According to this agreement, the income a bishop earned during his first year in office still went to the Vatican, but in effect, Francis now controlled the French Church. Its enormous patronage was at his disposal, and he could use it to reward servants or raise money. Since he had reached an agreement with the pope, he did not need to break with Rome in order to obtain the authority over the clergy that Henry VIII was soon to achieve in England.

▶ *Anonymous Miniature*
FRANCIS I AND HIS COURT, FROM THE MANUSCRIPT OF ANTOINE MACAULT'S TRANSLATION OF DIODORUS SICULUS, CA. 1532
The splendor and the patronage of learning for which the "new monarchs" were known are evoked by this tiny painting of the French king. He sits at a table with his three sons, surrounded by his courtiers and listening to the author reading the very manuscript (a translation of an ancient Greek historian) that this picture illustrates.

The Advance of Centralization In the 1520s Francis also began a major reorganization of the government. He legalized the sale of offices, and the purchasers gradually replaced local nobles as the administrators of the various regions of France. He also formed an inner council, more manageable than the large royal council, to act as the chief executive body of the realm. As part of this streamlining, in 1523 all tax-gathering and accounting responsibilities were centralized in one agency. Against the parlements, meanwhile, the king invoked the *lit de justice,* a prerogative that allowed him to appear in person before an assembly that was delaying the registration of any of his edicts or ordinances and declare them registered and therefore law. The Estates General was no threat because it did not meet between 1484 and 1560.

By the end of Francis' reign, royal power was stronger than ever before; but signs of disunity had begun to appear that would intensify in the years to come. The Reformation was making gains in the Holy Roman Empire, and one of its movements, Calvinism, was soon to cause religious divisions and social unrest in France. As the reign of Francis' son Henry II (1547–1559) came to a close, the Italian wars finally ended in a French defeat, badly damaging royal prestige. The civil wars that followed came perilously close to destroying all that France's kings had achieved during the previous 100 years.

UNITED SPAIN

The Iberian peninsula in the mid-fifteenth century was divided into three very different kingdoms. Portugal, with some 1.5 million inhabitants, was in the midst of its overseas expansion. Castile, in the center, with a population of more than 8 million, was the largest and richest area. Sheep farming was the basis of its prosperity, and its countryside was dominated by powerful nobles. Castile was the last kingdom still fighting Muslims on its southern frontier, and in this ceaseless crusade the nobles played a leading part. They had built up both a great chivalric tradition and considerable political strength as a result of their exploits, and their status was enhanced by the religious fervor that the long struggle had inspired. The third kingdom, Aragon, approximately the same size as Portugal, consisted of three areas: Catalonia, the heart of the kingdom and a great commercial region centered on the city of Barcelona; Aragon itself, which was little more than a barren hinterland to Catalonia; and Valencia, a farming and fishing region south of Catalonia along the Mediterranean coast.

In October 1469, Isabella, future queen of Castile, married Ferdinand, future king of Sicily and heir to the throne of Aragon. Realizing that the marriage would strengthen the crown, the Castilian nobles opposed the union, precipitating a 10-year civil war. But the two monarchs emerged victorious, and they created a new political entity: the Kingdom of Spain. They and their successors were to be as effective as the kings of England and France in centralizing power and establishing royal control over their realms.

FERDINAND AND ISABELLA

When Ferdinand and Isabella jointly assumed the thrones of Castile in 1474 and Aragon five years later, they made no attempt to create a monolithic state. Aragon remained a federation of territories, administered by viceroys who were appointed by the king but who allowed local customs to remain virtually intact. The traditions of governing by consent and preserving the subjects' rights were particularly strong in this kingdom, where each province had its own representative assembly, known as the Cortes. Ferdinand left the system untouched, but he did make the viceroys a permanent feature of the government and created a special council for Aragonese affairs, through which he controlled the kingdom. In Castile, however, the two monarchs were determined to assert their superiority over all possible rivals to their authority. Their immediate aims were to restore the order in the countryside that had been destroyed by civil war, much as it had been in England and France, and to reduce the power of the nobility.

The first objective was accomplished with the help of the Cortes of Castile, an assembly dominated by urban representatives who shared the wish for order because peace benefited trade. The Cortes established special tribunals to pursue and try criminals, and by the 1490s it had succeeded in ending the widespread lawlessness in the kingdom.

The Centralization of Power To reinforce their authority, Ferdinand and Isabella sharply reduced the number of great nobles in the royal council and overhauled the entire administration, particularly the financial agencies, applying the principle that ability, rather than social status, should determine appointments. As the bureaucracy spread, the *hidalgo*, a lesser aristocrat who was heavily dependent on royal favor, became increasingly important in government. Unlike the great nobles, whose enormous wealth was little affected by reforms that reduced their political role, the *hidalgos* were hurt when they lost their tax exemptions. The new livelihood they found was in the service of the crown, and they became essential figures in the centralization of power in Castile as well as in the overseas territories.

The monarchs achieved greater leverage over their nobles in the 1480s and 1490s, when they gained control of the aristocracy's rich and powerful military orders. These organizations, which served almost as independent armies, run by Castile's most important aristocratic families, gave allegiance primarily to their own elected leaders. To take over their leadership required assertiveness and determination, especially by Isabella, Castile's inherited ruler. At one point she rode on horseback for three straight days in order to get to one of the order's elections and control the outcome. The great nobles could not be subdued completely; nor did the king and queen wish to destroy their power, because they were essential servants of the crown, especially in the army and in the higher levels of government. But like the kings of England and France, Ferdinand and Isabella wanted to reduce the nobles' autonomy to a level that did not threaten central authority, and for that reason it was crucial that they overcame the independence of the military orders by 1500.

The Church The rulers also succeeded in weakening Spain's bishops and abbots, who were as strong and wealthy as leading nobles. When Ferdinand and Isabella finally destroyed the power of the Muslims in southern Castile in 1492, the pope granted the monarchy the right to make major ecclesiastical appointments in the newly won territory, and this right was extended to the New World shortly thereafter. During the reign of Ferdinand and Isabella's successor, Charles I, the monarchy gained complete control over Church appointments, making Spain more independent of Rome than any other Catholic state.

Royal Administration Mastery over the towns and the Cortes of Castile proved easy to achieve. Where local rule was concerned, a minor royal officials, the *corregidor*, was given new powers and a position of responsibility within the administrative hierarchy. He was usually a *hidalgo*, and he became the chief executive and judicial officer in his region, rather like the justice of the peace in England; he also supervised town affairs. No major local decisions, such as the number of soldiers to be sent to the army, could be made without his (and hence royal) approval. The Cortes did not seriously restrict the crown because Spanish taxes, like French, could be raised without consent. The Castilian assembly met frequently and even provided additional funds for foreign wars, but it never challenged royal supremacy during this reign.

The king and queen supervised the system of justice directly, hearing cases personally once a week. As was true of most Roman law systems, all law was considered to come from the throne, and the monarchs had full power to overrule the decisions of local courts, often run by nobles. Centralized judicial machinery began to appear, and in a few decades Castilian law was organized into a uniform code—always a landmark in the stabilization of a state. The code remained in effect for centuries and was a tribute to the determination and effectiveness with which the crown had centralized its dominions.

Revenues Considering the anarchy at the start of their reign and the absence of central institutions, Ferdinand and Isabella performed greater wonders in establishing royal power than did any of the other new monarchs. A good index of the effectiveness of their growing bureaucracy is the increase in their revenues. As soon as the main administrative reforms were completed in the 1490s, the yield of the sales tax (the *alcabala*), which was the mainstay of royal income, began to rise dramatically. Total annual revenue is estimated to have soared from 80,000 ducats in 1474 to 2.3 million by 1504, the year Isabella died.

Religion Religious affairs, too, helped in the consolidation of royal authority. After the civil wars in Castile ended in 1479, the two monarchs sought to drive the Muslims from southern Castile. The reasons for the aggressive policy were clear: First, it complemented the drive for centralized power; second, war was a traditional interest for ambitious rulers, and it helped keep restless nobles occupied; and finally, the crusade stimulated the country's religious fervor, which in turn promoted enthusiasm for its rulers.

The religious zeal aroused by the fight with the Muslims intensified Spaniards' loyalty toward their rulers, and it is not surprising that the monarchy sought religious uniformity as a means of strengthening political uniformity. Nor did the campaign come to an end when the last Muslim stronghold in the south, Granada, capitulated in 1492. Later that year, all Jews were expelled from Spain. Some 150,000 of the country's most enterprising people—including prominent doctors, government officials, and other leaders of economic and cultural life—departed overnight. For rulers who sought all means to win their subjects' loyalty, there was much to be gained by targeting a visible and often persecuted minority; it was a popular move, and it stimulated the religious passion that helped sustain the crown's authority. The campaign against the Jews thus went hand in hand with the other efforts to extend royal power.

The Inquisition The same drive to consolidate their strength had prompted Ferdinand and Isabella to obtain permission from the pope in 1478 to establish their own Inquisition. Since 1483 this body had been run by a royal council and given a mandate to root out Marranos and Moriscos—Jews and Muslims who, usually under coercion, had pretended to accept Christianity but, in fact, retained their original beliefs. After the fall of Granada, the Spanish Church attempted to convert the conquered Muslims, and in 1502 those who had not accepted Christianity were expelled from the country. Nonetheless suspected Moriscos and Marranos kept the Inquisition busy. The persecution welded the country into a religious

unity that paralleled and supported the political centralization achieved by the monarchy. Religious policy was thus as much an instrument of political power as it was of ideological conformity.

FOREIGN AFFAIRS

The fall of Granada extended Spain's dominion southward, but there were also lands to be captured to the north and east. This undertaking was Ferdinand's responsibility, because men took command in war, and he focused on foreign affairs during the 12 years he ruled on his own after Isabella's death in 1504. His first success had come in 1493, when he regained the two provinces on the French border that Louis XI had taken 30 years before. Two years later, fearful that France's Italian invasion might threaten his Kingdom of Sicily, Ferdinand entered the war in Italy.

His achievements in the next two decades were due to a combination of military and diplomatic skills unusual even among the highly capable rulers of the age. A reorganization of Spain's standing army made it the most effective in Europe, and it soon achieved a commanding presence in Italy: By 1504 it had conquered Naples, and Spain had become a major power in the peninsula. Ferdinand also founded the finest diplomatic service of the sixteenth century, centered on five permanent embassies: at Rome, Venice, London, Brussels, and the Habsburg court. The ambassadors' reports and activities made him the best-informed and most effective maneuverer in the international politics of his reign.

Thus by the time of his death in 1516, the united Spain that he and Isabella created had gained both territory and authority at home and international power abroad. The successor to the throne inherited a monarchy fully as dynamic and as triumphant over its rivals as those of England and France.

CHARLES V, HOLY ROMAN EMPEROR

To bolster their dynasty, Ferdinand and Isabella had married their children to members of the leading families of Europe. Their daughter Joanna became the wife of the Habsburg Archduke Philip of Austria, and her son Charles became in turn heir to both the royal throne of Spain and the Habsburg dukedom.

The Revolt of the Communes Early in his reign as King of Spain, however, Charles (1516–1556) had to withstand a major onslaught on the crown's position. Educated in Flanders, he spoke no Castilian, and when he arrived in Spain late in 1517, he soon aroused the resentment of the local nobility, particularly when members of the large Flemish entourage he brought with him were given positions in the government. The young king stayed for two and a half years, during which time he was elected emperor of the Holy Roman Empire (1519). This enhanced his prestige, but it also intensified his subjects' fears that he would become an absentee ruler with little interest in their affairs. The Cortes, in particular, showed open hostility when Charles requested additional tax funds so that he could leave the country with Spanish troops to pursue his Europe-wide ambitions. As soon as he left in 1520, revolts began to break out in Spain's towns, and the risings of these communes racked the country for two years. The troubles Charles now endured were among the first of many major clashes during the next 150 years between the traditional dynastic aims of the leading European monarchs and the jealous sense of distinctiveness felt by their subjects.

Fortunately for the crown, the communes lacked clear aims; their resentments and hopes were deep but vague. They wanted to reverse the growth of royal power and to restore their traditional autonomy—a grievance that central governments were bound to encounter as they extended their authority. To this end, the communes asked for the removal of Flemish royal officials and a reduction in taxation, and at first they had the strong sympathy of the Spanish nobles, who particularly disliked the foreign ruler. But the movement soon revealed other aims, with social overtones: The communes launched attacks on the privileged orders of society, especially the nobility, and this lost the revolt its only chance for success. For the nobles now turned against the communes and defeated them in battle even before Charles returned to Spain.

Imperial Ambitions The king took warning from the uprisings and made sure that his administration was now kept entirely in Spanish hands. As calm returned, his subjects could channel their energies into imperial missions overseas, where the conquest of Mexico was under way, and against the Ottoman Turks in the Mediterranean. As in France, foreign excursions brought a monarch peace at home.

The one notable extension of royal power during Charles's reign was the large empire Spaniards were establishing in Central and South America. Closer to home, however, there was little that gave him or his Spanish subjects cause for pleasure. As Holy Roman Emperor, Charles was the official ruler of almost all of continental Europe west of Poland and the Balkans, with the major exception of France; and although his real power in the Empire was limited, he was almost ceaselessly at war defending his territories. In the Spaniards' view, most of the wars helped Charles's ambitions as emperor and were thus irrelevant to Spain. As far as they were concerned, aside from the widening acquisitions in the New World, Charles did little to further the expansion started by Ferdinand and Isabella.

Royal Government The recurrent crises and wars outside of Spain kept Charles away from his kingdom for more than two-thirds of his 40-year reign. He relied, during these absences, on a highly talented administrator, Francisco de los Cobos, who shaped and clarified the government's policies. De los Cobos confirmed the supremacy of the crown by enlarging the bureaucracy and elaborating the system of councils that Ferdinand and Isabella had begun. In the 1520s this structure, which was to survive for centuries, received its final form.

There were two types of council. One was responsible for each of the departments of the government: finance, war, the Inquisition, and so on. The other supervised each of the territories ruled by the crown: Aragon, Castile, Italy, the Indies, and (later in the century) the Low Countries. At the head of this system was the Council of State, the principal advisory group, consisting of leading officials from the lower councils. All these councils reported to the king or to his chief ministers, but since each one controlled its own bureaucracy, they were perfectly capable of running the empire in the monarch's absence.

Map 14.4 The Empire of Charles V
This map indicates both the vastness of Charles's empire and the extent of the fighting in which he became involved. Almost every battle his troops fought—against Spanish communes, German Protestants, the Turks, and the French—is included so as to show the full measure of the emperor's never-ending ordeal.

What emerged was a vast federation, with Castile at its heart but with the parts, though directed from the center, allowed considerable autonomy. A viceroy in every major area (there were nine altogether from Naples to Peru) ran the administration under the supervision of the *audiencia*—the territorial council—and while on the whole these officials were left to do as they wished, they had to report to Castile in minute detail at regular intervals and refer major decisions to the central government.

The Bureaucracy Although corruption was widespread and slow communications (it took over eight months to send a message from Castile to Peru) made the system unwieldy, the centralization gave the monarch the power he wanted. The huge bureaucracy was carefully staffed with *hidalgos* and townsmen, while great nobles were given viceroyalties or high army posts. Some local initiative was allowed, but through the hierarchy of loyal servants the crown could exercise full control. As a result, Spain's administrative machine was one of the most remarkably detailed (if not always efficient) structures ever devised for ruling so vast an empire.

THE FINANCIAL TOLL OF WAR

The only serious strain on Charles's monarchy was financial, the result of the Habsburgs' constant wars. A large portion of the money for the fighting came from Italy and the Low Countries, but Spain had to pay a growing share of the costs. During the sixteenth century, the Spaniards increasingly resented the siphoning away of their funds into foreign wars. It was the tragedy of their century of glory that so much of the fantastic wealth they discovered in South America was exported for hostilities that brought them little benefit.

The burden was by no means equally distributed. The more independent Cortes of Aragon was able to prevent substantial increases in taxation, which meant that Castile had to assume the brunt of the payments. To some extent this was balanced by a monopoly of trade with the New World that was granted to the inhabitants of Castile, but in the next century the basic inequality among different Spanish regions would lead to civil war.

New World Trade Charles's finances were saved from disaster only by the influx of treasure—mainly silver—from America. Approximately 40 percent of the bullion went into the royal coffers, while the rest was taken by merchants (mainly Genoese) in the Castilian port of Seville, which was the only city where ships carrying goods to and from America were permitted to load and unload. Charles was receiving some 800,000 ducats' worth of treasure each year by the end of his reign. Unfortunately, it was always mortgaged in advance to the Italian and German bankers whose loans sustained his armies.

The country and the monarchy faced increasing difficulties as the wars continued for more than a century and a half. Seville's monopoly on shipping prevented the rest of the nation from gaining a share of the new wealth, and foreigners—notably the Italian and German financiers—came to dominate its economy and its commerce.

Spain was squeezed dry by the king's financial demands, yet he only just kept his head above water. In 1557, early in the reign of Charles's successor, Philip II, the monarchy had to declare itself bankrupt, a self-defeating evasion of its mammoth debts that it had to repeat seven times in the next 125 years. There has never been a better example of the way that ceaseless war can sap the strength of even the most formidable nation.

IV. The Splintered States

THE HOLY ROMAN EMPIRE

If in England, France, and Spain the authority of kings had begun to replace that of the local lord, to the east of these three kingdoms such centralization advanced fitfully and only within small states. Especially in the largest of these territories, the Holy Roman Empire, weak institutions prevented the emergence of a strong central government. Members of the leading family of Central Europe, the Habsburgs, had been elected to the imperial throne since the thirteenth century, but they lacked the authority and machinery to halt the fragmentation of this large territory; indeed, except for their own personal domain in the southeast of the empire, they ruled most areas and princes in name only. In addition to about 2000 imperial knights, some of whom owned no more than four or five acres, there were 50 ecclesiastical and 30 secular princes, more than 100 counts, some 70 prelates, and 66 cities, all virtually independent politically though officially subordinate to the emperor.

Local Independence The princes, whose territories comprised most of the area of the Holy Roman Empire, rarely had any trouble resisting the emperor's claims; their main concern was to increase their own power at the expense of their subjects, other princes, and the cities. The cities themselves also refused to remain subordinate to a central government. In 1500, 50 of them contained more than 2000 inhabitants—a sizable number for this time—and 20 had over 10,000. Their wealth was substantial because many were situated along a densely traveled trade artery, the

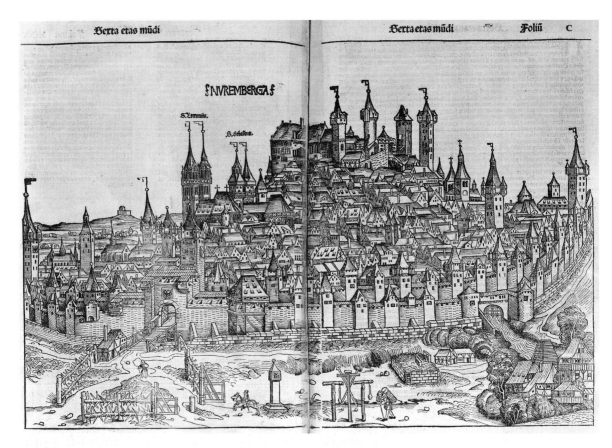

▶ *Hartmann Schedel*
THE NUREMBERG CHRONICLE, 1493
**This lavishly illustrated book, a history of the
world since the creation, is one of the earliest
masterpieces of the printer's art. It took about four
years to produce and contains dozens of elaborate
woodcuts, most of which are recognizable views of
European cities. This one depicts the proud and
independent German city where the book was
printed, Nuremberg, a major center of art and
craftsmanship.**

Rhine River, and many were also political powers. But their fierce independence meant that the
emperor could rarely tap their wealth or the services of their inhabitants.

The only central institution alongside the emperor was the Diet, which consisted of three assemblies: representatives of the cities, the princes,
and the electors (the seven princes, including
three archbishops, who elected each new emperor). Given this makeup, the Diet became in
effect the instrument of the princes; with its leg-

islation they secured their position against the
cities and the lesser nobility within their own
domains.

By the end of the fifteenth century, most of the
princes had achieved considerable control over
their own territories. Their success paralleled the
accomplishments of monarchs in England,
France, and Spain except that the units were
much smaller. Although the Habsburgs tried to
develop strong central authority, they exercised
significant control only over their personal domain, which in 1500 consisted of Austria, the Low
Countries, and Franche-Comté. To the rulers of
other states of the empire, they were feudal overlords in theory but powerless in practice.

Attempts at Centralization Nevertheless, the
need for effective central institutions was recognized in the late fifteenth century, especially in
the west and southwest of the Holy Roman
Empire. In 1495 the emperor created a tribunal to
settle disputes between local powers. Controlled
and financed by the princes, the chief benefici-

aries of its work, it made considerable headway toward ending the lawlessness that had marked the fifteenth century—an achievement similar to the restoration of order in France, Spain, and England at the same time. The tribunal's use of Roman law had a wide influence on legislation and justice throughout the empire, but again only to the advantage of the princes, who interpreted its endorsement of a leader's authority as referring only to themselves.

Other attempts at administrative reform had little effect, as ecclesiastical and secular princes tightened their hold on the multitude of territories that constituted the empire. The religious dissensions of the Reformation worsened the rivalries, dividing the empire and making Charles V no more than the leader of one party, incapable of asserting his authority over his opponents. The sheer number of Charles's commitments repeatedly diverted him, but even when he won deci-

sive military victories, he could not break the empire's long tradition of local independence. His dream had been to revive the sweeping imperial grandeur of an Augustus or a Charlemagne, and his failure brought to an end the thousand-year ambition to restore in Europe the power of ancient Rome.

▶ *Titian*

CHARLES V AT THE BATTLE OF MÜHLBERG, 1548
Because a statue of an ancient Roman emperor showed him in this pose, it was thought in the sixteenth century that a ruler appeared at his most magnificent on a horse and in full armor. Equestrian sculptures appeared in the fifteenth century, but this portrait is the first such painting. Titian created a heroic Charles V, even though the emperor had not been present at the military victory of the previous year that the picture celebrates.

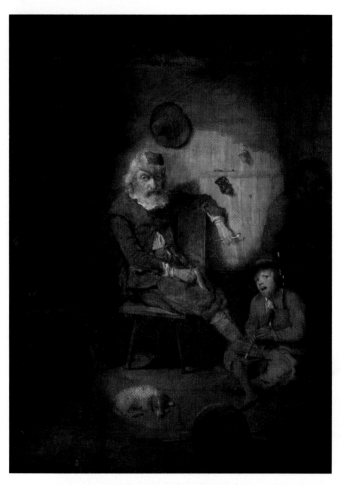

▷ *Christoph Paudiss*
PEASANTS IN A HUT
The sadness in the eyes of these two figures, even in a relaxed moment—the old man smoking a pipe, the boy playing the bagpipes—reflects the hardships of the peasants who were at the lowest level of European society and in eastern Europe were bound to the land as serfs.

EASTERN EUROPE

Hungary In the late fifteenth century, the dominant force in Eastern and Central Europe was the Kingdom of Hungary, ruled by Matthias Corvinus (1458–1490). He was in the mold of the other new monarchs of the day: He restrained the great nobles, expanded and centralized his administration, dramatically increased the yield of taxation, and established a standing army. The king's power thus grew spectacularly both at home and abroad. He gained Bohemia and some German and Austrian lands, and he made Vienna his capital in 1485.

Immediately after Matthias' death, however, royal authority collapsed. To gain Habsburg recognition of his right to the throne, his successor Ladislas II (1490–1516) gave up the conquests of Austrian and German territories and married his children to Habsburgs. This retreat provided the nobles of Hungary with an issue over which to reassert their position. First, by refusing the king essential financial support, they forced him to dissolve the standing army. Then, following a major peasant revolt against increasing repression by landowners, the nobles imposed serfdom on all peasants in 1514 at a meeting of the Hungarian Diet, the governing body, which was controlled by the aristocracy. Finally, they became the major beneficiaries of the conquest of Hungary by the Ottoman Empire over the next 30 years. That empire always supported any local leader who promised allegiance to Constantinople; by affirming loyalty to their new masters, the nobles were able to strengthen their power at the expense of both the old monarchy and the peasantry. By the middle of the sixteenth century, a revival of central authority had become impossible.

The Fragmentation of Poland Royal power in Poland began to decline in the 1490s, when the king was forced to rely on the lesser nobles to help him against the greater nobility. In return, he issued a statute in 1496 that strengthened the lower aristocrats against those below them, the townsmen and the peasants. The latter became virtual serfs, forbidden to buy land and deprived of freedom of movement. Once that was accomplished, the nobles united against the king. In 1505 the national Diet, consisting only of nobles, was made the supreme body of the land, and shortly thereafter it established serfdom officially. Since no law could now be passed without the Diet's consent, the crown's central authority was severely limited.

Royal and noble patronage produced a great cultural flowering around 1500 in Poland, which became an active center of Renaissance humanism and scholarship, most famously represented by the astronomer Nicolaus Copernicus. Yet the monarchy was losing influence steadily, as was revealed by the failure of its attempts to found a standing army. At the end of Sigismund II's reign (1548–1572), his kingdom was the largest in Europe; but his death ended the Jagellon dynasty, which had ruled the country for centuries. The Diet immediately made sure that succession to the crown, which technically had always been elective and in the hands of the nobles, would now depend entirely on their approval. Thus the aristocracy confirmed both its own dominance and the ineffectiveness of royal authority.

The Aristocracy   The political and social processes at work in Eastern and Central Europe thus contrasted starkly with developments in England, France, and Spain in this period. Nevertheless, although the trend was toward fragmentation in the East, one class, the aristocracy, did share the vigor and organizational ability that in the West was displayed by kings and queens. To that extent, therefore, the sense of renewed vitality in Europe during these years, spurred by economic and demographic growth, was also visible outside the borders of the new monarchies. But where nobles dominated, countries lost ground in the fierce competition of international affairs.

The Ottomans   Only in one state in Eastern Europe was strong central authority maintained in the sixteenth century: the Ottoman Empire. From his capital in Constantinople the sultan exercised unparalleled powers throughout the eastern Mediterranean and North Africa. He had a crack army of more than 25,000 men, who stood ready to serve him at all times, and within his domains his supremacy was unquestioned. He was both spiritual and temporal head of his empire, completely free to appoint all officers, issue laws, and raise taxes. But these powers, geared to military conquest and extending over enormous territories, never became a focus of cohesion among the disparate races of the Balkans, the Middle East, and North Africa, because the sultan left authority in the hands of local nobles and princes as long as his ultimate sovereignty was recognized. Whenever questions of loyalty arose (as they did sporadically in the Balkans), they revealed that the authority of the central government rested on its military might. That was more than enough,

though, to prevent any serious challenges to the power of the Ottomans until they began to lose ground to the Habsburgs in the eighteenth century.

The first signs of weakening at the center began to appear after the death in 1566 of the sultan whose conquests brought the empire to its largest size, Suleiman the Great. Suleiman had gained control of the Balkans with a victory at Mohacs in 1526, and he had even briefly laid siege to Vienna in 1529. Under his successors, the determined exercise of authority that had marked his rule began to decline; and harem intrigues, corruption at court, and the loosening of military discipline became increasingly serious. Yet the Ottomans remained an object of fear and hostility throughout the West—a constant threat to Central Europe from the Balkans and, despite naval setbacks, a formidable force in the eastern Mediterranean.

ITALY

Italy, the cultural and economic leader of Europe, had developed a unique political structure during the Renaissance. In the fifteenth century the five major states—Naples, the Papal States, Milan, Florence, and Venice—established a balance among themselves that was preserved without serious disruption from the 1450s to the 1490s. This long period of peace was finally broken in 1494, when Milan, abandoning a long tradition of the Italians settling problems among themselves, asked Charles VIII of France to help protect it against Florence and Naples. Thus began the Italian wars, which soon revealed that these relatively small territories were totally incapable of resisting the force that newly assertive monarchies could bring to bear.

Venice and Florence had long been regarded by Europeans as model republics—reincarnations of Classical city-states and centers of freedom governed with the consent of their citizens. In truth, Venice was controlled by a small merchant oligarchy and Florence by the Medici family, but the image of republican virtue was still widely accepted. Indeed, the political stability Venice had maintained for centuries was the envy of Europe. Tourists came not only to enjoy its many relaxations and entertainments but also

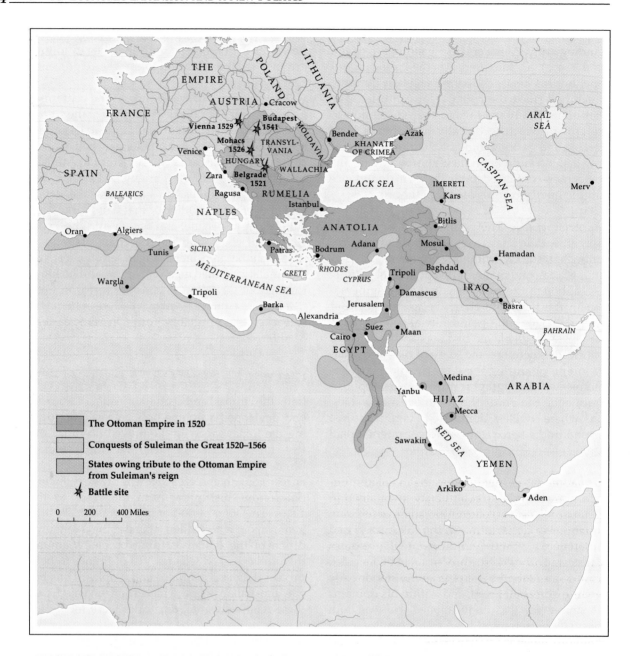

**Map 14.5 THE GROWTH OF THE OTTOMAN EMPIRE UNDER
SULEIMAN THE GREAT, 1520–1566**
The remarkable conquests of the Ottomans in North Africa,
the Middle East, and the Balkans terrified the rulers of Central
and Eastern Europe. Only the failure of the siege of
Vienna in 1529 halted the advance into Europe.

National Gallery, London

▶ *Titian*
THE VENDRAMIN FAMILY, 1547
The magnificence of the patrician families who ruled Venice is celebrated in this group portrait. Ostensibly, they are worshiping a relic of the true cross, but in fact they are displaying the hierarchy that rules their lives. Only men appear, dominated by the head of the family and his aged father, followed by his eldest son and heir, all of whom convey an image of wealth and power.

to marvel at the institutions that kept the city calm, powerful, and rich. Venice's leaders, elegant patricians who patronized some of the most sought-after artists of the sixteenth century, such as Titian, were thought of as the heirs of Roman senators. Throughout Europe, the Italians were regarded as masters not only of politics but also of culture and manners.

The Italian Wars It was a considerable shock, therefore, when the Italian states crumbled before the onslaught of French and then Spanish and Habsburg armies. Charles VIII's invasion led to the expulsion of the Medici from Florence in 1494 and the establishment of a new Florentine republic, but in 1512 the family engineered a return to power with the help of Ferdinand of Aragon, and eventually the Habsburgs set up the Medici as hereditary dukes of Tuscany. Ferdinand annexed Naples in 1504, and Emperor Charles V ultimately took over Milan. When the fighting ended in 1559, the Habsburgs controlled Italy and

would do so for the next century. Only Venice, Tuscany under the Medici, and the Papal States remained relatively independent—though Venice was no longer a force in European affairs after a series of defeats. The one major local beneficiary of the Italian wars was the papacy, as Julius II (1503–1513), known as the Warrior Pope, carved out a new papal territory in central and eastern Italy by force of arms.

The critical lesson of these disastrous events was that small political units could not survive in an age when governments were consolidating their authority in large kingdoms. No matter how brilliant and sophisticated, a compact city-state could not withstand such superior force. Italy's cultural and economic prominence faded only slowly, but by the mid-sixteenth century, except for the papacy, the international standing of its states was fading.

V. The New Statecraft

INTERNATIONAL RELATIONS

The Italian states of the fifteenth century, in their intensive political struggles and competition with one another, developed various new ways of pursuing foreign policy. During the Italian wars these techniques spread throughout Europe and caused a revolution in diplomacy. Any state hoping to play a prominent role in international affairs worked under a serious disadvantage if it did not conform. The Italians' essential innovation was the resident ambassador. Previously rulers had dispatched ambassadors to other states only for specific missions, such as to arrange an alliance, declare war, or deliver a message; but from the sixteenth century on, important states maintained representatives in every major capital or court at all times. The permanent ambassador could keep the home government informed of the latest local and international developments and could also move without delay to protect his country's interests. The Venetians, in particular, were masters of the new diplomacy. Leading patricians served as ambassadors, and they sent home brilliant political analyses that have remained crucial sources for historians ever since.

The New Diplomacy As states established embassies, procedures and organization became more sophisticated: A primitive system of diplomatic immunities (including freedom from prosecution for ambassadors and their households) evolved, formal protocol developed, and embassy officials were assigned different levels of responsibility and importance. Many advances were still to come, but by 1550 the outlines of the new diplomacy were already visible—yet another reflection of the growing powers and ambitions of central governments.

The great dividing line between older arrangements and the new diplomacy was the Italian wars, a Europe-wide crisis that involved rulers as distant as the English King Henry VIII and the Ottoman Sultan Suleiman II. Gradually all states recognized that it was in everybody's interest not to allow one power to dominate the rest. In later years this prevention of excessive aggression was to be known as the balance of power, but by the mid-sixteenth century the idea was already affecting alliances and peace treaties.

MACHIAVELLI AND GUICCIARDINI

As the Italian wars unfolded, political commentators began to seek theoretical explanations for the new authority and aggressiveness of rulers and the collapse of the Italian city-states. Turning from arguments based on divine will or contractual law, they treated effective government as an end in itself. The first full expression of these views came from the Italians, the pioneers of the methods and attitudes that were revolutionizing politics. When their small states proved unable to resist the superior forces of France and Spain, just as the ancient Greek city-states had succumbed to Macedonia and then to Rome, the Italians naturally wanted to find out why. The most disturbing answer was given by an experienced diplomat, Niccolò Machiavelli, who was exiled when the Medici took control of Florence in 1512. Barred from politics and bitter over the collapse of Italy, he set about analyzing exactly how power is won, exercised, and lost.

Machiavelli The result, *The Prince*, is one of the few radically original books in history. To move from his predecessors to Machiavelli is to see legal and moral thought transformed. Machiavelli swept away conventions as he sought, in an age of collapsing regimes, to understand how states function and how they affect their subjects. If he came out of any tradition, it was the Renaissance fascination with method that had produced manuals on cooking, dancing, fencing, and manners. But he wrote about method in an area that had never previously been analyzed in this way: power.

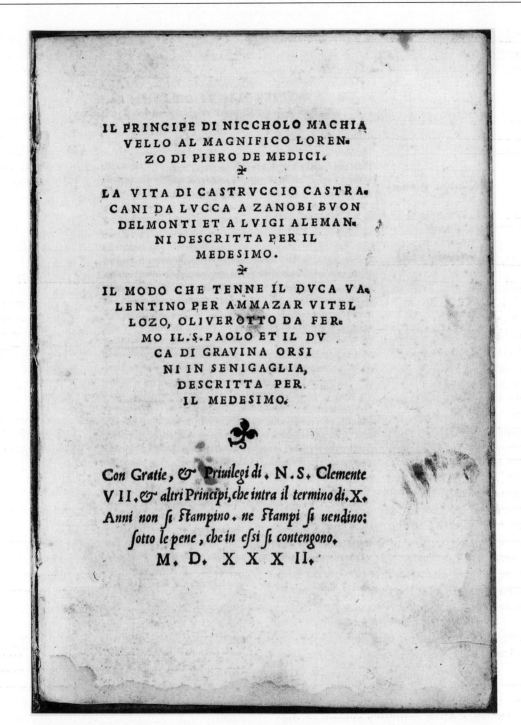

IL PRINCIPE DI NICCHOLO MACHIA
VELLO AL MAGNIFICO LOREN.
ZO DI PIERO DE MEDICI.

LA VITA DI CASTRVCCIO CASTRA.
CANI DA LVCCA A ZANOBI BVON
DELMONTI ET A LVIGI ALEMAN.
NI DESCRITTA PER IL
MEDESIMO.

IL MODO CHE TENNE IL DVCA VA.
LENTINO PER AMMAZAR VITEL
LOZO, OLIVEROTTO DA FER.
MO IL.S.PAOLO ET IL DV
CA DI GRAVINA ORSI
NI IN SENIGAGLIA,
DESCRITTA PER
IL MEDESIMO.

Con Gratie, & Priuilegi di, N.S. Clemente
V II. & altri Principi, che intra il termino di.X.
Anni non si stampino, ne stampi si uendino;
sotto le pene, che in essi si contengono,
M. D. X X X II.

► TITLE PAGE OF THE FIRST EDITION OF NICCOLO MACHIAVELLI'S THE PRINCE, 1532
This deceptively simple and elegant title page begins the brief but revolutionary book by
which Machiavelli is usually remembered. It remained unpublished for nearly 20 years after
it was written (and for 5 years after its author's death), probably because of concern over the
stir it would cause. And indeed, within 25 years of appearing in print, *The Prince* was
deemed sufficiently ungodly to be added to the index of books that Catholics were
forbidden to read.

Machiavelli showed not why power does or should exist but how it works. In the form of advice to a prince and without reference to divine, legal, or natural justification, the book explains what a ruler needs to do to win and maintain complete control over his subjects. Machiavelli did not deny the force of religion or law; what concerned him was how they ought to be *used* in the tactics of governing—religion for molding unity and contentment, and devotion to law for building the ruler's reputation as a fair-minded person. *The Prince* outlines the methods to be used by conquerors or legitimate heirs, as well as the proper ways to deal with insurrection and the many other problems that rulers encounter. Fear and respect are the bases of their authority, and they must exercise care at all times not to relax their control over potential troublemakers or over their image among the people.

Very few contemporaries of Machiavelli dared openly to accept so harsh a view of politics, but he did not hesitate to expand his analysis in his other masterpiece, the *Discourses*. This book developed a cyclical theory of every government moving inexorably from tyranny to democracy and back again. His conclusion, drawn particularly from a study of Roman history, is that healthy government can be preserved only by the active participation of all citizens in the life of the state. And the state in turn, he suggested, is the force that keeps people civilized. As he put it in the *Discourses*, "Men act rightly only when compelled. The law makes men good." But there were better and worse states. Machiavelli took the Roman Republic as his ideal, and it was this model, together with his Italian patriotism (rather than his cynicism), that was largely responsible for his long-lasting influence on European political thought.

Guicciardini The *History of Italy*, written in the 1530s by another Florentine, Francesco Guicciardini, was the first major work of history to rely heavily on original documents rather than secondhand accounts. If the conclusions he reached seem dauntingly cynical—he attributed even less to underlying historical forces than did Machiavelli, and like Thucydides, he argued dispassionately that fate determines everything—the reasons for his pessimism are not far to seek. The actions of rulers during his generation hardly gave much room for optimism, and shrewd observers like Machiavelli and Guicciardini must therefore have found it difficult to avoid pessimism about public events.

It was appropriate that the political theorists of the sixteenth century should have emphasized the obsession with power that dominated the age in which they lived. The relentless pragmatism and ambition of kings and princes as they extended their authority both at home and abroad reshaped institutions and governments throughout Europe. Given the assertiveness of these rulers and the rising fanaticism generated by religious dispute, it is not surprising that there should have begun in the mid-sixteenth century a series of wars of a ferocity and destructiveness that Europe had never before seen.

Recommended Reading

▼

Sources

*Guicciardini, Francesco. *The History of Italy and Other Selected Writings*. Cecil Grayson (tr.). 1964.

*Machiavelli, Niccolò. *The Prince* and the *Discourses*. Luigi Ricci (tr.). 1950.

*Parry, J. H. (ed.). *The European Reconnaissance: Selected Documents*. 1968.

Studies

Bonney, Richard. *The European Dynastic States 1494–1660*. 1991. An excellent overview.

Cipolla, Carlo M. *Guns, Sails, and Empires: Technological Innovation and the Early Phases of European Expansion 1400–1700*. 1965. This is a lively study of the reasons the expansion succeeded, with particular emphasis on weaponry.

*Crosby, Alfred W. *The Columbian Exchange: Biological and Cultural Consequences of 1492*. 1972. A fascinating study of plants, diseases, and other exchanges between the Old World and the New World.

*Elliott, J. H. *The Old World and the New 1492–1650*. 1970. A survey of the impact on Europe of the overseas discoveries.

Gilbert, Felix. *Machiavelli and Guicciardini: Politics and History in Sixteenth-Century Florence*. 1965. The standard account of the birth of new ideas in political theory and history.

*Jeannin, Pierre. *Merchants of the 16th Century*. Paul Fittingoff (tr.). 1972. A lucid introduction to sixteenth-century economic life.

*Kamen, Henry. *Spain 1469–1714: A Society of Conflict*. 1983. A clear and compact survey that gives a comprehensive account of Spanish history.

*Knecht, R. J. *French Renaissance Monarchy: Francis I & Henry II*. 1984. A lively introduction, with illustrative documents, to the development of governmental powers in France in the sixteenth century.

———, *Renaissance Warrior and Patron: The Reign of Francis I*. 1994.

*Mattingly, Garrett. *Renaissance Diplomacy*. 1971. An elegant account of the changes that began in international relations during the fifteenth century.

*Rady, Martin. *The Emperor Charles V*. 1988. An excellent overview, with illustrative documents, of the reign of the most powerful ruler in Europe.

*Rice, Eugene F., Jr. *The Foundations of Early Modern Europe, 1460–1559*. 1970. One of the best short surveys of the period, with three pages of suggested readings.

Scammell, G. V. *The First Imperial Age: European Overseas Expansion c. 1400–1715*. 1989. The best recent survey.

Scarisbrick, J. J. *Henry VIII*. 1968. A detailed but vivid biography of one of the most forceful of the new monarchs.

*Skinner, Quentin. *Machiavelli*. 1981. An excellent brief introduction to the man and his thought.

Strauss, Gerald. *Law, Resistance and the State*. 1986. A suggestive exploration of the development of legal and political thought.

Wilford, John Noble. *The Mysterious History of Columbus: An Exploration of the Man, the Myth, the Legacy*. 1991. A judicious account, both of Columbus' career and of the ways it has been interpreted.

*Williams, Penry. *The Tudor Regime*. 1981. The most recent comprehensive assessment of the workings of England's government.

*Wrigley, E. A. *Population and History*. 1969. An introduction to the methods and findings of historical demography by one of the pioneers of the field.

*Available in paperback.

Francois Dubois
THE MASSACRE OF ST. BARTHOLOMEW'S DAY
Although it makes no attempt to depict the
massacre realistically, this painting by a Protestant
does convey the horrors of religious war. As the
victims are hanged, disemboweled, decapitated,
tossed from windows, bludgeoned, shot, or
drowned, their bodies and homes are looted.
Dubois may have intended the figure dressed in
widow's black, and pointing at a pile of corpses
near the river at the back, to be a portrait of
Catherine de Medici, who many thought inspired
the massacre.

CHAPTER FIFTEEN

WAR AND CRISIS

IN the wake of the rapid and bewildering changes of the early sixteenth century—the Reformation, the rises in population and prices, the overseas discoveries, and the dislocations caused by the activities of the new monarchs—Europe entered a period of fierce upheaval. Such radical alterations were taking place in so many elements of society that conflict became inevitable. Many people, often led by nobles who saw their power dwindling, revolted against their monarchs. The poor launched hopeless rebellions against their social superiors. And the two religious camps struggled relentlessly to destroy each other. From Scotland to Russia, the century following the Reformation, from about 1560 to 1660, was dominated by warfare; and the constant military activity had widespread effects on politics, economics, society, and thought. The fighting was, in fact, a crucial element in the long and painful process whereby Europeans came to terms with the revolutions that had begun about 1500. Almost imperceptibly, fundamental economic, political, social, and religious changes took root; and troubled Europeans found ways to accept their altered circumstances.

I. Wars of Religion in the Age of Philip II

Although many other issues were involved in the wars that plagued Europe from the 1560s to the 1650s, religion was the burning motivation, the one that inspired fanatical devotion and the most vicious hatred. A deep conviction that heresy was dangerous to society and hateful to God made Protestants and Catholics treat one another brutally. Even the dead were not spared: Corpses were sometimes mutilated to emphasize how dreadful their sins had been. These emotions gave the fighting a brutality and a relentlessness that was unprecedented in European history.

THE CRUSADES OF PHILIP II

During the second half of the sixteenth century, international warfare was ignited by the leader of the Catholics, Philip II of Spain (1556–1598), the most powerful monarch in Europe. He ruled the Iberian peninsula, much of Italy, the Netherlands, and a huge overseas empire; but his main obsessions were the two enemies of his church, the Muslims and the Protestants. Against the Muslims in the Mediterranean area, Philip's campaigns seemed to justify the financial strains they caused. In particular, his naval victory at Lepanto, off the Greek coast, in 1571 made him a Christian hero at the same time as it reduced Muslim power. But elsewhere he fared less well.

Philip tried to prevent a Protestant, Henry IV, from succeeding to the French crown, and after he failed, he continued to back the losing side in France's civil wars even though Henry converted to Catholicism. Spain's policy toward England was similarly ineffective. After the Protestant Queen Elizabeth I came to the throne in 1558, Philip remained uneasily cordial toward her for about 10 years. But relations deteriorated as England's sailors and explorers threatened Philip's wealthy New World possessions. Worse, in 1585 Elizabeth began to help the Protestant Dutch who were rebelling against Spanish rule.

The Armada   Philip decided to end all these troubles with one mighty blow: In 1588 he sent a mammoth fleet—the Armada—to the Low Countries to pick up a Spanish army, invade England, and crush his Protestant enemies. By this time, however, English mariners were among the

National Gallery, London

▶ *El Greco*
THE DREAM OF PHILIP II, 1578
Characteristic of the mystical vision of El Greco is this portrayal of the devout, black-clad figure of Philip II. Kneeling alongside the doge of Venice and the pope, his allies in the victory of Lepanto over the Turks, Philip adores the blazing name of Jesus that is surrounded by angels in heaven, and he turns his back on the gaping mouth to hell.

best in the world; and their ships, which had greater maneuverability and fire power than the Spaniards', made up in tactical superiority what they lacked in size. After several skirmishes, the English set fire to a few of their own vessels with loaded cannons aboard and sent them drifting toward the Spanish ships, anchored off Calais. The Spaniards had to raise anchor in a hurry, and some of the fleet were lost. The next day the remaining Spanish ships retreated up the North Sea. The only way home was around Ireland; and wind, storms, and the pursuing English ensured that less than half the fleet reached Spain safely. This shattering reversal was comparable in scale and unexpectedness only to Xerxes' disaster at Salamis over 2000 years earlier.

THE DUTCH REVOLT

Philip's most serious reversal was the revolt of the provinces he inherited from his father, the Emperor Charles V, in the Netherlands. Here his single-mindedness provoked a fierce reaction that grew into a successful struggle for independ-

▶ *Anonymous*
THE ARMADA
This depiction suggests the sheer splendor of the scene as Philip II's fleet sailed through the channel on its way to invading England. The opposing ships were never this close, but the colorful flags (red cross English, yellow cross Spanish) and the elaborate coats of arms must have been dazzling. The firing cannon and the sinking ship remind us that, amidst the display, there was also death and destruction.

ence—the first major victory in Western Europe by subjects resisting their monarch's assertions of authority.

Causes of Revolt The original focus of opposition was Philip's reorganization of the ecclesiastical structure so as to gain control over the country's Catholic Church, a change that deprived the aristocracy of important patronage. At the same time, the billeting of troops aroused the resentment of ordinary citizens. In this situation, the local nobles, led by William of Orange, warned of mass disorder, but Philip kept up the pressure:

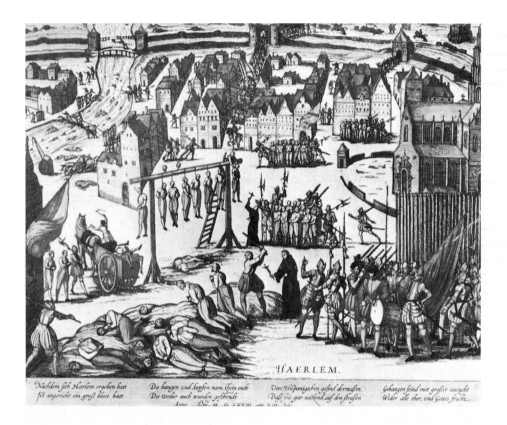

HAERLEM.

Nachdem sich Harlem ergeben hatt   *Da hangen vnd köpfen nam sein endt*   *Von Hispanischen gesind dermassen*   *Gehangen seind mit grosser onzucht*
ist angericht ein gross bluit batt   *Die weiber auch wurden geschendt*   *Dass sie gar nackend auf den strassen*   *Wider alle eher, vnd Gottes frucht.*
Anno Dni. M. D. LXXIII am XIII Iuly

He put the Inquisition to work against the Calvinists, who had begun to appear in the Netherlands, and also summoned the Jesuits to combat the heretics. These moves were disastrous because they further undermined local autonomy and made the Protestants bitter enemies of the king.

Philip's aggressiveness provoked violence in 1566: Although the Protestants were still a tiny minority, they formed mobs in a number of cities, assaulted Catholics, and sacked churches. In response, Philip tightened the pressure, appointing as governor the ruthless duke of Alba, whose Spanish troops were now used to suppress heresy and treason. Protestants were hanged in public, rebel groups were hunted down, and two nobles who had been guilty of nothing worse than demanding that Philip change his policy were executed.

Organized revolt broke out in 1572, when a small group of Dutch sailors flying the flag of William of Orange seized the fishing village of Brill, on the North Sea. The success of these "sea beggars," as the Spaniards called them, stimu-

▶ *Anonymous*

ENGRAVING OF THE SPANIARDS IN HAARLEM
This engraving was published to arouse horror at Spanish atrocities during the Dutch revolt. As the caption indicates, after the Spanish troops (on the right) captured the city of Haarlem, there was a great bloodbath (*ein gross bliut batt*). Blessed by priests, the Haarlemites were decapitated or hung, and then tossed in a river so that the city would be cleansed of them. The caption states that even women and children were not spared.

lated uprisings in towns throughout the Low Countries. The banner of William of Orange became the symbol of resistance, and under his leadership full-scale rebellion erupted. By 1576, when Philip's troops mutinied and rioted in Antwerp, 16 out of the 17 provinces in the Netherlands had united behind William. The next year, however, Philip offered a compromise to the Catholic nobles, and the 10 southern provinces returned to Spanish rule.

The United Provinces In 1579 the remaining seven provinces formed the independent United

Provinces. Despite the assassination of William in 1584, they managed to resist Spain's army for decades, mainly because they could open dikes, flood their country, and thus drive the invaders back. Moreover, Philip was often diverted by other wars and, in any case, never placed total confidence in his commanders. The heart of the resistance was the Calvinists, who (though still a minority) had the most to lose: They sought freedom for their religion as well as for their country. William never showed strong religious commit-

▶ *Pieter Brueghel the Elder*
THE MASSACRE OF THE INNOCENTS, CA. 1560
Probably to avoid trouble, Brueghel hid his critique of the Spanish rulers of the Netherlands in this supposed portrayal of a biblical event. It would have been clear to anyone who saw it, however, that this was a scene of Spanish cruelty toward the local inhabitants in the harsh days of winter, as soldiers tear babies from their mothers and kill them.

ments, but his son, Maurice of Nassau, a brilliant military commander who won a series of victories in the 1590s, embraced Calvinism and helped make it the country's official religion. Unable to make any progress, the Spaniards agreed to a 12-year truce in 1609, but they did not recognize the independence of the United Provinces until the Peace of Westphalia in 1648. The new state demonstrated that warfare could have positive effects in this period: It could unite a people and give them the means to achieve dignity and full autonomy.

CIVIL WAR IN FRANCE

The warfare that religion inspired had no such redeeming effects in France. By the 1550s Calvinism was widespread among the peasants and in the towns of the south and southwest, and its leaders had virtually created a small semi-independent state. To meet this threat, a great noble

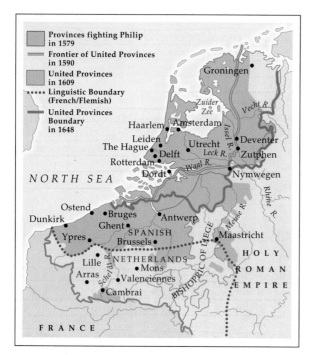

Map 15.1 THE NETHERLANDS, 1579–1609
The 17 provinces making up the Netherlands, or the
Low Countries, were detached from the Holy
Roman Empire when Charles V abdicated in 1556.
As the map indicates, their subsequent division
into two states was determined not by the linguistic
difference between French-speaking people of the
south and Dutch-speaking people of the north but
rather by geography. The great river systems at the
mouth of the Rhine eventually proved to be the
barriers beyond which the Spaniards could not
penetrate.

family, the Guises, assumed the leadership of the
Catholics; and in response the Bourbons, another
noble family, championed the Calvinists, about a
twelfth of the population. Their struggle split the
country apart.

It was ominous that in 1559—the year that
Henry II, France's last strong king for a generation, died—the Calvinists (known in France as
Huguenots) organized their first national synod,
an indication of impressive strength. During the
next 30 years, the throne was occupied by Henry's three ineffectual sons. The power behind the
crown was Henry's widow, Catherine de Medici
(see the genealogical table below), who tried desperately to preserve royal authority. But she was
often helpless because the religious conflict intensified the factional struggle for power between
the Guises and the Bourbons, both of whom were
closely related to the monarchy and hoped one
day to inherit the throne.

The Wars   Fighting started in 1562 and lasted for
36 years, interrupted only by short-lived peace
agreements. Catherine switched sides whenever
one party became too powerful; and she may
have approved the notorious massacre of St.
Bartholomew's Day—August 24, 1572—which
started in Paris, spread through France, and destroyed the Huguenots' leadership. Henry of
Navarre, a Bourbon, was the only major figure
who escaped. When Catherine switched sides
again and made peace with the Huguenots in
1576, the Guises formed the Catholic League,

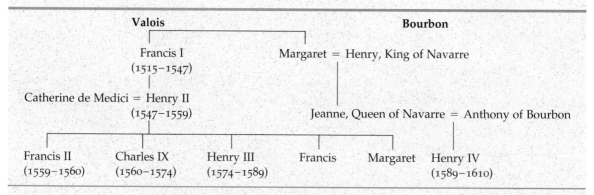

THE KINGS OF FRANCE IN THE SIXTEENTH CENTURY

Valois				Bourbon	
Francis I (1515–1547)			Margaret = Henry, King of Navarre		
Catherine de Medici = Henry II (1547–1559)			Jeanne, Queen of Navarre = Anthony of Bourbon		
Francis II (1559–1560)	Charles IX (1560–1574)	Henry III (1574–1589)	Francis	Margaret	Henry IV (1589–1610)

which for several years dominated the eastern half of the country. In 1584 the league allied with Spain's Philip II to attack heresy in France and deny the Bourbon Henry's legal right to inherit the throne.

The defeat of the Armada in 1588 proved to be the turning point in the French civil wars, for the duke of Guise lost his principal support, Spain, and was soon assassinated. Within a few months Henry of Navarre inherited the throne as Henry IV (1589–1610), though he had few advantages as he began to reassert royal authority. The Huguenots and Catholics ran almost independent governments in large sections of France. The Catholic League was in command of the east, including the capital, Paris; the Huguenots dominated the south and southwest, remote from the central government. In addition, the royal administration was in a sorry state because the crown's oldest rivals, the great nobles, could now resist all outside interference in their domains.

Peace Restored   Yet largely because of the assassination of the duke of Guise, Henry IV was able to restore order. The duke had been a forceful leader, a serious contender for the throne. His replacement was a Spanish candidate for the crown who had little chance of success. The distaste for a possible foreign ruler, combined with war weariness, destroyed much of the support for the Catholic League, which finally collapsed as a result of revolts against it in eastern France in the 1590s. These uprisings, founded on a demand for peace, increased in frequency and intensity after Henry IV renounced Protestantism in 1593 in order to win acceptance by his Catholic subjects. The following year Henry had himself officially crowned, and all of France rallied to the king as he beat back a Spanish invasion—Spain's final, rather weak, attempt to put its own candidate on the throne.

When Spain finally withdrew and signed a peace treaty in 1598, the fighting came to an end. To complete the reconciliation, Henry issued (also in 1598) the Edict of Nantes, which granted limited toleration to the Huguenots. Although it did not create complete religious liberty, the edict made Calvinist worship legal, protected the rights of the minority, and opened public office to Huguenots.

Map 15.2 CATHOLIC AND PROTESTANT POWERS IN THE LATE SIXTEENTH CENTURY
The heart of the Catholic cause in the wars of religion was the Spain of Philip II. Spanish territories surrounded France and provided the route to the Netherlands where the Protestant Dutch had rebelled against the Spaniards. The Armada was launched to help that cause by crushing the ally of the Dutch, Protestant England. In the meantime, the surrounded French had problems of their own with the Huguenots, who protected their Protestantism in a network of fortified towns.

Political Thought But the effects of decades of strife could not be brushed aside. A basic change in political thought, for example, was an inevitable response to the civil wars. The Huguenots had found ways to justify resistance to a monarch, and the Catholics used a similar justification when they were fighting the king. Even when order was restored, however, the advocates of peace and national unity, known as *politiques*, still had to argue forcefully for stability and a more powerful central government.

Their most famous representative, Jean Bodin, made his case by examining the basic structure of the state, and his analysis influenced political theorists for centuries. His principal work is *The Six Books of the Republic* (1576), in which he defines the nature and limits of the sovereignty exercised by governments. By seeking a balance between power and restraint, Bodin hoped to find a principle for restoring order in an age of shattering upheaval. But in the process, he also exposed the dilemma that has been the primary focus of political theory ever since: control versus freedom, the need for authority and yet the equal need for subjects' rights.

II. War and International Crisis

THE THIRTY YEARS' WAR

In the Holy Roman Empire, religious hatreds were especially disruptive because the empire lacked a central authority and unifying institutions. Small-scale fighting broke out repeatedly after the 1550s, always inspired by religion. And though in most of Western Europe the first two decades of the seventeenth century were a time of relative peace, which seemed to signal a decline of conflict over faith, in the empire the stage was being set for the bloodiest of all the wars fired by religion.

Known as the Thirty Years' War, this ferocious struggle began in the Kingdom of Bohemia in 1618 and continued until 1648. The principal battleground, the empire, was ravaged by the fighting, which eventually involved every major ruler in Europe. At first it was a renewed struggle between Protestants and Catholics, but eventually it became a fight among political rivals who were eager to take advantage of the fragmentation of

▶ "THE HANGING TREE," ENGRAVING FROM JACQUES CALLOT'S MISERIES OF WAR, 1633
An indication of the growing dismay over the brutality of the Thirty Years' War was the collection of 16 prints produced by the French engraver Callot, depicting the life of the soldier and the effects of armies on civilian populations. His soldiers destroy, loot, and rape, and only a few of them receive the punishments they deserve, like this mass hanging.

Ifrael ex. Cum Priul. Reg.

A la fin ces Voleurs infames et perdus ,   *Monftrent bien que le crime (horrible et noire engeance)*   *Et que cest le Deftin des hommes vicieux*
Comme fruits malheureux a cet arbre pendus   *Eft luy mefme inftrument de honte et de vengeance ,*   *Defprouuer tôft ou tard la iuftice des Cieux .* **1)**

the empire to advance their own ambitions. As the devastation spread, international relations seemed to be sinking into total chaos; but the chief victims were the Germans, who, like the Italians in the sixteenth century, found themselves at the mercy of well-organized states that used another country as the arena for settling their quarrels.

The First Phase, 1618–1621   The immediate problem was typical of the situation in the empire. In 1609 Emperor Rudolf II promised toleration for Protestants in Bohemia, one of his own domains. When his cousin Ferdinand, a pious Catholic, succeeded to the Bohemian throne in 1617, he refused to honor Rudolf's promise, and the Bohemians rebelled in 1618. Since the crown was elective, they declared Ferdinand deposed, replacing him with the leading Calvinist of the empire, Frederick II of the Palatinate. Frederick accepted the crown, an act of defiance whose only possible outcome was war.

The first decade or so of the war was a time of victories for the Catholics, and in particular the Habsburgs. Ferdinand became emperor (1619–1637), and the powerful Catholic Maximilian of Bavaria put an army at his disposal. Within a year the imperial troops won a stunning victory over the Bohemians at the Battle of the White Mountain. Leading rebels were executed or exiled, and Ferdinand II confiscated all of Frederick's lands. Maximilian received half as a reward for his army, and the remainder went to the Spaniards, who occupied it as a valuable base for their struggle with the Dutch. In this first round, the Catholic and imperial cause had triumphed.

The Second Phase, 1621–1630   When the truce between the Spaniards and the Dutch expired in 1621, and warfare resumed in Germany as well as in the Netherlands, the Protestants made no progress for 10 years. A new imperial army was raised by Albrecht von Wallenstein, a minor Bohemian nobleman and remarkable opportunist who had become one of the richest men in the empire. In 1624 Wallenstein, realizing that the emperor remained weak because he lacked his own army, offered to raise a force if he could billet it and raise its supplies wherever it happened

Die ficht man die 12. Köpff auff den Prager Bruckenthurn aufgesteckt.

▶ **"Heads of the Bohemian Rebels," Engraving from Mathäus Merian, *Theatrum Europaeum*, ca. 1630**
Since the scene had not changed when the engraving was made, this illustration is probably a fairly accurate representation of the punishment in 1621 of the leaders of the Bohemian rebellion. Twenty-four rebels were executed, and the heads of twelve of them were displayed on long poles at the top of the tower (still standing today) on the bridge over Prague's river. The heads were kept there for 10 years.

to be stationed. Ferdinand agreed, and by 1627 Wallenstein's army had begun to conquer the northern region of the empire, the last major center of Protestant strength. To emphasize his supremacy, Ferdinand issued the Edict of Restitution in 1629, ordering the restoration to Catholics of all the territories they had lost to Protestants since 1552.

But these Habsburg successes were more apparent than real, because it was only the extreme disorganization of the empire that permitted a mercenary captain like Wallenstein to achieve such immense military power. Once the princes realized the danger he posed to their independence, they united (Catholic as well as Protestant) against the Habsburgs, and in 1630 they made Ferdinand dismiss Wallenstein by threatening to keep his son from the imperial succession. The emperor's submission proved fatal to his cause, for Sweden and France were preparing to unleash new aggressions against the Habsburgs, and Wallenstein was the one military leader who might have been able to beat back the onslaught.

The Third Phase, 1630–1632   The year 1630 marked the beginning of a change in fortune for the Protestants and also a drift toward the purely political aim (of resisting the Habsburgs) that was coming to dominate the war. Although France's king was a Catholic, he was ready to join with Protestants against other Catholics so as to undermine Habsburg power. Early in 1630 the French attacked the duke of Savoy, a Habsburg ally, and occupied his lands. Then, in 1631, they allied with Gustavus Adolphus of Sweden, who, dismayed by Ferdinand's treatment of Protestants and fearing a Habsburg threat to Swedish lands around the Baltic Sea, had invaded the empire in 1630. The following year Gustavus destroyed an imperial army at Breitenfeld in one of the few decisive battles of the war. The tide had turned against the Habsburgs.

Ferdinand hastily recalled Wallenstein, whose troops met the Swedes in battle at Lützen in 1632. Although Gustavus' soldiers won the day, he himself was killed, and his death saved the Habsburg dynasty from being destroyed by Sweden. Nothing, however, could restore Ferdinand's former position. The emperor was forced by the princes to turn against Wallenstein once more; A few months later he had him assassinated. The removal of the great general marked the end of an era, for he was the last leader in more than two centuries who was capable of establishing unified authority in what is now Germany.

The Fourth Phase, 1632–1648   Gustavus' success opened the final phase of the war, as political ambitions—the quest of the empire's princes for independence, and the struggle between the Habsburgs and their enemies—almost completely replaced religious aims. The Protestant princes began to raise new armies, and by 1635 Ferdinand had to make peace with them. In return for their promise of assistance in driving out the Swedes, Ferdinand agreed to suspend the Edict of Restitution and to grant amnesty to all but Frederick of the Palatinate and a few Bohemian rebels. Ferdinand was renouncing most of his ambitions, and it seemed that peace might return at last.

But the French could not let matters rest. In 1635 they finally declared war on Ferdinand. For the next 13 years, the French and Swedes rained unmitigated disaster on Germany. Peace negotiations began in 1641, but not until 1648 did the combatants agree to lay down arms and sign the treaties of Westphalia. Even thereafter the war between France and Spain, pursued mainly in the Spanish Netherlands, continued for another 11 years; and hostilities around the Baltic among Sweden, Denmark, Poland, and Russia, which had started in 1611, did not end until 1661.

The Effect of War   The wars and their effects (such as the diseases spread by armies) killed off over a third of Germany's population. The conflict caused serious economic dislocation because a number of princes—already in serious financial straits—sharply debased their coinage. This worsened the continentwide trade depression that had begun around 1620 and had brought the great sixteenth-century boom to an end, causing the first drop in prices since 1500. Few contemporaries perceived the connection between war and economic trouble, but nobody could ignore the drain on men and resources or the destructive effects of the conflict.

THE PEACE OF WESTPHALIA

By the 1630s it was becoming apparent that the fighting was getting out of hand and that it would not be easy to bring the conflicts to an end. There had never been such widespread or devastating warfare, and many diplomats felt that the settlement had to be of far greater scope than any negotiated before. And they were right. When at last the treaties were signed in 1648, after seven years of negotiation in the German province of Westphalia, a landmark in international relations was passed—remarkable not

▶ *Jan Asselyn*

THE BATTLE OF LÜTZEN

Although it is not an accurate rendition of the scene, this painting of Gustavus Adolphus (the horseman in a brown coat with sword raised) shot by a gunman in red does give the flavor of seventeenth-century battle. Because of the chaos, the smoke, and the poor visibility that often obscured what was happening, Gustavus' escort did not notice when he was in fact hit by a musket shot that shattered his left arm and caused his horse to bolt. Further shots killed him, and not until hours after the battle was his seminaked body found, stripped of its finery.

only because it brought an anarchic situation under control but because it created a new system for dealing with wars.

The most important innovation was the gathering at the peace conference of all the participants in the Thirty Years' War, rather than the usual practice of bringing only two or three belligerents together. The presence of ambassadors from Bavaria, Brandenburg, Denmark, France, the Holy Roman Empire, Saxony, Spain, Sweden, Switzerland, and the United Provinces made possible, for the first time in European history, a series of all-embracing treaties that dealt with nearly every major international issue at one stroke. Visible at the meetings was the emergence of a state system. These independent states recognized that they were creating a mechanism for controlling their relations with one another. Although some fighting continued, the Peace of Westphalia in 1648 became the first comprehensive rearrangement of the map of Europe in modern times.

The Peace Terms   The principal beneficiaries were France and Sweden, the chief aggressors during the last decade of the war. France gained the provinces of Alsace and Lorraine, and Swe-

National Gallery, London

▶ *Gerard Terborch*
THE PEACE OF WESTPHALIA, 1648
The artist was an eyewitness to this scene, the formal signing of peace between the United Provinces and Spain in Münster on May 15, 1648. The two leaders of the Spanish delegation on the right put their hands on a Bible as they swear to uphold the terms of the treaty, and the Dutch on the left all raise their hands as they declare "So help me God." Terborch himself, dressed in brown, is looking out at the viewer on the far left.

den obtained extensive territories in the Holy Roman Empire. The main loser was the House of Habsburg, since both the United Provinces and the Swiss Confederation were recognized as independent states, and the German princes, who agreed not to join an alliance against the emperor, were otherwise given almost complete independence.

The princes' autonomy was formally established in 1657, when they elected as emperor Leopold I, the head of the House of Habsburg, in return for two promises. First, Leopold would give no help to his cousins, the rulers of Spain; and second, the empire would be a state of princes, in which each ruler would be free from imperial interference. This freedom permitted the rise of Brandenburg-Prussia and the growth of absolutism—the belief that the political authority of the ruler was unlimited—within the major principalities. Moreover, the Habsburgs' capitulation prepared the way for their reorientation toward the east along the Danube River—the beginnings of the Austro-Hungarian Empire.

The Effects of Westphalia For more than a century, the settlement reached at Westphalia was regarded as the basis for all international negotiations. Even major new accords, such as the one that ended yet another series of wars in 1713, were seen mainly as adjustments of the decisions of 1648. In practice, of course, multinational conferences were no more effective than brief, limited negotiations in reducing tensions among states. Wars continued to break out, and armies grew in size and skill. But diplomats did believe that international affairs were under better control and that the chaos of the Thirty Years' War had been replaced by something more stable and more clearly defined.

This confidence was reinforced as it became clear after 1648 that armies were trying to improve discipline and avoid the excesses of the previous 30 years. As religious passions waned, combat became less vicious and the treatment of civilians became more orderly. On battlefields, better discipline reduced the casualty rate from 1 death per 3 soldiers in the 1630s to 1 death in 7, or even 1 in 20, during the early 1700s. And the aims of war also changed significantly.

Changed International Relations The most obvious differences after the Peace of Westphalia were that France replaced Spain as the continent's dominant power and that northern countries—especially England and the Netherlands,

Map 15.3 TERRITORIAL CHANGES. 1648–1661
This map shows the territorial changes that took place after the Thirty Years' War. The treaties of Westphalia (1648) and the Pyrenees (1659) arranged the principal transfers, but the settlements in the Baltic were not confirmed until the treaties of Copenhagen, Oliva (both 1660), and Kardis (1661).

where growth in population and in commerce resumed more quickly than elsewhere—took over Europe's economic leadership. But behind this outward shift a more fundamental transformation was taking place. What had become apparent in the later stages of the Thirty Years' War was that Europe's states were prepared to fight only for economic, territorial, or political advantages. Dynastic aims were still important, but supranational goals like religious causes could no longer determine a state's foreign policy.

The Thirty Years' War was the last major international conflict in Europe in which two religious camps organized their forces as blocs. After 1648 such connections gave way to more purely national interests. This shift marked the decisive stage of a process that had been under way since the Late Middle Ages: the emergence of the state as the basic unit and object of loyalty in Western civilization. That it had taken a major crisis, a descent into international anarchy, to bring about so momentous a change is an indication of how profoundly the upheavals of the mid-seventeenth century affected European history. Indeed, the reshaping of the relations among Europe's states for centuries to come that was achieved at Westphalia is but one example of the multiple military and political consequences of this age of crisis.

III. The Military Revolution

▼

WEAPONS AND TACTICS

The constant warfare of the sixteenth and seventeenth centuries brought about dramatic changes in the ways battles were fought and armies were organized. Gunpowder, which had been used occasionally and to little effect since the 1330s, now came to occupy a central place in warfare. The result was not only the creation of a new type of industry, cannon and gun manufacture, but also a transformation of tactics. Individual castles could no longer be defended against explosives; even towns had to build heavy and elaborate fortifications if they were to resist the new fire power. Sieges became compli-

cated, expensive operations, whose purpose was to bring explosives right up to a town wall so that it could be blown up. This required an intricate system of trenches, because walls were built in star shapes so as to multiply angles of fire and make any approach dangerous. Although they became increasingly costly, sieges remained essential to the strategy of warfare until the eighteenth century.

Tactics In open battles, the effects of gunpowder were equally expensive. The new tactics that appeared around 1500, perfected by the Spaniards, relied on massed ranks of infantry, organized in huge squares, that made the traditional cavalry charge obsolete. Interspersed with the gunners were soldiers carrying pikes. They fended off horses or opposing infantry while the men with guns tried to mow the enemy down. The squares with the best discipline usually won, and for over a century after the reign of Ferdinand of Aragon, the Spaniards had the best army in Europe. Each square had about 3000 troops, and to maintain enough squares at full strength to fight all of Spain's battles required an army numbering approximately 40,000. The cost of keeping that many men clothed, fed, and housed, let alone equipped and paid, was enormous. But worse was to come: New tactics emerged in the early seventeenth century that required even more soldiers.

Since nobody could outdo the Spaniards at their own methods, a different approach was developed by their rivals. The first advance was made by Maurice of Nassau, who led the Dutch revolt against Spain from the 1580s. He relied not on sheer weight and power but on flexibility and mobility. Then Sweden's Gustavus Adolphus, one of the geniuses of the history of warfare, found a way to achieve mobility on the field without losing power. His main invention was the salvo: Instead of having his musketeers fire one row at a time, like the Spaniards, he had them all fire at once. What he lost in continuity of shot he gained in a fearsome blast that, if properly timed, could shatter enemy ranks. Huge, slow-moving squares were simply no match for smaller, faster units that riddled them with well-coordinated salvos.

THE ORGANIZATION AND SUPPORT OF ARMIES

These tactical changes brought about steady increases in the size of armies, because the more units there were, the better they could be placed on the battlefield. Although the Spanish army hardly grew between 1560 and 1640, remaining at 40,000 to 60,000 men, the Swedes had 150,000 by 1632; and at the end of the century, Louis XIV considered a force of 400,000 essential to maintain his dominant position in Europe.

This growth had far-reaching consequences. One was the need for conscription, which Gustavus introduced in the late 1620s. At least half his army consisted of his own subjects, who were easier to control than foreign mercenaries. Because it also made sense not to disband such huge forces each autumn, when the campaigning season ended, most armies were kept permanently ready. The need to maintain so many soldiers the year round caused a rapid expansion of supporting administrative personnel. Taxation mushroomed. All levels of society felt the impact but especially the lower classes, who paid the bulk of the taxes and provided most of the recruits. To encourage enlistment, rulers made military service as attractive as possible—a task made easier by the problems many people faced in finding regular meals, clothing, housing, and wages. Social distinctions were reduced; an able young man could rise high in the officer corps, though the top ranks were still reserved for nobles. Even the lower echelons were given important responsibilities because the new system of small, flexible units gave considerable initiative to the junior officers who led them.

New Ranks Other changes followed. Maneuverability on the field demanded tighter discipline, which was achieved by the introduction of drilling and combat training. The order of command was clarified, and many ranks familiar today—major, colonel, and the various levels of general—appeared in the seventeenth century. The distinctions were reinforced by uniforms, which became standard equipment. These developments created a sense of corporate spirit among military officers, an international phenomenon that was to occupy an important place in European society for three centuries.

THE LIFE OF THE SOLDIER

For the average soldier, who was now a common sight in Europe, life in the army began with recruitment. Some genuinely wanted to join up. They had heard stories of adventure, booty, and comradeship, and they were tempted by free

▶ *Anonymous Engraving after Jacques de Gheyn*
WAFFENHANDLUNG
The expansion of armies and the professionalization of war in the seventeenth century were reflected in the founding of military academies and the growing acceptance of the notion that warfare was a science. There was now a market for published manuals, especially if they had illustrations like this one, which shows how a pikeman was supposed to crouch and hold his weapons (stabilizing his pike against his foot) when facing a cavalry charge.

Map 15.4 AREAS OF FIGHTING, 1618–1660
The endemic fighting of this age of crisis engulfed most of Central Europe
and involved soldiers from every country.

food and clothing. But in many cases the "volunteers" did not want to go, for they had also heard of the hardship and danger. Unfortunately for them, recruiting officers had quotas, and villages had to provide the numbers demanded of them. Community pressure, bribery, enlistment of drunken men, and even outright kidnapping helped fill the ranks.

Joining an army did not necessarily mean cutting oneself off from friends or family. Men from a particular area enlisted together, and in some cases, wives came along. There were dozens of jobs to do aside from fighting, because soldiers needed cooks, laundresses, peddlers, and other tradespeople. It has been estimated that an army in the field might need five people for every soldier. The large majority of the troops, though, were on their own. For companionship, they looked to camp followers or the women of the town they were occupying. Few barracks had been built, and therefore, unless they were on the march or out in the open on a battlefield, they were housed (or billeted) with ordinary citizens. Since soldiers almost never received their wages on time—delays could be as long as a year or more—they rarely could pay for their food and housing. Local civilians therefore had to supply their needs, or risk the thievery that was universal. It was no wonder that the approach of an army was a terrifying event.

Military Justice   Officially, there were severe penalties for misbehavior—imprisonment, flogging, or, for crimes like desertion, execution. Yet discipline, though harsh, was only occasionally

▶ *Sebastian Vrancx*
A MILITARY CAMP
Vrancx was himself a soldier, and the many military scenes he painted during the Thirty Years' War give us a sense of the life of the soldier during the many months when there were no campaigns or battles. Conditions could be grim, but there were many hours when one could simply nap, chat, or play dice.

enforced, because men were needed for combat and it was easy to slip away from an army. Troops had their own law and courts, but the main goal of their officers was to maintain an effective fighting force. And disputes with civilians rarely ended in a judgment against a soldier. Punishments were rare even for corruption at an army's upper levels (for instance, when officers who were paid to raise troops listed phantom recruits and kept their wages).

Discomforts   The relatively light legal restrictions did not mean that military life was easy. Soldiers suffered constant discomfort. A garrison might be able to settle into a town in reasonable conditions for a long stretch; but if it was besieged, it became hungry, fearful, and vulnerable. Days spent on the march could be grim, exhausting, and uncertain; and even in camps soldiers were often filthy and wet. Real danger was not common, though it was intense during battles and occasionally during sieges. Even a simple wound could be fatal, because medical care was generally appalling. Yet the most persistent discomfort for the soldier was boredom. Sieges dragged, and even the hard labor of digging trenches or dragging cannons must have been a relief from the tedious waiting. Despite traditional recreations—drink, gambling, and the brawls common among soldiers—the attractions were limited; and most military men had few regrets when they returned to civilian life.

IV. Revolution in England

In the 1640s and 1650s the growing burdens of war and taxation, and the mounting assertiveness of governments, sparked upheavals throughout Europe that were the equivalent in domestic politics of the crisis in international relations. In country after country, people rose up in vain attempts to restore the individual and regional autonomies that were being eroded by powerful central governments. Only in England, however, did the revolt become a revolution—an attempt to overturn the social and political system and create a new structure for society.

ELIZABETH I

Before 1630, no such eruption could have been foreseen. With few wars, and those largely at sea, England was less affected than other countries by the fighting of the age. In addition, the people were united by such common bonds as the institution of Parliament and a commitment to the international Protestant cause that was carefully promoted by Queen Elizabeth I (1558–1603).

Elizabeth is an appealing figure because she combined shrewd hardheadedness and a sense of the possible with a disarming appearance of frailty. Her qualities were many: her dedication to the task of government; her astute choice of advisers; her civilizing influence at court, where she encouraged elegant manners and the arts; her tolerance of religious dissent as long as it posed no political threat; and her ability to feel the mood of her people, to catch their spirit, to inspire their enthusiasm. Although social, legal, and economic practices usually subordinated women to men in this age, inheritance was respected; thus a determined woman with a recognized claim to authority could win complete acceptance. Elizabeth was the most widely admired and most successful queen of her time, but she was by no means alone: Female rulers also shaped the histories of France, Sweden, and the southern Netherlands in the sixteenth and seventeenth centuries.

Royal Policy   Elizabeth could be indecisive, notably where the succession was concerned. Her refusal to marry caused serious uncertainties, and it was only the shrewd planning of her chief minister, Robert Cecil, that enabled the king of Scotland, James Stuart, to succeed her without incident in 1603. Similar dangers arose from her indecisive treatment of England's remaining Catholics. They hoped that Mary Queen of Scots, a Catholic, would inherit the throne; and since she was next in line, they were not above plotting against Elizabeth's life. Eventually, in 1587, Elizabeth had Mary executed and the plots died away. But her reluctance to take firm positions was also apparent in her choice of advisers. Some advocated caution, inaction, and discretion in international affairs; whereas others favored an aggressive foreign policy. Yet Elizabeth showed

Queen Elizabeth's Armada Speech

Elizabeth's ability to move her subjects was exemplified by the speech she gave to her troops as they awaited the fight with the Spanish Armada. She understood that they might have doubts about a woman leading them in war, but she turned that issue to her own advantage in a stirring cry to battle that enhanced her popularity at the time and her legendary image thereafter.

"My loving People: We have been persuaded by some that are careful of our safety, to take heed how we commit ourselves to armed multitudes, for fear of treachery; but I assure you, I do not desire to live to distrust my faithful and loving people.

"Let tyrants fear; I have always so behaved myself, that, under God, I have placed my chiefest strength and safeguard in the loyal hearts and good will of my subjects, and therefore I am come amongst you, as you see, at this time, not for my recreation . . . but being resolved in the midst and heat of the battle, to live or die amongst you all, to lay down for my God, and for my kingdoms, and for my people, my honour and my blood, even in the dust.

"I know I have the body of a weak and feeble woman; but I have the heart and stomach of a king, and of a king of England too; and think foul scorn that . . . Spain, or any prince of Europe should dare to invade the borders of my realm; to which rather than any dishonour shall grow by me, I myself will take up arms, I myself will be your general, judge, and rewarder of every one of your virtues in the field. . . . By your concord in the camp, and your valour in the field, we shall shortly have a famous victory over those enemies of my God, of my kingdoms, and of my people."

From Walter Scott (ed.), *A Collection of Scarce and Valuable Tracts, on the Most Interesting and Entertaining Subjects: but Chiefly Such as Relate to the History and Constitution of these Kingdoms*, vol. I (London, 1809), pp. 429–430.

great skill in balancing the contrasting viewpoints, and her adroit maneuvering assured her of her ministers' loyalty at all times.

She also inspired the devotion of her subjects by traveling throughout England to make public appearances: by brilliant speeches (*see box, above*); and by shaping her own image, even regulating how she was to be depicted in portraits. She thus retained her subjects' allegiance despite the profound social changes that were eroding traditional patterns of deference and order. England's nobility, for instance, no longer dominated the military and the government; nearly all Elizabeth's ministers were new in national life, and the House of Commons was beginning to exert more political influence within Parliament than the House of Lords. The nobles, less directly involved in commerce, did not benefit as much as other sections of society from England's rising prosperity; and in general they were losing their hold over the power, wealth, and goverment of the country.

The Gentry The gentry, the new group that joined the nobles at the head of society, ranged from people considered great in a parish or other small locality to courtiers considered great throughout the land. There were never more than 60 nobles during Elizabeth's reign, but the gentry may have numbered close to 20,000 by the time she died. Most of these gentry were doing well economically, profiting from their agricultural holdings as well as from crown offices. A number also became involved in industrial activity, and hundreds invested in new overseas trading and colonial ventures. The gentry's participation in commerce made them unique among the landed classes of Europe, whose members were tradi-

▶ *William Segar* (attrib.)
PORTRAIT OF ELIZABETH I, 1585
Elizabeth I was strongly aware of the power of propaganda, and she used it to foster a dazzling public image. Legends about her arose in literature. And in art she had herself portrayed in the most elaborate finery imaginable. Here, she is every inch the queen, with her magnificent dress, the trappings of monarchy, and the symbol of virginity, the ermine.

tionally contemptuous of business affairs, and it testified to the enterprise and vigor of England's social leaders. Long important in local administration, they flocked to the House of Commons to express their views of public matters. Their ambitions eventually posed a serious threat to the monarchy, especially when linked with the effects of rapid economic change.

Economic Advance   In Elizabeth's reign, thanks to a general boom in trade, England's merchants, helped by leading courtiers, began to transform the country's economy. They opened commercial links throughout Europe and parts of Asia and began English expansion overseas. At home, there was significant industrial development. Mining and manufacture developed rapidly, and shipbuilding became a major industry. The production of coal increased 14-fold between 1540 and 1680, creating fortunes and an expertise in industrial techniques that took England far ahead of its neighbors.

The economic vigor and growth that ensued gave the classes that benefited most—gentry and merchants—a cohesion and a sense of purpose that made it dangerous to oppose them when they felt their rights infringed. They increasingly regarded themselves as the leaders of the nation, second only to the nobility. They wanted respect for their wishes, and they bitterly resented the economic interference and political high-handedness of Elizabeth's successors.

The Puritans   Heightening this unease was the sympathy many of the gentry felt toward a small but vociferous group of religious reformers, the Puritans. Puritans believed that the Protestant Anglican Church established by Elizabeth was still too close to Roman Catholicism, and they wanted further reductions in ritual and hierarchy. Elizabeth refused, and although she tried to avoid a confrontation, in the last years of her reign she had to silence the most outspoken of her critics. As a result, the Puritans became a disgruntled minority. By the 1630s, when the government tried to repress such religious dissent more vigorously, there were many in England, non-Puritan as well as Puritan, who felt that the monarchy was leading the country astray and was ignoring the wishes of its subjects. Leading parliamentarians in particular soon came to believe that major changes were needed to restore good government in England.

PARLIAMENT AND THE LAW

The place where the gentry made their views known was Parliament, the nation's supreme legislative body. Three-quarters of the House of Commons consisted of gentry. They were better educated than ever before, and nearly half of them had legal training. Since the Commons had to approve all taxation, the gentry had the leverage to pursue their grievances.

The monarchy was still the dominant force in

the country when Elizabeth died in 1603, but Parliament's demand to be heard was gathering momentum. Although the queen had been careful with money, in the last 20 years of her reign her resources had been overtaxed by war with Spain and an economic depression. Thus she bequeathed to her successor, Scotland's James Stuart, a huge debt—£400,000, the equal of a year's royal revenue—and the struggle to pay it off gave the Commons the means to seek changes in royal policy.

James I   Trouble began in the reign of James I (1603–1625), who had a far more exalted view of his own powers than Elizabeth had had and who did not hesitate to tell his subjects, in the most tactless way, that he considered his authority almost unlimited. As a result, gentry opposed to royal policies dominated parliamentary proceedings, and they engaged in a running battle with the king. They blocked the union of England with Scotland that James sought. They drew up an "Apology" explaining his mistakes and his ignorance, as a Scotsman, of English traditions. They forced two of his ministers to resign in disgrace. And they wrung repeated concessions from him, including the unprecedented right for Parliament to discuss foreign policy.

Law   The Commons used the law to justify their resistance to royal power. The basic legal system of the country was the common law—justice administered on the basis of precedents and parliamentary statutes, and relying on the opinions of juries. This system stood in contrast to Roman law, prevalent on the continent, where royal edicts could make law and decisions were reached by judges without juries. Such practices existed in England only in a few royal courts of law, such as Star Chamber, which, because it was directly under the crown, came to be seen as an instrument of repression.

The common lawyers, whose leaders were also prominent in the Commons, resented the growing business of the royal courts and attacked them in Parliament. Both James and his successor were accused of pressuring judges, particularly after they won a series of famous cases involving a subject's right to criticize the monarch. Thus the crown could be portrayed as disregarding not only the desires of the people but the law itself.

The king still had broad powers, but when he exercised them contrary to Parliament's wishes, his actions seemed to many to be taking on the appearance of tyranny.

RISING ANTAGONISMS

The confrontation between Parliament and king grew worse during the 1620s, especially in the reign of James's son, Charles I (1625–1649). At the Parliament of 1628–1629, the open challenge to the crown reached a climax in the Petition of Right, which has become a landmark in constitutional history. The petition demanded an end to imprisonment without cause shown, to taxation without the consent of Parliament, to martial law in peacetime, and to the billeting of troops among civilians. Charles agreed, in the hope of gaining much-needed subsidies, but then broke his word. To many, this betrayal seemed to threaten Parliament's essential role in government alongside the king. Seeking to end discussion of these issues in the Commons, Charles ordered Parliament dissolved, but with great daring, two members denied the king even this hallowed right by holding the speaker of the House in his chair while they passed a final angry resolution denouncing Charles's actions.

Resentful subjects were clearly on the brink of openly defying their king. Puritans, common lawyers, and disenchanted country gentry had taken over the House of Commons; and Charles avoided further trouble only by refusing to call another session of Parliament. This he managed to do for 11 years, all the while increasing the repression of Puritanism and using extraordinary measures (such as reviving crown rights to special taxes that had not been demanded for a long time) to raise revenues that did not require parliamentary consent. But in 1639, the Calvinist Scots took up arms rather than accept the Anglican prayer book, and the parliamentarians had their chance. To raise funds for an army to fight the Scots, Charles had to turn to Parliament, which demanded that he first redress its grievances. When he resisted, civil war followed.

CIVIL WAR

The Parliament that met in 1640 began with a two-hour speech by John Pym, a prominent critic of the monarch, who outlined long-standing grievances against both church and government. Charles refused to change his policies, the Commons refused to grant a subsidy, and the king angrily dissolved the session. But there was no way to pay for an army without taxes. By the summer of 1640, the Scots occupied most of northern England, and Charles had to summon a new Parliament. This one sat for 13 years, earning the appropriate name of the Long Parliament.

In its first year, the House of Commons abolished the royal courts, such as Star Chamber, and made mandatory the writ of habeas corpus (which prevented imprisonment without cause shown); it declared taxation without parliamentary consent illegal; and it ruled that Parliament had to meet at least once every three years. Meanwhile, the Puritans in the Commons prepared to reform the church. Oliver Cromwell, one of their leaders, demanded abolition of the Anglican Book of Common Prayer and strongly attacked the institution of episcopacy. The climactic vote came the next year when the Commons passed a Grand Remonstrance, which outlined for the king all the legislation they had passed and asked that bishops be deprived of votes in the House of Lords.

The Two Sides   This was the prelude to a more revolutionary Puritan assault on the stucture of the Church, but in fact the Grand Remonstrance passed by only 11 votes. A moderate group was detaching itself from the Puritans, and it was to become the nucleus of a royalist party. The nation's chief grievances had been redressed, and there was no longer a uniform desire for change. Still Charles misjudged the situation and tried to arrest five leaders of the Commons, supposedly for plotting treason with the Scots. But Parliament resisted, and the citizens of London, openly hostile to Charles, sheltered the five. England now began gradually to split in two. By late 1642 both the royalists and the antiroyalists had assembled armies, and the Civil War was under way.

What made so many people overcome their habitual loyalty to the monarchy? We know that the royalists in Parliament were considerably younger than their opponents, which suggests that it was long experience with the Stuarts and

nostalgia for Elizabeth that created revolutionaries. Another clear divide was regional. The south and east of England were primarily antiroyalist, while the north and west were mostly royalist. This indicated that the more cosmopolitan areas, closer to the continent and also centers of Puritanism, were largely on Parliament's side. The decision was often a personal matter: A prominent family and its locality chose one side because its rival, a nearby family, had chosen the other. The Puritans were certainly antiroyalist, but they were a minority in the country and influential in the House of Commons only because they were so vociferous and determined. Like all revolutions, this one was animated by a small group of radicals (in this case, Puritans) who alone kept the momentum going.

Independents and Presbyterians   As the fighting began, a group among the Puritans known as Independents urged that the Anglican Church be replaced by a congregational system, in which each local congregation, free of all central authority, would decide its own form of worship. The most important leader of the Independents in Parliament was Oliver Cromwell. Opposed to them, but also considered Puritans, were the Presbyterians, who wanted to establish a strictly organized Calvinist system, like the one in Scotland, where local congregations were subject to centralized authority, though laypeople did participate in church government. Since both the Scots, whose alliance was vital in the war, and a majority of the Puritans in the Commons were Presbyterians, Cromwell agreed to give way, but only for the moment. There was also a quarrel over the goals of the war because the antiroyalists were unsure whether they ought to defeat Charles completely. This dispute crossed religious lines, though the Independents were in general more determined to force Charles into total submission, and eventually they had their way.

As the fighting continued, Cromwell persuaded the Commons to allow him to reorganize the antiroyalist troops. His New Model Army—whipped to fervor by sermons, prayers, and the singing of psalms—became unbeatable. At Naseby in 1645, it won a major victory, and a year later Charles surrendered. The next two years were chaotic. The Presbyterians and Independ-

▶ *Anonymous*
ENGRAVING OF THE EXECUTION OF CHARLES I
This contemporary Dutch engraving of the
execution of Charles I shows the scaffold in front of
the Banqueting House in Whitehall—a building
that still can be seen in London. On the far right of
the scaffold, the executioner displays the severed
head for the crowd.

ents quarreled over what to do with the king, and finally Civil War resumed. This time the Presbyterians and Scots backed Charles against the Independents. But even with this alliance the royalists were no match for the New Model Army; Cromwell soon defeated his opponents and captured the king.

The King's Fate At the same time, in 1647, the Independents abolished the House of Lords and removed all Presbyterians from the House of Commons. This "Rump" Parliament tried to negotiate with Charles but discovered that he continued to plot a return to power. With Cromwell's approval, the Commons decided that their monarch, untrustworthy and a troublemaker, would have to die. A trial of dubious legality was held, and though many of the participants refused to sign the death warrant, the "holy, anointed" king was executed by his subjects in January 1649, to the horror of all Europe and most of England.

ENGLAND UNDER CROMWELL

Oliver Cromwell was now master of England. The republic established after Charles's execution was officially ruled by the Rump Parliament, but a Council of State led by Cromwell controlled policy with the backing of the army. And they had to contend with a ferment of political and social ideas. One group, known as the Levellers, demanded the vote for nearly all adult males and parliamentary elections every other year. The men of property among the Puritans, notably Cromwell himself, were disturbed by the egalitarianism of these proposals and insisted that only men with an "interest" in England—that is, land—should be qualified to vote.

Radical Ideas Even more radical were the Diggers, a communistic sect that sought to implement the spirit of primitive Christianity by abolishing personal property; the Society of Friends, which stressed personal inspiration as the source of faith and all action; and the Fifth Monarchists, a messianic group who believed that the "saints"—themselves—should rule because the Day of Judgment was at hand. People of great ability, such as the famous poet John Milton, contributed to the fantastic flood of pamphlets and suggestions for reform that poured forth in these years, and their ideas inspired future revolutionaries. But at the time, they merely put Cromwell on the defensive, forcing him to maintain control at all costs.

Cromwell's Aims Cromwell himself fought for two overriding causes: religious freedom (except for the Anglican and Catholic churches) and constitutional government. But he achieved neither, and he grew increasingly unhappy at the Rump Parliament's refusal to enact reforms. When the assembly tried to prolong its own existence, he dissolved it in 1653 (the final end of the Long Parliament), and during the remaining five years of his life he tried desperately to lay down a new constitutional structure for his government. Cromwell always hoped that Parliament itself would establish the perfect political system for England, but he refused to influence its proceedings. The result was that he ignored the realities of politics and could never put his ideals into practice.

Cromwell was driven by noble aspirations, but in the end he had to rule by military dicta-torship. From 1653 on he was called lord protector and ruled through 11 major generals, each responsible for a different district of England and supported by a tax on the estates of royalists. To quell dissent, he banned newspapers, and to prevent disorder, he took such measures as enlisting innkeepers as government spies.

Cromwell was always a reluctant revolutionary; he hated power and sought only limited ends. Some revolutionaries, like Lenin, have a good idea of where they would like to be carried by events; others, like Cromwell, move painfully, hesitantly, and uncertainly to the extremes they finally reach. It was because he sought England's benefit so urgently and because he considered the nation too precious to abandon to irreligion or tyranny that Cromwell remained determinedly in command to the end of his life.

The End of the Revolution Gradually, more traditional political forms reappeared. The Parliament of 1656 offered Cromwell the crown, and

---

Oliver Cromwell's Aims

When Parliament in late 1656 offered to make Oliver Cromwell the king of England as a way of restoring political stability, he hesitated before replying. He soon came to realize, however, that this was a solution that went against his deepest principles. When he finally came to Parliament with his reply on April 13, 1657, he turned down the offer of a crown and explained in a long speech—from which a passage follows—why he felt it would be wrong to reestablish a monarchy in England.

"I do think you ought to attend to the settling of the peace and liberties of this Nation. Otherwise the Nation will fall in pieces. And in that, so far as I can, I am ready to serve not as a King, but as a Constable. For truly I have, before God, often thought that I could not tell what my business was, save comparing myself to a good Constable set to keep the peace of the parish. And truly this hath been my content and satisfaction in the troubles I have undergone. . . . I was a person who, from my first employment, was suddenly lifted up from lesser trusts to greater. . . . The Providence of God hath laid aside this Title of King; and that not by sudden humor, but by issue of ten or twelve years Civil War, wherein much blood hath been shed. I will not dispute the justice of it when it was done. But God in His severity hath eradicated a whole Family, and thrust them out of the land. And God hath seemed providential not only in striking at the family but at the Name [of king]. It is blotted out. God blasted the very Title. I will not seek to set up that which Providence hath destroyed, and laid in the dust: I would not build Jericho again."

From Thomas Carlyle (ed.), *Oliver Cromwell's Letters and Speeches* (London, 1908), vol. III, pp. 230, 231, and 235.

though he refused, he took the title of "His Highness" and ensured that the succession would go to his son. Cromwell was monarch in all but name, yet only his presence ensured stability (*see box*, p. 484). After he died, his quiet, retiring son Richard proved no match for the scheming generals of the army, who created political turmoil. To bring an end to the uncertainty, General George Monck, the commander of a well-disciplined force in Scotland, marched south in 1660, assumed control, and invited the son of Charles I, Charles II, to return from exile and restore the monarchy.

Only the actions taken during the first months of the Long Parliament—the abolition of royal courts, the prohibition of taxation without parliamentary consent, and the establishment of the writ of habeas corpus—persisted beyond the revolution. Otherwise, everything seemed much the same as before: Bishops and lords were reinstated, religious dissent was again repressed, and Parliament was called and dissolved by the monarch. But the tone and balance of political relations had changed for good.

Henceforth the gentry could no longer be denied a decisive voice in politics. In essence, this had been their revolution, and they had succeeded. When in the 1680s a king again tried to impose his wishes on the country without reference to Parliament, there was no need for another major upheaval. A quiet bloodless coup reaffirmed the new role of the gentry and Parliament. Thus a new settlement was reached after a long period of growing unease and open conflict. The crisis had been resolved, and the English settled into a system of rule that with only gradual modification remained in force for some two centuries.

V. Revolts in France and Spain

THE FRANCE OF HENRY IV

In the 1590s Henry IV resumed the strengthening of royal power that had been interrupted by the civil wars that had begun in the 1560s. He mollified the traditional landed aristocracy, known as the nobility of the sword, with places on his Council of Affairs and large financial settlements. The principal bureaucrats, known as the nobility of the robe, controlled the country's administration, and Henry made sure to turn their interests to his benefit. Since all crown offices had to be bought, he used the system both to raise revenues and to guarantee the loyalty of the bureaucrats. He not only accelerated the sales of offices but also invented a new device, an annual fee known as the *paulette*, which ensured that an officeholder's job would remain in his family when he died. This increased royal profits (by the end of Henry's reign in 1610, receipts from the sales accounted for one-twelfth of crown revenues), and also reduced the flow of newcomers and thus strengthened the commitment of existing officeholders to the crown.

By 1610 Henry had imposed his will throughout France, and he was secure enough to plan an invasion of the Holy Roman Empire. Although he was assassinated as he was about to join his army, his heritage, especially in economic affairs, long outlived him. France's rich agriculture may have had one unfortunate effect—successful merchants abandoned commerce as soon as they could afford to move to the country and buy a title of nobility (and thus gain exemption from taxes)—but it did ensure a solid basis for the French economy. Indeed, agriculture suffered little during the civil wars, though the violence and the rising taxes did cause uprisings of peasants (the main victims of the tax system) almost every year from the 1590s to the 1670s.

Mercantilism By restoring political stability Henry ended the worst economic disruptions, but his main legacy was the notion that his increasingly powerful government was responsible for the health of the country's economy. This view was justified by a theory developed mainly in France: mercantilism, which became an essential ingredient of absolutism. Mercantilism was more a set of attitudes than a systematic economic theory. Its basic premise—an erroneous one—was that the world contained a fixed amount of wealth and that each nation could enrich itself only at the expense of others. To some thinkers, this meant hoarding bullion (gold and

▶ *Anonymous*

THE SEINE FROM THE PONT NEUF, CA. 1635
Henry IV of France, celebrated in the equestrian statue overlooking the Seine that stands in Paris to this day, saw the physical reshaping of his capital as part of the effort to restore order after decades of civil war. He laid out the first squares in any European city, and under the shadow of his palace, the Louvre, he built the Pont Neuf (on the right)—the first open bridge (without houses on it) across the Seine.

silver); to others, it required a favorable balance of trade—more exports than imports. All mercantilists, however, agreed that state regulation of economic affairs was necessary for the welfare of a country. Only a strong, centralized government could encourage native industries, control production, set quality standards, allocate resources, establish tariffs, and take other measures to promote prosperity and improve trade. Thus mercantilism was as much about politics as economics and fitted in perfectly with Henry's restoration of royal power. In line with their advocacy of activist policies, the mercantilists also approved of war. Even economic advance was linked to warfare in this violent age.

LOUIS XIII

Unrest reappeared when Henry's death left the throne to his nine-year-old son, Louis XIII (1610–1643). The widowed queen, Marie de Medicis, served as regent and soon faced revolts by Calvinists and disgruntled nobles. In the face of these troubles, Marie summoned the Estates General in 1614. This was their last meeting for 175 years, until the eve of the French Revolution; and the weakness they displayed, as various groups within the Estates fought one another over plans for political reform, demonstrated that the monarchy was the only institution that could unite the nation. The session revealed the impotence of those who opposed royal policies, and Marie brought criticism to an end by declaring her son to be of age and the regency dissolved. In this absolutist state, further protest could be defined as treason.

Richelieu For a decade, the monarchy lacked energetic direction; but in 1624, one of Marie's favorites, Armand du Plessis de Richelieu, a churchman who rose to be a cardinal through her favor, became chief minister and took control of the government. Over the next 18 years, this ambitious and determined leader resumed Henry IV's assertion of royal authority (*see box*, p. 487).

The monarchy had to manage a number of vested interests as it concentrated its power, and Richelieu's achievement was that he kept them under control. The strongest was the bureaucracy, whose ranks had been swollen by the sale of office. Richelieu always paid close attention to the views of the bureaucrats, and one reason he had such influence over the king was that he acted as the head and representative of this army of royal servants. He also reduced the independence of traditional nobles by giving them positions in the regime as diplomats, soldiers, and officials without significant administrative responsibility. Finally, he took on the Huguenots in a military campaign that led to the capture of their chief bastion, the port of La Rochelle, in 1628. Following the victory he abolished most of the guarantees in the Edict of Nantes and ended the Huguenots' political independence.

Royal Administration   Under Richelieu the sale of office broke all bounds: By 1633 it accounted for approximately one-half of royal revenues. Ten years later more than three-quarters of the crown's direct taxation was needed to pay the salaries of the officeholders. It was a vicious circle, and the only solution was to increase the taxes on the lower classes. As this financial burden grew, Richelieu had to improve the government's control over the realm to obtain the revenue he needed. He increased the power of the *intendants*, the government's chief agents in the localities, and established them (instead of the nobles) as the principal representatives of the monarchy in each province of France. Unlike the nobles, the *intendants* depended entirely on royal favor for their position; and so it was with enthusiasm that they recruited for the army, arranged billeting, supervised the raising of taxes, and enforced the king's decrees. They soon came to be hated figures, both because of the rising taxes and because they threatened the power of the nobles. The result was a succession of peasant uprisings, often led by local notables who resented the rise of the *intendants* and of royal power.

POLITICAL CRISIS

France's foreign wars made the discontent worse, and it was clear that eventually the opponents of the central government would reassert themselves. But the amassing of centralized power by the crown had been so successful that when trou-

Richelieu on Diplomacy

The following passages are taken from a collection of the writings of Cardinal Richelieu that was put together after his death and published in 1688 under the title **Political Testament.** *The book is presented as a work of advice to the king and summarizes what Richelieu learned of politics and diplomacy as one of Europe's leading statesmen during the Thirty Years' War.*

"One cannot imagine how many advantages States gain from continued negotiations, if conducted wisely, unless one has experienced it oneself. I admit I did not realize this truth for five or six years after first being employed in the management of policy. But I am now so sure of it that I dare say boldly that to negotiate everywhere without cease, openly and secretly, even though one makes no immediate gains and future gains seem unlikely, is absolutely necessary for the good of the State. . . . He who negotiates all the time will find at last the right moment to achieve his aims, and even if he does not find it, at least it is true that he can lose nothing, and that through his negotiations he knows what is happening in the world, which is of no small consequence for the good of the State. . . . Important negotiations must not be interrupted for a moment. . . . One must not be disheartened by an unfortunate turn of events, because sometimes it happens that what is undertaken with good reason is achieved with little good fortune. . . . It is difficult to fight often and always win. . . . It is often because negotiations are so innocent that one can gain great advantages from them without ever faring badly. . . . In matters of State one must find an advantage in everything; that which can be useful must never be neglected."

From Louis André (ed.), *Testament Politique* (Paris, 1947), pp. 347–348 and 352. Translated by T. K. Rabb.

ble erupted, in a series of revolts known as the Fronde (or "tempest"), there was no serious effort to reshape the social order or the political system. The principal actors in the Fronde came from the upper levels of society: nobles, townsmen, and members of the regional courts and legislatures known as parlements. Only occasionally were these groups joined by peasants, and there was little foretaste of the revolution that was to overtake France in 1789.

Mazarin   The death of Louis XIII, in 1643, followed by a regency because Louis XIV was only five years old, offered an opportunity to those who wanted to reverse the rise of absolutism. Louis XIII's widow, Anne of Austria, took over the government and placed all the power in the hands of an Italian, Cardinal Giulio Mazarin. He used his position to amass a huge fortune, and he was therefore a perfect target for the anger caused by the encroachment of central government on local authority

Early in 1648 Mazarin sought to gain a respite from the monarch's perennial financial trouble by withholding payment of the salaries of some royal officials for four years. In response, the members of various institutions in Paris, including the Parlement, drew up a charter of demands. They wanted the office of *intendant* abolished, no new offices created, power to approve taxes, and enactment of a habeas corpus law. The last two demands reflected what the English Parliament was seeking at this very time, but the first two were long-standing French grievances.

THE FRONDE

Mazarin reacted by arresting the Paris Parlement's leaders, thus sparking a popular rebellion in the city that forced him and the royal family to flee from the capital—an experience the young Louis XIV never forgot. In 1649, Mazarin promised to redress the parlementaires' grievances, and he was allowed to return to Paris. But the trouble was far from over; during that summer uprisings spread throughout France, particularly among peasants and in the old Huguenot stronghold, the southwest.

For the next three years there was political chaos, mainly as a result of intrigues and shifting alliances among the nobility. As it became clear

that the perpetual unrest was producing no results, Mazarin was able to take advantage of the disillusionment among the nobles and the parlementaires to reassert the position of the monarchy. He used military force and threats of force to subdue Paris and most of the rebels in the countryside, and he brought the regency to an end by declaring the 14-year-old Louis of age in 1652. Although peasants continued their occasional regional uprisings for many years to come, the Fronde was over and the crown was established as the basis for order in the realm. As surely as England, France had surmounted its crisis and found a stable solution for long-standing conflicts.

SOURCES OF DISCONTENT IN SPAIN

For Spain the crisis that swept much of Europe in the mid-seventeenth century—with revolt in England and France, and war in the empire—meant the end of the country's international power. Yet the difficulties the monarchy faced had their roots in the sixteenth century. Philip II (1556–1598) had already found it difficult to hold his sprawling empire together, despite his elaborate bureaucracy. Obsessively suspicious, he maintained close control over all administrative decisions, and government action was therefore agonizingly slow. Moreover, the bureaucracy was run by Castilian nobles, who were resented as outsiders in other regions of the empire. And the standing army, though essential to royal power, was a terrible financial drain.

Philip did gain wide admiration in Spain for his devoutness. He persecuted heresy, encouraged the Inquisition, and for a while was even suspicious of the great flowering of Spanish mysticism, led by St. Teresa. Philip's commitment to religion undoubtedly promoted political cohesion, but the economic strains caused by relentless religious warfare eventually undermined Spanish power.

Economic Difficulties   Spain was a rich country in Philip's reign, but the most profitable activities were monopolized by limited groups. Because royal policy valued convenience above social benefit, the city of Seville (dominated by foreign bankers) received a monopoly over shipping to and from the New World; and other lucrative

INQVISITION

▶ *Anonymous Engraving*
THE SPANISH INQUISITION, 1560
The burning of heretics was a major public event in sixteenth-century Spain. Aimed mainly at people who practiced Judaism or Islam secretly, and in a few cases at Protestants, the Inquisition's investigations usually led to imprisonment or lesser punishments. The occasional executions of those who determinedly refused to accept Catholic teachings, even after torture, were carried out by secular authorities, and they attracted huge crowds.

pursuits, such as wool and wine production, were also controlled by a small coterie of insiders. The only important economic activities that involved large numbers of Spaniards were shipping and the prosperous Mediterranean trade, centered in Barcelona, which brought wealth to much of Catalonia.

Thus the influx of silver into Spain was not profitably invested within the country. Drastically overextended in foreign commitments, Philip had to declare himself bankrupt three times. For a while it seemed that the problems might ease because there was peace during the reign of Philip's son, Philip III (1598–1621). But,

in fact, Philip III's government was incompetent and corrupt, capable neither of dealing with the serious consequences of the spending on war nor of broadening the country's exports beyond wool and wine. And when the flow of treasure from the New World began to dwindle after 1600, the crown was deprived of a major source of income that it was unable to replace (see table below).

IMPORTS OF TREASURE TO SPAIN FROM THE NEW WORLD, 1591–1660

Decade	Total Value*
1591–1600	85,536,000
1601–1610	66,970,000
1611–1620	65,568,000
1621–1630	62,358,000
1631–1640	40,110,000
1641–1650	30,651,000
1651–1660	12,785,000

*In ducats.

Adapted from J. H. Elliott, *Imperial Spain 1469–1716*, New York, 1964, p. 175.

The decline was caused partly by a growing use of precious metals in the New World colonies but also by the depletion of the mines.

In the meantime, tax returns at home were shrinking. The most significant cause of this decrease was a drop in the population of Castile and Aragon as a result of severe plagues—from 10 million in 1600 to 6 million in 1700. No other country in Europe suffered a demographic reversal of this proportion during the seventeenth century. In addition, sheep farming took over huge tracts of arable land, and Spain had to rely increasingly on the importation of expensive foodstuffs to feed its people.

When Spain resumed large-scale fighting against the Dutch and French under Philip IV (1621–1665), the burdens became too much to bear. The effort to maintain the commitment to war despite totally inadequate finances was to bring the greatest state in Europe to its knees.

REVOLT AND SECESSION

The final crisis was brought about by the policies of Philip IV's chief minister, the count of Olivares. His aim was to unite the realm so that all the territories shared equally the burden of maintaining Spanish power. Although Castile would no longer dominate the government, it would also not have to provide the bulk of the taxes and army. Olivares' program was called the Union of Arms, and while it seemed eminently reasonable, it caused a series of revolts in the 1640s that split Spain apart.

The reason was that Castile's dominance had made the other provinces feel that local independence was being undermined by a centralized regime. They saw the Union of Arms, imposed by Olivares, as the last straw. Moreover, the plan appeared at a time when Spain's military and economic fortunes were in decline. France had declared war on the Habsburgs in 1635, the funds to support an army were becoming harder to raise, and in desperation Olivares pressed more vigorously for the Union of Arms. But all he accomplished was to provoke revolts against the Castilians in the 1640s by Catalonia, Portugal, Naples, and Sicily. By 1641 both Catalonia and Portugal had declared themselves independent republics and placed themselves under French protection. Plots began to appear against Oli-

vares, and Philip dismissed the one minister who had understood Spain's problems but who, in trying to solve them, had made them worse.

The Revolts The Catalonian rebellion continued for another 11 years, and it was thwarted in the end only because the peasants and town mobs transformed the resistance to the central government into an attack on the privileged and wealthy classes. When this happened, the Catalan nobility abandoned the cause and joined the government side. About the same time, the Fronde forced the withdrawal of French troops from Catalonia. When the last major holdout, Barcelona, fell to a royal army in 1652, the Catalan nobles could regain their rights and powers, and the revolt was over.

The Portuguese had no social upheaval; as a result, though not officially granted independence from Spain until 1668, they defended their autonomy easily and even invaded Castile in the 1640s. But the revolts that the people of Sicily and Naples directed at their Castilian rulers in 1647 took on social overtones. In Naples the unrest developed into a tremendous mob uprising, led by a local fisherman. The poor turned against all the representatives of government and wealth they could find, and chaos ensued until the leader of the revolt was killed. The violence in Sicily, the result of soaring taxes, was aimed primarily at government officials. In both Naples and Sicily, however, a forceful response enabled the government to regain control within a few months.

The effect of all this unrest was finally to end the Spanish government's international ambitions and thus the worst of its economic difficulties. Like England and France, Spain found a new way of life after its crisis, as a stable second-level state, heavily agricultural, run by its nobility.

VI. Political Change in an Age of Crisis

THE UNITED PROVINCES

The Dutch did not escape the struggles against the power of centralized governments that created an atmosphere of crisis in much of Europe

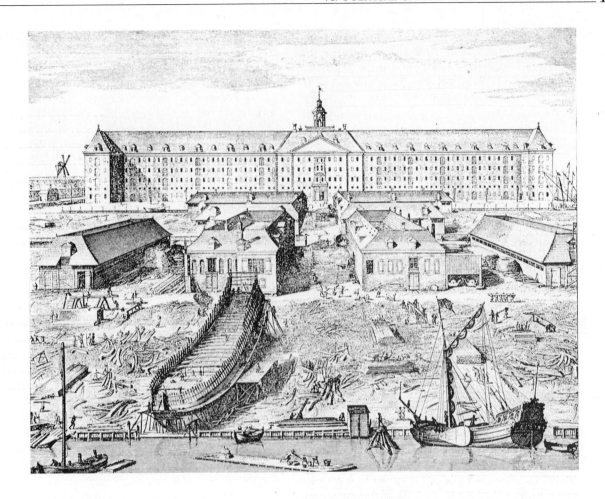

during the middle decades of the seventeenth century. Despite the remarkable fluidity of their society, the Dutch, too, became embroiled in a confrontation between a ruling family seeking to extend its authority and citizens defending the autonomy of their local regions. The outcome determined the structure of their government for over a century.

The United Provinces were unique in a number of ways. Other republics existed in Europe, but they were controlled by small oligarchies; the Dutch, who had a long tradition of a strong representative assembly, the Estates General, had created a nation in which many citizens participated in government through elected delegates. Although powerful merchants and a few aristocrats close to the House of Orange did create a small elite, the social differentiation was less than elsewhere in Europe. The resulting openness and homogeneity underlay the economic mastery and cultural brilliance of the United Provinces.

▶ *Anonymous*
ENGRAVING OF A DUTCH SHIPYARD
The Dutch became the best shipbuilders in Europe in the seventeenth century; the efficiency of their ships, which could be manned by fewer sailors than those of other countries, was a major reason for their successes in trade and commerce.

Commerce and Tolerance The most striking accomplishment of the Dutch was their rise to supremacy in the world of commerce. Amsterdam displaced Antwerp as the continent's financial capital and gained control of the trade of the world's richest markets. In addition, the Dutch rapidly emerged as the cheapest international shippers. As a result, by the middle of the seventeenth century they had become the chief carriers of European commerce.

The openness of Dutch society permitted the freest exchange of ideas of the time. The new state gave refuge to believers of all kinds, whether extreme Protestant radicals or Catholics who wore their faith lightly, and Amsterdam became the center of a brilliant Jewish community. This freedom attracted some of the greatest minds in Europe and fostered remarkable artistic creativity. The energy that produced this outpouring reflected the pride of a tiny nation that was winning its independence from Spain.

Two Political Parties   Yet there was a basic split within the United Provinces. The two most urbanized and commercial provinces, Holland and Zeeland, dominated the Estates General because they supplied a majority of its taxes. Their representatives formed a mercantile party, which advocated peace abroad so that their trade could flourish unhampered, government by the Estates General so that they could make their influence felt, and religious toleration so that their cities could attract enterprising people of all faiths. In opposition to this mercantile interest was the House of Orange: the descendants of William of Orange, who sought to establish their family's leadership of the Dutch. They were supported by the more rural provinces and stood for war because their authority and popularity derived from their command of the army, for centralized power to enhance the position of the family, and for the strict Calvinism that was upheld in the rural provinces.

The differences between the two factions led Maurice of Nassau to use religion as a pretext for executing his chief opponent, Jan van Oldenbarneveldt, the main representative of the province of Holland, in 1618. Oldenbarneveldt opposed war with Spain, and his removal left the House of Orange in full control of the country. Maurice resumed the war in 1621, and for more than 20 years, his family remained in command, unassailable because it led the army in wartime. Not until 1648—when a new leader, William II, tried to prolong the fighting—could the mercantile party reassert itself by insisting on peace. As a result, the Dutch signed the Treaty of Westphalia, which officially recognized the independence of the United Provinces. It now seemed that Holland and Zeeland had gained the upper hand. But their struggle with the House of Orange continued (there was even a threat by Orange troops to besiege Amsterdam) until William II suddenly died in 1650, leaving as his successor a baby son, William III.

Jan De Witt   The mercantile interest now assumed full power, and Jan De Witt, the representative of the province of Holland, took over the government in 1653. De Witt's aims were to leave as much authority as possible in the hands of the provinces, particularly Holland; to weaken the executive and prevent a revival of the House of Orange; to pursue trading advantage; and to maintain peace so that the economic supremacy of the Dutch would not be endangered. For nearly 20 years, he guided the country in its golden age. But in 1672 French armies overran the southern provinces, and De Witt lacked the military instinct to fight a dangerous enemy. The Dutch at once turned to the family that had led them to independence; a mob murdered De Witt; and the House of Orange, under William III, resumed the centralization that henceforth was to characterize the political structure of the United Provinces. The country had not experienced a midcentury upheaval as severe as those of its neighbors, but it had nevertheless been forced to endure unrest and violence before the form of its government was securely established.

SWEDEN

The Swedes, too, settled their political system in the mid-seventeenth century. In 1600 Sweden, a Lutheran country of a million people, was one of the backwaters of Europe. A feudal nobility dominated the countryside, a barter economy made money almost unknown, and both trade and towns were virtually nonexistent. Moreover, the country lacked a capital, central institutions, and government machinery. The royal administration consisted of the king and a few courtiers; other officials were appointed only to deal with specific problems as they arose.

Gustavus Adolphus (1611–1632) transformed this situation. He won over the nobles by giving them dominant positions in a newly expanded bureaucracy, and he reorganized his army. Thus equipped both to govern and to fight, Gustavus embarked on a remarkable series of conquests abroad. By 1629 he had made Sweden the most powerful state in the Baltic area. He then entered the Thirty Years' War, advancing victoriously through the Holy Roman Empire until his death, in 1632, during the showdown battle with Wallenstein. Although without their general the Swedes could do little more than hang on to the gains they had made, they were now a force to be reckoned with in international affairs.

Government and Economy The system of government that Gustavus and his chief adviser, Axel Oxenstierna, established was to be the envy of other countries until the twentieth century. At the heart of the system were five administrative departments, each led by a nobleman, with the most important—the Chancellery, for diplomacy and internal affairs—run by Oxenstierna. An administrative center emerged in Stockholm, and the new bureaucracy proved that it could run the nation, supply the army, and implement policy even during the last 12 years of Gustavus' reign, when the king himself was almost always abroad.

A major cause of Sweden's amazing rise was the development of the domestic economy, stimulated by the opening up of copper mines and the development of a major iron industry. The country's traditional tar and timber exports were also stepped up, and a fleet was built. By 1700 Stockholm had become an important trading and financial center, growing in the course of the century from fewer than 5000 to more than 50,000 inhabitants.

The Nobles The one source of tension amidst this remarkable progress was the position of the nobles. After Gustavus died, they openly challenged the monarchy for control of government and society. Between 1611 and 1652 they more than doubled the proportion of land they owned in Sweden, and much of this growth was at the expense of the crown, which granted away or sold lands to help the war effort abroad. Both peasants and townspeople viewed these developments with alarm, because the nobility usually pursued its own rather than public interests. The concern intensified when, in 1648, the nobles in neighboring Denmark took advantage of the

death of a strong king to gain control of the government. Two years later the showdown came in Sweden.

Political Confrontation The monarch now was Gustavus' daughter Christina, an able but erratic young queen who usually allowed Oxenstierna

CHRONOLOGY OF AN AGE OF CRISIS, 1618–1660

1618	Revolt in Bohemia, beginning of Thirty Years' War.
1621	Resumption of war between Spanish and Dutch.
1629	Edict of Restitution—high point of Habsburg power.
1630	Sweden enters war against Habsburgs.
1635	France declares war on Habsburgs.
1639	Scots invade England.
1640	Revolts in Catalonia and Portugal against Spanish government.
1642	Civil War in England.
1647	Revolts in Sicily and Naples against Spanish government.
1648	Peace of Westphalia ending Thirty Years' War. Outbreak of Fronde in France. Coup by nobles in Denmark. Revolt of Ukraine against Poland. Riots in Russian cities.
1650	Constitutional crisis in Sweden. Confrontation between William of Orange and Amsterdam in Netherlands.
1652	End of Catalan revolt.
1653	End of Fronde.
1655	War in Baltic region.
1659	Peace of the Pyrenees between France and Spain.
1660	End of English revolution. Treaties ending war in Baltic.

to run the government. For some time, she had hoped to abdicate her throne, become a Catholic, and leave Sweden—an ambition she fulfilled in 1654. She wanted her cousin Charles recognized as her successor, but the nobles threatened to create a republic if she abdicated. The queen therefore summoned the Riksdag, Sweden's usually weak representative assembly, in 1650; she encouraged the townspeople and peasants to raise their grievances and allowed them to attack the aristocracy. Very soon these groups were demanding the return of nobles' lands to the crown, freedom of speech, and real power; and under this pressure the nobility gave way and recognized Charles X as successor to the throne.

The political upheaval of 1650 was short-lived. Once Christina had her way, she turned her back on the Riksdag and rejected the demands of the lower estates. Only gradually did power shift away from the great nobles toward a broader elite of lesser nobles and bureaucrats, but the turning point in Sweden, as elsewhere, was during the crisis years of the mid-seventeenth century.

EASTERN EUROPE AND THE "CRISIS"

In Eastern Europe, too, long-term patterns became clear in this period. The limits of Ottoman rule were reconfirmed when an attack on Vienna failed in 1683. Poland's weak central government lost all claim to real authority when it proved unable to stop a group of nobles in the rich province of the Ukraine, who rebelled in 1648, from switching allegiance from the king of Poland to the tsar in Moscow. And in Russia, following a period of disorder known as the Time of Troubles (1584–1613), the new Romanov dynasty began consolidating its power. The nobility was won over, the last possibilities for escaping serfdom were closed, the legal system was codified, the church came under the tsar's control, and the revolts that erupted against these changes between 1648 and 1672 were brutally suppressed. As elsewhere in Europe, long-standing conflicts between centralizing regimes and their opponents were resolved, and a new political system, supported by the government's military power, was established for centuries to come.

Because these struggles were so widespread, historians have called the midcentury period an age of "general crisis." In country after country, people tried to resist the growing ambitions of central governments. These confrontations reached crisis proportions in almost all cases during the 1640s and 1650s, and then subsided, at the very time that the anarchy of warfare and international relations seemed to be getting out of hand, only to be resolved by the Peace of Westphalia. As a result, the sense of settlement after 1660 contrasted sharply with the turmoil of the preceding decades. Moreover, the progression in politics from turbulence to calm had its analogies in the cultural and social developments of the sixteenth and seventeenth centuries.

Recommended Reading

Sources

Bodin, Jean. *On Sovereignty.* Julian H. Franklin (ed. and tr.). 1992. An abridgment of Bodin's *Six Books of the Republic.*

*Franklin, Julian H. (ed. and tr.). *Constitutionalism and Resistance in the Sixteenth Century: Three Treatises by Hotman, Beza, & Mornay.* 1969. Three of the most radical tracts of the period, each justifying rebellion.

*Available in paperback.

Kossmann, E. H., and A. E. Mellink. *Texts Concerning the Revolt of the Netherlands.* 1974. A collection of Spanish and Dutch documents which reveal the different political and religious goals of the two sides.

Studies

*Aston, Trevor (ed.). *Crisis in Europe 1560–1660: Essays from Past and Present.* 1965. This is a collection of the essays in which the "general crisis" interpretation was initially put forward and discussed.

Brummett, Palmira. *Ottoman Seapower and Levantine Diplomacy in the Age of Discovery.* 1993.

*DeVries, Jan. *The Economy of Europe in an Age of Crisis, 1600–1750.* 1976. The standard introduction to the economic history of the period.

*Elliott, J. H. *Richelieu and Olivares.* 1984. A comparative study of the two statesmen who dominated Europe in the 1620s and 1630s, this book also analyzes the changing nature of political authority.

*Forster, Robert, and Jack P. Green (eds.). *Preconditions of Revolution in Early Modern Europe.* 1972. An excellent series of essays on resistance to central governments, and its causes, in a number of European countries.

*Hale, J. R. *War and Society in Renaissance Europe 1450–1620.* 1985. A vivid account of what it meant to be a soldier.

Hellie, Richard. *Enserfment and Military Change in Muscovy.* 1971. This study shows the links between military affairs and social change in Russia during the early modern period.

Hirst, Derek. *Authority and Conflict: England, 1603–1658.* 1986. The most recent survey of the revolution and its origins.

Lupinin, N. B. *Religious Revolt in the Seventeenth Century: The Schism of the Russian Church.* 1984. A thorough account of a major feature of Russia's crisis in this period.

Maczak, Antoni, Henryk Samsonowitz, and Peter Burke (eds.). *East-Central Europe in Transition: From the 14th to the 17th Century.* 1985. Essays on the history of Eastern Europe in this period.

*Mattingly, Garrett. *The Armada.* 1959. This beautifully written book, which was a best-seller when it first appeared, is a gripping account of a major international crisis.

Moote, A. Lloyd. *The Revolt of the Judges: The Parlement of Paris and the Fronde 1643–1652.* 1971. This is the most detailed account of the causes of the Fronde and its failures.

*Palliser, D. M. *The Age of Elizabeth: England under the Later Tudors 1547–1603.* 1983. A comprehensive history of English society and government.

Parker, Geoffrey. *The Dutch Revolt.* 1977. This brief book gives a good introduction to the revolt of the Netherlands and the nature of Dutch society in the seventeenth century.

———. *The Military Revolution: Military Innovation and the Rise of the West, 1500–1800.* 1988. The most recent history of the transformation of warfare in this period.

———. *The Thirty Years' War.* 1984. The most up-to-date history of the war.

Pierson, Peter. *Philip II of Spain.* 1975. A clear and lively biography of the dominant figure of the second half of the sixteenth century.

*Rabb, Theodore K. *The Struggle for Stability in Early Modern Europe.* 1975. An assessment of the "crisis" interpretation, including extensive bibliographic references.

Roberts, Michael. *Gustavus Adolphus and the Rise of Sweden.* 1973. This is the best biography of the Swedish king, emphasizing especially his military and administrative achievements.

Salmon, J. H. M. *Society in Crisis: France in the Sixteenth Century.* 1975. A clearly written overview, focusing mainly on the religious wars and Henry IV.

*Skinner, Quentin. *The Foundations of Modern Political Thought.* 1978. The standard account of the political theories of the fifteenth and sixteenth centuries.

Stone, Lawrence. *The Causes of the English Revolution, 1529–1642.* 1972. A short but comprehensive assessment of the reasons for the outbreak of the seventeenth century's most far-reaching revolution.

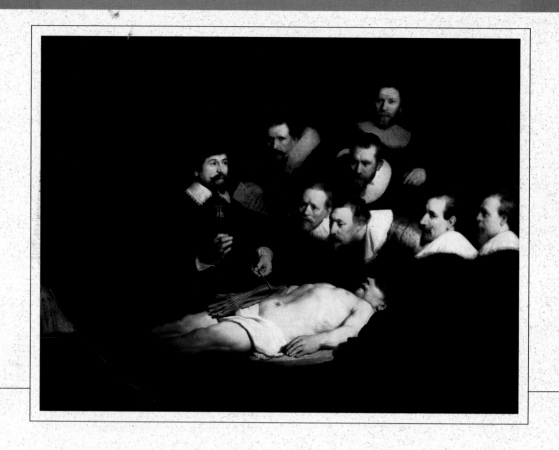

Rembrandt van Rijn
THE ANATOMY LESSON OF DR. NICOLAAS TULP
(1632)
Among the many representations of the public anatomy lessons so popular in seventeenth-century Holland, the most famous is one of Rembrandt's greatest paintings, *The Anatomy Lesson of Dr. Nicolaas Tulp.*

CULTURE AND SOCIETY IN THE AGE OF THE SCIENTIFIC REVOLUTION

O F all the many changes of the sixteenth and seventeenth centuries, none had a more far-reaching impact than the scientific revolution. By creating a new way of understanding how nature worked—and by solving long-standing problems in physics, astronomy, and anatomy—the theorists and experimenters of this period convinced their contemporaries that they had discovered new knowledge. They were not merely adapting the ideas of the revered figures of Greece and Rome; they had gone further than the ancients. Although their revolution began with disturbing questions but few clear answers about traditional ideas, they ended up by offering a promise of certain knowledge and truth that was eagerly embraced by a society that had been racked by decades of religious and political turmoil and the horrors of war. Indeed, it is remarkable how closely intellectual and cultural patterns paralleled the progression from struggle and uncertainty to stable resolution that marked the political developments of these years. In international and domestic politics a series of clashes grew ever more intense until, following a major crisis in the mid-seventeenth century, Europe's states were able to create more settled conditions. Similarly, in the realms of philosophy and the study of nature, a long period of searching, anxiety, and dispute (epitomized by the confrontation of one scientist, Galileo Galilei, with traditional authority) was resolved in the mid-seventeenth century by scientists whose discoveries and self-assurance helped restore a sense of order in intellectual life. And in literature, the arts, and social relations, a time of insecurity and doubt gave way to an atmosphere of confidence and calm.

I. The Scientific Revolution

ORIGINS OF THE SCIENTIFIC REVOLUTION

The Importance of Antiquity Until the sixteenth century, the study of nature in Europe was inspired by the ancient Greeks. Their work shaped subsequent research in three main fields: Aristotle in physics, Ptolemy in astronomy, and Galen in medicine. The most dramatic advances during the scientific revolution came in these fields, to some extent because it was becoming evident that the ancient theories could not account for new observations without highly complicated adjustments.

For instance, Aristotle's belief that all objects in their natural state are at rest created a number of problems, such as explaining why an arrow kept on flying after it left a bow. Similarly, Ptolemy's picture of the heavens, in which all motion was circular around a central earth, did not readily explain the peculiar motion that observers noticed in some planets, which at times seemed to be moving backward. And Galen's anatomical theories were often shown by dissections to be wrong.

Still, it is not likely that scientists (who in the sixteenth and seventeenth centuries were still known as "natural philosophers," or seekers of wisdom about nature) would have abandoned their cherished theories—they far preferred making adjustments to accepted theories than beginning anew—if it had not been for other influences at work in this period. One such stimulus to rethinking was the humanists' rediscovery of a number of previously unknown ancient scientists, who had not always agreed with the theories of Aristotle or Ptolemy. A particularly important rediscovery was the work of Archimedes, whose writings on dynamics helped inspire new ideas in physics.

"Magic" Another influence was a growing interest in what we now dismiss as "magic," but which at the time was regarded as a serious intellectual enterprise. There were various sides to magical inquiry. Alchemy was the belief that matter could be understood and transformed by mixing substances and using secret formulas. A famous sixteenth-century alchemist, Paracelsus, suggested that metals as well as plants might have medicinal properties, and he helped demonstrate that mercury (if carefully used) could cure syphilis. Another favorite study was astrology, which suggested that natural phenomena could be predicted if planetary movements were properly interpreted.

What linked these "magical" beliefs was the conviction that the world could be understood through simple, comprehensive keys to nature. The theories of Neoplatonism—an influential school of thought during the Renaissance, based

► *Peter Brueghel*
THE ALCHEMIST, ENGRAVING
This down-to-earth portrayal, typical of Brueghel's art, shows the alchemist as an undisciplined figure. He is surrounded by a chaos of instruments and half-finished experiments, and his helpers resemble witches. Like Brueghel, most people thought it unlikely that this disorganized figure would make a major contribution to the understanding of nature.

on Plato's belief that truth lay in essential but hidden "forms"—supported this conviction, as did some of the mystical ideas that attracted attention at the same time. One of the latter, derived from a system of Jewish thought known as *cabala*, suggested that the universe might be built around magical arrangements of numbers. The ancient Greek mathematician Pythagoras had also suggested that numerical patterns might connect all of nature, and his ideas now gained new attention. For all its irrational elements, it was precisely this interest in new and simple solutions for long-standing problems that made natural philosophers capable, for the first time, of discarding the honored theories they had inherited from antiquity, trying different ones, paying greater attention to mathematics, and eventually creating an intellectual revolution.

Observations, Experiments, and Instruments
Two other influences deserve mention. The first was Europe's fascination with technological invention. The architects, navigators, engineers, and weapons experts of the Renaissance were important pioneers of a new reliance on measurement and observation that affected not only how domes were built or heavy cannon were moved but also how problems in physics were addressed. A second, and related, influence was the growing interest in experiment among anatomists. In particular, the medical school at the university of Padua became famous for its dissections and direct observations of nature; many leading figures in the scientific revolution were trained there.

It was not too surprising, therefore, that important new instruments were invented in the sixteenth and seventeenth centuries which helped make scientific discovery possible: the telescope, the vacuum pump, the thermometer, the barometer, and the microscope. These instruments encouraged the development of a scientific approach that was entirely new in the seventeenth century: It did not go back to the ancients, to the practitioners of magic, or to the engineers. It was to be pioneered by the Englishman Francis Bacon (1561–1626—see p. 505) and consisted of the belief that in order to make nature reveal its secrets, it had to be made to do things it did not do normally: In Bacon's phrase, one had to "twist the lion's tail." What this meant was that one did not simply observe phenomena that occurred normally in nature—for instance, the way a stick seems to bend when it is placed in a glass of water—but created conditions that were *not* normal. With the telescope, one saw secrets hidden to the naked eye; with the vacuum pump, one could understand the properties of air.

THE BREAKTHROUGHS

The earliest scientific advances came in anatomy and astronomy, and by coincidence they were announced in two books published in 1543, which was also the year when the earliest printed edition of Archimedes appeared. The first book, *The Structure of the Human Body* by Andreas Vesalius (1514–1564), a member of the Padua faculty, pointed out errors in the work of Galen, the chief authority in medical practice for over a thousand years. Using dissections, Vesalius produced anatomical descriptions that opened a new era of careful observation and experimentation in studies of the body.

Copernicus The second book, *On the Revolutions of the Heavenly Spheres* by Nicolaus Copernicus (1473–1543), a Polish cleric who had studied at Padua, had far greater consequences. A first-rate mathematician, he felt that the calculations of planetary movements under Ptolemy's system had grown too complex. In Ptolemaic astronomy, the planets and the sun, attached to transparent, crystalline spheres, revolved around the earth. All motion was circular, and irregularities were accounted for by epicycles—movement around small revolving spheres that were attached to the larger spheres. Influenced by Neoplatonic ideas, Copernicus believed that a simpler picture would reflect more accurately the true structure of the universe. In good Neoplatonic fashion, he argued that the sun, as the most splendid of celestial bodies, ought rightfully to be at the center of an orderly and harmonious universe. The earth, no longer immobile, would thus circle the sun.

Copernicus' system was, in fact, scarcely simpler than Ptolemy's—the spheres and epicycles were just as complex—and he had no way of demonstrating the superiority of his theory. But he was such a fine mathematician that his suc-

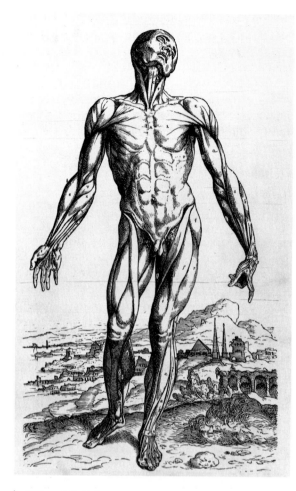

▶ *Titian* (attrib.)
ENGRAVING ILLUSTRATING ANDREAS VESALIUS,
THE STRUCTURE OF THE HUMAN BODY (1543)
Almost as remarkable as the findings themselves
were these illustrations of the results of Vesalius'
dissections. Traditionally, professors of anatomy
read from textbooks to their students while lowly
barber-surgeons cut up a cadaver and displayed the
parts being discussed. Vesalius did his dissections
himself, and thus could observe directly such
structures as the musculature. Here his illustrator
displays the muscles on a gesturing figure and
places it in a stretch of countryside near Padua,
where Vesalius taught.

cessors found his calculations of planetary motions indispensable. His ideas thus became part
of intellectual discussion, drawn on when Pope
Gregory XIII decided to reform the calendar in
1582. The Julian calendar, in use since Roman

times, counted century years as leap years, thus
adding extra days that caused Easter—whose
date is determined by the position of the sun—to
drift farther and farther away from its normal occurrence in late March. The reform produced the
Gregorian calendar, which we still use. Ten days
were simply dropped: October 5, 1582, became
October 15; and since then only one out of every
four century years has been counted as a leap
year (1900 had no February 29, but 2000 will have
one). The need for calendar reform had been one
of the motives for Copernicus' studies, which
thus proved useful even though his theories remained controversial.

Theories in Conflict The effect of *Revolutions* for
more than half a century was to cause growing
uncertainty, as the scholarly community argued
over the validity of the new ideas and the need
to abandon the old ones. The leading astronomer
of the period, the Dane Tycho Brahe (1546–1601),
produced the most remarkable observations of
the heavens before the invention of the telescope
by plotting the paths of the moon and planets
every night for decades. But the only theory he
could come up with was an uneasy compromise
between the Ptolemaic and Copernican systems.
There was similar indecision among anatomists,
who admired Vesalius but were not ready to dis-
card Galen. As late as 1600 or so, it seemed that
scientists were creating more problems than answers. But then two brilliant discoverers—Johannes Kepler (1571–1630), a German disciple of
Brahe, and Galileo Galilei, an Italian professor of
mathematics—made major advances on the work
of Copernicus and helped resolve the uncertainties that had arisen in the field of astronomy.

KEPLER AND GALILEO

Kepler Like Copernicus, Kepler believed that
only the language of mathematics could describe
the movements of the heavens. He was a famous
astrologer and an advocate of magical theories,
but he was also convinced that Copernicus was
right. He threw himself into the task of confirm-
ing the sun-centered (heliocentric) theory, and by
studying Brahe's observations, he discovered
three laws of planetary motion (published in 1609
and 1619) that opened a new era in astronomy.

Kepler was able to prove that the orbits of the planets are ellipses and that there is a regularity, based on their distance from the sun, that determines the movements of all planets. So revolutionary were these laws that few astronomers accepted them until Isaac Newton used them 50 years later as the basis for a new system of the heavens.

Galileo A contemporary of Kepler's, the Italian Galileo Galilei (1564–1642) took these advances a stage further when he became the first to perceive the connection between planetary motion and motion on earth. His studies revealed the importance to astronomy not only of observation and mathematics but also of physics. Moreover, he was the first to bring the new understanding of the universe to the attention of a reading public beyond the scholarly world. Galileo's self-consciousness about technique, argument, and evidence marks him as one of the first investigators of nature to approach his work in essentially the same way as a modern scientist.

Physics The study of motion inspired Galileo's most fundamental scientific contributions. When he began his investigations, the Aristotelian view that a body is naturally at rest and needs to be pushed constantly to keep moving dominated the study of dynamics. Galileo broke with this tradition, developing instead a new type of physical explanation that was perfected by Isaac Newton half a century later. Much of Galileo's work was based on observation. From watching how workers at the Arsenal in Venice used pulleys and other devices to lift huge weights, he gained insights into physics; adapting a Dutch lens maker's invention, he built himself a primitive telescope that was essential to his studies of the heavens; and his seemingly mundane experiments, such as swinging a pendulum or rolling balls down inclined planes, were crucial means of testing his theories. Indeed, it was by moving from observations to abstraction that Galileo arrived at the first wholly new way of understanding motion since Aristotle: the principle of inertia.

This breakthrough could not have been made by observation alone. For the discovery of inertia depended on mathematical abstraction, the ability to imagine a situation that cannot be created experimentally: the motion of a perfectly smooth ball across a perfectly smooth plane, free of any outside forces, such as friction. Galileo's conclusion was that "any velocity once imparted to a moving body will be rigidly maintained as long as external causes of acceleration and retardation are removed. . . . If the velocity is uniform, it will not be diminished or slackened, much less destroyed." This insight overturned the Aristotelian view. Galileo had demonstrated that only mathematical language could describe the underlying principles of nature.

Astronomy Galileo's most celebrated work was in astronomy. He first became famous in 1610, when he published his discoveries with the telescope that Jupiter has satellites and the moon has mountains. Both these revelations were further blows to traditional beliefs, which held that the earth is changing and imperfect while the heav-

▶ *Galileo Galilei*
THE MOON, 1610
This sketch of the moon's surface appeared in Galileo's *Starry Messenger* (1610). It shows what he had observed through the telescope and had interpreted as proof that the moon had a rugged surface because the lighted area within the dark section had to be mountains. These caught the light of the setting sun longer than surrounding lower terrain and revealed, for example, a large cavity in the lower center of the sketch.

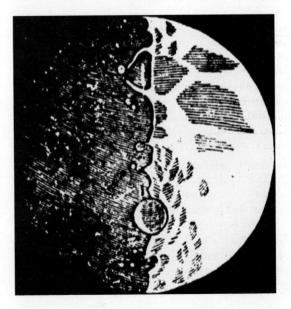

ens are immutable and unblemished. Now, however, it seemed that other planets had satellites, just like the earth, and that these satellites might have the same rough surface as the earth.

This was startling enough, but Galileo also argued that the principles of terrestrial physics could be used to explain phenomena in the heavens. He calculated the height of the mountains on the moon by using the geometric techniques of surveyors, and he described the moon's secondary light—seen while it is a crescent—as a reflection of sunlight from the earth. Galileo was treating his own planet simply as one part of a uniform universe. Every physical law, he was saying, is equally applicable on earth and in the heavens, including the laws of motion. As early as 1597 Galileo had admitted (in a letter to Kepler) that some of his discoveries in physics could be explained only if the earth were moving, and during the next 30 years he became the most famous advocate of Copernicanism in Europe (*see box,* below).

Galileo made a powerful case. Why, he asked, was it necessary to say that the entire universe revolved around the earth when all celestial motions could be explained by the rotation of a single planet, the earth? When academic and religious critics pointed out that we would feel the earth moving, or that the Bible said Joshua made the sun stand still, he reacted with scorn. In response to religious objections, he asserted that "in discussions of physical problems we ought to begin not from the authority of scriptural passages, but from sense experience and necessary demonstrations."

Conflict with the Church For all the brilliance of his arguments, Galileo was now on dangerous ground. Although traditionally the Catholic Church had not concerned itself with investigations of nature, in the early seventeenth century the situation was changing. The Church was deep in the struggle with Protestantism, and it responded to the challenge to its authority by try-

---

Galileo and Kepler on Copernicus

In 1597 Kepler sent Galileo a copy of his **New Astronomy,** *which argued for the Copernican theory of the heavens and asked the Italian for his opinion. The exchange of letters that followed, with Galileo cautious and Kepler urging him on, reflects an age when the new ideas were not yet proved and also gives a hint, in Kepler's last comments, of the troubles that lay ahead.*

Galileo to Kepler: "Like you, I accepted the Copernican position several years ago. I have written up many reasons on the subject, but have not dared until now to bring them into the open. I would dare publish my thoughts if there were many like you; but, since there are not, I shall forbear."

Kepler's Reply: "I could only have wished that you, who have so profound an insight, would choose another way. You advise us to retreat before the general ignorance and not to expose ourselves to the violent attacks of the mob of scholars. But after a tremendous task has been begun in our time, first by Copernicus and then by many very learned mathematicians, and when the assertion that the Earth moves can no longer be considered something new, would it not be much better to pull the wagon to its goal by our joint efforts, now that we have got it under way, and gradually, with powerful voices, to shout down the common herd? Be of good cheer, Galileo, and come out publicly! If I judge correctly, there are only a few of the distinguished mathematicians of Europe who would part company with us, so great is the power of truth. If Italy seems a less favorable place for your publication, perhaps Germany will allow us this freedom."

From Giorgio de Santillana, *The Crime of Galileo* (Chicago: University of Chicago Press, 1955), pp. 11 and 14–15.

ing to control potentially questionable views. And Galileo's biting sarcasm toward other scientists antagonized Jesuit and Dominican astronomers. These two orders were the chief upholders of orthodoxy in the Church. They referred Galileo's views to the Inquisition and then guided the attack on Copernicanism by seeking to condemn the brilliant advocate who had made the theory famous throughout Europe.

In 1616 the Inquisition forbade Galileo, within certain limits, to teach the heretical doctrine that the earth moves. When one of his friends was elected pope in 1623, however, Galileo thought he would be safe in writing a major work on astronomy, as long as he remained within the limits set in 1616. The result was Galileo's masterpiece, the *Dialogue on the Two Great World Systems*, published in 1632 (with the approval, probably accidental, of the Church). A marvelously witty, elegant book, the *Dialogue* is one of the few monuments in the history of science that the layperson can read with pleasure. And so it was intended. Galileo wrote it in Italian, not the Latin that had always been used for scholarly works, because he wanted it to reach the widest possible audience.

In April 1633 he was brought before the Inquisition for having defied the order not to teach Copernicanism. To establish their case, his accusers used a forged document that suggested the 1616 limits were stricter than they were. In a trial that has caused controversy ever since, the aged astronomer, under threat of torture, abjured the "errors and heresies" of believing that the earth moved. But he did not remain docile for the remainder of his life, though he was kept under house arrest and progressively lost his eyesight. He had his principal work on physics, the *Two New Sciences*, published in tolerant Holland in 1638, while many of his letters ridiculed his opponents.

Galileo's Legacy Galileo's condemnation discouraged further scientific activity by his compatriots. Italy had been a leader of the new investigations, but now major further advances were to be made by the English, Dutch, and French. Yet this shift showed merely that the rise of science, once begun, could not be halted for long. By the late 1630s no self-respecting astron-

omer could deny the correctness of the Copernican theory.

The new studies of nature may have started out by causing tremendous bewilderment, as scientists struggled with the ideas of pioneers like Copernicus and Vesalius. But in the end these investigations created a renewed sense of certainty about the physical world that was to have a far-reaching influence. And this was true not only in physics and astronomy but also in anatomy, where, in 1628, another genius of the scientific revolution, the English doctor William Harvey, revolutionized the understanding of the human body when he identified the function of the heart and proved that the blood circulates.

ISAAC NEWTON

The culmination of the scientific revolution was the work of Isaac Newton (1642–1727), who made decisive contributions to mathematics, physics, astronomy, and optics and brought to a climax the changes that had begun with Copernicus. He united physics and astronomy in a single system to explain all motion, he helped transform mathematics by the development of the calculus, and he established some of the basic laws of modern physics.

Part of the explanation of his versatility lies in the workings of the scientific community at the time. Newton was a retiring man who nevertheless got into fierce arguments with such prominent contemporaries as the learned German scholar and scientist Wilhelm von Leibniz, who was working on the calculus. If not for his active participation in meetings of scientists at the recently founded Royal Society of London (see p. 509) and the effort he had to make to demonstrate his views to his colleagues, Newton might never have pursued his researches to their conclusion. He disliked the give-and-take of these discussions, but he felt forced in self-justification to prepare some of his most important papers for the Royal Society. Such institutions were now being established throughout Europe to promote the advance of science, and their creation indicates how far the scientific community had come since the days of Copernicus, who had worked largely in isolation.

The Principia Newton's masterpiece, *The Mathematical Principles of Natural Philosophy* (1687)—usually referred to by the first word of its Latin title, the *Principia*—was the last widely influential book to be written in Latin, the traditional language of scholarship. Latin was still useful to Newton, who wanted as many experts as possible to read the book because he was seeking to refute the approach to science associated with the widely admired French philosopher and mathematician René Descartes (see p. 506). In contrast to Descartes, who emphasized the powers of the mind and pure reason in investigating nature, Newton felt that mere hypotheses, constructions of logic and words, were not the tools of a true scientist. As he put it in a celebrated phrase, "*Hypotheses non fingo*" ("I do not posit hypotheses"), because everything he said was proved by experiment or by mathematics.

The most dramatic of Newton's findings was the solution to the ancient problem of motion. Building on Galileo's advances and overturning Aristotle's theories once and for all, Newton defined his system in three laws: first, in the absence of force, motion continues in a straight line; second, the rate of change of the motion is determined by the forces acting on it (such as friction); and third, action and reaction between two bodies are equal and opposite. To arrive at these laws, he defined the concepts of mass, inertia, and force in relation to velocity and acceleration as we know them today.

Newton extended these principles to the entire universe by demonstrating that his laws govern the motions of the moon and planets too. Using the concept of gravity, he provided the explanation of the movement of objects in space that is the foundation for current space travel. There is a balance, he said, between the earth's pull on the moon and the forward motion of the satellite, which would continue in a straight line were it not for the earth's gravity. Consequently the moon moves in an elliptical orbit in which neither gravity nor inertia gains control. The same pattern is followed by the planets around the sun (as Kepler had shown).

The Influence of Newton It was largely on the basis of the uniformity and the systematic impersonal forces Newton described that the view of the universe as a vast machine gained ground. According to this theory, all motion is a result of precise, unvarying, and demonstrable forces. There is a celestial mechanics just like the mechanics that operates on earth. It was not far from this view to the belief that God is a great watchmaker who started the marvelous mechanism going but intervenes only when something goes wrong and needs repair. The general philosophical implication that the world was stable and orderly was as important as the specific discoveries in making Newton one of the idols of his own and the next centuries. The educated applauded Newton's achievements, and he was the first scientist to receive a knighthood in England. Only a few decades after the appearance of the *Principia*, the poet Alexander Pope summed up the public feeling:

> Nature and nature's law lay hid in night;
> God said, "Let Newton be!" and all was light.

So overpowering was Newton's stature that in physics and astronomy the remarkable advances of 150 years slowed down for more than half a century after the publication of the *Principia*. There was a general impression that somehow Newton had done it all, that no important problems remained. There were other reasons for the slowdown—changing patterns in education, an inevitable lessening of momentum—but none was so powerful as the reverence for Newton, who became the intellectual symbol of his own and succeeding ages.

A NEW EPISTEMOLOGY

Galileo had stressed that his discoveries rested on a way of thinking that had an independent value, and he refused to allow traditional considerations, such as common sense or theological teachings, to interfere with his conclusions. Scientists were now moving toward a new epistemology, a new theory of how to obtain and verify knowledge. They stressed experience, reason, and doubt; they rejected all unsubstantiated authority; and they developed a revolutionary way of determining what was a true description of physical reality.

The process the scientists said they followed,

after they had formulated a hypothesis, consisted of three parts: first, observations; second, a generalization induced from the observations; and third, tests of the generalization by experiments whose outcome could be predicted by the generalization. A generalization remained valid only as long as it was not contradicted by the experiments specifically designed to test it. The scientist used no data except the results of strict observation—such as the time it took balls to roll down Galileo's inclined planes, or the path Kepler saw the plants following—and scientific reasoning was confined to the perception of the laws, principles, or patterns that emerged from the observations. Since measurement was the key to the data, the observations had a numerical, not a subjective, value; and the language of science naturally came to be mathematics.

In fact, scientists rarely reach conclusions in the exact way this idealized scheme suggests. Galileo's perfectly smooth balls and planes, for instance, did not exist, but Galileo understood the relevant physical theory so well that he knew what would have happened if one had rolled across the other, and he used this "experiment" to demonstrate the principle of inertia. In other words, experiments as well as hypotheses can occur in the mind; the essence of scientific method still remains a special way of looking at and understanding nature.

THE WIDER INFLUENCE OF SCIENTIFIC THOUGHT

The principles of scientific inquiry received attention throughout the intellectual community only gradually; it took time for the power of the scientists' method to be recognized. For decades, as Galileo found out, even his fellow astronomers continued to use what he would have considered irrelevant criteria, such as the teachings of the Bible, in judging scientific work. If the new methods were to be accepted, then their effectiveness would have to be demonstrated to more than a few specialists. This wider understanding was eventually achieved by midcentury as much through the efforts or ardent propagandizers like Francis Bacon as through the writings of the great innovators themselves. Gradually, they were able to convince a broad, educated public that science,

▶ *Anonymous*
PORTRAIT OF ISAAC NEWTON
The increasingly common portraits of scientists in the seventeenth century—Descartes was even painted by one of the leading artists of his age, Frans Hals—testify to their growing fame. In this case, the intensity of Newton's gaze hints at the power of scientific insight that contemporaries thought he embodied.

after first causing doubts by challenging ancient truths, now offered a promise of certainty that was not to be found anywhere else in an age of general crisis.

BACON AND DESCARTES

Bacon Although he was not an important scientist himself, Francis Bacon was the greatest of science's propagandists, and he inspired a whole generation with his vision of what it could accomplish for humanity. His description of an ideal society in the *New Atlantis*—published in

1627, the year after his death—is a vision of science as the savior of the human race. It predicts a time when those doing research at the highest levels will be regarded as the most important people in the state and will work on a vast government-supported project to gather all known facts about the physical universe. By a process of gradual induction, this information will lead to universal laws that, in turn, will enable people to improve their lot on earth.

Bacon's view of research as a collective enterprise inspired a number of later scientists, particularly the founders of the Royal Society of London. By the mid-seventeenth century, his ideas had entered the mainstream of European thought, an acceptance that testified to the broadening interest in science.

Descartes The Frenchman René Descartes (1596–1650) made the first concentrated attempt to apply the new methods of science to theories of knowledge, and, in so doing, he laid the foundations for modern philosophy. The impulse behind his work was his realization that for all the importance of observation and experiment, people can be deceived by their senses. In order to find some solid truth, therefore, he decided to apply the principle of doubt—the refusal to accept any authority without strict verification—to all knowledge. He began with the assumption that he could know unquestionably only one thing: that he was doubting. This allowed him to proceed to the observation "I think, therefore I am," because the act of doubting proved he was thinking, and thinking, in turn, demonstrated his existence.

The heart of his philosophy was his statement that whatever is clearly and distinctly thought must be true. This was a conclusion drawn from the proof of his own existence, and it enabled him to construct a proof of God's existence. We cannot fail to realize that we are imperfect, he argued, and we must therefore have an idea of perfection against which we may be measured. If we have a clear idea of what perfection is, then it must exist; hence there must be a God.

This proof may have served primarily to show that the principle of doubt did not contradict religious belief, but it also reflected the emphasis on the power of the mind in his great work, *Dis-course on the Method of Rightly Conducting the Reason and Seeking Truth in the Sciences* (1637). Thought is a pure and unmistakable guide, and only by reliance on its operations can people hope to advance their understanding of the world.

Descartes developed this view into a fundamental proposition about the nature of the world—a proposition that philosophers have been wrestling with ever since. He stated that there is an essential divide between thought and extension (tangible objects) or, put another way, between spirit and matter. Bacon and Galileo had insisted that science, the study of nature, is separate from and unaffected by faith or theology, the study of God. But Descartes turned this distinction into a far-reaching principle, dividing not only science from faith but even the reality of the world from our perception of that reality. There is a difference, in other words, between a chair and how we think of it as a chair.

The Influence of Descartes The emphasis Descartes placed on the operations of the mind gave a new direction to epistemological discussions. A hypothesis gained credibility not so much from external proofs as from the logical tightness of the arguments used to support it. The decisive test was how lucid and irrefutable a statement appeared to be to the thinking mind, not whether it could be demonstrated by experiments. Descartes thus applied what he considered to be the methods of science to all knowledge. Not only the phenomena of nature but all truth had to be investigated according to what he regarded as the strict principles of the scientist.

At the same time, his insistence on strict definitions of cause and effect helped create a general scientific and intellectual theory known as *mechanism*. In its simplest form, mechanism holds that the entire universe, including human beings, can be regarded as a complicated machine and thus subject to strict physical principles. The arm is like a lever, the elbow is like a hinge, and so on. Even an emotion is no more than a simple response to a definable stimulus. This view was to influence philosophers for generations.

Descartes' contributions to the scientific research of his day were theoretical rather than experimental. In physics, he was the first to perceive the distinction between mass and weight; and in mathematics, he was the first to apply algebraic notations and methods to geometry, thus founding analytic geometry. Above all, his emphasis on the principle of doubt undermined forever such traditional assumptions as the belief in the hierarchical organization of the universe. And the admiration he inspired indicated how completely the methods he advocated had captured his contemporaries' imagination.

BLAISE PASCAL

At midcentury only one important voice still protested against the new science and, in particular, against the materialism of Descartes. It belonged to a Frenchman, Blaise Pascal, a brilliant mathematician and experimenter. Before his death at the age of 39 in 1662, Pascal's investigations of probability in games of chance produced the theorem that still bears his name, and his research in conic sections helped lay the foundations for integral calculus. He also helped discover barometric pressure and invented a calculating machine. In his late twenties, however, Pascal became increasingly dissatisfied with scientific research, and he began to wonder whether his life was being properly spent. His doubts were reinforced by frequent visits to his sister, a nun at the Abbey of Port-Royal, where he came into contact with a new spiritual movement within Catholicism known as *Jansenism.*

Jansenism, which insisted that salvation was entirely in the hands of an all-powerful God and that unswerving faith was the only path to salvation, was not a particularly popular movement. But it guided the nuns at Port-Royal; and Pascal was profoundly impressed by their piety, asceticism, and spirituality. Moved by a growing concern with faith, Pascal had a mystical experience in November 1654 that made him resolve to devote his life to the salvation of his soul. He adopted the austere doctrines of Jansenism, and wrote a series of devastating critiques of the more worldly Jesuits, accusing them of irresponsibility and, as he phrased it, of placing cushions under sinners' elbows.

The **Pensées**   During the few remaining years of his life, Pascal put on paper a collection of reflec-

tions—some only a few words long, some many pages—that were gathered together after his death and published as the *Pensées* (or "reflections"). These writings revealed not only the beliefs of a deeply religious man but also the anxieties of a scientist who feared the growing influence of science. He did not wish to put an end to research; he merely wanted people to realize that the truths uncovered by science were limited and not as important as the truths perceived by faith. As he put it in one of his more memorable *Pensées*, "The heart has its reasons that reason cannot know."

Pascal was warning against the replacement of the traditional understanding of humanity and its destiny, gained through religious faith, with the conclusions reached by the methods of the scientists. The separation between the material and the spiritual would be fatal, he believed, because it would destroy the primacy and even the importance of the spiritual. Pascal's protest was unique, but the fact that it was put forward at all indicates how high the status of the scientist and his methods had risen by the 1650s. Just a quarter-century earlier, such a dramatic change in fortune would have been hard to predict. But now the new epistemology, after its initial disturbing assault on ancient views, was offering one of the few promises of certainty in an age of upheaval and general crisis. In intellectual matters as in politics, turmoil was gradually giving way to assurance.

SCIENCE INSTITUTIONALIZED

There were many besides Bacon who realized that scientific work should be a cooperative endeavor and that information should be exchanged among all its practitioners. A scientific society founded in Rome in 1603 made the first major effort to apply this view, and it was soon followed up in France, where in the early seventeenth century a friar named Marin Mersenne became the center of an international network of correspondents interested in scientific work. He also spread news by bringing scientists together for discussions and experiments. Contacts that were developed at these meetings led eventually to a more permanent and systematic organization of scientific activity.

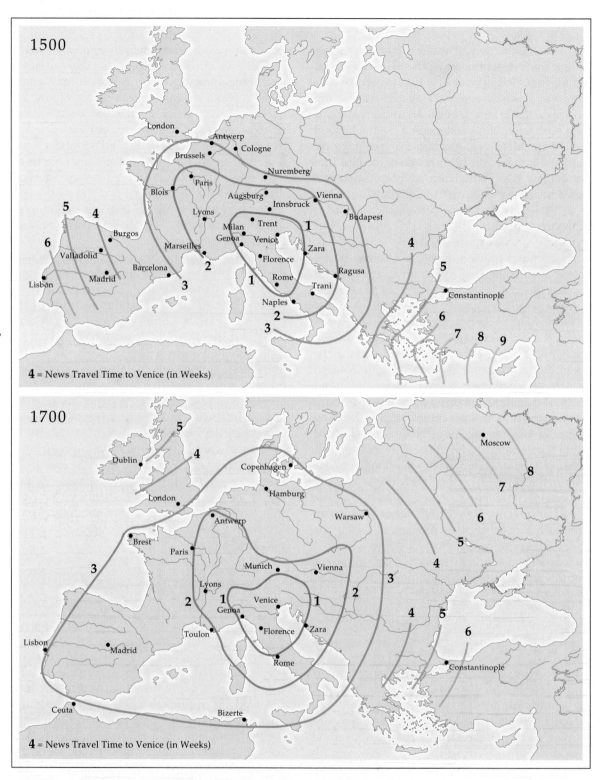

1500

London
Antwerp
Cologne
Brussels
Nuremberg
Blois
Paris
Augsburg
Vienna
Lyons
Innsbruck
Budapest
Trent
Milan
Genoa
Venice
Burgos
Marseilles
Zara
Valladolid
Florence
Ragusa
Barcelona
Rome
Madrid
Lisbon
Trani
Naples
Constantinople

5 4
6
2
3
1 1
2
3
4
5
6
7 8 9

4 = News Travel Time to Venice (in Weeks)

1700

Dublin
Moscow
Copenhagen
London
Hamburg
Antwerp
Warsaw
Brest
Paris
Munich
Vienna
Lyons
Venice
Genoa
Florence
Zara
Toulon
Lisbon
Madrid
Rome
Constantinople
Ceuta
Bizerte

5 4
3
2 1 1 2 3
8
7
6
5
4
5
6
4

4 = News Travel Time to Venice (in Weeks)

Map 16.1 SPEED OF NEWS TRAVELING TO VENICE IN 1500 AND 1700
Although the dramatic advances in communications lay in the future, by 1700
improved roads and canals and more efficient shipping did bring about
significant advances in the distance news could travel in two or three weeks.

The Royal Society In England, the first steps toward such organization were taken at Oxford during the Civil War in the 1640s, when the revolutionaries captured the city and replaced those at the university who taught traditional natural philosophy. A few of the newcomers formed what they called the Invisible College, a group that met to exchange information and discuss one another's work. The group included only one first-class scientist, the chemist Robert Boyle; but in 1660 he and 11 others formed an official organization, the Royal Society of London for Improving Natural Knowledge, with headquarters in the capital. In 1662 it was granted a charter by Charles II—the first sign of a connection with political authority that not only boosted science but also indicated the growing presence of central governments in all areas of society.

The Royal Society's purposes were openly Baconian. Its aim for a few years—until everyone realized it was impossible—was to gather all knowledge about nature, particularly if it had practical uses. For a long time the members offered their services for the public good, helping in one instance to develop the science of social statistics ("political arithmetic," as it was called) for the government. Soon, however, it became clear that the society's principal function was to serve as a headquarters and clearing center for research. Its secretaries maintained an enormous correspondence to encourage English and foreign scholars to send in news of their discoveries. And in 1665 the society began the regular publication of *Philosophical Transactions*, the first professional scientific journal.

Imitators were soon to follow. In 1666 Louis XIV gave his blessing to the founding of a French Royal Academy of Sciences, and similar organi-

▶ *Charles-Nicolas Cochin*
THE ACADÉMIE ROYALE DES SCIENCES, PARIS, ENGRAVING, 1698
This celebration of the work done by one of the first scientific societies suggests the variety of research that these organizations promoted. In contrast to the students of theology who merely read books (as we see through the arch on the right), the geographers, engineers, astronomers, physicists, and anatomists of the scientific academy examine the real world.

L'ACADEMIE DES SCIENCES ET DES BEAUX ARTS
DEDIEE AU ROY

zations were established in Naples and Berlin by 1700. Membership in these societies was limited and highly prized, a sign of the glamour that was beginning to attach itself to the new studies. By the 1660s there could be no doubt that science, secure in royal patronage, had become a model for all thought. Its practitioners were extravagantly admired, and throughout intellectual and high social circles, there was a scramble to apply its methods to almost every conceivable activity.

The Wider Appeal of Science Descartes himself had applied the ideas of science to philosophy in general; Bacon had put them at the service of social thought. But the applications were not only on these high levels. Formal gardens were designed to show the order, harmony, and reason that science had made such prized qualities. And methods of fortification and warfare were affected by the principles of the new investigations, such as the need for accurate measurement.

As the scientists' activities became more popular and fashionable, even aristocrats began to spend time playing at science. Herbariums and small observatories were added to country estates, and parties featured an evening of star gazing. Science also fascinated the general populace. Among the most eagerly anticipated occasions in seventeenth-century Holland was the public anatomy lesson. The body of a criminal would be brought to an enormous hall that was packed with students and a fascinated public. A famous surgeon would dissect the cadaver, announcing and displaying each organ as he removed it.

On the whole, the reverence for science and its methods did not develop from an understanding of its actual accomplishments or its potential consequences. Rather, it was caused by the fame of the spectacular discoveries that had offered new and convincing solutions to centuries-old problems in astronomy, physics, and anatomy. Here was a promise of certainty and order in a world that otherwise was bedeviled by conflict and doubt. As a result, the protests of Pascal could be ignored, and the new discipline could be given unblemished admiration. The entire world was coming to be viewed through the scientist's eyes—a striking achievement for a recently minor member of the intellectual community—and the qualities of regularity and harmony associated with science began to appear in the work of artists and writers.

II. *Literature and the Arts*

We have seen that the late sixteenth and early seventeenth centuries were a time of political turbulence, culminating in a general crisis in the mid-seventeenth century from which a more settled Europe emerged. Not only did the development of science follow a similar pattern—with decades of uncertainty as old truths were challenged, followed by a new sense of assurance in the mid-seventeenth century—but so too did the concerns of literature and the arts.

MANNERISM

One response that was provoked by the upheavals of the sixteenth century was the attempt to escape reality, an effort that was echoed by some of the painters of the age, known as Mannerists. The Mannerists and their patrons cultivated artificial and esoteric images of the world; they undermined perspective, distorted human figures, and devised unnatural colors and lighting to create startling effects.

El Greco Mannerism was embodied in El Greco (1541–1614), a Greek who was trained in Italy and settled in Spain. His compelling and almost mystic canvases created an otherworldly alternative (reminiscent of St. Teresa's visions) to the troubles of his time. El Greco's elongated and often agonized human beings, cool colors, and eerie lighting make him one of the most distinctive painters in the history of art (see p. 462). Increasingly after 1600, though, painters were to reject the Mannerists' flight from reality; eventually the arts, too, were to reflect the sense of settlement that descended over European civilization in the mid-seventeenth century.

MICHEL DE MONTAIGNE

In the world of literature, the concerns of the age were most vividly expressed by the Frenchman

Michel de Montaigne (1533–1592). Obsessed by the death he saw all around him and determined to overcome his fears, he retired in 1570 to his country home in order to "essay," or test, his innermost feelings by writing short pieces of prose even about subjects he did not fully comprehend. In the process he created a new literary form, the essay, that also helped shape the modern French language. But his chief influence was philosophical: He has inspired the search for self-knowledge ever since.

At first Montaigne's anxieties led him to the radical doubt about the possibility of finding truth that is known as *Skepticism;* this inspired the total uncertainty of his motto *"Que sais-je?"* ("What do I know?"). Eventually, however, Montaigne struggled toward a more confident view, taking as his model the ancient saying "Know thyself." By looking into one's own person, one can find values that hold true at least for oneself, and these will reflect the values of all humanity. Montaigne came close to a morality without theology, because good and self-determination were more important to him than doctrine, and he saw everywhere religious people committing inhuman acts. Trying to be an angel is wrong, he said; being good is enough.

Neostoicism A more general application of some of these ideas was a theory known as *Neostoicism,* inspired by the ancient Stoics' emphasis on self-knowledge and a calm acceptance of the world. The most influential of the Neostoics, a Dutch writer named Justus Lipsius, argued that public leaders ought to be guided by profound self-examination. Lipsius urged rulers to be restrained and self-disciplined, and he was much admired by the kings and royal ministers of the seventeenth century.

CERVANTES AND SHAKESPEARE

Cervantes In Spain the disillusionment that accompanied the political and economic decline of Europe's most powerful state was perfectly captured by Miguel de Cervantes (1547–1616). He was heir to a brilliant satirical tradition that had already produced in the sixteenth century the writings of Erasmus and Rabelais. Cervantes saw the wide gap between the hopes and the realities of his day—in religion, in social institutions, in human behavior—and made the dichotomy the basis of scathing social satire in his novel *Don Quixote.*

At one level, Cervantes was ridiculing the excessive chivalry of the Spanish nobility in his portrayal of a knight who was ready to tilt at windmills, though he obviously admired the sincerity of his well-meaning hero and sympathized with him as a perennial loser. On another level, the author brought to life the Europe of the time—the ordinary people and their hypocrisies and intolerances—with a liveliness rarely matched in literature. His view of that society, however, was far from cheery. "Justice, but not for my house," says Don Quixote. Cervantes avoided politics, but he was clearly directing many of his sharpest barbs at the brutality and disregard for human values that were characteristic of his fanatical times. And in England another towering figure was grappling with similar problems.

Shakespeare For the English-speaking world, the most brilliant writer of this and all other periods was William Shakespeare (1564–1616), whose characters bring to life almost every conceivable mood: searing grief, airy romance, rousing nationalism, uproarious humor. Despite his modest education his imagery shows a familiarity with subjects ranging from astronomy to seamanship, from alchemy to warfare. It is not surprising, therefore, that some have doubted that one man could have produced this amazing body of work.

Shakespeare started writing in the 1590s, when he was in his late twenties, and continued until his death in 1616. During most of this time, he was also involved with a theatrical company, where he often had to produce plays on short notice. He thus had the best of all possible tests—audience reactions—as he gained mastery of theatrical techniques.

Shakespeare's plays made timeless statements about human behavior: love, hatred, violence, sin. Of particular interest to the historian, however, is what he tells us about attitudes that belong especially to his own era. For example, the conservatism of his characters is quite clear. They believe firmly in the hierarchical structure of society, and throughout the long series of historical plays, events suggest that excessive ambition does not pay. Again and again, legality and stability are shown as fundamental virtues amidst turbulent times. Shakespeare's expressions of patriotism are particularly intense; when in *Richard II* the king's uncle, John of Gaunt, lies dying, he pours out his love for his country in words that have moved the English ever since:

> This royal throne of kings, this scepter'd isle,
> This earth of majesty, this seat of Mars,
> This other Eden, demi-paradise, . . .
> This happy breed of men, this little world,
> This precious stone set in the silver sea, . . .
> This blessed plot, this earth,
>   this realm, this England.
>
> *RICHARD II*, ACT 2, SCENE 1

As in so much of the art and writing of the time, instability is a central concern of Shakespeare's plays. His four most famous tragedies—*Hamlet, King Lear, Macbeth,* and *Othello*—end in disillusionment: The heroes are ruined by irresoluteness, pride, ambition, or jealousy. Shakespeare was exploring a theme that had absorbed playwrights since Euripides—the fatal flaws that destroy the great—and producing dramas of revenge that were popular in his day; but the plays also demonstrate his deep understanding of human nature. Whatever one's hopes, one cannot forget human weakness, the inevitability of decay, and the constant threat of disaster. The contrast appears with compelling clarity in a speech delivered by Hamlet:

> What a piece of work is man! How noble in reason! how infinite in faculties! in form and moving how express and admirable! in action how like an angel! in apprehension how like a god! the beauty of the world, the paragon of animals! And yet to me what is this quintessence of dust? Man delights not me.
>
> *HAMLET*, ACT 2, SCENE 2

Despite such pessimism, despite the deep sense of human inadequacy, the basic impression Shakespeare gives is of immense vigor, of a restlessness and confidence that recall the many achievements of the sixteenth century. Yet a sense of decay is never far absent. Repeatedly, people seem utterly helpless, overtaken by events they cannot control. Nothing remains constant or dependable, and everything that seems solid or reassuring, be it the love of a daughter or the crown of England, is challenged. In this atmosphere of ceaseless change, where landmarks easily disappear, Shakespeare conveys the tensions of his time.

THE BAROQUE: GRANDEUR AND EXCITEMENT

After 1600, the arts began to move toward the assurance and sense of settlement that was descending over other areas of European civilization. A new style, the Baroque, sought to drown the uneasiness of Mannerism in a blaze of grandeur. Passion, drama, mystery, and awe were the qualities of the Baroque: Every art form—from music to literature, from architecture to opera—had to involve, arouse, and uplift its audience.

The Baroque style was closely associated with the Counter Reformation's emphasis on gorgeous display in Catholic ritual. The patronage of leading Church figures made Rome a magnet for the major painters of the period. Elsewhere, the Baroque flourished primarily at the leading Catholic courts of the seventeenth century, most notably the Habsburg courts in Madrid, Prague, and Brussels. Few periods have conveyed so strong a sense of grandeur, theatricality, and ornateness.

Caravaggio   The artist who first shaped the new aesthetic, Caravaggio (1571–1610), lived most of his life in Rome. Although he received commissions from high Church figures and spent time in a cardinal's household, he was equally at home among the beggars and petty criminals of Rome's dark back streets. These ordinary people served as Caravaggio's models, which shocked those who felt it inappropriate for such humble characters to represent the holy figures of biblical scenes. Yet the power of Caravaggio's paintings—their depiction of highly emotional moments, and the drama created by their sharp contrasts of light and dark—made his work much prized. He had to flee Rome after he killed someone in a brawl, but he left behind a body of work that influenced an entire generation of painters.

National Gallery, London

▶ *Caravaggio*
THE SUPPER AT EMMAUS, CA. 1597
By choosing moments of high drama and using
sharp contrasts of light, Caravaggio created an
immediacy that came to be one of the hallmarks of
Baroque painting. This is the moment during the
supper at Emmaus when his disciples suddenly
recognized the resurrected Christ. The force of their
emotions and their almost theatrical gestures
convey the intensity of the moment, but many at
the time objected to the craggy, tattered appearance
of the disciples. These were not idealized figures, as
was expected, but ordinary people at a humble
table.

Rubens Among those who came to Rome to
study Caravaggio's art was Peter Paul Rubens
(1577–1640), the principal ornament of the brilliant Habsburg court at Brussels. His major
themes typified the grandeur that came to be the
hallmark of Baroque style: glorifications of great
rulers and also of the ceremony and mystery of
Catholicism. Rubens' secular paintings convey

enormous strength; his religious works overwhelm the viewer with the majesty of the Church
and excite the believer's piety by stressing the
power of the faith.

Velázquez Other artists glorified rulers through
idealized portraiture. The greatest court painter
of the age was Diego Velázquez (1599–1660). His
portraits of members of the Spanish court depict
rulers and their surroundings in the stately atmosphere appropriate to the theme. Yet occasionally Velázquez hinted at the weakness of an
ineffective monarch in his rendering of the face,
even though the basic purpose of his work was
always to exalt royal power. And his celebration
of a notable Habsburg victory, *The Surrender of
Breda*, managed to suggest the sadness and emp-
tiness as much as the glory of war.

Bernini GianLorenzo Bernini (1598–1680)
brought to sculpture and architecture the qualities that Rubens brought to painting, and like Ru-

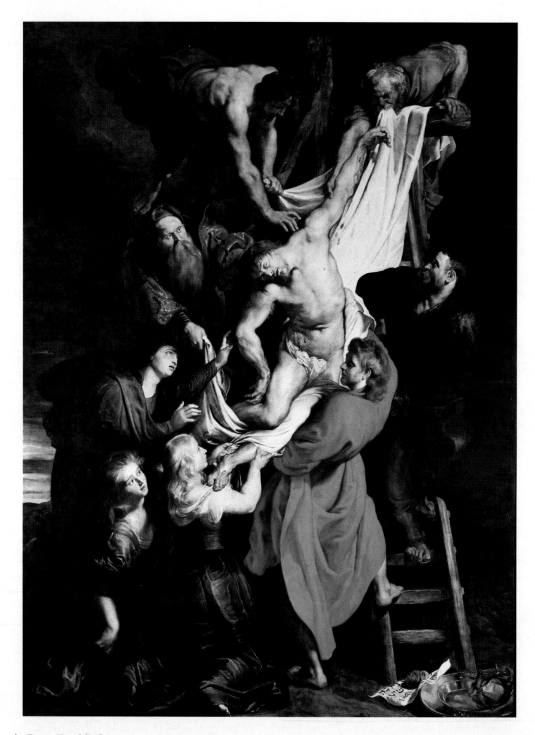

▶ *Peter Paul Rubens*
THE DESCENT FROM THE CROSS, 1612
This huge altarpiece was one of the first pictures Rubens painted after he returned to his native Antwerp, after spending most of his twenties developing his art in Italy. The ambitious scale, the strong emotions, the vivid lighting, and the dramatic action showed the artist's commitment to the Baroque style that had recently evolved in Italy, and the powerful impact of the altarpiece helped make him one of the most sought-after painters of the day.

bens he was closely associated with the Counter Reformation. Pope Urban VIII commissioned him in 1629 to complete both the inside and the outer setting of the basilica of St. Peter's in Rome. For the interior Bernini designed a splendid papal throne that seems to float on clouds beneath a burst of sunlight, and for the exterior he created an enormous plaza, surrounded by a double col-

onnade, that is the largest such plaza in Europe. Similarly, his dramatic religious works reflect the desire of the Counter Reformation popes to electrify the faithful. The sensual and overpowering altarpiece dedicated to the Spanish mystic St. Teresa makes a direct appeal to the emotions of the beholder that reveals the excitement of Baroque at its best.

▶ *Diego Velázquez*
THE SURRENDER OF BREDA, 1635
The contrasting postures of victory and defeat are masterfully captured by Diego Velázquez in *The Surrender of Breda*. The Dutch soldiers droop their heads and lances, but the victorious Spaniards hardly show triumph, and the gesture of the victorious general, Ambrogio Spinola, is one of consolation and understanding.

Music   The seventeenth century was significant, too, as a decisive time in the history of music. New instruments, notably in the keyboard and string families, enabled composers to create richer effects than had been possible before. Particularly in Italy, which in the sixteenth and seventeenth centuries was the chief center of new ideas in music, musicians began to explore the

▷ *GianLorenzo Bernini*
ST. PETER'S SQUARE AND CHURCH, ROME
The magnificent circular double colonnade that Bernini created in front of St. Peter's is
one of the triumphs of Baroque architecture. The church itself was already the largest
in Christendom (markers in the floor still indicate how far other famous churches
would reach if placed inside St. Peter's), and it was topped by the huge dome
Michelangelo had designed. The vast enclosed space that Bernini built reinforced the
grandeur of a church that was the pope's own.

▶ *GianLorenzo Bernini*
The Ecstasy of St. Teresa, 1652
Bernini's sculpture is as dramatic an example of Baroque art as the paintings of Caravaggio. The moment that St. Teresa described in her autobiography when she attained mystic ecstasy, as an angel repeatedly pierced her heart with a dart, became in Bernini's hands the centerpiece of a theatrical tableau. He placed the patrons who had commissioned the work on two walls of the chapel that houses this altarpiece, sitting in what seem to be boxes and looking at the stage on which the drama unfolds.

potential of a form that first emerged in these years: the opera. Drawing on the resources of the theater, painting, architecture, music, and the dance, an operatic production could achieve splendors that were beyond the reach of any one of these arts on its own. The form was perfectly attuned to the courtly culture of the age, to the love of display among the princes of Europe, and to the Baroque determination to overwhelm one's audience.

The dominant figure in seventeenth-century music was the Italian Claudio Monteverdi (1567–1643), one of the most innovative composers of all time. He has been called with some justification the creator of both the operatic form and the orchestra. His masterpiece *Orfeo* (1607) was a tremendous success, and in the course of the next century operas gained in richness and complexity, attracting composers, as well as audiences, in ever increasing numbers.

CLASSICISM: GRANDEUR AND RESTRAINT

Classicism, the other major style of the seventeenth century, attempted to recapture (though on a much larger scale than Renaissance imitations of antiquity) the aesthetic values and the strict forms that had been favored in ancient Greece and Rome. Like the Baroque, Classicism aimed for grandiose effects, but unlike the Baroque, it achieved them through restraint and discipline within a formal structure. The gradual rise of the Classical style in the seventeenth century echoed the trend toward stabilization that was taking place in other areas of intellectual life and in politics.

Poussin The epitome of disciplined expression and conscious imitation of Classical antiquity is the work of Nicolas Poussin (1594–1665), a French artist who spent much of his career in Rome. Poussin was no less interested than his contemporaries in momentous and dramatic subjects, but the atmosphere is always more subdued than in the work of Velázquez or Rubens. The colors are muted, the figures are restrained, and the settings are serene. Peaceful landscapes, men and women in togas, and ruins of Classical buildings are features of his art.

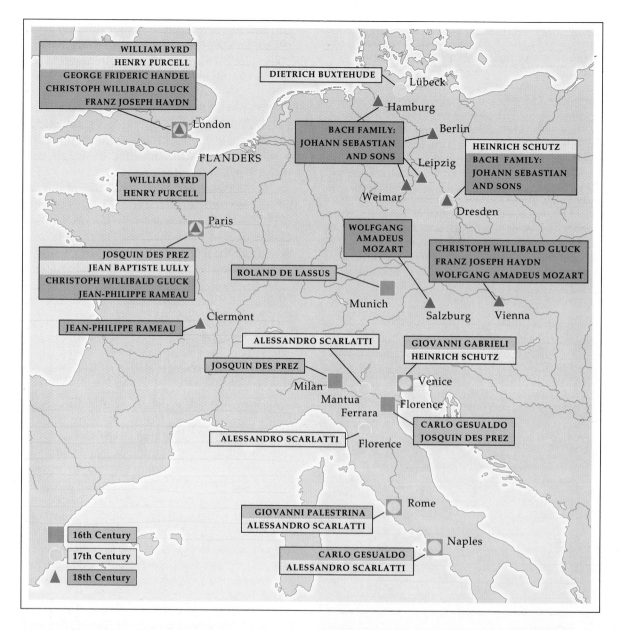

WILLIAM BYRD
HENRY PURCELL
GEORGE FRIDERIC HANDEL
CHRISTOPH WILLIBALD GLUCK
FRANZ JOSEPH HAYDN

London

DIETRICH BUXTEHUDE — Lübeck

Hamburg

FLANDERS

Berlin

BACH FAMILY:
JOHANN SEBASTIAN
AND SONS

Leipzig

HEINRICH SCHUTZ
BACH FAMILY:
JOHANN SEBASTIAN
AND SONS

WILLIAM BYRD
HENRY PURCELL

Weimar

Dresden

Paris

JOSQUIN DES PREZ
JEAN BAPTISTE LULLY
CHRISTOPH WILLIBALD GLUCK
JEAN-PHILIPPE RAMEAU

WOLFGANG
AMADEUS
MOZART

CHRISTOPH WILLIBALD GLUCK
FRANZ JOSEPH HAYDN
WOLFGANG AMADEUS MOZART

ROLAND DE LASSUS

Munich

Salzburg   Vienna

JEAN-PHILIPPE RAMEAU — Clermont

ALESSANDRO SCARLATTI

GIOVANNI GABRIELI
HEINRICH SCHUTZ

JOSQUIN DES PREZ

Milan

Venice

Mantua
Ferrara

Florence

CARLO GESUALDO
JOSQUIN DES PREZ

ALESSANDRO SCARLATTI

Florence

GIOVANNI PALESTRINA
ALESSANDRO SCARLATTI

Rome

Naples

CARLO GESUALDO
ALESSANDRO SCARLATTI

16th Century
17th Century
18th Century

Map 16.2 CENTERS OF MUSIC, 1500–1800
This map indicates the shifting centers of new ideas in music from Flanders and Italy in the sixteenth century; to Italy in the seventeenth; and on to Germany, England, and France in the eighteenth.

The Dutch In the United Provinces different forces were at work, and they led to a style that was much more intimate than the grandiose outpourings of a Rubens or a Velázquez. Two aspects of Dutch society, Protestantism and republicanism, had a particular influence on its painters. The Reformed Church frowned on religious art, which reduced the demand for paintings of biblical scenes. Religious works therefore tended to express personal faith. And the absence of a court meant that the chief patrons of art were sober merchants, who were far more interested in precise, dignified portraits than in ornate displays. The result, notably in the profound and moving works of Rembrandt, was a compelling art whose beauty lies in its calmness and restraint.

Rembrandt Rembrandt van Rijn (1606–1669) explored an amazing range of themes, but he was particularly fascinated by human character, emo-

▶ *Nicolas Poussin*
THE INSPIRATION OF THE EPIC POET, CA. 1628
Whereas Baroque art emphasized emotion, the Classical style sought to embody reason. Poussin, the leading Classical artist of his time, believed that painting, like poetry, had to elevate the minds of its audience. The poet was thus a particularly apt subject for him—a noble and serious theme that could be presented as a scene from antiquity, with formal figures, muted colors, and ancient symbols like the laurel wreath. Poussin's views became the official doctrine of the academy of art founded in France with royal approval, and they influenced generations of painters.

tion, and self-revelation. Whether children or old people, simple servant girls or rich burghers, his subjects are presented without elaboration or idealization; always the personality speaks for itself. Rembrandt's most remarkable achievement in portraiture—and one of the most moving series of canvases in the history of art—is his depiction of the changes in his own face over his lifetime. The brash youth turns into the confident, successful, middle-aged man, one of the most sought-after painters in Holland. But in his late thirties the sorrows mounted: He lost his beloved wife, and commissions began to fall off. Sadness fills the eyes in these pictures. The last portraits move from despair to a final, quiet resignation as his sight slowly failed. Taken together, these paintings bear comparison with Montaigne's es-

▷ *Rembrandt*
Self-Portrait with Palette, 1660
Over 60 self-portraits by Rembrandt have survived; though all are penetrating explorations of human character, those from his last years are especially moving. We see him here in his mid-fifties with the tools of his trade. Adapting Caravaggio's interest in light, he uses different shades of brown and the illumination of the face to create a somber and reflective mood. The very act of thinking is captured in this canvas, not to mention the full life that is etched in Rembrandt's wrinkles.

says as monuments to the exploration of one's own spirit—a searching appraisal that brings all who see it to a deeper understanding of human nature.

One could argue that Rembrandt cannot be fitted into either of the dominant styles of his time. Except for his powerful use of light, his work is far more introspective than most of the Baroque. Nor did he adopt the forms of antiquity, as did

Poussin and other Classical painters. Yet, like the advocates of Classicism, Rembrandt in his restraint seemed to anticipate the art of the next generation. After his death in 1669, serenity, calm, and elegance became the watchwords of European painting. An age of repose and grace was succeeding a time of upheaval as surely in the arts as in other spheres of life.

Drama   By the middle of the seventeenth century, the formalism of the Classical style was also being extended to literature, especially drama. This change was most noticeable in France, but it soon moved through Western Europe, as leading critics insisted that new plays conform to the structure laid down by the ancients. In particular, they wanted the three Classical unities observed: unity of place, which required that all scenes take place without change of location; unity of time, which demanded that the events in the play occur within a 24-hour period; and unity of action, which dictated simplicity and purity of plot.

Corneille   The work of Pierre Corneille (1606–1684), the dominant figure in the French theater during the midcentury years, reflects the rise of Classicism. His early plays were complex and involved, and even after he came into contact with the Classical tradition, he did not accept its rules easily. His masterpiece *Le Cid* (1636), based on the legends of a medieval Spanish hero, technically observed the three unities, but only by compressing an entire tragic love affair, a military campaign, and many other events into one day. The play won immediate popular success, but the critics, urged on by the royal minister Cardinal Richelieu, who admired the regularity and order of Classical style, condemned Corneille for imperfect observance of the three unities. Thereafter he adhered to the Classical forms, though he was never entirely at ease with their restraints.

Passion was not absent from the Classical play; the works of Jean Racine (1639–1699), the model Classical dramatist, generate some of the most intense emotion ever seen on the stage. But the exuberance of earlier drama was disappearing. Nobody summed up the values of Classicism better than Racine in his eulogy of Corneille:

You know in what a condition the stage was when he began to write. . . . All the rules of art, and even those of decency and decorum, broken everywhere. . . . Corneille, after having for some time sought the right path and struggled against the bad taste of his day, inspired by extraordinary genius and helped by the study of the ancients, at last brought reason upon the stage.

Paul Mesnard (ed.), *Oeuvres de J. Racine*, IV (1886), p. 366, translated by T. K. Rabb

This was exactly the progression—from turbulence to calm—that was apparent throughout European culture in this period.

III. Social Patterns and Popular Culture

POPULATION TRENDS

The sixteenth-century rise in Europe's population was succeeded by a period of decline that in most areas lasted long after the political and intellectual upheavals subsided. The rise had been fragile, because throughout these centuries only one child in two reached adulthood. Each couple had to give birth to four children merely to replace themselves, and since they had to wait until they were financially independent to marry—usually in their mid-twenties—they rarely had the chance to produce a big family. Women in this period lost the capacity to bear children in their late thirties, and on the average, therefore, a woman had some 12 years in which to give birth to four children to maintain the population. Because lactation delayed ovulation, the mean interval between births was almost two and a half years, which meant that most couples were only just capable of raising two adults. As soon as there was outside pressure—such as plague, famine, or war—population growth became impossible.

The worst of these outside pressures in the seventeenth century was the Thirty Years' War, which alone caused the death of more than 5 million people. It also helped plunge Europe into a debilitating economic depression, which, in turn, decreased the means of relieving famine. Disasters of such magnitude could not easily be absorbed. Only when better times returned could population increase resume. Because they led in economic recovery, England and the Netherlands experienced a demographic revival long before their neighbors; indeed, the rise in their numbers, which began in the 1660s, accounted for almost all of the slight population increase the whole of Europe was able to achieve in this difficult century.

SOCIAL STATUS

The determinants of status in modern times—wealth, education, and family background—were viewed rather differently in the seventeenth century. Wealth was significant chiefly to merchants, education was important mainly among professionals, and background was vital primarily to the nobility. But in this period the signifi-

EUROPE'S POPULATION, 1600–1700, BY REGIONS

Region	1600*	1700	Percentage Change
Spain, Portugal, and Italy	23.6	22.7	− 4
France, Switzerland, and Germany	35.0	36.2	+ 3
British Isles, Low Countries, and Scandinavia	12.0	16.1	+34
Total	70.6	75.0	+ 6

*All figures are in millions.

Source: Jan de Vries, *The Economy of Europe in an Age of Crisis, 1600–1750*, Cambridge, 1976, p. 5.

cance of these three social indicators began to shift. Wealth became a more general source of status, as ever-larger numbers of successful merchants bought offices, lands, and titles that allowed them to enter the nobility. Education was also becoming more highly prized; throughout Europe attendance at institutions of higher learning soared after 1550, bringing the sons of artisans as well as nobles to universities. And although background was being scrutinized ever more defensively by old-line nobles, who regarded family lineage as the only criterion for acceptance into their ranks, their resistance to change was futile as the "new" aristocrats multiplied.

In general, it was assumed that everyone occupied a fixed place in the social hierarchy and that it was against the order of nature for someone to move to another level. The growing social importance of wealth and education, however, indicates that mobility was possible. Thanks to the expansion of bureaucracies, it became easier to move to new levels, either by winning favor at court or by buying an office. High status conferred important privileges: Great landowners could demand services and fees from their tenants; those with political rights in cities, nobles, and bureaucrats were often exempt from taxes; and courtiers controlled portions of the vast patronage that the government disbursed. At each level, however, women were always considered subordinate: In many countries, even the widows of aristocrats could not inherit their husbands' estates; an abbess could never become prominent in Church government; and the few women allowed to practice a trade were excluded from the leadership of their guild. Nevertheless, there were businesswomen and female artists, writers, and even scientists among the growing numbers of successful self-made people in this period.

MOBILITY AND CRIME

The Peasant The remarkable economic advances of the sixteenth century helped change attitudes toward wealth, but they brought few benefits to the lower levels of society. Peasants throughout Europe were, in fact, entering a time of increasing difficulty at the end of the sixteenth century. Their taxes were rising rapidly, but the prices they got for the food they grew were stabilizing. Moreover, landowners were starting what has been called the "seigneurial reaction"— making additional demands on their tenants, raising rents, and squeezing as much as they could out of the lands they owned. The effects of famine and war were also more severe at this level of society. The only escapes were to cities or armies, both of which grew rapidly in the seventeenth century. Many of those who fled their villages, however, remained on the road, part of the huge bodies of vagrants and beggars who were a common sight throughout Europe.

A few of those who settled in a town or city improved their lot, but for the large majority, poverty in cities was even more miserable and hungry than poverty on the land. Few could become apprentices, and day laborers were poorly paid and usually out of work. As for military careers, armies were carriers of disease, frequently ill fed, and subject to constant hardship.

Crime For many, therefore, the only alternative to starvation was crime. One area of London in the seventeenth century was totally controlled by the underworld. It offered refuge to fugitives and was never entered by respectable citizens. Robbery and violence—committed equally by desperate men, women, and even children—were common in most cities. As a result, social events like dinners and outings, or visits to the theater, took place during the daytime because the streets were unsafe at night.

If caught, Europe's criminals were treated harshly. In an age before regular police forces, however, catching them was difficult. Crime was usually the responsibility of local authorities, who depended on part-time officials (known in England as *constables*) for law enforcement. Only in response to major outbreaks, such as a gang of robbers preying on travelers, would the authorities recruit a more substantial armed band (rather like a posse in the American West) to pursue criminals. If such efforts succeeded in bringing offenders to justice, the defendants found they had few rights, especially if they were poor, and that punishments were severe. Torture was a common means of extracting confessions; various forms of maiming, such as chopping off a hand or an ear, were considered acceptable

▶ *Artemisia Gentileschi*
JUDITH SLAYING HOLOFERNES, CA. 1620
Women artists are rare in the seventeenth century because they were not allowed to
become apprentices. But Artemisia (1593–1652) was the daughter of a painter who
happened to be a friend of Caravaggio, and she had the opportunity to become a
gifted exponent of Baroque style. Known throughout Europe for her vivid portrayals
of dramatic scenes (she painted the murder of Holofernes by the biblical heroine
Judith at least five times), she practiced her chosen profession with considerable
success, despite the trauma of being raped at 17 by a friend of her father's—an act of
violence that may be reflected (and avenged) in this painting.

penalties; and repeated thefts could lead to execution.

Society's hierarchical instincts were apparent even in civil disputes, where nobles were usually immune from prosecution and women often could not start a case. If a woman were raped, for example, she had to find a man to bring suit. In one famous case in Italy, a girl's father sued the rapist because it was *his* honor that had been damaged by the attack.

CHANGE IN THE VILLAGE

Over three-quarters of Europe's population still lived in small village communities, but their structure was not what it once had been. In Eastern Europe, peasants were being reduced to serfdom; in the West—our principal concern—familiar relationships and institutions were changing.

The essence of the traditional village had been its isolation. Cut off from frequent contact with the world beyond its immediate region, it had been self-sufficient and closely knit. Everyone knew everyone else, and mutual help was vital for survival. There might be distinctions among villagers—some more prosperous, others less so—but the sense of cohesiveness was powerful. It extended even to the main "outsiders" in the village, the priest and the local lord. The priest was often indistinguishable from his parishioners: almost as poor and sometimes hardly more literate. He adapted to local customs and beliefs, frequently taking part in semipagan rituals so as to keep his authority with his flock. The lord could be exploitative and demanding; but he considered the village his livelihood, and he therefore kept in close touch with its affairs and did all he could to ensure its safety, orderliness, and well-being.

Forces of Change The main intrusions onto this scene were economic and demographic. As a result of the boom in agricultural prices during the sixteenth century, followed by the economic difficulties of the seventeenth, differences in the wealth of the villagers became more marked. The richer peasants began to set themselves apart from their poorer neighbors, and the feeling of village unity began to break down. These divi-

sions were exacerbated by the rise in population during the sixteenth century, which strained resources and forced the less fortunate to leave in search of better opportunities in cities, and by the pressures of "seigneurial reaction," plague, and famine during the more difficult times of the seventeenth century.

Another intrusion which undermined the traditional cohesion of the community was the increased presence of royal officials. For centuries, elected councils, drawn from every part of the population, had run village affairs throughout Europe. In the late seventeenth century, however, these councils began to disappear as outside forces—in some cases a nearby lord, but more often government officials—asserted their control over the localities. Tax gatherers and army recruiters were now familiar figures throughout Europe. Although they were often the target of peasant rebellions, they were also welcomed when, for example, they distributed food during a famine. Their long-term influence, however, was the creation of a new layer of outside authority in the village, which was another cause of the division and fragmentation that led many to flee to the city.

As these outside intrusions gathered force, the interests of the local lord, who traditionally had defended the village's autonomy and had offered help in times of need, also changed. Nobles were beginning to look more and more to royal courts and capital cities, rather than to their local holdings, for position and power. The natural corollary was the "seigneurial reaction," with lords treating the villages they dominated as sources of income and increasingly distancing themselves from the inhabitants. Their commitment to charitable works declined, and they tended more and more to leave the welfare of the local population to church or government officials.

CITY LIFE

As village life changed, the inhabitants who felt forced to leave headed for the city—an impersonal place where, instead of joining a cohesive population, they found themselves part of a mingling of peoples that was breaking down the isolation of local areas. The growing cities needed ever wider regions to provide them with food

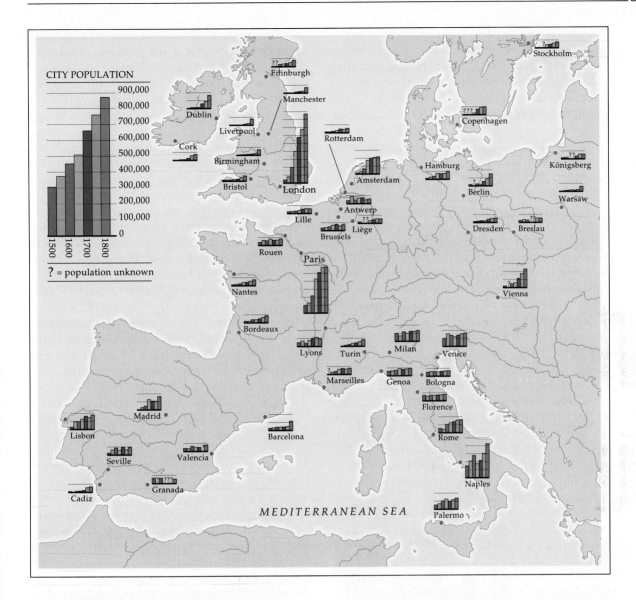

Map 16.3 THE GROWTH OF CITIES, 1500–1800
In addition to the remarkable rise in the population of Europe's cities, particularly after 1550, this map reveals the northward shift in the distribution of the largest cities: in 1500, three of the four largest were in Italy; in 1700, only one.

and goods, and they attracted the many who could not make ends meet in the countryside. Long-distance communications became more common, especially as localities were linked into national market and trade networks, and in the cities the new immigrants met others from distant villages.

There was no question that a city was far a more chaotic place than a rural community. Even if one of its areas, such as a parish, seemed distinct and even cohesive—some parishes, for example, were associated with a single trade—urban society in general was fragmentary and disorganized. A city's craft guilds gave structure to artisans and shopkeepers, regulating their lives and providing welfare, but less than half the population could join a guild. The rest did odd jobs or turned to crime.

The chief attraction of cities was the wide variety of economic opportunity: for women, in such areas as selling goods and processing food;

for men, in construction, on the docks, and in delivery services. But employment was unpredictable, and citizens did not have community support to fall back on in hard times as they did in the village. Even the forms of recreation and enjoyment were different in the city.

POPULAR CULTURE IN THE CITY

One major difference between country and town was the level of literacy. Only in urban areas were there significant numbers of people who could read: It has been estimated that in cities perhaps a third of adult males were literate by 1700. Not only was reading necessary for commerce but it had been strongly encouraged by the Reformation, with its insistence that the faithful read the Bible for themselves. This stimulus ensured that literacy also rose among women, who increasingly became pupils at the growing number of schools in Europe (though they were still not admitted to universities). It has been estimated that as many as 20 percent of the adult women in cities were able to read.

These changes had a notable effect on urban life. There was now a readership for newspapers, which became common in the late seventeenth century, as did the coffeehouses in which they were often read. Theater and opera became popular entertainments, with women for the first time taking stage roles and able to obtain performances for plays they had written. When the English royal official Samuel Pepys hired a new servant in the 1660s, he made sure she could play an instrument so that she could take part in the family's musical evenings. Sales of books multiplied, often because they served a popular audience, and they gave wide circulation to traditional favorites like travel stories and lives of saints as well as to the latest ideas of science.

MAGIC AND RITUALS

Although in the countryside cultural patterns looked different—with lower literacy, simpler recreations, and more visible religiosity—there was one area of popular culture in which the outlook of the city and the village was remarkably similar: the belief in magic. The townspeople may have seemed more sophisticated, but the basic assumption they shared with their country cousins was that nature and their own lives were controlled by mysterious forces, and there was little they could do to ensure their own well-being. The world was full of spirits, and all one could do was

Der Kramer und der newe Zeitung.

*Ihr lieb gutte fromme Herren.
Die ihr hört Neuwe Zeittung gern.
Habt ring ihr euch ein gangenhaussen.
Die wil ich euch al har verkauffen.
Halles war teuls nichts erlogen.
Darte Sawerkramer nit betrogen.
Groß wunder jtzt auch neuw Zeittung
Von der war nit aber dieser seiten.
Aus Frauckreich vnd aus Jngellandt.
Geb ich bericht euch aller handt.*

*Ich trag nicht brieff wie ander botten.
Die euch ver irren vnd euwer spotten.
Was ich hab ist nach allem lust.
Drey tag ver logen vor der quit.
Dieß mag ihr alles glauben frey.
Will allen noch ist frisch vnd neuw.
Auch geb geb euch so leichten sin.
Weil ich des gelts bedarff so wach.
Mein eyn waar ist sehr boß vnd schwach.
Ist zeit des ist ein anders machs.*

*Auff das geh ich die waar mehr.
Von der Hertzog von giesen sehr.
Dab ich mit ganzem fleiß gethan.
Der auch frantzösisch hosen an.
Drei das ir weiß so wil ich ich.
Die bleiben seien lang kramen nich.
Drumb sind euch mein fuchsschwantz gewiß.
Kauff heim das ist so euwer geld.
Au sehern ist der gangen schern.
Was ich mein für ein vogel sein.*

Gedruckt bey Jacob Kempner

► *Anonymous Woodcut*
THE NEWSVENDOR
The ancestor of the regularly published newspaper was the occasional single sheet describing the latest news or rumors. Printers would produce a few hundred copies and have them sold by street vendors whenever they had an event of some importance to describe: a battle, the death of a ruler, or some fantastic occurrence like the birth of a baby with two heads. As cities and the potential readership grew, the news sheets expanded; by the seventeenth century they had distinctive names and began to appear every week.

encourage the good, defend oneself against the evil, and hope that the good would win. Nothing that happened—a calf dying, lightning striking a house—was accidental. Everything had a purpose. Any unusual event was an omen, part of a larger plan, or the action of some unseen force.

"Charivari" To strengthen themselves against trouble, people used whatever help they could find. They organized special processions and holidays to celebrate good times such as harvests, to lament misfortunes, to complain about oppression, or to poke fun at scandalous behavior. These occasions, known as "rough music" in England and "charivari" in France, often used the theme of "the world turned upside down" to make their point. In the set pieces in a procession, a fool might be dressed up as a king, a woman might be shown beating her husband, or a tax collector might appear hanging from a tree. Whether ridiculing a dominating wife or lamenting the lack of bread, the community was expressing its solidarity in the face of difficulty or distasteful behavior through these rituals. It was a way of letting off steam and declaring public opinion.

The potential for violence was always present at such gatherings, especially when religious or social differences became entangled with other resentments. The viciousness of ordinary Protestants and Catholics toward one another—it was not uncommon for one side to mutilate the dead bodies of the other—revealed a frustration and aggressiveness that was not far below the surface. When food was scarce or new impositions had been ordered by their rulers, peasants and townspeople needed little excuse to show their anger openly. Women took the lead, not only because they had firsthand experience of the difficulty of feeding a family but also because troops were more reluctant to attack them. This tradition was still alive in 1789, in the early days of the French Revolution, when a band made up primarily of women marched from Paris to the royal court at Versailles to demand bread.

The Belief in Magic Ordinary people also had other outlets for their frustrations. Recognizing their powerlessness in the face of outside forces, they resorted to their version of the magic that

the literate were finding so fashionable at this very time. Where the sophisticated patronized astrologers, paying handsomely for horoscopes and advice about how to live their lives, the peasants and the poor consulted popular almanacs or sought out "cunning men" and wise women for secret spells, potions, and other remedies for their anxieties. Even religious ceremonies were thought of as being related to the rituals of the magical world, in which so-called white witches—the friendly kind—gave assistance when a ring was lost, when a new bride could not become pregnant, or when the butter would not form out of the milk.

WITCHCRAFT

Misfortunes, in other words, were never just plain bad luck; rather, there was intent behind everything that happened. Events were *willed*, and if they turned out badly, they must have been willed by the good witch's opposite, the evil witch. Such beliefs often led to cruel persecutions of innocent victims—usually helpless old women, able to do nothing but mutter curses when taunted by neighbors and easy targets if someone had to be blamed for unfortunate happenings.

This quest for scapegoats naturally focused on the most vulnerable members of society, such as Jews or, in the case of witches, women. Accusations were often directed at a woman who was old and alone, with nobody to defend her. She was feared because she seemed to be an outsider, or not sufficiently deferential to her supposed betters. It was believed that witches read strange books and knew magic spells, an indication of what many regarded as inappropriate and dangerous levels of literacy and learning for a woman.

Witch-hunts In the sixteenth and seventeenth centuries, the hunt for witches intensified to levels never previously reached. This has been called the era of "the great witch craze," and for good reason. There were outbursts in every part of Europe, and tens of thousands of the accused were executed. Dozens of men, most of them clerics, made witch-hunting a full-time profession, and persuaded civic and other government au-

▶ *Hans Baldung Grien*
Witches, Woodcut
This woodcut, by the German artist Grien, shows the popular image of witches in early
modern Europe. One carries a potion while flying on a goat. The others put together
the ingredients for a magic potion in a jar inscribed with mystical symbols. The fact that
witches were thought to be learned women who could understand magic was another
reason they were feared by a Europe that expected women to be uneducated.

thorities to devote their resources to stamping out this threat to social and religious stability. Suspects were almost always tortured, and it is not too surprising that they usually "confessed" and implicated others as servants of the devil. The practices that were uncovered varied—in some areas witches were said to dance with the devil, in others to fly on broomsticks, in others to be possessed by evil spirits who could induce dreadful (and possibly psychosomatic) symptoms—but the punishment was usually the same: burning at the stake. And the hysteria was infectious. One accusation could trigger dozens more until entire regions were swept with fear and hatred.

FORCES OF RESTRAINT

By the middle of the seventeenth century the wave of assaults on witches was beginning to recede (*see box,* below). Social and political leaders came to realize how dangerous to authority campaigns against witches could become, especially when accusations were turned against the rich and privileged classes. Increasingly, therefore, cases were not brought to trial, and when they were, lawyers and doctors (who approached the subject from a different point of view than the clergy) cast doubt on the validity of the testimony. Gradually, excesses were restrained and control was reestablished; by 1700 there was only a trickle of new incidents.

The decline in accusations of witchcraft reflected not only the more general quieting down of conflict and upheaval in the late seventeenth century but also the growing proportion of Europe's population that was living in cities. Here, less reliant on the luck of good weather, people could feel themselves more in control of their own fates. If there were unexpected fires, there were fire brigades; if a house burned down, there might even be insurance—a new protection for

A Witness Analyzes the Witch Craze

Although for most Europeans around 1600 witchcraft was real—a religious problem caused by the devil—there were a few observers who were beginning to think more analytically about the reasons for the rapid spread of accusations. One such observer was a clergyman named Linden, who was attached to the cathedral of the great city of Trier in western Germany. His description of a witch-hunt in the Trier region ignored the standard religious explanations.

"Inasmuch as it was popularly believed that the continued sterility of many years was caused by witches, the whole area rose to exterminate the witches. This movement was promoted by many in office, who hoped to gain wealth from the persecution. And so special accusers, inquisitors, notaries, judges, and constables dragged to trial and torture human beings of both sexes and burned them in great numbers. Scarcely any of those who were accused escaped punishment. So far did the madness of the furious populace and the courts go in this thirst for blood and booty that there was scarcely anybody who was not smirched by some suspicion of this crime. Meanwhile, notaries, copyists and innkeepers grew rich. The executioner rode a fine horse, like a noble of the court, and dressed in gold and silver; his wife competed with noble dames in the richness of her array. A direr pestilence or a more ruthless invader could hardly have ravaged the territory than this inquisition and persecution without bounds. Many were the reasons for doubting that all were really guilty. At last, though the flames were still unsated, the people grew poor, rules were made and enforced restricting the fees and costs of examinations, and suddenly, as when in war funds fail, the zeal of the persecutors died out."

From George L. Burr (ed.), "The Witch Persecutions," *Translations and Reprints from the Original Sources of European History,* III (Philadelphia: University of Pennsylvania, 1902), pp. 13–14.

individuals that was spreading in the late 1600s. A process that has been called the "disenchantment" of the world—growing skepticism about spirits and mysterious forces, and greater self-reliance—was under way.

Religious Discipline The churches played an important part in the suppression of the traditional reliance on magic. In Catholic countries the Counter Reformation produced better-educated priests who were trained to impose official doctrine instead of tolerating unusual local customs. Among Protestants, ministers were similarly well educated and denounced magical practices as idolatrous or superstitious. And both camps treated passion and enthusiasm with suspicion. Habits did not change overnight, but gradually ordinary people were being persuaded to abandon old fears and beliefs.

Even at the level of popular culture, therefore, Europeans had reason to feel, by the late seventeenth century, that a time of upheaval and uncertainty was over. A sense of confidence and orderliness was returning, and in intellectual circles the optimism seemed justified by the achievements of science. In fact, there arose a scholarly dispute around 1700, known as "the battle of the books," in which one side claimed, for the first time, that the "moderns" had outshone the "ancients." Using the scientists as their chief example, the advocates of the "moderns" argued—in a remarkable break with the reverence for the past that had dominated medieval and Renaissance culture—that advances in thought were possible and that one did not always have to accept the superiority of antiquity. Such self-confidence made it clear that, in the world of ideas as surely as in the world of politics, a period of turbulence had given way to an era of renewed assurance and stability.

Recommended Reading

Sources

*Drake, Stillman (tr. and ed.). *Discoveries and Opinions of Galileo*. 1957. The complete texts of some of Galileo's most important works.

*Hall, Marie Boas (ed.). *Nature and Nature's Laws: Documents of the Scientific Revolution*. 1970. A good collection of documents by and about the pioneers of modern science.

Studies

Braudel, Fernand. *Capitalism and Material Life 1400–1800*. Miriam Kochan (tr.). 1973. A classic, pioneering study of the structure of daily life in early modern Europe.

*Burke, Peter. *Popular Culture in Early Modern Europe*. 1978. A lively introduction to the many forms of expression and belief among the ordinary people of Europe.

*Available in paperback.

*Butterfield, Herbert. *The Origins of Modern Science*. 1949. An elegantly written history of the scientific revolution that conveys its excitement.

Drake, Stillman. *Galileo*. 1980. The standard biography of a central figure in the scientific revolution.

Frame, Donald M. *Montaigne: A Biography*. 1965. The best biography of this influential thinker.

*Ginzburg, Carlo. *The Cheese and the Worms: The Cosmos of a Sixteenth-Century Miller*. John and Ann Tedeschi (trs.). 1980. A remarkable account, focusing on the beliefs of a man who lived in a small northern Italian town, which brings to life the extraordinary variety of the popular culture of the time.

*Gutmann, Myron P. *Toward the Modern Economy: Early Industry in Europe 1500–1800*. 1988. A clear survey of recent work on economic development in this period.

*Hibbard, Howard, *Bernini*. 1965. A graceful account of the life and work of the artist who was the epitome of the Baroque.

*Krailsheimer, Alban. *Pascal*. 1980. The best brief biography, with good discussions of the life, the science, and the turn to religion.

*Kuhn, Thomas S. *The Structure of Scientific Revolutions.* 1962. A suggestive interpretation of the reasons the scientific revolution developed and took hold.

*Ladurie, Emmanuel Le Roy. *The Peasants of Languedoc.* John Day (tr.). 1966. A brilliant evocation of peasant life in France in the sixteenth and seventeenth centuries.

*Levack, Brian P. *The Witch-Hunt in Early Modern Europe.* 1987. An excellent survey of the belief in witchcraft and its consequences.

Maland, David. *Culture and Society in Seventeenth-Century France.* 1970. This survey of art, drama, and literature contains a good discussion of the rise of Classicism.

Palisca, Claude. *Baroque Music.* 1968. The best survey of this period in the history of music.

*Popkin, Richard H. *The History of Scepticism from Erasmus to Descartes.* 1964. Taking one strand in European thought as its subject, this lively study places both Montaigne and Descartes in a new perspective.

Rabb, Theodore K. *Renaissance Lives.* 1993. Brief biographies of 15 people, both famous and obscure, who lived just before and during this period.

*Shearman, John. *Mannerism.* 1968. The best short introduction to a difficult artistic style.

Tapié, V. L. *The Age of Grandeur: Baroque Art and Architecture.* A. R. Williamson (tr.). 1960. Although concentrating primarily on France and Austria, this is the most comprehensive survey of this period in art.

*Thirsk, Joan. *Economic Policy and Projects: The Development of a Consumer Society in Early Modern England.* 1978. A fascinating study of changing social and economic patterns.

*Thomas, Keith. *Religion and the Decline of Magic.* 1976. The most thorough account of popular culture yet published, this enormous book, while dealing mainly with England, treats at length such subjects as witchcraft, astrology, and ghosts in a most readable style.

*Westfall, Richard S. *The Construction of Modern Science: Mechanisms and Mechanics.* 1971. A cogent analysis of a central theme in the history of the scientific revolution.

———. *Never at Rest: A Biography of Isaac Newton.* 1980. The best introduction to the life and work of the great scientist.

White, Christopher. *Rembrandt and His World.* 1964. A brief but wide-ranging introduction to the artist's work and life.

———. *Rubens and His World.* 1968. As good on Rubens as the previous title is on Rembrandt.

LOUIS XIV AND HIS FAMILY
Louis XIV (seated) is shown here in full regal
splendor surrounded by three of his heirs. On his
right is his eldest son, on his left is his eldest
grandson, and, reaching out his hand, his eldest
great-grandson, held by his governess. All three of
these heirs died before Louis, and thus they never
became kings of France.

CHAPTER SEVENTEEN

THE EMERGENCE OF THE EUROPEAN STATE SYSTEM

THE acceptance of the strong central governments that emerged out of the crisis of the mid-seventeenth century was a victory not merely for kings but for an entire way of organizing political structures. As a result of huge increases both in the demands of warfare and in the availability of resources, bureaucracies had mushroomed, and their presence was felt throughout Europe. Yet no central administration, however powerful, could function without the support of the nobles who ruled the countryside. Regional loyalties had dominated European society for centuries, and only a regime that drew on those loyalties could hope to maintain the support of its subjects. The political structures that were developed during the century following the 1650s were therefore as much the work of a nobility that had long been accustomed to exercising authority, but was now prepared to find new ways of exerting its influence, as they were the product of ambitious princes. There were conflicts between monarchs and their subjects, to be sure, but it was clear to the leaders of society during the century following the crisis of the 1640s and 1650s that state building required a common effort to create political, social, military, financial, and religious structures that would enable governments to function more effectively. The result was the emergence of a set of institutions and practices that have remained essential to the functioning of the modern state ever since.

I. The Creation of Absolutism in France

VERSAILLES

The setting in which a central government operated often told a great deal about its power and its methods. Philip II in the late sixteenth century had created, at the Escorial outside Madrid, the first isolated palace that controlled a large realm. A hundred years later, the French King Louis XIV (1643–1715) created at Versailles, near Paris, a far more elaborate court as the center of an even larger and more intrusive bureaucracy than Philip's. It was as if the isolation of government and the exercise of vast personal power went hand in hand.

The king moved the court out of the capital in the 1680s and eventually, at a cost of half a year's royal income, transformed a small château his father had built at Versailles, 12 miles from Paris, into the largest building in Europe. There he could enjoy in peace the splendor and the daily round of ceremonies, centered on himself, which exalted his majesty. His very name, "Sun King" was a means of self-aggrandizement, symbolized by coins that showed the rays of the sun falling first on Louis and then by reflection onto his subjects, who thus owed life and warmth to their monarch.

Louis himself was almost never alone. Every nobleman of any significance in France spent time each year at Versailles, not only to maintain access to royal patronage and governmental af-

▶ **THE PALACE OF VERSAILLES IN 1668**
This painting shows Versailles not long before Louis decided to move there; he was soon to begin an enormous expansion into the gardens at the back which more than doubled the size of the buildings. In this scene, the royal coach, with its entourage, is just about to enter the château.

fairs but also to demonstrate the countrywide support for the system of rule Louis was developing. Historians have called this process the domestication of the aristocracy, in which great lords who had once drawn their status primarily from their lineage or their lands came to regard service to the throne as the best route to power. But the benefits cut both ways. The king gained the services of qualified and influential administrators, and they gained privileges and rewards without the uncertainties that had accompanied their traditional resistance to central control.

Absolutism   The belief that the monarch was absolute—that all power emanated from his unlimited authority—was based on a widely held theory known as the divine right of kings. This theory, which derived from the fact that kings were anointed with holy oil at their coronations, had long asserted that the monarch was God's representative on earth. Taken to an extreme, as it was at Versailles, this view justified absolute power and regarded treason as blasphemy. The leading advocate of the theory, Bishop Bossuet, called Louis God's lieutenant and argued that the Bible itself endorsed absolutism. In reality, the king worked in close partnership with the nobles to maintain order, and he often (though not always) felt obliged to defend their local authority as a reinforcement of his own power. Nevertheless, the very notion that the king not only was supreme but could assert his will with armies and bureaucracies of unprecedented size gave absolutism both an image and a reality that set it apart from previous systems of monarchical rule. This was, at last, a force that could hold together and control the increasingly complex interactions of regions and interest groups that made up a state.

Court Life   The visible symbol of Louis' absolutism was his court at Versailles. Here the leaders of France assembled, and around them swirled the most envied social circles of the time. From the court emanated the policies and directives that increasingly affected the lives of the king's subjects and also determined France's relations with other states.

At Versailles, too, French culture was shaped by the king's patronage of those artists and writers who appealed to the royal taste. For serious drama and history, Louis turned to the playwright and writer Racine (1639–1699); for comedy, to the theatrical producer and playwright Molière (1622–1673); and for opera and the first performances of what we now call ballet, to the composer Lully (1632–1687). Moreover, all artistic expression, from poetry to painting, was regulated by royal academies that were founded in the seventeenth century; backed by the king's authority, they laid down rules for what was acceptable in such areas as verse forms or architectural style. When the famous Italian sculptor and architect Bernini, for example, came to Paris to design part of a royal palace and fashion a sculpture of the king, both works were rejected as overly ornate. Official taste was all that counted. The dazzling splendor of Versailles had to be achieved in strict conformity to rules of dignity and gravity that were considered the only means of exalting the king. Yet everything was done on a scale and with a magnificence that no other European ruler could match, though many tried.

Paris and Versailles   The one alternative to Versailles as a center of society and culture was Paris, and indeed it has been suggested that the split between the court and the capital was one of the divisions between government and people that was eventually to lead to the French Revolution. A particularly notable difference was in the role of women. Versailles was overwhelmingly a male society. Women achieved prominence only as royal mistresses in Louis' early years, or as the creators of a rigidly pious atmosphere in his last years. They were also essential to the highly elaborate rituals of civility and manners that developed at Versailles. But they were allowed no independent initiative in social or cultural matters. In Paris, by contrast, women established and dominated the salons that promoted easy conversation, a mixture of social backgrounds, and forms of expression—political discussion and ribald humor, for example—that were not acceptable at the staid and sober court. Yet the contrasts were not merely between the formalities of a palace and the relaxation of a salon. Even before the king moved to Versailles, he banned as improper one of Molière's comedies, *Tartuffe*, which mocked excessive religious devoutness. It took

▶ *Antoine Watteau*
FÊTE IN THE PARK, 1718
The luxurious life of the nobility during the eighteenth century is captured in this scene of men and women in fine silks, enjoying a picnic in a lovely park setting.

five years of reworking by Molière before Louis would allow the play to be performed (1669), and it then became a major hit in Paris; significantly, though, it was never to be a favorite at court.

GOVERNMENT

Absolutism was not merely a device to satisfy royal whims, for Louis was a gifted administrator and politician who used his power for state building. In creating or reorganizing government institutions, he strengthened his authority at home and increased his ascendancy over his neighbors. The most durable result of the absolutist regime he commanded was that the French state won control over three crucial activities: the use of armed force, the formulation and execution of laws, and the collection and expenditure of revenue. These functions, in turn, depended on a centrally controlled bureaucracy responsive to royal orders and efficient enough to carry them out in distant provinces over the objections of local groups.

Although it was impossible to suppress all vested interests and local loyalties, an absolute monarch's bureaucracy was supposed to be insulated from outside pressure by the king's power to remove and transfer appointees. This independence was also promoted by training programs, improved administrative methods, and the use of experts wherever possible—both in the central bureaucracy and in provincial offices. Yet the system could not have functioned without the cooperation of local aristocrats, who were encouraged to use the power and income they derived from official positions to strengthen central authority.

Louis as King At the head of this structure, Louis XIV carried off successfully a dual function that few monarchs had the talent to sustain: He was both king in council and king in court. Louis the administrator coexisted with Louis the courtier, who hunted, cultivated the arts, and indulged in huge banquets. In his view, the two roles went together, and he held them in balance. Among his numerous imitators, however, the easier side of absolutism, court life, consumed an excessive share of a state's resources and became an end in itself. The effect was to give prestige to the leisure pursuits of the upper classes while sapping the energies of influential figures. Louis was one of the few who avoided sacrificing affairs of state to regal pomp.

Like court life, government policy under Louis XIV was tailored to the aim of state building. As he was to discover, there were limits to his absolutism; the resources and powers at his disposal were not endless. But until the last years of his reign, they served his many purposes extremely well (*see box*, below). Moreover, Louis had superb support at the highest levels of his administration—ministers whose viewpoints differed but whose skills were carefully blended by their ruler.

Colbert and Louvois The king's two leading advisers until the late 1680s were Jean-Baptiste Colbert and the marquis of Louvois. Colbert was a financial wizard who regarded a mercantilist policy as the key to state building. He believed that the government should give priority to increasing France's wealth. As a result, he felt that the chief danger to the country's well-being was the United Provinces, Europe's great trader state, and that royal resources should be poured into the navy, manufacturing, and shipping. By contrast, Louvois, the son of a military administrator, consistently emphasized the army as the foundation of France's power. He believed that the country was threatened primarily by land—by the Holy Roman Empire on its flat, vulnerable northeast frontier—and thus that resources should be allocated to the army and to border fortifications.

Louis XIV on Kingship

From time to time, Louis XIV put on paper brief accounts of his actions: For example, he wrote some brief memoirs in the late 1660s. These reflections about his role as king were intended as a guide for his son and indicate both his high view of kingship and the seriousness with which he approached his duties. The following are extracts from his memoirs and other writings.

"Homage is due to kings, and they do whatever they like. It certainly must be agreed that, however bad a prince may be, it is always a heinous crime for his subjects to rebel against him. He who gave men kings willed that they should be respected as His lieutenants, and reserved to Himself the right to question their conduct. It is His will that everyone who is born a subject should obey without qualification. This law, as clear as it is universal, was not made only for the sake of princes: it is also for the good of the people themselves. It is therefore the duty of kings to sustain by their own example the religion upon which they rely; and they must realize that, if their subjects see them plunged in vice or violence, they can hardly render to their person the respect due to their office, or recognize in them the living image of Him who is all-holy as well as almighty.

"It is a fine thing, a noble and enjoyable thing, to be a king. But it is not without its pains, its fatigues, and its troubles. One must work hard to reign. In working for the state, a king is working for himself. The good of the one is the glory of the other. When the state is prosperous, famous, and powerful, the king who is the cause of it is glorious; and he ought in consequence to have a larger share than others do of all that is most agreeable in life."

From J. M. Thompson, *Lectures on Foreign History, 1494–1789* (Oxford: Blackwell, 1956), pp. 172–174.

FOREIGN POLICY

Louis tried to balance these goals within his overall aims—to expand France's frontiers and to assert his superiority over other European states. Like the magnificence of his court, his power on the international scene served to demonstrate "la gloire" (the glory) of France. But his effort to expand that power prompted his neighbors to form coalitions and alliances of common defense, designed to keep him in check. From this response was to emerge the concept of a state system and the notion of a balance of power among the states of Europe.

In his early years Louis relied heavily on Colbert, who moved gradually toward war with the Dutch when all attempts to undermine their control of French maritime trade failed. But the war (1672–1678) was a failure, and so the pendulum swung toward Louvois. In the early 1680s Louis adopted the marquis' aims and asserted his right to a succession of territories on France's northeast border. No one claim seemed important enough to provoke his neighbors to military action, especially since the Holy Roman Emperor, Leopold I, was distracted by a resumption in 1682 of war with the Turks in the East. The result was that France was able to annex large segments of territory until, in 1686, a league of other European states was formed to restrain Louis' growing power (see Map 17.1).

Map 17.1 THE WARS OF LOUIS XIV
A. Louis XIV's aggressive aims took his troops to many areas of Europe.
B. The main conflict was on France's eastern border, where Louis made small but significant gains.

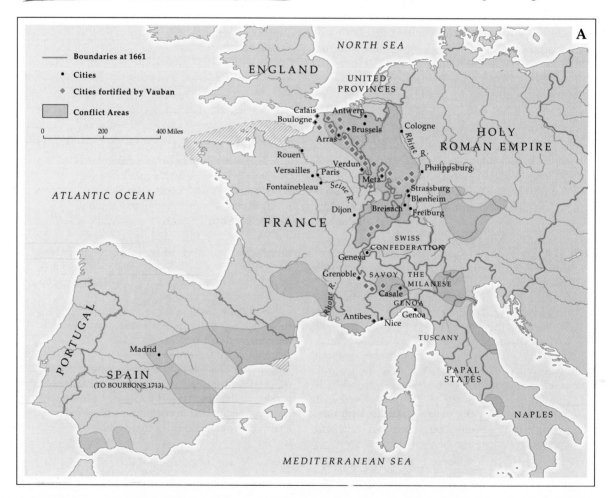

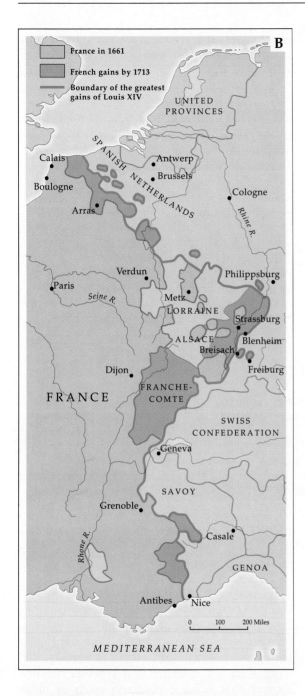

B

France in 1661

French gains by 1713

Boundary of the greatest gains of Louis XIV

UNITED PROVINCES

SPANISH NETHERLANDS

Calais
Antwerp
Brussels
Boulogne
Cologne
Arras
Rhine R.

Verdun
Philippsburg
Paris
Seine R.
Metz
LORRAINE
Strassburg
ALSACE
Blenheim
Breisach
Dijon
Freiburg
FRANCHE-COMTE

FRANCE

SWISS CONFEDERATION

Geneva

SAVOY

Grenoble

Rhone R.

Casale

GENOA

Antibes
Nice

0   100   200 Miles

MEDITERRANEAN SEA

Louis versus Europe The leaders of the league were William III of the United Provinces and Emperor Leopold. Leopold was prepared to join the struggle because, even though his war with the Turks was to continue until 1699, the fighting turned in his favor after 1683, when his troops broke a Turkish siege of Vienna. And six years later William became a far more redoubtable foe when he gained the English throne. The league finally went to war to put an end to French expansion in 1688, and when Louis began to lose the territories he had gained in the 1680s, he decided to seek peace and remove Louvois from power in 1690, though the war did not end until 1697. But the respite did not last long. Four years later France became involved in a bitter war that brought famine, wretched poverty, and humiliation. Louis was now seeking the succession to the Spanish throne for his family, with no regard for the terrible consequences of the fighting. This final, ruinous enterprise revealed both the new power of France and its limits. By launching an all-out attempt to establish his own and his country's supremacy in Europe, Louis showed that he felt capable of taking on the whole of the continent; but by then he no longer had the economic and military base at home or the weak opposition abroad to ensure success.

Economic strains had begun to appear in the 1690s, when shattering famines throughout France reduced tax revenues and the size of the work force, even as enemies began to unite abroad. Louis had the most formidable army in Europe—400,000 men by the end of his reign—but both William and Leopold believed he could be defeated by a combined assault, and they led the attack in the final showdown when the Habsburg king of Spain, Charles II, died without an heir in 1700.

There were various possible claimants to the Spanish throne, and Charles himself had changed his mind a number of times, but at his death his choice was Philip, Louis XIV's grandson (see the genealogical table on p. 540). Had Louis been willing to agree not to unite the thrones of France and Spain and to allow the Spanish empire to be opened (for the first time) to foreign traders, Charles's wish might well have been respected. But Louis refused to compromise, and in 1701 William and Leopold created the so-called Grand Alliance, which declared war on France the following year. The French now found themselves fighting virtually all of Europe in a war over the Spanish succession, not only at home but also overseas, in India, Canada, and the Caribbean.

Led by two brilliant generals—the English-

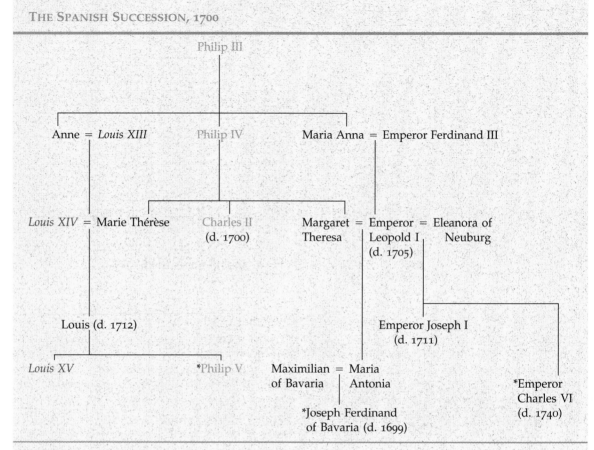

THE SPANISH SUCCESSION, 1700

Note: Names in blue = Kings of Spain; Names in red = Kings of France.
*People designated at various times as heirs of Charles II.

man John Churchill, duke of Marlborough, and the Austrian Prince Eugène—the Grand Alliance won a series of smashing victories. France's hardships were increased by a terrible famine in 1709. Although the criticism of his policies now became fierce, and dangerous rebellions erupted, the Sun King retained his hold over his subjects. Despite military disaster he was able to keep his nation's borders intact and the Spanish throne for his grandson (though he had to give up the possibility of union with France and end the restrictions on trade in the Spanish empire) when peace treaties were signed at Utrecht in 1713 and 1714. When it was all over, Louis' great task of state building, both at home and abroad, had withstood the severest of tests: defeat on the battlefield.

DOMESTIC POLICY

The assertion of royal supremacy at home was almost complete by the time Louis came to power, but he extended centralized control to religion and social institutions. Both the Protestant Huguenots and the Catholic Jansenists interfered with the spiritual and confessional uniformity that Louis considered essential in an absolutist state. As a result, pressures against them mounted steadily. In 1685 Louis revoked the Edict of Nantes, now almost a century old, which had granted Protestants limited toleration, and he forced France's 1 million Huguenots either to leave the country (four-fifths did) or to convert to Catholicism. This was a political rather than a religious step, taken to promote unity despite the economic consequences that followed the departure of a vigorous and productive minority.

Jansenism was more elusive. It had far fewer followers, and it was a movement that emphasized spiritual values within Catholicism. But the very fact that it challenged the official Church emphasis on ritual and was condemned by Rome made it a source of unrest. Even more unsettling was its success in gaining support among the magistrate class—the royal officers in the parlements, who had to register all royal edicts before they became law. The Parlement of Paris was the only governmental institution that offered Louis any real resistance. The issues over which it caused trouble were usually religious, and the link between parlementaire independence and Jansenism gave Louis more than enough reason for displeasure. He razed the Jansenists' headquarters, the Abbey of Port-Royal, and persuaded the pope to issue a bull condemning Jansenism. He was prevented from implementing the bull—over parlementaire opposition—only by his death in 1715.

Control and Reform The drive toward uniformity that prompted these actions was reflected in all of domestic policy. Louis kept in check what little protest arose in the parlements and either forbade or overruled their efforts to block his decrees; major uprisings by peasants in central France in the 1690s and 1700s were ruthlessly suppressed, as were all disturbances; Parisian publishers came under bureaucratic supervision; and the *intendants*, the government's chief provincial officers, were given increased authority, particularly to supply the ever-growing money and recruitment needs of the army.

At the outset of his rule, Louis used his power to improve France's economy. In this, he followed a pattern familiar from earlier monarchs' reigns: an initial burst of reform measures designed to cure the country's economic ills, which were gradually forgotten because foreign policy demanded instant funds. In the early years, under Colbert's ministry, major efforts were made to stimulate manufacturing, agriculture, and home and foreign trade. Some industries, notably those involving luxuries, like the silk production of Lyons, received considerable help and owed their prosperity to royal patronage. Colbert also tried, not entirely effectively, to reduce the crippling effects of France's countless internal tolls. These were usually nobles' perquisites, and they could multiply the cost of goods shipped any distance. The government divided the country into a number of districts, within which shipments were to be toll-free, but the system never removed the worst abuses. Louis also tried to boost foreign trade, at first by financing new overseas trading companies and later by founding new port cities as naval and commercial centers. He achieved notable success only in the West Indies, where sugar plantations became a source of great wealth.

THE CONDITION OF FRANCE

Louis' success in state building was remarkable, and France became the envy of Europe. Yet ever since the Sun King's reign, historians have recalled the ruination caused by famine and war during his last years and have contrasted his glittering court with the misery of most French people. Taxes and rents rose remorselessly, and in many regions the hardships were made worse by significant declines in the population. Particularly after the famines of the 1690s and 1709, many contemporaries remarked on the dreadful condition of France's peasants.

The reign of Louis XIV can thus be regarded as the end of an era in the life of the lower classes. By pushing his need for resources to its limits, he inflicted a level of suffering that was not to recur, because governments increasingly came to realize that state building depended on the welfare and support of their people. In the eighteenth century, though there was still much suffering to come, the terrible subsistence crises, with their cycles of famine and plague, came to an end, largely because of official efforts to distribute food in starving areas and to isolate and suppress outbreaks of plague. Thus, although the hand of the central government was heavier in 1715 than a hundred years before, it was becoming more obviously a beneficent as well as a burdensome force. And the Counter Reformation Church, growing in strength since the Council of Trent, also had a more salutary influence as religious struggles died away, for it brought into local parishes better-educated and more dedicated priests who, as part of their new commitment to service, exerted themselves to calm the outbreaks of witchcraft and irrational fear that had swept the countryside for centuries. Despite the strains Louis had caused, therefore, his absolutist authority was now firmly in place and could ensure a dominant European role for a united and powerful France.

FRANCE AFTER LOUIS XIV

Although the Sun King created a model for absolutism in partnership with his nobility, the traditional ambitions of the nobles reasserted themselves after he died in 1715, leaving a child as his heir. The duke of Orléans, Louis XIV's nephew, who became regent until 1723, was committed to giving authority to the aristocracy. He also restored the parlements to political power and replaced royal bureaucrats with councils composed of leading members of the nobility. The scheme was a failure because the councils were unable to govern effectively. The parlements, however,

would never again surrender their power to veto royal legislation. They became a rallying point for those who opposed centralization and wished to limit the king's powers.

Finance was also a serious problem for the government, because of the debts left by Louis XIV's wars. A brilliant Scottish financier, John Law, suggested an answer: a government-sponsored central bank that would issue paper notes,

▶ *P. D. Martin*
PROCESSION AFTER LOUIS XV'S CORONATION AT RHEIMS, 1722
This magnificent scene, in front of the cathedral where French kings traditionally were crowned, gives one a sense of the throngs who came to celebrate the day in 1722 when Louis XV officially came of age and received his crown. Paintings depicting royal virtue were erected around the cathedral, and Louis himself (in red on a white horse just to the right of center) was preceded by a flag covered with his symbol, the fleur-de-lis. The other flags remind us that this was an occasion for international pageantry.

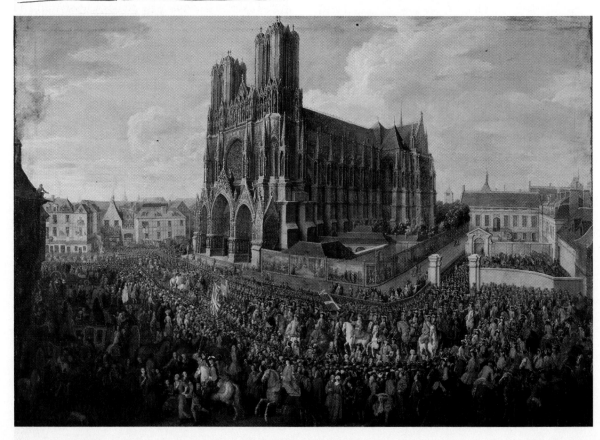

expand credit, and encourage investment in a new trading company for the French colonies. By tying the bank to this company, the Company of the Occident, a venture that promised subscribers vast profits from the Louisiana territory in North America, Law set off an investment boom. But the public's greed soon pushed prices for the company's stock to insanely high levels. A bust was inevitable, and when it came, in 1720, the entire scheme of bank notes and credit collapsed.

Fleury   The same political and financial problems were to plague France, in different forms, throughout the eighteenth century, until the leaders of the French Revolution sought radical ways to solve them in the 1790s. Yet the uncertainties of the regency did give way to a long period of stability after 1726, when Louis XV gave almost unlimited authority to his aging tutor and adviser, Cardinal Fleury. Cautious, dedicated to the monarchy, and surrounded by talented subordinates, Fleury made absolutism function quietly and effectively, and enabled France to recover from the setbacks that had marked the end of Louis XIV's reign. Fleury's tenure coincided with abundant harvests, slowly rising population, and increased commercial activity.

Political Problems   Fleury was able to contain the ambitions of the governing class. When he died in 1743 at the age of 90, these pressures exploded. War hawks immediately plunged France into the first of several unsuccessful wars with its neighbors that strained French credit to the breaking point. At home royal authority likewise deteriorated. Having no one to replace Fleury as unofficial prime minister, Louis XV put his confidence in a succession of advisers, some capable and some mediocre. But he did not back them when attacks from factions at court became uncomfortable. Uninterested in government, the king avoided confrontations and neglected affairs of state, devoting his energy instead to the pleasures of the hunt and court ceremony.

Although Louis XV provided weak leadership, France's difficulties were not simply personal but rather structural. The main problems—special privileges, political power, and finance—posed almost impossible challenges. Governments that levy new taxes arbitrarily seem despotic, even if the need for them is clear

and the distribution equitable. One of France's soundest taxes was the *vingtième*, or twentieth, which was supposed to tap the income of all parts of French society roughly equally. The nobility and clergy, however, all but evaded the tax. Naturally, aggressive royal ministers wanted to remedy that situation. In the 1750s, for example, an effort was made to put teeth into the *vingtième*'s bite on the clergy's huge wealth. But the effort merely ruined the career of the capable royal official who devised it. The clergy resisted furiously; and the parlements joined the attack against the "despotism" of a crown that would arbitrarily tax its subjects. Thus the privileged groups not only blocked reforms but also made the monarch's position more difficult by taking up opposition and a rhetoric of liberty as they fought to limit royal absolutism.

Despite the demands of these special interests, the eighteenth century was a time of notable advance for Europe's most populous and wealthy state. As we will see, France in this period experienced remarkable expansion in population, in the rural economy, in commerce, and in empire building. No one knew at the time that the failures of reforming royal ministers in the mid-1700s foretold a stalemate that would help bring the old regime crashing down.

II. The Creation of Absolutism outside of France

THE HABSBURGS AT VIENNA

The pattern set at Versailles was repeated at the court of the Habsburg Leopold I, the Holy Roman Emperor (1658–1705). Heir to a reduced inheritance that gave him control over only Bohemia, Austria, and a small part of Hungary, Leopold still maintained a splendid establishment. His plans for a new palace, Schönbrunn, that was to have outshone Versailles were modified only because of a lack of funds. And his promotion of the court as the center of all political and social life turned Vienna into what it had never been before: a city for nobles as well as small-time traders.

Nevertheless, Leopold did not display the pretensions of the Sun King. He was a younger son and had come to the throne only because of the death of his brother. Indecisive, retiring, and deeply religious, he had no fondness for the bravado Louis XIV enjoyed. He was a composer of some talent, and his patronage laid the foundation for the great musical culture that was to be one of Vienna's chief glories. But he did inherit considerable royal authority, which he sought to expand—though unlike Louis XIV he relied on a small group of leading nobles to devise policy and run his government.

Government Policy   The Thirty Years' War that ended in 1648 had revealed that the elected head of the Holy Roman Empire could no longer control the princes who nominally owed him allegiance. In his own dominions, however, he could maintain his control with the cooperation of his nobility. The Privy Council, which in effect ran Leopold's domain, was filled largely with members of aristocratic families, and his chief advisers were always prominent nobles. To make policy, he carefully consulted each of his ministers and then, even when all of them agreed, came to decisions with agonizing slowness.

Unlike the other courts of Europe, Schönbrunn did not favor only native-born aristocrats. The leader of Austria's armies during the Turks' siege of Vienna in 1683 was Charles, duke of Lorraine, whose duchy had been taken over by the French. His predecessor as field marshal had been an Italian, and his successor was to be one of the most brilliant soldiers of the age, Prince Eugène of Savoy. They became members of the Austrian nobility only when Leopold gave them titles within his own dominions, but they all fitted easily into the aristocratic circles that controlled the government and the army.

Eugène   Prince Eugène (1663–1736) was a spectacular symbol of the aristocracy's continuing dominance of politics and society. A member of one of Europe's most distinguished families, he had been raised in France but found himself passed over when Louis XIV awarded army commissions, perhaps because he had been intended for the Church. Yet he was determined to have a military career, and he volunteered to serve the

Austrians in the war with the Turks that, following the siege of Vienna, was to expand Habsburg territory in the Balkans by the time peace was signed in 1699 (see Map 17.2). Eugène's talents quickly became evident: He was field marshal of Austria's troops by the time he was 30. Over the next 40 years, as intermittent war with the Turks continued, he became a decisive influence in Habsburg affairs. Though foreign-born, he was the minister primarily responsible for the transformation of Vienna's policies from defensive to aggressive.

Until the siege of Vienna by the Turks in 1683, Leopold's cautiousness kept Austria simply holding the line, both against Louis XIV and against the Turks. In the 1690s, however, he tried a bolder course at Eugène's urging and in the process laid the foundations for a new Habsburg empire along the Danube River: Austria-Hungary. He helped create the coalition that defeated Louis in the 1700s, intervened in Italy so that his landlocked domains could gain an outlet to the sea, and began the long process of pushing the Turks out of the Balkans. Leopold did not live to see the advance more than started, but by the time of Eugène's death, the Austrians' advances against the Turks had brought them within a hundred miles of the Black Sea.

Yet the local power of the aristocracy tempered the centralization of Leopold's dominions. Louis XIV supported his nobles if they worked for him; Leopold, by contrast, gave them influence in the government without first establishing control over all his lands. The nobility did not cause the Habsburgs as much trouble as they had during the Thirty Years' War, but Leopold had to limit his ambitions outside Austria. Moreover, as Austrians came increasingly to dominate the court, the nobles of Hungary and Bohemia reacted by clinging stubbornly to their local rights. Thus Leopold's was an absolutism under which the nobility retained far more autonomous power—and a far firmer base of local support—than was the case in France, despite the centralization he achieved during his reign.

THE HABSBURGS AT MADRID

In Spain the Habsburgs had little success in state building either at home or abroad. The king,

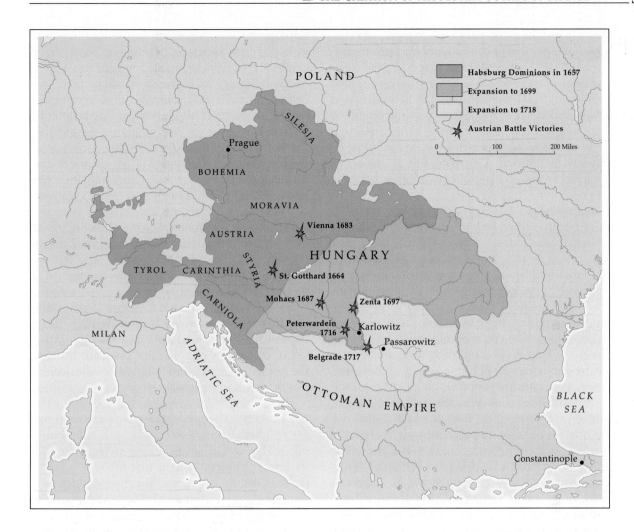

Map 17.2 THE AUSTRIAN EMPIRE, 1657–1718
The steady advance of the Habsburgs into the Balkans was marked by a succession of victories; their gains were confirmed by treaties with the Turks at Karlowitz (1699) and Passarowitz (1718).

Charles II (1665–1700), was a sickly man, incapable of having children; and the War of the Spanish Succession seriously reduced the inheritance he left. Both the southern Netherlands and most of Italy passed to the Austrian Habsburgs, and Spain's overseas possessions often paid little notice to the homeland.

The Spanish nobility was even more successful than the Austrian in turning absolutism to its advantage. In 1650 the crown had been able to recapture Catalonia's loyalty only by granting the province's aristocracy virtual autonomy, and this pattern recurred throughout Spain's territories. Parasitic, unproductive nobles controlled the regime, often for personal gain. The country fell into economic and cultural stagnation, subservient to a group of powerful families, with its former glory visible in the eighteenth century only in its strong navy.

THE HOHENZOLLERNS AT BERLIN

The one new power that emerged to prominence during the age of Louis XIV was Brandenburg-Prussia, and here again state building was made possible by a close alliance between a powerful ruler and his nobles. Frederick William of Hohenzollern (1640–1688), known as the "great elector," ruled scattered territories that stretched 700 miles from Cleves, on the Rhine, to a part of Prussia on the Baltic. That so fragmented and disconnected a set of lands could be shaped into a major European power was a testimony to the political abilities of the Hohenzollerns. The process began when, taking advantage of the uncertainties that followed the Thirty Years' War, Frederick William made his territories the dominant principality in northern Germany and at the same time strengthened his power over his subjects.

Foreign Policy His first task was in foreign affairs, because when he became elector, the troops of the various states that were fighting the Thirty Years' War swarmed over his possessions at will. Frederick William realized that by determination and intelligent planning, even a small prince could emerge from these disasters in a good position *if* he had an army. With some military force at his disposal, he could become a useful ally for the big powers, who could then help him against his neighbors; while at home he would have the strength to crush his opponents.

By 1648 Frederick William had 8000 troops, and he was backed by both the Dutch and the French as a possible restraint on Sweden in northern Europe during the negotiations leading to the treaty of Westphalia in that year. Without having done much to earn new territory, he did very well in the peace settlement, and he then took brilliant advantage of wars around the Baltic in the 1650s to confirm his gains by switching sides at crucial moments. In the process, his army grew to 22,000 men, and he began to use it to impose his will on his own lands. The fact that the army was essential to all Frederick William's successes—both at home and abroad—was to influence much of Prussia's and thus also Germany's subsequent history.

Domestic Policy The role of the military in establishing the elector's supremacy was apparent throughout Brandenburg-Prussia's society. In 1653 the Diet of Brandenburg met for the last time, sealing its own fate by giving Frederick William the right to raise taxes without its consent. The War Chest, the office in charge of financing the army, took over the functions of a treasury department and collected government revenue even when the state was at peace. The

implementation of policies in the localities was placed in the hands of war commissars—who originally were responsible for military recruitment, billeting, and supply in each district of Brandenburg-Prussia, but who now became the principal agents of all government departments.

Apart from the representative assemblies, Frederick William faced real resistance only from the long-independent cities of his realm. Accustomed to going their own way because authority had been fragmented in the empire for centuries, and especially during the Thirty Years' War, city leaders were dismayed when the elector began to intervene in their affairs. Yet once again sheer intimidation swept opposition aside. The last determined effort to dispute his authority arose in the rich city of Königsberg, which allied with the Estates General of Prussia to refuse to pay taxes. But this resistance was crushed in 1662, when Frederick William marched into the city with a few thousand troops. Similar pressure brought the towns of Cleves into submission after centuries of proud independence.

The Junkers The nobles were the main supporters and beneficiaries of the elector's state building. It was, in fact, an alliance between the nobility and Frederick William that made it possible for the Diet, the cities, and the representative assemblies to be undermined. The leading families saw their best opportunities for the future in cooperation with the central government, and both in the representative assemblies and in the localities, they worked to establish absolutist power—that is, to remove all restraints on the elector. The most significant indicator of the nobles' success was that by the end of the century, two tax rates had been devised, one for cities and one for the countryside, to the great advantage of the latter.

Not only did the nobles staff the upper levels of the elector's army and bureaucracy, but they also won new prosperity for themselves. Particularly in Prussia, the support of the elector enabled them to reimpose serfdom and consolidate their land holdings into vast, highly profitable estates. This was a major grain-producing area, and they made the most of its economic potential. To maximize profits, they eliminated intermediaries not only by growing but also by distributing their produce themselves. Efficiency became their hallmark, and their wealth was soon famous throughout the Holy Roman Empire. Known as Junkers (from the German for young lord, *jung herr*), these Prussian entrepreneurs were probably the most successful group of European aristocrats in pursuing economic and political power.

Frederick III Unlike Louis in France, Frederick William had little interest in court life. The Berlin court became the focus of society only under his son, Elector Frederick III, who ruled from 1688. The great elector himself was more interested in organizing his administration, increasing tax returns, building his army, and imposing his authority at home and abroad. He began the development of his capital, Berlin, into a cultural center—he founded what was to become one of the finest libraries in the world, the Prussian State Library—but this was never among his prime concerns. His son, by contrast, had little interest in state building, but he did enjoy princely pomp and he encouraged the arts with enthusiasm.

Frederick III lacked only one attribute of royalty: a crown. When Emperor Leopold I, who still had the right to confer titles in the empire, needed Prussia's troops during the War of the Spanish Succession, he gave Frederick, in return, the right to call himself "king in Prussia," and the title soon became "king of Prussia." At a splendid coronation in 1701, Elector Frederick III of Brandenburg was crowned King Frederick I, and thereafter his court could feel itself the equal of the other monarchical settings of Europe.

Frederick determinedly promoted social and cultural glitter. He made his palace a center of art and polite society to compete, he hoped, with Versailles. A construction program beautified Berlin with new churches and huge public buildings. He also established an Academy of Sciences and persuaded the most famous German scientist and philosopher of the day, Gottfried Wilhelm von Leibniz, to become its first president. All these activities obtained generous support from state revenues, as did the universities of Brandenburg and Prussia. By the end of his reign in 1713, Frederick had given his realm a throne, celebrated artistic and intellectual activity, and an elegant aristocracy at the head of social and political life.

PETER THE GREAT AT ST. PETERSBURG

One of the reasons the new absolutist regimes of the late seventeenth and eighteenth centuries seemed so different from their predecessors was that many of them consciously created new settings for themselves. Versailles, Schönbrunn, and Berlin were all either new or totally transformed sites for royal courts. But only one of the autocrats of the period went so far as to build an entirely new capital: Tsar Peter I (the Great) of Russia (1682–1725), who named the new city St. Petersburg after his patron saint.

The Tsar's Rule None of the state-building rulers of the period had Peter's terrifying energy or ruthless determination to exercise absolute control. This he made clear when he destroyed ecclesiastical independence in one stunning gesture: He simply did not replace the patriarch of the Russian Church when he died in 1700. The government took over the monasteries, using their enormous income for its own purposes, and appointed a procurator (at first an army officer) to supervise all religious affairs. The church was, in effect, made a branch of government.

In ruling, Peter virtually ignored the Duma, the traditional advisory council, and concentrated instead on his bureaucracy. He carried out change after change until he had created an administrative complex many times larger than the one he had inherited. In this effort he determinedly copied Western models—notably Prussia, where nobles ran the bureaucracy and the army, and Sweden, where a complex system of government departments had been created. Peter organized his administration into similar departments: Each had either a specialized function, such as finance, or responsibility for a geographic area, such as Siberia. The result was an elaborate but unified hierarchy of authority, rising from local agents of the government through provincial officials up to the staffs and governors of 11 large administrative units and finally to the leaders of the regime in the capital. Peter began the saturating bureaucratization that characterized Russia from that time on.

Russian Society The tsar's policies laid the foundations for a two-class society that persisted until the twentieth century. Previously, a number of ranks had existed within both the nobility and the peasantry, and a group in the middle was seen sometimes as the lowest nobles and sometimes as the highest peasants. Under Peter such mingling disappeared. All peasants were reduced to one level, subject to a new poll tax, military conscription, and forced public work, such as the building of St. Petersburg. Below them were serfs, whose numbers were increased by legislation restricting their movement. Peasants had a few advantages over serfs, such as the freedom to move, but their living conditions were often equally dreadful. Serfdom itself spread throughout all areas of Peter's dominions and became essential to his state building, because on royal lands as well as the estates of the nobles, serfs worked and ran the agricultural enterprise that was Russia's economic base.

At the same time, Peter created a single class of nobles by substituting status within the bureaucracy for status within the traditional hierarchy of titles. In 1722 he issued a table of bureaucratic ranks that gave everyone a place according to the office he held. Differentiations still existed, but they were no longer unbridgeable, as they had been when family was the decisive determinant of status. The result was a more controlled social order and greater uniformity than in France or Brandenburg-Prussia. The Russian aristocracy was the bureaucracy, and the bureaucracy the aristocracy.

▶ **PETER THE GREAT AT ST. PETERSBURG**
In the eighteenth century Peter the Great of Russia outstripped the grandeur of other monarchs of the period by erecting an entirely new city for his capital. St. Petersburg was built by forced labor of the peasants under Peter's orders; they are shown here laying the foundations for the city.

The Nobility But this was not a voluntary alliance between nobles and government, such as existed in the West; in return for his support and his total subjection of the peasantry, Peter *required* the nobles to provide officials for his bureaucracy and officers for his army. When he began the construction of St. Petersburg, he also demanded that the leading families build splendid mansions in his new capital. In effect, the tsar offered privilege and wealth in exchange for conscription into public service. Thus there was hardly any sense of partnership between nobility and throne: The tsar often had to use coercion to ensure that his wishes were followed.

On the other hand, Peter did a good deal to build up the nobles' fortunes and their ability to control the countryside. It has been estimated that by 1710 he had put under the supervision of great landowners more than 40,000 peasant and serf households that had formerly been under the crown. And he was liberal in conferring new titles—some of them, such as count and baron, copies of German examples.

Western Models In creating an aristocratic society at his court, Peter mixed imitations of what he admired in the West with native developments. He sought to apply Western models because he felt that Russia had much to learn from the advances its neighbors had made. To observe these achievements at firsthand, Peter traveled secretly through France, England, and the Netherlands in 1697 and 1698, paying special attention to economic, administrative, and military practices (such as the functioning of a Dutch shipyard). Many of his initiatives derived from this journey, including his importation of Western court rituals and his founding of an Academy of Sciences in 1725. Italian artists were brought to Russia, along with Scandinavian army officers, German engineers, and Dutch shipbuilders, not only to apply their skills but also to teach them to the Russians. St. Petersburg, the finest example of a city built in eighteenth-century Classical style, is mainly the work of Italians. But gradually, the Russians took over their own institutions—military academies produced native officers, for example—and by the end of Peter's reign the nobles had little need of foreign experts to help run the government. Peter the Great had laid the foundations for the aristocratic society that would rule his people for 200 years.

The purpose of these radical internal changes was to assert the tsar's power both at home and abroad. Peter established a huge standing army, more than 300,000 strong by the 1720s, and imported the latest military techniques from the West. One of Peter's most cherished projects, the creation of a navy, had limited success, but there could be no doubt that he transformed Russia's capacity for war and its position among European states. He extended Russia's frontier to the south and west, beginning the destruction of Sweden's empire at the battle of Poltava in 1709 and following this triumph by more than a decade of advance into Estonia, Livonia, and Poland. The very vastness of his realm justified Peter's drive for absolute control, and by the time of his death he had made Russia the dominant power in the Baltic and a major influence in European affairs.

III. *Alternatives to Absolutism*

THE TRIUMPH OF THE GENTRY IN ENGLAND

The absolutist regimes provided one model of political and social organization, but an alternative model—equally committed to uniformity, order, and state building—was also created in the late seventeenth century: governments dominated by aristocrats or merchants. The contrast between the two was noted by contemporary political theorists, especially opponents of absolutism, who compared France unfavorably with England. And yet the differences were often less sharp than the theorists suggested, mainly because the position of the aristocracy was similar throughout Europe.

England's King Charles II (1660–1685), for example, seemed to have powers similar to those of his father, Charles I. He still summoned and dissolved Parliament, he made all appointments in the bureaucracy, and he signed every law. But he no longer had royal prerogative courts like Star Chamber, he could not arrest a member of

Parliament, and he could not create a new seat in the Commons. Even two ancient prerogatives, the king's right to dispense with an act of Parliament for a specific individual or group and his right to suspend an act completely, proved to be empty when Charles II tried to exercise them. Nor could he raise money without parliamentary assent: Instead, he was given a fixed annual income, financed by a tax on beer.

The Gentry and Parliament   The real control of the country's affairs had by this time passed to the group of substantial landowners known as the *gentry*. In a country of some 5 million people, perhaps 15,000 to 20,000 families were considered gentry—leaders of the various localities throughout England, though they had neither titles of nobility nor special privileges. They represented about 2 percent of the population, a proportion that was probably not much different from the percentage of titled and privileged nobles in the populations of other states.

The gentry were distinguished from the nobles of other countries by the right they had won in England's civil war to determine national policy through Parliament. Whereas in France, Austria, Brandenburg-Prussia, and Russia nobles depended on the monarch for power and were subservient to him, the English revolution had made the gentry an independent force. Their authority was now hallowed by custom, upheld by law, and maintained by the House of Commons, a representative assembly that was both the supreme legislature and the body to which the executive government was ultimately responsible.

Not all the gentry took a continuing, active interest in affairs of state, and no more than a few of their number sat in the roughly 500-member House of Commons. Even the Commons did not exercise a constant influence over the govern-

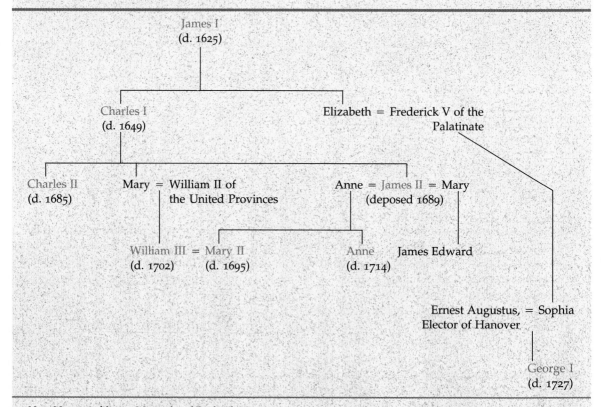

THE ENGLISH SUCCESSION FROM THE STUARTS TO THE HANOVERIANS

James I
(d. 1625)

Charles I
(d. 1649)

Elizabeth = Frederick V of the
Palatinate

Charles II
(d. 1685)

Mary = William II of
the United Provinces

Anne = James II = Mary
(deposed 1689)

William III = Mary II
(d. 1702)   (d. 1695)

Anne   James Edward
(d. 1714)

Ernest Augustus, = Sophia
Elector of Hanover

George I
(d. 1727)

Note: Names in blue = Monarchs of England.

ment; nevertheless, the ministers of the king had to be prominent representatives of the gentry, and they had to be able to win the support of a majority of the members of the Commons. Policy was still set by the king and his ministers. But the Commons had to be persuaded that the policies were correct; without parliamentary approval, a minister could not long survive.

The Succession Despite occasional conflicts, this structure worked relatively smoothly throughout Charles II's reign. But the gentry feared that Charles's brother, James, next in line for the succession and an open Catholic, might try to restore Catholicism in England. To prevent this, they attempted in 1680 to force Charles to exclude James from the throne. But in the end the traditional respect for legitimacy, combined with some shrewd maneuvering by Charles, ensured that there would be no tampering with the succession.

Soon, however, the reign of James II (1685–1688) turned into a disaster. Elated by his acceptance as king, James rashly attempted the very encouragement of Catholicism that the gentry feared. This was a direct challenge to the gentry's newly won power, and in the fall of 1688, seven of their leaders—including members of some of the oldest families in the realm—invited the Protestant ruler of the United Provinces, William III, to invade the country and take over the throne. Although William landed with an army half the size of the king's, James, uncertain of his support, decided not to risk battle and fled to exile in France.

William and Mary The new king gained what little title he had to the crown through his wife, Mary (see the genealogical table on p. 550), and the couple were proclaimed joint monarchs by Parliament early in 1689. The Dutch ruler had taken the throne primarily to bring England into his relentless struggles against Louis XIV, and he willingly accepted a settlement that confirmed the essential position of Parliament in the government. A Bill of Rights settled the future succession to the throne, defined Parliament's powers, and established basic civil rights; an Act of Toleration put an end to all religious persecution, though members of the official Church of England were still the only people allowed to vote,

The Metropolitan Museum of Art

▶ *Sir Joshua Reynolds*
LADY SMITH AND HER CHILDREN
The quiet serenity and assurance of England's gentry in the eighteenth century is apparent in all their portraits, whether the head of the household is present or, as in this case, only his wife and children.

sit in Parliament, hold a government office, or attend a university; and in 1694 a statute laid down that Parliament had to meet and new elections had to be held at least once every three years.

Despite the restrictions on his authority, William exercised strong leadership following this so-called Glorious Revolution.* He guided England into a new, aggressive foreign policy, picked the ministers favorable to his aims, and

---

*It got its name because it was bloodless and confirmed the supremacy of Parliament once and for all.

never let Parliament sit when he was out of the country to pursue the war or to oversee Dutch affairs. In his reign, too, the central government grew significantly, creating new positions, new powers, and new opportunities for political patronage. But unlike James, William recognized his limits. He tried to have the Bill of Rights reversed and a standing army established, but he gave up when these efforts provoked major opposition. By and large, therefore, the gentry were content to let the king rule as he saw fit. For they had shown by their intervention in 1688 that ultimately they controlled the country.

POLITICS AND PROSPERITY

The political system in England now reflected the social system: A small elite controlled both the country's policy and its institutions. This group was far from united, however, as was apparent when a party system began to appear in Parliament during Charles II's reign. On one side were the Whigs, who opposed royal prerogatives and Catholicism and were largely responsible for the attempt to exclude James II from the throne. Their rivals, the Tories, stood for the independence and authority of the crown and favored a ceremonial and traditional Anglicanism.

Party Conflict Because the Whigs had been the main advocates of the removal of James II, they controlled the government for most of William III's reign. They supported his war against Louis XIV (1689–1697), since France harbored both James and his followers, the romantic but ill-fated Jacobites, who kept trying to restore James's line to the throne. This was a relatively nonpartisan issue, but the Tories and Whigs still competed fiercely for voters. Because the qualification for voting—owning land worth 40 shillings a year in rent—had become less restrictive as a result of inflation (which made 40 shillings a fairly modest sum) and was not to be raised to a higher minimum until the late 1700s, England now had what would be its largest electorate before the 1860s. Almost 5 percent of the population (more than 15 percent of adult males) could vote, and although results were usually determined by powerful local magnates, fierce politicking was common. And in the election of 1700 there was a major upset: The Tories won by opposing a resumption of war against Louis XIV, who seemed to have been contained since the end of the previous war in 1697.

Within two years, however, and despite William's death in 1702, England was again at war with France, this time over the Spanish succession; and soon the Whigs were again in control of the government. The identification of the parties with their attitude toward war continued until 1710, when weariness over the fighting brought the Tories back into power. They persuaded Queen Anne, William's successor, to make peace with France at Utrecht in 1713; and it was only because the Tories made the mistake of negotiating with the rebel Jacobites after Anne died in 1714 without an heir that they lost power. Anne's successor was a German prince, the elector of Hanover, who founded the new Hanoverian dynasty as George I (1714–1727). Since they firmly supported his succession, the Whigs regained control of the government when George came to the throne. They then entrenched themselves, and under the leadership of Robert Walpole, they began almost a century of political ascendancy.

The Sea and the Economy At the same time, England was winning for itself unprecedented prosperity and laying the foundations of its world power. Its navy made it the premier force on the sea, the decisive victor over France during the worldwide struggle of the early eighteenth century. Overseas, new colonies were founded, and the empire expanded steadily. When England and Scotland joined into one kingdom in 1707, the union created a Great Britain ready to exercise a worldwide influence.

The economic advances were equally remarkable. A notable achievement was the establishment of the Bank of England in 1694. The bank was given permission to raise money from the public and then lend it to the government at a favorable 8 percent interest. Within 12 days its founders raised more than a million pounds, demonstrating not only the financial security and stability of England's government but also the commitment of the elite to the country's political structure. London was becoming the financial capital of the world, and British merchants were gaining control over maritime trade from East Asia to North America. Significantly, the benefits of this boom also helped the lower levels of society.

English Society There is little doubt that with the possible exception of the Dutch, ordinary English people were better off than their equivalents elsewhere in Europe. Compared with the sixteenth century, there was little starvation. The system of poor relief may often have been inhumane in forcing the unfortunate to work in horrifying workhouses, but it did provide them with the shelter and food that they had long lacked. It is true that thousands still found themselves unable to make a living in their home villages each year and were forced by poverty to take to the roads. And the many who ended up in London hardly improved their situation. The stream of immigrants was driving the capital's population toward half a million, and the city contained frightful slums and miserable crime-ridden sections. Even a terrible fire in London in 1666 did little to improve the appallingly crowded living conditions because the city was rebuilt much as before, the only notable additions being a series

▸ *William Hogarth*
THE POLLING, 1754

Despite the high reputation of the polling day as the central moment in the system of representative government, Hogarth's depiction of it in this scene suggests how corrupt and disheveled the process of voting was. The sick and the foolish are among the mob of voters; the central figure looks bewildered as he is told what to do; on the right a bloated official cannot decide whether a voter should be allowed to take his oath on the Bible with a wooden hand; and all ignore the distress of Britannia, the symbol of Britain, in her coach on the left.

The Metropolitan Museum of Art

▶ *Samuel Scott*
THE BUILDING OF WESTMINSTER BRIDGE, CA. 1742
The elegance, but not the squalor, of city life in the
eighteenth century is suggested by this view of
Westminster.

of splendid churches. But the grimness should not be overdrawn.

After more than a century of inflation, the laborer could once again make a decent living, and artisans were enjoying a growing demand for their work. Higher in the social scale, more men had a say in the political process than before, and more found opportunities for advancement in the rising economy—in trade overseas, in the bureaucracy, or in the expanding market for luxury goods. It has been estimated that in 1730 there were about 60,000 adult males in what we would recognize as the professions. England also had better roads than any other European country and a more impartial judicial system.

Yet none of these gains could compare with those that the gentry made. In fact, many of the improvements, such as fair administration of justice, were indirect results of what the upper classes had won for themselves. The fruits of progress clearly belonged primarily to the gentry.

ARISTOCRACY IN THE UNITED PROVINCES, SWEDEN, AND POLAND

In the Dutch republic, the succession of William III to the offfice of Stadholder in 1672 seemed to be a move toward absolutism. As he led the successful resistance to Louis XIV in war (1672–1678), he increasingly concentrated government in his own hands. Soon, however, the power of merchants and provincial leaders in the Estates General reasserted itself. William did not want to sign a peace treaty with Louis when the French invasion failed. He wanted instead to take the war into France and reinforce his own authority by keeping the position of commander in chief. But the Estates General, led by the province of Holland, ended the war.

A decade later it was only with the approval of the Estates General that William was able to seek the English throne, and he had to leave the representative assemblies that governed the two countries separate. When William died without an heir, his policies were continued by his close friend Antonius Heinsius, who held the same position of grand pensionary of Holland that Jan de Witt had once occupied; but the government was in effect controlled by the Estates General.

This representative assembly now had to preside over the decline of a great power. In finance and trade, the Dutch were gradually overtaken by the English, while in the war against Louis XIV, they had to support the crippling burden of maintaining a land force, only to hand command over to England. Within half a century Frederick II of Prussia was to call the republic "a dinghy boat trailing the English man-of-war."

Dutch Society The aristocrats of the United Provinces differed from the usual European pattern. Instead of ancient families and bureaucratic dynasties, they boasted merchants and mayors. The prominent citizens of the leading cities were the backbone of the Dutch upper classes. Moreover, social distinctions were less prominent than in any other country of Europe. The elite was composed of hard-working financiers and traders, richer and more powerful but not essentially more privileged or leisured than those farther down the social ladder. The inequality discussed in much eighteenth-century political writing—the special place nobles had, often including some immunity from the law—was far less noticeable in the United Provinces. There was no glittering court, and although here as elsewhere a small group controlled the country, it did so for largely economic ends and in different style.

Sweden The Swedes created yet another nonabsolutist model of state building. Here the nobles emerged from a long struggle with the king as the country's dominant political force. During the reign of Charles XI (1660–1697) the monarchy was able to force the great lords to return to the state the huge tracts of land they had received as rewards for loyalty earlier in the century. Since Charles stayed out of Europe's wars, he was able to conserve his resources and avoid relying on the nobility as he strengthened the smoothly running bureaucracy he had inherited from Gustavus Adolphus.

His successor, Charles XII (1697–1718), however, revived Sweden's tradition of military conquest. He won land from Peter the Great, but then made the fatal decision to invade Russia. Defeated at the battle of Poltava in 1709, Charles had to retreat and watch helplessly as the Swedish empire was dismembered. By the time he was killed in battle nine years later, his neighbors had

begun to overrun his lands, and in treaties signed from 1719 to 1721, Sweden reverted to roughly the territory it had had a century before.

Naturally the nobles took advantage of Charles XII's frequent absences to reassert their authority. They ran Sweden's highly efficient government while he was campaigning and forced his successor, Queen Ulrika, to accept a constitution that gave the Riksdag effective control over the country. The new structure was consciously modeled on England's political system, and the nobility came to occupy a position like England's gentry—leaders of society and the shapers of its politics. A splendid court arose, and Stockholm became one of the more elegant and cultured aristocratic centers in Europe.

Warsaw fared less well. In fact, the strongest contrast to the French political and social model in the late seventeenth century was Poland. The sheer chaos and disunity that plagued Poland until it ceased to exist as a state in the late eighteenth century were the direct result of continued dominance by the old landed aristocracy, which blocked all attempts to centralize the government. There were highly capable kings in this period—notably John III, who achieved Europewide fame by relieving Vienna from the Turkish siege in 1683. These monarchs could quite easily gather an enthusiastic army to fight, and fight well, against Poland's many foes: Germans, Swedes, Russians, and Turks. But once a battle was over, the ruler could exercise no more than nominal leadership. Each king was elected by the assembly of nobles and had to agree not to interfere with the independence of the great lords, who were growing rich from serf labor on fertile lands. The crown had neither revenue nor bureaucracy to speak of, and so the country continued to resemble a feudal kingdom, where power remained in the localities.

CONTRASTS IN POLITICAL THOUGHT

The intensive development of both absolutist and antiabsolutist forms in the seventeenth century stimulated an outpouring of ideas about the nature and purposes of government. Two Englishmen, in particular, developed theories about the basis of political authority that have been influential ever since.

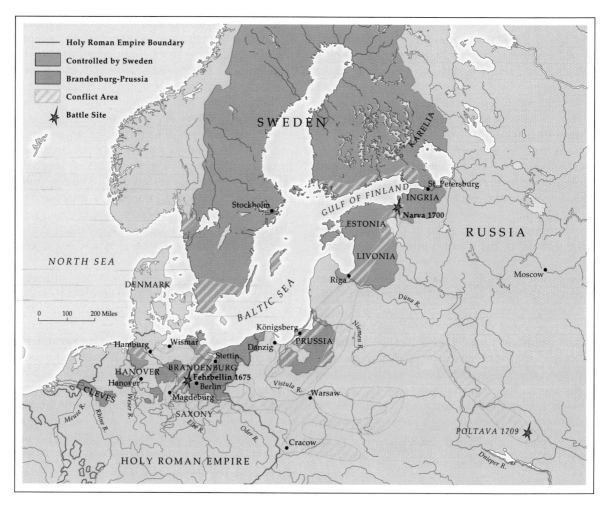

Map 17.3 **CONFLICT IN THE BALTIC AREA, 1660–1721**
The fighting around the Baltic eventually destroyed Sweden's power in northern Europe; the new powers were to be Brandenburg-Prussia and Russia.

Hobbes A story has it that Thomas Hobbes, a brilliant scholar from a poor family who earned his livelihood as the tutor to aristocrats' sons, once picked up a copy of Euclid's *Elements* and opened the book in the middle. The theorem on that page seemed totally without foundation, but it rested on a proof in the preceding theorem. Working his way backward, Hobbes discovered himself finally having to accept no more than the proposition that the shortest distance between two points is a straight line. He thereupon resolved to use the same approach to analyze political behavior. The story is probably apocryphal because as a young man Hobbes was secretary to Francis Bacon, who doubtless gave him a taste for science. Yet it does capture the essence of his masterpiece, *Leviathan* (1651), which began with a few premises about human nature from which Hobbes deduced major conclusions about political forms.

Hobbes's premises, drawn from his observation of the strife-ridden Europe of the 1640s and 1650s, were stark and uncompromising. People, he asserted, are selfish and ambitious; consequently, unless they are restrained, they fight a perpetual war with their fellows. The weak are more cunning and the strong more stupid. Given these unsavory characteristics, the state of nature—which precedes the existence of society—is a state of war, in which life is "solitary, poor, nasty, brutish, and short." Hobbes's conclusion was that the only way to restrain this instinctive aggressiveness is to erect an absolute and sovereign power that will maintain peace. Everyone should submit to the sovereign because the alternative is the anarchy of the state of nature. The moment of submission is the moment of the birth of orderly society.

In a startling innovation, Hobbes suggested that the transition from nature to society is accomplished by a contract that is implicitly accepted by all who wish to end the chaos. The unprecedented feature of the contract is that it is not between ruler and ruled; it is binding only on the ruled. They agree among themselves to submit to the sovereign; the sovereign is thus not a party to the contract and is not limited in any way. A government that is totally free to do whatever it wishes is best equipped to keep the peace, and peace is always better than the previous turmoil.

The power of Hobbes's logic, and the endorsement he seemed to give to absolutism, made his views enormously influential. But his approach also aroused hostility. Although later political theorists were deeply affected by his ideas, many of Hobbes's successors denounced him as godless, immoral, cynical, and unfeeling. It was dislike of his message, not weaknesses in his analysis, that made many people unwilling to accept his views.

Locke John Locke, a quiet Oxford professor who admired Hobbes but sought to soften his conclusions, founded his political analysis in a general theory of knowledge. Locke believed that at birth a person's mind is a *tabula rasa*, a clean slate; nothing, he said, is inborn or preordained. As human beings grow, they observe and experience the world. Once they have gathered enough data through their senses, their minds begin to work on the data. Then, with the help of reason, they perceive patterns, discovering the order and harmony that permeate the universe. Locke was convinced that this underlying order exists and that every person, regardless of individual experi-

Locke on the Origins of Government

The heart of John Locke's **Second Treatise of Civil Government,** *written in the mid-1680s before England's Glorious Revolution but published in 1690, is its optimism about human nature—as opposed to Hobbes's pessimism. In this passage Locke explains why, in his view, people create political systems.*

"If man in the state of nature be so free, if he be absolute lord of his own person and possessions, equal to the greatest, and subject to nobody, why will he part with his freedom, and subject himself to the dominion and control of any other power? To which it is obvious to answer, that though in the state of nature he hath such a right, yet the enjoyment of it is very uncertain, and constantly exposed to the invasions of others. This makes him willing to quit this condition, which, however free, is full of fears and continual dangers; and it is not without reason that he seeks out and is willing to join in society with others, who have a mind to unite, for the mutual preservation of their lives, liberties, and estates, which I call by the general name, property. The great and chief end, therefore, of men's putting themselves under government, is the preservation of their property.

"But though men when they enter into society give up the equality, liberty, and power they had in the state of nature into the hands of society; yet it being only with an intention in every one the better to preserve himself, his liberty, and property, the power of the society can never be supposed to extend further than the common good. And all this to be directed to no other end but the peace, safety, and public good of the people."

From John Locke, *The Second Treatise of Civil Government,* Thomas P. Peardon (ed.) (Indianapolis: Bobbs-Merrill, 1952), Chapter IX, pp. 70–73.

ences, must reach the same conclusions about its nature and structure.

When Locke turned his attention to political thought, he put into systematic form the views of the English gentry and other antiabsolutists throughout Europe. The *Second Treatise of Civil Government*, published in 1690, was deeply influenced by Hobbes. From his great predecessor Locke took the notions that a state of nature is a state of war and that only a contract among the people can end the anarchy that precedes the establishment of civil society. But his conclusions were decidedly different.

Using the principles of his theory of knowledge, Locke asserted that the application of reason to politics demonstrates the inalienability of the three rights of an individual: life, liberty, and property. Like Hobbes, he believed that there must be a sovereign power, but he argued that it has no power over these three natural rights of its subjects without their consent. Moreover, this consent—for levying taxes, for example—must come from a representative assembly of men of property, such as the English Parliament.

The affirmation of property as one of the three natural rights (it was changed to "the pursuit of happiness" in the more egalitarian American Declaration of Independence) is significant. Here Locke revealed himself as the spokesman of the gentry. Only people with a tangible stake in their country have any right to control its destiny, and that stake must be protected as surely as their life and liberty. The concept of liberty remained vague, but it was taken to imply the sorts of freedom, such as freedom from arbitrary arrest, that were outlined in the English Bill of Rights. All Hobbes allowed a person to do was protect his or her life. Locke permitted the overthrow of the sovereign power if it infringed on the subjects' rights—a course the English followed with James II and the Americans with George III.

Locke's prime concern was to defend the individual against the state, a concern that has remained essential to liberal thought ever since (*see box*, p. 557). But it is important to realize that Locke's emphasis on property served the elite better than the mass of society. With Locke to reassure them, the upper classes put their stamp on eighteenth-century European civilization.

IV. The State in the Eighteenth Century

STATE BUILDING

It sometimes seems as if international competition was the main preoccupation of eighteenth-century rulers. But, in fact, competition among states went hand in hand with internal state building. Conflict with rival powers compelled rulers to assert their sovereignty as forcefully as possible within their own borders in order to expand their revenues, armies, and bureaucracies. With the exception of Britain, countries where absolutism failed to develop—such as Sweden and the Netherlands—lost international influence. And Poland was partitioned three times by Russia, Austria, and Prussia, until in 1795 it ceased to exist as a sovereign state. The political consolidation of the eighteenth century, and the state system that was created, put a premium on military and economic power. In the process, the basic map of modern Europe emerged and the centralized character of the major states was confirmed.

The relationship between international rivalry and internal development is well illustrated by Prussia and Austria. In the mid-eighteenth century these two powers were vying to dominate Central Europe, and they instituted reforms so as to wage their struggle more effectively. Each was governed by absolute rulers who built their states by increasing the size of their armies, collecting larger revenues, and developing bureaucracies for their war effort. It did not seem to matter whether the ruler was a modern pragmatist like Frederick II of Prussia or a pious traditionalist like Maria Theresa of Austria. In their own way both understood the demands of the state system.

THE PRUSSIA OF FREDERICK WILLIAM I

Prussia's Frederick William I (1713–1740) was relentless in his pursuit of a strengthened absolutism at home and European-wide influence abroad. Strikingly different from his refined father, this spartan ruler approached affairs of state as all business and little pleasure. He disdained court life, dismissed numerous courtiers, and cut the salaries of those who remained. Uncluttered by royal ceremonies, his days were regulated in timetable fashion as he attempted to supervise everything himself.

Map 17.4 The Expansion of Russia and the Partition of Poland
All three of the powers in Eastern Europe—Prussia, Russia, and Austria—gained territory from the dismemberment of Poland. At the same time, Russia was expanding to the south and east.

The Emphasis on the Military It has been said that Frederick William I organized his state to serve his military power. During his reign the army grew from 38,000 to 83,000, making it the fourth largest in Europe, behind France, Russia, and Austria. While still relying on foreign mercenaries for one-third of his troops, he also instituted a form of conscription. And all his soldiers had to undergo intensive drilling and wear standardized uniforms. Determined to build an effective cadre of professionals, he forbade his subjects to serve in foreign armies and compelled the

sons of nobles to attend cadet schools to learn martial skills and attitudes.

In this military state Frederick William I was the number one soldier. A colorful commander in chief, he maintained a personal regiment of towering grenadiers and always wore a uniform, declaring that he would be buried in it. But he did not intend to die in battle. For all his involvement with military life, he avoided committing his army to battle, and he therefore passed it on intact to his son, Frederick II.

The process of centralization kept pace with the growth of the army. In 1723 a government superagency was created; called the General Directory of Finance, War, and Domains, it united the administration of all functions except justice, education, and religion. Its main task was to coordinate the collection of revenue, expenditures (mostly military), and local administration. The king also put resources into education so as to give the population the basic instruction they needed to serve the state. He made education compulsory for all children where schools existed, and where there were none, he instructed local communities and parents to set them up, though he made no attempt to enforce these decrees. The educational policy was thus more theoretical than practical and had few social consequences. Teachers, for example, were often clergy who held their jobs as sidelines. Uninterested in intellectual pursuits for their own sake, the king allowed the universities to decline; they did not fit his relentless vision of how to build his state.

FREDERICK THE GREAT

Frederick William I's most notable triumph, perhaps, was the grooming of his successor. This was no mean task. Frederick II (1740–1786) seemed opposite in temperament to his father and little inclined to follow in his footsteps. The father was a God-fearing German Protestant. The son disdained German culture and was a deist (see p. 611). Sentimental and artistically inclined, Frederick II was a composer of music who played the flute, wrote poetry, and greatly admired French culture. He even wrote philosophical treatises and corresponded with leading European intellectuals.

Since the Prussian monarchy was mobilizing all its subjects for the tasks of state building, however, the young prince was not exempted. On the contrary, he was forced to work at all levels of the state apparatus so as to experience them directly, from shoveling hay on a royal farm to marching with the troops. The father trained his son for kingship, reshaping his personality, giving him a sense of duty, and toughening him for leadership. Despite Frederick's prolonged resistance, this hard apprenticeship succeeded. In the end, as a modern psychiatrist would put it, the prince identified with the aggressor.

Frederick's Rule When he assumed the throne in 1740, Frederick II was prepared to lead Prussia in a ruthless struggle for power and territory. While his intellectual turn of mind caused him to agonize over moral issues and the nature of his role, he never flinched from exercising power. He did, however, attempt to justify absolutism at home and aggression abroad. He claimed undivided power for the ruler, not because the dynasty had a divine mission but because only absolute rule could bring results. The monarch, he stated, was the first servant of the state. In the long run, he hoped, an enlightened monarch might lead his people to a more rational and moral existence. Some of these objectives, such as religious toleration and judicial reform, could be reached immediately, and in implementing them Frederick gained a reputation as an "enlightened" absolutist.

But these were minor matters. The paramount issue, security, provided the best justification for absolutism. Success here required Prussia to improve its vulnerable geographic position by acquiring more territory, stronger borders, and the power to face other European states as an equal. Until that was achieved, Frederick would not consider the domestic reforms that might disrupt the flow of taxes or men into the army, or provoke his nobility. The capture of territory was his most singular contribution to the rise of Prussia and what earned him his title of Frederick the Great.

By coincidence, the year 1740, when Frederick II came to the throne, was the year when a suitable task for his army presented itself—an attack on the Habsburg province of Silesia. Prussia had no claim to the province; it was simply a wealthy neighboring domain that would expand Prussia's territory and that the Habsburgs were un-

able to defend. Yet the conquest of Silesia brought to a new level the state building begun in Prussia by the great elector in 1648; the reaction also shaped state building in the Habsburg empire.

THE HABSBURG EMPIRE UNDER ATTACK

The Habsburg empire in the eighteenth century was like a dynastic-holding company uniting diverse territories under one crown: Austria, Bohemia, Hungary, and other possessions like the Austrian Netherlands, Lombardy, and Tuscany. The emperors hoped to integrate Austria, Bohemia, and Hungary into a Catholic, centralized, German-speaking superstate. But the traditional representative assemblies in these provinces resisted such centralization.

International Rivalry and War   In the reign of Charles VI (1711–1740), yet another problem complicated the destiny of this multinational empire, for his only heir was his daughter, Maria Theresa. In 1713 Charles drafted a document

▶ *E. F. Cunningham*
THE RETURN OF FREDERICK II
FROM A MANEUVRE, 1787
Were it not for the richly embroidered saddle cover and the fine white horse, it would be hard to spot Frederick the Great among his officers. Nor is there anything to indicate that the two men on the black and brown horses behind him are his son and grandson. This sober evocation of a king as a professional soldier contrasts strikingly with earlier glorifications (see plate on p. 451).

known as the Pragmatic Sanction, declaring that all Habsburg dominions would pass intact to the eldest heir, male or female; and for the next 25 years he sought recognition of the Pragmatic Sanction from the European powers. By making all kinds of concessions and promises, he won this recognition on paper. But when he died in 1740, his daughter found that the commitments were worthless: The succession was challenged by force from several sides. Concentrating on diplomacy alone, Charles had neglected the work of state building, leaving an empty treasury, an inadequately trained army, and an ineffective bureaucracy.

In contrast to Austria, Prussia had a full treasury, a powerful army, and a confident ruler, Frederick II, who seized the Habsburg province of Silesia without qualm. His justification was simply "reasons of state" combined with the Habsburgs' faltering fortunes. And Maria Theresa had her hands more than full, because the French declared war on her to support their ally Bavaria's claim to the Habsburg throne. Meanwhile, Spain hoped to win back control of Austria's Italian possessions. Worse yet, Maria Theresa faced a rebellion by the Czech nobles in Bohemia. Her position would probably have been hopeless if Hungary's Magyar nobles had followed suit. But Maria Theresa promised them autonomy within the Habsburg empire, and they offered her the troops she needed to resist the invaders.

In the War of Austrian Succession (1740–1748) that followed, Maria Theresa learned the elements of state building. With her Hungarian troops and with financial help from her one ally, Britain, she fought her opponents to a stalemate. Frederick's conquest of Silesia proved to be the only significant territorial change produced by this major war. Even for England and France, who fought the war mainly in their overseas colonies, it was a standoff. But Maria Theresa now regarded the recovery of Silesia and the humiliation of Prussia as esential. These aims, in turn, required determined state building within Habsburg domains.

MARIA THERESA

The woman whose authority was established not by her father's negotiations but by force of arms was a marked contrast to her archenemy, Frederick. The Prussian king was practical and irreligious; Maria Theresa was moralistic and pious. While Frederick barely tolerated a loveless marriage, the Habsburg ruler enjoyed a happy domestic life, bearing numerous children and taking great personal interest in their upbringing. Her personality and her ruling style were deceptively traditional, for she was a shrewd innovator in the business of building and reasserting the power of her state.

Unlike Frederick, or for that matter her own son and successor, Joseph II, Maria Theresa had a strong regard for her dynasty. In this respect her being a woman made no difference to the policies or government of the empire. She believed in the divine mission of the Habsburgs and conscientiously attended to the practical needs of her realm. It was because she put the state's interests first that this most pious of Catholic sovereigns—who disdained religious toleration and loathed atheists—felt obliged to reform the Church. Responding to waste and self-interest in her monasteries, she forbade the founding of new establishments. She also abolished the clergy's exemptions from taxes, something the French king found impossible to do.

A new bureaucratic apparatus was constructed on the models of French and Prussian absolutism. In Vienna, reorganized central ministries recruited staffs of experts. In the provinces, new agents were appointed who were largely divorced from feudal and local interests, though some concession did have to be made to the regional traditions of the Habsburg realm. The core domains (excluding Hungary and the Italian possessions) were reorganized into 10 provinces, each subdivided into districts directed by royal officials. With the help of these officials, the central government could wrest new taxes from the local diets. Meanwhile, Maria Theresa brought important nobles from all her domains to Vienna to participate in its social and administrative life. She also reformed the military, improving the training of troops and establishing academies to produce a more professional officer corps. Thus did international needs help shape domestic political reforms.

THE GROWTH OF STABILITY IN GREAT BRITAIN

It was not only absolutists who strengthened their states. Britain, too, expanded its government and its international power in the eighteenth century. This was the work not so much of a monarch as of the "political nation"—the landowners and leading townsmen who made up about 5 percent of the population of Great Britain yet who elected almost all the members of Parliament. Their control of the nation was symbolized

▶ *M. van Meytens*
Maria Theresa and her Family, 1750
Although the setting is just as splendid, the portrayal of Maria Theresa with her husband and 11 of her 16 children suggests a domesticity that is absent from Louis XIV's family portrait of half a century before (see chapter opening plate on p. 532).

by the fact that the distribution of the 558 seats in the House of Commons bore little relation to the size of constituencies. In 1793, for example, 51 English and Welsh boroughs, which contained fewer than 1500 voters, elected 100 members of Parliament, nearly a fifth of the Commons. Many of these districts were safely in the pocket of a prominent local family; and election campaigns elsewhere were often determined by bribery, influence, and intimidation. On a national scale, loose party alignments did exist. The Whigs wanted a strong Parliament and generally preferred commercial to agricultural interests. The Tories usually supported the king and policies that favored large landholders. But the realities of politics were based on small factions within these larger groups, and politics revolved around the control of patronage and office.

As the financial and military needs and capabilities of the government expanded, Parliament now created a thoroughly bureaucratized state. Britain had always prided itself on having a smaller government and lower taxes than its neighbors, largely because, as an island, it had avoided the need for a standing army. All that now came to an end. Starting with the struggle against Louis XIV, wars required constant increases in resources, troops, and administrators. A steadily expanding navy had to be supported, as did an army that reached almost 200,000 men by the 1770s. Before the 1690s, public expenditures rarely amounted to £2 million a year; by the 1770s, they were almost £30 million, and most of that was spent on the military. In this period, as a result, Britain's fiscal bureaucracy more than tripled in size. The recruiting officer became a regular sight, and so too did the treasury men who were imposing increasingly heavy tax burdens.

Unlike their counterparts on the continent, however, the wealthier classes in Britain paid considerable taxes to support this state building, and they maintained more fluid relations with other classes. The landed gentry and the commercial class, in particular, were often linked by

▶ **New Gallows at the Old Bailey, Engraving** It was an indication of the severity of English criminal justice that the gallows erected near the chief court in London, the Old Bailey, in the mid-eighteenth century were specially constructed so that 10 condemned criminals, both men and women, could be executed at once.

▶ WILLIAM PITT IN THE COMMONS
WILLIAM PITT IN THE COMMONS
William Pitt the younger is shown here addressing the House of Commons. Like his father during the Seven Years' War, Pitt provided firm leadership against France in the 1790s.

marriage and by financial or political associations. Even great aristocrats sometimes had close ties with the business leaders of London. For the lower levels of society, however, the barriers were as high as they had ever been. For all of Britain's prosperity, the lower third of society remained poor and often desperate. As a result, despite the severity of the system of justice and the frequency of capital punishment, crime was endemic in both country and town. The eighteenth century was the heyday of that romantic but violent figure, the highwayman.

The Age of Walpole The first two rulers of the Hanoverian dynasty, George I (1714–1727) and George II (1727–1760), could not speak English fluently. The language barrier and their concern for their German territory of Hanover left them often uninterested in British politics, and this was one reason Parliament grew in authority. Its dominant figure for over 20 years was Sir Robert Walpole, who rose to prominence because of his skillful handling of fiscal policy during the panic following the collapse of an overseas trading company in 1720. This crash, known as the South Sea Bubble, resembled the failure of John Law's

similar scheme in France, but it had less effect on government finances. Thereafter, Walpole controlled British politics until 1742, mainly by dispensing patronage liberally and staying at peace.

Many historians have called Walpole the first prime minister, though the title was not official. He insisted that all ministers inform and consult with the House of Commons as well as with the king, and he himself continued to sit in Parliament in order to recruit support for his decisions. Not until the next century was it accepted that the Commons could force a minister to resign. But Walpole took a first step toward ministerial responsibility and thus shaped the future structure of British government.

In Great Britain as in France, the economic expansion of the eighteenth century increased the wealth and the social and political weight of the commercial and financial middle class. Although Londoners remained around 11 percent of the population, the proportion of the English who lived in other sizable towns doubled in the eighteenth century; and by 1800 some 30 percent of the country's inhabitants were urbanized. Walpole's policy of peace pleased the large landlords but angered this growing body of merchants and businesspeople, who feared the growth of French commerce and colonial settlements. They found their champion in William Pitt, later earl of Chatham, the grandson of a man who had made a fortune in India. Eloquent, self-confident, and infused with a vision of Britain's imperial destiny, Pitt began his parliamentary career in 1738 by attacking the timid policies of the government and demanding that France be driven from the seas. Although Walpole's policies continued even after his resignation in 1742, Pitt's moment finally came in 1758, when Britain became involved in the Seven Years' War (see p. 569). This conflict was to be a testing time throughout Europe for the advances of the previous century in state building and the development of the international system.

V. The International System

While rulers built up their states by enlarging their bureaucracies, strengthening governmental institutions, and expanding their resources, they also had to consider how best to deal with their neighbors. In an age that emphasized reasoned and practical solutions to problems, there was hope that an orderly system could be devised for international relations. If the reality fell short of the ideal, there were nevertheless many who thought they were creating a more impersonal and organized structure for diplomacy and warfare.

DIPLOMACY AND WARFARE

One obstacle to the creation of an impersonal international system was the continuing influence, in eighteenth-century diplomacy, of traditional dynastic interests. Princes and their ministers tried to preserve a family's succession, and they arranged marriages to gain new titles or alliances. Part of the reason that those perennial rivals, Britain and France, remained at peace for nearly 30 years until 1740 was that the rulers in both countries felt insecure on their thrones and thus had personal motives for not wanting to risk aggressive foreign policies.

Gradually, however, dynastic interests gave way to policies based on a more impersonal conception of the state. Men like Frederick II of Prussia and William Pitt of Britain tried to shape their diplomacy to what they considered the needs of their states. "Reasons of state" centered on security, which could be guaranteed only by force. Thus the search for defensible borders and the weakening of rivals became obvious goals. Eighteenth-century statesmen believed that the end (security and prosperity) justified the means (the use of power). Until a country was completely invulnerable, its leaders felt justified in using the crudest tactics in dealing with its neighbors.

The Diplomatic System   If there was any broad, commonly agreed principle at work, it was that hegemony, or domination by one state, had to be resisted because it threatened international security. The concern aroused by Louis XIV's ambitions showed the principle at work, when those whom he sought to dominate joined together in order to frustrate his designs. Their aim was to establish equilibrium in Europe by a balance of power, with no single state achieving hegemony. From the War of Spanish Succession until the rise of Napoleon, that balance was maintained, though the means could be unsavory.

The diplomats who were responsible for implementing "reasons of state" and the balance of power knew there were times when they had to deceive. They might fabricate a claim to a province or a princely title, and it was known that ambassadors were spies by vocation. They offered the bribes that were a part of foreign policy and negotiated treaties that they sometimes expected their prince to violate. Yet there was also a more stabilizing side to diplomacy: The eighteenth century marks its growth as a serious profession, parallel to the rationalization of the state itself. Foreign ministries were staffed with experts and clerks, and kept extensive archives, while the heads of the diplomatic machine, the

▶ **Engraving from the Westminster Magazine, 1774**
Political cartoons were standard fare in eighteenth-century newspapers and magazines. This one shows a weeping king of Poland and an angry Turk (who made no gains) after Poland was carved up in 1772 by Frederick the Great, the Austrian emperor, and the Russian empress. Louis XV sits by without helping his ally Poland, and all are urged on by the devil under the table.

ambassadors, were stationed in permanent embassies abroad. This routinized management of foreign relations helped foster a sense of collective identity among Europe's states despite their endless struggles. Linguistically and socially, diplomats gave a sugar coating to international relations. French was now the common language of diplomacy; by 1774 even a treaty between Turks and Russians was drafted in that language. And socially the diplomats were aristocratic and cosmopolitan. Regardless of the ruler they served, all ambassadors saw themselves as members of the same fraternity.

In general, the great powers dominated international agreements, usually at the expense of the smaller states. For example, Prussia, Austria, and Russia satisfied their territorial ambitions by agreeing to partition Poland among themselves. Ignoring the Poles, they declared in 1772 that "whatever the limits of the respective claims, the acquisitions which result must be exactly equal." Resolving disputes by negotiation could be as amoral as war.

ARMIES

Despite the settlement of some conflicts by diplomacy, others led to war. If Britain emphasized its navy, on the continent the focus of bureaucratic innovation and monetary expenditure was the standing army, whose growth was striking. France set the pace. After 1680 the size of its forces never fell below 200,000. In Prussia the army increased in size from 39,000 to 200,000 men between 1713 and 1786. But the cost, technology, and tactics of these armies served to limit the devastation of eighteenth-century warfare. The expenses led rulers to husband their armies carefully. Princes were quick to declare war but slow to deploy their armies at full strength or commit them to battle. And casualties also became less numerous as discipline improved and the ferocity that had been caused by religious passions died away.

Tactics and Discipline The techniques of building and besieging fortifications continued to preoccupy military planners, even though the impregnable fortresses that the French engineer Sebastian Vauban had built to protect France's northeastern border were simply bypassed by the English general Marlborough when he pursued the French army in the War of the Spanish Succession. The decisive encounter was still the battle between armies, where the majority of the troops—the infantry—used their training to

▶ *L. N. van Blarenberghe*
THE BATTLE OF FONTENOY, 1745
**This panorama shows the English and Dutch
assaulting the French position in a battle in present-
day Belgium. The French lines form a huge
semicircle from the distant town to the wood on the
left. The main attacking force in the center,
surrounded by gunfire, eventually retreated, and
news of the victory was brought to Louis XV, in red
on the right, by a horseman in blue who is doffing
his hat.**

maneuver and fire in carefully controlled line formations. The aim of strategy was not to annihilate but to nudge an opposing army into abandoning its position in the face of superior
maneuvers. This improved organization also
served to reduce brutality. Better supplied by a
system of magazines, more tightly disciplined by
constant drilling, troops were less likely to desert
or plunder than they had been during the Thirty
Years' War.

As these military practices took hold, some encounters were fought as if they were taking place
on a parade ground, and pitched battles in open
fields were increasingly avoided. Even important
victories might be nullified if a winning army returned to its home bases for winter camp. And
no victor ever demanded unconditional surrender. The same was true of naval battles. Commanders were cautious in combat and rarely pursued a defeated squadron.

The officer corps of the military were generally
the preserve of the European nobility, though
they also served as channels of upward social
mobility for wealthy sons of middle-class families who purchased commissions. In either case,
the officer ranks tended to be filled by men who
lacked the professional training for effective leadership. Officers were likely to be long on martial
spirit but short on technical skills. The branches
of service that showed the most progress were
the artillery and the engineers, in which competent middle-class officers played an unusually
large role.

A final limit on the scale of war in the eighteenth century was the inherent weakness of coalitions, which formed whenever a general war
erupted. On paper these alliances looked formidable. On the battlefield, however, they were

hampered by primitive communications and lack of mobility even at the peak of cooperation. Moreover, the partnerships rarely lasted very long. The competitiveness of the state system bred distrust among allies as well as enemies. Sudden abandonment of coalitions and the negotiation of separate peace treaties mark the history of almost every major war.

THE SEVEN YEARS' WAR

The pressures created by the competition of states, dynasties, and empires finally exploded in midcentury in a major war, the Seven Years' War (1756–1763). Its roots lay in a realignment of diplomatic alliances that began at Austria's prodding. Previously, the Bourbon-Habsburg rivalry had been the cornerstone of European diplomacy. But by the 1750s two other sets of antagonisms had taken over: French competition with the British in the New World and Austria's vendetta against Prussia over Silesia. For Austria, the rivalry with Bourbon France was no longer important. Its position in the Holy Roman Empire depended now on humbling Prussia. France was not yet concerned over Prussia, but French hostility to Austria had lessened. Austria was therefore free to lead a turnabout in alliances—a diplomatic revolution—in order to forge an anti-Prussian coalition with France and Russia. Russia was the key. Aside from her personal loathing of Frederick II, the pious Empress Elizabeth of Russia saw him as an obstacle to Russian ambitions

▶ ENGRAVING OF A MILITARY ACADEMY, FROM H. F. VON FLEMING, VOLKOMMENE TEUTSCHE SOLDAT, 1726
This scene, of young men studying fortifications and tactics in a German academy, would have been familiar to the sons of nobles throughout Europe who trained for a military career in the eighteenth century.

in Eastern Europe. Geographical vulnerability also made Prussia an inviting target, and so the stage was set for a diplomatic revolution.

Prussia was active in trying to compensate for that vulnerability. But its countermoves only alienated the other powers. Frederick sought to stay out of the Anglo-French rivalry by coming to terms with both these states. He had been France's ally in the past, and he now sought to negotiate a treaty with England. England—seeking to protect the royal territory of Hanover—willingly signed a neutrality accord, the Convention of Westminster, with Prussia in January 1756. Frederick had no intention of repudiating his friendship with France, but to the French—who had not been informed in advance of these negotiations—the Convention seemed an insult, if not an actual betrayal. The accord with France's mortal enemy, England, seemed the act of an untrustworthy ally. France overreacted, turned against Prussia, and thus fell into Austria's design (*see box*, p. 571). Russia too considered the Convention of Westminster a betrayal by *its* supposed ally England. English bribes and diplomacy could no longer keep Russia from actively joining Austria to plan Prussia's dismemberment.

Map 17.5 Prussia and the Austrian Empire, 1721–1772
The steady territorial advances of Prussia had created a major power in northern and Eastern Europe, alongside the Austrian Empire, by the time of the first partition of Poland in 1772.

Maria Theresa in Vehement Mood

The animosities and ambitions that shaped international relations in the eighteenth century were exemplified by the Empress Maria Theresa. Her furious reaction to the event that destroyed Europe's old diplomatic system—England's signing of the Convention of Westminster with Maria Theresa's archenemy, Frederick the Great— suggests how deep were the feelings that brought about the midcentury conflagration. After learning the news and deciding (in response) to ally herself with France, she told the British ambassador on May 13, 1756, exactly where she stood.

"I have not abandoned the old system, but Great Britain has abandoned me and the system, by concluding the Prussian treaty, the first intelligence of which struck me like a fit of apoplexy. I and the king of Prussia are incompatible; and no consideration on earth will ever induce me to enter into any engagement to which he is a party. Why should you be surprised if, following your example in concluding a treaty with Prussia, I should now enter into an engagement with France?

"I am far from being French in my disposition, and do not deny that the court of Versailles has been my bitterest enemy; but I have little to fear from France, and I have no other recourse than to form such arrangements as will secure what remains to me. My principal aim is to secure my hereditary possessions. I have truly but two enemies whom I really dread, the king of Prussia and the Turks; and while I and Russia continue on the same good terms as now exist between us, we shall, I trust, be able to convince Europe, that we are in a condition to defend ourselves against those adversaries, however formidable."

From William Coxe, *History of the House of Austria*, vol. III (London: Bohn, 1847), pp. 363–364.

The Course of War Fearing encirclement, Frederick gambled on a preventive war through Saxony in 1756. Although he easily conquered the duchy, his plan backfired, for it activated the coalition that he dreaded. Russia and France met their commitments to Austria, and a combined offensive against Prussia began.

For a time Frederick's genius as a general brought him success. His forces won a spectacular victory at Rossbach in late 1757 over a much larger French-Austrian army. Skillful tactics and daring surprise movements would bring other victories, but strategically the Prussian position was shaky. Frederick had to dash in all directions across his provinces to repel invading armies whose combined strength far exceeded his own. Each successive year of the war, he faced the prospect of Russian attacks on Brandenburg in the north and Austrian thrusts from the south through Silesia and Saxony. Disaster was avoided mainly because the Russian army returned east for winter quarters regardless of its gains, but even so, the Russians occupied Berlin. On the verge of exhaustion, Prussia at best seemed to face a stalemate with a considerable loss of territory; at worst, the war would continue and bring about a total Prussian collapse. But the other powers were also war-weary, and Frederick's enemies were becoming increasingly distrustful of one another.

In the end, Prussia was saved by one of those sudden changes of reign that could cause dramatic reversals of policy in Europe. In January 1762 Empress Elizabeth died and was replaced temporarily by Tsar Peter III, a passionate admirer of Frederick. He quickly pulled Russia out of the war and returned Frederick's conquered eastern domains of Prussia and Pomerania. In Britain, meanwhile, William Pitt was replaced by the more pacific earl of Bute, who brought about a reconciliation with France; both countries then ended their insistence on the punishment of Prussia. Austria's coalition had collapsed.

The terms of the Peace of Hubertusburg (1763), settling the continental phase of the Seven Years' War, were therefore surprisingly favorable to Prussia. Prussia returned Saxony to Austria but paid no compensation for the devastation of the duchy, and the Austrians recognized Silesia as Prussian. In short, the status quo was restored. Frederick could return to Berlin, his dominion preserved partly by his army but mainly by luck and the continuing fragility of international alliances.

> If, amidst the state building of the eighteenth century, many of Europe's regimes were able quite easily to sustain a major war even if it brought about few territorial changes, that was not simply because of the expansion of government and the disciplining of armies. It was also the result of remarkable economic advances and the availability of new resources that were flowing into Europe from the development of overseas empires. In politics, this was primarily an age of consolidation; in economics, it was a time of profound transformation.

Recommended Reading

Sources

*Hobbes, Thomas. *Leviathan*. 1651. Any modern edition.

*Locke, John. *Second Treatise of Civil Government*. 1690. Any modern edition.

Luvvas, J. (ed.). *Frederick the Great on the Art of War*. 1966.

Saint-Simon, Louis. *Historical Memoirs*. Lucy Norton (ed. and tr.). 2 vols. 1967 and 1968. Lively memoirs of the court at Versailles.

Studies

*Alexander, John T. *Catherine the Great: Life and Legend*. 1988.

Anderson, M. S. *Historians and Eighteenth-Century Europe, 1715–1789*. 1979. Past and current viewpoints on a number of fundamental issues.

Baxter, S. B. *William III and the Defense of European Liberty 1650–1702*. 1966. A solid and straightforward account of the career of the ruler of both England and the Netherlands.

*Behrens, C. B. A. *Society, Government, and the Enlightenment: The Experience of Eighteenth-Century France and Prussia*. 1985.

Brewer, John. *The Sinews of Power: War, Money and the English State. 1688–1783*. 1989. The work that demonstrated the importance of the military and the growth of bureaucracy in eighteenth-century England.

——— and John Styles (eds.). *An Ungovernable People: The English and Their Law in the Seventeenth and Eighteenth Centuries*. 1980. A rich collection of essays on crime and the administration of justice.

*Carsten, F. L. *The Origins of Prussia*. 1954. The standard account of the background to the reign of the great elector, Frederick William, and the best short history of his accomplishments and the rise of the Junkers.

Corvisier, André. *Armies and Societies in Europe, 1494–1789*. 1979. A comparative study, strongest on the French army.

Duffy, Christopher. *The Army of Frederick the Great*. 1974. A comprehensive account of everything from recruitment to tactics.

*Goubert, Pierre. *Louis XIV and Twenty Million Frenchmen*. Anne Carter (tr.). 1970. This is not so much a history of the king's reign as a study of the nature of French society and politics during Louis' rule.

Hatton, R. N. *Charles XII of Sweden*. 1968. A thorough and well-written biography that does justice to a dramatic life.

*———. *Europe in the Age of Louis XIV*. 1969. A beautifully illustrated and vividly interpretive history of the period that Louis dominated.

---

*Available in paperback.

Hay, D., P. Linebaugh, and E. P. Thompson. *Albion's Fatal Tree: Crime and Society in Eighteenth-Century England.* 1975. A pioneering study.

*Henshall, Nicholas. *The Myth of Absolutism: Change and Continuity in Early Modern European Monarchy.* 1992. A comparison, mainly of England and France, which argues that the term *absolutism*, a later invention, ignores the emphasis on tradition and continuity during the 1660–1789 period.

*Holmes, Geoffrey. *The Making of a Great Power: Late Stuart and Early Georgian Britain, 1660–1722*; and *The Age of Oligarchy: Pre-industrial Britain, 1722–1783.* 1993. The best detailed survey.

Linebaugh, Peter. *The London Hanged: Crime and Civil Society in the Eighteenth Century.* 1991. A detailed study of crime and criminals.

Mettam, Roger. *Power and Faction in Louis XIV's France.* 1988. An analysis of government and power under absolutist rule.

*Plumb, J. H. *The Growth of Political Stability in England, 1675–1725.* 1969. A brief, lucid survey of the developments in English politics that helped create Britain's modern parliamentary democracy.

———. *Sir Robert Walpole* (2 vols). 1956–1961. A masterly biography.

Raeff, Marc. *The Well-Ordered Police State: Social and Institutional Change through Law in the Germanies and Russia, 1600–1800.* 1983.

Rowen, Herbert H. *The King's State: Proprietary Dynasticism in Early Modern France.* 1980. An incisive study of the origins and elaboration of the theory by which Louis XIV ruled France.

Shennan, J. H. *Louis XIV.* 1986. A good introduction to the king and his reign.

Stoye, John. *The Siege of Vienna.* 1964. An exciting account of the last great threat to Christian Europe from the Turkish empire.

*Sumner, B. H. *Peter the Great and the Emergence of Russia.* 1950. This short but comprehensive book is the best introduction to Russian history in this period.

*Tuck, Richard. *Hobbes.* 1989. A clear and compact introduction to Hobbes's thought.

Weigley, R. F. *The Age of Battles: The Quest for Decisive Warfare from Breitenfeld to Waterloo.* 1991. The best military history of the age.

The docks of Marseilles in Southern France.

CHAPTER EIGHTEEN

THE WEALTH OF NATIONS

I N the early eighteenth century the great majority of Europe's people still lived directly off the land. With a few regional exceptions, the agrarian economy remained "immobile": It seemed to have no capacity for dramatic growth. People were aided in their labors by animals, wind, and water, but their technology, social arrangements, and management techniques offered little prospect of improvement. Several new developments, however, were about to touch off a remarkable surge of economic advance. The first sign of this new situation was the sustained growth of Europe's population, which depended in turn on an expansion of the food supply. While changes in agrarian output on the continent were modest but significant, in England innovations in the control and use of land dramatically increased food production and changed the entire structure of rural society.

The exploitation of overseas colonies provided another critical stimulus for European economic growth. Colonial trade in slaves, sugar, tobacco, and other raw materials radiated from port cities like London and Bristol in England and Bordeaux and Nantes in France. An infrastructure of supportive industries and processing facilities developed around these ports and fed trade networks for the reexport across Europe of finished colonial products. The colonies, in turn, offered new markets for goods manufactured in Europe, such as cotton fabrics.

The growing demand for cotton cloth at home and abroad touched off an urgent drive among English textile merchants for changes in the organization and technology of production. It was in English cotton manufacturing that dramatic structural change heralded the economic transformation known as industrialization. By the start of the nineteenth century, fundamental changes in the methods of raising food and producing goods were well under way in Britain and were beginning to spread to the continent. This chapter explores the character of economic development, the impediments to that process, and some of the consequences of the economic transformations that began in the eighteenth century.

I. Demographic and Economic Growth

A NEW DEMOGRAPHIC ERA

In the relationship between people and the land, between demography and agriculture, European life before the eighteenth century showed little change. Levels of population seemed to flow like the tides, in cyclical or wave-like patterns. Population might increase substantially over several generations, but eventually crop failures or the ravages of plague and other contagious diseases would drive the level of population down once again. In extreme cases, a lack of able-bodied workers led to the abandonment of land, and entire villages disappeared altogether. Such dramatic population losses had last occurred in seventeenth-century Germany, Poland, and Mediterranean Europe (the southern parts of Italy, Spain, and France).

For centuries Europe's population had been vulnerable to subsistence crises. Successions of poor harvests or crop failures might leave the population without adequate food and would drive up the price of grain and flour beyond what the poorest people could afford. If actual starvation did not carry them off, undernourishment made people more vulnerable than usual to disease. Such crises could also set off a chain of side effects, from unemployment to pessimism, that made people postpone marriage and childbearing. Thus subsistence crises could drive down the birthrate as well as drive up the death rate, causing in combination a substantial loss in population.

Population Growth   A new era in Europe's demography began around 1730, and by 1800 Europe's population had grown by at least 50 percent and probably by more. (Since the first censuses were not taken until the early nineteenth century, all population figures prior to that time are only estimates.) During the eighteenth century (which is considered, demographically, to have begun around 1730), Europe's estimated population jumped from about 120 million to about 180 or 190 million. Europe had probably never before experienced so rapid and substantial an increase in the number of its people. Prussia and Sweden may have doubled their populations, while Spain's grew from 7.5 million to about 11.5 million. Even higher growth rates in England and Wales raised the population there from an estimated 5 million people in 1700 to more than 9 million in 1801, the date of the first British census. The French, according to the best estimates, numbered about 19 million at the death of Louis XIV in 1715, and probably about 26 million in 1789. France was the most densely populated large nation in Europe in the late eighteenth century and, with the exception of the vast Russian Empire, the most populous state, which no doubt helps to explain its remarkable military preponderance in the revolutionary and Napoleonic eras.

Europe's population growth of the eighteenth century continued and indeed accelerated during the nineteenth century, thus breaking once and for all the tide-like cycles and "immobility" of Europe's demography. What caused this fundamental transformation in the underlying structure of European history?

Death Rates and Birthrates   There are two possible explanations for rapid population growth: a fall in death rates or a rise in birthrates. The consensus among historians is that a decline in mortality rates, rather than a rise in birthrates, accounts for most of the population growth in the eighteenth century, although England seems to have been an exception. Declines in the death rate did not occur because of improvements in medical science or hygiene, which became important factors in driving down mortality only in the late nineteenth century. Instead, Europe was beginning to enjoy a stabler and better food supply, perhaps owing to a mild improvement in average climate compared with that of the seventeenth century, which some historians regard as a "little ice age" of unusually cold and wet weather. The opening of new agricultural land in Poland, Hungary, and Russia helped increase Europe's food supplies, as did incremental advances in transportation networks (which made it easier to move regional grain surpluses to where they were most needed) and agrarian changes in England (to be discussed below).

Europe's population remained extremely vul-

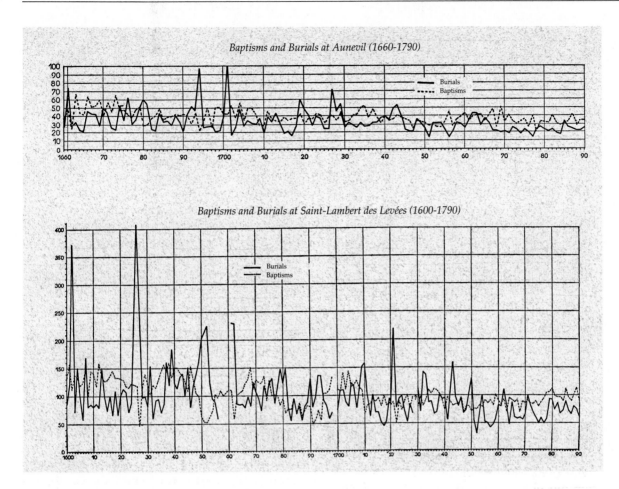

Baptisms and Burials at Aunevil (1660-1790)

Baptisms and Burials at Saint-Lambert des Levées (1600-1790)

nerable to disease. Endemic diseases such as tuberculosis, typhoid, and malaria still ravaged the populations of many regions. Periodic epidemics of dysentery (which attacked the digestive system), influenza (lethal to the respiratory systems of the elderly), typhus (a lice-borne disease that flourished in the conditions of poverty), and smallpox (which assaulted rich and poor alike) continued to take their toll. But a better-nourished population could perhaps stand up to those assaults with greater success.

With the exception of England, in most regions of Europe birthrates do not seem to have increased in the eighteenth century. A high average age at marriage, with women typically well into their twenties and men in their mid- to late twenties, served to check population growth. Since the birth of illegitimate children remained relatively rare, late marriages kept women from becoming pregnant during some of their most fecund years;

▶ **In these two French parishes, the seventeenth century came to a close with severe food shortages and sharp surges of mortality. In a more favorable economic climate, by contrast, the later eighteenth century brought an almost consistent annual surplus of births over deaths.**

they therefore had fewer babies altogether. In England, however, where greater geographic mobility and economic opportunities may have encouraged young couples to start families earlier, the average age at marriage came down and birthrates increased, helping to explain Britain's explosive population growth.

PROFIT INFLATION: THE MOVEMENT OF PRICES

The population grew in eighteenth-century Europe in tandem with an increasing pace and scale of economic activity. Europe's overall wealth expanded, though not steadily and consistently. While the economy experienced periods of fluctuation, of growth and decline, the long-term, or secular, trend was positive, compared with the stagnation and economic difficulty that prevailed (outside of England) during the "long seventeenth century," until roughly 1730. Scholars have made particularly rigorous studies of the economic cycles in France as revealed through the history of prices, and there is reason to believe that economies elsewhere in Europe behaved comparably to France's.

During the first decades of the eighteenth century, prices generally remained stable, perpetuating the long depression of the seventeenth century and no doubt reflecting the exhaustion of the European states from the War of the Spanish Succession. As with Europe's demographic growth, significant economic growth began around 1730 and lasted up until the peace settlements that followed the Napoleonic wars in 1815. Inflation in prices dominated the era. Since French money was kept stable after 1726, the upward movement of prices must be attributed to other causes. Primarily, the rise in prices reflected the stimulus and pressures of a growing population in France and a growing demand for food, land, goods, and employment.

Gently rising prices and gradual, mild inflation usually stimulate the economy—unlike sharp spikes of inflation that create hard times. This nearly century-long cycle of "profit inflation" generated economic growth. There were of course periodic reversals or countercyclical trends. In France, for example, prosperity leveled off around 1770, ushering in two decades of falling profits, unemployment, and hard times. The difficulties were compounded by a succession of crop failures and sharply rising grain prices in 1788–1789—coincident with the outbreak of the French Revolution. After the 1790s, however, profit inflation resumed until the end of the Napoleonic era.

The Impact of Inflation   Over the long term, the inflation did not affect all products, all sectors of the economy, or all segments of society equally. Prices in France between 1726 and 1789 increased by an average of about 65 percent. The cost of grains, the basic food for the poor, rose slightly more than the average and considerably more than other agricultural products, such as wine and meat. Rents rose sharply, suggesting a shortage of available land; in relation to averages for the decade of the 1730s, money rents had grown by 98 percent in the 1780s. Real wages, on the other hand, increased by a meager 22 percent in the same period, which points to a glut of workers competing for employment and to hard times for many wage earners.

These differentials had important social and economic effects. High rents in the countryside and low wages in the city took wealth from the poor and delivered it to the landlord and employer. Inflation helped drive many tenants from the soil, to the advantage of their better-off neighbors, who were eager to expand their holdings. In the city, inflation enabled merchants and manufacturers to sell goods for more and pay workers relatively less. Finally, inflation hurt the French government because its revenues did not grow as fast as its expenditures. Since a portion of French lands owned by the nobles and the Church was exempt from the land tax, the government relied heavily on sales and excise taxes that weighed on ordinary consumers. This inadequate and regressive tax base eventually contributed to a financial crisis for the French monarchy in the 1780s.

PROTOINDUSTRIALIZATION

Agriculture alone could not ensure economic growth in a heavily populated country like England, France, or the Netherlands. The excess of people to land in such countries meant that many rural people could not actually earn their livelihood in agriculture. One solution for needy families was domestic manufacturing. Traditionally, artisans in urban guilds manufactured the cloth fabrics used by Europeans, but textiles could also be produced through the putting-out system, whereby merchants distributed raw materials like wool or flax to rural households. Men and women would spin the raw material into yarn on hand-powered spinning machines; rural weavers working on looms in their cottages would then weave the yarn into cloth.

Protoindustrialization is the name historians

give to a type of economic development that occurred before the rise of the factory system in the late eighteenth century. In this phase, the volume of domestic rural manufacturing increased under the putting-out system, as more rural families devoted more time to industrial work—primarily spinning, weaving, or finishing textiles. A "thickening of the countryside" (a growth in population and in the pace of economic activity) occurred under protoindustrialization. This trend was particularly noticeable in certain regions of the Netherlands, Belgium, the Rhineland, France, and England, where the towns remained sources of capital, materials, and marketing services, but where merchants employed labor in the countryside.

Protoindustrialization had important economic, social, and demographic repercussions. Economically, it strengthened marketing networks, spurred capital accumulation that could be reinvested in production, generated additional revenue for needy rural families, and thereby increased their demand for products and services. Socially, it familiarized rural inhabitants with industrial processes and cash relationships. Demographically, it may have loosened restraints on marriages and births, which in turn might have led to increased immigration into the cities and thus to urban growth. On the other hand, protoindustrialization did not lead to significant technological improvements or to marked advances in productivity; it could not sustain continuous economic growth.

▶ In contrast to textile work, common artisanal trades such as shoemaking, tailoring, dressmaking, furniture making, and food services would continue to be conducted in small workshops down through the nineteenth century.

II. The New Shape of Industry

The transformation of manufacturing hinged above all on increasing the productivity of labor. This could occur through two kinds of innovations: the development of more efficient tools and machines, and the exploitation of new sources of energy. Economists call this process *factor substitution*, whereby capital, represented by the new tools and machines, is substituted for the skills or power of workers. In certain sectors of industry, the new tools were cheap and simple enough to be used by artisans in the home or in small workshops. But the growing complexity of machinery, especially when coupled with new sources of power, called into being a new social institution: the factory.

TOWARD A NEW ECONOMIC ORDER

In analyzing any economic system—traditional or modern, capitalist or socialist—economists distinguish between performance and structure. Performance is measured by output: the total or gross product, and the amount produced per individual in the community. This per capita productivity is, in fact, the best measure of an economy's performance. A particularly distinctive feature of an industrial economy is its capacity for sustained growth. Structure refers to all those characteristics of a society that support or affect performance. Economic, legal, and political institutions; tax policies; technology; demographic movements; even culture and ideology—all make up the structure underlying the economy.

Industrialization required innovations in technology, which dramatically raised per capita productivity. But new technology alone does not entirely explain the advent of industrialism. Social structure itself influences technological development in any age. To ask why dramatic change occurred in industry is thus to pose two deeper questions: What were the structural obstacles to technological innovation and entrepreneurship in traditional European society? And what structural changes in that society, from the late eighteenth century onward, promoted and rewarded innovation?

Impediments to Economic Innovation One major obstacle to innovation was the small size of most European markets, which were cut off from one another by physical barriers, political frontiers, tariff walls, and different laws, moneys, and units of measurement. Small markets slowed the growth of specialized manufacture and limited the mobility of capital and labor. Similarly, the highly skewed distribution of wealth typical of many European communities distorted the structure of demand. In many countries, a narrow aristocracy absorbed most disposable income, and the economy organized itself largely to serve the wealthy few. Catering to the desires of the rich, the economy produced expensive luxury goods, often exquisite in quality and workmanship but always in small quantities. Such small markets and skewed demand dampened the incentive to manufacture an abundance of relatively cheap goods.

Also crucial to the industrializing process was the question of property rights and privileges—whether they would encourage a high rate of return on innovation or impede it. Many institutions in traditional Europe worked against innovation. For instance, through feudal or seigneurial rents and tolls, lords throughout Europe collected payments for which they rendered no service in return. Increased production was thus likely to benefit these parasites as much as the entrepreneurs. In the towns, the guilds presented a major obstacle to economic innovation. Guild regulations, or government regulation of the economy enforced by the guilds, prescribed the techniques to be used in production and often dictated the terms and conditions under which goods could be sold, apprentices taken on, or workers hired. Out of simple self-interest, given their stake in existing arrangements, the guilds favored traditional technology and managerial techniques.

Governments, too, helped sustain these restrictive practices, principally by exploiting them for their own fiscal benefit. Governments typically collected substantial fees from guilds and other privileged institutions and groups. They also restricted economic activity by licensing monopoly companies with exclusive rights to trade in certain regions, such as the East Indies, or to manufacture certain products, such as fine por-

Laissez-Faire Ideology

At the heart of Adam Smith's laissez-faire ideology was a belief that individual self-interest is the motor of economic progress, a notion epitomized in this selection by Smith's reference to the "invisible hand." By the same token, each region or country should pursue what it does best, an argument against protective tariffs for domestic industry.

"Every individual is continually exerting himself to find out the most advantageous employment for whatever capital he can command. . . . But it is only for the sake of profit that any man employs a capital in the support of industry; and he will always, therefore, endeavor to employ it in the support of that industry of which the produce is likely to be of the greatest value, or to exchange for the greatest quantity either of money or of other goods. . . . [In so doing] he generally neither intends to promote the public interest, nor knows how much he is promoting it . . . he intends only his own security; and by directing that industry in such a manner as its produce may be of the greatest value, he intends only his own gain. [But] he is in this, as in many other cases, led by an invisible hand to promote an end which was not part of his intention. By pursuing his own interest he frequently promotes that of the society more effectually than when he really intends to promote it.

"What is the species of domestic industry which his capital can employ, and of which the produce is likely to be of the greatest value, every individual, it is evident, can, in his local situation, judge much better than any statesman or lawgiver can do for him. . . . To give the monopoly of the home market to the produce of domestic industry, in any particular art or manufacture, is in some measure to direct private people in what manner they ought to employ their capitals, and must, in almost all cases, be either a useless or hurtful regulation. If the produce of domestic can be brought there as cheaply as that of foreign industry, the regulation is evidently useless. If it cannot, it must generally be hurtful. . . . If a foreign country can supply us with a commodity cheaper than we ourselves can make it, better buy it from them with some part of the produce of our own industry."

From A. Smith, *An Inquiry into the Nature and Causes of the Wealth of Nations* (1776), Ch. II.

celain. With assured markets and profits, these companies were not likely to assume the risks of new ventures, and they blocked others from doing so. Cultural attitudes may also have discouraged entrepreneurial efforts. Many persons, particularly in the aristocratic classes, still regarded money made in trade or manufacture as somehow tainted. The highest aspiration of a successful businessperson seems often to have been the purchase of a noble title.

Adam Smith Although these institutions and attitudes still marked European life in the eighteenth century, they were subject to ever sharper criticisms. From midcentury on, certain French social thinkers denounced guild control of pro-

duction in the towns and economic privilege and monopoly in all forms. But the seminal work in this new school of economic thought was *The Wealth of Nations* (1776) by the Scottish philosopher Adam Smith (*see box*, above). Smith believed that economic progress required that each individual be allowed to pursue his or her own self-interest freely, without restriction by guilds, the state, or tradition. He argued that on all levels of economic activity—from the manufacturing process to the flow of international trade—a natural division of labor should be encouraged. High tariffs, guild restrictions, mercantilist restraints on free trade all artificially obstructed economic activity. Smith became a founding father of *laissez-faire* economic theory, meaning in effect: let individuals freely pursue their own economic interests—a battle cry that would be taken up vigorously by businesspeople and factory owners in the nineteenth century.

Such arguments slowly affected policy. Guilds were already growing weaker in most towns and were relatively powerless in towns of recent growth, like Manchester and Birmingham in England, where new industries such as cotton manufacturing escaped guild supervision altogether. This trend reached its culmination when the government of revolutionary France permanently dissolved all guilds and restrictive trade associations in 1791. Similarly, the British Parliament revoked the laws regulating apprenticeships in the 1790s. Legally and socially, the entrepreneur was winning greater freedom.

THE ROOTS OF ECONOMIC TRANSFORMATION IN ENGLAND

Of all the nations of Europe, England was the first to develop a social structure strongly supportive of innovation and economic growth. England's advantages were many, some of them deeply rooted in geography and history. This comparatively small realm contained an excellent balance of resources. The plain to the south and east, which contained the traditional centers of English settlement, was fertile and productive. The uplands to the north and west possessed rich deposits of coal and iron, and their streams had powered flour mills since the Middle Ages.

Proximity to the sea was another natural advantage. No part of the island kingdom was distant from the coast. At a time when water transport offered the sole economical means for moving bulky commodities, the sea brought coal close to iron, raw materials close to factories, and products close to markets. Above all, the sea gave Britain's merchants access to the much wider world beyond their shores.

Efficiency of transport was critical in setting the size of markets. During the eighteenth century, Britain witnessed a boom in the building of canals and turnpikes by private individuals or syndicates. By 1815 the country possessed some 2600 miles of canals linking rivers, ports, and other towns. In addition, there were few institutional obstructions to the movement of goods.

United under a strong monarchy since the Middle Ages, Britain was free of internal tariff barriers, unlike prerevolutionary France, Germany, or Italy. Merchants everywhere counted in the same money, measured their goods by the same standards, and conducted their affairs under the protection of the common law.

The English probably had the highest standard of living in Europe and generated strong consumer demand for manufactured goods. English society was less stratified than that on the continent, the aristocracy powerful but much smaller. Primogeniture (with the family's land going to the eldest son) was the rule among both the peers (the titled members of the House of Lords) and the country gentlemen or squires. Left without lands, younger sons had to seek careers in other walks of life, and some turned toward commerce or manufacturing. They frequently recruited capital for their ventures from their landed fathers and elder brothers. English religious dissenters, chiefly Calvinists and Quakers, formed another pool of potential entrepreneurs; denied careers in government because of their religion, many turned their energies to business enterprises.

British Financial Management　A high rate of reinvestment is critical to any takeoff into industrialization; reinvestment, in turn, depends on the skillful management of money by both individuals and public institutions. Here again, Britain enjoyed advantages. Early industrial enterprises could rely on Britain's growing banking system to meet their capital needs. In the seventeenth century the goldsmiths of London had assumed the functions of bankers. They accepted and guarded deposits, extended loans, transferred upon request credits from one account to another, and changed money. In the eighteenth century banking services became available beyond London; the number of country banks rose from 300 in 1780 to more than 700 by 1810. English businesspeople were familiar with bank notes and other forms of commercial papers, and their confidence in paper facilitated the recruitment and flow of capital.

The founding of the Bank of England in 1694 marked an epoch in the history of European finance. The bank took responsibility for managing

England's public debt, sold shares to the public, and faithfully met the interest payments due to the shareholders, with the help of government revenue (such as the customs duties efficiently collected on Britain's extensive foreign trade). When the government needed to borrow, it could turn to the Bank of England for assistance. This stability in government finances ensured a measure of stability for the entire money market and, most important, held down interest rates in both the public and private sectors. In general, since the "Glorious Revolution" of 1688, England's government had been sensitive to the interests of the business classes, who in turn had confidence in the government. Such close ties between money and power facilitated economic investment.

THE CONTOURS OF THE FRENCH ECONOMY

Structural obstacles to economic growth were more deeply entrenched in France than in England. The kingdom of France in the early modern period did not form a single national market; rather, it was a federation of regional markets.

France was large, and transportation grew more expensive with distance. Inadequate waterways and miserable roads (except for some military highways built during Louis XIV's reign) acted as a restraint on trade. In 1664 Louis' minister Colbert had created an area of free trade in the monarchy's central provinces, but beyond this zone, internal tolls and tariffs at provincial borders burdened commerce. Guilds and other forms of monopoly held back commercial innovation, but they protected their interests by paying fees to the monarchy in return for their privileges. Differences in provincial legal systems and in weights and measures further complicated and slowed exchange. As the writer Voltaire sarcastically remarked, the traveler crossing France by coach changed laws as frequently as horses.

Despite these obstacles, the French economy was far from stagnant during the eighteenth cen-

▶ Incremental improvements in road and water transportation facilitated economic growth in the eighteenth century. In France the government enlisted peasants periodically to work on the upkeep of major highways under a system of forced labor known as the royal *corvée.*

tury, as we have seen. Indeed the government improved communications arteries by building canals that linked rivers in northern and in central France, and in 1777 work began on the Burgundy Canal, which would eventually allow barges to move from the English Channel to the Mediterranean. The improvement of France's main highways, with labor provided by peasants, was even more impressive. Around midcentury the government founded the School of Bridges and Roads, which soon became a model engineering institute.

The collapse of a government-sanctioned investment scheme by John Law in 1720, however, had a regressive effect on French banking and credit. French investors developed a deep suspicion of banks, paper money, and joint-stock companies. Businesspeople tended to rely instead on resources that they or their close relatives could muster and preferred to deal in hard cash rather than commercial paper. On the other hand, stable coinage aided the financing of enterprises. In 1726 the government fixed the value of the principal gold coin and kept it stable thereafter—a notable feat in light of the monarchy's desperate financial needs. On balance, although limited capital and conservative management held back French business enterprises, they dampened but did not suppress the expansion of the economy. France remained a leader in producing wool and linen cloth as well as iron, but it seemed more inclined to produce luxury items or very cheap, low-quality goods. On the other hand, England (with its higher standard of living and strong domestic demand) was more adept at producing standardized products of reasonably good quality.

COTTON: THE BEGINNING OF INDUSTRIALIZATION

The process of early industrialization in England was extremely complex and remains difficult to explain. What seems certain is that a strong demand for cheap goods was growing at home and abroad in the eighteenth century, and important segments of the English community perceived this opportunity and responded to it.

The market for cotton goods was the most propulsive force for change in industrial production. Thanks to slave labor in plantation colonies, the supply of raw cotton was rising dramatically. On the demand side, lightweight cotton goods were durable, washable, versatile, and cheaper than woolen or linen cloth. Cotton therefore had a bright future as an item of mass consumption. But traditional textile manufacturing centers in England (the regions of protoindustrialization such as East Anglia and the Yorkshire districts) could not satisfy the growing demand. The organization and technology of the putting-out system had reached its limits. For one thing, the merchant was limited to the labor supply in his own district; the farther he went to find cottage workers, the longer it took and the more cumbersome it became to pass the materials back and forth. Second, he could not adequately control his workers. Clothiers were bedeviled with embezzlement of raw materials, poor workmanship, and lateness in finishing assigned work. English clothiers were therefore on the lookout for technological or organizational innovations to help them meet a growing demand for textiles.

Machines and Factories   Weavers could turn out large amounts of cloth thanks to the invention of the fly shuttle in the 1730s, which permitted the construction of larger and faster handlooms. But traditional methods of spinning the yarn caused a bottleneck in the production process. Responding to this problem, inventors built new kinds of spinning machines that could be grouped in large factories or mills. Richard Arkwright's water frame drew cotton fibers through rollers and twisted them into thread. Not simply an inventor but an entrepreneur (one who combined the various factors of production into a profitable enterprise), Arkwright initially housed his machines in a large factory sited near a river so that his machines could be propelled by waterpower.

At around the same time, James Watt had been perfecting the technology of steam engines—machinery originally used to power suction pumps that would evacuate water from the pits of coal mines. The earliest steam engine had produced a simple up-and-down motion. Watt not only redesigned it to make it far more efficient and powerful but also developed a system of gears to harness the engine's energy into rotary motion that could drive other types of machines. In 1785 Arkwright became one of Watt's first customers when he switched from water power to steam engines as the means of driving the spinning machines in his new cotton factory. With Arkwright (who became a millionaire) and Watt, the modern factory system was launched (*see box*, p. 586).

Spinning factories, however, disrupted the equilibrium between spinning and weaving in the other direction: Yarn was now abundant, but handloom weavers could not keep up with the pace. This created a brief golden age for the weavers, but merchants were eager to break the new bottleneck. In 1784 Edmund Cartwright de-

▶ *Right:* Richard Arkwright not only invented this power-driven machine to spin cotton yarn but proved to be a highly successful entrepreneur with the factory he constructed at Cromford in the Lancashire region.

▶ *Below:* The engineering firm of Bolton & Watt became famous for its steam engines, whose complex mechanisms of cams, gears, and levers could harness the power of steam to a variety of uses in industry and transportation.

Richard Arkwright's Achievement

This celebration of British industrialization, the factory system, and entrepreneurship begins by extolling Richard Arkwright's accomplishments in the 1780s.

"When the first water-frames for spinning cotton were erected at Cromford, about sixty years ago, mankind were little aware of the mighty revolution which the new system of labour was destined by Providence to achieve, not only in the structure of British society, but in the fortunes of the world at large. Arkwright alone had the sagacity to discern, and the boldness to predict in glowing language, how vastly productive human industry would become, when no longer proportioned in its results to muscular effort, which is by its nature fitful and capricious, but when made to consist in the task of guiding the work of mechanical fingers and arms, regularly impelled with great velocity by some indefatigable physical power [such as a steam engine].

"The main difficulty did not lie so much in the invention of a proper self-acting mechanism for drawing out and twisting cotton into a continuous thread, as in the distribution of different members of the apparatus into one co-operative body ... and above all, in training human beings to renounce their desultory habits of work, and to identify themselves with the unvarying regularity of the complex automaton. To devise and administer a successful code of factory discipline, suited to the necessities of factory diligence, was the Herculean enterprise, the noble achievement of Arkwright. ... It required, in fact, a man of Napoleonic nerve and ambition to subdue the refractory tempers of work-people accustomed to irregular paroxysms of diligence, and to urge on his multifarious and intricate constructions in the face of prejudice, passion, and envy."

From Andrew Ure, *The Philosophy of Manufactures* (1835).

---

signed a power-driven loom. Small technical flaws, and the violent opposition of handloom weavers, retarded the widescale adoption of power looms until the early nineteenth century, but then both spinning and weaving were totally transformed. Power-driven machinery boosted the output of yarn and cloth astronomically, while merchants were able to assemble their workers in factories and scrutinize their every move to maximize production. In a factory, one small boy could watch over two mechanized looms whose output was 15 times greater than that of a skilled handloom weaver.

In 1760 Britain imported only 2.5 million pounds of raw cotton; by 1830 it was importing 366 million pounds. Cotton textiles had become the single most important industrial product in terms of output, capital investment, and number of workers. Its production was almost exclusively organized in factories using power-driven machinery at all stages. In the process, the price of cotton yarn fell to about one-twentieth of what it had been in the 1760s. Lancashire, with its abundant waterways and coal deposits to fuel steam engines, became the center of a booming cotton cloth industry, and Manchester, its leading city, became the cotton capital of the world.

III. Innovation and Tradition in Agriculture

In England in 1700, an estimated 80 percent of the population lived directly from agriculture; a century later that portion had fallen to approximately 40 percent. This massive shift of labor and resources from agriculture would have been inconceivable had the countryside not been able to supply a greater abundance of food. English farmers introduced significant improvements in their methods of cultivation, which enabled the countryside to supply the industrial towns with food as well as labor, capital, and markets. On the continent, however, peasant cultivators generally clung tenaciously to traditional ways in agriculture as their only form of security.

CONVERTIBLE HUSBANDRY

A central problem in any agricultural system is the way repeated harvests on the same land eventually rob the soil of its fertility. Since the Early Middle Ages, the usual method of restoring a field's fertility involved letting the land lie fallow for a season (that is, resting it by planting nothing) every second or third year. This allowed bacteria in the soil to take needed nitrogen from the air. A quicker and better method, heavy manuring, could not be used widely because most farmers were unable to support sufficient livestock to produce the manure. Feeding farm animals, particularly with fodder during the winter, was beyond the means of most peasants.

But fallowing was an extremely inefficient and wasteful method of restoring the soil's fertility. One key to improving agricultural productivity therefore lay in eliminating the fallow periods, which in turn required that more animals be raised to provide fertilizer. In a given year, instead of taking it out of cultivation, a field could be planted not with grain but with turnips or with nitrogen-fixing grasses that could supply fodder for livestock. The grazing livestock would in turn deposit abundant quantities of manure on those fields. Thus by the end of that season the soil's fertility would be greater, and next year's grain crop was likely to produce a higher yield than it would have if the field had simply been left fallow the year before.

In the 1730s Charles Townshend (known as "Turnip Townshend") showed the value of planting turnips and other fodder crops in such a rotation system instead of letting the land lie fallow. One of the first British landlords to adopt this approach on a broad scale was Jethro Tull, an agriculturist and inventor. Tull's zeal in conducting his experiments and advocating new farming methods proved infectious. By the late eighteenth century, Norfolk, in the east of England, had achieved particular prominence for

such techniques, known as *convertible husbandry*.

With convertible husbandry, innovative or "improving" landlords never let their land lie fallow but always put it to some productive use. They also experimented with techniques designed to enhance the texture of the soil. Where soil was normally too thin to retain water effectively, they added clays or marl to help bind the soil. In those regions where the soil had the opposite problem of clumping too rigidly after rainfalls, farmers lightened the soil by adding chalk and lime to inhibit the clotting.

Eighteenth-century agrarian innovators also experimented with the selective breeding of animals. Some improved the quality of pigs, while others developed new breeds of sheep and dramatically increased the weight of marketed cattle. Soil management and livestock breeding did not depend on any high-tech knowledge or machinery but simply on a willingness to experiment in the management of one's land, and to invest capital to achieve higher yields.

THE ENCLOSURE MOVEMENT IN BRITAIN

To make use of such new methods, farmers had to be free to manage the land as they saw fit. This was all but impossible under the open-field system, which had dominated the countryside in Europe since the Middle Ages. Under the open-field system, even the largest landlords usually held their property in numerous elongated strips that were mixed in with and open to the land of their neighbors. Owners of contiguous strips had to follow the same routines of cultivation. One farmer could not raise grasses to graze cattle when another was raising wheat or leaving the land fallow. The village as a whole determined what routines should be followed and thus effectively managed each holding. The village also decided such matters as how many cattle each member could graze on common meadows and how much wood each could take from the forest. The open-field system froze the technology of cultivation at the levels of the Middle Ages.

Landowners who wished to form compact farms and apply new methods could do so only by enclosing their own properties. Both common law and cost considerations, however, worked against fencing the numerous narrow strips, un-

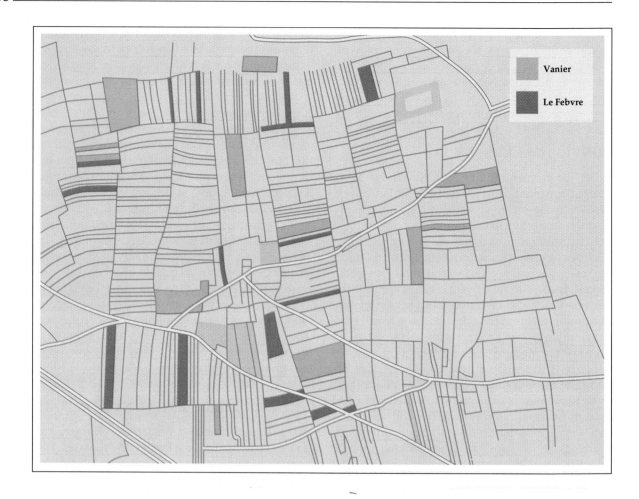

Map 18.1 AN OPEN FIELD VILLAGE IN FRANCE
The land in this Northern French village, originally blocked out in large fields, was subsequently subdivided into small strips owned by individual landowners or peasants. The scattered holdings of two large owners (Vanier and LeFebvre) are indicated by separate colors.

less the property of the entire village could be rearranged, which required the agreement of all the community. Such voluntary "enclosures" were nearly impossible to organize. In England, however, there was an alternative: An act of Parliament, usually passed in response to a petition by large landowners, could order the enclosure of all agrarian property in a village even against the opposition of some of its inhabitants. Then large landowners could fence in their land and manage it at their discretion.

Enclosing properties in a village was difficult and expensive. The lands of the village had to be surveyed and redistributed, in compact blocks, among the members in proportion to their former holdings. But over the course of the eighteenth century, the high rents and returns that could be earned with the new farming methods made enclosures very desirable investments. Numerous acts authorizing enclosure in a village had been passed by Parliament in earlier periods, but a new wave of such acts began to mount around the middle of the eighteenth century. Parliament passed 156 individual acts of enclosure in the decade of the 1750s; from 1800 to 1810 it passed 906 acts. Cumulatively, the enclosure movement all but eradicated the traditional open-field village from the British countryside.

The Impact of Enclosure While enclosure was clearly rational from an economic standpoint, it brought much human misery in its wake. The redistribution of the land deprived the poor of their traditional rights to the village's common land (which was usually divided among the villagers as well) and often left them with tiny, unprofitable plots. Frequently, they were forced to sell their holdings to their richer neighbors and seek employment as laborers or urban workers. However, no massive rural depopulation occurred in the wake of enclosures. For one thing, the actual work of fencing the fields required a good deal of labor, and some of the new husbandry techniques were also labor-intensive. In fact, the new industrial labor force drew as much on small-town artisans and casual laborers as on the dislodged rural poor.

The enclosure movement transformed the English countryside physically and socially, giving it the appearance it retains today of large verdant fields, neatly defined by hedges and fences. Enclosures in Britain led to the domination of rural society by great landlords and their prosperous tenant farmers, who usually held their farms under long leases. Conversely, they resulted in the near disappearance in England of the small peasant-type cultivators still typical of Western Europe. If enclosures did not abruptly push people to the towns, neither did they encourage

▶ Livestock and people could range freely over the land in open-field villages after the crops were harvested. The regrouping of scattered parcels and the enclosure of those consolidated properties would put an end to an entire rural way of life.

growth in rural settlements. They were therefore a major factor in the steady shift of population from countryside to city and in the emergence of the first urban, industrial economy.

SERFS AND PEASANTS ON THE CONTINENT

On the continent, peasants continued to work their small plots of land—whether owned or rented—in the village of their ancestors. In Eastern Europe, however, the peasants' status was defined by a system of serfdom similar to that which prevailed in Western Europe during the Middle Ages.

Lords and Serfs in Eastern Europe In most of Central and Eastern Europe, nobles retained a near monopoly on the ownership of land and peasants remained serfs, their personal freedom severely limited by the lord's supervision. Serfs could not marry, move away, or enter a trade without their lord's permission. This personal servitude ensured that peasants would be available to provide the labor that the lord required. In return the peasants received access to plots of land (which they did not actually own) and perhaps some rudimentary capital, such as seed for their crops. Much of their time, however, was spent in providing unpaid labor on their lord's domain, the amount of labor service determined by custom rather than law. Labor service often

The Condition of the Serfs in Russia

For publishing this unprecedented critique of the miseries and injustices of serfdom,
the author was imprisoned by Catherine II.

"A certain man left the capital, acquired a small village of one or two hundred souls [i.e., serfs], and determined to make his living by agriculture.... To this end he thought it the surest method to make his peasants resemble tools that have neither will nor impulse; and to a certain extent he actually made them like the soldiers of the present time who are commanded in a mass, who move to battle in a mass, and who count for nothing when acting singly. To attain this end he took away from his peasants the small allotment of plough land and the hay meadows which noblemen usually give them for their bare maintenance, as a recompense for all the forced labor which they demand from them. In a word, this nobleman forced all his peasants and their wives and children to work every day of the year for him. Lest they should starve, he doled out to them a definite quantity of bread.... If there was any real meat, it was only in Easter Week.

"These serfs also received clothing befitting their condition.... Naturally these serfs had no cows, horses, ewes, or rams. Their master did not withhold from these serfs the permission, but rather the means to have them. Whoever was a little better off and ate sparingly, kept a few chickens, which the master sometimes took for himself, paying for them as he pleased.

"In a short time he added to his two hundred souls another two hundred as victims of his greed, and proceeding with them just as with the first, he increased his holdings year after year, thus multiplying the number of those groaning in his fields. Now he counts them by the thousands and is praised as a famous agriculturalist.

"Barbarian! What good does it do the country that every year a few thousand more bushels of grain are grown, if those who produce it are valued on a par with the ox whose job it is to break the heavy furrow? Or do we think our citizens happy because our granaries are full and their stomachs empty?"

From Alexander Radischev, *A Journey from St. Petersburg to Moscow* (1790).

---

took up three days a week, and even more during harvest time. In Russia it was said that the peasants worked half the year for their master and only half for themselves (*see box*, above).

The degree of exploitation in European serfdom naturally varied. In Russia, Poland, Hungary, and certain small German states, the status of the serf scarcely differed from that of a slave. Russian and Polish serfs were in effect chattels who could be sold or traded at their lords' discretion, independent of the land they lived on or their family ties. In Russia the state itself owned many peasants and could assign them to work in the mines and factories of the Ural Mountains. Russian and Polish lords could inflict severe corporal punishment—up to 40 lashes—on their serfs, or six months in prison. Peasants had no right of appeal to the state against such punishments.

Serfdom was not as severe in Prussia or the Habsburg Monarchy, and the state did assure peasants of certain basic legal rights. In theory, peasants could not be expelled from their plots so long as they paid all their dues and rendered all the services they owed, although in practice the lords could usually remove them if they wished to. Since it was increasingly profitable for the lords to farm large domains directly, many felt an incentive to oust peasants from their tenures or to increase peasant labor services beyond customary limits.[1]

---

[1]In certain regions of Spain and southern Italy this situation had existed for centuries; noble lords monopolized the ownership of land in vast estates, or *latifundia*, on which their nominally free peasants provided the labor.

Lords and Peasants in the West   In Western Europe, by contrast, serfdom had waned. Most peasants were personally free and were free to buy land if they could afford it. Peasants were not necessarily secure or prosperous, however. There was not enough land to satisfy the needs of all peasant families, and lack of real independence was the rule. Moreover most French, German, Spanish, and Italian peasants still lived under the authority of a local noble in a system called *seigneurialism.* The peasants owed these lords various dues and obligations on their land, even if the peasants otherwise owned it. Seigneurial fees and charges (for example, a proportion of the harvest, somewhere between 5 and 15 percent) could be a considerable source of income for the lord and an oppressive burden to the already hard-pressed peasant. In addition, the lords administered petty justice in both civil and criminal matters; enjoyed the exclusive privilege of hunting rights across the lands of the village, no matter who owned them; and profited from monopolies on food-processing operations such as flour mills, bread ovens, and wine presses.

Concerned as they were with securing their basic livelihood, few peasants worried about trying to increase productivity with new farming methods. Satisfied with time-tested methods of cultivation, they could not risk the hazards of novel techniques. Along with growing grain for their own consumption, peasant households had to meet several obligations as well: royal taxes, rents, seigneurial dues, the tithe to the local

▶ **In Poland and Russia rural lords had direct control over their serfs without intervention by the state. Their powers included the right to inflict corporal punishment.**

church, and interest payments on their debts. In short, most peasant households in Western Europe were extremely insecure and relied on custom and tradition as their surest guides.

Peasant Survival Strategies   Every peasant household in Western Europe hoped to control enough land to ensure its subsistence and meet its obligations. Ideally, it would own this land. But most peasants did not own as much land as they needed and were obliged to rent additional plots or enter into sharecropping arrangements. Peasants therefore hated to see the consolidation of small plots into large farms, for this meant that the small plots that they might one day afford to buy or lease were becoming scarcer. The lords and the most prosperous peasants, on the other hand, were interested in extending their holdings, just like the "improving landlords" across the English Channel.

When the land that small peasants owned and rented did not meet their needs, they employed other survival strategies. Peasants could hire out as laborers on larger farms or migrate for a few months to other regions to help with grain or wine harvests. They might practice a simple rural handicraft or weave cloth for merchants on the putting-out system. Some engaged in illegal activities such as poaching game on restricted land or smuggling salt in avoidance of royal taxes. When all else failed, a destitute peasant family might be forced to take to the road as beggars.

In their precarious situation, peasants depended on strong family bonds. A peasant holding was a partnership between husband and wife, who usually waited until they had accumulated enough resources, including the bride's dowry, to establish their own household. Men looked for physical vigor and domestic skills in their prospective brides. ("When a girl knows how to knead and bake bread, she is fit to wed," went a French proverb.) In peasant households the wife's domain was inside the cottage, where she cooked, repaired clothing, and perhaps spent her evenings spinning yarn. Wives were also responsible for the small vegetable gardens or the precious hens and chickens that peasants tried to maintain to raise cash to help meet their obligations. The husband's work was outside: gathering fuel, caring for draft animals (if the family owned any), plowing the land, planting the fields, and nurturing the crops. But at harvest time everyone worked in the fields.

Peasants also drew strength from community solidarity. Many villages possessed common lands open to all residents. Poorer peasants could forage there for fuel and building materials, and could inexpensively graze whatever livestock they owned. Since villagers generally planted the same crops at the same times, after the harvest livestock was allowed to roam over the arable fields and graze on the stubble of the open fields, a practice known as vacant pasture. All in all, insecurity and the scarcity of land in continental villages made it risky and improbable that peasants would adopt innovative methods or agree to the division of common land.

The Limits of Agrarian Change on the Continent
Change therefore came more slowly to the continental countryside than it did to England. The regions that experienced the most active development were the Netherlands, the Paris basin and the northeast of France, the Rhineland, and the Po valley of Italy—all areas of dense settlement where high food prices encouraged landlords with large farms to invest in agricultural improvements and to adopt innovative English methods.

Like their English counterparts, innovating continental farmers waged a battle for managerial freedom, though the changes they sought were not as sweeping as the English enclosure movement. Most French villages worked the land under an open-field system in which peasants followed the same rhythms and routines of cultivation as their neighbors, with the village also determining the rights of its members on common lands. From the middle of the century on, the governing institutions of several provinces banned obligatory vacant pasture and allowed individual owners to enclose their land; some authorized the division of communal lands as well. But the French monarchy did not adopt enclosure as national policy, and after the 1760s provincial authorities proved reluctant to approve or enforce enclosure ordinances against the vigorous opposition of peasants. Traces of the medieval village thus lasted longer in France and Western Europe than in England.

▶ **In contrast to England as well as Russia, the small-holding peasant remained the most typical social type in France. In the peasant "family economy," husband and wife each made vital contributions to the household's productivity.**

In France in 1789, on the eve of the Revolution, probably 35 percent of the land was owned by the peasants who worked it. In this regard, the French peasants were more favored than those of most other European countries. But this society of small peasant farms was vulnerable to population pressures and was threatened by sharp movements in prices—two major characteristics of eighteenth-century economic history, as we have seen. The pattern of land distribution in France and the character of rural society, super-ficially favorable to the peasant, were thus also a source of acute tension in the countryside.

In the regions close to the Mediterranean Sea, such as southern Italy, difficult geographical and climatic conditions—the often rugged terrain, thin soil, and dearth of summer rain—did not readily allow the introduction of new techniques either, although many peasants improved their income by planting market crops like grapes for wine or olives for oil instead of grains for their own consumption. But most peasants continued to work their lands much as they had in the Late Middle Ages and for the same poor reward. Fertile areas near the Baltic Sea, such as east Prussia, benefited from the growing demand for grains in Western countries, but on the whole, Eastern Europe did not experience structural agrarian change until the next century.

IV. Eighteenth-Century Empires

After 1715 a new era began in the saga of European colonial development. The three pioneers in overseas expansion had by now grown passive, content to defend domains already conquered. Portugal, whose dominion over Brazil was recognized at the Peace of Utrecht in 1715, retired from active contention. Likewise, the Dutch could scarcely compete for new footholds overseas and now protected their interests through cautious neutrality. Although Spain continued its efforts to exclude outsiders from trade with its vast empire in the New World, it did not pose much of a threat to others. The stage of active competition was left to the two other Atlantic powers, France and Britain.

MERCANTILE AND NAVAL COMPETITION

The Decline of the Dutch   The case of Dutch decline is an instructive counterexample to the rise of French and British fortunes. In the seventeenth century the United Provinces, or Dutch Netherlands, had been Europe's greatest maritime power. But this federated state emerged from the wars of Louis XIV in a much weakened position. The country had survived intact, but it now suffered from demographic and political stagnation. The population of 2.5 million failed to rise during the eighteenth century, thus setting the Dutch apart from their French and British rivals. As a federation of loosely joined provinces, whose seven provincial oligarchies rarely acted in concert, the Netherlands could barely ensure the common defense of the realm.

The Dutch economy suffered when French and English merchants sought to eliminate them as the middlemen of maritime commerce, and when their industry failed to compete effectively. Heavy indirect taxes on manufactured goods and the high wages demanded by Dutch artisans forced up the price of Dutch products. What kept the nation from slipping completely out of Europe's economic life was its financial institutions. Dutch merchants shifted their activity away from actual trading ventures into the safer, lucrative areas of credit and finance. Their country was the first to perfect the uses of paper currency, a stock market, and a central bank. Amsterdam's merchant-bankers loaned large amounts of money to private borrowers and foreign governments, as the Dutch became financial instead of trading brokers.

The British and French Commercial Empires
Great Britain, a nation that had barely been able to hold its own against the Dutch in the seventeenth century, now began its rise to domination of the seas. Its one serious competitor was France, the only state in Europe to maintain both a large army and a large navy. Their rivalry played itself out in four regions. The West Indies, where both France and Britain had colonized several sugar-producing islands, constituted the fulcrum of both empires. The West Indian plantation economy, in turn, depended on slave-producing West Africa. The third area of colonial expansion was the North American continent, where Britain's 13 colonies became centers of settlement, whereas New France remained primarily a trading area. Finally, both nations sponsored powerful companies for trade with India and other Asian lands. These companies were supposed to compete for markets without establishing colonies.

The two colonial systems had obvious differences and important similarities. French absolutism fostered a centralized structure of control for its colonies, with intendants and military governors ruling across the seas as they did in the provinces at home. Britain's North American colonies, by contrast, remained independent from each other and to a degree escaped direct control from the home government, although crown and Parliament both claimed jurisdiction over them. British colonies each had a royal governor but also a local legislature of sorts, and most developed traditions of self-government. Nonetheless, the French and British faced similar problems and achieved generally similar results. Both applied mercantilist principles to the regulation of colonial trade, and both strengthened their navies to protect it.

Mercantilism   Mercantilist doctrine supported the regulation of trade by the state in order to increase the state's power against its neighbors (see Chapter 15). Mercantilism was not limited to the Atlantic colonial powers. Prussia was guided by mercantilism as much as were Britain and France, for all regarded the economic activities of their subjects as subordinate to the interests of the state.

Mercantilist theory advocated a favorable balance of trade as signified by a net inflow of gold and silver, and it assumed that a state's share of bullion could increase only at its neighbor's expense. Colonies could promote a favorable balance of trade by producing valuable raw materials or staple crops for the parent country, and by providing protected markets for the parent country's manufactured goods. Foreign states were to be excluded from these benefits as much as possible. By tariffs, elaborate regulations, bounties, or prohibitions, each government sought to channel trade between its colonies and itself. Spain, for example, restricted trade with its New World colonies exclusively to Spanish merchant vessels, although smugglers and pirates made a mockery of this policy.

Europe's governments sought to exploit overseas colonies for the benefit of the parent country and not simply for the profit of those who invested or settled abroad. But most of the parties

▶ **Commerce increased dramatically in the Atlantic ports of England and France as ships embarked for Africa, the Caribbean, North America, and Spanish America, as well as other parts of Europe. Businesses that supplied those ships or that processed colonial products brought back to Europe grew apace. Shown here, the port of Bristol in England.**

to this commerce prospered. The large West Indian planters made fortunes, as did the most successful merchants, manufacturers, and shipowners at home who were involved in colonial trade. Illicit trade also brought rewards to colonial merchants; John Hancock took the risk of smuggling food supplies from Boston to French West Indian planters in exchange for handsome profits.

Empire generally meant "trade," but this seaborne commerce depended on naval power: merchant ships had to be protected, trading rivals excluded, and regulations enforced. This reciprocal relationship between the expansion of trade and the deployment of naval forces added to the competitive nature of colonial expansion. Naval vessels needed stopping places for reprovisioning and refitting. This meant that ports had to be secured in strategic locations—such as Africa, India, and the Caribbean—and denied to rivals whenever possible.

THE PROFITS OF EMPIRE

The call of colonial markets invigorated European economic life. Colonial commerce provided new products, like sugar, and stimulated new consumer demand, which in turn created an impetus for manufacturing at home. It is estimated that the value of French commerce quadrupled during the eighteenth century. By the 1770s commerce with their colonies accounted for almost one-third of the total volume of both British and French foreign trade. The West Indies trade (mainly in sugar) bulked the largest, and its expansion was truly spectacular. The value of French imports from the West Indies increased more than tenfold between 1716 and 1788, from 16 million to 185 million livres.

The West Indies seemed to be ideal colonies. By virtue of their tropical climate and isolation from European society, which made slavery possible, the islands produced valuable crops difficult to raise elsewhere: tobacco, cotton, indigo, and especially sugar—a luxury that popular European taste soon turned into a necessity. Moreover, the islands could produce little else and therefore depended on exports from Europe. They could not raise an adequate supply of food animals or grain to feed the vast slave population, they could not cut enough lumber for build-

THE GROWTH OF ENGLAND'S FOREIGN TRADE IN THE EIGHTEENTH CENTURY Three-year averages of combined imports and exports.

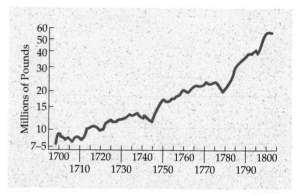

(Adapted from Dean, Phyllis, and Cole, W. A., *British Economic Growth, 1688–1959*, 1964, p. 49.)

ing, and they certainly could not manufacture the luxury goods demanded by the planter class.

Numerous variations of "triangular trade" (between the home country and two colonial areas) revolved around the West Indies. One pattern began with a ship departing from a British port with a cargo of manufactured products—paper, knives, pots, blankets, and the like—destined for the shopkeepers of North America. Landing at Marblehead, Massachusetts, or Philadelphia, the ship might exchange its goods for New England fish oil, fish, beef, and timber. These would then be transported to Jamaica or Barbados to be traded for sugar that would be turned over to British refineries many months later. Another variation might see a ship set out from Newport, Rhode Island (the chief slaving port in North America), with a cargo of New England rum. Landing in West Africa, it would acquire slaves in exchange for the rum and then sail to the Indies to sell the slaves—for bills of exchange or for molasses, from which more rum could be distilled. French and British manufacturers in the port cities made fortunes by refining or finishing colonial products such as sugar, indigo, tobacco, and furs and reexporting them to other European markets. For colonial commerce was superimposed on a complex pattern of European trade in which the Atlantic states carried off the lion's share of the profits.

SLAVERY, THE FOUNDATION OF EMPIRE

Much of this dynamic global trade rested on slavery. Only endless, backbreaking labor could transform a favorable climate and the investment of speculators into harvested plantation crops (*see box*, below). As a publication of the chamber of commerce of Nantes, France's chief slaving port, publicly argued, without slavery there would be no French colonial commerce at all. At the height of the Atlantic slave traffic, about 88,000 blacks were removed from Africa annually—half in British ships, a quarter in French, and the rest in Dutch, Portuguese, Danish, and American ships (see table on slavery). Over 600,000 slaves were imported into the island of Jamaica in the eighteenth century. The population of Saint-Domingue around 1790 comprised about half a million slaves compared with 35,000 whites of all nationalities and 28,000 mulattoes and free blacks.

MAGNITUDE OF THE SLAVE TRADE

The following figures represent the best current estimate of the number of persons removed from Africa and transported as slaves to the New World during the entire period of the Atlantic slave trade.

British Caribbean	1,665,000
British North America (to 1786)	275,000
United States (after 1786)	124,000
French Caribbean	1,600,000
Dutch Caribbean	500,000
Brazil	3,646,000
Spanish America	1,552,000

Source: Philip D. Curtin, *The Atlantic Slave Trade: A Census*, 1969.

A British Defense of Slavery and the Plantation Economy

"The most approved judges of the commercial interests of these Kingdoms have ever been of the opinion that our West-Indies and African Trades are the most nationally beneficial of any we carry on. It is also allowed on all hands that the Trade to Africa is the branch which renders our American Colonies and Plantations so advantageous to Great Britain; that traffic only affording our plantations a constant supply of Negroe-servants [slaves] for the culture of their lands in the produce of *sugars, tobacco, rice, rum, cotton, pimento*, and all others our plantations produce. So that the extensive employment of our shipping in, to, and from America, the great brood of seamen consequent thereupon, and the daily bread of the most considerable part of our British Manufacturers, are owing primarily to the labor of Negroes; who, as they were the first happy instrument of raising our Plantations, so their labor only can support and preserve them, and render them still more and more profitable to their Mother-Kingdom.

"The Negroe-Trade therefore, and the natural consequences resulting from it, may be justly esteemed an inexhaustible fund of Wealth and Naval Power to this Nation. And by the overplus of Negroes above what have served our own Plantations, we have drawn likewise no inconsiderable quantities of treasure from the Spaniards.... What renders the Negroe-Trade still more estimable and important is that near nine-tenths of those Negroes are paid for in Africa with British produce and manufactures only. We send no specie of bullion to pay for the products of Africa.... And it may be worth consideration, that while our Plantations depend only on planting by Negroes, they will neither depopulate our own Country, become independent of her Dominion, or any way interfere [i.e., compete] with the interests of the British Manufacturer, Merchant, or Landed Gentleman."

From Malachy Postlethwayt, *The National and Private Advantages of the African Trade Considered* (London, 1746).

A European commercial settlement on the Guinea coast of Africa in the early 18th century. The four compounds belong to Portugal (left), France (centre), England (right) and Holland (right foreground). In the left foreground the French director (numbered 14) returns with his train of servants. (4)

▶ **An early eighteenth-century European commercial settlement on the west coast of Africa consisted of four national compounds: Portuguese, French, English, and Dutch.**

Trafficking in slaves was competitive and risky but highly profitable. The demand for slaves in the West Indies, Brazil, Venezuela, and the southern colonies of North America kept rising, pushing up prices. In both Britain and France, chartered companies holding exclusive rights from the crown originally monopolized the slave trade. They did not actually colonize or conquer African territory but instead established forts, or "factories," on the West African coast for the coordination and defense of their slaving expeditions. Gradually, the monopolies were challenged by other merchants and investors who combined to launch their own ships on slaving voyages. The West Indian planters, who needed more slaves, welcomed all additional sources. The independent traders clustered in port cities like Bristol and Liverpool in England, and by the 1730s they had broken the monopoly on the slave trade.

The Ordeal of Enslavement   Europeans alone did not condemn black Africans to slavery. In this period, Europeans scarcely penetrated the interior of the continent; the forbidding topography and the resistance of the natives confined them to coastal areas. The actual enslavement took place in the interior at the hands of aggressive local groups whose chiefs became the intermediaries of this commerce. The competition among European traders for the slaves tended to drive up the prices that African middlemen could command in hardware, cloth, liquor, or guns. In response, some traders ventured into new areas where the blacks might be more eager to come to terms. Increasing demand, rising prices, and competitiveness spread the slave trade and further marred the future of West African society.

Many blacks failed to survive the process of enslavement at all. Some perished on the forced marches from the interior to the coast or on the nightmarish "middle passage" across the Atlantic, which has been compared to the transit in freight cars of Jewish prisoners to Nazi extermination camps in World War II. Since the risks of slaving ventures were high and the time lag between investment and return somewhere from one to two years, the traders sought to maximize their profits by jamming as many captives as possible onto the ships. Medium-sized ships carried as many as 500 slaves on a voyage, all packed below deck in only enough space for each person to lie at full length pressed against neighboring bodies, and with only enough headroom to crawl, not to stand. Food and provisions were held to a minimum. The mortality rate that resulted from these conditions was a staggering 10 percent or more on average, and in extreme cases exceeded 50 percent.

Agitation against slavery by reformers in Britain and France focused initially on the practices of the slave trade rather than on slavery itself. After the 1780s participation in the Atlantic slave trade tapered off, and the supply of slaves was replenished mainly from children born to slaves already in the New World. A dismal chapter in Europe's relations with the outside world dwindled to an end, although the final suppression of slaving voyages did not come for several more decades.

MOUNTING COLONIAL CONFLICTS

In the New World, the population of Britain's North American colonies reached about 1.5 million by midcentury. Some colonists pushed the frontier westward, while others clustered around the original settlements, a few of which—like Boston, New York, and Philadelphia—could now be called cities. The westward extension of the frontier and the growth of towns gave a vitality to the British colonial world that New France appeared to lack. Since there was little enthusiasm among the French for emigration to the Louisiana Territory or Canada, the French remained thinly spread in their vast dominions. Yet France's colonies were well organized and profitable. French West Indian planters underpriced the sugar of their British competitors, while the French trading company in India seemed more effective than its British rival in expanding its operations.

As French fishermen and fur traders prospered in Canada, French soldiers established a series of strongholds to support them, including the bastion of Fort Louisbourg at the entrance to the Gulf of St. Lawrence and a string of forts near the Great Lakes (see Map 18.2), which served as bridgeheads for French fur traders and as a security buffer for Quebec province. In Louisiana, at the other end of the continent, New Orleans guarded the terminus of the Mississippi River. On their side, the British established their first large military base in North America at Halifax, Nova Scotia, contesting French penetration of the fishing grounds and waterways of the St. Lawrence Gulf.

The unsettled Ohio valley was a second focus of colonial rivalry in North America. Pushing south from their Great Lakes trading forts and north from their posts on the Mississippi, the French began to assume control over that wil-

▶ **This diagram of "tight packing" below deck conveys the horror of the trans-Atlantic slaving voyages, known as the "middle passage." The drawing was circulated by British antislavery reformers.**

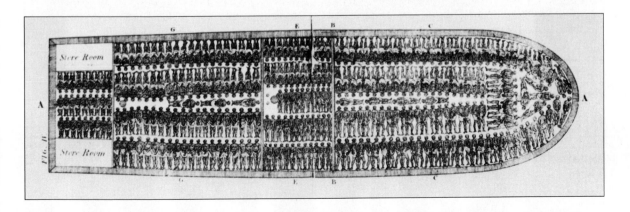

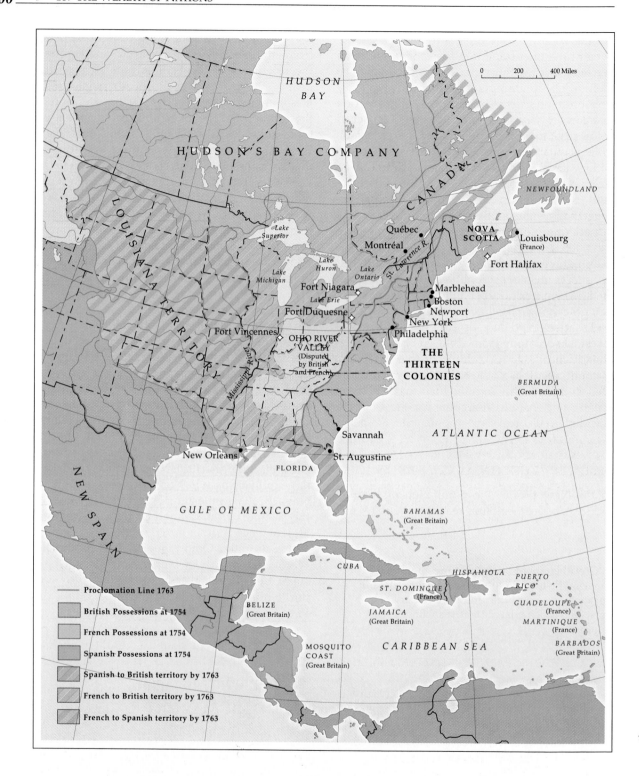

**Map 18.2 ANGLO-FRENCH RIVALRY IN NORTH AMERICA
AND THE CARIBBEAN AS OF 1756**

derness. A new string of forts formed pivots for potential French domination of the whole area between the Appalachian Mountains and the Mississippi—territory claimed and coveted by British subjects in the 13 colonies. The threat grew that the French might completely cut off the westward expansion of these colonies. On their side, the French feared that British penetration of the Ohio valley would lead to encroachments on their Canadian territory.

In jockeying for position, both sides sought the allegiance of the American Indians, and in this respect the French gradually gained the upper hand. Because they were traders only, not settlers, the French did not force the Native Americans from their traditional hunting grounds as the British had done repeatedly. Hence the American Indians were willing to cooperate with the French in sealing off the Ohio valley. A large land investment company, the Ohio Company of Virginia, faced ruin with that prospect, and in 1745 it attempted to break the French and Indian hold on the Ohio valley by sending an expedition against Fort Duquesne. Led by a young militiaman named George Washington, the raid failed.

Contrary to a British tradition of letting settled colonies pay for themselves, the home government eventually shouldered the burden of colonial defense. An expedition of British army regulars was sent to do the job that the colonial militia could not accomplish. Limited skirmishes were about to give way to a full-scale war, as each side began to reinforce its garrisons and naval squadrons. In May 1756, after several years of unofficial hostilities, Britain and France formally declared war.

THE GREAT WAR FOR EMPIRE

The pressures created by the competition of states, dynasties, and colonial empires in the eighteenth century exploded in midcentury in Europe's last large-scale war before the French Revolution. Its continental phase, known as the Seven Years' War, centered on the bitter rivalry between Austria and Prussia, but enmeshed Russia, France, and Britain as well. As we saw in Chapter 17, this protracted war ended in 1763 with a peace treaty that essentially restored the status quo. The other phase of this midcentury conflagration revolved around Anglo-French competition for empire in North America, the West Indies, and India. Historians call it the Great War for Empire, and its North American sector was known as the French and Indian War. It was this great global confrontation that produced the most striking changes when the smoke cleared.

The Great War for Empire was one of Britain's high moments in history, the stuff of patriotic legends. The conflict started, however, in quite another fashion. Jumping to the initiative on several fronts, the better-coordinated French struck the first blows. Calcutta in India, the Mediterranean island of Minorca, and several key British forts on the Great Lakes all fell to the French. At the same time, Britain's expeditionary force to the continent, fighting in alliance with Prussia, suffered humiliating defeats. Yet the French had disadvantages that would show in the long run. Spread so thinly in North America, they would be hard put to follow their early success in the French and Indian War. More important, France depended on naval support to reinforce, supply, and move its troops; unfortunately for France, a fairly even naval matchup in the 1740s had turned into clear British naval superiority by the 1750s. British ships of the line outnumbered French ships almost two to one.

Pitt's Strategy   When William Pitt became Britain's prime minister in 1758, the tide was about to turn in the Great War for Empire. Pitt, later the Earl of Chatham, was the grandson of a man who had made a fortune in India. Eloquent, supremely self-confident, infused with a vision of Britain's imperial destiny, Pitt had begun his career in Parliament in 1738 by denouncing the timid policies of the government and demanding that France be driven from the seas. Now he had his chance to lead Britain in the battle against its arch rival. Pitt brought single-mindedness and vigor to his task. Although he honored Britain's commitment to Prussia, he attached highest priority to defeating France in the colonial world. His strategy involved an immediate series of offensives and an imaginative use of the British navy. He assigned the largest segment of the British fleet to cover the French home fleet, and he waited.

The French hoped to invade the British Isles

as the surest method of bringing the enemy to the peace table, and the French fleet was ordered to prepare the way. In 1759 major battles were joined between French squadrons from Brest and Toulon and the British ships assigned to cover them. The British decimated the French fleet in these naval battles and thus decided the fate of colonial empires. Henceforth the British had an almost free hand at sea and could prevent France from deploying its superior military forces in the colonial world. Unable to transport men and supplies to its colonies, France could no longer reinforce its garrisons or repel amphibious landings by the British. In every theater of the war, French colonial possessions fell to the British, thanks to Britain's naval supremacy.

In the French and Indian War, for example, Britain's General Wolfe defeated France's General Montcalm in the battle of Quebec in September 1759. Had the French been able to reinforce Montreal, which they still held, they could have launched a counterattack against Wolfe's over-extended lines. But Pitt's successful naval strategy had made it impossible for the French to reinforce their overseas garrisons. By September 1760 this last outpost of French power in North America capitulated to the British, who had already ousted the French from the Ohio valley and the Great Lakes area. The same pattern unfolded in India, where soldiers in the employ of the British East India Company enlisted native allies and roundly defeated the French garrison and its allies. Finally, in the West Indies the long duel between the two powers turned into a rout. One by one Britain seized the French islands.

The Peace of Paris In the peace negotiations that followed (concluded by the Treaty of Paris in 1763) Britain did not insist on retaining all its conquests. A war-weary British government was

▶ **British naval power is shown here laying siege to the French stronghold of Louisbourg in July 1758.**

prepared to return certain colonies to France in exchange for an end to the fighting. Since British West Indian planters feared the added competition from the inclusion of the French islands in the British trading system, the British government returned several of them. But France did surrender Canada, which Britain chose to retain, perhaps unwisely; the British occupation of Canada removed the threat of French power, which had actually been an important factor in keeping the restive British colonists loyal to Britain. (On that front, France would soon have its revenge, when it came to the aid of the rebellious colonies in the War for American Independence.)

In the long run, India proved to be Britain's most important colonial domain. Its domination

▶ **This painting depicts a British District Officer in 1799 in Madras, one of the regions of the Indian subcontinent where the British began to exercise control after they ousted the French and defeated native forces that challenged them. The official's main function was to supervise the collection of taxes, which he did with the cooperation of local Indian princes and merchants.**

of India began with the Treaty of Paris, which excluded French troops from the subcontinent and left only British influence to have any force. Within a few decades the British moved from organizing profitable commerce in India to occupying and governing much of its territory.

French and English merchants capitalized aggressively on the commercial opportunities afforded by overseas colonies, plantation economies, and slavery, but these traders required backing by their states in the form of naval power. The growth of the British and French empires thus reflected the dynamics of the competitive state system. Those empires also propelled the growth of a global maritime economy and thus became a major factor in the economic dynamism of the eighteenth century. It is well to remember, however, that two totally disenfranchised groups supported the entire structure of state power and mercantile profit: the slaves in the colonies and the serfs, peasants, or agricultural laborers in Europe. Their toil produced the food supplies, staple commodities, and revenues that sustained the merchants, landowners, rulers, armies, and navies of the great powers. The economic future, however, lay not with slavery, serfdom, or seigneurialism but with innovations in agriculture and industrial production that would yield sustained economic growth and whose roots in England we have sketched. Along with the intellectual and cultural transformations to be discussed in the next chapter, these agricultural and industrial innovations heralded the dawn of the modern era.

Recommended Reading

Sources

*Young, Arthur. *Travels in France during the Years 1787, 1788, 1789.* 1972. A critical view of French agriculture by an English expert.

Radischev, Alexander. *A Journey from St. Petersburg to Moscow* [1790]. 1958. The first major exposé of the miseries of Russian serfdom.

*Smith, Adam. *An Inquiry into the Nature and Causes of the Wealth of Nations* [1776]. 1961.

Studies

*Ashton, T. S. *The Industrial Revolution, 1760–1830.* 1962. A brief, classic account of early industrialization in Britain.

*Berg, Maxine. *The Age of Manufactures: Industry, Innovation and Work in Britain, 1700–1820.* 1986. An important revisionist view, emphasizing the persistence of domestic and workshop manufacturing alongside the new factory system.

*Blum, Jerome. *The End of the Old Order in Rural Europe.* 1976. A valuable trove of information on rural conditions, particularly in the regions of serfdom.

Chambers, J. D., and G. E. Mingay. *The Agricultural Revolution, 1750–1880.* 1966. A reliable overview and interpretation.

Coleman, D. C. (ed.). *Revisions in Mercantilism.* 1969. An anthology of views about the nature of mercantilism in early modern Europe.

Crafts, N. F. R. *British Economic Growth during the Industrial Revolution.* 1985. A revisionist statistical study, emphasizing the gradual pace of industrialization.

Craton, Michael. *Sinews of Empire: A Short History of British Slavery.* 1974. An excellent synthesis.

*Davis, David B. *The Problem of Slavery in Western Culture.* 1966. And *The Problem of Slavery in the Age of Revolutions.* 1975. A comparative history of Western attitudes toward slavery, from ancient times to the nineteenth century.

Davis, Ralph. *The Rise of the Atlantic Economies.* 1973.

*De Vries, Jan. *The Economy of Europe in an Age of Crisis, 1600–1750.* 1976. A reliable survey of the European economy before the industrial revolution.

———. *European Urbanization, 1500–1800.* 1984. The development of major cities across Europe.

*Flandrin, Jean-Louis. *Families in Former Times: Kinship, Household and Sexuality.* 1979. From demographic history to the history of marriage and the family.

*Flinn, M. W. *The European Demographic System, 1500–1820.* 1981. A concise overview of the historical demography of early modern Europe.

Forster, Robert. *The House of Saulx-Tavanes: Versailles and Burgundy, 1700–1830.* 1971. A brilliant portrait of an aristocratic family and the peasant communities that supported its life style.

*Available in paperback.

Glass, D. V., and D. Eversley (eds.). *Population in History*. 1964. A collection of pioneering articles in historical demography.

*Gutmann, Myron. *Toward the Modern Economy: Early Industry in Europe*. 1988. Another fine synthesis illustrating the complexity of the European economy.

Hohenberg, Paul M., and Lynn Holen Lees. *The Making of Urban Europe, 1000–1950*. 1985. The impact of protoindustrialization and industrialization on cities.

Hufton, Olwen. *The Poor of Eighteenth-Century France*. 1974. A luminous study of the survival strategies of the indigent who could not sustain themselves on the land, and of the institutions which aided or confined them.

*Landes, David S. *The Unbound Prometheus: Technological Change and Industrial Development in Western Europe from 1750 to the Present*. 1969. A broad and engaging synthesis, emphasizing technological change.

Link, Edith M. *The Emancipation of the Austrian Peasantry, 1740–1789*. 1949. Traces the efforts and frustration of Habsburg agrarian reformers.

*Mantoux, Paul. *The Industrial Revolution in the Eighteenth Century*. 1962. A classic account, emphasizing the early inventions and factories.

*Mathias, Peter. *The First Industrial Nation: An Economic History of Britain, 1700–1914* (2d ed.). 1983. A reliable survey of quantitative and descriptive analysis.

North, Douglass C. *Structure and Change in Economic History*. 1981. Stresses the importance of supportive legal institutions in the coming of industrialism.

*Parry, J. H. *Trade and Dominion: The European Overseas Empires in the Eighteenth Century*. 1971. A panoramic overview.

Price, Roger. *The Economic Modernization of France, 1730–1870*. 1975. A good survey of economic trends and institutions in France.

Ringrose, David. *Transportation and Economic Stagnation in Spain, 1750–1850*. 1970. The factors that impeded economic growth in Spain—a counterexample to British economic growth.

Wilson, Charles. *England's Apprenticeship, 1603–1767*. 1965. An economic history of England before the agricultural and industrial revolutions began.

Wright, William E. *Serf, Seigneur and Sovereign: Agrarian Reform in Eighteenth-Century Bohemia*. Minneapolis, 1966. On the agrarian problem in the Czech domains of the Habsburg Empire.

*Wrigley, E. A. *Population and History*. 1969. A fascinating introduction to the field of historical demography.

Wrigley, E. A., and R. S. Schofield. *The Population History of England, 1541–1871: Studies in Social and Demographic History*. 1981. A reconstruction of population movements.

Joseph II's private orchestra performing after a
royal banquet in Vienna, 1760.

CHAPTER NINETEEN

THE AGE OF ENLIGHTENMENT

ALTHOUGH sharp breaks in the intellectual and cultural history of Europe have been rare, the seventeenth, eighteenth, and nineteenth centuries represent three relatively distinct phases of Western cultural development. The seventeenth century, as we have seen, was an age of genius in European thought, a period of great scientific and philosophical innovation. It was also an elitist age in that the audience for cultural activity remained small, while artists and writers generally depended on aristocratic patronage. If we jump ahead to the nineteenth century, we find a thriving middle-class cultural life in Europe's cities and the beginnings of mass literacy. Obviously, then, the eighteenth century was transitional.

During the eighteenth century the impact of scientific knowledge and the growth of religious skepticism matured into a naturalistic world view divorced from religion. There were now important thinkers who no longer believed in Christianity and wished to reduce its influence in society. They argued that there was no reality beyond human society, no afterlife to divert humanity from worldly concerns. Intellectuals developed a strong, sometimes arrogant, sense of their own power to guide society and point it toward change.

Although they were critics of their society, most eighteenth-century intellectuals lived comfortably amid Europe's high culture. They utilized its organized institutions, benefited from a dramatic expansion of publishing, and enjoyed its new literary and musical genres. They had little interest in or understanding of popular culture, however. Their growing sense of "public opinion" referred only to the educated elites of the aristocracy and the middle classes.

I. The Enlightenment

Building on seventeenth-century science, on skepticism in matters of religion, and on a heightened appreciation of the culture of Classical antiquity, eighteenth-century intellectuals approached their role in a new spirit. They believed that human behavior and institutions could be studied rationally, like Newton's universe, and that their faults could be corrected. They saw themselves as participants in a movement—which they called the Enlightenment—that could make educated men and women more understanding, tolerant, and virtuous.

THE BROADENING REVERBERATIONS OF SCIENCE

It is hard to think of two men less revolutionary in temperament than the seventeenth century's René Descartes and Isaac Newton. Both were conservative on matters outside the confines of science, had relatively little concern for social institutions, remained practicing Christians, and wrote only for small learned audiences. Yet their legacy of insight into the world of nature produced in succeeding generations what has been described as "a permanent intellectual insurrection," which unfolded in a spirit undreamed of by either man.

The Popularization of Science While eighteenth-century scientists pondered the cosmologies of Descartes and Newton, nonscientists in England and on the continent applied the methodologies of Descartes, Newton, and the philosopher John Locke to other realms of human thought. They fused the notion of methodical doubt and naturalistic explanations of phenomena into a scientific or mathematical spirit, which at bottom simply meant confidence in reason and a skeptical attitude toward accepted dogmas. They attempted to popularize scientific method, with the aim of transforming the values of Western civilization. Writers translated the discoveries of scientists into clear and even amusing general reading. The literary talents of these enthusiasts helped make household words of Newton and Descartes among educated Europeans.

A more calculating and ambitious propagandist of the scientific spirit was François-Marie Arouet, who wrote under the pen name of Voltaire and was the Frenchman who is virtually synonymous with the Enlightenment. While his chief talents lay in literature and criticism, Voltaire also spent some time studying Newton's work. In 1738 he published a widely read popularization called *Elements of the Philosophy of Newton*. However dry the study of physics, Voltaire argued, it frees the mind from dogma, and its experimental methods provide a model for the liberation of human thought. Moreover, Voltaire related Newton's achievement to the environment of a liberal England that also produced Francis Bacon and Locke, the three of whom Voltaire adopted as his personal Trinity. In his *Philosophical Letters on the English* (1734)—a celebration of English toleration and an indirect attack on religious bigotry, censorship, and social snobbery in France—Voltaire had already noted the respect enjoyed in England by its writers and scientists. He saw this recognition of talent as a crucial component of a free society and as a condition for the achievements of a man like Newton.

Popularizations of scientific method stimulated public interest in science, as mathematicians, cartographers, and astronomers made notable advances in their fields. But further scientific progress was far from automatic. In chemistry, for example, the traditions of alchemy persisted, and phenomena such as fire long escaped objective analysis. At the end of the century, however, a major breakthrough occurred when the Englishman Joseph Priestley isolated oxygen and the Frenchman Antoine Lavoisier analyzed the components of air and water and came close to explaining the process of combustion.

The vogue for science also had a dubious side, apparent, for example, in the great popularity of mesmerism. This pseudoscience of magnetic fields purported to offer its wealthy devotees relief from a variety of ailments by the use of special "electrical" baths and treatments. Although repeatedly condemned by the Academy of Sciences in Paris, mesmerism continued to attract educated followers.

Natural History The most widely followed scientific enterprise in the eighteenth century was

▶ French chemist Lavoisier conducts an experiment in his laboratory to study the composition of air during the process of respiration.

natural history, the science of the earth's development—a combination of geology, zoology, and botany. This field of study was easy for the nonscientist to appreciate. Its foremost practitioner was G. L. Buffon, keeper of the French Botanical Gardens—a patronage position that allowed him to produce a multivolume *Natural History of the Earth* between 1749 and 1778. Drawing on a vast knowledge of phenomena such as fossils, Buffon went beyond previous attempts to classify the data of nature and provided both a description and a theory of the earth's development.

Although he was a nonbeliever, Buffon did not explicitly attack religious versions of such events as the Creation; he simply ignored them, an omission of obvious significance to his readers. Similarly, while he did not specifically contend that human beings have evolved from beasts, he implied it. "It is possible," he wrote, "to descend by almost insensible degrees from the most perfect creature to the most formless matter." Buffon's earth did not derive from a singular act of divine creation that would explain the origins of human beings. The readers of his *Natural History* or its numerous popularizations in several languages

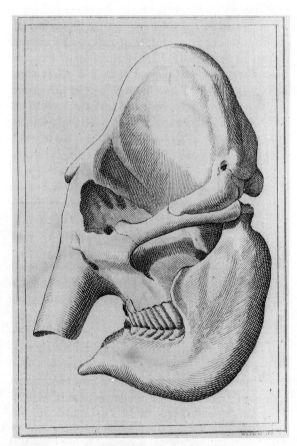

▶ A plate from the section on fossil remains in Buffon's *Natural History* illustrating the skull of an elephant from India.

thus encountered a universe that had developed through evolution.

BEYOND CHRISTIANITY

The erosion of biblical revelation as a source of authority is one hallmark of the Enlightenment. This shift derived some of its impetus from seventeenth-century scientists and liberal theologians who were themselves believing Christians but who opposed religious superstition or "enthusiasm," as they called it. They had hoped to accommodate religion to new philosophical standards and scientific formulations by eliminating the superstitious imagery that could make religion seem ridiculous, and by treating the world of nature as a form of revelation in which God's majesty could be seen. The devil, for example, could be considered as a category of moral evil rather than as a specific horned creature with a pitchfork. They hoped to bolster the Christian religion by deemphasizing miracles and focusing on reverence for the Creator and on the moral teachings of the Bible. Their approach did indeed help educated people adhere to Christianity during the eighteenth century. In the final analysis, however, this kind of thinking diminished the authority of religion in society.

Toleration One current of thought that encouraged a more secular outlook was the idea of toleration, as propounded by the respected French critic Pierre Bayle. Consciously applying methodical doubt to subjects that Descartes had excluded from such treatment, Bayle's *Critical and Historical Dictionary* (1697) put the claims of religion to the test of critical reason. Certain Christian traditions emerged from this scrutiny as the equivalent of myth and fairy tale, and the history of Christianity appeared as a record of fanaticism and persecution. Bayle's chief target was Christianity's attempts to impose orthodoxy at any cost (for example, the Spanish Inquisition and Louis XIV's revocation of the Edict of Nantes and persecution of French Protestants). Though a devout Calvinist himself, Bayle advocated complete toleration,

▶ **In 1745, the Habsburg Monarchy expelled an estimated 70,000 Jews from Prague to appease anti-Semitic sentiment.**

Joseph II on Religious Toleration

Between 1765 and 1781 Joseph II was joint ruler of the Habsburg Empire with his pious mother, Empress Maria Theresa. Joseph advocated a utilitarian approach to religious toleration (Document I) but made little headway against Maria Theresa's traditional insistence that the state must actively combat religious dissent. Soon after Maria Theresa's death Joseph promulgated a series of decrees on religion, including a landmark Toleration Edict for Protestants (Document II) and even a special, if somewhat less sweeping, edict of toleration for the Jews of his domains.

(I) LETTER TO MARIA THERESA, JULY 1777

"The word *toleration* has caused misunderstanding. . . . God preserve me from thinking it a matter of indifference whether the citizens turn Protestant or remain Catholics. . . . I would give all I possess if all the Protestants of your States would go over to Catholicism. The word *toleration* as I understand it, means only that I would employ any persons, without distinction of religion, in purely temporal matters, allow them to own property, practice trades, be citizens if they were qualified and if this would be of advantage to the State and its industry. . . . The undisturbed practice of their religion makes them far better subjects and causes them to avoid irreligion, which is a far greater danger to our Catholics. . . ."

(II) TOLERATION EDICT OF OCTOBER 1781

"We have found Ourselves moved to grant to the adherents of the Lutheran and Calvinist religions, and also to the non-Uniat Greek religion, everywhere, the appropriate private practice of their faith. . . . The Catholic religion alone shall continue to enjoy the prerogative of the public practice of its faith. . . . Non-Catholics are in future admitted under dispensation to buy houses and real property, to acquire municipal domicile and practice as master craftsmen, to take up academic appointments and posts in the public service, and are not to be required to take the oath in any form contrary to their religious tenets. . . . In all choices or appointments to official posts . . . difference of religion is to be disregarded."

From C. A. Macartney (ed.), *The Habsburg and Hohenzollern Dynasties* (Harper Torchbook, 1970), pp. 151 and 155–157.

which would allow any person to practice any religion or none at all. An individual's moral behavior rather than his or her creed is what mattered, according to Bayle. Ethics, he argued, do not depend on the Bible; a Muslim, a Confucian, a Jew, even an atheist can be moral.

The most striking success of the eighteenth-century campaign for toleration came with the Edict of Toleration issued by the Habsburg emperor Joseph II on his ascendancy to the throne in 1781. For the first time a Catholic Habsburg ruler recognized the right of Protestants and Jews in his realm to worship freely and to hold property and public office (*see box, above*). Joseph also tried to reduce the influence of the Catholic Church by ordering the dissolution of numerous monasteries on the grounds that they were use-

less and corrupt. Part of their confiscated wealth was used to support the medical school at the University of Vienna.

Deism   Voltaire became the Enlightenment's most vigorous antireligious polemicist. This prolific writer was one of the century's most brilliant literary stylists, historians, and poets. Those talents alone would have assured his fame. But Voltaire was also a dedicated antagonist of Christianity. For tactical reasons, much of his attack against *l'infame* ("the infamous thing"), as he called Christianity, targeted such practices as monasticism or the behavior of priests. His ultimate target, though, was Christianity itself, which, he declared, "every sensible man, every honorable man must hold in horror."

Voltaire's masterpiece, a best-seller called *The Philosophical Dictionary* (1764), had to be published anonymously and was burned by the authorities in Switzerland, France, and the Netherlands. Modeled after Bayle's dictionary, it was far blunter. Of theology, he wrote, "We find man's insanity in all its plenitude." Organized religion is not simply false but pernicious, he argued. Voltaire believed that religious superstition inevitably bred fanaticism and predictably resulted in bloody episodes like the Saint Bartholomew's Day Massacre.

Voltaire hoped that educated Europeans would abandon Christianity in favor of deism, a belief that recognized God as the Creator but held that the world, once created, functions according to natural laws without interference by God. Humanity thus lives essentially on its own in an ordered universe, without hope or fear of divine intervention and without the threat of damnation or the hope of eternal salvation. For deists, religion should be a matter of private contemplation rather than public worship and mythic creeds. Although certain figures in the Enlightenment went beyond deism to a philosophical atheism, which rejected any concept of God as unprovable, Voltaire's mild deism remained a characteristic view of eighteenth-century writers. At bottom, however, this form of spirituality was essentially secular. Broad-minded clergy could accept many of the arguments of eighteenth-century science and philosophy, but they could not accept deism.

THE PHILOSOPHES

Science and secularism became the rallying points of a group of French intellectuals known as the *philosophes.* Their traditionalist opponents employed this term to mock the group's pretensions, but the philosophes themselves used that label with pride. For they saw themselves as a vanguard, the men who raised the Enlightenment to the status of a self-conscious movement.

The leaders of this influential coterie of writers were Voltaire and Denis Diderot. Its ranks included mathematicians Jean d'Alembert and the marquis de Condorcet, the magistrate baron de Montesquieu, the government official Jacques Turgot, and the atheist philosopher baron d'Hol-

bach. Thus, the French philosophes came from both the aristocracy and the middle class. Outside of France their kinship extended to a group of brilliant Scottish philosophers, including David Hume and Adam Smith; to the German playwright Gotthold Lessing and the philosopher Immanuel Kant; to the Italian economist and penal reformer the marquis of Beccaria; and to such founders of the American Philosophical Society as Benjamin Franklin and Thomas Jefferson.

Intellectual Freedom The philosophes shared above all else a critical spirit, the desire to reexamine the assumptions and institutions of their societies and expose them to the tests of reason, experience, and utility. Today this might sound banal, but it was not so at a time when almost everywhere religion permeated society. Asserting the primacy of reason meant turning away from faith, the essence of religion. It meant a decisive break with the Christian worldview, which placed religious doctrine at the center of society's values. The philosophes invoked the paganism of ancient Greece and Rome, where the spirit of rational inquiry prevailed among educated people. They ridiculed the Middle Ages as the "Dark Ages" and contrasted the religious spirit of that era to their own sense of liberation and modernity. In *The Decline and Fall of the Roman Empire* (1776–1788), the historian Edward Gibbon declared that Christianity had eclipsed a Roman civilization that had sought to live according to reason rather than myths.

The inspiration of antiquity was matched by the stimulus of modern science and philosophy. The philosophes laid claim to Newton, who made the universe intelligible without the aid of revelation, and Locke, who uncovered the workings of the human mind. From Locke they went on to argue that human personality is malleable: its nature is not fixed, let alone corrupted by original sin. People are therefore ultimately responsible to themselves for what they do with their lives. Existing arrangements are no more nor less sacred than experience has proved them to be. As the humanists had several centuries before, the philosophes placed human beings at the center of thought. Unlike most humanists, however, they placed thought in the service of change and launched a noisy public movement.

They appeared clamorous to their contemporaries because they had to battle entrenched authority. Religious traditionalists and the apparatus of censorship in almost all countries threatened the intellectual freedom they demanded. The philosophes often had to publish their works clandestinely and anonymously. Sometimes they were pressured into withholding manuscripts from publication altogether or into making humiliating public apologies for controversial books. Even with such caution, almost all philosophes saw some of their publications confiscated and burned. A few were forced into exile or sent to jail: Voltaire spent several decades across the French border in Switzerland, and Voltaire and Diderot both spent time in prison. Although the notoriety produced by these persecutions stimulated the sale of their works, the anxiety took its toll.

By the 1770s, however, the philosophes had survived their running war with the authorities. Some of them lived to see their ideas widely accepted and their works acclaimed. Thus, even if they had contributed little else to the Western experience, their struggle for freedom of expression would merit them a significant place in its history.

Social Science But the philosophes achieved far more. In their scholarly and polemical writings, they investigated a wide range of subjects and pioneered in several new disciplines. Some philosophes—Voltaire, for example—were pathbreaking historians. Moving beyond traditional chronicles of battles and rulers' biographies, they studied culture, social institutions, and government structures in an effort to understand past societies as well as describe major events. Practically inventing the notion of social science, they investigated the theoretical foundations of social organization (sociology) and the workings of the human mind (psychology). On a more practical level, they proposed fundamental reforms in such areas as the penal system and education.

The philosophes embedded their study of social science in questions of morality and the study of ethics. Enlightenment ethics were generally utilitarian. Such philosophers as David Hume tried to define good and evil in pragmatic terms;

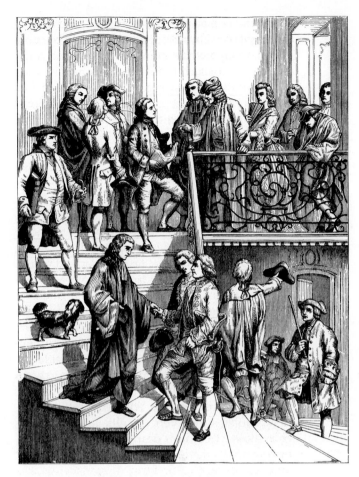

▶ An English engraving entitled "Voltaire's Staircase" suggests how the great writer stood at the center of Europe's literary and intellectual life. The fifth figure from the right at the top, Voltaire is bidding good-bye to d'Alembert.

they argued that social utility should become the standard for public morality. This approach to moral philosophy in turn raised the question of whether any human values were absolute and eternal. Among the philosophers who grappled with this challenge, Kant tried to harmonize the notion of absolute moral values with practical reason.

Political Liberty The most influential work of social science produced by the Enlightenment was probably *The Spirit of the Laws* (1748) by the French magistrate Montesquieu. The book offered a comparative study of governments and societies. On the one hand, Montesquieu introduced the perspective of relativism: He tried to analyze the institutions of government in relation to the special customs, climate, religion, and commerce of various countries. He thus argued that no single, ideal model of government existed. On the other hand, he deeply admired his own idealized version of the British system of government; he thereby implied that all societies could learn from the British about liberty.

Montesquieu's sections on liberty won a wide readership in Europe and in America, where the book was influential among the drafters of the United States Constitution. Political liberty, said Montesquieu, requires checks on those who hold power in a state, whether that power is exercised by a king, an aristocracy, or the people. Liberty can thrive only with a balance of powers, preferably by the separation of the executive, the legislative, and the judicial branches of government. Montesquieu ascribed a central role to aristocracies as checks on royal despotism. Indeed, many eighteenth-century writers on politics considered strong privileged groups, independent from both the crown and the people, as the only effective bulwarks against tyranny. To put it another way, Montesquieu's followers thought that the price for a society free from despotism was privilege for some of its members.

Liberal Economics French and British thinkers of the Enlightenment transformed economic theory with attacks against mercantilism and government regulation. We have earlier noted in Chapter 18 Adam Smith's critique of artificial restraints on individual economic initiative. In France, the *physiocrats* similarly argued that economic progress depended on freeing agriculture and trade from restrictions. Since in their view land was the only real source of wealth, they also called for reforms in the tax structure with a uniform and equitable land tax. In opposition to a traditional popular insistence on government intervention to maintain supplies of grain and flour at fair prices, the physiocrats advocated freedom for the grain trade to operate according to the dictates of supply and demand. The incentive of higher prices would encourage growers to expand productivity, they believed, and in this way the grain shortages that plagued Europe could eventually be eliminated, although at the cost of temporary hardship for most consumers.

DIDEROT AND THE ENCYCLOPEDIA

The Enlightenment thus produced not only a new intellectual spirit but also a wide range of critical writings on various subjects. In addition, the French philosophes collectively generated a single work that exemplified their notion of how knowledge could be useful: Diderot's *Encyclopédie* (*Encyclopedia*).

Denis Diderot never achieved the celebrity of his friend Voltaire, but his career proved equally central to the Enlightenment. The son of a provincial knife maker, Diderot was educated in Jesuit schools, but at the first opportunity he headed for Paris. Continuing to educate himself while living a bohemian existence, Diderot developed an unshakable sense of purpose: to make himself into an independent and influential intellectual.

Within a few years, he had published a remarkable succession of writings—novels and plays, mathematical treatises, an attack on inept medical practices, and several works on religion and moral philosophy. His most original writings examined the role of passion in human personality and in any system of values derived from an understanding of human nature. Specifically, Diderot affirmed the role of sexuality, arguing against artificial taboos and repression. As an advocate of what was sometimes called "the natural man," Diderot belies the charge leveled against the philosophes that they overemphasized reason to the neglect of feeling. The thread of religious criticism in these works was also notable. Starting from a position of mild skepticism, Diderot soon passed to deism and ended up in the atheist camp.

Diderot's unusual boldness in getting his works published brought him a considerable reputation but also some real trouble. Two of his books were condemned by the authorities as contrary to religion, the state, and morals. In 1749 he spent 100 days in prison and was released only after making a humiliating apology. At about that time, Diderot was approached by a publisher to translate a British encyclopedic reference work into French. After a number of false starts, he persuaded the publisher to sponsor instead an entirely new and more comprehensive work that would reflect the interests of the philosophes.

The Encyclopedia The *Encyclopedia, or Classified Dictionary of the Sciences, Arts, and Occupations,* an inventory of all fields of knowledge from the most theoretical to the most mundane, constituted an arsenal of critical concepts. As the preface stated: "Our Encyclopedia is a work that could only be carried out in a philosophic century. . . . All things must be examined without sparing anyone's sensibilities. . . . The arts and sciences must regain their freedom." The ultimate purpose of the Encyclopedia, wrote its editors, was "to change the general way of thinking." Written in this spirit by an array of talented collaborators, the expensive 28-volume *Encyclopedia* (1752–1772) fulfilled the fondest hopes of its editors and 4000 initial subscribers.

In such a work, religion could scarcely be ignored, but neither could it be openly attacked. Instead, the editors treated religion with artful satire or else relegated it to a philosophical or historical plane. Demystified and subordinated, religion was probed and questioned like any other subject, much to the discomfort of learned but orthodox critics.

Science stood at the core of the *Encyclopedia,* but the editors emphasized the technological or practical side of science with numerous articles and plates illustrating machines, tools, and manufacturing processes. They praised the roles of mechanics, engineers, and artisans in society and stressed the benefits of efficient production in the advance of civilization. Such emphasis implied that technology and artisanal skills constituted valuable realms of knowledge comparable to theoretical sciences such as physics and mathematics.

On economic topics the encyclopedists tended to echo the physiocratic crusade against restrictions on trade and agriculture. But the opinions and aspirations expressed were those of the elites, whose prerogatives, especially in matters of property, were not being threatened. Articles that might reflect the concerns of the popular masses on such issues as wages or affordable food prices were notably absent. Nor did the *Encyclopedia* take a novel line on questions of government. The authors generally endorsed abso-

▶ **Diderot's *Encyclopedia* focused much of its attention on technology. Illustrations of mechanical processes, such as the one shown here for making plate glass, filled 11 folio volumes.**

lute monarchy, provided it was reasonably efficient and just. The major political concerns of the editors were civil rights, freedom of expression, and the rule of law.

In retrospect, after the French Revolution, the *Encyclopedia* does not seem very revolutionary. Yet in the context of the times, it assuredly was. The revolution that Diderot sought was intellectual. As he wrote in a letter to a friend, the encyclopedists were promoting "a revolution in the minds of men to free them from prejudice." Judging by the reaction of religious and government authorities, they were eminently successful. "Up till now," commented one French bishop, "hell has vomited its venom drop by drop." Now, he concluded, it could be found assembled between the *Encyclopedia*'s covers.

After allowing the first three volumes to appear, the government banned the *Encyclopedia* in 1759 and revoked the bookseller's license to issue the remaining volumes. As the attorney general of France put it: "There is a project formed, a society organized to propagate materialism, to destroy religion, to inspire a spirit of independence, and to nourish the corruption of morals." Most of the *Encyclopedia*'s contributors prudently withdrew from the project, but Diderot went underground and continued the herculean task until the subscribers received every promised volume, including 11 magnificent folios of illustrations. By the time these appeared, the persecutions had receded. Indeed, the *Encyclopedia* was reprinted in cheaper editions (both legal and pirated) that sold out rapidly, earning fortunes for their publishers. This turn of events ensured the status of Diderot's project as the landmark of its age.

JEAN-JACQUES ROUSSEAU

Arguably the most original and influential eighteenth-century thinker, Jean-Jacques Rousseau stood close to but self-consciously outside the coterie of the philosophes. For Rousseau provided in his life and writing a critique not only of the status quo but of the Enlightenment itself. Obsessed with the issue of moral freedom, Rousseau found society far more oppressive than most philosophes would admit, and he considered the philosophes themselves to be part of the problem.

Young Rousseau won instant fame when he submitted a prize-winning essay in a contest sponsored by a provincial academy on the topic, "Has the restoration of the arts and sciences had a purifying effect upon morals?" Unlike most respondents, Rousseau answered that it had not. He argued that the lustrous cultural and scientific achievements of recent decades were producing pretension, conformity, and useless luxury. Most scientific pursuits, he wrote, "are the effect of idleness which generate idleness in their turn." The system of rewards in the arts produces "a servile and deceptive conformity . . . the dissolution of morals . . . and the corruption of taste." Against the decadence of high culture, he advocated a return "to the simplicity which prevailed in earliest times"—manly physical pastimes, self-reliance, independent citizens instead of fawning courtiers.

Rousseau had no wish to return to a state of nature, a condition of anarchy where force ruled and people were slaves of appetite. But the basis of morality, he argued, was conscience, not reason. "Virtue, sublime science of simple minds: are not your principles graven on every heart?" This became one of his basic themes in two popular works of fiction, *Julie, or the New Heloise* (1761), and *Emile, or Treatise on Education* (1762).

In the first novel Julie is educated in virtue by her tutor St. Preux but allows herself to fall in love with and be seduced by him. In the second half of the novel, Julie breaks away from St. Preux and marries Monsieur de Wolmar, her father's wealthy friend. She maintains a distant friendship with her old lover and rears her children in exemplary fashion, overseeing their education. In the end she overcomes her past moral lapse and sacrifices her own life to save one of her children. Wolmar then brings in the chastened St. Preux to continue the children's education. This tale of love, virtue, and motherhood won an adoring audience of male and female readers who identified with the characters, shed tears over their moral dilemmas, and applauded Rousseau for this superb lesson in the new sensibility.

Emile recounts the story of a young boy raised to be a moral adult by a tutor who emphasized experience over book learning and who considered education a matter of individual self-development. This new kind of man of course required a comparably sensitive wife, attuned to practical matters and without vain aristocratic pretenses. Sophie, the girl in question, received a very different type of education, however, one concerned with virtue but far more limited in its scope. Rousseau depicted men and women liberating themselves from stultifying traditional values, yet in the new relationships he portrayed in these novels, women held a decidedly subordinate position. Their virtues were to be exclusively domestic in character, while the men would be prepared for public roles—a distinction that deeply troubled feminist thinkers in the future (*see box, below*).

Rousseau himself was by no means a saint. His personal weaknesses—including the illegitimate child that he fathered and abandoned—doubtless contributed to his preoccupation with morality and conscience. Nonetheless, his rebellious life as well as his writings greatly impressed the generation of readers and writers coming of age in the 1770s and 1780s. Not only did he quarrel with the repressive authorities of Church and

Mary Wollstonecraft on the Education of Women

The sharpest challenge to Rousseau's widely shared attitude toward women came only in 1792, with the publication of Mary Wollstonecraft's **A Vindication of the Rights of Woman.** *Inspired by the French Revolution's doctrine of natural rights, this spirited writer deplored the fact that society kept women (in her words) frivolous, artificial, weak, and in a perpetual state of childhood. While men praised women for their beauty and grace, they hypocritically condemned them for a concern with vanity, fashion, and trivial matters, yet refused to treat them as rational human beings who could contribute to society as much as men. Her book emphasized the need for educational reform that would allow women to develop agile bodies and strong minds. Along the way Wollstonecraft took particular aim at Rousseau's* **Emile.**

"The conduct and manners of women, in fact, evidently prove that their minds are not in a healthy state; for, like the flowers which are planted in too rich a soil, strength and usefulness are sacrificed to beauty. . . . One cause of this barren blooming I attribute to a false system of education, gathered from the books written on this subject by men who, considering females rather as women than human creatures, have been more anxious to make them alluring mistresses than affectionate wives and rational mothers. The understanding of the sex has been so bubbled by this specious homage, that the civilized women of the present century, with a few exceptions, are only anxious to inspire love, when they ought to cherish a nobler ambition, and by their abilities and virtues exact respect.

"[T]he most perfect education, in my opinion, is such an exercise of the understanding as is best calculated to strengthen the body and form the heart. Or, in other words, to enable the individual to attain such habits of virtue as will render it independent. In fact, it is a farce to call any being virtuous whose virtues do not result from the exercise of its own reason. This was Rousseau's opinion respecting men: I extend it to women, and confidently assert that they have been drawn out of their sphere by false refinement, and not by an endeavour to acquire masculine qualities. Still the regal homage which they receive is so intoxicating, that till the manners of the times are changed, and formed on more reasonable principles, it may be impossible to convince them that the illegitimate power, which they obtain by degrading themselves, is a curse, and that they must return to nature and equality. . . ."

From Sandra M. Gilbert and Susan Gubar (eds.), *The Norton Anthology of Literature by Women: The Tradition in English* (W. W. Norton, 1985).

▶ **The French revolutionaries acclaimed both Voltaire and Rousseau and transferred their remains to a new Pantheon. But Rousseau was the man considered by many French people to be the Revolution's spiritual father, as suggested by his position in this allegorical painting of 1793, filled with the new symbolism of liberty and equality.**

state—who repeatedly banned his books—but he also attacked the pretensions of his fellow philosophes, whom he considered arrogant, cynical, and lacking in spirituality. By the 1770s the commanding figures of the Enlightenment, such as Voltaire and Diderot, had won their battles and had become masters of the most prestigious academies and channels of patronage. In a sense, they had themselves become the establishment. For younger writers frustrated by the existing distribution of influence and patronage, Rousseau became the inspiration.

Rousseau's Concept of Freedom What proved to be Rousseau's most enduring work, *The Social Contract*, published in 1762, became famous only after the French Revolution dramatized the issues that the book had raised. (The Revolution, it could be said, did more for the book than Rousseau did for the Revolution, which he neither prophesied nor advocated.) *The Social Contract* was not meant as a blueprint for revolution but rather as an ideal standard against which readers might measure their own society. Rousseau did not expect that this standard could be achieved in practice, since existing states were too large and complex to allow the kind of participation that he considered essential.

For Rousseau, a government distinct from the individuals over whom it claims to exercise authority has no validity. Rousseau denied the almost universal idea that some people are meant to govern and others to obey. In the ideal polity, Rousseau said, individuals have a role in making the law to which they submit. By obeying it, they are thus obeying themselves as well as their fellow citizens. For this reason, they are free from arbitrary power. To found such an ideal society, each citizen would have to take part in creating a social contract laying out the society's ground rules. By doing so, these citizens would establish themselves as "the sovereign." This sovereign—the people—then creates a government that will carry on the day-to-day business of applying the laws.

Rousseau was not advocating simple majority rule but rather a quest for consensus as to the best interests of all citizens. Even if it *appears* contrary to the welfare of some or even many citizens, he believed, the best interest of the community must be every individual's best interest as well, since that individual is a member of the community. Rousseau called this difficult concept "the general will." Deferring to the general will means that an individual ultimately must do what one *ought*, not simply what one *wants*. This commitment derives from conscience, which must do battle within the individual against passion, appetite, and mere self-interest. Under the social contract, to use Rousseau's most striking phrase, the individual "will be forced to be free" (*see box,* p. 619). Thus for Rousseau, individual freedom depends on a political framework involving consent and participation as well as subordination of individual self-interest to the commonweal. More than any of the philosophes, Rousseau argued that individual freedom depends on the arrangements governing the collectivity.

II. Eighteenth-Century Elite Culture

The Enlightenment was merely one dimension of Europe's cultural life. Europe's economic expansion and relative prosperity, discussed in the previous chapter, were matched by a marked increase in publishing activity that served diverse audiences and by the creation of new cultural forms and institutions. Although the aristocracy still dominated society, men and women of lesser social status participated prominently in cultural life. Eighteenth-century elite culture was cosmopolitan, spilling across national borders as well as certain social class lines.

COSMOPOLITAN HIGH CULTURE

As the expansive, cosmopolitan aspects of European high culture are described here, it must be remembered that the mass of Europe's peasants and workers remained virtually untouched by these developments, insulated within their local environments and traditions. But the educated and wealthy, the numerically small and influential elites, enjoyed a sense of belonging to a common European civilization. French was the international language of this culture; even King Frederick II of Prussia favored French over German. Whatever the effects of Frederick's attitude might have been—the German dramatist Lessing, for one, considered it a deplorable cultural prejudice—the widespread knowledge of French meant that ideas and literature could circulate easily past language barriers.

Travel Europeans sharpened their sense of common identity through travel literature and by their appetite for visiting foreign places. Although transportation was slow and uncomfortable, many embarked on a "grand tour," whose

Rousseau's Concept of the General Will

"The essence of the social compact reduces itself to the following terms: Each of us puts his person and all his power in common under the supreme direction of the general will, and, in our collective capacity, we receive each member as an indivisible part of the whole....

"In fact, each individual, as a man, may have a particular will contrary or dissimilar to the general will which he has as a citizen. His particular interest may speak to him quite differently from the common interest: his absolute and naturally independent existence may make him look upon what he owes to the common cause as a gratuitous contribution, the loss of which will do less harm to others than the payment of it is burdensome to

himself.... He may wish to enjoy the rights of citizenship without being ready to fulfill the duties of a subject. The continuance of such an injustice could not but prove the undoing of the body politic.

"In order then that the social compact may not be an empty formula, it tacitly includes the undertaking, which alone can give force to the rest, that whoever refuses to obey the general will shall be compelled to do so by the whole body. This means nothing less than that he will be forced to be free; for this is the condition which, by giving each citizen to his country, secures him against all personal dependence. In this lies the key to the working of the political machine...."

From *The Social Contract*, Book I, chs. 6–7.

highlights included visits to Europe's large cities (such as London, Paris, Rome, and Vienna) and to the ruins of antiquity—to the glories of the modern and the ancient worlds.

Kings, princes, and municipal authorities were embellishing their towns with plazas, public gardens, theaters, and opera houses. Toward the end of the century, amenities such as street lighting and public transportation began to appear in a few cities, with London leading the way. From the private sector came two notable additions to the urban scene: the coffeehouse and the storefront window display. Coffeehouses, where customers could chat or read, and enticing shop windows, which added to the pleasures of city walking (and stimulated consumer demand), enhanced the rhythms of urban life for tourists and residents alike. When a man is tired of London, Samuel Johnson remarked, he is tired of life.

Travelers on tour invariably passed from the attractions of bustling city life to the silent monuments of antiquity. As the philosophes recalled the virtues of pagan philosophers like Cicero, in-

terest grew in surviving examples of Greek and Roman architecture and sculpture. Many would have agreed with the German art historian Johann Winckelmann that Greek sculpture was the most worthy standard of aesthetic beauty in all the world.

The Republic of Letters   Among writers, intellectuals, and scientists, the sense of a cosmopolitan European culture devolved into the concept of a "republic of letters." The phrase, introduced by sixteenth-century French humanists, was popularized by Pierre Bayle (noted earlier as a pro-

▶ **This painting of Mme. Geoffrin's Salon in 1755, which dates from 1814, reflects the artist Lemonnier's imagination rather than historical reality. His canvas depicts an assemblage of all the major philosophes and their patrons that never actually took place. Yet it does accurately convey the social atmosphere and serious purpose of the Parisian salons. At the center is a bust of Voltaire, who lived in exile at the time.**

ponent of religious toleration), who published a critical journal that he called *News of the Republic of Letters*. The title implied that the realm of culture and ideas stretched across Europe's political borders. In one sense it was an exclusive republic, limited to the educated; but it was also an open society to which people of talent could belong regardless of their social origins. For this reason, European intellectuals felt that their "republic of letters" was a model for a "public sphere" in which political and social issues could be debated freely as well.

Aside from the medium of the printed word, the republic of letters was organized around the salons and the academies. Both institutions encouraged social interchange by bringing together socially prominent men and women with talented writers. The philosophes themselves exemplified this social mixture, for their "family" was composed in almost equal measures of nobles (Montesquieu, Holbach, Condorcet) and commoners (Voltaire, Diderot, d'Alembert). Voltaire, while insisting that he was as good as any aristocrat, had no desire to topple the aristocracy from its position; rather he sought amalgamation. As d'Alembert put it, talent on the one hand and birth and eminence on the other both deserve recognition.

The salons, usually organized and led by women of wealthy bourgeois or noble families, sought to bring together important writers with the influential persons they needed for favors and patronage. The salon of Madame Tencin, for example, helped launch Montesquieu's *Spirit of the Laws* in the 1740s, while the salon of Madame du Deffand in the 1760s became a forum where the philosophes could test their ideas (see figure, p. 620). The salons also helped to enlarge the audience and contacts of the philosophes by introducing them to a flow of foreign visitors, ranging from German princes to Benjamin Franklin. Private newsletters kept interested foreigners and provincials abreast of activities in the Parisian salons when they could not attend personally, but salons also operated in Vienna, London, and Berlin.

The salons placed a premium on elegant conversation and wit. The women who ran them insisted that intellectuals make their ideas lucid and comprehensible to laypeople, which increased the likelihood that their thought and writings would have some impact. The salons were also a forum where men learned to take women seriously, and they constituted a unique cultural space for women between the domestic and public spheres. But the salons' emphasis on style over substance led Rousseau to denounce them as artificial rituals that prevented the display of genuine feeling and sincerity.

Throughout Europe, freemasonry was another important form of cultural sociability that often crossed the lines of class and (less commonly) of gender. Operating in an aura of secretiveness and symbolism, the masonic lodges fostered a curious mixture of spirituality and rationalism. Originating as clubs or fraternities dedicated to humane values, they attracted a wide range of educated nobles, commoners, and liberal clergy, while a few lodges accepted women as well. But toward the end of the century, freemasonry was torn by sectarian controversies and its influence seemed to be diminishing.

The Learned Academies As important for the dissemination of ideas in the eighteenth century as the salons were the learned academies. These ranged from the Lunar Society in Birmingham, a forum for innovative British industrialists and engineers, to state-sponsored academies in almost every capital of Southern and Central Europe, which served as conduits for advanced scientific and philosophical ideas coming from Western Europe. In France, moreover, academies were established in more than 30 provincial cities, most of which became strongholds of advanced thinking outside the capital.

These provincial academies were founded after the death of Louis XIV in 1715, as if in testimony to the liberating effect of his demise. Most began as literary institutes, concerned with upholding traditional values such as purity of literary style. A few academies adhered to such goals well into midcentury, but most gradually shifted their interests from literary matters to scientific and practical questions in such areas as commerce, agriculture, and local administration. They became offshoots, so to speak, of the *Encyclopedia*'s spirit. Indeed, when a Jesuit launched an attack against the *Encyclopedia* in the Lyons

Academy, many members threatened to resign unless he retracted his remarks. By the 1770s the essay contests sponsored by the provincial academies and the papers published by their members had turned to such topics as population growth, capital punishment and penology, education, poverty and welfare, the grain trade, the guilds, and the origins of sovereignty.

A parallel shift in membership occurred. The local academies began as privileged corpora-

▶ **The title page of Samuel Johnson's pioneering** *Dictionary of the English Language* **(1755 edition), one of the masterpieces of eighteenth-century literature.**

A

DICTIONARY

OF THE

ENGLISH LANGUAGE:

IN WHICH

The WORDS are deduced from their ORIGINALS,

AND

ILLUSTRATED in their DIFFERENT SIGNIFICATIONS

BY

EXAMPLES from the best WRITERS.

TO WHICH ARE PREFIXED,

A HISTORY of the LANGUAGE,

AND

AN ENGLISH GRAMMAR.

BY SAMUEL JOHNSON, A.M.

IN TWO VOLUMES.

VOL. I.

Cum tabulis animum censoris sumet honesti ;
Audebit quæcunque parum splendoris habebunt,
Et sine pondere erunt, et honore indigna ferentur,
Verba movere loco ; quamvis invita recedant,
Et versentur adhuc intra penetralia Vestæ :
Obscurata diu populo bonus eruet, atque
Proferet in lucem speciosa vocabula rerum,
Quæ priscis memorata Catonibus atque Cethegis,
Nunc situs informis premit et deserta vetustas. Hor.

LONDON
Printed by W. STRAHAN,
For J. and P. KNAPTON ; T. and T. LONGMAN ; C. HITCH and L. HAWES ;
A. MILLAR· and R. and J. DODSLEY.
MDCCLV.

tions, dominated by the nobility of the region. Associate membership was extended to commoners from the ranks of civil servants, doctors, and professionals. Gradually, the distinction between regular and associate participants crumbled. The academies admitted more commoners to full membership, and a fragile social fusion took place.

PUBLISHING AND READING

The eighteenth century saw a notable rise in publishing that was geared to several kinds of readers. Traveling circulating libraries originated in England around 1740 and opened untapped markets for reading material; by the end of the century almost 1000 traveling libraries had been established. "Booksellers," or publishers—the intermediary between author and reader—combined the functions of a modern editor, printer, salesperson, and (if need be) smuggler. Their judgment and marketing techniques helped create as well as fill the demand for books, since they conceived and financed a variety of works. The *Encyclopedia* originated as a bookseller's project; so, too, did such enduring masterpieces as Samuel Johnson's *Dictionary*, a monumental lexicon that helped purify and standardize the English language. Booksellers commissioned talented stylists to write popular versions of serious scientific, historical, and philosophical works. Recognizing a specialized demand among women readers, they increased the output of fictional romances and fashion magazines, and also began to publish more fiction and poetry by women. In general, the entertainment and instruction of a diverse but educated audience became the focus of most publishers.

Journals and Newspapers Eighteenth-century publishing was notable for the proliferation of periodicals. In England, which pioneered in this domain, the number of periodicals increased from 25 to 158 between 1700 and 1780. In one successful model, Addison and Steele's *Spectator* (1711), each issue consisted of a single essay that sought in elegant but clear prose to raise the reader's standards of morality and taste. Their goal was "to enliven Morality with Wit, and to temper

Wit with Morality. . . . To bring Philosophy . . . to dwell in clubs and assemblies, at tea-tables and coffeehouses." Eliza Haywood adapted this format in her journal, *The Female Spectator* (1744–1756), where she avocated improvement in the treatment of women and greater "opportunities of enlarging our minds." (A comparable periodical in France, the *Journal des Dames*, which appeared in 1759, propagated the writings of the Enlightenment but also raised the question of women's place in society.) Another type of journal published extracts and summaries of books and covered current events and entertainment; one such journal, the *Gentleman's Magazine*, reached the impressive circulation of 15,000 in 1740. More learned periodicals specialized in book reviews and serious articles on science and philosophy.

Most important for the future of reading habits in Europe was the daily newspaper, which originated in England. Papers like the *London Chronicle* at first provided family entertainment and then took on classified advertisements (thereby spurring consumerism and the notion of fashion). English newspapers of course published news of current events, but only after strenuous battles for permission from a reluctant government did they win the right to report directly on parliamentary debates. In France, a handful of major Parisian newspapers enjoyed privileged monopolies in exchange for full compliance with government censorship. This severely restricted their ability to discuss government and politics, although other periodicals published outside France's borders helped satisfy the demand for such coverage in France. With the Revolution of 1789, however, a politically aroused French citizenry provided unimagined opportunities for the growth of political journalism.

"Bad Books" The demand for books and the dynamism of the publishing industry created new employment opportunities for men and women. Although the number of would-be writers swelled, relatively few could develop their talents without constraint or achieve financial independence without patronage. Many remained poverty-stricken and frustrated.

Publishers thus could hire legions of otherwise unemployed writers to turn out the kinds of books for which they sensed a great demand: potboilers, romances, salacious pamphlets, and gossip sheets, which pandered to low tastes. Paid for quantity and speed rather than quality, these hack writers led a precarious, humiliating existence. Booksellers and desperate writers saw money to be made in sensational pamphlets assailing the character of notorious aristocrats, in partisan pamphlets attacking a particular faction in court politics, and in pornography. Sometimes they combined character assassination and pornography in pamphlets dwelling on the alleged perversions of rulers or courtiers. For all its wild exaggeration, such material helped "desacralize" monarchy and created a vivid image of a decadent aristocracy.

To satisfy the public's demand for gossip, character assassination, and pornography in violation of laws regulating the book trade in France, publishers located just across the French border marketed such books and pamphlets clandestinely. They smuggled this material into France—along with banned books by writers like Voltaire and Rousseau—using networks of couriers and distributors. In their sales lists of what they called Philosophic Books, the clandestine publishers lumped together banned books by serious writers along with such illicit publications as *The Scandalous Chronicles*, *The Private Life of Louis XV*, and *Venus in the Cloister* (a pornographic account of the alleged perversions of the clergy). The police made the same judgment. In attempting to stop the flow of "bad books," they scarcely distinguished between a banned work by Voltaire assaulting religious bigotry and a libelous pamphlet depicting the queen as a corrupt pervert.

LITERATURE, MUSIC, AND ART

Unlike the artistic style of the seventeenth century, generally classified as Baroque, that of the eighteenth century cannot be given a single stylistic label. The nature of the audience and the sources of support for writers and composers also varied considerably. But several artistic trends proved to be of lasting importance: the rise of the novel in England, the birth of romantic po-

▶ One of the leading French portrait painters, and the most successful female artist of the era anywhere, was Élisabeth Vigée-Lebrun, who enjoyed the patronage of Queen Marie Antoinette. Shown here is one of several portraits that she painted of the French queen.

etry, the development of the symphony in Austria, and the changing social context of French painting late in the century.

The Rise of the Novel   The modern novel had its strongest development in England, where writers and booksellers cultivated a growing middle-class reading public. The acknowledged pioneer of this new genre was Samuel Richardson, a bookseller as well as a writer. With a series of letters telling the story, Richardson's *Pamela, or Virtue Rewarded* (1740) recounted the trials and tribulations of an honest if somewhat hypocritical servant girl. Pamela's sexual virtue is repeatedly challenged but never conquered by her wealthy employer, Mr. B., who finally agrees to marry her. An instant success, this melodrama broke from the standard forms and heroic subjects of most narrative fiction. Richardson dealt with recognizable types of people.

Pamela's apparent hypocrisy, however, prompted a playwright and lawyer named Henry Fielding to pen a short satire called *Shamela*, which he followed with his own novel *Joseph Andrews*. Here comedy and adventure replaced melodrama; Fielding prefaced *Joseph Andrews* with a manifesto claiming that the novel was to be "a comic epic in prose." Fielding realized the full potential of his bold experimentation with literary forms in *Tom Jones* (1749), a colorful, robust, comic panorama of English society featuring a gallery of brilliantly developed characters and vivid depictions of varied social environments.

The novel was thus emerging as a form of fiction that told its story and treated the development of personality in a realistic social context. It seemed to mirror its times better than other forms of fiction, and like the dramas that filled the stage in the second half of the century, most novels focused on family life and everyday problems of love, marriage, and social relations. Novelists could use broad comedy, or they could be totally serious; they could experiment endlessly with forms and techniques and could deal with a wide range of social settings.

In *Evelina or A Young Lady's Entrance into the World* (1778), the writer Fanny Burney used the flexibility of the novel to give a woman's perspective on eighteenth-century English social life. In the form of letters, like *Pamela* and *Julie*, *Evelina* traces a provincial girl's adventures in London as she discovers her true father and finds a suitable husband. While falling back on conventional melodrama, in which marriage is the only happy ending for a young woman, Burney also uses social satire to suggest how society restricts, and even endangers, an independent woman's life. If Burney was ambivalent about the possibilities for female independence in the social world, her own writing, together with other women writers of the period, demonstrated the opportunities for female artistic achievement.

Meanwhile, writers with more didactic objectives perfected a satiric genre called the philosophical tale, as exemplified by the great Irish satirist Jonathan Swift in his *Gulliver's Travels* (1726). The French philosophes favored this form of satire because it allowed them to criticize their society covertly and avoid open clashes with the censors. Thus Montesquieu created a range of mythical foreign settings and travelers from the Levant to ridicule contemporary European morality in *The Persian Letters* (1721). Voltaire similarly achieved great success in his tale *Candide* (1759), a critique of the notion that this was the best of all possible worlds. His exotic characters and incidents disguised an Enlightenment tract against the idiocy and cruelty that he saw in European society.

The Birth of Romantic Poetry

During most of this century of innovation in prose fiction, poetry retained its traditional qualities. Still the most prized form of literary expression, poetry followed unchanging rules on what made good literature. Each poetic form had its particular essence and rules; but in all types of poems diction was supposed to be elegant and the sentiments refined. Poets were expected to transform the raw materials of emotion into delicate language and references that only the highly educated could appreciate. In this Neoclassical tradition, art was seen to echo eternal standards of truth and beauty. The poet was not permitted to unburden his soul or hold forth on his own experience. The audience for poetry was the narrowest segment of the reading public—"the wealthy few," in the phrase of William Wordsworth, who criticized eighteenth-century poets for pandering exclusively to that group.

By the end of the century, however, the restraints of Neoclassicism finally provoked rebellion in the ranks of English and German poets. Men like Friedrich von Schiller and Wordsworth defiantly raised the celebration of individual feeling and inner passion to the level of a creed, which came to be known as Romanticism. These young poets generally prized Rousseau's writings, seeing the Genevan rebel as someone who had forged a personal idiom of expression and who valued inner feeling, moral passion, and the wonders of nature. Hoping to appeal to a much broader audience, these poets decisively changed the nature of poetic composition and made this literary form, like the novel, a flexible and more accessible vehicle of artistic expression.

Goethe

The writer who came to embody the new ambitions of poets, novelists, and dramatists was Johann von Goethe, whose long life (1749–1832) spanned the beginnings and the high point of the Romantic movement. A friend of Schiller and many of the German writers and philosophers of the day, he soon came to tower over all of them. Goethe first inspired a literary movement known as *Sturm und Drang* (Storm and Stress), which emphasized strong artistic emotions and gave early intimations of the Romantic temperament. The best-known work of *Sturm und Drang* was young Goethe's *The Sorrows of Young Werther* (1774), a novel about a young man driven to despair and suicide by an impossible love.

Courted by many of the princes and monarchs of Germany, Goethe soon joined the circle of the duke who ruled the small city-state of Weimar, where he remained for the rest of his life. There flowed from his pen an astonishing stream of works—lyrical love poetry, powerful dramas, art and literary criticism, translations, philosophic reflections, an account of his travels in Italy, and studies of optics, botany, anatomy, and mathematics. Even though he held official posts in the duke's court, Goethe's literary output never flagged. His masterpiece, *Faust*, occupied him for nearly 50 years and revealed the progress of his art. The first part (published in 1808) imbued with romantic longing the somewhat autobiographical story of a man who yearns to master all of knowledge and who makes a pact with the devil to achieve his goal. But the second part (1831) emphasized the renunciation and determination that came to be Goethe's credo. The final lines are:

> He only earns his freedom and existence
> Who daily conquers them anew.

What had begun in the youthful exuberance and energy of Romanticism ended in an almost classical mood of discipline. No wonder that Goethe seemed to his contemporaries the last "universal man," the embodiment of conflicting cultural values and Western civilization's struggle to resolve them.

The Symphony For Europe's elites, music offered the supreme form of entertainment, and the development of the symphony in music paralleled the rise of the novel in literature. It must be noted at once, however, that a great deal of eighteenth-century music was routine and undistinguished. For much of the century, composers still served under royal, ecclesiastical, or aristocratic patronage. They were bound by rigid formulas of composition and by prevailing tastes tyrannically insistent on conventions. Most listeners wanted little more than pleasant melodies in familiar forms; instrumental music was often commissioned as background fare for balls or other social occasions.

The heartland of Europe's music tradition shifted during the eighteenth century from Italy and France to Austria. Here a trio of geniuses transformed the routines of eighteenth-century composition into original and enduring masterpieces. True, the early symphonies of Franz Joseph Haydn and young Wolfgang Amadeus Mozart were conventional exercises. As light and tuneful as its audience could wish, their early music had little emotional impact. By the end of their careers, however, these two composers had altered the symphonic form from three to four movements, had achieved extraordinary harmonic virtuosity, and had brought a deep if restrained emotionalism to their music. Haydn and Mozart had changed the symphony radically from the elegant trifles of earlier years.

Ludwig van Beethoven consummated this development and assured that the symphony, like the novel and romantic poetry, would be an adaptable vehicle for the expression of creative genius. In each of his nine symphonies, as well as in his five piano concertos, Beethoven progressively modified the standard formulas, enlarged the orchestra, and wrote movements of increasing intricacy. His last symphony burst the bonds of the form altogether. Beethoven introduced a large chorus singing one of Schiller's odes to conclude his Ninth Symphony (1824),

making it a celebration in music of freedom and brotherhood. Laden with passion, the music is nevertheless recognizable as an advanced form of the classical symphony. Thus it provides a bridge between the music of two periods: eighteenth-century Classicism and nineteenth-century Romanticism.

Aristocratic and court patronage remained the surest foundation for a career in music during the eighteenth century. Haydn, for example, worked with mutual satisfaction as the court composer for one prince from 1761 to 1790. At the end of his long life, however, Haydn moved out on his own, having won enough international recognition to sign a lucrative contract with a London music publisher who underwrote performances of his last 12 symphonies. In contrast, Mozart had an unhappy experience trying to earn his living by composing. After a few miserable years as court composer for the Archbishop of Salzburg, Mozart escaped to Vienna but could not find a permanent employer. He was obliged to eke out an inadequate living by teaching, filling private commissions, and giving public concerts. Beethoven did much better at freeing himself from dependence on a single patron through individual commissions and public concerts.

The Social Context of Art Unlike the situation in literature and music, there were no notable innovations in the field of painting during most of the eighteenth century. With the exception of the Frenchman Jacques-Louis David, eighteenth-century painters were overshadowed by their predecessors. Neoclassicism remained a popular style in the late eighteenth century, with its themes inspired by antiquity and its timeless conceptions of form and beauty, comparable to the rules of Neoclassical poetry.

The social context of painting, however, was changing. Most commissions and patronage still depended on aristocrats and princes, but the public was beginning to claim a role as the judge of talent in the visual arts. Public opinion found its voice in a new breed of art critics, unaffiliated with official sources of patronage, who reached their new audience through the press in the second half of the century. The Royal Academy of Art in France created the opening for this new

▶ **The kind of art held in high esteem in eighteenth-century France included the sensuous and ornate scenes of aristocratic life in the so-called Rococo style painted by J.-H. Fragonard, such as *Blind Man's Bluff*, shown here (detail).**

voice by sponsoring an annual public exhibition, or "salon," starting in 1737. People could view the canvases chosen by the Academy for these exhibitions and could reach their own judgments about the painters. In this way a "public sphere" of cultural discourse came into being, where once the official word of the Academy had determined the matter of taste and reputation in painting.

David, a brilliant painter in the Neoclassical style, won the greatest renown in this arena of public opinion during the 1780s. He skillfully celebrated the values of the ancient world in such historical paintings as *The Oath of the Horatii* (see figure, bottom of p. 628), *The Death of Socrates*, and *Brutus*. Discarding many of the standard conventions for history painting (and thereby drawing criticism from the Academy), David overwhelmed the public with his vivid imagery and the emotional force of his compositions. His paintings of the 1780s unmistakably conveyed a yearning for civic virtue and patriotism that had yet to find its political outlet in France. Not surprisingly, David became the most engaged and triumphant painter of the French Revolution.

In an entirely different vein, a few eighteenth-century artists chose more mundane and "realistic" subjects or themes for their canvases, parallel in some respects to what novelists and playwrights were doing. Jean-Baptiste Greuze, for example, made a hit in the Parisian exhibitions of the 1770s with his sentimentalized paintings of ordinary people in family settings caught in a dramatic situation, such as the death of a father or the banishment of a disobedient son. William Hogarth, a superb London engraver who worked through the medium of prints and book illustrations, went further down the social pyramid with his remarkable scenes of life among the working classes and the poor.

▶ Instead of the aristocrats or classical figures that most artists chose for their subjects, Jean-Baptiste Greuze painted ordinary French people. His portraits and dramatic scenes (such as *The Father's Curse*) seemed to echo Rousseau's call for honest, "natural" feeling.

▶ The greatest innovation in French painting came in reaction to the artificiality of Baroque and Rococo styles and subject matter, with a return to favor of "noble simplicity and calm grandeur." This Neoclassical style found its supreme expression in the work of Jacques-Louis David. Such history paintings as *The Oath of the Horatii* evoked the ideal of civic virtue in ancient Greek and Roman civilization.

III. *Popular Culture*

While the cultural world of aristocratic and middle-class elites has been extensively studied, the cultures of artisans, peasants, and the urban poor remain more dimly illuminated. In those sectors of society, culture primarily meant recreation and was essentially public and collective. Popular culture had its written forms, but they were relatively unimportant compared to the oral tradition of songs, folktales, and sayings, which have left fewer firsthand traces in the historical record. Nonetheless, it is possible to suggest the rich variety of cultural and recreational practice among working people.

POPULAR LITERATURE

Far removed from the markets for Voltaire and the *Gentleman's Magazine*, there existed a distinct world of popular literature—the reading matter consumed by journeymen and peasants, the poor and the almost poor, those who could barely read and those who could not read at all. From the seventeenth through the early nineteenth century, but particularly in the eighteenth century, publishers produced for this audience small booklets written anonymously, printed on cheap paper, and costing only a few pennies. These brochures were sold by itinerant peddlers who knew the tastes of their customers; presumably the booklets were often read aloud by those who could read to those who could not.

This popular literature took three major forms. Religious material included devotional tracts, saints' lives, catechisms, manuals of penitence, and Bible stories, all written simply and generously laced with miracles. Readers who were preoccupied with fears of death and damnation sought reassurance in these works that a virtuous life would end in salvation. Almanacs constituted a second type of popular literature, which appealed to the readers' concern for getting along in this life. Almanacs and how-to-live-successfully pamphlets discussed things like the kinds of potions to take for illnesses and featured astrology—how to read the stars and other signs for clues about the future. The third type of pop-

▶ **A page from an English almanac of 1769 on the month of July includes saints' days, information about likely weather patterns, and advice about agricultural matters and health care.**

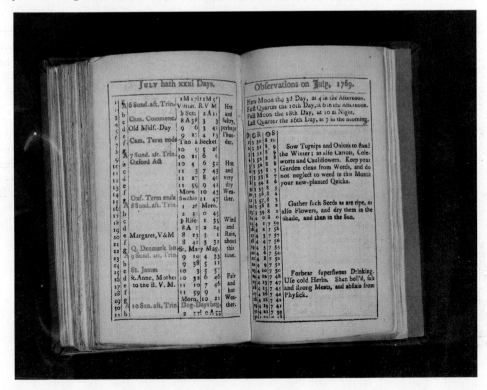

ular literature provided entertainment: tales and fables, burlesques and crude satires, mixtures of fiction and history in which miraculous events frequently helped bring the story to a satisfactory conclusion.

Although useful information may have trickled down through these booklets, most of them were escapist. The religiosity and supernatural events of popular literature separate it from the growing rationalism and secularism of elite culture. Moreover, it could be argued that by ignoring such problems as food shortages, high taxes, and material insecurity, popular writings fostered submissiveness, a fatalistic acceptance of a dismal status quo. Glimpsing the content of this popular literature helps us understand why Voltaire had no hope of extending his ideas on religion to the masses.

Oral Tradition Almanacs and pamphlets for working people were produced by outsiders, printers and writers who were themselves well educated. Oral tradition encompassed more authentic forms of popular culture: folktales told at

Map 19.1 **Estimated Regional Variations in French Literacy (1780s)**

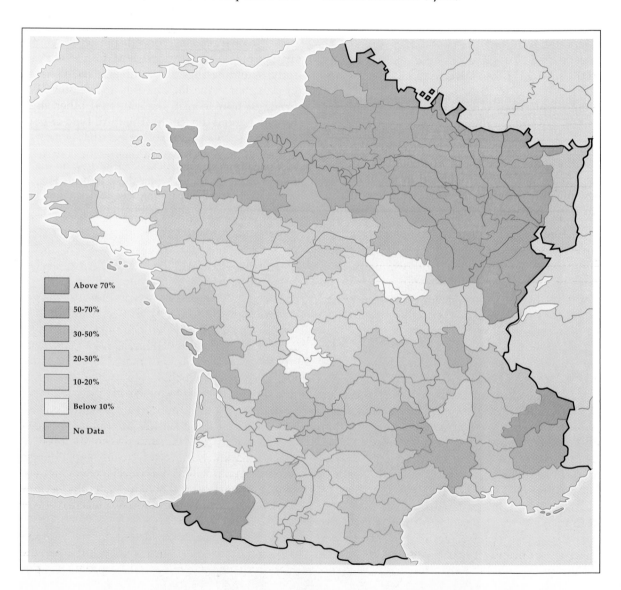

the fireside on long winter nights, songs passed on from generation to generation, sayings that embodied the conventional wisdom of the people.

Themes touching on hunger, sex, or oppression were more likely to turn up in songs or oral tales than in booklets. Songs and tales expressed the joyful bawdiness of ordinary men and women but also the ever-present hardships and dangers of daily life: the endless drudgery of work in the fields, the gnawing ache of an empty stomach, the cruelty of parental neglect or mean stepparents, the desperation of beggars on the road. The most fantastic tales evoked a threatening world where strangers might turn out to be princes or good fairies but might just as well turn into wolves or witches. Oral tradition also celebrated the shrewdness and cunning of ordinary people struggling for survival, in the spirit of the saying: "Better a knave than a fool." Often rendered in local dialects, these tales or songs would have been incomprehensible to an educated Parisian, Londoner, or Viennese.

LITERACY AND PRIMARY SCHOOLING

The Wars of Religion had spurred the spread of literacy and elementary schooling in Europe. Protestantism explicitly promoted literacy so that Christians could read their Bibles directly; strongly Protestant societies such as Scotland, Switzerland, and Sweden had unusually high rates of literacy by the eighteenth century. The Catholic Church, as well, believed that the spread of literacy would serve its cause in the battle against heresy. While teaching reading, Catholic schoolmasters could provide religious instruction and could socialize children into the beliefs and behavior of a Catholic way of life.

A unique study of literacy in France carried out in the late nineteenth century, based on signatures versus X's on parish marriage registers all across the country, indicates a national literacy rate (meaning the ability to read) in 1686 of about 21 percent, which reached 37 percent a century later. These national averages, however, conceal striking regional and social disparities. The south of France had much lower rates than the north/northeast (see Map 19.1), and rural literacy rates lagged significantly behind those of the towns. While agricultural laborers rarely could read, ur-

ban artisans were generally literate. The widest gap of all, however, separated men from women, the rates in 1786 being 47 and 27 percent, respectively. Similarly, estimates for England suggest a male literacy rate of slightly under 60 percent and a female rate of about 40 percent.

Primary Education Schooling was not intended to transform society or lift the mass of people out of the situations into which they were born. On the contrary, it was supposed to maintain the social order and reinforce the family in promoting piety and decent behavior among the young. Many among the elites (including Voltaire) were skeptical about the value of education for peasants and laborers. Might it not confuse them, or make it more difficult for them to accept the drudgery to which they seemed destined? Peasant or laboring parents might well have shared such skepticism about educating their young. Education could seem a waste of time when their children could be contributing to the family's livelihood; they might especially begrudge spending the money on tuition that most elementary schooling required.

A village usually hired a schoolmaster in consultation with the pastor or priest; schools usually straddled community and church, since the schoolmaster often served as the pastor's aide. Except in towns that had charitable endowments to support schooling, the parents, the village, or some combination of the two paid the schoolmaster, and for that reason numerous villages did without any schooling. Even a modest tuition could deter impoverished parents from hiring a master, enrolling their children, or keeping them in school for a sufficient time. Since schoolmasters taught reading first and writing separately and later, many pupils, especially girls, were not kept in school long enough to learn how to write anything but their names. Schooling, in other words, was largely demand-driven, the product of a community's level of wealth and interest. When a region achieved a critical mass of literacy, however, interest in schooling generally became more widespread and gradually reached lower down the social scale.

While England and France left primary schooling entirely to the chance of local initiative, the Habsburg Monarchy seriously promoted pri-

▶ Most eighteenth-century elementary school teachers used the extremely inefficient individual method of instruction, where pupils read to the teacher from whatever book they happened to bring from home, while the other pupils occupied themselves as best they could.

mary education and thereby became the first Catholic realm to do so. The Habsburg General School Ordinance of 1774 authorized state subsidies, in combination with local funds, for the support of a school in almost every parish. Attendance was supposed to be compulsory, though the state had no way to enforce this. The state also intended to train future teachers at institutions called normal schools. A similar two-pronged strategy was adopted in Prussia under Frederick II at about the same time, although little was done to implement it.

In Prussia, as in most of Europe, schoolmasters remained barely competent and poorly paid. Frederick II indeed had a limiting vision of popular education: "It is enough for the country people to learn only a little reading and writing. . . . Instruction must be planned so that they receive only what is most essential for them but which is designed to keep them in the villages and not influence them to leave." As elsewhere in Europe, the goals of elementary schooling were to inculcate religion and morality, propagate the virtues of hard work, and promote sobriety and deference to one's superiors.

SOCIABILITY AND RECREATION

If the educated elites had their salons, masonic lodges, and learned academies, the common people also formed organized cultural groups. Many journeyman artisans, for example, belonged to secret societies that combined fraternal and trade-union functions. Young unmarried artisans frequently traveled the country, stopping periodically to work with comrades in other towns in order to hone their skills. Artisans also relied on their associations for camaraderie and ritual celebrations. Rivalries among federations of artisan associations occasionally led to pitched battles, however—a far cry from the nineteenth-century ideal of labor solidarity. Married artisans often joined religious confraternities, which honored a patron saint and assured a dignified funeral when they died, or mutual aid societies to which they contributed small monthly dues to pay for assistance if illness or accident should strike.

Corresponding to the coffeehouses of the urban middle classes were the taverns in working-class neighborhoods. These noisy, crowded places catered to a poor clientele, especially on Sunday and on Monday, which working people often took as a day off, honoring (as they put it) "Saint Monday." The urban common people were first beginning to consume wine in the eighteenth century, still something of a luxury except in its cheapest watered form. In England gin was the poor person's drink, cheap and plentiful until the government levied a hefty excise tax after realizing that too many people were drinking themselves into disability and death—a concern depicted in Hogarth's etchings.

More commonly, drinking was not done in that morbid fashion but as part of a healthy and vibrant outdoor life. In England, before the spread of industrialization changed the cultural as well as physical landscape, popular pastimes followed a calendar of holidays that provided occasions for group merrymaking, eating, drinking, dressing-up, contests, and games. Local festivals were particularly comfortable settings for single young men and women to meet each other. The highlight of a country year usually came in early autumn after the summer harvest was in, when most villages held a public feast that lasted several days. In Catholic countries similar festivities

▶ **In his "Gin Lane" etching of 1750, Hogarth depicted the results of excessive gin drinking by the English common people as death, apathy, and moral decay. A cheerful companion piece called "Beer Street," however, suggested that drinking in moderation was an acceptable practice.**

GIN LANE. BEER STREET.

were often linked with church rituals. Popular observances included the commemoration of local patron saints, pilgrimages to holy places, and the period of Carnival before Lent.

Sports A growing "commercialization of leisure" in the eighteenth century supported new spectator sports, such as horseracing and boxing matches. Blood sports, constituted a more prevalent popular recreation. Bullbaiting, for example, involved setting loose a pack of dogs on a tethered steer. These events were usually collaborations between a butcher (who provided the steer, its meat to be sold later) and an innkeeper (whose yard served as the arena and who sold refreshments to the spectators). Cockfighting, similar in its gory results, attracted gentlemen and commoners alike, who enjoyed wagering on the outcome.

In early modern Europe, gentlefolk and commoners had been accustomed to mixing in recreational and religious settings: fairs and markets, sporting events, village or town festivals, Carnival in Catholic countries. But in the eighteenth century, as aristocrats and bourgeois alike became more concerned with good manners and refinement, these elite groups began to distance themselves from the bawdy and vulgar behavior of ordinary people. With growing intolerance they censured popular recreational culture in the hope of "reforming" the people into a more sober and orderly life style. Social status was based on birth or wealth, but cultural taste was becoming its behavioral marker.

The philosophes, celebrated members of Europe's cultural establishment by the 1770s, hoped that their society would gradually reform itself under their inspiration. Although these writers criticized their society, they were not its subverters. Distrustful of the uneducated masses—and afraid of popular emotion, superstition, and disorder—they were anything but democrats. Nonetheless, the Enlightenment challenged basic traditional values of European society: from Voltaire's polemics against Christianity through the sober social science of Diderot's *Encyclopedia* to the impassioned writings of Rousseau. Along with a flood of "bad books"—the pornography and scandal sheets of the clandestine publishers—booksellers, writers, and journalists disseminated critical ideas among Europe's educated men and women. The philosophes challenged the automatic respect for convention and authority, promoted the habit of independent reflection, and implanted the conviction that the reform of institutions was both necessary and possible. They promoted a climate in which the status quo was gradually put on the defensive and in which revolution—when provoked under particular circumstances—would not be unthinkable.

Recommended Reading

Sources

Crocker, Lester (ed.). *The Age of Enlightenment.* 1969.
Gendzier, Stephen (ed.). *Denis Diderot: The Encyclopedia: Selections.* 1967.
Mohl, Mary R., and Helene Koon (eds.). *The Female Spectator: English Women Writers Before* 1800. 1977.

*Rousseau, Jean-Jacques. *The Social Contract and Discourses.* 1950.

*Voltaire. *The Portable Voltaire.* 1949, 1977.

Studies

*Baker, Keith. *Condorcet, from Natural Philosophy to Social Mathematics.* 1975. A study of a philosophe who lived to participate in the French Revolution.
Bernard, Paul. *Jesuits and Jacobins: Enlightenment and*

*Available in paperback.

Enlightened Despotism in Austria. 1971. Liberalization and conflict in the Habsburg domain.

Bruford, W. H. *Germany in the Eighteenth Century: The Social Background of the Literary Revival.* 1952.

Capp, Bernard. *English Almanacs, 1500–1800: Astrology and the Popular Press.* 1979. A probing study of the most important genre of popular literature.

*Cassirer, Ernst. *The Question of Jean-Jacques Rousseau.* 1963. Brief and reliable.

*Chartier, Roger. *The Cultural Origins of the French Revolution.* 1991. A synthesis of recent research on publishing, the "public sphere," and the emergence of a new political culture.

*Cragg, G. R. *The Church and the Age of Reason, 1648–1789.* 1966.

Cranston, Maurice. *Jean-Jacques* (2 vols.). 1983, 1991. The most recent study of Rousseau's life and work.

*Crow, Thomas. *Painters and Public Life in Eighteenth-Century Paris.* 1985. A pioneering work on the development of a "public sphere" of critical discourse about art.

Darnton, Robert. *The Business of Enlightenment: A Publishing History of the Encyclopedia.* 1979. The "biography of a book" and of the century's most influential publishing venture.

*———. *The Great Cat Massacre and Other Essays in French Cultural History.* 1984. A notable collection of essays on "the social history of ideas" and on the "mentalities" of peasants and workers.

*———. *The Literary Underground of the Old Regime.* 1982. A pathbreaking book on the clandestine world of hack writers, publishers, and smugglers of illegal books.

Furet, François, and Jacques Ozouf. *Reading and Writing: Literacy in France from Calvin to Jules Ferry.* 1982. An overview of literacy and primary schooling based on quantitative sources.

*Gay, Peter. *The Enlightenment: An Interpretation* (2 vols.). 1966–1969. A masterly, full-bodied exposition of Enlightenment thought.

*———. *Voltaire's Politics: The Poet as Realist.* 1959. A lively and sympathetic portrait.

*Hahn, Roger. *The Anatomy of a Scientific Institution: The Paris Academy of Sciences, 1666–1803.* 1971. The rise and problems of a scientific "establishment."

*Hampson, Norman. *A Cultural History of the Enlightenment.* 1969. A good general introduction.

Herr, Richard. *The Eighteenth-Century Revolution in Spain.* 1958. The reverberations of the Enlightenment in Spain—a case study not discussed in the present text.

*Isherwood, Robert. *Farce and Fantasy: Popular Entertainment in Eighteenth-Century Paris.* 1986. A cultural and institutional history of fairs and popular theater.

Joeres, Ruth-Ellen, and Mary Jo Maynes (eds.). *German Women in the Eighteenth and Nineteenth Centuries.* 1986. Essays on women's writings and women's roles.

Kors, Alan. *D'Holbach's Coterie: An Enlightenment in Paris.* 1976. Focuses on the circle of a leading French atheist.

Korshin, P. J. (ed.). *The Widening Circle: Essays on the Circulation of Literature in Eighteenth-Century Europe.* 1976.

Malcolmson, R. W. *Popular Recreations in English Society, 1700–1850.* 1973. A good survey of a neglected subject.

Melton, James Van Horn. *Absolutism and the Eighteenth-Century Origins of Compulsory Schooling in Prussia and Austria.* 1988. An excellent comparative study.

Palmer, Robert R. *Catholics and Unbelievers in Eighteenth-Century France.* 1939. The response of Catholic intellectuals to the century's philosophic thought.

*Paulson, Ronald. *Hogarth: His Life, Art, and Times* (abridged ed.). 1974.

Payne, Harry. *The Philosophes and the People.* 1976. An analysis of the Enlightenment's liberal elitism.

*Roche, Daniel. *The People of Paris: An Essay on Popular Culture in the Eighteenth Century.* 1987. On the material culture and aspirations of ordinary Parisians.

Schackleton, Robert. *Montesquieu.* 1961. A biography of the French thinker with influence on both sides of the Atlantic.

*Spencer, Samia (ed.). *French Women and the Age of Enlightenment.* 1984. A pioneering collection of essays on a variety of literary and historical themes.

Venturi, Franco. *Italy and the Enlightenment.* 1972. Essays on important Italian philosophes by a leading historian.

*Watt, Ian. *The Rise of the Novel: Studies of Defoe, Richardson, and Fielding.* 1957. The view from England.

Wilson, Arthur. *Diderot.* 1972. An exhaustive, reliable biography of the consummate French philosophe.

The storming of the Bastille.

CHAPTER TWENTY

THE FRENCH REVOLUTION

MOST eighteenth-century monarchs and princes still claimed to hold their authority directly from God and presided over realms composed of distinct orders of citizens, or *estates*, each with its own rights, privileges, and obligations. But forces for change had been building during the century. In France Enlightenment writers, who rarely questioned the basic forms of government, had nonetheless helped to create a "public sphere" of political discourse outside the framework of official monarchical institutions. In contrast, self-confident monarchs in Austria, Prussia, and Russia cultivated a new style of ruling as they imposed reforms from above. Royal innovations there and elsewhere, however, usually met with resistance from aristocracies or local oligarchies who resented encroachments on their privileges. Conflicts over political exclusion and empowerment also erupted in Britain, and in Britain's American colonies local resentments exploded into outright rebellion.

Without question, however, the pivotal event of European history in the eighteenth century was the French Revolution. From its outbreak in 1789, the Revolution transformed the social values and political system of France and resonated across the borders of other European states. When war broke out in 1792, French armies carried revolutionary ideology into neighboring states. Both at home and abroad the new regime faced formidable opposition, and its struggle for survival propelled it in unanticipated directions. The French Revolution's ideals defined the basic aspirations of modern liberal society, but its bloody events dramatized the brutal dilemma of ends versus means.

I. Reform and Political Crisis

"ENLIGHTENED ABSOLUTISM" IN CENTRAL AND EASTERN EUROPE

During the late nineteenth century, German historians invented the concept of "enlightened absolutism" to describe the Prussian and Habsburg monarchies of the eighteenth century. Critical of the ineptitude and weakness of French monarchs in that period, these historians argued that the strength of an enlightened ruler had been the surest basis for progress in early modern Europe. A king who ruled in his subjects' interest, they implied, avoided violent conflicts like those of the French Revolution. Earlier strong monarchs such as Philip II of Spain and France's Louis XIV (who had once declared: "I am the state") had been irresponsible; in contrast, these German historians argued, Frederick II of Prussia symbolized the "enlightened" phase of absolutism with his comment that the ruler is merely the "first servant of the state."

Earlier chapters, however, have demonstrated that monarchs dealt with the same fundamental issues during all stages of absolutism. They always strove to assert their authority over their subjects and to maximize the power of their state in relation to other realms, principally by means of territorial expansion. Any notion that Enlightenment thinking caused monarchs to desist from these efforts is misleading. Still, several eighteenth-century monarchs did initiate reforms from above and did modify their styles of ruling in order to appear more modern or enlightened. Frederick II of Prussia and Catherine II of Russia, for example, lavished praise on Voltaire and Denis Diderot, and those philosophes returned the compliment. For these rulers it may have been simply a question of public relations. Yet the fact that they found it desirable to seem supportive of such controversial writers suggests that absolutism had indeed adopted a new image.

Catherine the Great (who reigned from 1762 to 1796) played this game to its limit. In 1767 she announced a new experiment in the direction of representative government—a policy hailed as a landmark by her philosophe admirers, who were too remote from St. Petersburg to see its insincerity. Catherine convened a Legislative Commission, a body of delegates from various strata of Russian society who were invited to present grievances, propose reforms, and then debate the proposals. In the end, however, she sent the delegates home under the pretext of having to turn her attention to a war with Turkey. Little came of the Legislative Commission except some good publicity for Catherine. In fact, she later promulgated a Charter of the Nobility, which, instead of limiting the nobility's privileges, strengthened their corporate status and increased their control over their serfs in exchange for their loyalty to the throne.

Conceptions of Enlightened Rule in Germany In justification of absolute monarchy, eighteenth-century German writers depicted the state as a machine and the ruler as its mainspring. Progress came from sound administration, through an enlightened monarch and well-trained officials. In keeping with this notion, German universities began to train government bureaucrats, and professors offered courses in the science of public finance and administration called *cameralism*. Before long the governments of Prussia and Austria introduced the rudiments of a civil service system.

The orders for the bureaucracy came from the monarchs, who were expected to dedicate themselves to the welfare of their subjects in return for their subjects' obedience. The framework for this command-obedience chain was to be a coherent body of public law, fairly administered by state officials. According to its advocates, this system would produce the rule of law, a *Rechtsstaat*, without the need for a written constitution or a representative parliament. The ruler and his or her officials, following their sense of public responsibility and rational analysis, would ensure the citizen's rights and well-being.

JOSEPH II AND THE LIMITS OF ABSOLUTISM

Joseph II—coruler of the Habsburg Empire with his mother, Maria Theresa, from 1765 and sole ruler in the 1780s—vigorously promoted reform from above. Unlike Frederick or Catherine, he did not openly identify with the philosophes, and he maintained his own Catholic faith. But Joseph proved to be the most innovative of the century's major rulers, as well as one of its most autocratic personalities. It was a problematic combination.

Sound rule for Emperor Joseph involved far more than the customary administrative and financial modernization necessary for survival in the competitive state system. With startling boldness he implemented several reforms long advocated by Enlightenment thinkers: freedom of expression, religious toleration, greater state control over the Catholic Church, and legal reform. A new criminal code, for example, reduced the use of the death penalty, ended judicial torture, and allowed for no class differences in the application of the laws. By greatly reducing royal censorship, Joseph made it possible for Vienna to become a major center of literary activity. And we have already noted Joseph's remarkable Edicts of Religious Toleration for Protestants and for Jews. But Joseph's religious policies did not stop there. To make the Catholic Church serve its parishioners better, Joseph forced the clergy to modernize its rituals and services. Most of his Catholic subjects, however, preferred their traditional ways to Joseph's streamlined brand of Catholicism. These "reforms" proved extremely unpopular.

Agrarian Reform Joseph's most ambitious policies aimed to transform the economic and social position of the peasants. In this respect the Habsburg emperor acted far more boldly than any other eighteenth-century sovereign. Agrarian reform was generally the weak side of "enlightened absolutism," since Frederick II and Catherine II did little to improve the lot of the peasants or serfs in their realms. Joseph, however, set out to eradicate serfdom and to convert Habsburg peasants into free individuals in command of their persons and of the land they cultivated.

By royal decree Joseph abolished personal servitude and gave peasants the right to move, marry, and enter any trade they wished. He then promulgated laws to secure peasants' control over the land they worked. Finally and most remarkably, he sought to limit the financial obligations of peasant tenants to their lords and to the state. All land was to be surveyed and subject to a uniform tax. Twelve percent of the land's annual yield would go to the state and a maxi-

▶ **Joseph II, shown here visiting a peasant's field, actually promulgated his momentous agrarian reform edicts without any significant consultation with the peasants before or after the fact.**

mum of 18 percent would go to the lord, in place of previous seigneurial obligations in which peasants owed service to their lord that could consume more than 100 days' labor a year.

Joseph ordered these reforms in an authoritarian fashion, with little consultation and no consent from any quarter. Predictably, they provoked fierce opposition among the landowning nobles. But they also perplexed most peasants, who already distrusted the government because of its arbitrary religious policies. Joseph made no effort to build support among the peasants by carefully explaining the reforms, let alone by modifying their details after getting feedback from the grass roots. As a sympathetic chronicler of Joseph's reign observed, "He brought in his beneficial measures in an arbitrary manner."

His arbitrary manner, however, was not incidental. Joseph acknowledged no other way of doing things, no limitation on his own sovereignty. In reaction to the opposition that his reforms aroused he moved to suppress dissent in the firmest possible way. Not only did he restore censorship in his last years, but he elevated the police department to the status of an imperial ministry and gave it unprecedented powers. By the time he died, in 1790, Joseph was a disillusioned man. His realm resembled less a *Rechtsstaat* than a police state, and his successors quickly restored serfdom.

CONSTITUTIONAL CRISES IN THE WEST

While "enlightened absolutists" reigned in Austria, Prussia, and Russia, political tension and spirited debate over the institutions of government erupted in several Western European countries. To understand these crises we must recall the role of *estates* in European history. The term is both a social and a political signifier. Socially, every person belonged to one legally distinct order or another. The clergy usually constituted the First Estate of the realm, the nobles formed the Second Estate, and both maintained a common aristocratic viewpoint. The remainder of the population constituted the Third Estate. In the past the estates had sent representatives to national and provincial assemblies or diets, which shared in making government decisions. But absolutism had drastically curtailed the political role of the estates, as we have seen in previous chapters. It was the Third Estate's new bid for prominence and power in several countries at the expense of the dominant aristocratic orders that made the late eighteenth century, as one historian calls it, "the age of the democratic revolution."

Monarchs and Aristocrats On one level monarchs and the privileged orders were perennial and natural rivals. The rights and privileges of various groups, especially but not solely the aristocratic orders, reduced the fiscal resources of kings and princes and hampered their ability to pursue internal reform. The privileges and monopolies enjoyed by provinces, towns, and guilds restrained trade, hampered economic growth, and militated against the common welfare. Eighteenth-century struggles over political power often began when rulers initiated changes in traditional political or economic arrangements. While monarchs might wish to allocate a smaller place to nobles in the business of government, nobles would not willingly cede the privileges they held and might demand an even larger share in the exercise of power.

Aristocracies all over Europe thus sought to advance their fortunes and consolidate their roles in their country's traditional or unwritten constitutions. Armed perhaps with the ideas of the French philosophe Montesquieu, who held that privilege is the bulwark of liberty, nobles claimed that they had the exclusive right to serve as ministers of the king as well as the obligation to lead the community in the conduct of its important affairs. In the last decades of the century, the nobility continued to enjoy a near monopoly over high offices in the state, the army, and the Church. In 1781, for example, officers' commissions in the French army were limited almost exclusively to those who could prove descent from four generations of nobility. Aristocrats in several countries demanded that local assemblies of estates, which they expected to dominate, be granted a larger share of political power.

Upheavals over such issues erupted in the Austrian Netherlands (Belgium) and in the Dutch Netherlands, where provincial oligarchies rebelled against the centralizing reforms of their princes: Joseph II in Belgium and the Prince of Orange in the Dutch Netherlands. In each case a more democratic element of unprivileged commoners, including urban artisans, turned these conflicts into triangular struggles, as they took up arms to oppose both princely tyranny and oligarchic privilege. To a certain extent, these Dutch and Belgian "patriots," as they called themselves, provided a foretaste of the French Revolution. Their suppression, in turn, suggested that "counterrevolution" was a force to be reckoned with.

UPHEAVALS IN THE BRITISH EMPIRE

An aggressive monarch, George III, helped ignite political unrest in Great Britain. Unlike his Hanoverian predecessors George I and George II, this king had been born in England and knew its language and its political system well. He was intent on advancing royal authority, but rather than bypass Parliament altogether he simply tried, as Whig ministers had before him, to control its members through patronage and influence. The Whig aristocrats saw this operation as a threat to their own traditional power. Not only did they oppose the king and his ministers in Parliament, but they enlisted the support of citizens' groups outside of Parliament as well. These organizations were calling for political reform, including representation in Parliament proportionate to population, stricter laws against political corruption, and greater freedom of the press.

"Wilkes and Liberty" John Wilkes, a member of Parliament and a journalist, became the center of this rising storm. Wilkes viciously attacked the king's prime minister, and by implication the king himself, over the terms of the Treaty of Paris, which ended the Seven Years' War in 1763. The government arrested him for seditious libel on a general warrant. When the courts quashed the indictment, the government then accused Wilkes of having authored a libelous pornographic poem, and this time he fled to France to avoid prison. He stayed there for four years; but in 1768, still under indictment, he returned to stand once more for Parliament. Three times he was re-elected, and three times the House of Commons refused to seat him. With the ardent support of radicals and to the acclaim of crowds in London, who marched to the chant of "Wilkes and Liberty," Wilkes finally took his seat in 1774.

Agitation for parliamentary reform drew support primarily from "solid citizens": shopkeepers, artisans, and property owners who had the franchise in a few districts but were denied it in most others. Thus even without a right to vote, English citizens could engage in politics and mobilize the power of public opinion, in this case by rallying to Wilkes. Most radicals called only for political reform, not for the overthrow of the British political system. They retained a measure of respect for the nation's political traditions, which ideally guaranteed the rights of "freeborn Englishmen."

Rebellion in America Great Britain did face revolutionary action in her 13 North American colonies. George III and his prime minister, Lord North, attempted to force the colonies to pay the costs, past and present, of their own defense. The policy would have meant an increase in taxes and a centralization of authority in the governance of the British empire. Colonial landowners, merchants, and artisans of the eastern seaboard organized petitions and boycotts in opposition to the proposed fiscal and constitutional changes.

The resistance in North America differed fundamentally from comparable movements in Europe. American political leaders did not appeal to a body of privileges that the actions of the monarchy were allegedly violating. Instead they appealed to traditional rights supposedly enjoyed by all British subjects, regardless of status, and to theories of popular sovereignty and natural rights advanced by John Locke and other English libertarian writers. When conciliation and compromise with the British government failed, the American Declaration of Independence in 1776 gave eloquent expression to those concepts. The lack of a rigid system of estates and hereditary privileges in American society, the fluid boundaries that separated the social strata, and the traditions of local government in the colonies—from town meetings in New England to the elected legislatures that had advised colonial governors—blunted the kinds of conflicts between aristocrats and commoners that derailed incipient revolutionary movements in Ireland, Belgium, and the Dutch Netherlands.

These differences help to explain the unique character of the American rebellion, which was

▶ The committee that drafted the American Declaration of Independence included John Adams, Thomas Jefferson, and Benjamin Franklin, all shown here standing at the desk.

simultaneously a war for independence and a political revolution. The theories that supported the rebellion, and the continuing alliance between social strata, made it the most democratic revolution of the eighteenth century before 1789. The American Revolution created the first state governments, and ultimately a national government, in which the exercise of power was grounded not on royal sovereignty or traditional privilege but on the participation and consent of the citizens (apart from the numerous black slaves, whose status did not change). Even more important as an historical precedent, perhaps, it was the first successful rebellion by overseas colonies against their European masters.

II. 1789: The French Revolution

Although the rebellion in America stirred sympathy and interest across the Atlantic, it seemed remote from the realities of Europe. The French Revolution of 1789 proved to be the turning point in European history. Its sheer radicalism, creativity, and claims of universalism made it unique. Its ultimate slogan—"Liberty, Equality, Fraternity"—expressed social and civic ideals that became the foundations of modern Western civilization. In the name of individual liberty, French revolutionaries swept away the institutionalized constraints of the old regime: seigneurial charges upon the land, vestiges of feudalism, tax privileges, guild monopolies on commerce, and even (in 1794) black slavery overseas. The revolutionaries held that legitimate governments required written constitutions, elections, and powerful legislatures. They demanded equality before the law for all persons and uniformity of institutions for all regions of the country, denying the claims to special treatment of privileged groups, provinces, towns, or religions. The term *fraternity* expressed a different kind of revolutionary goal. Rousseauist in inspiration, it meant that all citizens regardless of social class or region shared a common fate in society and that the nation's well-being could override the interests of individual citizens.

ORIGINS OF THE REVOLUTION

Those who made the Revolution believed they were rising against despotic government, in which citizens had no voice, and against inequality and privilege. Yet the government of France at that time was no more tyrannical or unjust than it had been in the past. On the contrary, a process of reform had been under way for several decades. What, then, set off the revolutionary upheaval? What had failed in France's long-standing political system?

An easy answer would be to point to the incompetence of King Louis XVI (who reigned from 1774 to 1792) and his queen, Marie Antoinette. Louis was good-natured but weak and indecisive, a man of limited intelligence who lacked self-confidence and who preferred hunting deer to supervising the business of government. By no stretch of the imagination was he an "enlightened absolutist." Worse yet, his young queen, a Habsburg princess, was frivolous, meddlesome, and tactless. But even the most capable ruler could not have escaped challenge and unrest in the 1780s. It is the roots of the political crisis, not its mismanagement, that claim the historian's attention.

The Cultural Climate In eighteenth-century France, as we have seen, intellectual ferment preceded political revolt. For decades the philosophes had questioned accepted political and religious beliefs. They undermined the old confidence that traditional ways were the best ways. But the philosophes harbored deep-seated fears of the uneducated masses and did not question the notion that educated and propertied elites should rule society; they wished only that the elites should be more enlightened and more open to new ideas. Indeed, the Enlightenment had become respectable by the 1770s, a kind of intellectual establishment. Rousseau damned that establishment and wrote of the need for simplicity, sincerity, and virtue, but the word *revolution* never flowed from his pen either.

More subversive perhaps than the writings of Enlightenment intellectuals were the "bad books," the clandestine flow of gossip sheets, libels, and pornography that indirectly, at least, portrayed the French aristocracy as decadent and the monarchy as a ridiculous despotism. Royal officials and philosophes alike regarded the authors of this material as "the excrement of literature," as Voltaire put it. And writers forced to earn their living by turning out such stuff must have been embittered by their plight. Their resentment at being stuck on the bottom rung in the world of letters would explode once the Revolution began in 1789, and many became radical journalists either for or against the new regime. In itself, however, this "literary underground" of the old regime did not cause the Revolution.

Class Conflict? Did the structure of French society, then, provoke the Revolution? Karl Marx, and the many historians inspired by him, certainly believed so. Marx saw the French Revolution as the necessary break marking the transition from the aristocratic feudalism of the Middle Ages to the era of middle-class capitalism. In the words of historian Georges Lefebvre, "The clergy and nobility preserved the highest rank in the legal structure of the country, but in reality economic power, personal abilities and confidence in the future had passed largely to the bourgeoisie. Such a discrepancy never lasts forever. The Revolution of 1789 restored the harmony between fact and law." In this view, the French bourgeoisie, or middle classes, had been gaining in wealth during the eighteenth century and resented the privileges of the nobility, which placed obstacles in the path of their ambition. Though they framed their ideology in universal terms in 1789, the middle classes led the Revolution in order to change the political and social systems in their own interests.

Three decades of research have rendered this

theory of the Revolution's origins untenable. Whether a sizable and coherent capitalist middle class actually existed in eighteenth-century France is questionable. In any case, the leaders of the Revolution in 1789 were lawyers, administrators, and liberal nobles, and rarely merchants or industrialists. Moreover, the barrier between the nobility of the Second Estate and the wealthy and educated members of the Third Estate was porous, the lines of social division frequently (though not always) blurred. Many members of the middle class identified themselves on official documents as "living nobly"—as substantial property owners who did not work for a living. Conversely, wealthy nobles often invested in mining, overseas trade, and finance—activities usually associated with the middle classes. Even more important, the gap between the nobility and the middle classes was as nothing compared with the gulf that separated both from the working people of town and country. In this revisionist historiography, the bourgeoisie did not make the Revolution, so much as the Revolution made the bourgeoisie.

Yet numerous disruptive pressures were at work in French society. A growing population left large numbers of young people in the countryside and the towns struggling to attain a stable place in society. New images and attitudes rippled through the media of the day, despite the state's efforts to censor material it deemed subversive. The nobility, long-since banished by Louis XIV from an independent role in monarchical government, chafed at its exclusion, while the prosperous middle classes too aspired to a more active role. The monarchy struggled to contain these forces within the established social and political systems. Until the 1780s it succeeded, but then its troubles began in earnest.

FISCAL CRISIS AND POLITICAL IMPASSE

When he took the throne in 1774, Louis XVI tried to conciliate elite opinion by recalling the Parlements, or sovereign law courts, that his grandfather had banished in 1770 for their opposition to his policies. This concession to France's traditional "unwritten constitution" did not suffice to smooth the new sovereign's road. Louis' new controller-general of finances, Jacques Turgot, en-

countered a storm of opposition from privileged groups to the modest reforms he proposed.

Turgot, an ally of the philosophes and an experienced administrator, hoped to encourage economic growth by a policy of nonintervention, or laissez-faire, that would give free play to economic markets and allow individuals maximum freedom to pursue their own economic interests. He proposed to remove all restrictions on commerce in grain and to abolish the guilds. In addition, he tried to cut down on expenses at court and to replace the obligation of peasants to work on the royal roads (the *corvée*) with a small new tax on all landholders. Privately, he also considered establishing elected advisory assemblies of landowners to assist in local administration. Vested interests, however, viewed Turgot as a dangerous innovator. When agitation against him mounted in the king's court at Versailles and in the Paris Parlement, Louis took the easy way out and dismissed his contentious minister. With Turgot went perhaps the last hope for significant reform in France under royal leadership.

Deficit Financing The king then turned to Jacques Necker, a banker from Geneva who had a reputation for financial wizardry. Necker had a shrewd sense of public relations. To finance the heavy costs of France's aid to the rebellious British colonies in North America, Necker avoided new taxes, which gained him wide popularity, and instead floated a series of large loans at exorbitant interest rates as high as 10 percent. (England, through sound management of its public finances and public confidence in the government, financed its war effort with loans at only 3 or 4 percent interest.)

By the 1780s royal finances hovered in a state of permanent crisis. Direct taxes on land, borne mainly by the peasants, were extremely high but were levied inequitably. The great variations in taxation from province to province and the numerous exemptions for privileged groups were regarded by those who benefited from them as traditional liberties. Any attempt to revoke these privileges therefore appeared to be tyrannical. Meanwhile indirect taxes on commercial activity (customs duties, excise or sales taxes, and royal monopolies on salt and tobacco) hit regressively at consumers, especially in the towns. Any tax increases or new taxes imposed by the monarchy at this point would be bitterly resented. At the same time, the cycle of borrowing—the alternative to increased taxes—had reached its limits. New loans would only raise the huge interest payments already being paid out. By the 1780s those payments accounted for about half of the royal budget and created additional budget deficits of perhaps 150,000,000 livres each year!

Calonne and the Assembly of Notables When the king's new controller-general, Charles Calonne, pieced all this information together in 1787, he warned that, contrary to Necker's rosy projections, the monarchy was facing outright bankruptcy. Though no way had yet been found to win public confidence and forge a consensus for fiscal reform, the monarchy had to act and could no longer rely on old expedients. Bold innovations were essential. Calonne accordingly proposed to establish a new tax, called the *territorial subvention*, to be levied on the yield of all landed property without exemptions. At the same time, he proposed to convene *provincial assemblies* elected by large landowners to advise royal officials on the collection and allocation of revenues.

Certain that the Parlements would reject this scheme, Calonne convinced the king to convene an Assembly of Notables, comprising about 150 influential men, mainly but not exclusively from the aristocracy, who might more easily be persuaded to support the reforms. To Calonne's shock, the Assembly of Notables refused to endorse the proposed decrees. Instead, they denounced the lavish spending of the court and insisted on auditing the monarchy's financial accounts. To save the day, Louis dismissed Calonne and appointed one of the notables, Archbishop Brienne, in his place. Brienne now submitted Calonne's proposals to the Parlement, which not only rejected them but also demanded that Louis convene the Estates General, a body representing the clergy, nobility, and Third Estate, which had not met since 1614. Louis responded by sending the members of the Parlements into exile. But a huge outcry in Paris and in the provinces against this arbitrary act forced the king to back down: After all, the whole purpose of Calonne's proposals had been to build public confidence in the government.

Facing bankruptcy and unable to float new loans in this atmosphere, the King recalled the Parlements, reappointed Necker, and agreed to convene the Estates General in May 1789. In the opinion of the English writer Arthur Young, who was visiting France, the kingdom was "on the verge of a revolution, but one likely to add to the scale of the nobility and clergy." The aristocracy's determined opposition was putting an end to absolutism in France. But it was not clear what would take its place.

FROM THE ESTATES GENERAL TO THE NATIONAL ASSEMBLY

The calling of the Estates General in 1789 created extraordinary excitement across the land. The king invited his subjects to express their opinions about this great event, and thousands did so in pamphlet form. Here the "patriot," or liberal, ideology first took shape. Self-styled patriots came from the ranks of the nobility and clergy as well as from the middle classes; they opposed traditionalists, whom they labeled as "aristocrats." Their top priority was the method of voting to be used in the Estates General. While the king accorded the Third Estate twice as many delegates as the two higher orders, he refused to promise that the deputies would all vote together (by head) rather than separately in three chambers (by order). Voting by order would mean that the two upper chambers would outweigh the Third Estate no matter how many deputies it had. Patriots had hoped that the lines dividing the nobility from the middle class would crumble in a common effort by France's elites at reform. Instead, it appeared as if the Estates General might sharpen the lines of separation between the orders.

The Critique of Privilege It did not matter that the nobility had led the fight against absolutism. Even if they endorsed new constitutional checks on absolutism and accepted equality in the allocation of taxes, nobles would still hold vastly disproportionate powers if the Estates General voted by order. In the most influential pamphlet about the Estates General, Emmanuel Sieyès posed the question "What is the Third Estate?"

▶ Thousands of pamphlets were published to discuss the calling of the Estates General in 1789, but the grievances and claims of the Third Estate translated most readily into vivid imagery and caricature; this print was titled "The Awakening of the Third Estate."

and answered flatly "Everything." "And what has it been until now in the political order?" he asked. Answer: "Nothing." The nobility, he claimed, monopolized all the lucrative positions in society while doing little of its productive work. In the manifestos of Sieyès and other patriots, the enemy was no longer simply absolutism but privilege as well.

Unlike reformers in England, or the Belgian rebels against Joseph II, or even the American revolutionaries of 1776, the French patriots did not simply claim that the king had violated historic traditions of liberty. Rather, they contemplated a complete break with a discredited past.

As a basis for reform, they would substitute reason for tradition. It is this frame of mind that made the French Revolution so radical.

Cahiers and Elections   For the moment, however, the patriot spokesmen stood far in advance of opinion at the grass roots. The king had invited all citizens to meet in their local parishes to elect delegates to district electoral assemblies and to draft grievance petitions (*cahiers*) setting forth their views. The great majority of rural *cahiers* were highly traditional in tone and complained only of particular local ills or high taxes, expressing confidence that the king would redress them. Only a few *cahiers* from cities like Paris invoked concepts of natural rights and popular sovereignty, or demanded that France must have a written constitution, that sovereignty belonged to the nation, or that feudalism and regional privileges should be abolished. It is impossible, in other words, to read in the *cahiers* the future course of the Revolution. Still, these gatherings of citizens promoted reflection on France's problems and encouraged expectations for change. They thereby helped raise the nation's political consciousness.

So too did the local elections, whose royal ground rules were remarkably democratic. Virtually every adult male taxpayer was eligible to vote for electors, who, in turn, met in district assemblies to choose representatives of the Third Estate to the Estates General. The electoral assemblies were a kind of political seminar, where articulate local leaders emerged to be sent by their fellow citizens as deputies to Versailles. Most of these deputies were lawyers or officials, without a single peasant or artisan among them. In the elections for the First Estate, meanwhile, parish priests rather than Church notables formed a majority of the deputies. And in the elections for the Second Estate, about one-third of the deputies could be described as liberal nobles or patriots, the rest traditionalists.

Deadlock and Revolution Popular expectation that the monarchy would provide leadership in reform proved to be ill-founded. When the deputies to the Estates General met on May 5, Necker and Louis XVI spoke to them only in generalities and left unsettled whether the estates would vote by order or by head. The upper two estates proceeded to organize their own chambers, but the deputies of the Third Estate balked. Vainly inviting the others to join them, the Third Estate took a decisive revolutionary step on June 17 by proclaiming that it formed a "National Assembly." A few days later over a third of the deputies from the clergy joined them. The king, on the other hand, decided to cast his lot with the nobility and locked the Third Estate out of its meeting hall until he could present his own program. But the deputies moved to an indoor tennis court and swore that they would not separate until they had given France a constitution.

The king ignored this act of defiance and addressed the delegates of all three orders on June 23. He promised equality in taxation, civil liber-

▶ **When the king opened the meeting of the Estates General, the deputies for each estate were directed to sit in three separate sections of the hall.**

▶ Jacques-Louis David's depiction of the Tennis Court Oath, one of the great historical paintings, captures the deputies' sense of idealism and purpose.

ties, and regular meetings of the Estates General at which, however, voting would be by order. France would be provided with a constitution, he pledged, "but the ancient distinction of the three orders will be conserved in its entirety." He then ordered the three estates to retire to their individual meeting halls, but the Third Estate refused to move. "The assembled nation cannot receive orders," declared its spokesman. Startled by the determination of the patriots, the king backed down. For the time being, he recognized the National Assembly and ordered deputies from all three estates to join it.

Thus the French Revolution began as a nonviolent, "legal" revolution. By their own will, delegates elected by France's three estates to represent their own districts to the king became instead the representatives of the entire nation. As such, they claimed to be the sovereign power in France—a claim that the king now seemed powerless to contest. In fact, however, he was merely biding his time until he could deploy his army to subdue the capital and overwhelm the deputies at Versailles. Twenty thousand royal troops were ordered into the Paris region, due to arrive sometime in July.

THE CONVERGENCE OF REVOLUTIONS

The political struggle at Versailles was not occurring in isolation. The mass of French citizens, politically aroused by elections to the Estates General, was also mobilizing over subsistence issues. The winter and spring of 1788–89 had brought severe economic difficulties, as crop failures and grain shortages almost doubled the price of flour and bread on which the population depended for subsistence. Unemployed vagrants filled the roads, angry consumers stormed grain convoys and marketplaces, and relations between town and country grew tense. Economic anxieties merged with rage over the obstructive behavior of aristocrats in Versailles. Parisians believed that food shortages and royal troops would be used to intimidate the people into submission. They feared an "aristocratic plot" against the National Assembly and the patriot cause.

The Fall of the Bastille   When the King dismissed the popular Necker on July 11, Parisians correctly assumed that a counterrevolution was about to begin. They prepared to resist, and most of the king's military units pulled back. On July 14 Parisian crowds searching for weapons and ammunition laid siege to the Bastille, an old fortress that had served as a royal prison, where gunpowder was stored. The small garrison resisted, and a fierce firefight erupted. Although the troops soon capitulated, dozens of citizens were hit, providing the first martyrs of the Revolution, and the infuriated crowd massacred several soldiers as they left the fortress. Meanwhile,

patriot electors ousted royal officials of the Paris city government, replaced them with a revolutionary municipality, and organized a citizens' militia to patrol the city. Similar municipal revolutions occurred in 26 of the 30 largest French cities, thus ensuring that the defiance in the capital would not be an isolated act.

The Parisian insurrection of July 14 not only saved the National Assembly but altered the Revolution's course by giving it a far more popular dimension. Again the king capitulated. He traveled to Paris on July 17 and, to please the

▶ The fall of the Bastille was understood at the time to be a great turning point in history, and July 14 eventually became the French national holiday. Numerous prints and paintings evoke the daunting qualities of the fortress, the determination of the besieging crowd, and the heroism of individuals in that crowd.

people, donned a ribbon bearing three colors: white for the monarchy and blue and red for the capital. This *tricolor* would become the emblem of the new regime.

Rural Revolt and the August 4 Decree

These events did not pacify the anxious and hungry people of the countryside. Peasants had numerous and long-standing grievances. Population growth and the parceling of holdings reduced the margin of subsistence for many families, while the purchase of land by rich townspeople further shrank their opportunities for economic advancement. Seigneurial dues and church tithes weighed heavily on many peasants. Now, in addition, suspicions were rampant that nobles were hoarding grain in order to stymie the patriotic cause. In July peasants in several regions sacked the castles of the nobles and burned the documents that recorded their feudal obligations.

This peasant insurgency blended into a vast movement known to historians as "the Great Fear." Rumors abounded that the vagrants who swarmed through the countryside were actually "brigands" in the pay of nobles, who were marching on villages to destroy the new harvest and cow the peasants into submission. The fear was baseless, but it stirred up the peasants' hatred and suspicion of the nobles, prompted armed mobilizations in hundreds of villages, and set off new attacks on manor houses.

Peasant insurgency worried the deputies of the National Assembly, but they decided to appease the peasants rather than simply denounce their violence. On the night of August 4, therefore, certain deputies of the nobility and clergy dramatically renounced their ancient privileges. This set the stage for the Assembly to decree "the abolition of feudalism" as well as the end of the church tithe, the sale of royal offices, regional tax privileges, and social privilege of all kinds. Later, it is true, the Assembly clarified the August 4 decree to ensure that property rights were maintained. While personal servitudes such as hunting rights, manorial justice, and labor services were suppressed outright, the Assembly decreed that most seigneurial dues would end only after the peasants had paid compensation to their lords. Peasants resented this onerous requirement, and most simply refused to pay the dues;

pressure built until all seigneurial dues were finally abolished without compensation by a more radical government in 1793.

The Declaration of the Rights of Man

By sweeping away the old web of privileges, the August 4 decree permitted the Assembly to construct a new regime. Since it would take months to draft a constitution, the Assembly drew up a Declaration of the Rights of Man and Citizen to indicate its intentions (*see box*, p. 651). The Declaration was the death certificate of the old regime and a rallying point for the future. It affirmed individual liberties but also set forth the basic obligation of citizenship: obedience to legitimate law. The Declaration enumerated natural rights such as freedom of expression and freedom of religious conscience but stipulated that even these rights could be circumscribed by law. It proclaimed the sovereignty of the nation and sketched the basic criteria for a legitimate government, which the constitution would eventually amplify, such as representation and the separation of powers. The Declaration's concept of natural rights meant that the new regime would be based on the principles of reason rather than history or tradition.

In his *Reflections on the Revolution in France*, published in 1790, the Anglo-Irish statesman Edmund Burke condemned this attitude, as well as the violence of 1789. In this influential counter-revolutionary tract, Burke argued that France had passed from despotism to anarchy in the name of misguided, abstract principles. Burke distrusted the simplicity of reason that the Assembly celebrated. In his view the complexity of traditional institutions served the public interest. Burke attacked the belief in natural rights that guided the revolutionaries; something was natural, he believed, only if it resulted from long historical development and habit. Trying to wipe the slate of history clean was a grievous error, he wrote, since society "is a contract between the dead, the living, and the unborn." Society's main right, in Burke's view, was the right to be well-governed by its rulers. Naturally this argument did not go unchallenged, even in England. Mary Wollstonecraft countered with *A Vindication of the Rights of Man*, while Thomas Paine's *The Rights of Man*, published in 1792 to refute Burke, won a larger readership than Burke's tract.

Two Views of the Rights of Man

The radical theoretical and practical implications of French revolutionary ideology are suggested in a comparison of two essentially contemporaneous documents. The Prussian General Code, a codification initiated by Frederick the Great and issued in its final form in 1791 after his death, reinforced the traditional prerogatives of the nobility under an umbrella of public law. The National Assembly's Declaration of the Rights of Man and Citizen (1789) established the principle of civil equality, alongside the doctrines of national sovereignty, representation, and the rule of law. While the Prussian General Code exemplifies the old order against which French revolutionary ideology took aim, the Declaration became a foundational document of the liberal tradition.

EXCERPTS FROM "THE PRUSSIAN GENERAL CODE," 1791

- This general code contains the provisions by which the rights and obligations of inhabitants of the state, so far as they are not determined by particular laws, are to be judged.

- The rights of a man arise from his birth, from his estate, and from actions and arrangements with which the laws have associated a certain determinate effect.

- The general rights of man are grounded on the natural liberty to seek and further his own welfare, without injury to the rights of another.

- Persons to whom, by their birth, destination or principal occupation, equal rights are ascribed in civil society, make up together an *estate* of the state.

- The nobility, as the first estate in the state, most especially bears the obligation, by its distinctive destination, to maintain the defense of the state. . . .

- The nobleman has an especial right to places of honor in the state for which he has made himself fit.

- Only the nobleman has the right to possess noble property.

- Persons of the burgher [middle-class] estate cannot own noble property except by permission of the sovereign.

- Noblemen shall normally engage in no burgher livelihood or occupation.

EXCERPTS FROM THE FRENCH "DECLARATION OF THE RIGHTS OF MAN AND CITIZEN," 1789

1. Men are born and remain free and equal in rights. Social distinctions may be based only on common utility.

3. The principle of all sovereignty rests essentially in the nation. No body and no individual may exercise authority which does not emanate expressly from the nation.

4. Liberty consists in the ability to do whatever does not harm another; hence the exercise of the natural rights of each man has no limits except those which assure to other members of society the enjoyment of the same rights. These limits can only be determined by law.

6. Law is the expression of the general will. All citizens have the right to take part, in person or by their representatives, in its formation. It must be the same for all whether it protects or penalizes. All citizens being equal in its eyes are equally admissible to all public dignities, offices and employments, according to their capacity, and with no other distinction than that of their virtues and talents.

13. For maintenance of public forces and for expenses of administration common taxation is necessary. It should be apportioned equally among all citizens according to their capacity to pay.

14. All citizens have the right, by themselves or through their representatives, to have demonstrated to them the necessity of public taxes, to consent to them freely, to follow the use made of the proceeds, and to determine the shares to be paid, the means of assessment and collection and the duration.

III. The Reconstruction of France

▼

THE NEW CONSTITUTION

From 1789 to 1791, the National Assembly acted as a Constituent Assembly to produce a constitution for France. While recognizing the civil rights of all French citizens, it effectively transferred political power from the monarchy and the privileged estates to the body of propertied citizens; in 1790 nobles lost their titles and became indistinguishable from other citizens. The new constitution created a limited monarchy with a clear separation of powers. Sovereignty effectively resided in the representatives of the people, a single-house legislature to be elected by a system of indirect voting. The king was to name and dismiss his ministers, but he was given only a suspensive or delaying veto over legislation; if a bill passed the Assembly in three successive years, it would become law even without royal approval.

The Assembly limited the franchise to "active" citizens, defined as those who paid a minimal sum in taxes; the property qualification was higher for election to public office. Under this system about two-thirds of adult males had the right to vote for the electors who would then choose deputies to the legislature and local officials. Although it favored the propertied, the system was vastly more democratic than the political structure in Britain.

Gender and Race   Under the old regime women from prominent families had exercised considerable political influence behind the scenes. Now that the Assembly had established a public sphere of political action with clear ground rules based on elections, would women be admitted to this arena? In petitions to the Assembly and in pamphlets such as Olympe de Gouges' *Declaration of the Rights of Women* (1791), women's rights activists demanded suffrage for women without success. Sieyè spoke for most deputies when he claimed that women's emotional natures made them prone to being easily misled in public affairs. This weakness of character, Sieyès said,

made it imperative that women be kept out of public life and devote themselves to their nurturing and maternal roles.

The formal exclusion of women from politics did not mean that they remained passive spectators, however. Women actively engaged in local conflicts over the Assembly's religious policy (discussed below). In the towns they agitated over food prices, and in October 1789 Parisian women led a mass demonstration to Versailles that pressured the king into moving permanently to Paris. Women formed female auxiliaries to local political clubs and organized a handful of independent women's clubs; they participated in civic festivals and helped with relief for the poor. Nor was revolutionary policy indifferent to women's rights. A remarkably egalitarian inheritance law stipulated that all children regardless of gender were entitled to an equal share of a family's estate. And in 1794, an unprecedented system of free primary schools for girls as well as boys was enacted in which the state would pay the teachers' salaries.

As the Assembly excluded women from "active" citizenship without much debate, other groups posed challenges on how to apply "the rights of man" to French society. In eastern France, where most of France's 40,000 Jews resided, public opinion scorned them as an alien race not entitled to citizenship. Eventually, however, the Assembly rejected that argument and extended civil and political equality to Jews. A similar debate raged over the status of the free Negroes and mulattoes in France's Caribbean colonies. White planters, in alliance with the merchants who traded with the islands, were intent on preserving slavery and demanded local control over the islands' racial policy. The planters argued that they could not maintain slavery, which was manifestly based on race, unless free people of color were disenfranchised. When the Assembly accepted this view, the mulattoes rebelled. But their abortive uprising had the unintended consequence of helping to ignite a slave rebellion. Led by Toussaint-L'Ouverture, the blacks turned on their white masters and proclaimed the independence of the colony, which became known as Haiti. In 1794 the French revolutionary government belatedly abolished slavery in all French colonies.

Redividing the Nation's Territory Within France the Assembly obliterated the political identities of the country's historic provinces and instead divided the nation's territory into 83 departments of roughly equal size (see Map 20.1). Unlike the old provinces, each new department was to have exactly the same institutions. The departments were, in turn, subdivided into districts, cantons, and communes (the common designation for a village or town). On the one hand, this administrative transformation promoted local autonomy: The citizens of each department, district, and commune elected their own local officials, and in that sense political power was decentralized. On the other hand, these local governments were subordinated to the national legislature in Paris and became instruments for promoting national integration and uniformity.

The new administrative map also created the boundaries for a new judicial system. Sweeping away the parlements and law courts of the old regime, the revolutionaries established a justice of the peace in each canton, a civil court in each district, and a criminal court in each department. The judges on all tribunals were to be elected. The Assembly rejected the use of juries in civil cases but decreed that felonies would be tried by juries;

Map 20.1 REDIVIDING THE NATION'S TERRITORY IN 1789: FROM HISTORIC PROVINCES (*left*) TO REVOLUTIONARY DEPARTMENTS (*right*)

also, criminal defendants for the first time gained the right to counsel. In civil law, the Assembly encouraged arbitration and mediation to avoid the time-consuming and expensive processes of formal litigation. In general, the revolutionaries hoped to make the administration of justice faster and more accessible.

The Assembly's clearing operations extended to economic institutions as well. Guided by the dogmas of laissez-faire theory, and by its uncompromising hostility to privileged corporations, the Assembly sought to open up economic life to individual initiative, much as Turgot had attempted in the 1770s. Besides dismantling internal tariffs and chartered trading monopolies, it abolished merchants' and artisans' guilds and proclaimed the right of every citizen to enter any trade and conduct it freely. The government would no longer concern itself with regulating wages or the quality of goods. The Assembly also insisted that workers bargain in the economic marketplace as individuals, and it therefore banned workers' associations and strikes. The precepts of economic individualism extended to the countryside as well. At least in theory, peasants and landlords were free to cultivate their fields as they saw fit, regardless of traditional collective practices. In fact, those deep-rooted communal restraints proved to be extremely resistant to change.

THE REVOLUTION AND THE CHURCH

To address the state's financial problems, the National Assembly acted in a way that the monarchy had never dared contemplate. Under revolutionary ideology, the French Catholic Church could no longer exist as an independent corporation—as a separate estate within the state. The Assembly therefore nationalized Church property, placing it "at the disposition of the nation," and made the state responsible for the upkeep of the Church. It then issued paper notes called *assignats*, which were backed by the value of these "national lands." The property was to be sold by auction at the district capitals to the highest bidders. This plan favored the bourgeois and rich peasants with ready capital and made it difficult for needy peasants to acquire the land, though some pooled their resources to do so.

The sale of Church lands and the issuance of *assignats* had several consequences. In the short run, they eliminated the need for new borrowing. Second, the hundreds of thousands of purchasers gained a strong vested interest in the Revolution, since a successful counterrevolution was likely to reclaim their properties for the Church. Finally, after war broke out with an Austrian–Prussian coalition in 1792, the government made the *assignats* a national currency and printed a volume of *assignats* way beyond their underlying value in land, thereby touching off severe inflation and new political turmoil.

Religious Schism The issue of church reform produced the Revolution's first and most fateful crisis. The Assembly intended to rid the Church of inequities that enriched the aristocratic prelates of the old regime. Many Catholics looked forward to such healthy changes that might bring the clergy closer to the people. In the Civil Constitution of the Clergy (1790), the Assembly reduced the number of bishops from 130 to 83 and reshaped diocesan boundaries to conform exactly with those of the new departments. Bishops and parish priests were to be chosen by the electoral assemblies in the departments and districts, and were to be paid according to a uniform salary scale that favored those currently at the lower end. Like all other public officials, the clergy was to take an oath of loyalty to the constitution.

The clergy generally opposed the Civil Constitution because it had been dictated to them by the National Assembly; they argued that such questions as the selection of bishops and priests should be negotiated either with the Pope or with a National Church Council. But the Assembly asserted that it had the sovereign power to order such reforms, since they affected temporal rather than spiritual matters. In November 1790 the Assembly demanded that all clergy take the loyalty oath forthwith; those who refused would lose their positions and be pensioned off. In all of France only seven bishops and about 54 percent of the parish clergy swore the oath; but in the west of France only 15 percent of the priests complied. A schism tore through French Catholicism, since the laity had to take a position as well: Should parishioners remain loyal to their priests who had refused to take the oath (the nonjuring, or refractory, clergy) and thus be at odds with the state? Or should they accept the unfamiliar "constitutional clergy" designated by the districts to replace their own priests?

The Assembly's effort to impose reform in defiance of religious sensibilities and Church autonomy was a grave tactical error. The oath crisis polarized the nation. It seemed to link the Revolution with impiety and the Church with counterrevolution. In local communities, refractory clergy began to preach against the entire Revolution. Local officials fought back by arresting them and demanding repressive laws. Civil strife rocked thousands of communities.

COUNTERREVOLUTION, RADICALISM, AND WAR

Opposition to the Revolution had actually begun much earlier. After July 14 some of the king's relatives had left the country in disgust, thus becoming the first *émigrés*, or political exiles, of the Revolution. During the next three years thousands of nobles, including two-thirds of the royal army's officer corps, joined the emigration. Across the Rhine River in Coblenz, émigrés formed an army that threatened to overthrow the new regime at the first opportunity. The king himself publicly submitted to the Revolution, but privately he smoldered in resentment. Finally, in June 1791, Louis and his family fled in secret from Paris, hoping to cross the Belgian frontier and enlist the aid of Austria. But Louis was stopped at the French village of Varennes and was forcibly returned to Paris.

Moderates hoped that this aborted escape would finally end the king's opposition to the Revolution. The Assembly, after all, needed his cooperation to make its constitutional monarchy viable. It did not wish to open the door to a republic or to further unrest. Radicals such as the journalist Jean-Paul Marat, on the other hand, had long thundered against the treachery of the king and the émigrés, and against the Assembly itself for not acting vigorously against aristocrats and counterrevolutionaries. But the Assembly was determined to maintain the status quo and adopted the fiction that the king had been kidnapped. The Assembly reaffirmed the king's place in the new regime, but Louis' treasonous flight to Varennes ensured that radical agitation would continue.

The Outbreak of War When the newly elected Legislative Assembly convened on October 1, 1791, the questions of counterrevolution at home and the prospect of war abroad dominated its stormy sessions. Both the right and the left saw advantages to be gained in a war between France and Austria. The king and his court hoped that a military defeat would discredit the new regime and restore full power to the monarchy. Most members of the Jacobin Club—the leading radical political club in Paris—wanted war to strike down the foreign supporters of the émigrés and domestic counterrevolutionaries.

When Francis II ascended the throne of the Habsburg Monarchy in March 1792, the stage was set for war. Unlike his father, Leopold, who had rejected intervention in France's affairs, Francis fell under the influence of émigrés and bellicose advisers. He was determined to assist the French queen, his aunt, and he also expected to make territorial gains. With both sides thus eager for battle, France went to war in April 1792 against a coalition of Austria, Prussia, and the émigrés.

Each camp expected rapid victory, but both were deceived. The French offensive quickly faltered, and invading armies soon crossed France's borders. The Legislative Assembly ordered the arrest of refractory clergy and called for a special corps of 20,000 national guardsmen to protect Paris. Louis vetoed both measures and held to his decisions in spite of demonstrations against them in the capital. For all practical purposes, these were his last acts as king. The legislature also called for 100,000 volunteers to bolster the French army and defend the homeland.

The Fall of the Monarchy As Prussian forces began a drive toward Paris, their commander, the Duke of Brunswick, rashly threatened to level the city if it resisted or if it harmed the royal family. When Louis XVI published this Brunswick Manifesto, it seemed proof that he was in league with the enemy. Far from intimidating the revolutionaries, the threat drove them forward. Since a divided Legislative Assembly refused to act decisively in the face of royal obstructionism, Parisian militants, spurred on by the Jacobin Club, organized an insurrection.

On August 10, 1792, a crowd of armed Parisians stormed the royal palace at the Tuileries, literally driving the king from the throne. The Assembly then had no choice but to declare Louis XVI suspended. That night more than half the Assembly's members themselves fled Paris, making it clear that the Assembly too had lost its legitimacy. The deputies who remained ordered elections for a National Convention to decide the king's fate, to draft a republican constitution, and to govern France during the current emergency. What the events of 1789 in Versailles and Paris had begun, the insurrection of August 10, 1792 completed. The old regime in France had truly been destroyed.

IV. The Second Revolution

By 1792—just three years after the fall of the Bastille—the Revolution had profoundly altered the foundations of government and society in France.

▶ Like July 14, the assault on the Tuileries of August 10, 1792 led to a brief battle with numerous casualties among the besiegers and infuriated reprisals against the garrison after it surrendered. The event brought the end of the constitutional monarchy and led directly to the founding of the first French Republic.

The National Assembly swept away absolutism and introduced constitutional government, legislative representation, and local self-government. It repudiated aristocratic and corporate privilege and established civil equality and uniform institutions across the country. Peasants were freed from the seigneurial system, religious minorities from persecution. Yet the Revolution was far from over, and in the short view, one might say that it was only beginning. True, these changes ultimately proved to be the most significant. But they had been won at the price of great opposition, and the old order was far from vanquished. European monarchs and aristocrats encouraged refractory priests, émigrés, and royalists in France to resist, while many ordinary French citizens turned against the revolutionaries for a variety of reasons.

The patriots, threatened in 1792 by military defeat and counterrevolution, were themselves divided. Some became radicalized, while others grew alienated from the Revolution's increasingly radical course and joined its opponents. Each spasm of change produced new opponents at home and abroad, but each increment of opposition stiffened the resolve of the Revolution's partisans. Building on the momentum of August 1792, the Jacobins forged a coalition with urban militants known as the *sans-culottes* (literally, men who wore trousers rather than fashionable knee breeches). The sans-culottes sought to revolutionize the Revolution, to create a democratic republic based on a broadening definition of equality. But the government's responses to the crisis distorted this second revolution. To establish liberty, the Jacobins argued, coercion was required. The ideals of equality became confused with problems of national defense and with the impulse to repress opposition.

THE NATIONAL CONVENTION

The insurrection of August 10, 1792 created a vacuum of authority until the election of a National Convention was completed. A revolutionary Paris Commune, or city government, became one power center, but that bastion of radicalism could not control events even within its own domain. As thousands of volunteers left for the battlefront, Parisians nervously eyed the capital's jails, which overflowed with political prisoners and common criminals. Radical journalists like Jean-Paul Marat saw these prisoners as a counterrevolutionary striking force and feared a plot to open the prisons. A growing sense of alarm finally exploded early in September. For three days groups of Parisians invaded the prisons, set up "popular tribunals," and slaughtered more than 2000 prisoners. No official dared intervene to stop the carnage, known since as the September massacres.

The sense of panic eased, however, with the success of the French armies. Bolstered by units of volunteers, the army finally halted the invaders at the Battle of Valmy on September 20. Two months later it defeated the allies at Jemappes in the Austrian Netherlands, which the French now occupied. Meanwhile, the Convention convened and promptly declared France a republic.

Settling Louis XVI's fate proved to be extremely contentious. While the deputies unanimously found the ex-king guilty of treason, they divided sharply over the question of his punishment. Some argued for clemency, while others insisted that his execution was a necessary symbolic gesture as well as a fitting punishment for his betrayal. Finally, by a vote of 387 to 334, the Convention sentenced Louis to death and voted down efforts to reprieve this sentence or delay it for a popular referendum. On January 21, 1793, Louis was guillotined, put to death like an ordinary citizen. The deputies to the Convention had become regicides (king killers) and would make no compromise with the counterrevolution.

▶ Beset by invasion jitters, and fearing a plot to force open the capital's overcrowded jails, mobs of Parisians invaded the prisons and over the course of three days in September 1792 slaughtered over 2000 prisoners.

▶ After the National Convention concluded its trial of ex-King Louis XVI and voted to impose the death penalty without reprieve, "Louis Capet" was guillotined and the leaders of the Republic became regicides, king killers.

Factional Conflict From the Convention's opening day, two bitterly hostile groups of deputies vied for leadership and almost immobilized it with their rancorous conflict. One group became known as the *Girondins*, since several of its spokesmen were elected as deputies from the Gironde department. The Girondins were fiery orators and ambitious politicians who avocated provincial liberty and laissez-faire economics. They reacted hostilely to the growing radicalism of Paris and broke with or were expelled by the Jacobin Club, to which some had originally belonged. Meanwhile Parisian electors chose as their deputies leading members of the Jacobin Club such as Danton, Robespierre, and Marat. The Parisian deputation to the Convention became the nucleus of a group known as the *Mountain*, so-called because it occupied the upper benches of the Convention's hall. The Mountain attracted the more militant provincial deputies and attacked the Girondins as treacherous compromisers unwilling to adopt bold measures in the face of crisis. The Girondins, in turn, denounced the Mountain as would-be tyrants and captives of Parisian radicalism, and held them responsible for the September prison massacres.

Several hundred deputies stood between these two factions. These centrists (known as the *Plain*) were committed to the Revolution but were uncertain which path to follow. The Plain detested popular agitation, but they were reluctant to turn against the sans-culottes, who so fervently supported the Revolution. In the end they would support men or policies that promised to consolidate the Revolution.

THE REVOLUTIONARY CRISIS

By the spring of 1793 the National Convention faced a perilous convergence of invasion, civil war, and economic crises that demanded imaginative responses. Austria and Prussia had mounted a new offensive in 1793, their alliance strengthened by the addition of Spain, Piedmont, and Britain. Between March and September military reversals occurred on every front. The Convention reacted by introducing a military draft, but this, in turn, touched off a rebellion in western France by peasants and rural weavers, who had long resented the patriot middle class in the towns for monopolizing local political power and for persecuting their priests. In the isolated towns of the Vendée region, south of the Loire River, they attacked the Republic's supporters. Priests and nobles offered leadership to the rebels, who first organized into guerrilla bands and finally into a "Catholic and Royalist Army." The Vendée rebels briefly occupied several towns, massacred local patriots, and even threatened the port of Nantes, where British troops could have landed.

Meanwhile, economic troubles were provoking the Parisian sans-culottes. By early 1793 the Revolution's paper money, the *assignats*, had declined to 50 percent of its face value. Inflation was compounded by a poor harvest, food shortages, hoarding, and profiteering. Municipal authorities fixed the price of bread but could not always secure adequate supplies. Under these conditions the government could not even supply its armies.

Spokesmen for the sans-culottes declared that even the Convention and the Paris Commune were insufficiently responsive to popular opinion. They demanded that the Convention purge the Girondins and adopt a program of "public safety," including price controls for basic commodities, execution of hoarders and speculators, and forced requisitions of grain. Behind these demands lay the threat of armed insurrection. This

▶ **Bitter fighting in the Vendée between counterrevolutionaries and republicans caused a profound split in the loyalties of Western France, which endured for at least the next hundred years. Each side cultivated its own memories of the event and honored its own martyrs.**

pressure from the sans-culottes aided the Mountain in their struggle against the Girondins, but it could easily have degenerated into anarchy. In a sense, all elements of the revolutionary crisis hinged on one problem: the lack of an effective government that would not simply respond to popular pressures but would organize and master them. When the sans-culottes mounted a massive armed demonstration for a purge of the Girondins on June 2, centrist deputies reluctantly agreed to go along. The Convention expelled 23 Girondin deputies, who were subsequently tried and executed for treason.

Factionalism in the Convention reflected conflict in the provinces. Moderate republicans in several cities struggled with local Jacobin radicals and sympathized with the Girondin deputies in their campaign against the Parisian sans-culottes. In the south, local Jacobins lost control of Marseilles, Bordeaux, and Lyons to their rivals, who then repudiated the Convention. As in the Ven-

Map 20.2 CONFLICTS IN REVOLUTIONARY FRANCE

dée revolt, royalists soon took over the resistance in Lyons, France's second largest city. This was an intolerable challenge to the Convention. Labeling the anti-Jacobin rebels in Lyons and elsewhere as "federalists," the Convention dispatched armed forces to suppress them. In the eyes of the Jacobins, to defy the Convention's authority was to betray France itself.

THE JACOBIN DICTATORSHIP

Popular radicalism in Paris had helped bring the Mountain to power in the Convention. The question now was: Which side of this coalition between the Mountain and the sans-culottes would dominate the other? The sans-culottes seemed to believe that the sovereign people could dictate their will to the Convention. Popular agitation peaked on September 5, when a mass demonstration in Paris demanded new policies to ensure food supplies. To give force to the law, urged the sans-culottes, "Let terror be placed on the order of the day." The Convention responded with the Law of the Maximum, which imposed general price controls, and with the Law of Suspects, which empowered local revolutionary committees to imprison citizens whose loyalty they suspected.

Revolutionary Government In June the triumphant Mountain had drafted a new democratic constitution for the French Republic and had submitted it to an unprecedented referendum, in which almost 2 million citizens had overwhelmingly voted yes. But the Convention formally laid the constitution aside and proclaimed the government "revolutionary until the peace." Elections, local self-government, and guarantees of individual liberty were to be suspended until the Republic had defeated its enemies within and without. The Convention placed responsibility for military, economic, and political policy, as well as control over local officials, in the hands of a 12-man Committee of Public Safety. Spontaneous popular action was about to give way to revolutionary centralization.

Maximilien Robespierre emerged as the Committee's leading personality and tactician. An austere bachelor in his mid-thirties, Robespierre had been a provincial lawyer before the Revolu-

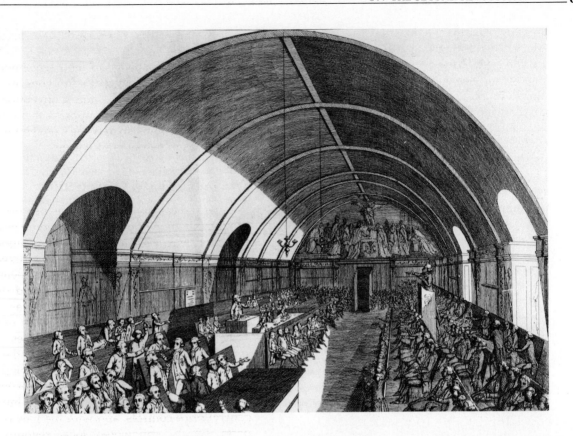

▶ **The Paris Jacobin Club began as a caucus for a group of liberal deputies to the National Assembly. During the Convention it became a bastion of democratic deputies and middle-class Parisian radicals, while continuing to serve as a "mother club" for affiliated clubs in the provinces.**

tion. As a deputy to the National Assembly he had ardently advocated greater democracy. His main political forum was the Paris Jacobin Club, which by 1793 he more or less dominated. In the Convention, Robespierre was inflexible and self-righteous in his dedication to the Revolution. He sought to appease the sans-culottes but also to control them, for he placed the Revolution's survival above any one viewpoint (*see box*, p. 662).

Local political clubs (numbering over 5000 by 1794) formed crucial links in the chain of revolutionary government. The clubs nominated citizens for posts on local revolutionary institutions, exercised surveillance over those officials, and served as "arsenals of public opinion." The clubs fostered the egalitarian ideals of the second revolution and supported the war effort. They also saw it as their civic duty to denounce fellow citizens for unpatriotic behavior, and thereby sowed fear and recrimination across the land.

For the Jacobins tolerated no serious dissent. The government's demand for unity during the emergency nullified the right to freedom of expression. Among those to fall were a group of ultrarevolutionaries led by Jacques-René Hébert, a leading radical journalist and Paris official. They were accused of a plot against the Republic and were guillotined. In reality, Hébert had questioned what he deemed the Convention's leniency toward "enemies of the people." Next came the so-called indulgents. Headed by Georges-Jacques Danton, a leading member of the Jacobin Club, they publicly argued for a relaxation of rigorous measures. For this dissent they were indicted on trumped-up charges of treason and were sentenced to death by the revolutionary tribunal. This succession of purges, which started with the Girondins and later ended with Robespierre himself, suggested, as one contemporary put it, that "revolutions devour their own children."

Robespierre's Justification of the Terror

"If the spring of popular government in time of peace is virtue, the springs of popular government in revolution are at once *virtue and terror*: virtue, without which terror is fatal; terror, without which virtue is powerless. Terror is nothing other than justice, prompt, severe, inflexible; it is therefore an emanation of virtue. . . . It is a consequence of the general principle of democracy applied to our country's most urgent needs.

"It has been said that terror is the principle of despotic government. Does your government therefore resemble despotism? Yes, as the sword that gleams in the hands of the heroes of liberty resembles that with which the henchman of tyranny are armed. Let the despot govern his brutalized subjects by terror; he is right, as a despot. Subdue by terror the enemies of liberty, and you will be right, as founders of the Republic. The government of the revolution is liberty's despotism against tyranny. Is force made only to protect crime?

"Society owes protection only to peaceable citizens; the only citizens in the Republic are the republicans. For it, the royalists, the conspirators are only strangers or, rather, enemies. This terrible war waged by liberty against tyranny—is it not indivisible? Are the enemies within not the allies of the enemies without? The assassins who tear our country apart, the intriguers who buy the consciences that hold the people's mandate; the traitors who sell them; the mercenary pamphleteers hired to dishonor the people's cause, to kill public virtue, to stir up the fire of civil discord, and to prepare political counter-revolution—are all those men less guilty or less dangerous than the tyrants [abroad] whom they serve?

"We try to control revolutions with the quibbles of the courtroom; we treat conspiracies against the Republic like lawsuits between individuals. Tyranny kills, and liberty argues. . . ."

From Robespierre's speech to the Convention on "The Moral and Political Principles of Domestic Policy," December 1793.

The Reign of Terror Most of those devoured by the French Revolution, however, were not its own children but an assortment of armed rebels, counterrevolutionaries, and unfortunate citizens who were swept into the vortex of war and internal strife. As an official policy, the Reign of Terror sought to organize repression so as to avoid anarchic violence like the September massacres. It reflected a state of mind that saw threats and plots everywhere (some real, some imagined). The laws of the Terror struck most directly at the people perceived to be enemies of the Revolution: Refractory priests and émigrés, for instance, were banned from the Republic upon threat of death. But the Law of Suspects also led to the incarceration of as many as 300,000 ordinary citizens for their opinions, past behavior, or social status.

The Terror produced its own atrocities: the brutal drowning of imprisoned priests at Nantes; the execution of thousands of noncombatants during the military campaigns of the Vendée; and the summary executions of about 2000 citizens of Lyons, more than two-thirds of them from the wealthy classes. ("Lyons has made war against liberty," declared the Convention, "thus Lyons no longer exists.") But except in the two zones of intense civil war—western France and the area of "federalist" rebellion in the south (see Map 20.2)—the Terror impressed by examples, not by the execution of entire social groups.

THE SANS-CULOTTES AND REVOLUTION FROM BELOW

The Parisian sans-culottes formed the crowds and demonstrations that produced the Revolution's dramatic turning points (see chart on p.

Air Ou Courez vous M.ʳ l'Abbé.
Ne redoutez plus les Brocards.
Gentes Nonettes beaux frocards

De la Metamorphose
He bien
L'Amour rit et pour cause
Et vous mentendez bien.

On me Raze ce Matin, Je me Marie ce Soir.

▶ **At the height of the "dechristianization" movement (which lasted for about eight months in the period 1793–1794), over 18,000 priests renounced their vocations. About a third were also pressured into marrying as a way of proving the sincerity of their resignations. ("They shave me in the morning and have me married by evening.")**

664), but they also threw themselves into a daily routine of political activism during the second revolution of 1792–1794. The sans-culottes were mainly artisans, shopkeepers, and workers— building contractors, carpenters, shoemakers, wine sellers, clerks, tailors, cafe keepers. Many owned their own businesses; others were wage earners. But they shared a strong sense of local community in the capital's varied neighborhoods.

Popular Attitudes The sans-culottes were obsessed with the availability and price of bread. As consumers, they faced inflation and scarcities with fear, distress, and rage, and demanded forceful government intervention to ensure the basic necessities of life. Sans-culotte militants believed in property rights, but they insisted that people did not have the right to misuse property by hoarding food or speculating. As one petition put it, "What is the meaning of freedom, when one class of men can starve another? What is the meaning of equality, when the rich, by their monopolies, can exercise the right of life and death over their equals?" The sans-culotte call for price controls clashed dramatically with the dogma of laissez-faire. By 1793, however, the Jacobins had acknowledged "the right to subsistence" in their new constitution and had instituted price controls under the Law of the Maximum to regulate the economy during the emergency.

Bitterly antiaristocratic, the sans-culottes displayed their social attitudes in everyday behavior. They advocated simplicity in dress and manners, and attacked opulence and pretension wherever they found or imagined them to be. Under their disapproving eye, high society and fancy dress generally disappeared from view. Vices like prostitution and gambling were attributed to aristocrats and were denounced in the virtuous society of the Revolution; drinking, the common people's vice, was tolerated. The revolutionaries symbolized their break with the past

TURNING POINTS IN THE FRENCH REVOLUTION

June 17, 1789	Third Estate declares itself a "National Assembly."
July 14, 1789	Storming of the Bastille and triumph of the patriots.
August 10, 1792	Storming of the Tuileries and the end of the monarchy (followed by the September prison massacres).
January 21, 1793	Execution of Louis XVI.
March 1793	Vendée rebellion begins.
June 2, 1793	Sans-culottes intimidate the Convention into purging the Girondin deputies. "Federalist" rebellion begins in Lyons.
September 5, 1793	Sans-culottes demonstrate for the enactment of economic controls and Terror.
October 1793	The Jacobin dictatorship and the Terror begin: The Convention declares that "the government is revolutionary until the peace."
9 Thermidor year II (July 27, 1794)	Fall of Robespierre.
1–2 Prairial year III (May 20–21, 1795)	Failed insurrection by Parisian sans-culottes for "Bread and the Constitution of 1793."
18 Brumaire year VIII (November 9, 1799)	Coup d'état by General Bonaparte and the "revisionists."

▶ The radical activists of the Paris sections—the *sans-culottes* and their female counterparts—made a point of their plebeian forms of dress, their freedom to bear arms, and their egalitarian insignias, such as the red liberty cap.

by changing the names of streets and public places to eliminate signs of royalism, religion, or aristocracy. The Palais Royal thus became the Palais d'Égalité ("Equality Palace"). Some citizens exchanged their Christian names for the names of secular heroes from antiquity, like Brutus. And all citizens were expected to drop honorifics like *monsieur* and *madame* in favor of the simple, uniform designation of *citizen*. Even the measurement of time was altered when the Convention decreed a new republican calendar in which the months were renamed, the seven-day week replaced by a ten-day *décadi*, and the year I dated from the establishment of the Republic in 1792.

Popular Politics   The Convention believed in representative democracy, with an active political life at the grass roots, but during the emergency it enacted a centralized revolutionary dictatorship. The sans-culottes preferred a more decentralized style of participatory democracy. They believed that the local assembly of citizens was the ultimate sovereign body. At the beginning of the year II (1793–1794), the 48 sections of

A Portrait of the Parisian Sans-Culotte

"A Sans-Culotte is a man who goes everywhere on his own two feet, who has none of the millions you're all after, no mansions, no lackeys to wait on him, and who lives quite simply with his wife and children, if he has any, on the fourth or fifth floor. He is useful, because he knows how to plough a field, handle a forge, a saw, or a file, how to cover a roof or how to make shoes and to shed his blood to the last drop to save the Republic. And since he is a working man, you will never find him in the Cafe de Chartres where they plot and gamble. . . . In the evening, he is at his Section, not powdered and perfumed and all dolled up to catch the eyes of the *citoyennes* in the galleries, but to support sound resolutions with all his power and to pulverize the vile faction [of moderates]. For the rest, a Sans-Culotte always keeps his sword with a sharp edge, to clip the ears of the malevolent. Sometimes he carries his pike and at the first roll of the drum, off he goes to the Vendée, to the Army of the Alps or the Army of the North."

From a pamphlet attributed to the sectional militant Vingternier: "A Reply to the Impertinent Question: But What Is a Sans-Culotte?" (1794).

Paris functioned almost as autonomous republics in which local activists ran their own affairs. Political life in Paris and elsewhere had a naive, breathless quality and made thousands of ordinary citizens feel that they held real political power (*see box,* above).

To Robespierre, this ideal of direct democracy appeared unworkable and akin to anarchy. The Convention watched the sans-culottes uneasily, supportive of democratic egalitarianism but fearful of the unpredictability, disorder, and inefficiency of this popular movement. The Mountain attempted to steer between encouraging civic participation and controlling it. From the 48 sections of Paris, however, came an endless stream of petitions, denunciations, and veiled threats to the government. In the spring of 1794 the Convention decided to curb the power of the sections with a series of decrees drastically restricting their rights and activities. By forcibly cooling down the ardor of the sans-culottes, however, the revolutionary government necessarily weakened its own base of support.

THE REVOLUTIONARY WARS

Ultimately, the Revolution's fate rested in the hands of its armies, although no one had thought in such terms in 1789. France's revolutionary ideology had initially posed no direct threat to the European state system. Indeed, the orators of the National Assembly had argued that the best foreign policy for a free society was peace, neutrality, and isolation from the diplomatic intrigues of monarchs. But peaceful intentions did not imply pacifism. When counterrevolution at home coalesced with threats from abroad, the revolutionaries were eager to fight against both. As in most major wars, however, the initial objectives were soon forgotten. As the war expanded, it brought revolution to other states.

The revolutionary wars involved timeless considerations of international relations as well as new and explosive purposes. On the one hand, France pursued the traditional aim of extending and rounding off its frontiers. On the other hand, France now espoused revolutionary principles such as the right of a people to self-determination. As early as September 1791, the National Assembly had declared that "the rights of peoples are not determined by the treaties of princes."

Foreign Revolutionaries and French Armies
Even before 1789 "patriots" in Geneva, the Dutch Netherlands, and the Austrian Netherlands (Belgium) had unsuccessfully challenged the traditional arrangements that governed their societies,

▶ Amidst elaborate arrays of symbolism, revolutionary iconography generally used the figure of a woman to represent its ideals. Briefly in the period 1793–1794, however, the Jacobins introduced the more aggressive masculine figure of Hercules to represent the Republic.

and the French Revolution rekindled those rebellious sentiments. Foreign revolutionaries were eager to challenge their governments again, and they looked to revolutionary France for assistance. Refugees from these struggles had fled to France and now formed pressure groups to lobby French leaders for help in liberating their own countries during France's war against Austria and Prussia. Some revolutionaries from areas contiguous to France (Belgium, Savoy, and the Rhineland) hoped that the French Republic might simply annex those territories. Elsewhere—in the

Dutch Netherlands, Lombardy, Ireland, and the Swiss Confederation—insurgents hoped that France would help establish independent republics by overthrowing the ruling princes or oligarchies.

Few French leaders were interested in leading a European crusade for liberty, but practical considerations led them to intervention. As the war spilled over into Belgium and the Rhineland, the French sought to establish support abroad by incorporating the principles of the Revolution into their foreign policy. Thus in December 1792 the Convention decided that feudal practices and hereditary privileges would be abolished wherever French armies prevailed. The people thus liberated, however, would have to pay for their liberation with special taxes and requisitions of supplies for French troops. By 1794 France had a permanent foothold in Belgium and soon annexed that territory to the Republic. Yet Robespierre was dubious about foreign entanglements; he believed that liberty had to be secured in France before it could be exported abroad. The Committee of Public Safety thus declined to support a distant Polish revolutionary movement, refused to invade Holland, and attempted to avoid any involvements in Italy.

The Armies of the Republic   The fighting men who defended France and carried its revolution abroad were a far different body from the old royal army. The National Assembly of 1789 retained the notion of a professional army but opened officers' careers to ordinary soldiers, especially after most of the royal officer corps emigrated or resigned. At the same time, the concept of the citizen-soldier was introduced in the newly organized national guard, which had elected officers. When the war against the coalition began in 1792 the government enrolled over 100,000 volunteers for short-term service at the front. But when the coalition launched its second offensive in 1793, the inadequacy of the French army demanded drastic innovations.

The Convention responded with the mass levy of August 1793 (*levée en masse*). All able-bodied unmarried men between the ages of 18 and 25 were drafted for military service, without the option of buying themselves a replacement. About 300,000 new recruits poured into the armies, while perhaps 200,000 draftees fled to avoid service. By the end of 1794 the French had almost 750,000 men under arms. With elected officers at their head, the citizen-soldiers marched off to the front under banners that read "The French people risen against the tyrants." The Convention merged these recruits with the regulars of line army into units called demibrigades, so that the professionals could impart their military skills to the new troops.

Military tactics in the field reflected a combination of revolutionary spirit and pragmatism. The new demibrigades did not have the training to be deployed in the well-drilled line formations of old-regime armies. Commanders instead favored mass columns that could move quickly without much drilling. Mass and mobility characterized the armies of the French Revolution. The Committee of Public Safety advised its commanders, "Act offensively and in masses. Use the bayonet at every opportunity. Fight great battles and pursue the enemy until he is destroyed."

The revolutionary government fostered new attitudes toward military life. The military was under civilian control. Discipline applied equally to officers and men, and wounded soldiers received generous veterans benefits. The Convention insisted that generals show not only military talent but the will to win. Many young officers rose quickly to command positions, but some generals fared badly. The commander of the defeated Rhine army in early 1793, for example, was branded a traitor, tried, and guillotined. Mean-

▶ **To bolster the professional troops of the line army in 1791 and again in 1792 after the war began, the government called for volunteers, one of whom is shown in this sentimental and patriotic portrait bidding farewell to his family. By 1793, the National Convention had to go further and draft all able-bodied young men.**

while, <u>economic mobilization at home produced the weapons, ammunition, clothing, and food necessary to support this mass army.</u>

In late 1793–early 1794 the armies of the Republic won a string of victories, culminating in the Battle of Fleurus in June 1794, which liberated Belgium for the second time. French armies also triumphed at the Pyrénées and the Rhine, and forced their enemies one by one to the peace table—first Spain and Prussia, then Piedmont. <u>An army crippled at the outset by treason and desertion, defeat, lack of training and discipline, and collapsing morale had been forged into a potent force in less than two years. Militarily, at least, the revolutionary government had succeeded brilliantly.</u>

To its most dedicated supporters, the revolutionary government had two major purposes: first, to surmount a crisis and steer the Republic to victory; and second, to democratize France's political and social fabric. Only the first objective, however, won widespread adherence. The National Convention held a polarized nation together, consolidated the Republic, and defeated its foreign enemies, but only at enormous and questionable costs. Moderates and ultrarevolutionaries alike resented the stifling political conformity imposed by the revolutionary government. Wealthy peasants and businesspeople chafed under the economic regimentation, and Catholics bitterly resented local "dechristianization" campaigns. The Jacobins increasingly isolated themselves, making enemies on every side. It is not surprising, then, that the security provided by the military victories of 1793–1794 would permit the Convention to end the Jacobin dictatorship and abandon its rhetoric of radical egalitarianism. But the question remained: What would take their place?

Recommended Reading

Sources

*Beik, Paul H. (ed.). *The French Revolution.* 1971.

*Burke, Edmund. *Reflections on the Revolution in France.* 1969. The most influential antirevolutionary book.

Kirchberger, Joe H. (ed.). *The French Revolution and Napoleon: An Eyewitness History.* 1989. Includes key documents and contemporary accounts of the principal events.

*Levy, Darlene, H. Applewhite, and M. Johnson (eds.). *Women in Revolutionary Paris, 1789–1795.* 1979. A documentary history of women activists.

Roland, Manon Jeanne. *The Private Memoirs of Madame Roland* (2d ed.). E. G. Johnson (ed.). 1976. By a woman deeply involved in revolutionary politics, guillotined in 1793 with the Girondins.

Stewart, J. H. *A Documentary Survey of the French Revolution.* 1951.

*Young, Arthur. *Travels in France during the Years 1787, 1788, 1789.* 1972. Invaluable eyewitness testimony by a keen British observer.

*Available in paperback.

Studies

*Bailyn, Bernard. *The Ideological Origins of the American Revolution.* 1967. A classic account of the impact of British libertarian thought on the American colonies.

Bertaud, Jean-Paul. *The Army of the French Revolution.* 1988. A pioneering political and social study of the soldiers and officers of the Republic's armies.

Blanning, T. C. W. *Joseph II and Enlightened Despotism.* 1970. A convenient synthesis on a fundamental subject.

*Chartier, Roger. *The Cultural Origins of the French Revolution.* 1990. On the emergence of a "public sphere" of political discourse in the old regime.

*Christie, Ian. *Great Britain and the American Colonies, 1754–1783.* 1966. A synthesis written from the British viewpoint.

*———. *Wars and Revolutions: Britain, 1760–1815.* 1982. Focuses on British government policy in the age of revolutions.

*Cobb, R. C. *The People's Armies.* 1987. On the paramilitary battalions of sans-culottes, an "instrument of the terror" in 1793–1794.

———. *The Police and the People: French Popular Protest.*

1970. A study of peasants and sans-culottes that should be compared to Soboul's work.

*De Tocqueville, Alexis. *The Old Regime and the French Revolution*. Stuart Gilbert (tr.). 1955. A classic interpretation of the Revolution's genesis first published in the 1850s.

*Doyle, William. *Origins of the French Revolution*. 1980. A reliable synthesis of revisionist historiography; should be compared to Lefebvre's treatment.

*———. *The Oxford History of the French Revolution*. 1989. A readable, detailed narrative.

Egret, Jean. *The French Pre-Revolution, 1787–88*. 1978. A masterly account of the unraveling of the old regime.

Forrest, Alan. *The French Revolution and the Poor*. 1982. A history of good intentions and disappointing results.

*———. *Soldiers of the French Revolution*. 1990. A deft synthesis of recent research.

Furet, François, and Mona Ozouf (eds.). *A Critical Dictionary of the French Revolution*. 1989. A collection of essays, some brilliant and some idiosyncratic, on selected events, actors, institutions, ideas, and historians of the French Revolution.

Gershoy, Leo. *Bertrand Barère, a Reluctant Terrorist*. 1962. Perhaps the best available biography of a revolutionary figure.

Greer, Donald. *The Incidence of the Terror during the French Revolution*. 1935. A statistical study of the geography and social composition of death sentences during the Terror.

*Hampson, Norman. *A Social History of the French Revolution*. 1963. A clear, concise history of the Revolution through 1795.

*Hunt, Lynn. *Politics, Culture, and Class in the French Revolution*. 1984. A pioneering analysis of the imagery and sociology of revolutionary politics.

*Jones, Peter. *The Peasantry in the French Revolution*. 1988. A comprehensive study of the impact of the Revolution on rural society.

*Kennedy, Emmet. *A Cultural History of the French Revolution*. 1989. The Revolution's impact on cultural institutions and artistic activity.

Kennedy, Michael. *The Jacobin Club of Marseilles*. 1973. On the second most important center of Jacobinism.

*Landes, Joan. *Women and the Public Sphere in the Age of the French Revolution*. 1988. A discussion of eighteenth-century thought on women, and of the "gendered republic" of the 1790s.

*Lefebvre, Georges. *The Coming of the French Revolution*. 1967. A classic interpretation dating from 1939 by a major French historian; should be compared to Doyle's treatment.

McManners, John. *The French Revolution and the Church*. 1970. A superb synthesis on a major issue.

*Palmer, Robert R. *The Age of the Democratic Revolution: A Political History of Europe and America, 1760–1800* (2 vols.). 1959–1962. Examines the origins of revolutionary movements in the eighteenth-century comparatively, from America to Poland.

———. *The Improvement of Humanity: Education and the French Revolution*. 1985. A history of good intentions and mixed results.

*———. *Twelve Who Ruled: The Year of the Terror in the French Revolution*. 1941. A modern classic, by far the best book on the subject.

*Popkin, Jeremy. *Revolutionary News: The Press in France 1789–1799*. 1990. An excellent analysis of journalism and the impact of journalists in the revolutionary decade.

*Rudé, George. *The Crowd in the French Revolution*. 1959. Description and analysis of popular participation in the Revolution's crucial turning points.

———. *Robespierre: Portrait of a Revolutionary Democrat*. 1975. An extremely admiring portrait.

———. *Wilkes and Liberty*. 1962. On popular movements for parliamentary reform in England.

Schama, Simon. *Patriots and Liberators: Revolution in the Netherlands 1780–1813*. 1977. An exhaustive but lively account.

Scott, H. M. (ed.). *Enlightened Absolutism: Reforms and Reformers in Later Eighteenth-Century Europe*. 1990. The latest and most comprehensive assessment.

*Soboul, Albert. *The Parisian Sans-Culottes and the French Revolution*. 1964. An abridgment of a landmark French thesis; should be compared to Cobb's treatment.

*Sutherland, Donald. *France 1789–1815: Revolution and Counter-revolution*. 1986. The best general history of the period.

Tackett, Timothy. *Religion, Revolution and Regional Culture in Eighteenth-Century France: The Ecclesiastical Oath of 1791*. 1986. An exhaustive study of the Revolution's first and most fateful crisis.

Venturi, Franco. *The End of the Old Regime in Europe, 1768–1776: The First Crisis*. 1989. Like Palmer's treatment, a comparative European perspective on the period.

*Vovelle, Michel. *The Fall of the French Monarchy, 1787–1792*. 1984. A good synthesis of recent research.

Woloch, Isser. *The New Regime: Transformations of the French Civic Order, 1789–1820s*. 1994. A thematic study of new civic institutions and how they fared, from the beginning of the Revolution to the Restoration of the Bourbons.

General Bonaparte, in an uncompleted portrait by
Jacques-Louis David.

CHAPTER TWENTY-ONE

THE AGE OF NAPOLEON

THE second phase of the French Revolution (1792–1794) remains a study in contradictions. On the one hand, the National Convention moved for the first time since ancient Athens to institute a democratic republic: a government without kings, based on universal male suffrage, where popular rights—for example, the right to subsistence and to education for all—were inscribed in the constitution. On the other hand, the Convention responded to the crisis of foreign military threats, internal rebellion, and intense factionalism by establishing a revolutionary dictatorship. Individual liberties disappeared, and terror against "enemies of the people" became the order of the day. With the crisis finally surmounted by repression and military victories in 1794, most members of the Convention wearied of those harsh policies and wished to terminate the Revolution as quickly as possible. They hoped to end the Terror, yet preserve the Revolution's positive gains.

But it proved extremely difficult to jettison the Terror without unraveling the revolutionary changes that had preceded or accompanied it. By 1794 too much blood had been spilled, too many people nursed deep wounds, frustrated aspirations, and social hatreds. The new regime could not easily be steered toward the safe harbor of republican liberty in such a polarized atmosphere. In the end the Revolution was terminated by a dictatorship, which the men of 1789 (schooled in the history of the Roman Republic) had feared from the start. But since the struggle for and against revolution had long since spilled across France's borders, this development held profound consequences throughout Europe as well. After the French Republic succumbed to the Napoleonic dictatorship, the public life of both France and Europe hinged to an unparalleled degree on the will of a single man. How would Napoleon Bonaparte use that power at home and abroad?

I. From Robespierre to Bonaparte

Relatively secure after the military victories of the year II (1793–1794), the National Convention repudiated the Terror and turned against the leading Jacobin terrorists. Jacobinism, however, was now a permanent part of the French political experience, along with antirevolutionary royalism. The political spectrum of modern European history had been created. The surviving revolutionaries attempted to command a centrist or moderate position within this range of opinions, but they proved inadequate to the task. During the four unsteady years of the Directory regime (1795–1799), however, French armies helped bring revolution to other parts of Western Europe, only to provoke a second anti-French coalition. This new challenge brought the weaknesses of the Republic to a head and opened the way to the seizure of power by an ambitious general.

THE THERMIDORIAN REACTION (1794–1795)

When the military victories of the year II over the coalition and the Vendée rebels eased the need for patriotic unity, long-standing clashes over personalities and policies exploded in the Convention. Robespierre prepared to denounce yet another group of unspecified intriguers, presumably to send them to the guillotine as he had Hébert and Danton. But his enemies made a preemptive strike and denounced Robespierre to the Convention as a tyrant. The Convention no longer needed Robespierre's uncompromising style of leadership. Moderate deputies now repudiated him along with his policies of terror. The Parisian sans-culottes might have intervened to keep Robespierre in power, but the Jacobins had alienated their one-time allies when they curbed the sans-culottes' political autonomy several months earlier. On July 27, 1794 (9 Thermidor year II in the revolutionary calendar), the Convention declared Robespierre an outlaw and he was guillotined the following day, along with several loyal associates.

Anti-Jacobinism　Robespierre's fall broke the Revolution's momentum. As the Convention dismantled the apparatus of the Terror, suspects were released from jail, the revolutionary committees that had spearheaded the Terror were

▶ With its field of guillotines, this Thermidorian caricature ("Robespierre Guillotining the Executioner") portrays Robespierre as a murderous tyrant who had depopulated France.

abolished, and some of their former members were arrested in turn. The Convention closed the Paris Jacobin Club, once the main forum for Robespierre's influence, while the political clubs in the provinces gradually withered away. The Convention also extended an amnesty to the surviving Girondins and arrested a few leading deputies of the Mountain. Those who had taken responsibility for the Terror in the year II now found themselves under attack. The anti-Jacobin thirst for retribution eventually produced a "white terror" against the Jacobins and the sans-culottes that resulted in arrests, assassinations, and, in the south of France, wholesale massacres.

Thermidor also released France from the social austerity of the year II. The Jacobins' insistence on public virtue gave way to the toleration of luxury, fancy dress, and self-indulgence among the wealthy. The titles *monsieur* and *madame* reappeared, replacing the republican designation of *citizen*. In keeping with laissez-faire ideology, the Thermidorians rescinded economic controls.

With the marketplace again ruled by supply and demand, skyrocketing inflation reignited. Worse yet, the harvest of 1795 proved mediocre, and many consumers suffered worse privations than those they had dreaded during the shortages of 1793. In near-famine conditions, mortality rates rose markedly; police reports spoke of little but popular misery.

The Last Revolutionary Uprising Former militants attempted to spark a political reversal and halt the Thermidorian reaction. In the spring of 1795 sans-culottes began to demonstrate in Paris with the slogan "Bread and the Constitution of 1793." The Thermidorians, however, were moving in the opposite direction. They viewed the Jacobin Constitution of 1793 as far too democratic and looked for an excuse to scrap it altogether. In May sans-culottes launched a poorly organized insurrection (the revolt of Prairial year III). In a grim and desperate gamble they invaded the

▶ The Parisian sans-culottes launched a futile rebellion in the spring of 1795 for "Bread and the Constitution of 1793" in response to hyperinflation and severe food shortages.

Convention's hall, where they won the sympathy of only a handful of deputies. Their hours were numbered. In two days of street fighting, government forces overwhelmed the insurgents. Afterward, 36 sans-culottes were executed, and 1200 more were imprisoned for their activism during the Terror. This proved to be the last mobilization of the Parisian revolutionary crowd and the final eclipse of the egalitarian movement.

THE DIRECTORY (1795–1799)

By the end of 1795, the remaining members of the Convention considered the Revolution over. The extremes had been vanquished, and the time for the "peaceable enjoyment of liberty" seemed at hand. The Thermidorians drafted a new constitution—the constitution of the year III (1795)—proclaimed a general amnesty, and hoped to turn a new page. The revolutionary government, which had replaced the fallen constitutional monarchy in 1793, gave way to a constitutional republic, known as the Directory after its five-man executive.

The Directory's proponents declared that the Republic should "be governed by the best citizens, who are found among the property-owning class." The new constitution said little about the popular rights proclaimed by the Constitution of 1793, like the right to subsistence, public assistance, or free education. The constitution also abandoned the universal male suffrage promised in 1793 and restored the propertied franchise of 1791 and the system of indirect elections. The regime's two-house legislature was designed to moderate the political process, while its five-man executive was meant to prevent the rise of a dictator. The Directory also feared a royalist resurgence. Since genuinely free elections at this point might be carried by the antirepublicans of the right, the outgoing Convention decided to coopt two-thirds of its members into the new legislature, thereby ensuring a substantial degree of political continuity. A royalist revolt against this power grab was easily crushed by government troops.

The Directory wished to command the center of the political spectrum, which one historian has aptly called "the mirage of the moderates." To maintain themselves in power, however, the di-

rectorials violated the liberties pledged in their own constitution. They repeatedly purged elected officials, and periodically suppressed political clubs and newspapers on the left and right. In general they refused to acknowledge the legitimacy of organized opposition of any kind. This explains the succession of coups and purges that marked the Directory's four years. Although the repressive measures were mild compared with those of the Terror—deportation usually being the harshest punishment meted out—they ultimately undermined the regime's viability. In the end many moderate republicans walked away from their own creation.

The Political Spectrum For all its repressive qualities, however, the Directory regime was democratic enough to allow most shades of the political spectrum some visibility. The full range of opinions in France, obscured previously by the Terror, was evident during the years of the Directory and would persist with some modifications into the twentieth century. The most important legacy of all, no doubt, was the apathy born of exhaustion or cynicism. Most citizens, especially peasants, had wearied of politics and distrusted all officials whatever government they served. Participation in the Directory regime's annual elections was extremely low.

Within this context of massive apathy, politically conscious minorities showed fierce partisanship. On the right, ultraroyalists (including émigrés, refractory priests, and armed rebels in western France) hoped to overthrow the Republic altogether. Some worked with the exiled Bourbon princes and with British secret agents. More moderate royalists hoped to win control of the Republic's political institutions lawfully, and then bring back the émigrés and refractory priests while stamping out the last vestiges of Jacobinism. (Since Napoleon later effected such changes on his own terms, they would form a major base of his support.)

On the left of the spectrum stood the Neo-Jacobins—democrats in their own eyes, anarchists to their opponents. The Neo-Jacobins adhered to the moderate Republic of 1795 but identified positively with the experience of 1793. They did not advocate a return to the Terror or the use of force to regain power. Instead, the Neo-

Jacobins promoted grass-roots activism through local political clubs, petition drives, newspapers, and electoral campaigns to keep alive the egalitarian ideals of the year II, such as free public education and progressive taxation.

At the far end of the spectrum stood a tiny group of radicals whose significance would loom larger in the next century than it did in 1796. Their leader was François-Noël Babeuf, who had changed his name to Gracchus Babeuf in 1793. The Babeuvists viewed the revolutionary government of the year II as a promising stage that had to be followed by a final revolution in the name of the masses. The Babeuvists advocated a vaguely defined material equality, or communism, for all citizens—a "community of goods," as they called it. They also assigned a key role to a small revolutionary vanguard in carrying out this final revolution. Regarding the present Republic as simply a new form of oppression by the elites, they conspired to overthrow it.

The Elusive Center The Directory's adherents stood somewhere in the center of this broad spectrum, hostile to royalists and Neo-Jacobins alike and ready to shift their ground with any change in the political balance. Thus, although the Neo-Jacobins had spurned Babeuf's calls for insurrection, after Babeuf's plot was exposed the Directory joined forces with the right. But when the first regular elections in the year V (1797) produced a royalist victory, the Directory reversed field. Backed by influential generals, the government purged newly elected royalist deputies, suppressed royalist newspapers, and allowed the Neo-Jacobins to open new clubs.

After a few months, however, the Directory grew fearful of the revived left. During the elections of the year VI (1798), Neo-Jacobins and Directorial moderates vied for influence in what almost amounted to party rivalry. But in the end the Directory would not risk the results of free elections. Again it intervened: closed down clubs and newspapers, manipulated electoral assemblies, and purged those neo-Jacobins who were elected anyway. Interestingly, at almost the same moment that France's government was quashing its political rivals, leaders of the American republic were reluctantly coming to accept opposition parties as legitimate. In France, however, the Directory would not tolerate organized opposition, and that rigidity contributed to the Republic's demise.

▶ "The Directory Falls between Two Stools" is a caricature depicting the political dilemma of the Directory, which vainly sought a centrist position between the left and right.

THE RISE OF BONAPARTE

Meanwhile, the Directory years provided unexpected impetus for revolutionary expansion in Europe, which brought into being a half dozen "sister republics" (see Map 21.1), including the Batavian Republic in the Netherlands and the Helvetic Republic in the Swiss Confederation. Revolutionary change also spread through the entire Italian peninsula, as French commanders

Map 21.1 France and Its Sister Republics, 1798

in the field began to make their own diplomacy. Among them was a young brigadier general named Napoleon Bonaparte.

Bonaparte personifies the world-historic individual—the rare person whose life decisively dominates the course of historical events. Born in 1769 of an impoverished but well-connected family on the French-controlled island of Corsica, Napoleon scarcely seemed destined to play such a historic role. His youthful ambitions and fantasies involved little more than leading Corsica to independence from France. Sent to French military academies, he proved a diligent student, adept at mathematics. Aloof from his aristocratic classmates, whose pretensions he resented, self-reliant and energetic, he became an expert on artillery.

After 1789 the young officer returned to Corsica, but his ambitions ran up against more conservative forces on the island. Eventually, local factional conflict drove him and his family off Corsica altogether. Bonaparte then moved onto a much larger stage. He rose steadily and rapidly through the military ranks, based in part on the luck of opportunities but equally on his ability to act decisively and effectively. While on leave in Paris in 1795, Bonaparte was assigned to the planning bureau of the war ministry. There he advocated a new strategy—the opening of a front in Italy to strike at Austrian forces and push into Germany from the south, while French armies on the Rhine pushed as usual from the west. The strategy was approved, and Bonaparte gained command of the Army of Italy in 1796.

The Making of a Hero   Austria's forces outnumbered the French in Italy, but Bonaparte moved his troops rapidly to achieve surprise and numerical superiority in specific encounters. The end result was a major victory that brought the French into the Habsburg domain of Lombardy and its capital, Milan. Bonaparte's overall plan almost miscarried, since the Army of the Rhine did not advance as planned. But this made his own triumphs all the more important to the Directory. And Bonaparte ensured his popularity with the government by making his campaign self-supporting through organized levies on the Italians.

Bonaparte brought a great sense of excitement and drama to the French occupation of Lombardy. His personal magnetism and his talent in manipulating people attracted many Italians. The general encouraged the Italians to organize their own revolutionary movement; the liberation of northern Italy, he believed, would solidify support for his army and enhance his own reputation. This policy distressed the Directory, since it had intended to trade back conquests in Italy in exchange for security on the Rhine frontier. But in the end the Directory endorsed the Treaty of

Campo Formio, in which Bonaparte personally negotiated a peace settlement with Austria in October 1797. Austria recognized a new, independent state in northern Italy, the Cisalpine Republic, and left the Rhine question to future negotiations. The Directory regime had found the hero it so desperately needed.

The French now focused their patriotic aspirations on defeating the last member of the first coalition: the hated British enemy. Bonaparte naturally yearned for the glory of accomplishing this feat, and he was authorized to prepare an invasion force. Previous seaborne landings directed at Ireland had failed, however, and Bonaparte too finally had to abandon the scheme because of France's insufficient naval force.

Instead, in the spring of 1798 Bonaparte launched an expedition to Egypt intended to strike at Britain's colonial interests, including the approaches to India. But British naval superiority, in the form of Admiral Horatio Nelson's fleet, turned the expedition into a debacle. The British destroyed the French fleet at the Battle of the Nile, thereby marooning a French army in North Africa. Worse yet, the French were beaten back in several engagements with Turkish forces. Only cynical news management prevented the full story of this defeat from reaching France; instead, the expedition's exotic details and scientific explorations held the attention of the French public. Bonaparte extricated himself from this mess by slipping off through the British blockade, in effect abandoning his army as he returned to France.

THE BRUMAIRE COUP

While Bonaparte floundered in Egypt, the Directory was faltering under political pressures at home. Charges of tyranny and ineptitude accumulated against the directors. Further French expansion into Italy, which produced new sister republics centered in Rome and Naples, precipitated a new coalition against France, consisting of Britain, Russia, and Austria. In June 1799 ill-supplied French forces were driven out of most of Italy and Switzerland.

Widespread discontent with the Directory led to the defeat of many government-sponsored candidates in the spring elections of 1799. The legislature then ousted four of the five directors and named Sieyès, a respected leader of the patriots in 1789, among the replacements. Sieyès and his supporters secretly wished to alter the constitution itself, for they had lost confidence in the regime's institutions, especially its annual elections. These "revisionists" wanted to redesign the Republic along more oligarchic lines, as against the Neo-Jacobins who wished to democratize the Republic. The centrist position had virtually disappeared. The revisionists blocked emergency measures proposed by the Neo-Jacobins in reaction to the new war crisis, and breathed a sigh of relief as French armies rallied and repulsed Anglo-Russian forces in the Batavian Republic and Switzerland. Most of Italy was lost for the time being, but the threat to France itself had passed. Sieyès and the revisionists moved against the Neo-Jacobins by closing their clubs and newspapers, and prepared for a coup.

A General Comes to Power Although no dire military threat remained to propel the country into the arms of a general, the revisionists wished to establish a more centralized, oligarchic republic, and they needed a general's support. Generals were the only national heroes in France, and only a general could organize the force necessary to ensure the coup's success. Bonaparte's return to France from Egypt thus seemed most timely. Bonaparte was not the revisionists' first choice, but he proved to be the best available one. On his trip up from the Mediterranean, people had cheered him warmly, since they knew little of the Egyptian fiasco and saw him in his role as victor of the Italian campaign.

Contrary to the intentions of Sieyès and his fellow conspirators, Bonaparte proved to be the tail that wagged the dog. Once the coup began, he proved to be far more ambitious and energetic than the other conspirators and thrust himself into the most prominent position. Bonaparte addressed the legislature to denounce a mythical Jacobin plot and to demand emergency powers for a new provisional government. Along with two former directors, he was empowered to draft a new constitution; a cooperative rump of the legislature subsequently approved the new arrangements. Thus unfolded the coup of 18 Brumaire year VIII (November 9, 1799).

The Brumaire coup had not been intended to install a dictatorship, but that was its eventual result. In the maneuvering among the revisionists, Bonaparte's ideas and personality prevailed. The plotters agreed to eliminate meaningful elections, which they saw as promoting political instability. They agreed also to enshrine the social ideals of 1789, such as civil equality, and to bury those of the year II, such as popular democracy. The vague notion of popular sovereignty gave way to concentrated authority. The general came out of the coup as the regime's strongman, and Sieyès' elaborate plans for a republican oligarchy ended in the wastebasket. On one other point, the plotters were particularly deceived. With General Bonaparte's assistance they hoped to achieve durable peace through military victory. Instead, the Napoleonic regime promoted unbounded expansion and endless warfare.

II. The Napoleonic Settlement in France

Bonaparte's prime asset in his rapid takeover of France was the resignation of its citizens. Most French people were so weary politically that they saw in Bonaparte what they wished to see.[1] The Committee of Public Safety had won grudging submission through its terroristic policies; Bonaparte achieved that result almost by default. As an effective propagandist for himself and a man of great personal appeal, he soothed a divided France. Ultraroyalists and dedicated Jacobins never warmed to his regime, but most citizens fell between those positions and could find comfort in the prospect of a return to order and stability.

THE NAPOLEONIC STYLE

Napoleon Bonaparte was not a royalist or a Jacobin, not a conservative or a liberal, though his attitudes were flavored by a touch of each view-

---

[1] It is customary to refer to "Bonaparte" until 1804, when the general crowned himself Emperor Napoleon I.

point. Authority, not ideology, was his great concern, and he justified his actions by their results. The revolutionaries of 1789 could consider Napoleon one of theirs because of his hostility toward the unjust and ineffective institutions of the old regime. He had little use for seigneurialism, the cumbersome institutions of Bourbon absolutism, or the congealed structures of aristocratic privilege, which the Revolution had destroyed. Napoleon valued the Revolution's commitment to equality of opportunity and continued to espouse that liberal premise. Other rights and liberties of 1789 he curtailed or disdained.

Ten years of upheaval had produced a grim paradox: The French Revolution had proceeded in the name of liberty, yet successive forms of repression had been mounted to defend it. Napoleon fit comfortably into this history; unlike the Directory, he made no pretense about it. The social gains of the Revolution would be preserved through political centralization and authoritarian control. Napoleon's field of action was in fact far greater than that of the most powerful eighteenth-century monarch, for no entrenched aristocracy existed to resist him. Thanks to the clearing operations of the Revolution, he could reconstruct at will.

Tragically, however, Napoleon drifted away from his own rational ideals. Increasingly absorbed in his personal power, he began to force domestic and foreign policies on France that were geared to his imperial ambitions. Increasingly he concentrated his government on raising men and money for his armies, and turned his back on revolutionary liberties.

POLITICAL AND RELIGIOUS SETTLEMENTS

Bonaparte gave France a constitution, approved in a plebiscite, that placed almost unchecked authority in the hands of a First Consul (himself) for 10 years. Two later constitutional revisions, also approved overwhelmingly in plebiscites, increased executive power and diminished the legislative branch until it became simply a rubber stamp. The first revision, in 1802, converted the consulship into a lifetime post; the second, in 1804, proclaimed Napoleon hereditary emperor. The task of proposing new laws passed from elected representatives to appointed experts in the Council of State. This new body advised the ruler, drafted legislation under his direction, and monitored public officials. Such government by experts stood as an alternative to meaningful parliamentary democracy for the next century.

The system of local government established by Bonaparte in 1800 came ironically close to the kind of royal centralization that public opinion had roundly condemned in 1789. Bonaparte eliminated the local elections that the Revolution had emphasized. Instead, each department was now administered by a *prefect* appointed by the ruler. The 400-odd subprefects on the district level as well as the 40,000 mayors of France's communes were likewise appointed. With minor changes the

▶ **Napoleon Bonaparte as First Consul, at the height of his popularity, painted by his admirer J.-B. Gros.**

unquestionably efficient prefectorial system survived in France for 150 years, severely limiting local autonomy and self-government.

Police-state methods finished what constitutional change began: the suppression of independent political activity. From the legislature to the grass roots, France was depoliticized. The government permitted no organized opposition, reduced the number of newspapers drastically, and censored the remaining ones. The free journalism born in 1789 gave way to government press releases and news management. In 1811 only four newspapers remained in Paris, all hewing to the official line. Political clubs were prohibited, outspoken dissidents deported, and others placed under police surveillance. All this silenced liberal intellectuals as well as former political activists.

The Concordat Napoleon's religious policies promoted tranquillity at home and a good image abroad. Before Brumaire the Republic tolerated Catholic worship in theory but severely restricted it in practice. Continued proscription of the refractory clergy; insistence on the republican calendar, with its 10-day weeks that made Sunday a workday; and a drive to keep religious instruction out of elementary schools curtailed the free and familiar exercise of Catholicism. These policies provoked wide resentment among the mass of citizens whose commitment to Catholicism remained intact throughout the Revolution.

Though not a believer himself, Napoleon judged that major concessions to Catholic sentiment were in order, provided that the Church remained under the control of the state. In 1801 he negotiated a Concordat, or agreement, with Pope Pius VII. It stipulated that Catholicism was the "preferred" religion of France but protected religious freedom for non-Catholics. The Church was again free to operate in full public view and to restore the refractory priests. Primary education would espouse Catholic values and use Catholic texts, as it had before the Revolution, and clerical salaries would be paid by the state. Though nominated by the ruler, bishops would again be consecrated by the pope. But as a major concession to the Revolution, the Concordat stipulated that land confiscated from the Church and sold during the Revolution would be retained by its purchasers. On the other hand, the government dropped the 10-day week and restored the Gregorian calendar.

The balance of church-state relations tilted firmly in the state's favor, for Napoleon intended to use the clergy as a major prop of his regime. The pulpit and the primary school became instruments of social control, to be used, as a new catechism stated, "to bind the religious conscience of the people to the august person of the Emperor." As Napoleon put it, the clergy would be his "moral prefects." Devout Catholics came to resent this subordination of the Church. Eventually Pope Pius renounced the Concordat, to which Napoleon responded by removing the pontiff to France and placing him under house arrest.

THE ERA OF THE NOTABLES

With civil equality established and feudalism abolished, Napoleon believed that the Revolution was complete. It remained to encourage an orderly hierarchical society to counteract what he regarded as the excessive individualism of revolutionary social policy. Napoleon intended to reassert the authority of the state, the elites, and, in family life, the father.

In the absence of electoral politics, Napoleon used the state's appointive powers to confer status on prominent local individuals, or *notables*, thus associating them with his regime. These local dignitaries were usually chosen from among the largest taxpayers: prosperous landowners, former nobles, businessmen, and professionals. Those who served the regime with distinction were honored by induction into the Legion of Honor, nine-tenths of whose members were military men. "It is with trinkets that mankind is governed," Napoleon once said. Legion of Honor awards and appointments to prestigious but powerless local bodies were precisely such trinkets, and they endured long after their creator was gone.

Napoleon offered more tangible rewards to the country's leading bankers when he chartered a national bank that enjoyed the credit power derived from official ties to the state. In education, Napoleon created elite secondary schools, or *lycées*, to train future government officials, engineers, and officers. The *lycées* embodied the concept of careers open to talent and became part of a highly centralized French academic system called the *University*, which survived into the twentieth century.

The Civil Code   Napoleon's most important legacy was a Civil Code regulating social relations and property rights. Baptized the Napoleonic Code in 1807, it was in some measure a revolutionary law code that progressives throughout Europe embraced. Wherever it was implemented, the Civil Code swept away feudal property relations and gave legal sanction to modern contractual notions of property. The code established the right to choose one's occupation, to receive equal treatment under the law, and to enjoy religious freedom. At the same time, it allowed employers to dominate their workers by prohibiting strikes and trade unions. Nor did the code match property rights with popular rights like the right to subsistence.

Revolutionary legislation had emancipated women and children by establishing their civil rights. Napoleon undid most of this by restoring the father's absolute authority in the family. "A wife owes obedience to her husband," said the code, which proceeded to deprive wives of property and juridical rights established during the 1790s and to curtail the right to divorce, while establishing a kind of double standard in the dissolution of a marriage (*see box*, below). The code also expanded the husband's options in disposing of his estate, although each child was still guaranteed a portion.

The prefectorial system of local government, the Civil Code, the Concordat, the University, the Legion of Honor, and the local bodies of *notables* all proved to be durable institutions. They fulfilled Napoleon's desire to create a series of "granite masses" on which to reconstruct French society. His admirers emphasized that these institutions contributed to social stability amid France's chronic political unrest. One can argue

Family and Gender Roles
under the Napoleonic Civil Code

"Art. 148. The son who has not attained the full age of 25 years, the daughter who has not attained the full age of 21 years, cannot contract marriage without the consent of their father and mother; in case of disagreement, the consent of the father is sufficient.

"Art. 212. Married persons owe to each other fidelity, succor, assistance.

"Art. 213. The husband owes protection to his wife, the wife obedience to her husband.

"Art. 214. The wife is obliged to live with her husband, and to follow him to every place where he may judge it convenient to reside: the husband is obliged to receive her, and to furnish her with everything necessary for the wants of life, according to his means and station.

"Art. 215. The wife cannot plead [in court] in her own name, without the authority of her husband, even though she should be a public trader . . . or separate in property.

"Art. 217. A wife . . . cannot give, alienate, pledge, or acquire by free or chargeable title, without the concurrence of her husband in the act, or his consent in writing.

"Art. 219. If the husband refuses to authorize his wife to pass an act, the wife may cause her husband to be cited directly before the court of first instance . . . which may give or refuse its authority, after the husband shall have been heard, or duly summoned.

"Art. 229. The husband may demand a divorce on the ground of his wife's adultery.

"Art. 230. The wife may demand divorce on the ground of adultery in her husband, when he shall have brought his concubine into their common residence.

"Art. 231. The married parties may reciprocally demand divorce for outrageous conduct, ill-usage, or grievous injuries, exercised by one of them towards the other."

that they were skillful compromises between revolutionary liberalism and an older belief in hierarchy and central authority. Detractors point out that they were class-oriented and excessively patriarchal. Moreover they fostered overcentralized, rigid structures that might have sapped the vitality of French institutions in succeeding generations. Whatever their merits or defects, these institutions took root, unlike Napoleon's attempt to dominate all of Europe.

III. *Napoleonic Hegemony in Europe*

After giving France a new government, Bonaparte's first task was to defeat the second anti-French coalition on the battlefield, especially in northern Italy. The outcome of this campaign against Austria would reinforce or destroy the settlement he had imposed on France after Brumaire. Napoleon's dictatorial tendencies became obvious enough within France, but it was in the arena of international relations that his ambitions lost all semblance of restraint. There he evolved from a general of the Revolution to an imperial conqueror. Napoleon's conquest of Italy, Germany, Spain, and other lands set contradictory responses of collaboration and resistance in motion. French expansion sparked nationalism abroad, but also liberalism and reaction.

MILITARY SUPREMACY AND THE REORGANIZATION OF EUROPE

Bonaparte's strategy in 1800 called for a repeat of the 1797 campaign: He would strike through Italy while the Army of the Rhine pushed eastward against Vienna. Following French victories at Marengo in Lombardy and Hohenlinden in Germany, Austria sued for peace. The Treaty of Lunéville (February 1801) essentially restored France to the position it had held after Bonaparte's triumphs in Italy in 1797.

▶ **Deputies from the Cisalpine Republic of Italy proclaim Napoleon Bonaparte their president in 1802.**

▶ **Admiral Nelson's heavily armed three-decker ship of the line, which inflicted such devastation on the French fleet at Trafalgar.**

In Britain a war-weary government now stood alone against France and decided to negotiate. The Treaty of Amiens (March 1801) ended hostilities and reshuffled territorial holdings outside Europe, such as the Cape Colony in South Africa, which passed from the Dutch to the British. But this truce proved precarious since it did not settle the future of French influence in Europe or of commercial relations between the two great powers. Napoleon abided by the letter of the treaty but soon violated its spirit. Britain and Austria alike were dismayed by further expansion of French influence in Italy, Switzerland, and North America. Most important, perhaps, France seemed determined to exclude British trade rather than restore normal commercial relations. Historians agree that the Treaty of Amiens failed to keep the peace because neither side was ready to abandon its century-long struggle for predominance.

The Third Coalition A third anti-French coalition soon took shape, a replay of its predecessors. France ostensibly fought to preserve the new regime at home and its sister republics abroad. The coalition's objectives included the restoration of the Netherlands and Italy to "independence," the limitation of French influence elsewhere, and, if possible, a reduction of France to its prerevolutionary borders. Like most such alliances, the co-

alition would be dismembered piecemeal.

French hopes of settling the issue directly by invading Britain proved impossible once again. At the Battle of Trafalgar (October 1805), Admiral Nelson's fleet crushed an outnumbered and outmanned French navy. Nelson was an innovative tactician who broke rule-book procedures on the high seas just as French generals did on land, and he ensured the security of the British Isles for the remainder of the Napoleonic era.

Napoleon then turned against the Austro-Russian forces. Moving 200,000 French soldiers with unprecedented speed across the continent, he took his enemies by surprise and won a dazzling succession of victories. After occupying Vienna he proceeded against the coalition's main army in December. Feigning weakness and retreat at the moment of battle, he drew his numerically superior opponents into an exposed position, crushed the center of their lines, and inflicted a decisive defeat. This Battle of Austerlitz was Napoleon's most brilliant tactical achievement, and it forced the Habsburgs to the peace table. The resulting Treaty of Pressburg (December 1805), extremely harsh and humiliating for

Austria, imposed a large indemnity and required the Habsburgs to cede their Venetian provinces.

France and Germany By now the French sphere of influence had increased dramatically to include most of southern Germany, which Napoleon reorganized into the Confederation of the Rhine, a client realm of France (see Map 21.2). France had kept Prussia neutral during the war with Austria by skillful diplomacy. Only after Austria made peace did Prussia recognize its error in failing to join with Austria to halt Napoleon. Belatedly, Prussia mobilized its famous but antiquated army; it was rewarded with stinging defeats by France in a number of encounters culminating in the Battle of Jena (October 1806). With the collapse of Prussian military power, the conquerors settled in Berlin and watched the prestige of the Prussian ruling class crumble. Napoleon was now master of northern Germany as well as the south. For a while it appeared that he might obliterate Prussia entirely, but he restored its sovereignty—after amputating part of its territory and imposing a crushing indemnity.

Napoleon was free to reorganize Central Europe as he pleased. After formally proclaiming the end of the Holy Roman Empire in 1806, he liquidated numerous small German states and merged them into two new ones: the Kingdom of Westphalia, with brother Jérôme on the throne, and the Grand Duchy of Berg, to be ruled by his brother-in-law Joachim Murat. His ally Saxony became a full-scale kingdom, while a new duchy of Warsaw was carved out of Prussian Poland. This "restoration" of Poland had propaganda value; it made the emperor appear as a champion of Polish aspirations, compared to the rulers of Prussia, Russia, and Austria, who had dismembered Poland in a series of partitions between 1772 and 1795. Moreover, Napoleon could now enlist a Polish army and use Polish territory as a base of operations against his remaining continental foe, Russia.

France and Russia In February 1807 Napoleon confronted the colossus of the East in the Battle of Eylau; the resulting carnage was horrifying but

▶ **Napoleon amidst the carnage on the battlefield of Eylau, the bloodiest engagement to date of the revolutionary-Napoleonic era, where the French and Russians fought each other to a stalemate in 1807.**

inconclusive. When spring came, only a dramatic victory could preserve his conquests in Central Europe and vindicate the extraordinary commitments of the past two years. Fortunately for the emperor, the Battle of Friedland in June was a French victory that demoralized Russia's Tsar Alexander I and persuaded him to negotiate.

Meeting at Tilsit, the two rulers buried their differences and agreed in effect to partition Europe into Eastern and Western spheres of influence. Each would support the other's conquests and mediate in behalf of the other's interests. The Treaty of Tilsit (July 1807) sanctioned new an-

nexations of territory directly into France and the reorganization of other conquered countries. The creation of new satellite kingdoms became the vehicle for Napoleon's domination of Europe. Like the French Republic, the sister republics became kingdoms between 1805 and 1807. And it happened that Napoleon had a large family of brothers ready to wear those new royal crowns.

The distorted shape of Napoleonic Europe is apparent on maps dating from 1808 to 1810 (see Map 21.2). His chief satellites included the King-

Map 21.2 **EUROPE AROUND 1810**

dom of Holland, with brother Louis on the throne; the Kingdom of Italy, with Napoleon himself as king and his stepson Eugène de Beauharnais as viceroy; the Confederation of the Rhine, including brother Jérôme's Kingdom of Westphalia; the Kingdom of Naples, covering southern Italy, with brother Joseph the ruler until Napoleon transferred him to Spain and installed his brother-in-law Murat; and the Duchy of War-

▶ Emperor Napoleon I on his imperial throne in 1806, by the great portrait painter Ingres. Note the dramatic contrast in appearance with the young, intense military hero of the Republic in David's portrait, which opens the chapter.

saw. Belgium, the Rhineland, Tuscany, Piedmont, Genoa, and the Illyrian provinces had been annexed to France. Switzerland did not become a kingdom, but the Helvetic Republic (as it was now called) received a new constitution dictated by France. In 1810, after yet another war with Austria, a marriage was arranged between the house of Bonaparte and the house of Habsburg. Having divorced Joséphine de Beauharnais, Napoleon married princess Marie Louise, daughter of Francis II, who bore him a male heir the following year.

NAVAL WAR WITH BRITAIN

For a time it seemed that Britain alone stood between Napoleon and his dream of hegemony over Europe. Since Britain was invulnerable to invasion, Napoleon hoped to destroy its influence by means of economic warfare. Unable to blockade British ports directly, he could try to close off the continent: keep Britain from its markets, stop its exports, and thus ruin its trade and credit. Napoleon reasoned that if Britain had nowhere to sell its manufactured goods, no gold would come into the country and bankruptcy would eventually ensue. Meanwhile overproduction would cause unemployment and labor unrest, which would turn the British people against their government and force the latter to make peace with France. At the same time, French advantages in continental markets would increase with the elimination of British competition.

The Continental System Napoleon therefore launched his "Continental System" to prohibit British trade with all French allies. Even neutral ships were banned from European ports if they carried goods coming from the British Isles. Britain responded in 1807 with the Orders in Council, which in effect reversed the blockade: It *required* all neutral ships to stop at British ports to procure trading licenses and pay tariffs. In other words, the British insisted on regulating all trade between neutral states and European ports. Ships that failed to obey would be stopped on the high seas and captured. In an angry response, Napoleon, in turn, threatened to seize any neutral ship that obeyed the Orders in Council by stopping at British ports.

Thus a total naval war between France and Britain enveloped all neutral nations. Indeed, neutral immunity virtually disappeared, since every ship was obliged to violate one system or the other and thus run afoul of naval patrols or privateers. While the British captured only about 40 French ships a year after 1807 (for few were left afloat), they seized almost 3000 neutral vessels a year, including many from the United States.

The Continental System did hurt British trade. British gold reserves dwindled, and 1811 saw widespread unemployment and rioting. France was affected, in turn, by Britain's counterblockade, which cut it off from certain raw materials necessary for industrial production. But the satellite states, as economic vassals of France, suffered the most. In Amsterdam, for example, shipping volume declined from 1350 ships entering the port in 1806 to 310 in 1809, and commercial revenues dropped calamitously. Out of loyalty to the people whom he ruled, Holland's King Louis Bonaparte tolerated smuggling. But this so infuriated Napoleon that he ousted his brother from the throne and annexed the Kingdom of Holland directly to France. Smuggling was in fact the weak link in the system, for it created holes in Napoleon's wall of economic sanctions that constantly needed plugging. This problem drove the emperor to ever more drastic actions.

THE NAPOLEONIC CONSCRIPTION MACHINE

One key to Napoleon's unrestrained ambitions in Europe was the creation of an efficient administrative state in France and its annexed territories. State penetration of the countryside under Napoleon achieved its most dramatic impact by creating a veritable conscription machine, which continuously replenished the ranks of the imperial army.

The National Convention's mass levy of August 1793 had drafted all able-bodied unmarried men between the ages of 18 and 25. But this unprecedented mobilization had been meant as a one-time-only emergency measure, a temporary "requisition." There was no implication that subsequent cohorts of young men would face conscription into the army as part of their civic obligations. When the war resumed in 1798, however, the Directory passed a conscription law that made successive "classes" of young men (that is, those born in a particular year) subject to a military draft should the need arise. The Directory immediately implemented this law and called up three classes, but local officials reported massive draft evasion in most of the departments. Many French youths found the prospect of military service repugnant. From this shaky foundation, however, the Napoleonic regime developed a successful conscription system.

After much trial and error with the details, timetables, and mechanisms, the system began to operate efficiently within a few years. The government assigned an annual quota of conscripts for each department. Using parish birth registers, the mayor of every community compiled a list of men reaching the age of 19 that year. These youths were then led by their mayor to the cantonal seat on a specified day for a draft lottery. Panels of doctors at the departmental capitals later verified or rejected claims for medical exemptions. In all, about a third of French youths legally avoided military service because they were physically unfit—too short, lame, deformed, or suffering from poor eyesight, chronic diseases, or other infirmities.

In the draft lottery, youths picked numbers out of a box; marriage could no longer be used as an exemption, for obvious reasons. Those with high numbers were spared (for the time being), while those who drew low numbers filled the local induction quota. Two means of avoiding service remained: The wealthy could purchase a replacement, and the poor could flee. True, the regime had a bad conscience about allowing draftees to hire replacements, because the practice made its rhetoric about the duties of citizenship sound hollow. But to placate wealthy notables and peasants with large holdings (who were sometimes desperate to keep their sons on the farm), the government permitted the hiring of a replacement under strict guidelines that made it difficult and expensive but not impossible. The proportion of replacements was somewhere between 5 and 10 percent of all draftees.

Draft Evasion For Napoleon's prefects, conscription levies were always the top priority

▶ **The departure of a group of conscripts from the "class" of 1807 in Paris.**

among their duties, and draft evasion was the number one problem. Dogged persistence, bureaucratic routine, and various forms of coercion gradually overcame this chronic resistance. From time to time, columns of troops swept through areas where evasion and desertion were most common and arrested culprits by the hundreds. But draft evaders usually hid out in remote places—mountains, forests, marshes—so coercion had to be directed against their families as well. Heavy fines assessed against the parents did little good since most were too poor to pay anything. A better tactic was to billet troops in the draft evaders' homes; if their families could not afford to feed the troops, then the community's wealthy taxpayers were required to do so. All this created pressure on the youths to turn themselves in. By 1811 the regime had broken the habit of draft evasion, and conscription was generally becoming accepted as a disagreeable civic obligation, much like taxes. In fact, just as draft calls were beginning to rise sharply, draft evasion fell dramatically. In 1812 prefects all over France reported that the year's levies were more successful than ever before.

Napoleon had begun by drafting 60,000 Frenchmen annually, but by 1810 the annual quotas had risen steadily to 120,000, and they continued to climb. Moreover, in 1810 the emperor ordered the first of many "supplementary levies," calling up men from earlier classes who had drawn high lottery numbers. In January 1813, to look ahead, Napoleon replenished his armies by calling up the class of 1814 a year early and by making repeated supplementary calls on earlier classes.

IV. Opposition to Napoleon

In 1808, with every major European power except Britain vanquished on the battlefield, Napoleon felt that nothing stood in his way. Since Spain and Russia seemed unable or unwilling to stop smuggling from Britain, the emperor decided to deal with each by force of arms, assuming that his design against Britain could then be pursued to its conclusion. On all counts he was mistaken.

Napoleon's confrontations with Spain and Russia proved that his reach had exceeded his grasp.

THE "SPANISH ULCER"

Spain and France shared a common interest in weakening British power in Europe and the colonial world. But the alliance they formed after making peace with each other in 1795 brought only troubles for Spain, including the loss of its Louisiana Territory in America and (at the Battle of Trafalgar) most of its naval fleet. The Spanish royal household, meanwhile, was mired in scandal. Prime Minister Manuel de Godoy, once a lover of the queen, was a corrupt opportunist and extremely unpopular with the people. Crown Prince Ferdinand despised Godoy and Godoy's protectors, the king and queen, while Ferdinand's parents actively returned their son's hostility.

Napoleon looked on at this farce with irritation. At the zenith of his power, he concluded that he must reorganize Spain himself to bring it solidly into the Continental System. As a pretext for military intervention, he set in motion a plan to invade Portugal, supposedly to partition it with Spain. Once the French army was well inside Spain, however, Napoleon intended to impose his own political solution to Spain's instability.

Napoleon brought the squabbling king and prince to France, where he threatened and bribed one and then the other into abdicating. The emperor then gathered a group of handpicked Spanish notables who followed Napoleon's scenario by petitioning him to provide a new sovereign, preferably his brother Joseph. Joseph was duly proclaimed king of Spain. With 100,000 French troops already positioned around Madrid, he prepared to assume his new throne, eager to rule under a liberal constitution and to believe his brother's statement that "all the better Spanish people are on your side." As he took up the crown, however, an unanticipated drama erupted.

▶ **Tricked and cajoled out of the Spanish throne by Napoleon, Ferdinand VII sits unhappily as a virtual prisoner in Bayonne, across the French border.**

Popular Resistance Faced with military occupation, the disappearance of their royal family, and the crowning of a Frenchman, the Spanish people rose in rebellion. It began on May 2, 1808, when an angry crowd in Madrid rioted against French troops, who responded with firing squads and brutal reprisals. This bloody incident, known as the Dos de Mayo and captured in Goya's famous paintings, has remained a source of Spanish national pride, for it touched off a sustained uprising against the French. Local notables created committees, or *juntas*, to organize resistance, mainly by peasants and monks, and to coordinate campaigns by regular Spanish troops. These troops were generally ineffective against the French, but they did produce one early victory: A half-starved French army was cut off and forced to surrender at Bailén in July 1808. This defeat broke the aura of Napoleonic invincibility.

The British saw a great opportunity to attack Napoleon in concert with the rebellious Spanish people. Landing an army in Portugal, the British actually bore the brunt of anti-French military operations in Spain, in what they called the Peninsular War. In a grueling war of attrition, their forces drove the French out of Portugal, and after five years of fighting and many reversals they pushed the French back across the Pyrénées in November 1813. The British commander, the Duke of Wellington, had grasped the French predicament when he said: "The more ground the French hold down in Spain, the weaker they will be at any given point."

▶ **The great Spanish artist Francisco Goya memorably captured the brutality of French reprisals against the citizens of Madrid who dared to rebel against the Napoleonic occupation on May 2, 1808.**

About 30,000 Spanish guerilla fighters helped wear down the French and forced the occupiers to struggle for survival in hostile country. The guerillas drew French forces from the main battlefields, inflicted casualties, denied the French access to food, and punished Spanish collaborators. In short, the Spanish fighters established the model for modern guerilla warfare. Their harassment kept the invaders in a constant state of anxiety, which led the French to adopt harsh measures in reprisal. But these "pacification" tactics

▶ In a relentlessly bleak series of drawings collectively entitled "The Horrors of War," Goya went on to record the savagery and atrocities committed by both sides of the struggle in Spain.

only escalated the war's brutality and further enraged the Spanish people.

Together, the juntas, the Spanish regulars, the guerillas, and the British expeditionary force kept a massive French army of up to 300,000 men pinned down in Spain. Napoleon referred to the

Spanish Liberals Draft a Constitution, 1812

"The general and extraordinary Cortes of the Spanish nation, duly organized . . . in order duly to discharge the lofty objective of furthering the glory, prosperity and welfare of the Nation as a whole, decrees the following political Constitution to assure the well-being and upright administration of the State.

"Art. 1: The Spanish Nation is the union of all Spaniards from both hemispheres.

"Art. 3: Sovereignty resides primarily in the Nation and because of this the right to establish the fundamental laws belongs to it exclusively.

"Art. 4: The Nation is obligated to preserve and protect with wise and just laws civil liberty, property and the other legitimate rights of all the individuals belonging to it.

"Art. 12: The religion of the Spanish Nation is and always will be the Catholic, Apostolic, Roman and only true faith. The Nation protects it with wise and just laws and prohibits the exercise of any other.

"Art. 14: The Government of the Spanish Nation is an hereditary limited Monarchy.

"Art. 15: The power to make laws resides in the Cortes with the King.

"Art. 16: The power to enforce laws resides in the King.

"Art. 27: The Cortes is the union of all the deputies that represent the Nation, named by the citizens.

"Art. 34: To elect deputies to the Cortes, electoral meetings will be held in the parish, the district, and the province.

"Art. 59: The electoral meetings on the district level will be made up of the electors chosen at the parish level who will convene at the seat of every district in order to name the electors who will then converge on the provincial capital to elect the deputies to the Cortes.

"Art. 338: The Cortes will annually establish or confirm all taxes, be they direct or indirect, general, provincial or municipal. . . .

"Art. 339: Taxes will be apportioned among all Spaniards in proportion to their abilities [to pay], without exception to any privilege."

From the Political Constitution of the Spanish Monarchy proclaimed in Cádiz March 19, 1812 (translated by James Tueller).

---

war as his "Spanish ulcer," an open sore that would not heal. Though he held the rebel fighters in contempt, other Europeans were inspired by their example of armed resistance to France.

The Spanish Liberals The war, however, proved a disaster for Spanish liberals. Torn between loyalty to Joseph, who would have liked to be a liberal ruler, and nationalist rebels, liberals faced a difficult dilemma. Those who collaborated with Joseph hoped to spare the people from a brutal war and to institute reform from above in the tradition of Spanish enlightened absolutism. But they found that Joseph could not rule independently; Napoleon gave the orders in Spain and relied on his generals to implement them. The liberals who joined the rebellion organized a provisional government by reviving the ancient Spanish parliament, or *Cortes,* in the southern town of Cádiz. Like the French National Assembly of 1789, the Cortes of Cádiz drafted a liberal constitution in 1812 (*see box,* above), which pleased the British and was therefore tolerated for the time being by the juntas.

In reality, most nationalist rebels despised the liberals. Most rebels were royalists who were fighting for the Catholic Church, the Spanish monarchy, and the old way of life. When in 1814 Wellington finally drove the French out of Spain and former crown prince Ferdinand VII took the throne, the joy of the Cádiz liberals quickly evaporated. As a royalist mob sacked the Cortes building, Ferdinand tore up the constitution of 1812, reinstated absolutism, restored the monasteries and the Inquisition, revived censorship, and arrested the leading liberals. Nationalist reactionaries emerged as the victors of the Spanish rebellion and the Peninsular War.

Independence in Spanish America The Creoles, descendants of Spanish settlers who were born in the New World, also profited from the upheaval in Spain. Spain had been cut off from its vast empire of American colonies in 1805, when the British navy won control of the Atlantic after the Battle of Trafalgar. In 1807 a British force attacked Buenos Aires in Spain's vice-royalty of the Río de la Plata (now Argentina). The Argentines—who raised excellent cattle on the *pampas*, or grassy plains—were eager to trade their beef and hides for British goods, but Spain's rigid mercantilism had always prevented such beneficial commerce. The Argentines welcomed the prospect of free trade, but not the prospect of British conquest. With Spain unable to defend them, the Creoles organized their own militia and drove off the invaders. Gaining confidence from this victory, they pushed aside the Spanish viceroy and his bureaucrats and took power into their own hands, though they still swore allegiance to the Spanish crown. The subsequent upheaval in Spain, however, led the Argentines to declare their independence. After Ferdinand regained the Spanish throne in 1814, he sent an army to reclaim the colony but the Argentines, under General José de San Martín, drove it off, and Argentina made good on its claim to full independence.

Rebellion spread throughout Spanish America, led above all by Simón Bolívar, revered in the hemisphere as "The Liberator." After Napoleon removed the king of Spain in 1808, the Creoles in Spain's vice-royalty of New Granada (encompassing modern-day Venezuela, Colombia, and Ecuador) elected a congress, which declared independence from Spain. An arduous, protracted war with the Spanish garrisons followed, and by 1816 Spain had regained control of the region. But Bolívar resumed the struggle and gradually wore down the Spanish forces; in one campaign his army marched 600 miles from the torrid Venezuelan lowlands over the snow-capped Andes Mountains to Colombia. Finally in 1819 the Spanish conceded defeat. Bolívar's dream of one unified, conservative republic of Gran Colombia soon disintegrated, under regional pressures, into several independent states, but not before Bolívar launched one final military campaign and liberated Peru, Spain's remaining colony in South America (see Maps 21.3a and b on pages 694 and 695).

THE RUSSIAN DEBACLE

Napoleon did not yet realize in 1811 that his entanglement in Spain would drain French military power and encourage resistance in Central Europe. On the contrary, never were the emperor's schemes more grandiose. Surveying the crumbling state system of Europe, he imagined that it could be replaced with a vast empire, ruled from Paris and based on the Napoleonic Code. He mistakenly believed that the era of the balance of power among Europe's nations was over and that nationalist sentiments need not constrain his actions.

Russia now loomed as the main obstacle to Napoleon's imperial reorganization and domination of Europe. Russia, a restive ally with ambitions of its own in Eastern Europe, resented the restrictions on its trade under the Continental System. British diplomats, anti-Napoleonic exiles such as Baron Stein of Prussia, and nationalist reactionaries at court all pressured the tsar to resist Napoleon. Russian court liberals, more concerned with domestic reforms, hoped on the contrary that Alexander would maintain peace with France, but by 1812 their influence on the tsar had waned. For his part, Napoleon wanted to enforce the Continental System and humble Russia. As he bluntly put it: "Let Alexander defeat the Persians, but don't let him meddle in the affairs of Europe." Once again two major powers faced each other with diminishing interest in maintaining peace.

Napoleon prepared for his most momentous military campaign. His objective was to annihilate Russia's army or, at the least, to conquer Moscow and chase the army to the point of disarray. To this end he marshaled a "Grand Army" of almost 600,000 men (half of them French, the

Map 21.3a **SPANISH AMERICA BEFORE INDEPENDENCE**

Map 21.3b SPANISH AMERICA AFTER INDEPENDENCE

remainder from his satellite states and allies) and moved them steadily by forced marches across Central Europe into Russia. The Russians responded by retreating in orderly fashion and avoiding a fight. Many Russian nobles abandoned their estates and burned their crops to the ground, leaving the Grand Army to operate far from its supply bases in territory stripped of food. At Borodino the Russians finally made a stand and sustained a frightful 45,000 casualties, but the remaining Russian troops managed to withdraw in order (see Map 21.4). Napoleon lost 35,000 men in that battle; but far more men and horses were dying from hunger, thirst, fatigue, and disease in the march across Russia's unending, barren territory (see plate on p. 697). The greatly depleted ranks of the Grand Army staggered into Moscow on September 14, 1812, but the Russian army was still intact and far from demoralized.

The Destruction of the Grand Army In fact, the condition of Moscow demoralized the French. They found the city deserted and bereft of badly needed supplies. The next night Moscow was

mysteriously set ablaze, causing such extensive damage as to make it unfit to be the Grand Army's winter quarters. Realistic advisers warned the emperor that his situation was dangerous, while others told him what he wished to hear— that Russian resistance was crumbling. For weeks Napoleon hesitated. Logistically it was imperative that the French begin to retreat immediately, but that would constitute a political defeat. Only on October 19 did Napoleon finally order a retreat, but the order came too late.

The delay forced an utterly unrealistic pace on the bedraggled army as it headed west. Supplies were gone, medical care for the thousands of wounded nonexistent, horses lacking. French officers were poorly prepared for the march, and the soldiers grew insubordinate. Food shortages compelled foraging parties to sweep far from the main body of troops, and these men fell prey to Russian guerillas. And there was the weather— a normal Russian winter in which no commander would wish to find himself facing a march of several hundred miles, laden with wounded and loot but without food, fuel, horses, or proper clothing. Napoleon's poor planning, the harsh weather, and the operation of Russian guerilla

Map 21.4 **THE RUSSIAN CAMPAIGN OF 1812**

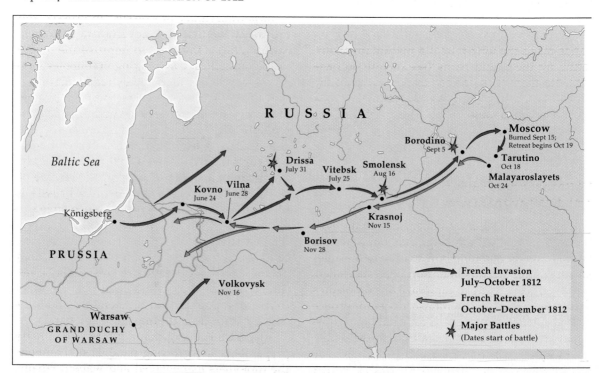

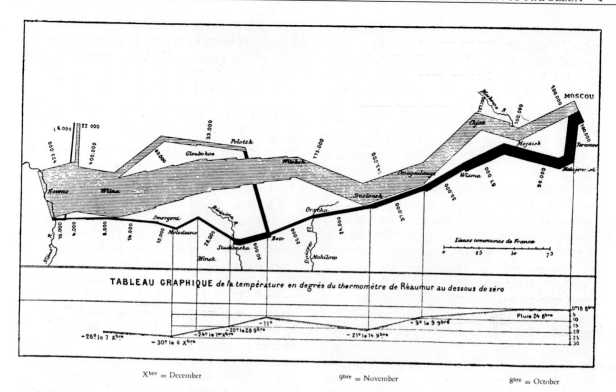

TABLEAU GRAPHIQUE de la température en degrés du thermomètre de Réaumur au dessous de zéro

Xᵇʳᵉ = December   9ᵇʳᵉ = November   8ᵇʳᵉ = October

▶ **This ingenious image, which dates from 1861, demonstrates graphically the attrition in the ranks of Napoleon's Grand Army on its way into and then out of Russia in 1812.**

bands made the long retreat a nightmare of suffering for the Grand Army (see picture on page 698). No more than 100,000 troops survived the ordeal. Worse yet, the Prussian contingent took the occasion to desert Napoleon, opening the possibility of mass defections and the formation of a new anti-Napoleonic coalition.

GERMAN RESISTANCE AND THE LAST COALITION

Napoleon was evidently impervious to the horror around him. On the sleigh ride out of Russia he was already planning how to raise new armies and set things aright. Other European statesmen, however, were ready to capitalize on Napoleon's defeat in Russia and demolish his empire once and for all. Provocative calls for a national uprising in the various German states to throw off the tyrant's yoke reinforced the efforts of diplomats like Prussia's Baron Stein and Austria's Klemens

von Metternich to revive the anti-Napoleonic coalition.

Reform from Above in Prussia In Prussia, after the defeat of 1806, the government had introduced reforms intended to improve the quality of the bureaucracy by offering non-nobles more access to high positions and by reducing some of the nobility's privileges. The monarchy hoped thereby to salvage the position of the nobility and the authority of the state. Prussian military reformers adopted new methods of recruitment to build up a trained reserve force that could be rapidly mobilized, along with a corps of reserve officers to take command of these units. Prussia, in other words, hoped to achieve French-style efficiency and military mobilization without resorting to new concepts of citizenship, constitutions, legislatures, or the abolition of seigneurialism. On the level of propaganda and the symbolic gesture, writers in Prussia and other German states called for a popular war of liberation under the slogan "With God for King and Fatherland."

Against this background of Prussian military preparation and growing nationalist sentiment, the diplomats maneuvered and waited. Finally,

▶ Just as Goya's drawings captured the unique ferocity of the Spanish campaign, this picture evokes the particular agonies of climate and logistics in the Russian debacle.

in March 1813, King Frederick William III of Prussia signed a treaty with Russia to form an offensive coalition against Napoleon. A great struggle for Germany ensued between the Russo-Prussian forces and Napoleon and his allies. Austria continued to claim neutrality and offered to mediate the dispute, but at a meeting in Prague, Napoleon rejected an offer of peace in exchange for restoring all French conquests since 1802.

In August, as Napoleon learned of new defeats in Spain, Habsburg Emperor Francis finally declared war on his son-in-law. Napoleon called up underage and overage conscripts and was able to field one last army, but his major southern German ally, Bavaria, finally changed sides. A great battle raged around Leipzig for three days

in October, and when the smoke cleared, Napoleon was in full retreat. As far as Germany was concerned, the war of liberation had been won. German states were free from Napoleon's domination, but Prussia's rulers were also free from the need to concede further reforms in the political and social order.

The Fall of Napoleon In the belief that he could rely on his conscription machine, Napoleon had rebuffed offers by the allies to negotiate peace in 1813. In fact, however, he reached the end of the line in November 1813 with a desperate call for 300,000 more men to defend France against the allies. Difficulties were inevitable, wrote one prefect, "when the number of men required exceeds the number available." Another reported: "There is scarcely a family that is not oppressed by conscription." Alongside sizable contingents of Italians, Germans, and other foreigners from the annexed territories and satellite states, nearly 2.5 million Frenchmen had been drafted by Napoleon. At least 1 million of those conscripts never returned.

With Napoleon driven back into France, British troops reinforced the coalition to ensure that it would not disintegrate once Central Europe had been liberated. The coalition offered final terms to the emperor: He could retain his throne, but France would be reduced to her "normal frontiers." (The precise meaning of this was left purposely vague.) Napoleon, still hoping for a dramatic reversal, chose to fight, and with some reluctance the allies invaded France. Napoleon led the remnants of his army skillfully but to no avail. The French had lost confidence in him, conscription has reached its limits, and no popular spirit of resistance to invasion developed as it had in 1792. Paris fell in March 1814. The price of this defeat was unconditional surrender and the emperor's abdication. Napoleon was transported to the island of Elba, between Corsica and Italy, over which he was granted sovereignty. After 22 years of exile, the Bourbon dynasty returned to France.

THE NAPOLEONIC LEGEND

For Napoleon, imperial authority—originating with him in France and radiating throughout Europe—represented the principle of rational progress. In his view, the old notion of balance of power among European states merely served as an excuse for the British to pursue their selfish interests. While paying lip service to the notion of Italian, Spanish, and Polish nationhood, he generally scorned patriotic opposition to his domination as an outmoded, reactionary sentiment—exemplified by the "barbaric" guerillas in Spain fighting for king and religion. Modern-minded Europeans, he believed, would see beyond historic, parochial traditions to the prospect of a new European order. Indeed, Napoleon's credibility with some reformers in Europe was considerable. The Bavarian prime minister, for instance, justified his collaboration with France in 1810 in these words: "The spirit of the new age is one of mobility, destruction, creativity. . . . The wars against France offer the [unfortunate] possibility of bringing back old constitutions, privileges, and property relations."

During his final exile, however, Napoleon came to recognize that nationalism was not necessarily reactionary—as one could plainly see in the nationalistic but liberal Cortes of Cádiz of 1812. Progressive thinking and nationalist aspirations could coexist. From exile Napoleon rewrote his life story to portray his career as a series of defensive wars against selfish adversaries (especially Britain) and as a battle in behalf of the

---

Napoleon Justifies Himself in 1815

"I have cleansed the Revolution, ennobled the common people, and restored the authority of kings. I have stirred all men to competition, I have rewarded merit wherever I found it, I have pushed back the boundaries of greatness. Is there any point on which I could be attacked and on which a historian could not take up my defense? My despotism? He can prove that dictatorship was absolutely necessary. Will it be said that I restricted freedom? He will be able to prove that license, anarchy, and general disorder were still on our doorstep. Shall I be accused of having loved war too much? He will show that I was always on the defensive. That I wanted to set up a universal monarchy? He will explain that it was merely the fortuitous result of circumstances and that I was led to it step by step by our very enemies. My ambition? Ah, no doubt he will find that I had ambition, a great deal of it—but the grandest and noblest perhaps, that ever was: the ambition of establishing and consecrating at last the kingdom of reason and the full exercise, the complete enjoyment, of all human capabilities!"

From B. Las Cases, ed., *Mémorial de Sainte-Hélène.*

nations of Europe against reactionary dynasties. In this way Napoleon brilliantly (if falsely) put himself on the side of the future.

These memoirs and recollections from exile formed the basis of the Napoleonic legend, as potent a force historically, perhaps, as the reality of the Napoleonic experience. The image they projected emphasized how General Bonaparte had consolidated what was best about the French Revolution while pacifying a bitterly divided nation and saving it from chaos. They cast the imperial experience in a deceptively positive light, glossed over the tyranny and unending military slaughter, and aligned Napoleon with pragmatism, efficiency, and modernity (*see box*, p. 699).

The Napoleonic legend also evoked a sense of grandeur and glory that moved ordinary people in years to come. Napoleon's dynamism and energy became his ultimate inspirational legacy to succeeding generations. In this way the Napoleonic legend fed on the romantic movement in literature and the arts. Many young romantics (including the poet William Wordsworth and the composer Ludwig van Beethoven) saw in the French Revolution a release of creativity and a liberation of the individual spirit. Napoleon's tyranny eventually alienated most such creative people. But the Napoleonic legend, by emphasizing the bold creativity of his career, meshed nicely with the emotional exaltation and sense of individual possibility that the romantics cultivated. Napoleon's retrospective justifications of his reign may not be convincing, but one can only marvel at the irrepressible audacity of the man!

In the confrontations between Napoleon and his European adversaries, France still embodied the specter of revolution. Even if the revolutionary legacy in France amounted by that time to little more than Napoleon's contempt for the inefficiency and outmoded institutions of the old regime, France after Brumaire remained a powerful challenge to the status quo. Napoleon intended to abolish feudalism, institute centralized administrations, and implant the French Civil Code in all of France's satellite states. But by 1808 his extravagant international ambitions relied on increasingly tyrannical and militaristic measures. These in turn provoked a range of responses, including nationalist rebellions. Britain and Russia, then Prussia and Austria, joined forces once more to bring the Napoleonic Empire down, to restore the balance of power in Europe, and to reinstall the Bourbons in France. But the clock could not really be set back from Europe's experience of revolution and Napoleonic transformation. The era of modern political and social conflicts had begun.

Recommended Reading (See Also Chapter 20)

Sources

De Caulaincourt, Armand. *With Napoleon in Russia.* 1935. A remarkable account of the diplomacy and warfare of the 1812 debacle by a man at Napoleon's side.

Herold, J. C. (ed.). *The Mind of Napoleon.* 1961.

Thompson, J. M. (ed.). *Napoleon Self-Revealed.* 1934.

*Walter, Jakob. *The Diary of a Napoleonic Foot Soldier.* 1991. A vivid and appalling account of the Russian campaign.

---

*Available in paperback.

Studies

Alexander, Don. *Rod of Iron: French Counterinsurgency Policy in Aragon during the Peninsular War.* 1985. A case study of French responses to Spanish guerilla warfare.

Anderson, Eugene. *Nationalism and the Cultural Crisis in Prussia, 1806–1815.* 1939. The intellectual roots of German resistance to Napoleon.

*Bergeron, Louis. *France under Napoleon.* 1981. A fresh and insightful evaluation of the Napoleonic settlement in France.

*Carr, Raymond. *Spain 1808–1975.* 1982. An authoritative general history with fine chapters on this period.

Chandler, David. *Napoleon's Marshals*. 1986. By a leading expert on Napoleonic military history.

Cobb, Richard. *Reactions to the French Revolution*. 1972. On the violent aftermath of the second revolution in the provinces.

*Connelley, Owen. *Blundering to Glory: Napoleon's Military Campaigns*. 1988. An irreverent but incisive account of Napoleon's military leadership.

———. *Napoleon's Satellite Kingdoms*. 1965. A study of the states conquered by France and ruled by the Bonaparte family.

Ellis, Geoffrey. *Napoleon's Continental Blockade: The Case of Alsace*. 1981. A case study of the period's economic warfare.

Forrest, Alan. *Conscripts and Deserters: The Army and French Society during the Revolution and Empire*. 1988. A study of popular resistance to revolutionary and Napoleonic conscription.

Gates, David. *The Spanish Ulcer: A History of the Peninsular War*. 1986. On the Spanish rebellion, the French response, and Wellington's expeditionary force.

Geyl, Pieter. *Napoleon, For and Against*. 1949. Napoleon and the historians, as reviewed by a Dutch scholar with no illusions.

*Herold, J. Christopher. *The Age of Napoleon*. 1963. A brilliant popular history of the era.

*Lefebvre, Georges. *Napoleon* (2 vols.). 1959. A general history of the period by a master historian.

———. *The Thermidorians*. 1964. A detailed narrative of 1794–1795.

Lucas, C., and G. Lewis (eds.). *Beyond the Terror: Essays in French Regional and Social History, 1794–1815*. 1983. Local studies by students of Richard Cobb.

*Lynch, John. *The Spanish American Revolutions, 1808–1826*. 1973. A comprehensive account of the independence movements in Spanish America and their aftermath.

Lyons, Martyn. *France under the Directory*. 1975. A brief topical survey of the Revolution's later, unheroic phase.

Marcus, G. J. *A Naval History of England, II: The Age of Nelson*. 1971. The standard history of British naval supremacy.

*Markham, Felix. *Napoleon*. 1966. Perhaps the best biography in English.

Mitchell, Harvey. *The Underground War against Revolutionary France: The Missions of William Wickham 1794–1800*. 1965. On British attempts to subvert the French Republic.

*Palmer, Robert R. *The World of the French Revolution*. 1971. Emphasizes the interplay of French power and indigenous revolutionary movements outside of France.

Rosenberg, Hans. *Bureaucracy, Aristocracy, and Autocracy: The Prussian Experience, 1660–1815*. 1958. On reform from above in Prussia that helped preserve the status quo.

Rothenberg, Gunther. *The Art of Warfare in the Age of Napoleon*. 1978. A good analysis of strategy and tactics.

*Sutherland, D. M. G. *France, 1789–1815: Revolution and Counterrevolution*. 1985. The best general history of France in this period.

Tulard, Jean. *Napoleon: The Myth of the Savior*. 1984. A synthesis by the leading French expert on Napoleon.

Woloch, Isser. *Jacobin Legacy: The Democratic Movement under the Directory*. 1970. On the ideas and practice of democratic activism after the Terror.

Woolf, Stuart. *A History of Italy, 1700–1860*. 1979. An authoritative general history, with fine chapters on this period.

*Woronoff, Denis. *The Thermidorian Regime and the Directory*. 1984. A relatively recent synthesis on France between Robespierre and Bonaparte.

PHOTO AND TEXT CREDITS

RMN ◆ p. 577: General Research Division, The New York Public Library. Astor, Lenox, and Tilden Foundations ◆ p. 579: Raspal, "Atelier de Couture en Arles." 1760. Photo Bulloz ◆ p. 583: J. Vernet, "Construction of a Road." Giraudon/Art Resource ◆ p. 585: Both, The Science Museum, London ◆ p. 591: Bettmann ◆ p. 593: Nicolas-Bernard Lépicié, "Cour de Ferme." Paris, Musée du Louvre. Photo RMN ◆ p. 595: City of Bristol Museum and Art Gallery/Bridgeman Art Library ◆ p. 598: From "Voyage du Chevalier des Marchais in Guinée" by J. B. Labat, 1730 ◆ p. 599: Courtesy of the New-York Historial Society ◆ p. 602: New Brunswick Museum ◆ p. 603: Thomas Hickey, "Colonel Kirkpatrick with Attendants." Courtesy of the National Gallery of Ireland **Chapter 19:** p. 606: Martin van Meytens, "Banquet for the Wedding of Joseph II and Isabella von Parma in 1760," 1763. Archiv für Kunst und Geschichte ◆ p. 609: Top, Bettmann. Bottom, from "Natural History General and Particular" by George Buffon. Courtesy Brooklyn Public Library ◆ p. 613: Bettmann ◆ p. 618: Nicolas H. Jeurat de Bertry, "Allegory of the Revolution with a Portrait Medallion of J. J. Rousseau." Giraudon/Art Resource ◆ p. 620: Lemonnier, "Salon of Mme. Geoffrin, 1725." Giraudon/Art Resource ◆ p. 622: Mary Evans Picture Library ◆ p. 624: Giraudon/Art Resource ◆ p. 627: Jean-Honore Fragonard, "Blindman's Buff," detail, c. 1765. Samuel H. Kress Collection. © 1995 National Gallery of Art, Washington ◆ p. 628: Jean-Baptiste Greuze, "The Paternal Curse." Giraudon/Art Resource ◆ p. 628: Jacques Louis David, "The Oath of the Horatii." Scala/Art Resource ◆ p. 629: New York Public Library, General Research Division, Astor, Lenox, and Tilden Foundations ◆ p. 632: Bibliothèque des Art Decoratif, Paris. Photo Jean-Loup Charmet. Tallandier ◆ p. 633: Hogarth's "Gin Lane" & "Beer Lane." The Metropolitan Museum of Art, Harris Brisbane Dick Fund, 1932 **Chapter 20:** p. 636: Musée Carnavalet/Photo Bulloz ◆ p. 639: Austrian Press & Information Service ◆ p. 642: John Trumbull, "The Declaration of Independence, 4 July 1776." Yale University Art Gallery, Trumbull Collection ◆ p. 646: Bibliothéque Nationale/Roger-Viollet ◆ p. 647: Bibliothéque Nationale/Photo Bulloz ◆ p. 648: Jacques Louis David, detail from "Oath of the Tennis Court at Versailles, June 20, 1789." Giraudon/Art Resource ◆ p. 649: Houet, "The Storming of the Bastille." Musée Carnavalet/Photo Bulloz ◆ p. 656: Jean Duplessi Bertaux, "Storming of the Tuileries, August 10, 1792." Giraudon/Art Resource ◆ p. 657: Musée Carnavalet/Photo Bulloz ◆ p. 658: Musée Carnavalet/Photo Bulloz ◆ p. 659: Jules Benoit-Levy, "Battle of Cholet" 1794. Giraudon/Art Resource ◆ p. 661: Masquelier, "A Session of the Jacobin Club." Giraudon/Art Re-

source ◆ p. 663: Bibliothéque Nationale ◆ p. 664: Photo Bulloz ◆ p. 666: Left, Photo Bulloz. Right, Collection Viollet ◆ p. 667: F. L. J. Watteau, "The Departure of the Volunteers." Musée Carnavalet/Bridgeman Art Library **Chapter 21:** p. 670: Jacques Louis David, "Napoleon Bonaparte" sketch. Giraudon/Art Resource ◆ p. 672: Giraudon/Art Resource ◆ p. 673: LeSeure, lack of bread in Paris 1795. Photothèque des Musées de la Ville de Paris, © Spadem 1995 ◆ p. 675: Musée Carnavalet/Photo Bulloz ◆ p. 679: Musée Légion d'Honneur/Photo Bulloz ◆ p. 682: Nicolas André Monsiau, "The Council of the Cisalpine Republic Proclaims Napoleon President," 1802. Giraudon/Art Resource ◆ p. 683: Nicholas Pocock, "Nelson's Flagships at Anchor." National Maritime Museum, London ◆ p. 684: C. Meynier, "The Day After the Battle of Eylau, February 9, 1807." Giraudon/Art Resource ◆ p. 686: J. A. D. Ingres, "Napoleon I Enthroned." Giraudon/Art Resource ◆ p. 688: Boilly, "The Departure of Conscripts at St. Denis," 1807. Musée Carnavalet/Photo Bulloz ◆ p. 689: Musée Carnavalet/Photo Bulloz ◆ p. 690: Erich Lessing/Art Resource ◆ p. 691: Francisco de Goya y Lucientes, "The Disasters of War: Populacho." Etching. Harris 148. 1st Edition. The Norton Simon Foundation ◆ p. 697: The Russian Campaign, by C. J. Minard ◆ p. 698: Photo Archives, Nationalbibliotek Austria.

TEXT

Chapter 11: p. 316: Boccaccio, Giovanni. Excerpt from *The Decameron.* In Ferdinand Schevill, ed. *The First Century of Italian Humanism.* New York: Russell & Russell, 1967, pp. 32–34. Reprinted by permission of Simon & Schuster. ◆ p. 334: Excerpt from *The Trial of Jeanne d'Arc,* 1438. In Bernard, Leonard & Hodges, Theodore B.; eds. *Readings in European History,* 1958, pp. 181–182. Copyright © 1958 by Macmillan College Publishing Company. Reprinted with the permission of Macmillan College Publishing Company. **Chapter 12:** p. 369: d'Este, Isabella. Letters, 1502, 1505, 1504. In D. S. Chambers, ed. *Patrons and Artists in the Italian Renaissance.* London: Macmillan, 1970, pp. 123–130 and 147–148. Reprinted by permission of The Macmillan Press Ltd. ◆ p. 379: Hus, Jan. Letter, 1415. In Matthew Spinka, ed. *The Letters of John Hus,* pp. 195–197. 1972 © Columbia University Press, New York. Reprinted with permission of the publisher. **Chapter 13:** p. 389: Table adapted from Febvre, Lucien & Martin, Henri-Jean. *The Coming of the Book: The Impact of Printing 1450–1800.* Trans. David Gerard, 1976, pp. 178–179 and 184–185. Reprinted by permission of Verso/New Left Books, London. ◆ p. 397: Luther, Martin. Preface, 1545. Trans. from the Latin by Theodore K. Rabb from

Otto Schell, ed. *Dokumente zu Luther's Entwicklung.* Tubingen: J. C. B. Mohr, 1929, pp. 191–192. Reprinted by permission ♦ p. 415: St. Theresa. Excerpt from her autobiography, begun 1562. In E. Ellison Peers, *The Life of Theresa of Jesus*, pp. 258–260, 273–274. Reprinted by permission of Sheed & Ward, Kansas City, MO. **Chapter 14:** p. 423: Elliott, John H. Table adapted from *Imperial Spain, 1469–1716.* London: Edward Arnold, publisher, 1964, p. 175. Reprinted by permission of Professor Sir John Elliott, Oriel College at Oxford University, England. ♦ p. 431: Morison, S. E. Excerpt from *Admiral of the Ocean Sea: A Life of Christopher Columbus,* 1942, pp. 670–671. Reprinted by permission of Little, Brown & Company. ♦ p. 431: Sale, Kirkpatrick. Excerpt from *The Conquest of Paradise: Christopher Columbus and the Columbian Legacy,* 1990, pp. 209–210 and 362. Reprinted by permission of Alfred A. Knopf, Inc. **Chapter 15:** p. 489: Elliott, John H. Table adapted from *Imperial Spain, 1469–1716.* London: Edward Arnold, publisher, 1964, p. 175. Reprinted by permission of Professor Sir John Elliott, Oriel College at Oxford University, England. **Chapter 16:** p. 502: Galileo Galilei and Kepler, Johannes. Letters dated from 1597. In Giorgio de Santillana, *The Crime of Galileo,* 1955, pp. 11, 14–15. Copyright © 1955. Reprinted by permission of the publisher, University of Chicago Press. ♦ p. 521: de Vries, Jan. Table from *The Economy of Europe in an Age of Crisis, 1600–1750,* 1976, p. 5. Reprinted by permission of Cambridge University Press. **Chapter 17:** p. 537: Louis XIV. Memoirs, c. 1665–1670. In Thompson, J. M., ed. *Lectures on Foreign History, 1494–1789,* 1956, pp. 172–174. Reprinted by permission of Blackwell Publishers, Oxford. ♦ p. 557: Locke, John. Excerpt from *The Second Treatise of Civil Government,* 1690. Thomas P. Peardon, ed. Reprinted with permission of Macmillan College Publishing Company. Copyright © 1952 by Macmillan College Publishing Company, Inc. **Chapter 18:** p. 596: Exhibit adapted from Dean, Phyllis, and Cole, W. A. *British Economic Growth, 1688–1959,* 1964, p. 49. Reprinted by permission of Cambridge University Press. **Chapter 19:** p. 611: Joseph II: Edict, 1781. In Macartney, C. A., ed. Excerpts from *The Habsburg and Hohenzollern Dynasties,* 1970. Copyright © 1970 by C. A. Macartney. Used by permission of HarperCollins Publishers, Inc. ♦ p. 617: Wollstonecraft, Mary. Excerpt from *A Vindication of the Rights of Woman,* 1792. From Sandra M. Gilbert and Susan Gubar, eds. *The Norton Anthology of Literature by Women: The Tradition in English.* Copyright © 1985 by Sandra M. Gilbert and Susan Gubar. Used by permission of W. W. Norton & Company, Inc. ♦ p. 619: Rousseau, Jean-Jacques. Excerpt from "Concept of the General Will." In G. D. H. Cole, ed. and trans. *The Social Contract,* Book I, Chapter 6: "The Sovereign." London: Everyman's Library, 1950. © David Campbell Publishers Ltd., London. **Chapter 21:** p. 692: Political Constitution of the Spanish Monarchy, 1812. Excerpt trans. James Tueller. Copyright James B. Tueller 1993. Reprinted by permission.

INDEX

CONTEMPORARY EUROPE

Reykjavik ⊛
ICELAND

NORWEGIAN SEA

```
0        200        400 Miles
```

⊛ Capital cities
• Other cities
– – – Commonwealth of Independent
       States boundary

SHETLAND ISLANDS

Trondheim •

NORWAY   **SWEDEN**   *Gulf of Bothnia*   **FIN**

Bergen •   Dal R.   Tammert

Oslo ⊛   *ALAND I.*   Helsin

Stockholm •   Gul
                Tallin ⊛
                         E

ORKNEY ISLANDS

SCOTLAND
Glasgow •
Edinburgh •

NORTH SEA   *Skagerrak*   Ålborg •   *Kattegat*   Göteborg •

Alborg   Copenhagen ⊛   **BALTIC SEA**   **LATVI**

NORTHERN IRELAND
Belfast ⊛
IRELAND   **UNITED KINGDOM**   **DENMARK** ⊛   Kaliningrad   **LITH**
                                                                (Königsberg) • (RUS.)

Dublin ⊛   **ENGLAND**   Hamburg •   Gdansk
Cork •   Liverpool •   (Danzig) •

ATLANTIC OCEAN

WALES • Birmingham   Elbe R.   Berlin •   *Vistula R.*   **POLAND**   Wars •

London ⊛   **NETHERLANDS**   **GERMANY**   Lodz •
           Amsterdam ⊛

English Channel   Antwerp •   Dusseldorf •   Oder R.
Brest •   Rouen •   **Brussels** ⊛   Köln •   Leipzig •   Dresden •   Prague ⊛   Krakow •
          NORMANDY   **BELGIUM**   Bonn •   Rhine R.   **CZECH REP.**
                                    LUX.   Frankfurt •
BRITTANY   Paris ⊛   Luxemburg ⊛   **SLOVAKIA**
             Orléans •   *LORRAINE*   Danube R.   Vienna ⊛   Bratislava •
Loire R.   *Seine R.*   Strassburg •   Munich •   **AUSTRIA**
Nantes •   Tours •   *ALSACE*   *BADEN*   **LIECHTENSTEIN**   Graz •   Budapest ⊛
                                                 Bern ⊛   **HUNGARY**
BAY OF BISCAY   **FRANCE**   *Saône R.*   **SWITZERLAND** ⊛ Vaduz   Ljubljana ⊛   RO
                                           Geneva •   **SLOVENIA**   Zagreb ⊛
Bordeaux •   Lyons •   *PIEDMONT*   Milan •   **LOMBARDY**   Trieste •   **CROATIA**
                      Rhône R.   *VENEZIA*   Venice •   Belgrade ⊛
GALICIA   Bilbao •   *GASCONY*   *LANGUEDOC*   Genoa •   *Po R.*
Porto •   **LEON**   *BASQUE COUNTRY*   *PROVENCE*   **SAN MARINO**   *ADRIATIC SEA*   Sarajevo ⊛
Douro R.   **OLD CASTILE**   *NAVARRE*   Marseilles •   **MONACO** ⊛   **SERBIA**   **YUGO-**
             ANDORRA   Toulon •   **BOSNIA-**   **SLAVIA**
PORTUGAL   *ARAGON*   *CATALONIA*   *CORSICA*   **TUSCANY**   Rome ⊛   *CAMPANIA*   **HERZEGOVINA**   **MONTE-**
                          Barcelona •   *(France)*   **VATICAN CITY**   Tiranë ⊛   **NEGRO**
Lisbon ⊛   Madrid ⊛   *Tagus R.*   *APULIA*   **ALBANIA**   Sk
          SPAIN   *NEW CASTILE*   Valencia •   *BALEARIC I.*   Naples •
          LA MANCHA   Palma •   *(Spain)*   *SARDINIA*   Corfu
Seville •   Cordoba •   *(Italy)*   **ITALY**
          ANDALUSIA
Ebro R.   Málaga •   Palermo •
Strait of Gibraltar   Gibraltar •   **G**
Tangier •   Ceuta •   Patras
Rabat •   Melilla •   Oran •   Algiers ⊛   *SICILY*
Casablanca •   *Pantelleria (Italy)*
MOROCCO   Tunis •   **MALTA**
                        Valetta ⊛
ALGERIA   **TUNISIA**   *MEDITERRANEAN S*
              Tripoli ⊛   **LIBYA**   *Gulf of Sidra*